The Ultimate Encyclopedia of
STEAM & RAIL

The Ultimate Encyclopedia of
STEAM & RAIL

COLIN GARRATT AND MAX WADE-MATTHEWS

southwater

This edition is published by Southwater, an imprint of Anness Publishing Ltd,
108 Great Russell Street, London WC1B 3NA; info@anness.com

www.southwaterbooks.com; www.annesspublishing.com

Anness Publishing has a new picture agency outlet for images for publishing, promotions
or advertising. Please visit our website www.practicalpictures.com for more information.

A CIP catalogue record for this book is available from the British Library

Publisher Joanna Lorenz
Editorial Manager Helen Sudell
Assistant Editor Emma Gray
Designer Michael Morey

This book has been written and picture researched by the Milepost Publishing
Production Team. Milepost also conserves and markets collections of railway
transparencies and negatives.

Milepost 92½, Newton Harcourt, Leicestershire, LE8 9FH, UK

For historical reasons, the measurements in this book are not always given with their
metric or imperial equivalent. See page 512 for a conversion chart.

PUBLISHER'S NOTE
Although the advice and information in this book are believed to be accurate and true at
the time of going to press, neither the authors nor the publisher can accept any legal
responsibility or liability for any errors or omissions that may have been made.

Contents

● **ABOVE**
An early photograph of a steam engine from the 1830s.

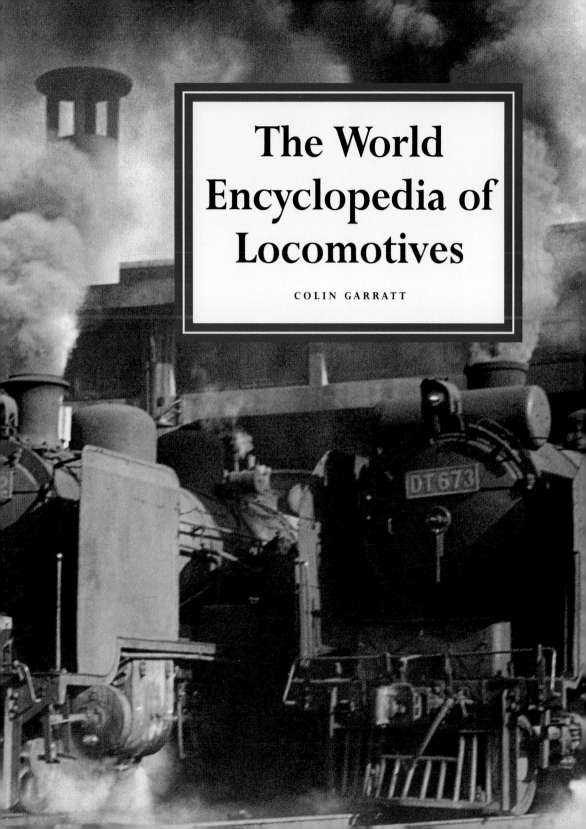

The World Encyclopedia of Locomotives

COLIN GARRATT

The Birth of the Railway

The following section looks at the development of the railway, from its very beginnings up to 1900, touching on both the technical changes it underwent and the role it played in societies and industries around the world. The text and photographs provide a comprehensive account of the railway pioneers and the machines and lines they created, while the technical boxes give an at-a-glance record of some of the most influential and innovative locomotives.

● OPPOSITE
Locomotion No. 1 – a working replica built in 1975. The first locomotive built at the Stephensons' Forth Street works, Newcastle upon Tyne, in 1825, it also established the advent of mechanical traction for public railways. The original locomotive survives in Darlington Railway Museum, County Durham, north-east England.

● ABOVE
A Puffing Billy-type engine built by William Hedley of Wylam Colliery, Northumberland, in 1813. From a painting by David Weston (born 1936).

FROM TRAMWAYS TO STEAM

● **BELOW**
Before railways, canals were the main means of moving heavy goods such as coal. With the coming of the railways, waterways fast fell into disuse. Today, they are basically used for pleasure.

In Britain, one of the first tramways was built about 1630 to serve collieries near Newcastle upon Tyne. The Tanfield Waggonway in County Durham was begun about 1725, and by 1727 included the Causey Arch, the world's first railway viaduct, built by Ralph Wood. At first, the rails were made of wood but these wore quickly, and in 1767 iron plates were affixed to them for durability. The first cast-iron plates were made by the Coalbrookdale Ironworks in Shropshire. Plate rails, that is iron-flanged rails, were introduced underground at Sheffield Park Colliery in 1787 and on the surface at Ketley Incline in 1788.

● **STAGECOACH IMPROVES ROADS**
Transportation in the 17th and 18th centuries was either by stagecoach or water. In 1658, the state of the roads was so bad that the stagecoach took two weeks to travel from London to Edinburgh. Even by the end of the 1700s, with responsibility for the maintenance of main roads handed from parishes to turnpike trusts, the state of the roads was not much better. In winter, they were blocked by snow or floods; in

summer, hard-baked ruts made journeys uncomfortable. This was acceptable while most travel was on horseback. With the ever-increasing use of coaches for public transport, however, the roads improved. By the 1750s the stagecoach had come into its own.

● **RAILWAYS REPLACE WATERWAYS**
With industrialization, however, the need for transportation of heavy goods remained. By about the mid-18th century, artificial canals came into being

as arteries for goods making their way to the larger rivers and to the sea for export to various parts of Britain. The waterways' half-century of posterity and public service ended, however, with the coming of the railways. Many became ruins or were bought by local railway companies. Turnpike roads ceased to be the chief arteries of the nation's lifeblood. Posting-inns were replaced by hotels springing up at railway termini. The Railway Era saw the demise of the public mailcoach and heavy family coach. In some instances, however, when such conservative-minded gentry as the Duke of Wellington travelled by rail, they sat in their coaches, which were placed on flat trucks. By 1840, with railways halving the cost of travel, canal and stagecoach were doomed.

● **THE FIRST RAILWAYS**
In 1804, the world's first public railway company, the Surrey Iron Railway Company, opened a horse-drawn line from Wandsworth Wharf, on the River Thames in south London, to Croydon in Surrey. The line was extended to Merstham, Surrey, but

● **RIGHT**
The Rocket – a working replica built in 1980. This represents the appearance of the locomotive as it competed in the Rainhill Trials.

● **FAR RIGHT**
Richard Trevithick (1771–1833): the great pioneer. The Cornish inventor and engineer graduated from building mines' pumping-engines in 1803–4 to construct the first steam locomotive to haul a load on iron rails.

● **OPPOSITE BELOW**
The packhorse bridge was a means of crossing rivers. Cutaways provided passing-points for approaching animals and people.

never reached its intended destination, Portsmouth in Hampshire.

● **RICHARD TREVITHICK**
Another landmark in the history of railways also occurred in 1804 when British engineer Richard Trevithick (1771–1833) tested his newly invented steam locomotive. This drew five wagons and a coach with 70 passengers along the ten miles of track from the Pen-y-Darren Ironworks to the Glamorganshire Canal. This historic event saw the world's first steam locomotive to run on rails hauling a train carrying fare-paying passengers.

Trevithick continued his experiments and in 1808 erected a circular track in Euston Square, London, on which he ran his latest production "Catch Me Who Can". The public was invited to pay a shilling, almost a day's wages for the average working man, to ride on this

novel method of transportation, but the venture failed financially and in a few weeks Trevithick had to close it.

● **GEORGE STEPHENSON**
Between 1814–21 Northumbrian engineer George Stephenson (1781–1848), born in Wylam, a village near Newcastle upon Tyne, built 17 experimental locomotives. Although he was not the first to produce a steam locomotive, he was the prime mover in introducing them on a wide scale. His turning-point came in 1821 when he was appointed engineer-in-charge of what became the 42 km (26 mile) long Stockton & Darlington Railway, between the County Durham towns of Stockton-on-Tees, a seaport, and Darlington, an industrial centre. It was opened in September 1825. Stephenson's Locomotion No. 1 drew the first train.

This historic event saw the world's first public railway regularly to use steam locomotives to haul wagons of goods (the main traffic was coal) and carriages of passengers. Passengers were carried in horse-drawn coaches until 1833.

In 1829, Lancashire's Liverpool & Manchester Railway, built mainly to carry cotton, offered a £500 prize to the winner of a competition for the best steam-locomotive design to work the line. The trials were held at Rainhill, near Liverpool. Of the three locomotives entered, George Stephenson's Rocket, gaily painted yellow, black and white, won at a speed of about 26 mph (42 kph).

ROCKET	
Date	1829
Builder	George Stephenson
Client	Liverpool & Manchester Railway (L&MR)
Gauge	4 ft 8½ in
Type	0-2-2
Capacity	2 cylinders outside 8 x 17 in inclined
Pressure	50 lb
Weight	4 tons 5 cwt

BRITISH LOCOMOTIVES OF THE 1830S

By 1830 almost 100 locomotives had been built in Britain. These early experimental engines were of two main types: those with inclined cylinders and those with vertical cylinders. Then, in 1830 George Stephenson introduced the 2-2-0 Planet type. This was a radical step forward from the Rocket and its derivatives and established the general form that all future steam locomotives were to take. Planet combined the multi-tubular boiler with a fully water-jacketed firebox and a separate smokebox. The cylinders were now inside and horizontally mounted, while the engine's boiler and motion were carried on a sturdy outside frame of oak beams sandwiched by iron plates. The first Planet was a passenger-engine with 5 ft driving wheels and 3 ft carrying wheels, but Stephenson was quick to see that the frame arrangement would allow him to substitute two pairs of coupled 4 ft 6 in wheels to create a heavy-goods locomotive. The resulting engines, Samson and Goliath, were supplied to the Liverpool & Manchester Railway (L&MR) in 1831.

● **ABOVE**
Robert Stephenson (1803–59): at the age of 20 he was put in charge of his father's locomotive works in Newcastle upon Tyne. He became the leading locomotive engineer of his day. He built railway bridges and viaducts, notably the tubular bridge over the Menai Strait between Anglesey and mainland Wales.

● **BELOW**
Lion, built in the same year as Samson, shows how far heavy-goods engine design had really progressed. The first engine built by Todd, Kitson & Laird, this 0-4-2 had 5 ft driving wheels and is still in working order.

PATENTEE	
Date	1833
Builder	Robert Stephenson
Client	Liverpool & Manchester Railway (L&MR)
Gauge	4 ft 8$^1/_2$ in
Type	2-2-2
Driving wheels	5 ft
Capacity	2 cylinders 12 x 18 in
Pressure	50 lb

Hackworth, meanwhile, was still firmly wedded to the archaic vertical cylinder arrangement. In 1831 he built six engines of the Majestic class for heavy-coal haulage on the Stockton & Darlington Railway (S&DR). Their cylinders were carried on an overhanging platform at the back of the boiler and drove a crankshaft carried on a bracket below. The crankshaft in turn drove the nearest pair of the six coupled wheels, allowing all axles to be sprung. The boilers combined Hackworth's longitudinal flue with a return multi-tubular arrangement intended to provide the best features of both layouts. In the event, the small grate area possible in the single flue severely limited the engines' steaming power. Also, they were heavy on fuel as well as being cumbersome in appearance with a tender at each end of the locomotive. Their ponderous performance in traffic was such that the line's rigid speed limit of 6 mph (9.7 kph) did not trouble them.

Edward Bury had intended his first locomotive, Liverpool, to take part in the Rainhill Trials but it was not ready in time. Noting Rocket's superior features,

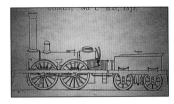

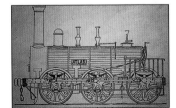

● **FAR LEFT**
George Stephenson (1781–1848): the world's
most well-known locomotive engineer. He
worked as an engineer for several railway
companies and built the first railway line to
carry passengers (1825).

● **ABOVE LEFT**
Comet was the first locomotive put into
service on the Leicester & Swannington
Railway (L&SR). On the inaugural run, in May
1832, the 13 ft high chimney was knocked
down in the Glenfield Tunnel, near Leicester,
covering the travelling dignitaries in soot.
Swannington, in Leicestershire, is 19 km
(12 miles) north-west of the county town.

● **BELOW LEFT**
Atlas was the first 0-6-0 goods engine built by
Robert Stephenson. It was delivered to the
L&SR in 1834. At the time, this was the largest,
heaviest and most powerful locomotive
running on any railway.

he was able to modify his design and
deliver the engine to the L&MR in 1830.
In its rebuilt form, it was bristling with
innovations and became an international
prototype. Most striking were the 6 ft
coupled wheels, bigger than any previously
made, but equally notable were the
multi-tubular boiler, inside bar-frames
and raised-dome firebox-casing. The
cylinders, too, were inside, inclined
slightly upwards to allow the piston rods
to pass beneath the leading axle. On the
line, Liverpool proved capable of hauling
an 18-wagon train at an average of
12$\frac{1}{2}$ mph (19 kph). In short, she was a
stunning little creation, topped off by a
small chimney with a procession of

cutout brass liver birds around its crown.
(The liver is a fanciful bird on the arms
of the city of Liverpool.)

With progress came the need for
more powerful locomotives, and it had to
be admitted that Planets were unsteady at
any speed and their firebox capacity was
limited. Robert Stephenson rectified this
by extending the frames rearwards,
adding a trailing axle behind a much-
enlarged firebox. Thus was born the
Patentee 2-2-2 Type, which became the
standard British express-engine for the
next four decades and was exported
widely to inaugurate railway services
across Europe. Stephenson's Patentees
also incorporated great improvements in

boiler construction and valve gear. All
had flangeless driving wheels.

The design could be varied to
incorporate coupled driving wheels, as
other manufacturers were quick to see.
Perhaps the best known front-coupled
Patentee is the 0-4-2 Lion, built for the
L&MR in 1838 by Todd, Kitson & Laird
of Leeds, Yorkshire.

● **BELOW**
Samson, built by Timothy Hackworth in 1838
for heavy-goods work on the Stockton &
Darlington Railway (S&DR), already looked
outdated by the standards of the time. Note
the fireman feeding the single-flue boiler from
the front end.

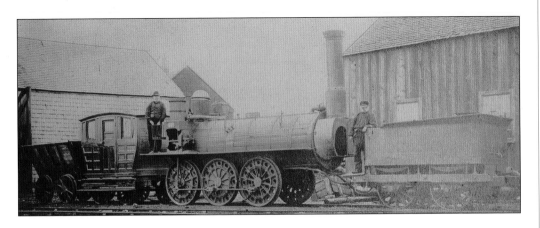

THE BATTLE OF THE GAUGES

Isambard Kingdom Brunel (1806–59) conceived railways on a grand scale. For his Great Western Railway (GWR), authorized in 1835, he dismissed the well-established 4 ft 8½ in gauge as inadequate to cope with the greater speeds, safety and smoother travel he planned for his relatively straight and level main line from London to Bristol. So he fixed his gauge at a spacious 7 ft. The main drawbacks were that this set the GWR apart from all other railways and meant that all goods and passengers had to change trains when travelling to or from areas not served by GWR trains.

The first GWR train steamed out of Paddington Station, west London, on 4 June 1838 behind the Stephenson 2-2-2 North Star, a large example of the Patentee type, which was originally built for the 5 ft 6 in gauge New Orleans Railway in the USA. A broken contract caused her to be altered to 7 ft gauge and to go to the GWR instead. A sister engine, Morning Star, entered service at the same time. North Star had 7 ft driving wheels and the inside-cylinders

A classic GWR broad-gauge single powers an express-train westwards through the Sonning Cutting, near Reading, Berkshire. It is late in the broad-gauge era for a third rail has been laid on each track to allow rolling stock of both gauges to operate.

were 16 x 16 in. Obsolescence was rapid in those days, but North Star was rebuilt with a large boiler and new cylinders in 1854, lasting in service for 33 years. When finally withdrawn, she was preserved at Swindon, Wiltshire, until, in an act of official vandalism, she was scrapped in 1906. In something of an atonement, GWR built a full-sized replica incorporating original parts in 1925. This is displayed at Swindon Railway Museum.

For the most part, the other original GWR broad-gauge locomotives were a collection of mechanical freaks, the best of a poor lot being six 2-2-2s with 8 ft driving wheels from Tayleur's Vulcan Foundry, which were Patentee copies but

IRON DUKE	
Date	1847
Builder	Daniel Gooch, Swindon, Wiltshire, England
Client	Great Western Railway (GWR)
Gauge	7 ft
Type	4-2-2
Driving wheels	8 ft
Capacity	2 cylinders 18 x 24 in
Pressure	100 lb later 120 lb
Weight	35 tons

● **ABOVE LEFT**
The importance of the broad gauge and its hitherto unimagined speeds caught the imagination of the populace. People flocked to experience this revolutionary form of travel in which speeds of 90 mph (145 kph) had been reported.

● **ABOVE RIGHT**
Tiny: built by Sara & Co., of Plymouth, Devon, in 1868, this broad-gauge locomotive went into service on England's South Devon Railway (SDR).

● **OPPOSITE MIDDLE**
Isambard Kingdom Brunel (1806–59), the 19th-century English engineer who pioneered the broad gauge of the Great Western Railways, between London and Exeter in Devon. His father was a French engineer in England, Sir Marc Isambard Brunel (1769–1849).

● **OPPOSITE BOTTOM**
Iron Duke (replica): built by Gooch, this 4-2-2 of the Duke Class was named after Arthur Wellesley, the first Duke of Wellington (1769–1852), on whose birthday – 1 May – it first ran.

with small low-pressure boilers. They were delivered from Manchester, Lancashire, to London by sea and then on to West Drayton, Middlesex, by canal. Among their more bizarre stablemates were two 2-2-2s from Mather & Dixon with 10 ft driving wheels fabricated from riveted iron plates.

There was much opposition to the broad gauge, and in July 1845 the Gauge Commission sat to choose between the rival claims of both gauges. High-speed trial runs were organized, the honours going to Daniel Gooch's 7 ft GWR single "Ixion", which achieved 60 mph (96.6

kph) hauling an 80 ton (81,284 kg) train. The best standard-gauge performance was 53 mph (85.1 kph) behind a brand new Stephenson 4-2-0 with 6 ft 6 in driving wheels. Although the Commission considered the 7 ft gauge in every way superior, the standard gauge was selected on the basis of the greater mileage already in use. In 1848, Parliament decided there should in future be only one gauge, the narrow, and eventually the GWR had to bow to the inevitable, laying a third rail to give 4 ft 8½ in throughout its system and abolishing the broad gauge altogether in May 1892.

● **RIGHT**
Rain, Steam and Speed (National Gallery, London): Turner (1775–1851), the English landscape painter, welcomed the Industrial Revolution of the 18th and 19th centuries and painted this picture of one of Gooch's singles crossing the Maidenhead Viaduct, Berkshire, during a squally storm in the Thames valley.

BRITISH LOCOMOTIVES
– 1840–60

● BELOW

Derwent: built by W.A. Kitching in 1845, this 0-6-0 went into service on the Stockton & Darlington Railway (S&DR) between Stockton-on-Tees port and Darlington, County Durham, the first passenger-carrying railway in the world (1825). This railway largely developed the industrial town.

In 1841, Robert Stephenson introduced the first of his "long-boilered" locomotives. In these, he sought to obtain greater boiler power by grouping all the axles in front of the firebox and having a much longer boiler barrel than usual. The necessarily short wheelbase was dictated by the small turntables of the period. "Long-boiler" engines also featured inside frames of iron-plate and the inside-cylinders shared a common steam-chest placed between them. The design could be built in almost any form: a 2-2-2 or 2-4-0 for passenger work and an 0-6-0 for goods-trains were the commonest configurations. But as line speeds rose, the passenger types were found to oscillate dangerously on their short wheelbase chassis and soon fell out of favour. For goods work, however, the design was an undoubted success and these were most numerous on Stephenson's home turf. The North Eastern Railway (NER), a successor to the Stockton & Darlington Railway (S&DR), had no fewer than 125 long-boiler 0-6-0s of the 1001 class built between 1852 and 1875. Fittingly, No. 1275 is preserved in the National Railway Museum at York.

Thomas Russell Crampton (1816–88) was an ambitious young engineer working at Swindon, Wiltshire, under Daniel Gooch. He began to develop his own ideas for an express-locomotive with a large boiler and driving wheels but low centre of gravity and took out his first patent in 1842. In his design, the driving axle was placed right at the base of the frame, behind the firebox. To keep the connecting-rods as short as possible, the cylinders were displaced rearwards outside the frames and fed from the smokebox by prominent outside steam-pipes. The motion and valve gear was all placed outside, allowing the boiler to

LARGE BLOOMER	
Date	1852
Builder	W. Fairbairn/ E.B. Wilson
Client	London & North Western Railway (LNWR)
Gauge	4 ft 8 1/2 in
Type	2-2-2
Driving wheels	7 ft 6 in
Capacity	2 cylinders 18 x 24 in
Pressure	150 lb
Weight	31 tons 4 cwt

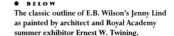

● **BELOW MIDDLE**
A 2-2-2 Single of 1851 built by Robert
Stephenson for LNWR.

● **BELOW**
The classic outline of E.B. Wilson's Jenny Lind
as painted by architect and Royal Academy
summer exhibitor Ernest W. Twining.

be sunk down in the frames but making
the engine very wide. Crampton left the
GWR to promote his design to a wider
market. His first two engines were built
by Tulk & Ley for the Liège & Namur
Railway, Belgium, in 1846.

One of the Cramptons destined for
Belgium was tested on the Grand
Junction Railway (GJR), leading the
London and North Western Railway
(LNWR) to build one for themselves at
Crewe, Cheshire, in 1847. This was the
4-2-0 Courier with 7 in driving wheels,
inside-frames and a boiler of oval cross-
section. At the same time, larger versions
with 8 in driving wheels, the 4-2-0
London by Tulk & Ley and the 6-2-0
Liverpool by Bury, Curtis & Kennedy,
were tried out by the LNWR, the latter
with great destructive effect on the track.
Cramptons could run at speeds
approaching 90 mph (145 kph), but they
never achieved great popularity in Britain
because of their rough riding caused by
the position of the driving axle. On the
Continent, it was a different matter and
the French Northern Railway in
particular gained its reputation for
lightweight fast expresses by the use of
Crampton locomotives. "Prendre le
Crampton" even entered the French

language as slang for "a quick getaway".
These French Cramptons had very strong
outside-frames, because the continental
loading-gauge left room for the resulting
enormous width over cylinders and
cranks. A British example built the same

way by J.E. McConnell of LNWR earned
the nickname "Mac's Mangle" following
the trail of broken platforms and lineside
structures left in its wake.

In 1847, from E.B. Wilson's Railway
Foundry in Leeds, Yorkshire, emerged
the first engine built to their most
famous design, the Jenny Lind class. This
2-2-2 passenger-engine was the
brainchild of the young chief
draughtsman, David Joy. Built at a cost of
about £2,500 each, the basic model had
6 in driving wheels powered by
15 x 20 in inside-cylinders, making it
capable of a mile-a-minute in regular
service. For the first time, railways could
buy an off-the-peg express locomotive of
peerless quality. This most elegant
machine, with its polished mahogany
boiler lagging and classically fluted bronze
dome and safety-valve casings, rapidly
became top-link motive power for many
of Britain's main lines. The largest Jenny
Lind was the Salopian built for
Shrewsbury & Birmingham Railway
(S&BR) in June 1849. It had a boiler
with more than 1,270 sq ft of heating
surface and a pressure of 120 lb
with $15^{1}/_{2}$ x 22 in cylinders driving
6 ft 6 in wheels.

● **OPPOSITE**
Built by W. Fairbairn
and E.B. Wilson for
the LNWR, this Large
Bloomer is pictured at
Milton Keynes Central
in 1992. The English
new town in Bucking-
hamshire was founded
in 1967.

● **RIGHT**
The inside-framed
Crampton Kinnaird,
built for Scotland's
Dundee & Perth
Junction Railway by
Tulk & Ley in 1848.

BRITISH LOCOMOTIVES – 1860–75

Patrick Stirling's early locomotives were cabless and had domed boilers. His first 2-2-2 was built for Scotland's Glasgow & South Western Railway (G&SWR) in 1857 and bore many of the design hallmarks that were refined into their finest flowering in his Great Northern 4-2-2 No. 1 of 1870. His crowning achievements were the 8 ft 4-2-2 singles, built at Doncaster, Yorkshire, from 1870 onwards, said to be one of the most handsome locomotives ever made. With modification these were used on all main-line trains for the next 25 years. In 1895, they took part in the railway Races to the North with average speeds of more than 80 mph (129 kph) between King's Cross Station, London, and York.

When William Stroudley became Locomotive Superintendent of the London, Brighton & South Coast Railway (LB&SCR) in 1870, he found a bizarre assortment of locomotives, which were

by no means a match for the work they had to do. Over the next two decades, he restocked with a fine series of soundly engineered machines for every purpose from express-passenger to branch-line

haulage. His smallest, yet most celebrated class, was the Terrier 0-6-0Ts of 1872. Fifty engines were built, originally for suburban work in south London but later widely dispersed to more rural

● **ABOVE**
William Stroudley's beautiful livery is captured to perfection on Terrier 0-6-0T No. 55 Stepney, built in 1875 and preserved in full working order on England's Bluebell Railway in Sussex.

● **LEFT**
Kirtley's double-framed 2-4-0 No. 158A breathes the spirit of the Midland Railway in the 19th century at the Midland Railway Centre, Butterley, Derbyshire. Butterley was a seat of ironworks and collieries.

● BELOW
A 4-2-2 Massey Bromley of 1879. Dübs & Co.
built ten for the Great Eastern Railway (GER).
Kitsons built ten more in 1881–2.

● BELOW
A 2-4-0 of Scotland's Highland Railway in
about 1877. Note the louvred chimney, which
produced a current of air with the object of
lifting the exhaust above the cab.

surroundings. They had 4 ft driving
wheels, a 150 lb boiler and 12 x 20 in
cylinders. Most were rebuilt with slightly
larger boilers without in any way spoiling
their appearance. Always useful, they
notched up a working life of more than
90 years. Today, nearly a dozen exist in
preservation.

Joseph Beattie of the London & South
Western Railway (L&SWR) was an
ingenious Irishman who sought to
increase the steaming power of the
locomotive boiler by incorporating
elaborate firebox arrangements. A typical
Beattie firebox had two compartments,
divided by a water-filled partition. Heavy
firing took place in the rear portion, the
forward fire being kept as far as possible
in an incandescent state. Like Kirtley, he
made great use of the 2-4-0 type, both in
tender form as an express-engine and as
a tank-engine for suburban work. He was
determined to obtain the maximum
steam output from every ounce of coal,
and his express 2-4-0s also featured
combustion chambers, thermic siphons
and auxiliary chimneys. His 2-4-0 tank-
engines carried their water supply in a
well-tank between the frames. In 1874,
88 entered service.

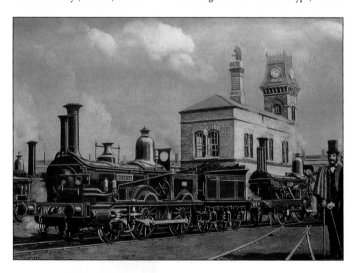

STIRLING SINGLE	
Date	1870
Builder	Doncaster, Yorkshire, England
Client	Great Northern Railway (GNR)
Gauge	4 ft 8½ in
Type	2-4-0
Driving wheels	8 ft 1 in
Capacity	2 cylinders 18 x 28 in outside
Pressure	140 lb
Weight	38 tons 9 cwt

● ABOVE
Joseph Beattie's L&SWR express 2-4-0 Medusa, fitted with double firebox and
auxiliary chimney, as captured by artist Cuthbert Hamilton Ellis (born 1909).

BRITISH LOCOMOTIVES – 1875–1900

In 1882 Francis William Webb designed a three-cylinder compound express-engine with uncoupled driving wheels – the 2-2-2-0. The engine, LNWR No. 66 Experiment, had two outside high-pressure cylinders driving the rear axle and one huge low-pressure cylinder between the frames driving the leading axle. The absence of coupling-rods meant that one pair of wheels could slip without the other, and it was not unknown for the driving wheels to revolve in opposite directions when attempts were made to start the train. The best of this type were the Teutonics introduced in 1889, with their larger boilers and 7 ft 1 in driving wheels.

The first main-line 0-8-0 tender-engine to run in Britain was introduced on the newly opened Barry Railway in 1889. Built by Sharp, Stewart of Glasgow, they proved ideal for hauling heavy South Wales coal-trains, with their 18 x 26 in outside-cylinders and 4 ft-3 in driving wheels.

● **ABOVE**
The Jones Goods engines of 1894 were Britain's first 4-6-0s. No. 103 shows off its immaculate Highland Railway livery and Jones's louvred chimney.

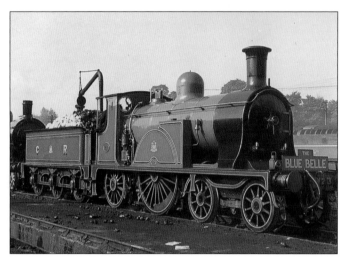

● **ABOVE**
F.W. Webb's LNWR Precedent 2-4-0s were introduced in 1874. By 1882, the Crewe works had built 90 examples. They performed prodigious feats of haulage, culminating in No. 790 Hardwicke's performance in the 1895 Race to the North. Although Webb tried to displace them from top-link work with his compounds, the little 2-4-0s were the most reliable of all 19th-century LNWR passenger types.

● **LEFT**
A Neilson & Co. 4-2-2 with 7 ft driving wheels. Built in 1886, it is seen here in 1963, before heading the Blue Belle excursion.

● **OPPOSITE**
This Johnson Single of the former Midland Railway is one of a class known as Spinners, regarded by many as the most beautiful locomotives of all time. With variations, the class totalled 95 engines, all in service by 1900.

● **ABOVE LEFT**
Ivatt's Great Northern No. 990 was the first British Atlantic 4-4-2 and was built at Doncaster Works, Yorkshire, in 1898. Ten more were in service by 1900. In 1902, a larger boiler version appeared, No. 251, which was the first of one of Britain's most successful express-passenger types. Both the original engines are preserved and are shown here running together.

● **ABOVE RIGHT**
Nicknamed Cauliflowers because of the appearance of the LNWR coat of arms on their driving splashers resembling that vegetable, these were F.W. Webb's 18 in express goods-engines, 310 of which were built between 1880 and the turn of the century.

A serious problem on many railways was the blowing back of the exhaust into the crew's faces as they descended gradients. To remedy this, in 1877 David Jones of the Highland Railway introduced locomotives with a louvred chimney. This produced a current of air that lifted the exhaust above the cab. Jones also introduced a counter-pressure brake to assist in controlling trains descending the formidable Highland gradients. His most famous locomotives were his 4-6-0s of 1894, the first engines of this wheel arrangement to work in the

British Isles. Sharp, Stewart built 15, which were, at the time, the most powerful main-line engines in Britain.

Few inside-cylinder 4-4-0s surpassed Dugald Drummond's famed T9s of 1899 for the London & South Western Railway (L&SWR). By extending the coupled wheelbase of his earlier designs to 10 ft, he made room in his T9s for a large firebox. The new engines were a success. With their 6 ft 7 in driving wheels, they were fast and able to haul heavy expresses over the difficult South Western main line west of Salisbury, Wiltshire.

CAULIFLOWER	
Date	1880
Builder	F.W. Webb, Crewe Works, Cheshire, England
Client	London & North Western Railway (LNWR)
Gauge	4 ft 8½ in
Type	0-6-0
Driving wheels	5 ft 2 in
Capacity	Cylinders 18 in x 24 in
Pressure	150 lb
Weight	36 tons

BRITISH BUILDERS OF THE 19TH CENTURY

Britain's railways were developed piece-meal by private companies with loco-motives coming from outside firms, but once the operating companies joined together to form larger organizations they established their own works for over-hauling and building. These company workshops caused places like Crewe (LNWR), Doncaster (GNR), Derby (MR) and Swindon (GWR) to become known as the Railway Towns. Tens of thousands of locomotives were built in these and other towns – over 7,000 in Crewe alone – all for home use rather than export.

The first centre of locomotive building in Britain was established in the mining town of Newcastle in 1821 when George Stephenson and his son Robert opened the world's first workshop dedicated solely to locomotive building. By 1855 the company had built more than 1,000 for Britain and the rest of the world. In 1899 the private company was shut down and a new limited company took its place.

One of the first builders of loco-motives in Leeds was Fenton, Murray & Wood. Founded in 1795, their first locomotive, "Prince Regent", was built for Middleton Colliery in 1812. Although the company only built five more

● **ABOVE LEFT**
Charles Beyer (1813–76) of the locomotive building partnership Beyer Peacock.

● **ABOVE RIGHT**
Richard Peacock of the locomotive building partnership Beyer Peacock.

● **LEFT**
Beyer Peacock letterhead.

● **ABOVE**
Works plate from Kitson & Co., Leeds, one of the Leeds builders who made that city famous across the world.

● **ABOVE**
Another great Glasgow builder, Sharp, Stewart, who had moved to Springburn from Great Bridgwater Street in Manchester.

● **ABOVE**
A plate of Falcon Engine and Car Works Company of Loughborough – the forerunner of the famous Brush Works, which continues the tradition of building hi-tech locomotives for today's railway.

● **RIGHT**
A 4-6-0 locomotive built by Robert Stephenson of Newcastle.

● **BELOW LEFT**
The Greek god of Fire used as the symbol for Charles Tayleur & Co., whose works became the famous Vulcan Foundry.

● **BELOW RIGHT**
James Naysmyth, legendary Victorian engineer and founder of Naysmyth Wilson Patricroft Locomotive Works.

locomotives, one of Murray's apprentices, Charles Todd, went on to found his own business, with James Kitson, in 1835. At first they built only parts, but by 1838 they had produced their first complete locomotive. It was so large that they had to pull down one of the workshop walls before it could be delivered.

One of the earliest manufacturers of locomotives in Manchester was William Fairbairn, who had founded an iron foundry in 1816 and who entered into locomotive building in 1839. In 1863, having built about 400 locomotives, the firm was taken over by Sharp, Stewart & Co., a firm which had been established in

● **ABOVE**
Dübs works plate from an early Spanish locomotive.

● **RIGHT**
Henry Dübs, one of the great Glasgow builders, whose works were in Polmadie.

1828 by Thomas Sharp and Richard Roberts. By the 1880s Sharp, Stewart had expanded so much that they left their Manchester foundries and relocated in Glasgow. In 1903 the three firms of Sharp, Stewart, Neilson Reid and Henry Dübs merged to become the North British Locomotive Company Ltd. Another of the great Manchester builders was Beyer, Peacock & Co., which, unlike the companies mentioned so far, had been founded, in 1854, purely as a locomotive building works.

One of the earliest building firms founded in Glasgow was that of Walter Neilson and James Mitchell. Although they had commenced the production of stationary engines in 1830, it was not

until 1843 that they produced their first locomotives. By 1860 the small works could not keep pace with orders, and a new foundry was built in Finniston. Even this factory soon became too small, and in 1861 work began on new premises in Springburn. The firm's locomotives were exported to many countries, including India, South Africa and Argentina. In 1864 Henry Dübs left the company to establish his own locomotive factory at Polmadie. Within three years the firm had achieved such a reputation that it was exporting to India, Cuba, Spain, Finland and Russia.

The great export trade that developed as Britain took railways to many parts of the world continued to be developed by private builders who in turn made cities like Manchester, Leeds, Newcastle and Glasgow famous throughout the world.

EARLY NORTH AMERICAN LOCOMOTIVES

Horse-drawn railways for hauling coal first appeared in the United States of America from about 1826. Then, having heard of events in England, in 1828 a commission of three American engineers visited the works of Robert Stephenson in Newcastle upon Tyne, the great engineering centre, and those of Foster, Rastrick & Co. in Stourbridge, a market-town and manufacturing centre in Worcestershire, west central England. The result of this visit was that, the next year, four locomotives were ordered, one from Stephenson and three from Foster, Rastrick. Stephenson's was delivered first in January 1829, but, for reasons which are unclear, it was not put into service. Foster, Rastrick's Stourbridge Lion arrived next and was the first steam-driven locomotive put into operation in the USA.

● **LEFT**
The York was Phineas Davis's winning entry in the 1831 Baltimore & Ohio locomotive competition. Like many early American designs, it featured a vertical boiler – but this style was called a "cheese".

● **MATTHIAS BALDWIN**

The second Stephenson locomotive sent to America, a six-wheeler built in 1829, had, like the first, bar-frames. This type of design, soon to be abandoned in

● **ABOVE**
Ross Winans built vertical-boiler, vertical-cylinder locomotives called "grasshoppers" for the Baltimore & Ohio line, at its Mount Claire Shops, Baltimore, Maryland. In 1927, for its "Fair of the Iron Horse", B&O posed the Andrew Jackson of about 1835 as the Thomas Jefferson.

Britain, remained the standard in America for many years. Stephenson's third, a Planet-type 2-2-0, was delivered to the Mohawk & Hudson Railway (M&HR) in 1832. This was examined by Matthias Baldwin who went on to build Old Ironside, which on its first run reached 30 mph.

At about the same time, Stephenson sent another locomotive to the Camden & Amboy Railroad & Transportation Co. (C&AR&TC). Camden is a seaport in New Jersey, which became a terminus in 1834, Amboy is in Illinois. The locomotive had a circular boiler and domed "haystack" firebox. A year after its arrival, its front wheels were removed and a four-wheeled bogie with a cowcatcher substituted, to make it suitable for local conditions. It entered service in November 1831 at Bordentown, New Jersey. The oldest complete locomotive in the USA, it was brought out of retirement in 1893 to haul a train of two 1836-type C&A passenger-coaches. The train did the 1,481 km (920 miles) from New York City to Chicago in five days.

● **LEFT**
The De Witt Clinton was built for the Mohawk & Hudson line by the West Point Foundry, New York, in 1831.

● PETER COOPER

In 1830, the Baltimore & Ohio (B&O) line put into service Peter Cooper's Tom Thumb, on the 21 km (13 mile) stretch across Maryland between Baltimore and Ellicott's Mill. This was more of a scientific model than a proper locomotive, but it convinced American business that steam traction was a practical thing. The same year, the West Point Foundry of New York City constructed the first all-American-built locomotive, "The Best Friend of Charleston", for the South Carolina Railroad (SCR). In 1832, the same foundry completed Experiment, later named Brother Jonathan. This, the first locomotive in the USA to incorporate a leading bogie, was also the

first to operate on a regular scheduled run. The locomotive came to a premature end when its vertical bottle-like boiler burst.

In 1831, the De Witt Clinton, built by the West Point Foundry, made her first journey on the M&HR line. The locomotive, with cylinders mounted either side of the footplate's rear, reached 15 mph on the Albany-Schenectady line, which had been built across New York state to connect the two eponymous rivers. It could not have been a successful engine, for it was scrapped in 1835.

● **ABOVE AND INSET**
Camden & Amboy's first locomotive, John Bull, was built by Stephenson in England. It was assembled in the USA by Isaac Dripps. He added a pilot, making it the first locomotive in America to employ a cowcatcher pilot.

TOM THUMB

Date	1830
Builder	Peter Cooper, New York, USA
Client	Baltimore & Ohio (B&O)
Gauge	4 ft 8½ in
Driving wheels	2-2-0
Capacity	2 cylinders 3 x 14 in

● **RIGHT**
In 1830, New York businessman Peter Cooper demonstrated the first American-built locomotive on the Baltimore & Ohio railroad. This locomotive was later named Tom Thumb. A 1926 replica poses here.

EARLY BALDWIN LOCOMOTIVES

In 1834, Baldwin, having already built Old Ironside, produced his second engine, the E.L. Miller. This was for the Charleston and Hamburg Railroad (C&HR). Old Ironside's composite wood-and-iron wheels had proved fragile, so Baldwin fitted his six-wheeled machine with solid bell-metal driving wheels of 4 ft 6 in in diameter. A sister locomotive, Lancaster, appeared in June the same year and promptly set an American record by hauling 19 loaded cars over Pennsylvania's highest gradients between Philadelphia and Columbia. This persuaded the railway's directors to adopt steam power instead of horse traction and they placed an order with Baldwin for five more locomotives. The first Baldwin engine to

● LEFT
This Class 152 2-6-0 is typical of early wagontop boilered Moguls from Baldwin. The usual array of fluted and flanged domes, diamond chimney, short smokebox, cross-head-driven boiler-feed pump with back-up injector is completed by a decorated headlight.

have outside-cylinders, the Black Hawk, was delivered to the Philadelphia & Trenton Railroad (P&TR) in 1835.

● POWER DEMANDED

Railways were now demanding more powerful locomotives. Baldwin considered there was no advantage in the eight-wheeled engine, arguing it would not turn a corner without slipping one or more pairs of wheels sideways. None the less, in May 1837, he built his first eight-wheeler. Baldwin's outside-cylindered 0-8-0 Ironton of 1846 had the two leading coupled axles on a flexible beam truck, allowing lateral motion and the relatively long wheelbase to accommodate itself to curves.

● CONCERNS ABOUT ADHESION

As railroads spread, so 1:50 gradients or steeper were met, bringing concerns about adhesion. Baldwin's initial response was to incorporate a supplementary pair of smaller-diameter wheels on an independent axle, driven by cranks from the main driving wheels. The first such engine was sold to the Sugarloaf Coal Co. in August 1841. On a trial run,

it hauled 590 tons across Pennsylvania from Reading to Philadelphia, a distance of 87 km (54 miles) in 5 hours 22 minutes, yet another American speed-and-haulage record.

Baldwin's classic locomotive development for heavy freightwork was the 2-6-0- Mogul. In this design, he substituted an extra pair of coupled wheels and single carrying-axle for the leading bogie of the classic American 4-4-0 passenger-engine. The result was a machine that could also be turned to passenger work in mountainous country.

Baldwin's earliest locomotives were built at Matty, his modest assembly-shop in Lodge Alley, Philadelphia. The company he formed became the world's largest locomotive-builder. In the 117-year history of Baldwin Locomotives' work more than 7,000 engines were built.

OLD IRONSIDES

Date	1832
Builder	Baldwin, Philadelphia, Pennsylvania, USA
Client	Camden & Amboy Railroad (C&AR)
Gauge	4 ft 8½ in
Driving wheels	4 ft 6 in
Capacity	2 cylinders 9½ x 18 in

● OPPOSITE TOP, INSET
The builder's plate of the Baldwin-built 2-6-0 Mogul No. 20, Tahoe.

● OPPOSITE TOP
Matty Baldwin's first locomotive-building shop, in Lodge Alley, Philadelphia.

● OPPOSITE BOTTOM
The Tahoe, a Baldwin-built 2-6-0 Mogul-type, once operated by the Virginia & Truckee (V&T) line in Nevada, displayed at the Railroad Museum of Pennsylvania, Stroudsburg, Pennsylvania.

● RIGHT
From the early years, Baldwin built many saddle-tanks of distinctive generic appearance. This veteran, working at the E.G. Lavandero Sugar Mill, Cuba, is typical.

AMERICAN LOCOMOTIVES – 1840–75

The years between 1840 and the American Civil War (1861–5) saw locomotive production treble. By the end of the 1850s, not only were there 11 main American builders but they had also progressed beyond the experimental stage to bulk production of well-defined standard types suited to local conditions.

With the development of the railroad over the Appalachian Mountains, separating the American East from the West, Richard Norris & Son of Philadelphia, Pennsylvania, extended the classic 4-4-0 by adding an extra coupled axle at the rear to become the 4-6-0 type ("Ten-Wheeler"). This allowed a much larger boiler and the extra pair of drivers gave 50 per cent extra adhesion to cope with steep gradients. The use of bar-frames by American locomotive builders allowed the simple enlargement of existing designs without needing to retool or create more workshop capacity.

● **RIGHT**
The Pioneer, a 2-2-2 single-driver "bicycle"-type built in 1851 by Seth Wilmarth for the Cumberland Valley Railroad. This was the first locomotive to operate in Chicago.

● **LEFT**
The railroad depot at Nashville, Tennessee, during the American Civil War.

● **BELOW**
This replica of the Central Pacific Railway's 4-4-0 Jupiter and Union Pacific Railroad's No. 119 stands at the Golden Spike National Monument, Promontory, Promontory Point, Utah.

● **RIGHT**
A typical American express train of the 1860s headed by a 4-4-0. This was the most important type of American locomotive providing the flexibility for running at speeds over lightly laid and often rough track beds.

● MOGULS AND CONSOLIDATIONS

Many American engineers became concerned that the increasing length of locomotive boilers interfered with the driver's view. In 1853 Samuel J. Hayes of the Baltimore & Ohio Railroad (B&OR) built a 4-6-0 with the cab perched on top of the boiler, surrounding the steam dome. It looked strange but the mechanical design was sound. The layout was copied by other builders.

In the 1860s, the New Jersey Railroad Co. (NJRC) was an early customer for the Baldwin 2-6-0 Mogul freight locomotives already described. As line speeds rose and trains became heavier still, an even larger freight engine was needed. In 1866, the Lehigh & Mahoning Railroad (L&MR), eponymous with rivers in Pennsylvania and Ohio, added a leading two-wheeled truck to the 0-8-0 design to create the Consolidation, the name by which heavy-freight 2-8-0s were henceforth known.

● **ABOVE**
The 1855 Brooks-built General, owned by the Western & Atlantic Railroad (W&AR), is famous for its role in the American Civil War. It was stolen from the Confederacy by Union spies and involved in a great chase. This is a typical 4-4-0 American-type of the period.

ATLAS	
Date	1846
Builder	Baldwin, Philadelphia, Pennsylvania, USA
Client	Philadelphia & Reading
Wheels	0-8-0
Capacity	Cylinders 16½ x 18½ in
Weight	23.7 tons

Transcontinental links were planned in 1862 as part of President Lincoln's aim to unite the North and preserve the Union. As the 1860s ended, the last rails of the Union Pacific Railroad (UPR) and the Central Pacific Railway (CPR) were joined at Promontory, near Ogden, Utah. CPR President Leland Stanford, who had built eastwards from California, drove in the gold spike to fasten the track when the two lines met to form the first American transcontinental railway on 10 May 1869. The event, commemorated by the Golden Spike Monument, linked the Atlantic and Pacific Oceans by rail and left the way open to the large and powerful locomotives that were to come, serving settlement of the West, which now leapt ahead.

AMERICAN LOCOMOTIVES – 1875–1900

Industrialization and modernization meant free time and more spending money for the American workforce to buy things such as day trips and holidays. To meet this demand, in the late 1870s heavy traffic developed, especially weekend travel between Philadelphia and New Jersey. This called for longer passenger-trains and faster schedules.

● AIR-BRAKES AND ANTHRACITE

Until the 1870s, the 4-4-0 engine proved ideal for American railroads. Then, faster, heavier traffic began to demand something larger. Bigger locomotives led to heavier rails, stronger bridges, bigger turntables, better cars, longer passing-loops and, most important of all, air-brakes. George Westinghouse's

● **ABOVE**
The 4-4-0 American type was the universal locomotive from about 1850 to 1895. More than 24,000 were built. On this high-drivered Philadelphia & Reading camelback-design 4-4-0, the engineer rides above the boiler, the fireman behind.

● **LEFT**
The 2-8-0 type was popular with narrow-gauge railroads for high adhesion on mountain rails. This 1881 Baldwin, built for the D&RG, is displayed at the Colorado Railroad Museum, Golden, Colorado.

CHICAGO BURLINGTON & QUINCY 2-4-2	
Date	1895
Builder	Baldwin, Philadelphia, Pennsylvania, USA
Client	Chicago Burlington & Quincy (CB&Q)
Gauge	4 ft 8½ in
Driving wheels	7 ft ¼ in
Capacity	Cylinders 19 x 26 in

● **LEFT**
This 1895 Baldwin-built 36 in gauge 2-8-0 Consolidation-type was typical of locomotives operating in Colorado before the turn of the century. It first operated on the Florence & Cripple Creek Railroad (F&CCR) and later on the Denver & Rio Grande (D&RG). It is displayed at Durango, Colorado.

● LEFT
When built in 1886, this Baldwin 2-10-0 "Decapod" was reported to be the world's largest locomotive. No. 500 and its sister No. 501 beat a temporary track across the mountains while a tunnel was being completed.

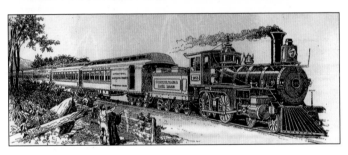

● ABOVE
A 4-4-0 on the Pennsylvania Railroad.

compressed air-brake replaced hand-brakes almost immediately after he introduced it in 1868, allowing the high speed of modern trains.

Baldwin's 5,000th production was the 4-2-2 Lovett Eames. Built in 1880, the locomotive was fitted with a wide-grate Wootten firebox for burning anthracite coal, a fuel fast replacing coke and wood. The 6 ft 6 in driving wheels made the locomotive well suited for high-speed passenger service: Baldwin guaranteed it would maintain a 60 mph average speed pulling four cars. It was to have been No. 507 of the Philadelphia & Reading Railroad (P&RR) but only ran trials before the railroad went bankrupt and returned it to her builder.

● "DECAPOD" – WORLD'S LARGEST LOCOMOTIVE

Six years later, Baldwin produced what was reported to be the largest locomotive in the world – a 2-10-0 "Decapod". Its

● BELOW
A 4-4-0 built in 1881 by Sharp, Stewart, of Glasgow, Scotland, for the St John & Maine Railroad (SJ&MR), linking St John and Maine.

ten 3 ft 9 in driving wheels were intended as much for spreading its great weight over as many axles as possible as they were for gaining adhesion on a temporary track over the mountains while a tunnel was being driven. To facilitate negotiating tight curves, the second and third pairs of drivers were flangeless. A rival claimant for the title of largest engine in the world was the 4-8-0 Mastodon heavyfreight engine of the 1890s.

The American type 4-4-0 was eclipsed on all major railroads by the end of the century. Its final flowering, in 1893, was the L Class of New York Central Railroad (NYCR). That year, No. 999 topped 100 mph at the head of the Empire State Limited between New York City and Buffalo.

AMERICAN LOCOMOTIVE BUILDERS

The first British locomotive was imported into the USA in 1829. Within a year the first American-built machine, "The Best Friend of Charleston", from the West Point Foundry of New York City, was on the rails. By the end of the 1830s, about a dozen workshops had tried their hands at locomotive-building. By 1840, as railways were being built or projected in all parts of the USA, the three main American builders – Baldwin, Norris and Rogers – had made 246 locomotives between them, the first two in Philadelphia, the third in New Jersey.

● STANDARDIZATION OF COMPONENTS

In the USA, as in Britain, there were operating-company workshops as well as private builders. Generally, company shops concentrated on repair and main-tenance, leaving building of complete locomotives to private companies. An exception was the Pennsylvania Railroad's Altoona Works, which began locomotive production in 1866 and quickly standardized components within classes. This was a great improvement because, at this time, locomotives were still mainly handbuilt, meaning it was rarely possible to interchange parts, even on locomotives of the same type from the same builder.

● ABOVE
Baldwin's erecting shop (*The American Railway*, 1892).

● BELOW
The William Crooks was the first locomotive to operate in Minnesota. It was built by the New Jersey Machine Works in Paterson, New Jersey, in 1861 for the St Paul & Pacific Railroad (SP&PR), a predecessor of American railway pioneering entrepreneur James J. Hill's Great Northern Railway (GNR). Hill was nicknamed "the Empire Builder".

Rogers Locomotive and Machine Works,

Of PATERSON, N. J.   *New York Office:* 44 EXCHANGE PLACE.

Manufacturers of

LOCOMOTIVE ENGINES AND TENDERS.

AND OTHER RAILROAD MACHINERY.

J. S. ROGERS, Pres't,
R. S. HUGHES, Sec'y,   } PATERSON, N. J.
WM. S. HUDSON, Sup't,

ROBT. S. HUCHES Treas.
44 Exchange Place New York.

Poor's Manual of Railroads, 1879.

- **LEFT**
Rogers Locomotive and Machine Works, of
New Jersey, one of the USA's most important.
The works produced 6,200 locomotives in the
76 years 1837–1913.

- **ABOVE RIGHT**
A Baldwin builder's plate dated 1878, found
on a locomotive shipped to Cuba.

- **BELOW LEFT**
Manchester Locomotives Works, of
Manchester, New Hampshire, built this high-
drivered 4-4-0 American type for the Boston &
Maine Railroad (B&MR).

- **BELOW**
Florence & Cripple Creek Railroad's No. 20, a
36 in gauge Schenectady-built 4-6-0, later used
by the Rio Grande Southern Railroad.

- **BOTTOM**
The numberplate for Duluth & Northern
Minnesota's No. 14, a Baldwin 2-8-2 Mikado-
type built in 1912.

• SPECIALISTS TAILOR-MADE FOR INDUSTRY

Apart from main-line railroads, rail
transport was spreading widely across
industry, and specialist locomotive-
manufacturers sprang up to tailor-make
machines for industry's needs. Doyen of
these was Ephraim Shay, a sawmill-owner
from Haring, Michigan. He brought
timber down from forests on temporary,
corkscrew tracks. As these could not
stand the weight of a conventional
locomotive, he designed his own. In
1880, he mounted a boiler in the centre
of a flat bogie-car. This was offset to one
side, to allow a pair of vertical cylinders
to drive a horizontal shaft turning along
the locomotive's right-hand side at
wheel-centre level. This engine was
nothing like a conventional locomotive,
but it was perfect for its job.

• VOLUME OUTPUT FROM FACTORIES

Before 1880, most American locomotives
were fairly small machines of weights
rarely exceeding 30 tons. This meant
they could be built in small workshops
without the need for big overhead cranes
and their bar-frame components could
be made by hand in an ordinary black-
smith's forge. However, by 1890, locomotives had grown so much in size that
traditional shops had become useless.
The largest builders, such as Baldwin and
Cook, set up multi-storied factories with
heavy-duty power cranes to build
locomotives on a volume-production
scale. Smaller firms could no longer
compete and collapsed financially.

CANADIAN LOCOMOTIVES

Canada's first railway was a wooden tramway in Quebec extending just more than 27 km (17 miles) between Laprairie and St Johns. The line, opened for traffic in 1832, was for combining rail and water transport via the Hudson and Richelieu rivers. In the first winter of operation, the wooden rails were torn up by adverse weather. The next spring, metal rails replaced them.

● AMERICAN ENGINES

In July 1836, the Champlain & St Lawrence Railroad (C&SLR) was opened. Its first train was pulled by horses because the Canadian engineer could not get the English-built locomotive, Stephenson's 0-4-0 Dorchester, nicknamed "Kitten", to work. An engineer from the USA found that all it needed was "plenty of wood and water", and eventually it built up steam and managed an "extraordinary" 20 mph.

Canadian steam locomotives displayed British and American characteristics and the classic American-outline 4-4-0 was popular. Canadian winter conditions could play havoc with the track, and the American design proved more satisfactory than the British-style 2-4-0 with its relatively rigid wheelbase. American 4-4-0s were supplied in quantities to Canada in the 1870s and were regarded as a general-service type.

● ABOVE
The Samson was built in 1838 by Hackworth, of Wylam, Northumberland, in England for use in Canada. It was the first locomotive to operate in Nova Scotia and one of the earliest used in Canada.

● BELOW
The Countess of Dufferin, a typically Canadian 4-4-0, was the first locomotive put into service on the Canadian Pacific Railway (CPR).

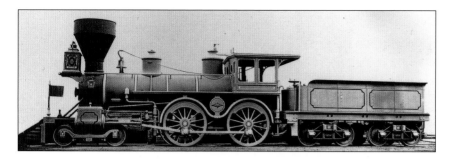

● **LEFT**
A 4-4-0 built in 1870 by Dübs, of Glasgow, Scotland, for the Canadian ICR. Note the ornate headlamp and wheel bosses.

● **RIGHT**
In 1868, a 4-4-0 was built by Neilson of Glasgow, Scotland, for the 5 ft 6½ in-gauge Canadian Grand Trunk Railway (CGTR). The massive spark-arrester chimney top was 6 ft wide.

● **COUNTESS OF DUFFERIN**

The Countess of Dufferin was built by Baldwin in 1872 and used on governmental contracts in Manitoba, Canada's easternmost Prairie Province, before going to the Canadian Pacific Railway (CPR) in 1883 – the same year the CPR built its first locomotive. Designed by the Scottish engineer F.R.F. Brown, it was a typical "American" type 4-4-0 with 5 ft-2 in coupled wheels. Canada followed American locomotive practice very closely, but there were subtle differences. The Countess featured a British-style parallel boiler, not the steeply coned American wagon-top pattern; the spark-arresting stack's shape bespoke Canadian rather than American design.

However, the wagon-top boiler did feature in the early Canadian 4-6-0 and 2-8-0 designs. Its provision for additional steam space over the firebox crown, the hottest part of the boiler, helped avoid priming, particularly when locomotives were tackling the 1:25 gradients of the CPR's Rocky Mountain section. On this section, passenger- and freight-trains were handled by small-wheeled 2-8-0s, loads often limited to no more than two bogie-cars per locomotive. When a long train had to be worked over the mountains, engines were interspersed through the train at two-car intervals. By the end of the 19th century, coal replaced wood as fuel, and the need for hitherto prominent spark-arrester chimneys ceased.

A 4-4-0	
Date	1868
Builder	Neilson, Glasgow, Scotland
Client	Canadian Grand Trunk Railway (CGTR)
Gauge	5 ft 6½ in
Driving wheels	4-4-0
Capacity	Cylinders

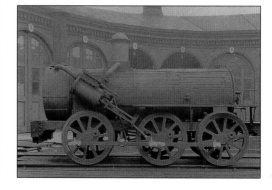

● **LEFT**
The Albion, often cited as the third locomotive to operate in Canada, was made by Rayne & Burn at Newcastle upon Tyne, England. This locomotive is often misrepresented as a Hackworth product.

EARLY EUROPEAN LOCOMOTIVES

The first locomotive built on mainland Europe was the unsuccessful Berliner Dampfwagen 1, a 0-4-0, constructed in Germany in 1816 for the horse-drawn Köningsgrube Tramway. The first successful steam trials in Europe were on the Saint-Etienne & Lyons Railway in 1828, using a pair of early Stephenson engines. In November 1829, French engineer Marc Séguin put his own engine into service on the line. It had a multi-tubular boiler with huge rotary fans, mounted on the tender and blowing fire through leather pipes. It could pull up to 18 tons but could not exceed 2 mph.

AJAX	
Date	1841
Client	Austrian North Railway
Gauge	1,435 mm
Driving wheels	0-6-0

● **BELOW**
Der Adler, the first steam locomotive used on the Nuremberg-Fürth Railway, Bavaria, on 7 December 1835.

● **ALTERNATING SAWS**
Séguin produced two more locomotives. They went into service but had problems with belt-driven bellows mounted in the tender. These continually broke down from lack of steam. To allow for this, a wagon with four horses always accompanied the locomotive to provide traction should it be needed. These faults were ironed out, and by 1835 Séguin had completed 12 more locomotives of the same type that, because of the action of the levers, were referred to as *scieurs de long*, "alternating saws".

FIRST IN GERMANY AND THE NETHERLANDS

The inaugural locomotive used in 1835 on Germany's first steam railway, in Bavaria, between Nuremberg and Fürth, was Der Adler. This 2-2-2 Patentee-type, built by Stephenson, had outside-frames and an enormously tall chimney of small diameter. It became popular in Europe and was the first locomotive introduced into several countries, including the Netherlands in 1839 when one opened the country's first line, in North Holland province, between Amsterdam, the commercial capital, and Haarlem 19 km (12 miles) west.

AUSTRIAN EMPIRE'S FIRST

The first steam railway in the Austrian Empire was the Kaiser Ferdinand Nordbahn, which opened in 1837 using two Stephenson Planet-type locomotives, the Austria and the Moravia. Robert Stephenson's assistant John Haswell (1812–97) accompanied the engines to Vienna and stayed on to take charge of the rail workshops there. He was responsible for much early Austrian locomotive development.

BRITISH INFLUENCE IN RUSSIA

Russia's first public railway was opened in 1837 between the royal centres of St Petersburg, the capital (1712–1914), and Tsarskoye Selo – "The Tsar's Village" summer residence 24 km (15 miles) south. Its first three locomotives were all Patentee 2-2-2s, one each from Timothy Hackworth, Robert Stephenson & Co. and Tayleur & Co. However, the first Russian-built engine was already at work on an industrial line in the Urals. This was a 2-2-0, built in 1833 by M. Cherepanov, a man who had seen early Stephenson locomotives in action in England.

● **ABOVE**
A Buddicom 2-2-2 locomotive built for the Paris-Rouen Railway in 1843. It could average 38 mph and is pictured arriving for display at the Festival of Britain in London in 1951.

● **BELOW**
Ajax, built by Isambard Kingdom Brunel in 1841 for the Austrian North Railway, entered service on the Floridsdorf-Stockerau stretch of the line, north out of Vienna.

37

EUROPE – MID-19TH CENTURY

The Alps are a mountain barrier in south Central Europe extending more than 1,000 km (650 miles) from the Mediterranean coast of France and north-west Italy through Switzerland, northern Italy and Austria to Slovenia. Their highest peak is 4,807 m (15,771 ft) Mont Blanc.

From 1844, the Austrian Government built the main line southwards from Vienna over the Alps via the Semmering Pass, 980 m (3,215 ft) above sea level. Engineer Karl Ghega used heavy gradients and severe curvature to conquer this barrier. The 29 km (18 mile) ascent from Gloggnitz to the summit is graded almost continually at 1:40. No existing locomotive was powerful enough to work trains over the pass, and it was at first thought that trains would have to be cable-hauled or worked by atmospheric power. Finally, a German technical magazine suggested a locomotive competition, on the lines of the Rainhill Trials, to find the best design of engine for mountain haulage. The Government Locomotive

● **ABOVE**
Wesel, built in 1851 by Borsig of Berlin, ran on the Cologne-Minden line across what since 1946 has been the Federal German state of North-Rhine Westphalia.

● **BELOW LEFT**
RENFE locomotive No. 030-2016, built by Kitson, Thomson & Hewitson, of Leeds in 1857, is seen here working as a station-pilot at Valencia, eastern Spain, in 1962.

● **BELOW RIGHT**
Gmunden was built in 1854 by Gunther, of the Lower Austrian town of Wiener Neustadt, for the narrow-gauge (1.106 metre) Linz-Gmunden line crossing Upper Austria.

Superintendent, Baron Engerth, agreed. The Semmering Trials were held in July 1851.

● **SEMMERING TRIALS**
Of the four entrants, three became milestone-makers in articulated-locomotive development. All four competitors more than fulfilled the test conditions, climbing the pass with the test-load faster than the required minimum speed. The winner of the first prize of 20,000 gold florins was the German entry Bavaria

● BELOW
Pfalz, a Crampton-type locomotive, was built
in 1853 by Maffei of Munich for the Bavarian
Palatine Railway. This replica is pictured in
front of locomotive sheds at Nuremberg,
Bavaria.

LIMMAT	
Date	1846
Builder	Emil Kessler, Karlsruhe, Baden, Germany
Client	Swiss Northern
Gauge	1,435 mm
Driving wheels	4-2-0
Capacity	Cylinders 14.25 x 22 mm

locally by Wilhelm Günther.

The railway bought all the engines, and Bavaria was rebuilt in 1852 by Engerth as an 0-6-0 with its tender-frames extended forward to support the firebox's weight. Thus was created the Engerth-type of semi-articulated locomotive, which became popular in Austria, France, Switzerland and Spain. Seraing was progenitor of the double-boiler Fairlie-type articulated. Wiener Neustadt's design led to the Meyer articulated-locomotive layout. Both types achieved worldwide acceptance.

built by Maffei of Munich, a 0-4-4-4 tender-locomotive with rod-coupled groups of driving wheels linked by roller chains. The other entries were Vindobona, a rigid-framed 0-8-0 by John Haswell of Vienna; Seraing, a double-boilered articulated machine by John Cockerill of Belgium; and Wiener Neustadt, a double-bogie articulated with a single boiler, built

● ANATOLE MALLET

The first compound engine was built by Swiss-born, French-educated engineer Anatole Mallet (1837–1919) in 1876 for the Bayonne and Biarritz Railway in south-western France. Steam was admitted to a single high-pressure cylinder from where it was exhausted into a larger-diameter low-pressure

cylinder, working twice over. The claimed advantage was fuel efficiency. Right to the end of steam operation, French Railways were strongly committed to compounds. Two-cylinder compounding was developed in Germany by von Borries of Hanover State Railways, who introduced his compound 2-4-0s for express work in 1880.

Limmat, a long-boilered engine built by Emil Kessler of Karlsruhe, Baden, in the German state of Württemberg, was the first locomotive to run from Zurich, Switzerland, to Baden, south-western Germany, on 19 August 1847. The line became known as the "Spanische Brötli Bahn" – a popular type of confectionery.

EUROPE TO 1900

● BELOW
This de Glehn compound running on France's Nord railway is typical of the closing years of the 19th century. Similar engines played a prolific part in express service across France and were also exported to many countries by French and other continental builders.

By 1879, the total track length on Russian railroads was 20,125 km (12,500 miles). Between 1860–90 the ever-growing demand for locomotives could not be met by Russian building alone, and many engines were imported from Britain, France, Germany and Austria. Two features of Russian locomotives of this period were the fully enclosed cabs, giving protection from harsh winters, and the promenade-deck effect, produced by handrails extending round the footplating on either side of the boiler to stop the crew slipping off in icy weather. In 1895, the first of 29 0-6-6-0 Mallet articulated-compound tender-engines was put into service, on the 3 ft 6 in gauge Vologda-Archangel railway in north Russia.

● **ALFRED DE GLEHN**
Alfred de Glehn (1848–1936), an inspired British engineer working in France as technical chief of Société Alsacienne, evolved a system of compounding using two high- and two low-pressure cylinders. His first locomotive was an advanced 4-2-2-0 in which the outside high-pressure cylinders were set well back in Crampton fashion and drove the rear-pair of uncoupled wheels. The low-pressure cylinders, set forward between the frames, drove the leading driving-axle. In partnership with Gaston du Bousquet (1839–1910), chief engineer of the Northern Railway of France, bigger, better and faster derivatives with coupled driving wheels were introduced in the 1890s, placing the Nord at the fore of high-speed locomotive performance. The first four-cylinder de Glehn compound was made in 1886 – the last in 1929.

● **KARL GÖLSDORF**
Compound locomotives were also developed in Austria by Karl Gölsdorf (1861–1916), engineer to Austrian State Railways – Österreichische Bundesbahnen (ÖBB). His earliest two-cylinder engines were freight 0-6-0s introduced

● **LEFT**
One of Europe's early, huge, heavy-hauling 0-8-0 tender-engines from the German builder Hartmann, exported to Spain in 1879.

● **ABOVE**
This Czech 0-8-0 was originally built in 1893 for the Austrian State Railways as their locomotive No. 73175, by STEG, of Vienna.

EMMETT 2-6-0T

Date	1886
Builder	Emil Kessler, Karlsruhe, Baden, Germany
Client	Portuguese CN Railway
Gauge	Metre
Driving wheels	3 ft 3½ in
Capacity	Cylinders 13 x 19 mm

● **LEFT**
In 1886 these Emmett light 2-6-0Ts were introduced by builder Emil Kessler, of Karlsruhe, capital of the then state of Baden, for Portugal's metre-gauge lines.

● **BELOW LEFT**
An early Portuguese Railways 5 ft 6 in gauge saddle-tank built by Beyer Peacock, of Manchester, England.

● **BELOW RIGHT**
This type 0-8-0 of the Volga Dam Railway was imported from Britain's Sharp, Stewart in 1871.

in 1893. Gölsdorf's main concern was to provide both passenger- and freight-engines capable of hauling trains over Alpine passes. His heavyfreight 2-8-0s, designed for the Arlberg Tunnel, and of which more than 900 were built, were so successful they lasted in service until the 1950s.

● **CAESAR FRESCOT**
In 1884, Caesar Frescot, chief mechanical engineer (CME) of the Upper Italian Railway, gave Europe its first standard-gauge 4-6-0 tender-locomotive, Vittorio Emanuele II. These locomotives, built at Turin's works, were intended for heavy passenger and freightwork over the 8 km (5 mile) long Giovi Pass railway tunnel at an altitude of 329 m (1,080 ft), across the Apennine mountain range of central Italy, linking Genoa, Turin and Milan in northern Italy. They had outside-cylinders and were decorated with much ornamental brasswork, though their appearance was spoilt by the short wheelbase bogie. They were built into the 1890s and lasted well into the 20th century.

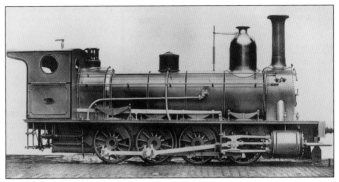

EUROPEAN BUILDERS OF THE 19TH CENTURY

One of Europe's first locomotive builders was Matthias von Schönner, the architect of the horse-drawn Budweis & Linz Railway linking the then German-named brewing city of České Budějovice, in southern Bohemia (now Czech Republic) and the Upper Austrian commercial city. Von Schönner visited America in the 1830s and was greatly influenced by the Philadelphian builder William Norris. He returned home to build the Vienna & Raub line which opened in 1842.

The Vienna & Gloggnitz Railway, immediately after opening in 1841,

● ABOVE
European builders, such as Kuntze & Jürdens of Germany, exported their locomotives as far afield as Cuba.

● ABOVE
One of Germany's most prolific locomotive builders was Henschel & Sohn whose works were in Kassel. The company built its first locomotive in 1848. Henschel produced for domestic railways and world export.

● ABOVE
Another prolific world-export market builder was Richard Hartmann, of Chemnitz, a town known as the "Saxon Manchester", standing at the base of the Erzgebirge, the "Ore Mountains" chain.

● ABOVE
The former German builder BMAG of Berlin was initially known as Schwartzkopff, as shown by this ornate maker's plate.

● ABOVE
A lesser-known German builder was Rheinische Metalfabrik of Düsseldorf, capital of North-Rhine Westphalia and commercial hub of the Rhine-Ruhr industrial area. Its name is pictured on a Class 20 2-6-0, built in 1922, of Yugoslav Railway – Jugoslovenske Železnice (JŽ).

● ABOVE
Borsig of Berlin was a prolific builder for home and export markets.

● ABOVE LEFT TO RIGHT
Orenstein & Koppel builder's plates.

● **RIGHT**
The Indian metre-gauge Class D 0-4-0 was a standard design comprising ten engines built at Sharp, Stewart's Great Bridgewater Street Foundry, Manchester, England, in 1873.

in what today is the state of Uttar Pradesh, ordered a 5 ft 6 in gauge version from Dübs of Glasgow in 1883. Despite different cab and valve arrangements, it closely resembled the Crewe original, right down to the uncoupled driving wheels.

● **BENGAL-NAGPUR LEADS DEVELOPMENT**

In the late 19th century, Indian broad-gauge locomotive practice often mirrored that on British main lines with 4-4-0s for passenger work and 0-6-0s for goods. Increasing train weights, however, pressed for the development of the small-wheeled six-coupled engine into something rather bigger for Indian conditions. Hence, the Bengal-Nagpur Railway, which linked Calcutta and the capital of the Central Provinces (later Madhya Pradesh) and was always at the fore of technical development, commissioned a class of mixed-traffic 4-6-0s, delivered between 1888–91. Aside from their headlamps and cowcatchers, they were of typical British appearance with straight running-plates, outside-cylinders and inside valve-gear.

● **LEFT**
The coat of arms of India's Bengal-Nagpur Railway (BNR).

● **LEFT**
The most celebrated of all Indian 2 ft gauge designs are the 0-4-0 saddle-tanks built for the Darjeeling Railway from 1889. The line took Bengal government officials to their hot-weather headquarters.

● **BELOW**
The metre-gauge O Class 4-4-0 was an outside-cylinder version of the early M Class. It was the standard passenger-engine on most lines. Some were superheated. The class totalled 297 examples, from six different builders between 1883–1912.

F CLASS 0-6-0	
Date	1874
Builder	Various: Britain, Germany, India
Client	Various: Indian State Railways
Gauge	Metre
Driving wheels	3 ft 6 in
Capacity	Cylinders 13 x 20 in
Weight in full working order	20 tons

CHINESE LOCOMOTIVES

China's first railway was opened in 1876 in the eastern province of Kiangsu. It was an 8 km (5 mile) long stretch of 2 ft 6 in gauge between Shanghai and Wusung, Shanghai's outport, that is a subsidiary port built in deeper water than the original port. The first locomotive on the line was the Pioneer, built by Ransomes & Rapier of Ipswich, Suffolk, England. Used by the railway's builders, this 1½ ton engine with 1 ft 6 in driving wheels had a service-truck attached on which the driver sat. The line had a short history. After it had operated for only a month, a local man was fatally injured. Riots ensued and the line was closed. A few months later, it was reopened with two 9 ton 0-4-2STs, Celestial Empire and Flowery Land, both with outside-cylinders and 2 ft 3 in wheels. On these locomotives the water-tanks, a combination of side and saddle, completely enveloped the boiler but left the smokebox clear. However, by the end

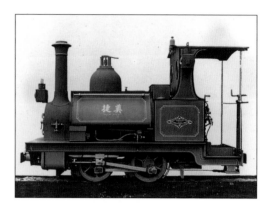

● LEFT
Built by Dübs of Glasgow, Scotland, in 1886, this 0-4-0 saddle-tank, Speedy Peace, Works No. 2254, was scrapped when more than 20 bound Chinese were thrown in the approaching engine's path as part of the uprising against railways. Note Dübs's ornately enhanced diamond workplate.

ROCKET OF CHINA	
Date	1881
Builder	C.W. Kinder
Client	Kaiping Tramway
Gauge	Narrow gauge
Driving wheels	0-6-0
Capacity	Cylinders 14.25 x 22 mm

of 1877, the Chinese authorities ordered line and engines dismantled.

● **KAIPING TRAMWAY**

The next attempt to provide a railway in China was in 1881 in the northern province of Hopeh. A mining company built the narrow-gauge Kaiping Tramway as an 8 km (5 mile) link between the Kaiping coalfield near Tangshan, north of Tientsin, and the canal that connected with the Pehtang River. At first, because of Chinese prejudices against steam locomotion, mule traction was used. C.W. Kinder, the company's resident engineer, decided nonetheless to build a steam locomotive. Using odds and ends recovered from various scrap-heaps, he secretly built a small 2-4-0 locomotive, which he named Rocket of China. When the Chinese authorities heard about the locomotive, they sent a commission to investigate. Forewarned of their imminent arrival, Kinder dug a pit and buried his engine.

● **THE CHINESE IMPERIAL RAILWAY**

In 1886 Dübs & Co. of Glasgow, Scotland, built two 0-4-0STs for a 2 ft gauge section of the Imperial Chinese Railway (ICR). Named Speedy Peace and Flying Victory, they were instantly opposed by the Chinese, who were convinced that the

● ABOVE
The Kaiping Tramway in Hopeh Province was China's first permanent railway. The 2-4-0 Rocket of China pictured here was built in China by British engineer C.W. Kinder and was the tramway's first locomotive.

● **RIGHT**
Sung Wu Railway
2-4-2T No. 2 was
built by Brooks
Locomotive Works,
Dunkirk, New York,
USA. This celebrated
American builder
produced more than
4,000 locomotives
until it combined
with seven others in
1901 to form the
American
Locomotive
Company (Alco).

● **RIGHT**
A 2-6-2 saddle-tank built by Dübs in 1887
entered service on the Tientsin Railway in
Hopeh Province.

"devil's machines" would desecrate
ancestral graves. To prevent this, many
trains were halted by Chinese being
thrown in front of the locomotives. Many
were run over and killed. After about 20
of these deaths, the line was eventually
closed and the locomotives scrapped.

● **BELOW**
This engine is an example of how American
locomotives exported to China exerted
permanent influence on developments. It was
built by Baldwin in 1899 and was No. 230 on
the Chinese Eastern Railway (CER). Although
the CER was operated by Russians, most of its
motive power was of American origin. No. 230
was one of 121 Vauclain compound 2-8-0s
built for the line by Baldwin in 1899. Samuel
Vauclain (1856–1940) worked for Baldwin for
51 years, becoming chairman in 1929. He
invented his compounding system in 1899.

EAST ASIAN RAILWAYS

In Malaya, the first train service started in 1885 in Perak State, between Taiping and Port Weld. Then, in 1886, the first section of the metre-gauge Perak Government Railway (PGR), the 11 km (7 mile) stretch between Kelung and Kuala Lumpur, Perak's capital, was opened. The railway came when the country was covered in dense jungle and transport was entirely by river. The first locomotive was a little 0-6-0 tank by Ransomes & Rapier, of Ipswich, Suffolk, England, similar to the Pioneer and one of the few built by the firm. Small tank-engines were the most suitable for the infant railway system, with the Class A 4-4-0Ts favoured. The larger B Class engines of 1890 were later developed into a tender-engine version. Malayan locomotives were distinguished by their huge headlight – a necessary item on line in dark jungle. Nonetheless, one of these locomotives was charged and derailed by a bull elephant, which lifted the tender clear off the track.

● **SINGAPORE-PENANG**

By 1909 passengers could travel by train between Singapore and Penang. Completion of the Johore Causeway in

● **RIGHT**
Indonesian State Railways (ISR) C12 Class 2-6-0 Tank No. C1206 was a two-cylinder compound built for the Staats Spoorwegen by Hartmann of Chemnitz, Germany, in 1895.

1923 brought the line into Singapore. Singapore had had a railway from Tank Road to Bukit Timah since 1903. In eastern Malaya, goods and passengers could go by train from Gemas to Kota Bharu from 1931.

● **BRITISH INFLUENCE IN JAPAN**
Japan's first line was built by British engineers in 1872. The first locomotive, a 14¼ ton 2-4-0T with 4 ft 3 in driving wheels, to run on the 3 ft 6 in gauge line was built in 1871 by the Vulcan Foundry of Newton-le-Willows, England. The early equipment on Japanese railways was almost entirely British and included some outside-cylinder 4-4-0s supplied by Dübs & Co. of Glasgow. Other British locomotives to run in Japan were made

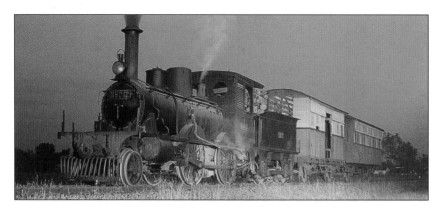

● **LEFT**
One of Java's Staats Spoorwegen B50 Class 2-4-0s, No. B5012, built by Sharp, Stewart of Great Bridgewater Street, Manchester, England, in 1884. When built, these were main-line passenger-engines for Java's 3 ft 6 in gauge lines.

by Sharp, Stewart of Manchester and by Kitson of Leeds.

One of Kitson's creations was a 0-6-0 goods-engine built in 1873, which three years later was rebuilt in the shops at Kobe, Honshu, as a 4-4-0, a type which became the standard Japanese passenger-locomotive. In 1876 Kitson built another 4-4-0, of typical British appearance, its only oriental feature being the small louvred shutter in the cab side. Class 1800s were introduced in 1881. These engines were fitted with smart copper-capped chimneys bearing the number in brass.

● AMERICAN INFLUENCE IN JAPAN
In 1897, Baldwin exported to Japan the Mikado-type. These were the first locomotives built with a 2-8-2 wheel arrangement with a tender. Named in honour of the Japanese head of state, these locomotives were designed to burn an inferior quality of coal,

requiring a large grate area and a deep, large firebox.

One of Japan's steepest railways, up to 1:40 gradient, was the Hakone line serving the eponymous mountain resort near Mount Fuji, on Honshu. For this, Moguls were bought from Rogers in 1897. Japanese railways were Americanized even more in 1900 by the introduction of Schenectady-built 4-4-0s.

● JAVA
Perhaps East Asia's most remarkable railway system was on Java whose network serving the islands was developed during the Dutch East Indies

period. The main lines were developed in the last 20 years of the 19th century. Innumerable feeder lines, known as steam tramways, joined them. A gauges battle occurred between the 3 ft 6 in gauge and the standard. For a while, a third rail was laid over the 4 ft 8½ in gauge to enable through 3 ft 6 in gauge trains to operate. The gauge was finally standardized at 3 ft 6 in.

The multiplicity of state and private enterprises that built Java's railways produced a wide diversity of motive power primarily of Dutch, German and British origin.

INDONESIAN STATE RAILWAYS (ISR) B50 CLASS 2-4-0	
Date	1880
Builder	Sharp, Stewart, Manchester, England
Client	Staats Spoorwegen
Gauge	3 ft 6 in
Driving wheels	1,413 mm
Capacity	Cylinders 381 x 457 mm

AUSTRALASIAN RAILWAYS

In the 19th century, Australia consisted of a series of separate colonies, all with administrations operating independently of each other. This, added to personalities and poor communications, led to the mess of gauge problems from which the country has suffered ever since.

The first steam locomotive to run in Australia was locally built by Robertson, Martin, Smith & Co. It entered service on the Colony of Victoria's Melbourne and Hobsons Bay Railway on 12 September 1854. New South Wales (NSW) followed by opening a 21 km (13½ mile) line from Sydney to Parramatta on 26 September 1855.

● DIFFICULT TERRAIN

Australian locomotive design was much governed by the difficult country to be traversed with mountainous country close to coast. The standard gauge in NSW had many 1:30 gradients with curves as tight as 8-chains radius on the main lines. Branch and narrow-gauge states' lines were even worse.

Early locomotives that became standards were generally of the 4-4-0 or 0-6-0 wheel arrangements and of British design or styling. Australia's most significant development was probably the

● **BELOW**
Baldwin supplied ten K(294) Class goods engines in 1885. They were put on lesser duties, including working water-trains between Lake Menindee and Broken Hill mining-town in NSW's dry west. The large wagon behind the locomotive is a 32,000 litre (7,000 gallon) water "gin" to augment the tender's supply.

● **ABOVE**
One of South Australia's Y Class "Colonial Moguls" introduced in 1886. This class originally totalled 134 examples, 58 of which were converted to YX Class with higher-pressure boilers from 1907.

CLASS K TANK	
Date	1892
Builder	Neilson Reid
Client	Western Australian Government Railways (WAGR)
Gauge	3 ft 6 in
Driving wheels	2-8-4
Capacity	Cylinders 19 x 24 in

● OPPOSITE TOP
"Number 10" was the first locomotive built in
NSW. She was a 2-4-0 designed on the
Stephenson long-boiler principle. Completed
in 1870, she was used as an express passenger-
locomotive. She is pictured at Picton Station,
south-west of Sydney, soon after entering
service.

● ABOVE
A New Zealand
Government
Railways (NZGR)
1873-built A Class
0-4-0 tank by Dübs.
These little engines,
nicknamed
"Dodos", worked
well and lasted into
the 1920s.

● RIGHT
One of 77 members
of the New South
Wales (NSW) A(93)
Class 0-6-0s,
shunting at Sydney's
Darling Harbour
goods yard.

4-6-0 type, well before Jones introduced
it to the Highland Railway in Britain. The
30 R Class was introduced from 1886 in
South Australia. The P6 Class introduced
in NSW in 1892 eventually numbered
191 units.

On the narrow gauge, Beyer, Peacock's
development of the "Colonial Mogul" had
the most impact, with 134 Y Class in
South Australia, 47 G Class in Western
Australia and 28 C Class in Tasmania.

● NEW ZEALAND'S GAUGES
New Zealand also started with a mess of
gauges. South Island had a 3 ft gauge
horse-drawn railway from Nelson, in
1862; a 5 ft 3in gauge steam railway from
Christchurch in 1863; a wooden-railed
line, worked unsuccessfully on the Davies

or Prosser principle, from Invercargill in
1864; and a 4 ft 8½ in gauge steam-line
from Invercargill in 1866. Finally, the 3 ft
6 in gauge was selected as standard and
introduced, with double Fairlie locomotives, at Dunedin in September 1872.

New Zealand had, as well as regular
designs, a great variety of types: vertical-
boilered locomotives, single- and double-
Fairlies, flangeless Prosser-types, Fell
locomotives and locally made curiosities.
Mainly, short lines radiated from coastal
ports, so the most significant design
would have been the 88-strong F Class
0-6-0T saddle-tanks.

American locomotives were more
successful in New Zealand, starting with
eight K Class supplied by Rogers
Locomotive works in 1878.

SOUTHERN AFRICAN RAILWAYS

South Africa's first public railway was a 3 km (2 mile) stretch in Natal between Durban and The Point, opened in June 1860. The locomotive was the "Natal". It was built by Carrett Marshall & Co., of Leeds, England, stripped down, crated and sent to Durban, where it was rebuilt by Henry Jacobs. The engine had a large dome cover and its chimney, of typical American design, incorporated a wire-mesh spark-arrester. This locomotive,

CLASS 6	
Date	1893
Builder	Dübs, of Glasgow, Scotland
Client	Cape Government Railway (CGR)
Gauge	3 ft 6 in
Driving wheels	4 ft 6 in
Capacity	Cylinders 17 x 26 in
Weight in full working order	80 tons

South Africa's first steam locomotive, which operated in Cape Province, was a contractor's engine for building the Cape Town – Wellington Railway in 1859. She was built by Hawthorn & Co.'s works in Leith, Scotland, as a 4 ft 8 in gauge 0-4-2. Here is the preserved veteran, proclaimed a national monument in 1936.

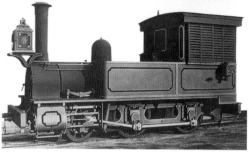

● LEFT
The first locomotive to serve the Ugandan Railway was this Dübs 2-4-0T, one of two locomotives bought secondhand from Indian State Railway (ISR). Dübs of Glasgow built 25 of these engines in 1871–2.

however, was not the first to run in South Africa, for in September 1859, E. & J. Pickering had imported a 0-4-2 built by Hawthorn & Co. of Leith, Scotland.

● KITSON VERSUS FAIRLIE
In 1875, the Cape Government Railway (CGR) introduced a back-to-back from Kitson & Co. of Leeds, Yorkshire, and a

0-6-0+0-6-0 Fairlie-type from Avonside Engine Co. of Bristol. In 1864, Robert Fairlie introduced his double-ender. This could be driven in either direction and was adopted in hilly countries where curves and gradients challenged ordinary locomotives. When the two machines were tested against each other, the Fairlie worked around curves with facility, up

● RIGHT
The Class 6s were one of the most important types in South African locomotive history. Between 1893–1904, almost all the 268 engines being built to a basic design came from Glasgow. They operated express passenger-trains across the entire republic, with the exception of Natal.

and down gradients, and the Kitson lurched badly descending a decline and was much heavier on fuel.

In 1887, Black Hawthorn, of Gateshead, County Durham, England, built a woodburning 0-4-2ST for the Cape of Good Hope & Port Elizabeth 3 ft 6 in gauge line. It had spark-arrester rails above the tank for wood storage, single slide-bars and Ramsbottom safety-valves with single exhaust.

EAST AFRICAN LINES

The two pioneer public railways in East Africa were Kenya's Mombasa & Nairobi laid in 1896 and the Usambara Railway through the eponymous highlands of

Tanga Province of German East Africa (later Tanganyika) on which work began in 1893 but was not completed until 1911. A private railway was built from Tanga to Sigi, to serve the logging interests of the Deutsche Holtzegesellschaft für Ostafrika. The first engine used on this line, naturally a woodburner, was a 0-4-2 tank built in 1893 by Vulcan of Stettin, then capital of Pomerania, a province of Prussia.

In May 1896 the first locomotives were delivered to the Ugandan Railway. They were secondhand 2-4-0Ts, bought from Indian State Railways (ISR), built in 1871 by Dübs of Glasgow, Scotland.

● **ABOVE**
The Cape Government Railway (CGR) Class 7 was a small-wheeled freight version of the Class 6 passenger-locomotive. It was introduced in 1892. More than 100 were built, all by the three Glasgow builders Dübs, Neilson and Sharp, Stewart.

● **BELOW**
These locomotives began as main-line 4-10-2Ts on the Natal Government Railway (NGR). They were among more than 100 engines built by Dübs in Polemadie, Glasgow. Replaced by tender-engines, they were converted to 4-8-2Ts for further use as shunting- and trip-engines.

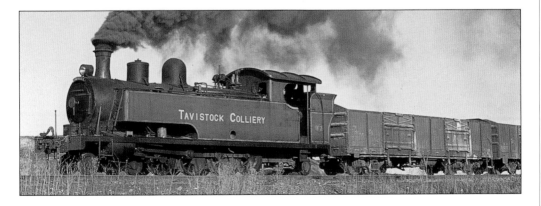

NORTHERN AFRICAN RAILWAYS

Although the first steam tramway in North Africa was built at Egypt's El Dikheila quarries near Alexandria as early as 1838, the first public railway in the region was the British-built Cairo-Alexandria line opened in 1854. By 1870, Egyptian State Railway (ESR) took delivery of a mixed collection of 241 locomotives of over 50 classes supplied by 16 builders from five countries. Besides the usual types, there were a few exotic 2-2-4T saloon locomotives to carry visiting royalty.

● F.H. TREVITHICK'S IN THE NILE VALLEY

British occupation of the Nile Valley in 1882 put railways under the direction of F. H. Trevithick, grandson of the Cornish pioneer. The first new locomotives he introduced were Great Western in concept, with inside-cylinders and strong double-frames. These frames were essential to negotiate Egypt's rough tracks. For the lightest and fastest duties, he ordered 25 2-2-2s from Kitson and the Franco-Belge Company of La Coyère. These sturdy locomotives were the last singles to work in Africa. Some were still in use in World War II.

MOGUL	2-6-0
Date	1891
Builder	Baldwin, Philadelphia, Pennsylvania, USA
Client	Bône-Guelma Railway, Algeria
Gauge	3 ft 6 in
Driving wheels	4 ft
Capacity	Cylinders 18 x 22 in

● **ABOVE**
A type 0-6-0 tender built by North British, of Glasgow, Scotland, for ESR. The driving wheels are 5 ft ¼ in diameter, the cylinders of 18 x 24 in capacity.

● BELOW
Built by Neilson, of Glasgow, Scotland, this design was on display at the Great Exhibition of 1862, where it was seen by Said Pasha, Viceroy of Egypt, who later ordered one for Egyptian State Railways (ESR).

● FRENCH DESIGN FOR ALGERIA

Algeria's railway development was put in the hands of the French Paris, Lyons & Mediterranean Company in 1863. Secondhand PLM 0-6-0s of characteristic French design were shipped to get services started. Some of these redoubtable 0-6-0 designs, as SNCFA classes 3B, 3E and 3F, were destined to last almost until the end of steam on the Algerian standard gauge. The Algiers-Oran main line opened in 1871 when more 0-6-0s were supplied, with the first of the successful 0-8-0 goods-engines of classes 4A and 4C for the 1:80 gradients up from Philippeville. Operations between Algeria and Tunisia were begun with 0-6-0s built by Batignolles. By 1883, 39 of these, assisted by 18 0-6-0Ts built by the same firm for shunting and banking, were in operation. On the 300 km (184 mile) of the Algerian Western, the sparse service was operated by 26 0-6-0s that were built by Fives Lille and SACM. These ultimately became SNCFA classes 3L and 3M. In 1899 the Bône-Guelma Railway in eastern Algeria turned to Baldwin for ten of its ready-made American-style Moguls. These performed well but were rebuilt as tank-engines in the early 20th century.

● BRITISH PRESENCE IN TUNISIA

Tunisia's first railway was built with British capital and equipment, as part of a move to extend British influence in the region. The standard-gauge line was opened from Tunis to La Marsa in 1874 using four little Sharp, Stewart 2-4-0 tanks. The Italians took over the line in 1876 and ran it until it was acquired by Algeria's Bône-Guelma Co. in 1898. In 1895, under Bône-Guelma's auspices, an extensive metre-gauge network was inaugurated along the coastal region south of Tunis. As motive power, a fleet of no fewer than 135 Mallet articulated engines was built – the largest concentration of these tank-engines in Africa. The first batch of eight 0-4-4-0s came from Batignolles to start services, and larger machines were delivered early in the new century.

SOUTH AMERICAN RAILWAYS

In 1836, three Baldwin locomotives were exported to Cuba, then a Spanish territory. These would have been for the line between the capital, Havana and the small town of Bejueal in La Habana Province. It opened in July 1837.

● LEFT
The 4-4-0 was the classic locomotive type in the first few decades of railroading in America, because it provided a good turn of speed and stability over inevitably roughly laid tracks. This example, from the 1840s-50s, was exported to Chile and is pictured in Santiago.

● **ARGENTINE CAUTION**
Railways came to Argentina in 1857 when a line opened between the towns of Parque and Floresta. The line manager had so little faith in his own product that he rode on horseback to the opening rather than trust himself to his own railway. The four-wheeled engine used on this occasion was La Portena, a locomotive which had been used in the Crimea, Ukraine.

● **AMERICAN INFLUENCE IN BRAZIL**
The first railway in Brazil, a short 5 ft 3 in gauge line in the neighbourhood of Rio de Janeiro, the then capital, opened in 1854. The inaugural train was hauled by the 2-2-2 Baroneza. The bulk of Brazil's railway track was laid to metre gauge, though in 1889 the Huain railway was built to the peculiar gauge of 3 ft 1¼ in. Most Brazilian woodburning locomotives of the 19th century were supplied by American builders. Typical was a series of relatively small 2-8-0s from Baldwin with driving wheels of only 3 ft 1 in diameter.

● BELOW
This classic 4-6-0 two-cylinder compound was built by Beyer, Peacock for the British-owned 5 ft 6 in gauge Buenos Aires and Great Southern Railway (BAGS). These locomotives were a principal express-passenger type for many years.

B CLASS	
Date	1906
Builder	Beyer, Peacock, Manchester, England
Client	Buenos Aires and Great Southern (BAGS)
Gauge	5 ft 6 in
Driving wheels	6 ft
Capacity	Cylinders 19 x 26 in (high pressure) 27½ x 26 in (low pressure)
Weight in full working order	115 tons

● LEFT
Another early 4-4-0, almost certainly of European origin and sporting a cowl, is pictured heading a tourist-train in the desert border region between Tacna in Peru and Arica in Chile, disputed territory until 1930.

● LEFT
Superficially
American in style,
this British engine
has no running-plate
but plate-frames,
splashers and a
brass dome. It was
built by Sharp,
Stewart at
Springburn Works,
Glasgow, Scotland,
in 1892 for Brazil's
metre-gauge
Mogiana Railway. It
hauled trains of
varnished teak
coaches through the
Atlantic seaboard's
lush tropical
scenery.

MEXICAN CHOICES

In Mexico, a 424 km (265 mile) line opened in 1873 between the capital Mexico City and the seaport Veracruz. The railway was an early user of double-boilered Fairlie 0-6-0 tanks. These were successful, unlike the totally impractical American-built Johnstone articulateds of 1888. These were so large they had to be partly dismantled to pass through the 2,608 m (8,560 ft) high Raton Tunnel, Colorado, during delivery. The Mexicans, ever willing to try another form of flexible wheelbase engine, in 1890 bought two Baldwin Mason-Fairlie articulated 2-6-6 tanks. This engine was essentially an American interpretation of the single Fairlie principle, with a power-bogie and a trailing-truck supporting a large boiler with deep firebox.

● ABOVE
Numberplate and worksplate of the
Leopoldina Railway.

● RIGHT
This metre-gauge
2-6-0 was one of a
class of 15 engines
built by Beyer,
Peacock of
Manchester,
England, at the end
of the 19th century
for Brazil's
Leopoldina Railway.
The Leopoldina
system, all on the
metre gauge, has
approximately
3,200 km
(2,000 miles) of
track and was
owned by the
British-controlled
Leopoldina
Railway Co.

The Golden Age
1900–50

The first half of the 20th century may truly be called the Golden Age
of railways. The railway was the primary form of transport for moving
people and freight. The railway was perceived as being the heartbeat of
society. Furthermore, throughout the period the vast majority of the
world's railways were powered by steam. The period began with a legacy
of modest 19th century locomotive designs, which rapidly gave way to
20th century concepts – larger, heavier and more powerful engines,
which by the advent of World War II had evolved almost to the ultimate
potential within the existing loading gauges. One of the many precepts
that accelerated the world change from steam to modern forms of
traction was that the necessary power and speeds demanded by railway
administrations were outstripping the capacity of steam within the
physical restrictions imposed on it.

BRITISH MAIN-LINE LOCOMOTIVES – PASSENGER

● BELOW
The 4-6-0 manifested in both inside- and outside-cylinder form. The former type shown here is one of Holden's Great Eastern engines introduced in 1911 with 6 ft 6 in-diameter wheels, which gave them speed over the flat lands of eastern England.

The turn of the century saw the elegance of the Atlantic-type locomotive established on the main lines of Britain. The type soon led to the Pacific, which in essence was an Atlantic with an extra pair of driving wheels. When Gresley introduced his A1 Pacifics to the Great Northern Railways (GNR) in 1922, they represented in terms of size and power as large an increase over the GN's biggest Atlantic as the first Atlantics of 1898 exerted over the earlier 4-4-2 singles. The Pacific represented the end of the evolutionary line. Nothing bigger ever appeared in Britain, apart from Gresley's incursions into huge 2-8-2 Mikados and his solitary 4-6-4.

The Pacific captured the popular imagination, especially during the competition for Scottish traffic over

Britain's East and West Coast routes in the early 1930s. Worldwide, the streamlined Pacifics of this decade generated much publicity. Gresley's A4s proved to be the "Concordes" of their day and have become the most celebrated British locomotive type. No. 4468

Mallard achieved the world speed record for steam traction of 126 mph in 1938.

The Pacific as an express passenger locomotive was backed up by the 4-6-0, which began to become profuse after the turn of the century. By 1923, the 4-6-0 in both two- and four-cylinder form was

● **RIGHT**
In the 1920s, need arose for an extra
passenger locomotive on Britain's Southern
Railway, one able to work a 500-ton train at an
average speed of almost one mile a minute. So,
four-cylinder Lord Nelsons were introduced.
They totalled a class of 16 engines named after
famous British Sea Lords. These engines
worked the Continental Expresses between
Victoria Station, London, and the English
channel port of Dover, and served the
south-western sections of Britain's
Southern network.

widespread, largely replacing the Atlantic.
Not until 1933 did the first Stanier
Pacific take the title of the most powerful
express-passenger-locomotive type away
from the 4-6-0. In 1930, the 4-4-0 made
its last flourish with Britain's Southern
Railway's three-cylinder Schools engine,
the most powerful of this wheel
arrangement ever to run in the country.

From the mid-1930s, the 4-6-0
became increasingly used as the basis for

powerful mixed-traffic types. In this guise,
it continued to play an important role in
main-line passenger duties. With Britain's
policy of frequent and relatively light
trains, the 4-6-0, despite its restrictive
firebox capacity, was sufficient, with the
quality of coal available, to provide the
necessary power and adhesion for most
express duties until the end of steam. The
next logical step, to the 4-8-0, although
proposed, was never taken.

● **BELOW**
Britain's Great Western Railway experimented
with compounding in 1903 when Churchward
introduced several engines on the De Glehn
system. The first engine was built at Belfort,
France, and named Le France. These compound
Atlantics did not convince the Great Western to
adopt the principle and they progressed to
ultimate success with conventional 4-6-0s of
two- and four-cylinder varieties.

PRINCESS CORONATION CLASS	
Date	1937
Builder	Crewe Works, Cheshire, England
Client	London, Midland & Scottish Railway
Gauge	Standard
Driving wheels	6 ft 9 in
Capacity	4 cylinders 16 x 28 in
Total weight in full working order	165 tons

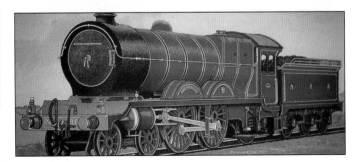

● **OPPOSITE**
William Stanier followed up his Princess Royal
Pacifics with the Princess Coronations
introduced in 1937. They hauled many of the
heaviest trains on Britain's West Coast route
until the end of steam.

● **ABOVE**
One of W.P. Read's Atlantics. These were the largest engines built for the North British
Railway. They were introduced in 1906 and given Scottish names such as Aberdonian,
Waverley and Highland Chief. They worked on the North British main lines, especially
on the heavily graded Waverley route between Edinburgh and Carlisle in Cumbria.

BRITISH MAIN-LINE LOCOMOTIVES – FREIGHT

● BELOW
Stanier's class 8F 2-8-0s were freight engines and provided Britain's LMS with a robust heavyfreight locomotive. They were a huge advance on the 0-6-0 and 0-8-0 types.

The freight locomotive's evolution was less dramatic than that of its express passenger-hauling counterpart. The inside-cylinder 0-6-0s and 0-8-0s so prolific in the late-19th century continued to be built into the 20th century, although a major advance occurred in 1903 when Churchward introduced his 2800 class 2-8-0s. The 2-8-0 was pre-eminent until the end of steam. Churchward's engines were followed by Robinson's 04s for the Great Central Railway in 1911. Two years later, the 2-8-0 was taken up by Gresley on the Great Northern Railway. The London, Midland and Scottish (LMS) built most 2-8-0s: Stanier's 8Fs for LMS totalled 772 locomotives.

The modest size of British freight engines was given a massive boost in 1927 when the LMS introduced its 2-6-6-2T Garratts. These were built by Beyer Peacock of Manchester, northern England, to alleviate the double-heading of inside-cylinder 0-6-0s on Britain's Midland main line. Of these four-cylinder giants, 33 went into operation and demonstrated a potency hitherto unknown on Britain's railways. Gresley turned to the 2-8-2 with his P1s of 1925. Two of these giants were built and hauled coal-trains weighing upwards of 2,000 tons.

The 2-8-2 was the next logical phase of development; as compared with the 2-10-1, it readily provided for a deep firebox with adequate space for the ashpan. Sadly, however, no further heavyfreight hauling 2-8-2s were ever built for use on the home railway, and the ultimate in British freight locomotives

● BELOW LEFT
Britain's first 2-10-0s were built for the Ministry of Supply in World War II by the North British works in Glasgow. With their more numerous 2-8-0 counterparts, they served in many countries during the war. The example shown here was taken into the stock of Greek State Railways.

● BELOW RIGHT
Gresley's V2 2-6-2 Green Arrow was one of the most successful classes in British locomotive history. They were true mixed-traffic engines capable of enormous haulage. They did monumental service in World War II and were popularly known in Britain as "the engines which won the war". Here, one is seen on the rollers of the British locomotive-testing plant at Swindon, Wiltshire.

was the 2-10-0. This was not truly established until the 1950s, under the British Railways (BR) standard locomotive scheme. The 2-10-0s had first appeared as an Austerity version of the World War II 2-8-0s used for military operations, but these were primarily for light-axle loadings rather than sustained heavy haulage. The BR 9Fs were mineral haulers in their own right and building continued until 1960. An engine of this design became the last main-line locomotive built for Britain. It was named Evening Star. The 9Fs had a very short life for by 1968 steam operation in Britain ceased. They went to the scrapyard with all earlier forms of British freight locomotives – inside-cylinder 0-6-0s and 0-8-0s and the main 2-8-0 types.

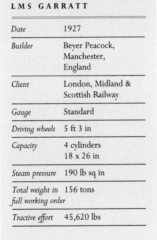

LMS GARRATT

Date	1927
Builder	Beyer Peacock, Manchester, England
Client	London, Midland & Scottish Railway
Gauge	Standard
Driving wheels	5 ft 3 in
Capacity	4 cylinders 18 x 26 in
Steam pressure	190 lb sq in
Total weight in full working order	156 tons
Tractive effort	45,620 lbs

● **ABOVE LEFT**
The inside-cylinder 4-6-0 appeared on Scotland's Caledonian Railway in 1902. Over the next 12 years, the company's chief mechanical engineer (CME) J. F. McIntosh produced six different designs totalling 42 locomotives.

● **ABOVE RIGHT**
One of Churchward's 2800-class 2-8-0s introduced in 1903. The design caused his successor, Collett, to produce more between 1938-42 with only slight variations. Very few classes in British locomotive history have been built over a period as long as 40 years.

● **BELOW**
The LMS Garratt was a most exciting development in British freight-locomotive history. The engines were built for the LMS by Beyer Peacock. The class totalled 33 engines and hauled coal-trains over the Midland main line between Toton (Nottingham) and Cricklewood (north London). They took the place of two inside-cylinder 0-6-0s.

BRITISH SHUNTERS AND INDUSTRIAL LOCOMOTIVES

The traditional main-line shunting tank has been either an 0-4-0 or, more commonly, an 0-6-0. Numerous designs were created, especially Britain's LMS Jinty 0-6-0, of which more than 500 were built, and the Great Western 5700-class 0-6-0 pannier tanks, totalling 863 examples. Many more classes of 0-6-0 and even 0-8-0 tanks would have been built for shunting had not these forms of locomotives been heavily supplemented by downgraded inside-cylinder 0-6-0s and 0-8-0s. These engines, important main-line freight haulers in the closing years of the 19th century, became ideal heavy shunters and tripping engines in their

later years. Wagons had grown bigger, loads much heavier and the abundance of these downgraded freight engines meant the traditional 0-6-0 tank-engine did not evolve to any great size, remaining largely unchanged for almost a century.

Some larger marshalling yards – especially those with humps – needed something bigger than the 0-6-0, so special designs evolved to fill this niche. The first of these giants appeared in 1907 when John George Robinson introduced a three-cylinder 0-8-4T for humping at the Great Central Railway's Wath Yards, in the North Riding of Yorkshire. Two years later, the ever-prolific Wilson

Worsdell, CME of the North Eastern Railway, put into traffic some three-cylinder 4-8-0Ts. The LNWR introduced the first 30 0-8-2Ts in 1911, followed by 30 0-8-4Ts. These two classes were, in effect, a heavy tank-engine version of their standard 0-8-0 freight engines.

The definitive industrial locomotive evolved as either a side or saddle tank, four- or six-coupled. Larger industrial locomotives invariably came in the form of former main-line engines, which had been sold out of service. This practice led to tender-engines appearing on industrial lines. These environments often gave a massive extension of life to engines that

GWR 5700 CLASS	
Date	1929
Builder	Swindon Works, Wiltshire, England
Client	Great Western Railway
Gauge	Standard
Driving wheels	4 ft 7 in
Capacity	2 cylinders 17 x 24 in
Steam pressure	200 lb sq in
Total weight in full working order	51 tons
Tractive effort	2,255 lbs

● LEFT
Britain's Great Western Railway adopted the pannier tank for shunting operations. GWR's ultimate design was Collett's 5700-class with 4 ft 7 in wheels. Between 1929-49, 863 engines were built. When building ended, they were the largest class in Britain.

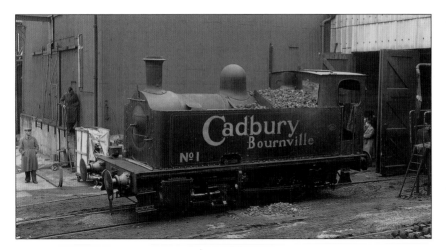

had outlived their normal life span on main lines.

The basic industrial engine changed little in its century of pre-eminence. One fascinating variation, however, occurred in the form of the Fireless, of which some 200 worked in Britain. These engines were a low-cost shunting unit for industries with a ready supply of high-pressure steam. They took their steam secondhand from the works' boilers.

Up until World War II, several thousand industrial engines were active the length and breadth of Britain. Many survived in their industrial habitats after main-line steam working ended in 1968. This was historically appropriate. The world's first steam locomotive, created in a South Wales ironworks in 1804, was an industrial.

● **BELOW LEFT**
Andrew Barclay & Son, locomotive builders of Kilmarnock, Strathclyde, south-west Scotland, were famous for a long range of 0-4-0 and 0-6-0 saddle-tanks, which formed a distinctive family of engines built almost unchanged over a 70-year period. Here, one of their 0-4-0s works on the Storefield Ironstone system in Northamptonshire, in the English Midlands, taking iron ore to the connection with British Railways' main line.

● **BELOW LEFT**
Britain's LMS Jinty 0-6-0s represented the ultimate manifestation of a long line of Midland Railway 0-6-0 shunting-tanks. They were found all over the English part of the LMS system in the years before most freight carriage was transferred from rail to road.

● **BELOW RIGHT**
Andrew Barclay pioneered the Fireless type in Britain and built many examples, both 0-4-0 and 0-6-0, for industrial establishments. The Fireless was arguably the most efficient and economical shunting unit ever devised.

BRITISH MAIN-LINE TANK ENGINES

The engines that worked suburban trains around Britain's great cities and conurbations were almost exclusively tank designs. The absence of a tender facilitated ease of running in either direction and cut out cumbersome and time-consuming turning. Also, the water's weight above the coupled wheels provided adhesion useful for rapid starts from stations. For similar reasons, tank-engines were favoured on branch lines across Britain.

In the 19th century, the urban and branch-line tank-engine evolved in many forms: 2-4-0, 4-4-0, 4-4-2, 0-4-2, 0-4-4 and 0-6-0.

The 0-4-4 was particularly favoured. It had flexibility to run in either direction. Its boiler and cylinder blocks were often interchangeable with sister inside-cylinder 0-6-0s and inside-cylinder 4-4-0 express-passenger engines.

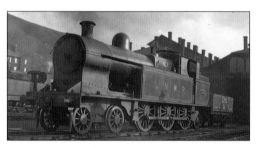

As the population of Britain's cities grew, so did the suburban tank's proportions. It graduated to the 4-4-2 and by the turn of the century, with the harmonious 4-4-4, in sheer aesthetic terms, reached its pièce de résistance, the ultimate in balanced proportions.

The most remarkable suburban engine was Holden's Decapod 0-10-0T for the Great Eastern Railway (GER). Advocates of electrification claimed that a 315-ton train could be accelerated to 30 mph in 30 seconds. Holden, in producing his Decapod, proved that this achievement could be bettered with steam. As a result, the proposed electrification of GER's suburban services from London's Liverpool Street Station was shelved.

● BELOW
An 0-6-0 shunting-tank of Britain's North Eastern Railway, from a class of 120 engines built between 1886–95. The type's suitability is shown by the introduction of a second and similar batch in 1898 of which 85 were built by 1925. Then, 28 more were built between 1949–51, under British Railways. This created the unique situation of a design being built over a 54-year period. Possibly no other class in world locomotive history has achieved this distinction.

● LEFT
The 0-4-4 T's flexibility was shown by this example from England's North Staffordshire Railway. Classified as "M", five examples of the type were built in 1907–8.

● BELOW
Britain's Great Western Railway (GWR) achieved excellent standardization in all categories of motive power. For suburban and branch-line work, Churchward introduced a range of 2-6-2s.

Alas, the Decapod was so heavy on the track that it never entered service.

Six-coupled engines in the form of 0-6-2s and 0-6-4s progressed to 2-6-2s and 2-6-4s, the preferred power from the 1930s onwards. Many of these engines were mixed-traffic types, equally suited for cross-country and branch-line work as well.

Electrification – especially of metropolitan and suburban services – progressively eroded the need for tank engines, particularly on Britain's Southern Railway. A partial erosion of need also occurred on branch lines, where demoted express-passenger designs of earlier years were used, 2-4-0s and 4-4-0s being especially common.

The tank-engine is popularly thought of as something of a plodding machine. In truth, many were extremely fast runners, and speeds of 70 mph were quite normal on many suburban and outer-suburban workings, some of which were very tightly timed and had to be fitted in between the paths of more important, longer-distance trains.

● BELOW
This engine belonged to a class of Ivatt 0-6-2Ts with 5 ft 8 in wheels, built for the Great Northern Railway (GNR) between 1906–12. The class totalled 56 engines. These appeared prolifically on suburban workings out of London's Kings Cross Station. Many had condensing apparatus for working through metropolitan tunnels. In their later years, many were found on suburban workings around Leeds and Bradford, in west Yorkshire.

LNER CLASS J72 0-6-0T	
Date	1898
Builder	Darlington Locomotive Works, Co. Durham, England
Client	North Eastern Railway; London & North Eastern Railway; British Railways
Gauge	4 ft 8 in
Driving wheels	4 ft 1 in
Capacity	2 cylinders 17 x 24 in
Steam pressure	140 lb sq in
Weight	43 tons
Tractive effort	16,760 lbs

BRITISH EXPORTS

The steam-locomotive was arguably Britain's greatest technological contribution to mankind. Her lead in railways ensured wide opportunities, and she became railway builder to her empire and the world. A vast locomotive industry developed quite separately from that of the famous railway towns, which served Britain's domestic needs. Legendary foundries in Glasgow, Scotland, and in the English provinces at Leeds in Yorkshire, Newcastle upon Tyne in Northumberland (now Tyne and Wear), Darlington in Durham, Manchester and other parts of Lancashire, and in Stafford, west central England, sent

● LEFT
● LEFT
Manning Wardle of Leeds, west Yorkshire, built this Crane Tank locomotive in 1903. It lifted tree trunks at an Indian sawmill, replacing elephants.

locomotives worldwide, often exporting the industrial revolution with them. Lands beyond the British Empire were served, including those having no political affinity with Britain. Exported locomotives reflected the designs of engines running in the mother country, and the types of engines seen rolling through the soft English countryside

were soon found crossing barren, rugged and jungle-clad landscapes in many countries of Africa, Australia, South-east Asia and South America.

Britain's role as locomotive-builder to the world remained largely unchallenged throughout the 19th century, but the early 20th saw serious competition for the first time, especially from America and, to a lesser extent, from builders in continental Europe. America's engines were a commercial threat and also challenged conventional British design. These, though produced by skilled craftsmen, nonetheless had deficiencies. These, not apparent in Britain, caused problems in the rough-and-tumble of world railways.

● LEFT
The lineage of these British build Pacifics is fully shown in this scene of a South African Railways 3 ft 6 in gauge 16CR heading over flood waters of the tidal Swartkops River in Port Elizabeth, Cape Province, South Africa.

● RIGHT
One of a group of Moguls built in 189 by Beyer Peacock of Manchester, Lancashire, for Brazil's Leopoldina Railway. This Mogu is an example of exported types being used abroad before coming into service in the country of manufacture.

● **RIGHT**
In East Africa, the scrublands of Tanzania resounded to the wail of British locomotives in the 1920s after the territory was mandated to Britain at the end of World War I, when it was known as Tanganyika. This light-axle 2-8-2 was ideal for riding the lightly laid and rough track beds common in Africa.

BAGNALL 2-8-2

Date	1947
Builder	Bagnall's of Stafford, Staffordshire, England
Client	Tanganyika Railway, East Africa
Gauge	Metre
Driving wheels	3 ft 7 in
Capacity	Cylinders 17 x 23 in
Steam pressure	180 lb sq in
Total weight full working order	100 tons
Tractive effort	25,050 lb

Most British locomotives had small fireboxes set between the frames, a restriction that caused steaming difficulties when inferior coal was used.

Traditional British plate frames gave problems when engines ran on the developing world's poor quality tracks. American engines had wide fireboxes suitable for inferior fuel. Their bar-frames enjoyed greater tolerance in adverse conditions. Some British loco-motives' limited bearing surfaces also gave trouble in rough conditions.

American engines' bearing proportions were more generous.

An immediate effect of America's aggressive export drive in the early 20th century was the amalgamation in 1903 of Glasgow's three big builders – Sharp Stewart, Neilson and Dübs – to form the North British Locomotive Company. Although there was a shift towards a more international design of locomotive, created in the light of world experience, British builders retained a significant role right to the end of the steam age.

● **RIGHT**
Britain's private loco-motive builders often built for companies in Britain whose works were unable to supply engines quickly enough. Here, at the North British Works in Glasgow, Scotland, an LNER class B1 4-6-0 is in the background, by a light-axle loaded 2-8-2 for East African Railways.

BRITISH RECORD-BREAKERS AND STREAMLINERS

The commonly held view that the steam-locomotive was replaced because it was slow is incorrect. Many of today's diesel and even electrically operated services are not appreciably faster than steam was 50 or more years ago.

The magical three-figure speed was reached in 1903 by the Great Western Railway's 4-4-0 City of Truro. This achieved 102.3 mph down Wellington Bank in Somerset, south-west England, with an Ocean Mails train, the first time any form of transport reached 100 mph.

GWR featured in another speed dash, with a Churchward Saint Class 4-6-0, which allegedly reached 120 mph while running light engine on a test trip after an overhaul at Swindon works in Wiltshire. This alleged achievement is not authenticated, but over the years authorities have claimed it to be true.

The 1930s, the "streamlined era", were a time of epic record-breaking runs all over the world. Streamlining was in vogue. It inspired and fascinated the public, but its usefulness in reaching high speeds was soon questioned.

The legendary speed records of the

LNER A4 PACIFIC	
Date	1935
Builder	Doncaster Works, south Yorkshire
Client	London & North Eastern Railway
Gauge	Standard
Driving wheels	6 ft 8 in
Capacity	3 cylinders 18 x 26 in
Total weight in full working order	167 tons
Steam pressure	250 lb sq in
Tractive effort	33,455 lb

● **LEFT**
The LNER's plaque affixed to the boiler of Mallard to commemorate its world record-breaking run in 1938.

● **BELOW**
The LNER class-A4 No.4468 Mallard, dubbed the world's fastest steam locomotive. Mallard's record may remain unbeaten.

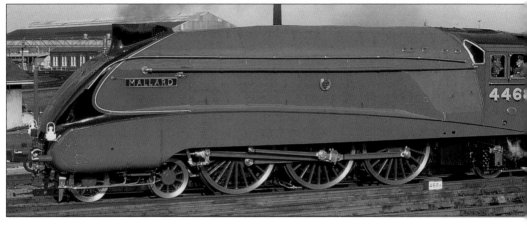

● **ABOVE**
Stanier's record-breaking Princess Royal
Pacific No. 6201 Princess Elizabeth, which in
1936 covered the 401 miles between Glasgow,
Scotland, and London Euston in 5 hours
44 minutes – an average speed of 70 mph.
Almost 60 years later, in November 1996, the
Daily Telegraph reported that many electrically
operated services on the West Coast route were
slower than Princess Elizabeth's epic run.

● **BELOW**
The Princess Royals
were followed by the
Princess
Coronations. One of
these engines,
streamlined, briefly
held the world
record for steam
traction of 114 mph.
Over the years after
World War II, all
streamlined
examples lost their
casing.

1930s were again the result of
competition between the East and West
Coast routes linking London and
Scotland. Both the LMS and the LNER
had brand new designs of Pacific
locomotives in service – streamlined
Coronations on the former and Gresley
A4s on the latter.

In terms of maximum speed, the
LMS bid for the world speed record on
29 June 1937 when a special run of the
Coronation Scot was made for the
press six days before the service's official
start. The locomotive, No. 6220
Coronation, reached 114 mph down
Madeley Bank on the approaches to
Crewe, Cheshire, in northern England.
Alas, the bank was not long enough and
the train was still doing 60-70 mph when
the platform signal came into sight and
rapid braking for a standstill in Crewe
Station smashed all the crockery in the
dining car.

The LNER would not countenance
the LMS taking the honour in this way.
Almost a year later, on 3 July 1938, the
A4 class Pacific Mallard, ostensibly on a
special run to test braking, achieved 126

mph on the descent of Stoke Bank,
between Grantham in Lincolnshire and
Peterborough in Cambridgeshire, eastern
England, thus beating the LMS and
setting a never-beaten world speed
record for the steam locomotive.

Non-streamlined activity in the
1930s was also exciting, not least with
the Cheltenham Flyer express, which was
booked to run the 77.3 miles from
Paddington, London, to Swindon,
Wiltshire, in 65 minutes. On one
occasion the distance was covered in
56 minutes. This involved a start-to-stop
average of 82 mph.

World War II ended any such
performances and in the postwar period
the railway network's recovery was slow.
Not until the 1950s did three-figure
speeds with steam reappear.

AMERICAN MIKADOS

The 2-8-2 Mikado-type locomotive was developed in 1897 for Japanese Railways by the Baldwin Locomotive Works, the largest and most prolific locomotive-builder in the United States of America.

● AN AMERICAN ENGINE FOR JAPAN

The Mikado-type locomotive derives its name from this first owner, though during World War II, when America was fighting Japan, American nationalists tried to change the name to "MacArthur-type". Many Americans call these locomotives "Mikes".

In 1905, the Northern Pacific Railway was the first railroad to embrace the Mikado in large numbers. The locomotive quickly caught on, and many were produced for many railroads until about 1930. Some 10,000 were built for domestic use, and more than 4,000 were built for export.

● A SOLID DESIGN

The 2-8-2 wheel arrangement was a natural progression from the popular 2-8-0 Consolidation-type and 2-6-2 Prairie-type. The Mikado's overall design was outstanding. It was well balanced, providing excellent tractive effort and a good ride. The trailing truck allowed for a larger firebox, therefore more steam capacity and larger cylinders, giving the engine greater power than earlier designs which it rendered obsolete. When technological advances such as superheating were developed, they were used on the Mikado to great success. The

locomotive's primary application was heavy freight service, though many railroads used lighter Mikes on branch lines.

● NARROW-GAUGE APPLICATION

The Mikado type was particularly well adapted to narrow-gauge freight service because of its balanced design and four sets of drivers. These provided the traction needed on heavy mountain grades, while producing only minimum wear and tear on lightweight track and right-of-way. In the West, Denver & Rio Grande Western (D&RGW) operated four classes of Mikado on its rugged mountain grades. Its

● **LEFT**
Pennsylvania
Railroad (PRR)
No. 1596, a Class-
L1s Mikado-type,
features a boxy
Belpaire-type
firebox, standard on
most late-era PRR
steam locomotives.
It is pictured near
the end of its active
life, at Enola,
Pennsylvania.

line over the 3,048 m (10,003 ft) high
Cumbres Pass, in the San Juan Mountains
of south Colorado, featured gruelling 4
per cent grades, which gave the 3 ft
narrow-gauge Mikado a real proving

ground. In the East, narrow-gauge coal
hauler East Broad Top also preferred the
Mikados, owning several from Baldwin.
Many of these narrow-gauge locomotives
are preserved in working order.

● **RIGHT**
The Duluth &
Northern
Minnesota's Mikado
No. 14 clips along
north of Duluth,
Minnesota. This
light Mikado was
built by Baldwin in
1913.

MISSOURI PACIFIC MIKADO TYPE	
Date	1923
Builder	American Locomotive Co. (Alco)
Client	Missouri Pacific
Gauge	4 ft 8½ in
Driving wheels	65 in
Capacity	2 cylinders 27 x 32 in
Steam pressure	200 lb
Weight	305,115 lb
Tractive effort	62,950 lb

● **RIGHT**
This 2-8-2 Mikado-
type was built by the
American
Locomotive
Company (Alco) at
its Brooks Works in
1920. It worked for
the Aberdeen &
Rockfish Railroad,
and serves the Valley
Railroad at Essex,
Connecticut, New
Maryland.

AMERICAN ARTICULATED LOCOMOTIVES

The Mallet-type compound articulated steam locomotive, named after Swiss inventor Anatole Mallet, had been popular in Europe for decades before its eventual introduction in the United States of America.

● **B&O EMPLOYS THE MALLET**

After the turn of the century, a need for greater tractive effort led American railroads to employ articulated steam locomotives with two sets of driving wheels. The compound articulated

● **OPPOSITE TOP**
The Baltimore & Ohio's articulated 2-8-8-2 Class KK1 was an experimental locomotive that featured a water-tube boiler (most American locomotives had fire-tube boilers). It delivered a 90,000 lb tractive effort.

● **LEFT**
Union Pacific (UP) 4-6-6-4 Challenger-type simple articulated No. 3985 at Portola, California. UP owned more than 100 locomotives of this type for heavy-freight service in western USA.

BALTIMORE & OHIO MALLET-TYPE NO. 2400 "OLD MAUD"	
Date	1904
Builder	American Locomotive Co. (Alco)
Client	Baltimore & Ohio Railroad
Gauge	4 ft 8½ in
Driving wheels	56 in
Capacity	4 cylinders: 2 (20 x 32 in) and 2 (32 x 32 in)
Steam pressure	235 lb
Weight	334,500 lb
Tractive effort	71,500 lb

engine reused steam from high-pressure cylinders, in low-pressure cylinders, to achieve maximum efficiency. On most Mallets, very large low-pressure cylinders were used at the first set of drivers, while high-pressure cylinders were used at the second.

In 1904, the American Locomotive Company (Alco) built the first American Mallet-type, a 0-6-6-0 compound articulated nicknamed "Old Maud", for the Baltimore & Ohio Railroad (B&O), a

coalhauler facing many steep grades. While Mallet-types were effective for slow-speed service, few railroads used them for general service on the main line.

● **THE SIMPLE ARTICULATED GAINS POPULARITY**

The articulated concept achieved greater popularity in a more traditional format. This was the simple articulated engine, which has two sets of cylinders but does not reuse steam. Most articulated engines

● **LEFT**
The Baltimore & Ohio's No. 2400 was the first American locomotive to use the Mallet design. It was built in 1904 by Alco and known as "Old Maud". It weighed 334,500 lb and had a 71,500 lb tractive effort.

built after about 1910 were not compounds and thus not true Mallets. While many railroads preferred simple articulated engines, the Norfolk & Western (N&WR) continued to perfect the Mallet. The N&WR class-Y6b built by the railroad's Roanoke shops in North Carolina for main-line service represented the zenith of the type. N&WR was one of the last American railroads to use Mallets in regular main-line service.

The development of articulated steam locomotives, combined with other improvements such as mechanical stokers and superheaters, eventually led to the building of the world's largest locomotives. Among the largest articulateds were the 2-8-8-4 Yellowstone type used by Northern Pacific and ore-hauler Duluth, Missabi & Iron Range (DM&IR); the 2-6-6-6 Allegheny type built by the Lima Locomotive works for the Chesapeake & Ohio and Virginian Railway, in 1941 and 1945 respectively; and the 4-8-8-4 Big Boy type built for Union Pacific lines between 1941–44.

● **SOUTHERN PACIFIC CAB FORWARD**

The Southern Pacific (SP) developed a unique variation of the articulated engine. The traditional steam locomotive configuration featuring the cab behind the boiler proved unsatisfactory on the big articulateds when operating in the long tunnels and snowsheds found on the 2,174 metre (7,135 ft) Donner Pass in California's Sierra Nevada. Crews suffered from smoke inhalation. So SP turned the engine around, placing the cab in front of the boiler. The first of SP's 256 cab-forward articulated was a Mallet-type built in 1910. The last were Baldwin-built articulated 2-8-8-4 types, the SP class-AC-12, built in 1944.

● **ABOVE**
Among the heaviest articulated steam locomotives ever built were 2-8-8-4 Yellowstone types made for Northern Pacific (NP) and Duluth, Missabi & Iron Range (DM&IR).

● **RIGHT**
Norfolk & Western continued to perfect the Mallet compound-articulated-locomotive design long after other railroads adopted the simple articulated. An N&WR Y6 Mallet 2-8-8-2 pictured near Blue Ridge Summit, West Virginia, in 1958.

AMERICAN PACIFICS

The 4-6-2 Pacific-type steam locomotive came into favour shortly after the turn of the century and was produced widely for many American railroads until the 1930s.

● **PREMIER PASSENGER POWER**

This locomotive followed the logical developmental progression from the 4-4-0 American-type, 4-4-2 Atlantic-type and, to a lesser extent, the 2-6-2 Prairie-type. Most Pacifics, designed for high-speed passenger service, had relatively large fireboxes and high drivers. By 1915, this type had supplanted 4-6-0 Ten Wheelers and 4-4-2 Atlantics on crack passenger-trains. All around America, flashy high-drivered Pacifics were hauling name trains. These included Northern Pacific's luxurious North Coast Limited, Southern Pacific's Sunset Limited and the Pennsylvania Railroad's Broadway Limited.

● **BELOW**
The Baltimore & Ohio's Pacific type, No. 5305.

● **OPPOSITE TOP**
The Louisville & Nashville's Pacific-type No. 152 was built by Alco's Rogers Works in January 1905. This locomotive served the railroad for nearly 50 years.

● **THE PACIFIC ADAPTS WELL TO NEW TECHNOLOGY AND STYLES**

The Pacific-type was well suited to technological improvements. Superheating, mechanical stokers and roller bearings were developed. Superheating recirculated hot steam through the engine's firetubes, allowing for more power and greater efficiency. These developments were applied to both new and existing Pacifics, dramatically improving the performance of the engines. In the 1930s, when streamlined trains became the latest thing in railroad style, some railroads dressed up their Pacifics in snazzy shrouds.

● **PENNSYLVANIA RAILROAD K4**

The best-known, most loved and perhaps the best-performing Pacific was the Pennsylvania Railroad's Class K4. PPR received its first Pacific-type from Alco in 1907, an experimental locomotive Class K28. This locomotive led to several other

classes of Pacific, with the culmination of design exhibited in the 1914 Class K4. A masterpiece of engineering, the K4 was an outstanding performer. Eventually, Pennsylvania rostered some 425 K4s, an exceptional number for a single class of locomotive. They were the railroad's preferred passenger locomotive for nearly 30 years. Some K4s were built by Baldwin but many were constructed at the railroad's Juniata Shops. Like many PRR steam locomotives, the K4 featured the boxy Belpaire-type firebox. The last K4 was retired from regular service in 1957.

● **LEFT**
The Southern Pacific's No. 2472 was one of 15 Class-P8 Pacific types in the railroad's passenger fleet. These 1912 Baldwin-built locomotives had a 43,660-lb tractive effort.

● **ABOVE**
A highly polished Pennsylvania Railroad K4 Pacific, No. 5475.

PENNSYLVANIA RAILROAD K4 PACIFIC

Date	1914 –28
Builder	Juniata Shops, Baldwin, Pennsylvania, USA
Client	Pennsylvania Railroad
Gauge	4 ft 8½ in
Driving wheels	80 in
Capacity	2 cylinders 27 x 28 in
Steam pressure	205 lb
Weight	468,000 lb
Tractive effort	44,460 lb

SHAYS AND SWITCHERS

American logging railroads had special locomotive requirements because their track, often crudely built, used very sharp curves and negotiated grades as steep as 10 per cent. Also, these railroads required locomotives that could haul relatively heavy loads at very slow speeds.

● **SHAYS AND OTHER GEARED LOCOMOTIVES**

To meet these requirements, three builders specialized in constructing flexible, high-adhesion steam locomotives that operated with a geared drive, rather than the direct drive used on conventional locomotives. These builders were Lima, at Ohio, with the Shay-type; Heisler Locomotive Works, at Eire, Pennsylvania, and Climax Locomotive and Machine Works at Corry, Pennsylvania. Each builder used the same basic principle – a cylinder-driven shaft that connected to the driving wheels using bevelled gears – but each approached the concept slightly differently.

● **ABOVE**
This is a stock Shay, built by Lima in 1928. It was sold to the Mayo Lumber Company and operated in British Columbia, Canada. It is preserved, with other Shays, at the Cass Scenic Railroad, West Virginia, USA.

Lima's Shay was the most popular type. It used a row of vertical cylinders on the fireman's side, that is the right-hand side of the engine, to power a shaft that connected two or three sets of driving wheels. Two-cylinder Shays had two sets of driving wheels; three-cylinder Shays had three sets of driving wheels. The Shay-type was first constructed in the 1880s.

Heisler used two cylinders facing one another crosswise, one on each side of the locomotive, forming a V-pattern. These cylinders turned a shaft to power two sets of driving wheels. Climax used two parallel, sharply inclined cylinders, one on each side of the locomotive, to power a shaft connecting two sets of driving wheels.

● **SWITCHERS**

Most railroads used specialized locomotives of a conventional design for switching service at yards, terminals and industrial sites. Because most switchers were relatively small locomotives, operated at slow speeds, and needed high adhesion to move long cuts of cars, they normally did not have pilot or trailing trucks – commonly used on road locomotives.

The smallest switchers were 0-4-0 types. This sort of locomotive, however,

had low adhesion and a notoriously bad-ride quality, so locomotives with more driving wheels were generally preferred. The 0-6-0 switcher was the most popular for general switching and about 10,000 were built. Some railroads used 0-8-0 switchers for heavier switching duties and, after the turn of the century, 0-10-0 switchers saw only limited service in hump yards.

Specialty tenderless switchers, with water-tanks built over the boilers, and "fireless" steam engines saw limited use in areas where conventional locomotives were inappropriate.

TYPICAL 0-6-0 SWITCHER

Date	About 1905
Builder	American Locomotive Co. (Alco)
Gauge	4 ft 8½ in
Driving wheels	51 in
Capacity	2 cylinders 19 x 24 in
Steam pressure	180 lb
Weight	163,365 lb
Tractive effort	26,510 lb

● **OPPOSITE**
Heisler's geared locomotives use two cylinders in a V position. This Heisler was built in 1912 for the Louise Lumber Company of Hawkes, Mississippi. It operates on the Silver Creek & Stephenson Railroad in Freeport, Illinois, USA.

● **RIGHT**
The last of the Lima-built Shay-types were heavy, three-cylinder locomotives built in 1945. The Western Maryland railroad in the USA owned several of these big Shays. They weighed 324,000 lb and generated a 59,740 lb tractive effort.

● **ABOVE**
Locomotive 2-8-0, No. 207 (formerly Southern 630), and North American Rayon Company's fireless 0-6-0T, No. 1, on the East Tennessee and Western North Carolina Railroad, USA.

● **BELOW**
Surrounded by lumber, this Ely Thomas Lumber Company's Lima-built Shay-type No. 2 waits for its next run in 1958 near Gauley, West Virginia, USA.

AMERICAN EXPORTS

Nations around the world relied on the locomotive prowess of the United States of America to supply their motive-power needs. Of some 175,000 steam locomotives built in the USA in the 120 years between 1830 and 1950, about 37,000, more than 20 per cent, were built specifically for export. Many varieties of locomotives were sold, depending on customers' needs, but five types were particularly popular in the export market and represented the lion's share of those sold.

● CONSOLIDATIONS

The most popular export model was the 2-8-0 Consolidation. More than 10,000 were sold outside the USA. This model was the second most-popular domestic locomotive, too. More than 22,000 were built for use in the USA where only the 19th-century 4-4-0 American-type was more popular.

A distant second to the Consolidation was the 2-8-2 Mikado-type. More than 4,000 were exported. This type was specifically designed by Baldwin

Locomotive Works for Japanese Railways in 1897. Later, it was adapted for domestic use. Many were used for freight service in the USA.

● DECAPODS FOR RUSSIA

The 2-10-0 Decapod was the third most-popular model. Many of the heavy locomotives went to Russia and to the Soviet Union during World Wars I and II. The Decapod was also popular in Germany, Greece, Poland and Turkey. Oddly, it was not very popular in the

MACARTHUR 2-8-2 USATC	
Builder	Baldwin Locomotive Company, Eddystone, Pennsylvania, USA
Client	United States Army Transport Corps (USATC)
Gauge	Metre
Driving wheels	4 ft
Capacity	Cylinders 16 x 24 in
Weight in full working order	112 tons

● LEFT
One of the last surviving MacArthur 2-8-2s. These metre-gauge engines were built for the United States Army Transport Corps (USATC) for operations during World War II. They saw wide service in India, Burma, Thailand and the Philippines. After the war, survivors remained active. In India, they were classified MAWD (McArthur War Department) and found in the country's Northeast Frontier region.

● **ABOVE**
Cuba's Manuel Isla sugar mill is host to this vintage Baldwin 0-4-2 tank believed to have been built in 1882. A retired employee at the mill, 88-year-old Jose Alfonso Melgoragio, remembers knowing the engine all his life. He worked on it for 25 years.

● **LEFT**
This classic American ten-wheeler, built by Rogers of New Jersey in 1896, pictured at the San Barnado Locomotive Works near Santiago, Chile, where the veteran was ending its days as work's pilot.

● **ABOVE LEFT**
A night scene in the mountains of the Philippines island of Negros. Two last survivors of their respective types are seen at the Insula Lumber Company. On the left, a Baldwin-built, four-cylinder compound Mallet; on the right, a vertical-cylinder Shay. These are classic American locomotives of the American Pacific Northwest.

● **LEFT**
A rare Baldwin 2-6-2 saddle-tank, known as the "Lavras Rose", which as Baldwin export order No. 372 of 1927 operated as a work's shunter at Lavras in Mina Gerais State, Brazil.

domestic market. Only the Santa Fe and Pennsylvania Railroad owned large numbers. The Frisco picked up Decapods intended for Russia and used them successfully for many years. Of the 4,100 American-built Decapods, 3,400 were exported around the world.

● **EXPORTS OF MOGULS AND TEN-WHEELERS**
Nearly 3,000 2-6-0 Mogul-types were built for export. This locomotive was popular for heavy freight in the mid-19th century. Some 1,600 4-6-0 ten-wheeler types were also exported, nearly 10 per cent of American production. Of 3,800 geared locomotives built in the USA for use on steep grades and for specialty railroads, such as logging, 600 were exported.

● **BELOW LEFT**
This classic American switcher once worked for the 5 ft 3 in gauge Paulista Railway serving the city and Pernambuco state in eastern Brazil. It was built by Baldwin of Philadelphia, Pennsylvania, USA, in 1896. The veteran is pictured here pensioned off to industrial service at the Cosim Steelworks at São Paulo, Brazil.

STREAMLINED STEAM

In 1934, at the height of the Great Depression, the Burlington railroad's Budd-built stainless-steel streamlined Pioneer Zephyr streaked across America.

● STREAMLINING TAKES OFF

Everywhere Pioneer Zephyr went, it inspired railroad managers and the riding public. In a similar vein, Union Pacific's streamlined City of Salina toured the West. These Winton engine-powered diesel articulated "trains of the future" soon resulted in the streamlining of a great many steam locomotives for passenger service. New locomotives, steam, diesel-electric and electric, were ordered as well, along with whole streamlined trains of luxurious passenger cars.

● DRESSING UP THE OLD GUARD

The railroads were quick to send crack passenger locomotives to shop for a fancy new dress. In 1936, Pennsylvania Railroad hired noted industrial designer

● **BELOW**
The Chesapeake & Ohio railroad operated four Class L1 streamlined 4-6-4 Hudson types in passenger service. These odd-looking, yellow and stainless-steel adorned locomotives were nicknamed "Yellowbellies".

Raymond Loewy to improve K4 No. 3768 aesthetically. The result was a flashy-looking locomotive. Many railroads dressed up their older locomotives with elaborate shrouding, though in some cases with less than superlative results. In many cases, shrouding hampered maintenance and was later removed.

● NEW STREAMLINERS

The Milwaukee Road was one of the first railroads to order new streamlined steam locomotives. In 1935, it ordered high-speed 4-4-2s with 84 in driving wheels and shrouds designed by Otto Kuhler. Assigned to its Hiawathas, these fast engines would regularly zip at more than 100 mph between Chicago, Illinois, and Milwaukee, Wisconsin.

Beginning in the late 1930s, Southern Pacific's fleet of semi-streamlined 4-8-4 Northern types, painted in its flashy orange, red and silver "Daylight" scheme, marched about California. The epitome of this famous class were the 30 GS-4s and GS-5s built by the Lima works in 1941–42. These powerful engines exhibited some of the finest styling found on any North American locomotive.

Among the last types of streamlined locomotive built were the Norfolk & Western's J Class 4-8-4s, for service with its passenger-trains.

● **RIGHT**
The Norfolk & Western Railroad's Class-J Northerns, Nos. 600 to 612, were its most famous streamliners. These powerful locomotives could operate to a top speed of 110 mph but rarely needed to. N&WR operated other streamline steam as well, including its 800 Series Class K-2, 4-8-2 Mountains. Two N&WR Js pause for servicing in 1958.

● **ABOVE**
Canadian National Railway 4-8-4 No. 6402
passing through Toronto.

● **BELOW**
Southern Pacific owned a fleet of semi-
streamlined, "Daylight"-painted 4-8-4
Northern types for fast passenger service. Of
these, the best performing and most
aesthetically pleasing were 30 Class GS-4s and
GS-5s built in 1941–42.

SOUTHERN PACIFIC GS-4	
Date	1941
Builder	Lima, Ohio, USA
Client	Southern Pacific
Gauge	4 ft 8½ in
Driving wheels	80 in
Capacity	2 cylinders 26 x 32 in
Steam pressure	300 lb
Weight	475,000 lb
Tractive effort	78,650 lb

THE NETWORK EXPANDS – DECAPODS, MOUNTAINS, SANTA FES AND OVERLANDS

The railroads of the United States of America had an insatiable appetite for ever-larger, more powerful and more efficient locomotives. It stemmed from their belief that more powerful locomotives would produce lower operating costs through the ability to haul more goods, faster, with fewer crews and locomotives.

In the 19th century, locomotive output was limited to the size of the firebox and the fireman's ability to shovel coal. Early attempts at producing big locomotives usually resulted in curious behemoths that did not steam well and languished for lack of power. The development of superheating (recirculation of steam through a locomotive's firetubes, significantly increasing power) and of the trailing truck (enabling an increase in firebox capacity) allowed for significant increases in practical locomotive size and for the development of several large new locomotive types. The further development of devices such as the mechanical stoker (moving coal from tender to firebox without a shovel) allowed for maximum performance from new larger locomotives.

CHESAPEAKE & OHIO CLASS J1 MOUNTAIN TYPE

Date	1911–12
Builder	American Locomotive Co. (Alco)
Client	Chesapeake & Ohio Railroad
Gauge	4 ft 8½ in
Driving wheels	62 in
Capacity	2 cylinders 29 x 28 in
Steam pressure	180 lb
Weight	499,500 lb
Tractive effort	58,000 lb

● **DECAPOD AND MOUNTAIN-TYPES**

The 2-10-0 Decapod-type, first introduced in 1870 by the Lehigh Valley Railroad, Pennsylvania, proved too big for its time. After 1900, it was built with limited success for several American railroads. It was most successful in the export market.

The 4-8-2 was introduced in about 1910 for use on the Chesapeake & Ohio railroad and soon proved a very popular design. This versatile type of locomotive was well suited for fast passenger-trains.

● **SANTA FE AND OVERLAND-TYPES**

Western railroads, which operated over great distances across the open plains, mountains and deserts, had a special need for large, powerful locomotives and

● **ABOVE**
The 2-10-0 Decapod type was not popular among American railroads, but Pennsylvania Railroad owned more than 500. The Decapod was used for heavy, slow-speed freight service.

● **RIGHT**
The Norfolk & Western Railroad operated streamlined 4-8-2 Mountain types in passenger service. These locomotives, Class K2, looked very similar to the J Class Northern types.

were better able to handle those with a long wheelbase. Shortly after the turn of the century, the Santa Fe Railway took delivery of 2-10-2 locomotives called Santa Fe types. This type did not attain popularity with other railroads until World War I, when changes in technology made it more appealing and the type was

mass produced. In the 1920s, the Union Pacific railroad took delivery of a three-cylinder 4-10-2 locomotive named after that railroad's primary corridor, the Overland Route. Southern Pacific also ordered this type and referred to it as the Southern Pacific type. The 4-10-2 was not very popular. Fewer than 100 were built.

● **ABOVE**
This Baltimore & Ohio railroad's 4-8-2 brand new Mountain type poses for its builder's photograph. This locomotive had 74 in driving wheels, 30 x 30 in cylinders, operated at 210 lb per sq in and produced a 65,000 lb tractive effort.

AMERICAN SUPERPOWER

American locomotive builders were constantly looking to improve the steam locomotives' output and fuel economy, and in doing so developed many important innovations.

● FOUR-AXLE TRAILING TRUCK KEY TO POWER

The development of the four-axle trailing-truck or -tender allowed for a larger firebox, and thus increased the heating surface and power. "Superpower" also took advantage of other improvements, such as automatic stokers, superheating and, later, roller bearings.

The first locomotive exhibiting the radial, outside-bearing, four-axle truck and enlarged firebox was a Lima 2-8-4 built in 1925 for the New York Central railroad. It was designed for heavyfreight service. NYC used its 2-8-4s on the Boston & Albany (B&A) line in western Massachusetts. This line featured the

steepest grades on NYC's system. As a result, this new type was named the "Berkshire", after the mountain range in which it operated. The Berkshire type was the logical progression from the Mikado type, long popular for freight service. NYC was pleased with the Berkshires' performance and ordered a fleet of them for service on the B&A line. There they served for more than 20 years, until the introduction of diesel-electric.

● SUPER PASSENGER POWER

The four-axle trailing-truck and larger firebox principle worked so well on the freight-hauling Berkshire that the same principle was tried on fast passenger locomotives. In 1927, NYC took delivery of its first 4-6-4 locomotive from Alco. This type was named after the Hudson River, NYC's famed Water Level Route, which runs parallel to the line between New York City and Albany, the state capital.

● LEFT
One of the most impressive types of steam locomotive ever built was Atchison, Topeka & Santa Fe's 2900 Series, 4-8-4 Northerns. They weighed 510,000 lb, operated at 300 lb per sq in and had 80 in driving wheels. They regularly ran at more than 100 miles an hour.

● **OPPOSITE**
In 1945, Reading Railroad built eight 4-8-4 Northerns, Class T1, at its shops in Reading, Pennsylvania. Designed for freight service, the T1 weighed 809,000 lb, had 70 in driving wheels and operated at 240 lb per sq in.

● **RIGHT**
The Baltimore & Ohio Railroad's 4-6-4 Hudson type. Many American railroads used Hudsons in passenger service. The superpowered Hudson was the natural progression from the Pacific type.

READING 4-8-4 NORTHERN TYPE CLASS T1

Date	1945
Builder	Reading Shops, Reading, Pennsylvania, USA
Client	Reading Railroad
Gauge	4 ft 8½ in
Driving wheels	70 in
Capacity	2 cylinders 27 x 32 in
Steam pressure	240 lb
Weight	809,000 lb
Tractive effort	68,000 lb

● **ABOVE**
Milwaukee Road took delivery of Class S-3 Northerns from Alco in 1944. These powerful locomotives were used for freight and passenger service but were too heavy to operate on some routes.

Continued development of the Hudson type produced some of the finest passenger locomotives ever built. About 500 Hudson types were built for service in America.

● **NORTHERNS**
The 4-8-4 Northern type was first developed in 1927 for the Northern Pacific. The Northern was an excellent locomotive for high-speed passenger service and fast freight service and remained in production throughout World War II. Some of the finest examples of the Northern type were

Union Pacific railroad's 800-class, built by Alco in 1937; Milwaukee Road's S-Class, built by Alco in 1944; Santa Fe's 2900 Series, built by Baldwin that same year; and NYC's 6000 Series locomotives, built in 1946 and usually referred to by the railroad as Niagaras rather than as Northerns.

Some Northerns were delivered in streamlined shrouds, notably Norfolk & Western Railroad's J Class and Southern Pacific's GS-2 to GS-6 Class. (SP's Class GS-1, GS-7 and GS-8 did not feature streamlining.)

More than 1,000 Northern types were built for North American railroads. Union Pacific has the distinction of maintaining a Northern well past the end of steam in the 1950s. In 1996 its famous Northern No. 844 emerged from a multi-million dollar overhaul and paraded around the system in excursion service.

● **RIGHT**
Union Pacific has maintained No. 844. While used mainly for excursion services, it occasionally hauls freight. In September 1989, it led a westbound freight across Nebraska from Omaha to North Platte.

AMERICAN ELECTRIC AND EARLY DIESELS

The first use of electric locomotives in the United States of America was in the Baltimore Railway Tunnel, by the Baltimore & Ohio Railroad (B&O) in 1895.

● ELECTRICS

Electrification gained popularity after the turn of the century and through the 1930s many American railroads electrified portions of their main lines. Most notable were the Pennsylvania Railroad (PPR) extensive 11,000-volt alternating current (a.c.) electrification in New York, New Jersey, Maryland and Pennsylvania; the New York Central (NYC) 660-volt direct current (d.c.) third-rail electrification; New Haven's 11,000-volt a.c. suburban main-line electrification in Connecticut; and Milwaukee Road's famous 3,000-volt d.c. overhead electrification through the mountains of Montana, Idaho and Washington State. PRR owned many classes of electric locomotives, from the

PENNSYLVANIA RAILROAD CLASS GG1 ELECTRIC LOCOMOTIVE	
Date	1934–43
Builder	Baldwin, General Electric, Juniata Shops
Client	Pennsylvania Railroad
Gauge	4 ft 8½ in
Voltage	11,000 volts a.c.
Power	4,680 hp
Weight	460,000 lb
Tractive effort	75,000 lb

small 0-C-0 switchers, Class B1, to the famous Raymond Loewy-styled 4-C+C-4, Class GG1. The GG1 served PRR and its successors for nearly 50 years.

NYC operated several classes of motors in the New York City area. Its first electric, Class S1, No. 6000, was in service from 1904 until the 1970s.

New Haven's electrics could operate from both 660-volt d.c. third rail and 11,000-volt a.c. overhead wire. New Haven used EF-class motors in freight service and EP-class motors in passenger service. Its last passenger electrics were 10 EP-5s, delivered by General Electric in 1955.

● BELOW
The PRR operated 139 GG1 electrics in freight and passenger service on its electrified lines. These Raymond Loewy-styled locomotives operated for nearly 50 years.

● ABOVE
A PRR GG1 leads a high-speed passenger-train through Frankford Junction, near Philadelphia, Pennsylvania, in 1959.

● LEFT
The Rio Grande Zephyr on the Denver & Rio Grande Western Railroad, seen at Thistle, Colorado, in 1982.

● **LEFT**
One of the New Haven railroad's EP-5 passenger electrics leads a train through Sunnyside Yard, in Queens, New York, in 1960. New Haven's 10 EP-5s, built by General Electric in 1955, were the railroad's last new passenger electrics.

Milwaukee Road's most famous electrics were its 6-D+D-6, Class EP-2, Bipolars, built by GE in 1918 for use on its Washington State lines; and its 1949 GE-built Little Joes for its Montana and Idaho lines. These double-ended, baby-faced locomotives were intended for operation in Russia but not delivered because of the start of the Cold War. Hence their nickname, after Joseph Stalin. Milwaukee discontinued the last of its electric operations in 1974, and six years later abandoned its tracks to the Pacific Coast.

● **DIESEL-ELECTRIC INTRIGUE**
America's first successful commercial diesel-electric was a 60 ton, 300 hp boxcab built by Alco-GE-Ingersol Rand for the Central Railroad of New Jersey in 1925. At first, the diesel-electric was primarily used for switching, but its passenger application became evident with the introduction of the Budd-built Pioneer Zephyr on the Burlington railroad in 1934. This articulated, streamlined, stainless-steel wonder changed the way railroads viewed the diesel-electric.

In 1939, General Motors Electro-Motive Corporation introduced the FT, a 1,350-hp, streamlined locomotive designed to be operated in sets of four in heavyfreight service. This amazing locomotive outperformed contemporary steam locomotives in nearly every service in which it was tested. The diesel had proved it could handle all kinds of service and, in most respects, in a more cost-efficient way than steam. Only World War II prolonged the inevitable. Following the war, the diesel-electric quickly took over from the steam locomotive. By the mid-1950s, many railroads had completely replaced

locomotive fleets with new diesels. By 1960, the steam locomotive was relegated to the status of a historical curiosity.

The diesel-electric enabled American railroads to "electrify" their lines without stringing wires. In some cases, the diesel-electric replaced true electric operations as well.

● **BELOW TOP**
The Electro-Motive E7 was one of the most popular passenger locomotives. More than 500 were built. Here, a pair of the Louisville & Nashville railroad's E7s rest at Louisville, Kentucky, in 1958.

● **BELOW BOTTOM**
Electro-Motive Corporation's EAs built in 1937 for the Baltimore & Ohio railroad were the first streamlined passenger diesel-electrics not part of an articulated-train set.

AMERICAN INTERURBANS

Between the 1890s and World War I, lightweight interurban electric railways were built throughout the United States of America. Their greatest concentration was in the Northeast and Midwest.

● INTERURBANS' PERFORMANCE ACROSS AMERICA

Interurbans were mainly passenger carriers, but many developed freight business as well. Interurbans were badly affected when automobile travel became popular, and very few interurban companies survived the Great Depression of the 1930s. A handful of interurban lines operated passenger services into the 1950s and early 1960s. Others survived as freight carriers. Only a few segments of the once-great interurban system exist today, mostly as freight carriers. Three are still electrified, and one line, the Chicago, South Shore & South Bend, still carries passengers.

● INTERURBAN CARS

Early interurban car design emulated that of steam railroad passenger cars. Ornate, heavyweight, wooden cars prevailed until about 1915 when steel cars became standard. Interurban cars were built by several companies including the American Car Company, Brill, Cincinnati Car Company, Holman Car Company and the Jewett Car Company, most of which also built street cars and elevated rapid-transit cars.

● ABOVE

The North Shore operated two articulated, streamlined electric train sets called Electroliners on its high-speed line between Chicago, Illinois, and Milwaukee, Wisconsin. An Electroliner is seen here on the streets of Milwaukee – on 19 July 1958.

● BELOW

The Chicago, South Shore & South Bend Railroad operated a fleet of Standard Steel Car interurban cars. Here, a typical South Shore interurban is seen at Gary, Indiana, in 1958.

The North Shore painted some of its heavyweight interurban cars to make it appear as if they were modern, stainless-steel, streamlined cars.

CHICAGO, SOUTH SHORE & SOUTH BEND INTERURBAN COACH	
Date	1929
Builder	Standard Steel Car
Client	South Shore & South Bend Interurban
Gauge	4 ft 8½ in
Voltage	1,500 d.c.
Axles	Four
Weight	133,600 lb
Propulsion	Westinghouse
Seating	48 seats

A few interurbans ordered high-speed, lightweight cars in the 1930s, notably the Fonda, Johnstown & Gloversville railroad in New York State, which acquired five streamlined Bullet cars from Brill in 1932; the Cincinnati & Lake Erie railroad, which acquired 20 high-speed cars from the Cincinnati Car Company in 1932; and the Northern Indiana Railway, which acquired ten lightweight cars from Cummings in 1930.

● ARTICULATED STREAMLINERS
The Chicago, North Shore & Milwaukee (the North Shore) received two streamlined, articulated interurban train sets from the St Louis Car Company in 1941. Named Electroliners, these flashy trains were painted in a unique emerald-and-salmon multistriped scheme. The North Shore was one of few interurbans integrated with a city rapid-transit system. For more than 20 years, the Electroliners zipped between Milwaukee, Wisconsin, and Chicago's "L" Loop. After the North Shore's demise in 1963, the Electroliners were sold to Philadelphia, where they operated for another ten years as Liberty Liners on the Norristown Highspeed Line (the former Philadelphia & Western). The Illinois Terminal also operated St Louis Car streamlined articulated interurbans.

The Chicago, Aurora & Elgin (CA&E) railroad's No. 20 was built by the Niles Car & Manufacturing Company in 1902. It weighs 85,000 lb and seats 52 passengers. The CA&E powered its cars by third-rail and overhead wire.

CANADIAN PASSENGER

In 1948, about 4,100 steam locomotives were serving Canada's two main railroads, Canadian National (CN) and Canadian Pacific (CP).

● LOCOMOTIVE BUILDERS

Two commercial Canadian builders provided most of these locomotives. The Montreal Locomotive Works (MLW), a subsidiary of the American Locomotive Company (Alco), built more than 3,600 steam locomotives between the turn of the century and the early-1950s when it switched to producing diesel-electric locomotives. The Canadian Locomotive Company (CLC), founded in the 1850s, built more than 2,500 steam locomotives, including about 500 export models. In 1950, CLC was given the licence to build Fairbanks-Morse diesel-electric locomotives.

● CANADIAN NATIONAL

The CN railroad introduced the 4-8-4 to Canada in 1927, only a few months after Northern Pacific first tried it in the United States of America. CN called the 4-8-4 the Confederation type and during 20 years ordered more than 200 for freight and passenger service. Of CN's 4-8-4s, 11 were streamlined. One of the most impressive types of 4-8-4 was CN's Class U-2-h, intended for dual service. They operated at 250 lb per sq in,

● ABOVE
Canadian Pacific's most famous locomotives were its Royal Hudsons, built by the Montreal Locomotive Works from 1938. Like many CP steam-locomotives, they were semi-streamlined and had recessed headlights.

● BELOW
Canadian Pacific Railway G-5 4-6-2s, Nos. 1246 and 1293, pictured at Brockways Mills, Vermont, USA.

weighed 400,300 lb, featured 73 in driving wheels, and produced a 56,000 lb tractive effort. CN also maintained a fleet of 4-8-2 Mountain types, many working exclusively in passenger service.

● **CANADIAN PACIFIC**

The late-era steam locomotives of CP feature several distinctive hallmarks. Most were semi-streamlined and featured centred, recessed headlights. As with CN locomotives, CP used vestibule cabs to give crews greater comfort when operating in extremely cold temperatures.

CP preferred 4-6-2 Pacific types and 4-6-4 Hudson types for its passenger service. It began buying Pacifics in 1906 and continued acquiring them until 1948. Its Hudsons were notable locomotives, with outstanding performance records and excellent aesthetic qualities. Some CP Hudsons regularly operated on 800-mile-long runs. Its best-known 4-6-4s were its H1 Royal Hudsons, so named because two of their class hauled the special trains that brought King George VI and Queen Elizabeth across Canada in 1939. The Royal Hudsons were decorated with an embossed crown.

CANADIAN PACIFIC CLASS H1D, 4-6-4 ROYAL HUDSON	
Date	1938
Builder	Montreal Locomotive Works
Client	Canadian Pacific
Gauge	4 ft 8½ in
Driving wheels	75 in
Capacity	2 cylinders 22 x 30 in
Steam pressure	275 lb
Weight	628,500 lb
Tractive effort	45,300 lb

● **ABOVE**
A Canadian National 4-8-4, No. 6218, races with a passenger excursion. CN owned more 4-8-4s than any other railroad.

● **ABOVE**
A Canadian National 4-8-4, No. 6218, rolls a passenger-train off a bridge in 1964.

● **LEFT**
Canadian National railroad preferred four-coupled steam locomotives and owned many Mikados, Mountains and Confederations (known elsewhere as Northerns). Here, a 4-8-2 Mountain Class N-7b, No. 6017, rests at Turcot Yard, Montreal.

CANADIAN FREIGHT

Canadian National was a publicly owned company formed in 1922 from a number of failing railroad lines. It was the larger line of the two Canadian systems and spanned Canada from coast to coast.

● **CANADIAN NATIONAL**

In the 1920s, the unified CN acquired many 4-8-2 Mountain types and smaller 2-8-2 Mikados. In 1927 it was one of the first railroads to adopt the 4-8-4 Northern type, which it called the Confederation type. CN and its American subsidiary, Grand Trunk Western (GTW), eventually owned more than 200 4-8-4s, far more than any other North American railroad. These high horsepower 4-8-4s were ideal suited for heavy freight service and passenger service.

In 1929, CN experimented with an alternative form of motive power. It ordered two diesel-electrics from Westinghouse and was the first North American railroad to use the diesel in main-line service. However, these experimental locomotives were unsuccessful and not duplicated.

● **LEFT**
While CN preferred four-coupled steam locomotives such as 4-8-2 Mountains, CP embraced three-coupled locomotives. CP had many 4-6-2 Pacifics and used them in all sorts of service. Here, a CP 4-6-2 leads a mixed train at Jackman, Maine, USA, in 1958.

● **LEFT**
A 40-ton Shay "Old One Spot", standard gauge, built in 1910: the last of the woodburners.

Ultimately, CN converted from steam to diesel operations, but at a more gradual rate than railroads in the USA.

● **CANADIAN PACIFIC**
Privately owned CP took a different approach to its freight locomotives

from CN. Where CN used many four-coupled locomotives, 4-8-2s, 4-8-4s, etc., CP preferred three-coupled locomotives for many applications. It owned many 4-6-2 Pacific types and 4-6-4 Hudson types. It used light Pacifics in branch-line freight service as

● **RIGHT**
A Canadian National 4-8-4, No. 6168, leads a mixed train near Brantford, Ontario, in 1959. CN used many 4-8-4s in freight and passenger service.

CANADIAN PACIFIC CLASS T1b, 2-10-4 SELKIRK TYPE

Date	1929–49
Builder	Montreal Locomotive Works
Client	Canadian Pacific
Gauge	4 ft 8½ in
Driving wheels	63 in
Capacity	2 cylinders 25 x 32 in
Steam pressure	285 lb
Weight	447,000 lb (engine only)
Tractive effort	76,905 lb

well as in passenger service. CP was also one of the few railroads to employ its Hudsons in freight service. Most railroads used this type exclusively for passenger trains.

CP did own some big locomotives. In 1928 it built two 4-8-4s but acquired no more. However, for heavy freight service in the Canadian Rockies, it owned 36 semi-streamlined 2-10-4 Texas-types that it called Selkirks. These locomotives were well suited for steep grades and heavy tonnage and performed well. In 1931, CP built an experimental three-cylinder 2-10-4. This locomotive was not particularly successful, CP did not bother to duplicate it and it was eventually scrapped.

● **ABOVE**
A Canadian National 2-8-0 Consolidation sits at Turcot Yard, Montreal. Most CN steam locomotives were built by Montreal Locomotive Works.

● **ABOVE**
A 45-ton, two-truck Climax logging locomotive, No. 9, built in 1912.

● **LEFT**
In the 1920s, the newly formed Canadian National began buying many 2-8-2 Mikados.

95

THE PRUSSIAN INFLUENCE

Prussian influence is seen by many to be confined to the large class of 4-6-0 locomotives known as the P8. After Germany's unification in 1871 as an imperial power, Prussia continued to go its own way in railway matters. Other states in the German Empire followed suit under Prussia's sway.

● THE EARLY DAYS

At the end of the 19th century, most railway locomotive authorities were trying to cope with the pace of advance in design, Prussia included. Because of the fairly level nature of Prussian territory, lightweight locomotives with a fair turn of speed lasted for many years and in various guises. Compounding was in fashion and classes were turned out seemingly almost at random, some being compound locomotives and others simple locomotives.

● **ABOVE**
The Prussian P8 also lasted to the end of the days of steam in West Germany. Here, in the late 1960s, No. 038 509-6 trundles under a bridge.

PRUSSIAN P8	
Date	1906
Builder	Schwarzkopff, Berlin
Client	Prussian State Railways
Gauge	1,435 mm
Class	Prussian P8; Deutsche Reichsbahn (DR) 38
Type	4-6-0
Driving wheels	1,750 mm
Capacity	2 cylinders 575 x 630 mm
Weight in working order	78.2 tonnes
Maximum service speed	100 kph

● THE SCHMIDT SUPERHEATER

Then came a most important event for Prussia and railway administrations worldwide. This was the development of a successful superheater. Steam was dried in a further set of tubes in the boiler to remove water drops in suspension. This superheated steam worked far more efficiently than those preceding it.

In the early 1890s, a Prussian physicist working in this field, Dr Wilhelm Schmidt, was encouraged to try out his results on the Prussian State Railways (PSR) system, by Mr Geheimiath Garbe of PSR. The first Schmidt superheater was fitted in 1897, but, as with many innovations, there were problems of lubrication and leaks. Further, locomotives fitted with superheaters cost more to build. In 1900, a simple 4-4-0 was fitted with the Schmidt superheater and achieved much interest and some success. Compared with nonsuperheated compound 4-4-0s of the same class, the nonsuperheated machines used 12 per cent more coal and 30 per cent more water.

● THE PRUSSIAN P8

The cost-savings of a simple machine against a compound being most

attractive, superheaters began to be fitted more widely and to more types of locomotive, including a class of sturdy 2-6-0 mixed-traffic locomotive. Compounding was not abandoned, however, for high-speed work. PSR had gained experience of the De Glehn compounds and developed their own compound 4-6-0 version. When a simple two-cylinder version for mixed traffic came out in 1906, the scene was set for the expansion of the Prussian Class P8. The first was built by Schwarzkopff of Berlin. Between 1906–21, the PSR bought 3,370 machines. Many others were constructed, including for export. More than 6,000 were built in total. After World War I, reparations demanded from Germany led to the arrival of the P8 in many other countries including Belgium and France.

● **THE WIDER IMPLICATIONS**
Several other classes of Prussian-designed locomotive were also distributed widely, including to Germany's allies, especially Turkey. This distribution and the reparations possibly extended Prussian influence far wider, and interest in these relatively

simple and robust designs grew. The German locomotive-building industry's need to gear up to replace stocks distributed elsewhere increased its design and production capacity. From this, German builders outside Prussia also benefited while, in Germany, the foundations were laid for German State Railways – the Deutsche Reichsbahn (DR) and, after 1945, the Deutsche Bundesbahn (DB).

● **BELOW LEFT**
The Deutsche Bundesbahn (DB) Class 078 4-6-4T lasted right to the end of the days of steam, in the early-1970s in then-West Germany. One of the class is pictured in a familiar role on a light passenger-train. This class, as Prussian Class T18, was built in batches between 1912-27.

● **BELOW**
Also on shed at Eregli in Turkey, in the 1970s, a driver is oiling round on a Prussian Type-G8 44071, an 0-8-0 dating from 1902, before moving off to pick up his train.

THE REICHSBAHN STANDARDS

After World War I, Germany's need to reorganize its railways led in 1920 to formation of a national system, the Reichsbahn. It is not surprising that Prussian management and methods were prominent.

● **RIGHT**
This unmodified 01-798 had a trailing load of 450 tonnes as it neared Grossenhain, in the then-East Germany, on the 06.37 hours express from Berlin to Dresden in 1977.

● **THE FOUNDATIONS**
An engineering-management centre was set up in Berlin. One of its decisions was to produce a series of locomotive classes that would operate across the network. A man called Wagner was placed in charge. In the years to 1939, at least, Wagner's stature as an engineer and manager grew.

● **FIRST STEPS**
One of his first decisions was to categorize all the locomotives from various sources under his control. This was so successful that its basic tenets were widely followed elsewhere in the operation. It pointed to strengths and weaknesses in the stock. Once more, Prussian influence emerged.

This is not to say that the other German States' railways had little to offer. Saxony and Württemberg were well advanced. Further, private locomotive builders contributed high technical input to many designs.

KRIEGSLOK – DEUTSCHE REICHSBAHN (DR) CLASS 52

Date	1942
Builder	Borsig of Berlin
Client	Deutsche Reichsbahn
Gauge	1,435 mm
Class	52
Type	2-10-0
Driving wheels	1,400 mm
Capacity	2 cylinders 500 x 600 mm (stroke)
Weight in working order	85.3 tonnes
Maximum service speed	80 kph

● **OPPOSITE**
A Kriegslok of Turkish State Railways (TCDD), No. 56533, pictured about to move off to pick up a freight train in the nearby yard.

● **RIGHT**
Class 01 Pacific 4-6-2s were still working between Berlin and Dresden, Saxony, in the then East Germany, in 1977, when this rural scene was briefly disturbed near Weinböhla.

● **RIGHT**
A Class 050 2-10-0, No. 050 383-9, pulling away from Freudenstadt Station in the Black Forest, in the then West Germany of the late 1960s.

● **DESIGN CRITERIA**

Compounding was on the way out. Two-cylinder, simple expansion locomotives were to be adopted, although, in the 1930s, three small specialist classes had three cylinders. Robust engineering was assisted by raising the axleload on main lines to 20.4 tonnes. Ease of maintenance was improved by mounting ancillaries on the boiler and adopting bar-frames as favoured by the locomotive-builders, J.A. Maffei of Munich. Commodious cabs eased the lot of footplate crews. Many other decisions affected components and fittings, some of which carried on

Prussian practice. Despite radical changes to external appearance, the Prussian style continued to dominate.

● **STANDARDS AT HOME AND ABROAD**

No fewer than 29 classes were brought into service between 1925–45. They ranged from small classes of 0-6-0T and 2-4-2T, to the 6,292 Class 52 Kriegslok introduced in 1942. These ranged far and wide across Europe, surviving well beyond designers' expectations.

Standard designs proved attractive to other countries. Some bought almost identical designs from German builders, or built them under licence in their own works. For example, Poland had modified Prussian P8s in 1922; Turkey had a range of types in regular use in the 1970s and, in small numbers, even later than this.

Many examples remained in regular use in the former East Germany until the late 1980s. A substantial number, especially of Kriegsloks, have been recovered for restoration and use on special trains in European countries.

GÖLSDORF AND THE AUSTRIAN EMPIRE

The Austro-Hungarian Empire, before its eventual collapse in 1918 as a result of World War I, was one of the most powerful political and economic entities in continental Europe.

● **BACKGROUND**

Its railways' main axis ran generally east-west with few topographical problems in the easterly direction from Vienna, in Austria, to Budapest, in Hungary. To the south, the only real geographical challenge between Vienna and Graz, in Austria, was surmounted by the opening in 1853 of the Trieste Railway line over the Austrian Alps and through the 980 m (3,215 ft) high Semmering Pass. A similar problem faced railway builders for the line going southward to Italy from Innsbruck in Austria. This crossed the mountains through the 1,369 m (4,494 ft) high Brenner Pass whose railroad was

completed 1867. Apart from the relatively level lines to the German border to the west, other lines westward tended to be regarded as secondary. Moreover, they faced the main European Alpine barrier. The best route was a single line through Austria's Tirol and Vorarlberg. This reached Buchs, Kanton St Gallen on the Swiss border, with hard climbing on both sides of the 1,798 m (5,900 ft) high Arlberg Tunnel, 6 km (3¾ miles) long and opened in 1884.

● **DR KARL GÖLSDORF**

Karl Gölsdorf was born into a railway family in 1861. By the age of 30 he was chief mechanical engineer (CME) of the Austrian State Railway. In the early 1900s, he was made responsible for all mechanical engineering under the purview of the Austrian Railway Ministry, which also influenced the notionally

independent Hungarian railways. His achievements include the rack-and-pinion Erzberg line. The 1,533 m (5,032 ft) high Erzberg Mountain, rich in iron ore, stands above the mining commune of Eisenerz in Austria's Styria province.

● **DESIGN PROBLEMS AND SOLUTIONS**

The empire's level routes required locomotives capable of sustained high speed, while the curving, mountainous lines called for machines capable of a long, hard slog. Both criteria needed free steaming. However, Gölsdorf faced the severe limitation of lightweight track and, consequently, a maximum axleload of no more than 14.5 tons.

He achieved high power:weight ratios by relatively high boiler pressures and by applying his own dictum that it is easier to save weight on each of a thousand

● **LEFT**
This scene in Strasshof locomotive depot north of Vienna in 1987 includes BBÖ, Bundesbahnen Österreich, class 30.33. This engine dates from 1895 and is sporting two steam domes and joining-pipe.

● **ABOVE LEFT AND RIGHT**
These locomotives are Gölsdorf designs or
derivatives active as late as the 1970s in what
was then Yugoslavia.

● **BELOW RIGHT**
The elegance of Gölsdorf's express passenger
locomotives is well known. Less well known is
this class of three rack-and-pinion locomotives.
Its life was spent mostly on trains loaded with
iron ore from the Erzberg, the Iron Mountain
at Eisenerz, in Austria's Styria province, to the
point where trains were handed over to pure
adhesion traction at Vordernberg.

GÖLSDORF'S DESIGN FOR THE RACK AND PINION ERZBERG LINE

Date	1912
Builder	Dr Karl Gölsdorf
Gauge	1,435 mm
Class	BBO 269; OBB 197
Type	BBO category F: Whyte notation 0-12-0T
Capacity adhesion:	2 cylinders 570 x 520 mm
pinion:	2 cylinders 520 x 450 mm
Coupled wheel diameter	1,030 mm
Weight in working order	88 tonnes
Maximum service speed	Adhesion, 30 kph; rack, 15 kph

small parts than on a few large ones. Wide
firegrates helped to ensure a plentiful
supply of steam. Very large driving wheels
on express locomotives, up to 7 ft in
diameter, gave the opportunity for high
speed. Up to 12 small coupled wheels
offered the adhesion and formed part of
the tractive-effort calculations for heavy
hauling in the mountains.

● **COMPOUNDING**
Gölsdorf's designs are often regarded as
unusual. One obvious feature was visible
early on. Two domes were mounted on
the boiler barrel, both to collect steam.
They were linked by a large pipe through
which steam from one passed to the
regulator in the other. More important

was a hidden device. Gölsdorf was a great
proponent of compounding, often using
just two cylinders, one high- and the
other low-pressure. Difficulty was often
experienced in starting compounds from
rest. Instead of the usual starting-valve
requiring skilled operation, high-pressure
steam was automatically admitted to the
low-pressure cylinder when the valve gear
was fully in fore or back gear.

His designs were generally adopted by
the Hungarian railways, although in some
cases they used simple machines based on
Gölsdorf's compounds. After the empire's
break-up, many of his numerous types of
locomotive could be found in Czechoslovakia, Hungary and Yugoslavia where,
as in Austria, some can be seen today.

THE FRENCH INFLUENCE – STEAM

1900 to 1950 truly was the "Golden Age" for steam in France. Designers were pushing at the frontiers of knowledge of locomotive design and performance. The age also bred a class of driver who not only had to learn about the new technology but also had to adapt driving techniques to take best advantage of it. The French *mécanicien* was an outstanding footplate technician.

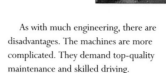

● **RIGHT**
French railways had a wide range of tank locomotives for local passenger and freight work. These Class 141TAs are former Paris-Orleans railway machines built between 1911–23.

● COMPOUNDING

To a railway historian, compounding is immediately identified with France and two names: Alfred De Glehn and André Chapelon. De Glehn was born in Britain.

Compounding works like this. A basic steam locomotive creates steam under pressure in its boiler. The steam expands in cylinders to drive the pistons and is then exhausted to the atmosphere. But a lot of power is still left in the exhausting steam. If this steam is channelled to a larger, low-pressure cylinder, this power, otherwise wasted, can be used to save fuel and water.

As with much engineering, there are disadvantages. The machines are more complicated. They demand top-quality maintenance and skilled driving.

● DESIGNERS AND THEIR WORK

Other French engineers who made great contributions to worldwide development included Gaston Du Bousquet, a contemporary of De Glehn, and, towards the end of the steam era, Mark de Caso. Chapelon always acknowledged Du Bousquet's groundwork, which led to some of his successes.

As always, locomotive designers had to work under constraints. In France, where railways have been strictly controlled since 1857, there was a requirement before World War II for the shortest possible journey-times to be achieved without exceeding 75 mph. This meant that uphill speeds with heavy loads had to be high. The De Glehn compounds built up to 1914, economical and free running, were more than adequate in their day. As loads increased and they had to be worked harder, however, efficiency fell away, and little real work was obtained from a four-cylinder compound's low-pressure cylinders.

● **LEFT**
Much painstaking work was required to restore this classic "Mountain", No. 241A 65, to working order. It was built by Fives-Lille (Works No. 4714/1931) and is shown on shed at St Sulpice, Neuchâtel, Switzerland, in 1994.

SNCF (ETAT) 241A	
Date	1927
Builder	Compagnie de Fives-Lille, Fives, France
Client	Société Nationale des Chemins de Fer (SNCF)
Gauge	1,435 mm
Type	241 (Whyte notation, 4-8-2)
Driving wheels	1,790 mm
Capacity	2 cylinders 510 x 650 mm 2 cylinders 720 x 700 mm
Weight in working order	114.6 tonnes
Maximum service speed	120 kph

● **REDOUBLING POWER AND
EFFICIENCY**

In the late 1920s, Chapelon began to
stand out as a great railway engineer. He
had entered railway service in 1919 but
in 1924 joined a telephone company. His
research abilities, recognized while he
was a student, then led to him accepting
an appointment in the Paris-Orleans
railway's research department. There,
Monsieur Paul Billet charged him to
improve specific machines' exhaust
systems. This was the platform on which
his career really began.

Studies had confirmed that power was
being wasted in getting steam from boiler
to cylinder. The reasons included

inadequate and indirect steam passages.
Redesign under Chapelon's expert
guidance led almost to redoubling the
power and efficiency of rebuilt
compound locomotives.

However, these improvements
applied equally to simple expansion
locomotives, and the techniques were
eagerly adopted across the world. They
strengthened the argument of those who
considered that simple locomotives with
high superheat were, overall, more
economical. To Chapelon's credit, he was
not a slavish devotee of compounding,
and he caused similar significant
improvements to classes of simple
expansion locomotives.

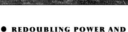

● **LEFT**
231 G 558 drifts into
the port of Le
Havre, northern
France, with a train
of 1930s stock. Were
it not for the
overhead-line
equipment, the
scene might have
been soon after
1935 when the SNCF
rebuilt this 1922-
constructed
Batignolles Pacific.
In fact, the picture
was taken in 1992.

THE FRENCH INFLUENCE – ELECTRIC

Most major European countries dabbled with electrification in the early 1900s with varying degrees of success.

In 1903, the 31 km (19 mile) long, steeply graded line from St Georges de Commiers to La Mure was electrified by Séchéron, the Swiss firm. It was the first high-tension main line electrified at 2,400 volt d.c. supplied through two wires to Bo-Bo locomotives which were capable of handling 110-tonne trains on the 1:38 gradients.

● THE EARLY YEARS

In 1910, French engineers Auvert and Ferrand together developed a single-phase a.c./d.c. 2Bo+Bo2 locomotive which was built by the Alioth works, Münchenstein. Current at 12,000-volt 25 Hz was fed through converters to vertically mounted traction motors. Trials proved successful and another locomotive was designed but not built.

Southern France's Midi Railway also saw electrification as a solution for effective traction in mountains. Between 1902-08, 12,000-volt a.c. single-phase 162/3 Hz was installed on the 54 km (34 mile) long metre-gauge line in the

Pyrénées Orientales of the Roussillon between Villefranche-de-Conflent and Bourg-Madame on the Franco-Spanish border and on the standard-gauge section between Villefranche and Ille-sur-Tet. Six locomotives were ordered from different builders for comparative trials. One established that regenerative braking with single-phase current was practicable. The builder, Jeumont of France, was one of two companies selected for a small production contract. The other was Westinghouse of the USA.

As for multiple-unit operation, the Paris Métropolitan (Métro), opened for

2-D-2 SERIES 5401-23 (ETAT 501-23)	
Date	1937
Builder	Fives-Lille, Fives, France
Client	SNCF
Gauge	1,435 mm
Class	2D2 5400
Type	2-D-2
Voltage	1,500v d.c.
Drive	Buechli
Length	17.78 m
Weight in working order	88 tonnes
Maximum service speed	140 kph

● **ABOVE**
BB 915, a former Etat Railway loco, built in 1935 by Alsthom, standing at Le Mans depot in 1970. It is one of a class of 35 and operates on 1,500-volt d.c.

● **LEFT**
The 253 trains of Luxembourg Railways were built by MTE in France in 1975 yet all showed the salient characteristics of the Budd cars referred to in the main text when introduced on the Le Mans line. One is pictured entering Esch Alzetle station, southern Luxembourg, in 1995.

● LEFT
BB 209, formerly on the Paris-Orleans line, was
built in 1938 by Alsthom and retains the very
angular bodywork of earlier years. It is pictured
shunting at Paris Austerlitz Station in 1970.

2-D-2 5100s. In the 1940s, the short
body with a generally rounded outline
established the French look, especially for
Bo-Bos. A final development was the cab
with a prominent top overhang, possibly
unique to French builders.

● **MULTIPLE UNITS**

In 1937, the Société Nationale des
Chemins de Fer (SCNF) ordered 27 sets
of multiple units for the Paris-Versailles-
Le Mans electrification, using the Budd
corrugated stainless-steel body
construction. This set a pattern that was
to last for many years, and similar units
can be seen today.

traffic on 14 July 1900, was early in the
field, two months after the Paris Invalides
to Les Molineaux services.

● **THE AGE OF DEVELOPMENT**

Between 1918–39, basic experimentation
gave way to the desire to achieve speed,
tractive power and efficiency using
technology that was growing apace.

A difficulty facing designers was the
disparity of current-supply systems. This
was largely created by haphazard development and the autonomy of the regional
railways. These showed little desire for
standardization. This may have been good
for Europe as a whole, because multicurrent locomotives were developed
capable of crossing boundaries between
countries whose electrical supplies
differed from those of France.

Locomotives' shapes and sizes were
legion. Various drive systems were
adopted. Again, as for steam locomotives,
the vehicles either looked awkward, being
boxes on wheels, or were the more
attractive bonnet-ended machines.

In the mid-1930s, softer outlines
appeared, as on the Paris-Orleans Type

● ABOVE
No. 2D2 5534, formerly on the Paris-Orleans
line, heading a train of postal vans at Paris
Austerlitz Station in 1970. It was built in 1934
by Compagnie-Electro-Mécanique, at Le
Havre, the Channel port in northern France.

● BELOW
Number 5406 about to leave Le Mans, a
railcar-production centre in north-western
France, on an express to Paris in 1961.

THE SWISS INFLUENCE – MOUNTAIN RAILWAYS

Mountain railways are usually powered either on the funicular principle (the weight of a descending car pulls another up) or on the "rack-and-pinion" principle of toothed rails.

● THE RIGGENBACH SYSTEM

The first successful rack-and-pinion system was developed not in Switzerland but in the USA. Development was proceeding in both countries, but neither of their two respective engineers knew of the other's work.

In Switzerland, Niklaus Riggenbach took out a patent on 12 August 1863 but did not develop it then. In 1869, he heard about the railway up 800 m (2,624 ft) high Mount Washington, in Berkshire County, USA, with its rack system designed by Sylvester Marsh. He visited that railway and on his return successfully developed his "ladder rack". Its first application was to a short quarry line at Ostermundigen, near Bern, in 1870. The locomotive that worked the

RIGI BAHN NO. 7	
Date	1873
Builder	Swiss Locomotive and Machine Works (SLM), Winterthur
Client	Rigi Bahn
Gauge	1,435 mm
Rack system	Riggenbach
Capacity	2 cylinders 270 x 400 mm
Weight in working order	15.1 tonnes (as built)
Maximum speed	7.5 kph

● **BELOW**
The first SLM-built steam railway locomotive, Rigi Bahn No. 7, was taken from Luzern Transport Museum in 1995 and restored by SLM for the 125th anniversary of Switzerland's Vitznau-Rigi Bahn (VRB) in 1996, when it was pictured pushing a fully loaded vintage coach from Rigi Staffel to Rigi Kulm summit station.

● **BELOW**
Switzerland's Vitznau-Rigi Bahn (VRB) owns two steam locomotives that regularly operate on vintage trains. H2/3 No. 17 built by SLM in 1925, is pictured at Rigi Kaltbad in 1986. The sturdy nature of Riggenbach's ladder rack is shown.

line, "Gnom", has been preserved.

The success was soon followed by another when his system was applied to the Vitznau-Rigi Bahn (VRB), a standard-gauge line linking Vitznau, on Lake Lucerne, with the isolated 1,800 m (5,906 ft) high Rigi Mountain. This line

● RIGHT
There is no difficulty in fitting pinion gear to electric vehicles. The 800 mm-gauge Wengernalp Bahn (WAB), which provides the intermediate stage of the journey from Interlaken to the 4,758 m (13,642 ft)-high Jungfrau Mountain in central Switzerland's Bernese Alps, uses the Riggenbach-Pauli rack to reach Kleine Scheidegg. These trains are pictured at Grindelwald Grund in 1989 before tackling their climb. Some stock dates from 1947.

● BELOW
The Locher rack's unique construction is shown in this picture, taken in 1991 from the traverser well at the Pilatus railway depot, Alpnachstad, at the foot of Mount Pilatus, near Luzern.

● LEFT
The opening of the Filisur-Bever section of Switzerland's Rhaetische Bahn in 1903 signalled the conquest of river, valley and mountain to reach a plateau at 1,800 m (6,000 ft). Steam was the original power but in 1921 the 61-tonne electric locomotives pictured here came on the scene.

or system celebrated its centenary in 1996 by operating one of the original vertical-boilered locomotives, No. 7, the first locomotive to be built by the Swiss Locomotive and Machine Works (SLM), of Winterthur, near Zürich.

● THE RIGGENBACH-LOCHER SYSTEM
It was Riggenbach who came up with the germ of an idea from the fitting of hooks that ran under the rails on the funicular from Territet to Glion near Montreux at the eastern end of Lake Geneva. The actual design is credited to Colonel Eduard Locher who became engineer to the Pilatus line in Unterwalden Canton, central Switzerland, with its 1:2 gradients. The design amounted to a pair of horizontally mounted guide pinion wheels with deep, plain flanges which run underneath the specially designed rack-rail. In effect, traction and guidance

were performed by the rack-rail and pinion wheels. The rails on which the carriage wheels run are merely for balance.

● ADHESION LINES
Numerous, mostly metre-gauge, lines wind their way into the mountains, in some cases tackling gradients of about 1:13 (7.7 per cent) without rack assistance. Two examples are popular with tourists. One is the Montreux-Oberland-Bernoise, which runs from Montreux through valley and alp to Zweisimmen. The other is the extensive spread of metre-gauge routes on the Rhaetische Bahn, which covers the Rhaetian Alps and Switzerland's largest canton, Graubünden (Grisons).
The Rhaetische Bahn offers spectacular scenery and benefits from remarkable engineering feats, which enable the line to reach the fertile flatlands of the Engadine, that is the 97 km (60 mile)

long valley of the River Inn, some 1,800 m (6,000 ft) above sea level. Much of the area is devoted to sports in winter when there is only one reliable means of access and egress – the railway. Spirals and tunnelling had to be used similar to that adopted by Swiss Federal Railways on two earlier lines. The section of the SFR over the St Gotthard Pass, with an inter-cantonal 15 km (9½ mile) long tunnel at 1,154 m (3,788 ft), completed in 1872–81, links Göschenen and Airolo and the Bern-Loetschberg-Simplon line between Frütigen and Brig with the Loetschberg Tunnel.
The 20 km (12½ mile) long Simplon Tunnel built in 1898–1905, between Brig and Domodossola, lies partly in Switzerland and partly in Italy. In its day it was the world's longest railway tunnel, famous for carrying the Simplon–Orient Express, with connections, from Calais, over the Alps at 705 m (2,313 ft), to Istanbul, Athens and Asia Minor.

SOUTHERN EUROPE – IBERIAN, ITALIAN AND GREEK PENINSULAS

The railways of Peninsular Europe – Iberia (Spain and Portugal), Italy and Greece – have long been concerned not only with national and international services but with intercontinental links between Europe and Africa, across the Western and Eastern Mediterranean Sea. Since 1869, proposals to build a rail-and-road fixed link between Spain and Morocco, across the Strait of Gibraltar, making Tangier the gateway to Africa, have been discussed. (Similarly, proposals to link Eurasia and North America by a rail tunnel across the Bering Strait, between Russia's Siberia and Alaska, have been discussed since 1905.)

● **SPAIN**

In Spain, locomotive design and construction was well developed and most steam locomotives not only entered the 20th century but continued to operate beyond the 1950s – apart from those most heavily used or taxed by mountainous terrain. Nevertheless, from the 1920s, many large and well-proportioned locomotives were obtained for the standard gauge from various domestic and foreign builders, the 4-8-2 wheel arrangement

● LEFT
A large Mallet-type metre-gauge 2-4-6-0T, pictured at Chaves, northern Portugal, in 1974.

● LEFT
In Greece, the sun glints on a chunky USA-built 2-8-0 of a general type familiar across Europe immediately after World War II.

● BELOW
Locomotives 2-8-2 No. 7108 and doubled-domed Es Class No. 7721 head a special train at Diakofto, Greece in 1980.

being preferred. There were even Garratts, built in 1930 for passenger work.

Electrification began in 1911 on 21 km (13 miles) of steeply graded line on the Spanish Southern Railway between Gérgal and Santa Fé de Montdújar, in the Sierra Nevada of Almeria province, and was slowly extended to Almeria town, on the coast, 44 km (27 miles) in all. Overhead-line a.c. 5.5kv 3 phase was used. Some massive locomotives were supplied for these lines, including 12 2CC2s in 1928 from Babcock & Wilcox-Brown Boveri.

Steady progress came to a grinding halt with the Civil War (1936–9), but new steam and electrics began operating fairly quickly thereafter. Further, the process of building new lines to make a more effective network continued, forming a firm base for the sound rail system Spain has today.

● **FAR RIGHT**
Visible on FS Italia
2-8-0 No. 741 046
are the Crosti
preheater drum,
beneath the
smokebox door, and
the exhaust
replacing the
conventional
chimney.

FS ITALIA CLASS 741

Date	1911 (rebuilt 1955)
Builder	Breda
Client	F.S. Italia (rebuild)
Gauge	1,435 mm
Class	741 (rebuilt from 740)
Driving wheels	140 (Whyte notation 2-8-0)
Capacity	2 cylinders 540 x 700 mm
Driving wheel diameter	1,370 mm
Weight in working order	68.3 tonnes
Maximum service speed	65 kph

● **BELOW**
This Alco 1,500 hp
diesel-electric,
delivered in 1948, is
one of 12 in the van
of Portugal's diesel
revolution. It is
pictured at Tunes,
Algarve, in 1996.

● **PORTUGAL**
At the turn of the century, Portugal's
steam-locomotive stock was varied and of
good lineage. It included De Glehn
compounds built in 1898-1903 and
typical Henschel outline 4-6-0s, built at
Kossel, Germany. Indeed, most European
builders of note were represented. It was
1924 before Pacifics arrived from
Henschel. Several series of 2-8-0s for
freight came into service between 1912-
24, built by Schwarzkopf of Berlin and
North British of the United Kingdom.
The first 4-8-0 arrived from Henschel in
1930. Tank locomotives ranging from
0-4-0T to 2-8-4T helped to cover
remaining duties, including suburban
passenger-train services.

The metre gauge had some fine
machines, many of them big Mallet
2-4-6-0T tanks. The suburban services

around Oporto, the country's second-
largest city, were shared by 0-4-4-0Ts and
2-8-2Ts dating from 1931.

● **ITALY**
Italy's steam development was reasonably
conventional for the period, subject to
disruption in World Wars I and II. The
unusual took the form of a novel and
effective preheating system for feed
water. Dr Ing Piero Crosti designed
boilers in which combustion gases pass in
the normal way through the main, simple
boiler and then in reverse direction
through a drum or drums. The feed
water introduced into the drum(s)
thereby captured more heat from flue
gases and reduced scale on the firebox
wall. This cut fuel costs but the
locomotives' conventional appearance
suffered. They had no obvious chimney

and exhaust gases were disposed of by a
series of pipes near the boiler's rear.

Italy is probably best known in the
diesel world for its export of railcars. The
names Fiat and Breda are on worksplates
across the world. These companies began
to develop in this field in the mid-1930s,
as did Ganz of Hungary. The Fiat railcar
started a vogue in 1935 for wheel spats
over the bogie wheels, as in aircraft of the
day. FS Italia Class Aln 56 was just
one example.

● **GREECE**
In Greece, locomotives were haphazardly
obtained from various builders and by
purchase of secondhand engines from
Germany, Austria and Italy. USA-built
locomotives were brought to Greece in
1914 and, again, after damage done to
the railways in World War II.

SCANDINAVIAN RAILWAYS

From 1900 the railways of the Scandinavian countries – Norway and Sweden forming the Scandinavian Peninsula and Denmark and Finland respectively to its south and east – were gradually extended, in some cases upgrading from metre to standard gauge, especially in Norway, and moved from steam to electrification, except for Finland whose 805-unit fleet included 766 steam locomotives (95 per cent) as late as 1958.

Apart from Denmark, whose insular component presented other physical difficulties, problems facing the railways were the same as in all cold countries. Frost heave disturbed the permanent way in the level wet areas. Heavy snow, with the ever-present risk of avalanche, was a burden in the mountains of Norway and northern Sweden.

● DENMARK

Denmark remains different from the other Scandinavian countries because of its islands, its population density and its closely sited communities. Here, speed and frequency of services became paramount together with the desire,

● **RIGHT AND OPPOSITE BOTTOM LEFT AND RIGHT** These pictures of steam in Finland capture the sense of an age long past and illustrate Russian design influence. The balloon stack and high stacking-rails on the tender of the wood-burner, No. 1163, can be seen.

● **BELOW RIGHT** The simple outlines of this 1-C-1 diesel, No. HP 15, of the Danish Hjörringer Privatbanen, the railway operating in north-east Jutland's Hjörring county, are appropriate for this workhorse. It was built in about 1935 by Frichs and is pictured at Randers, the east Jutland seaport.

gradually being achieved, to link the mainland Jutland Peninsula to all the islands and to the Scandinavian Peninsula at Malmo by bridge and tunnel rather than conveying trains on albeit very efficient train ferries.

In the 1930s, route length was 5,233 km (3,250 miles), of which only 2,512 km (1,560 miles), that is 48 per cent, was state-owned. The level terrain put no great demands on steam locomotives and it was the light diesel-

● **LEFT** This 2-6-0T No. 7 sports typical features of Danish steam locomotives, including the smokebox saddle and the national colours in the band around the chimney. Vintage coaches with clerestorey roofs and torpedo vents enhance the nostalgic scene at Helsingor, near Copenhagen, on the Danish island of Zeeland, in 1980.

● **LEFT**
One of the later
versions of the
Lyntog
("Lightning") train
pictured at Struen,
western Jutland,
Denmark, in 1980.
The four-car unit is
powered by a
Maybach diesel
engine with Voith
(Heidenheim,
Germany) hydraulic
transmission. The
power-car is Class
MA, No. 467.

railcar that became attractive for
passenger work as an alternative
to steam.

Electrification came late to Denmark,
starting with the suburban system in the
capital, Copenhagen, in 1934 employing
a line voltage of 1,500 dc. The state
system owned a good stock of steam
power, mostly built in Germany, but, to
develop high-speed services, three-car
diesel-electric units called Lyntog
("Lightning") were introduced, which
cut journey times dramatically.

● **FINLAND**
From 1809 to 1917, Finland was part of
what was then the Russian Empire and so
adopted the Russian 5 ft gauge for main
lines and 2 ft 5½ in gauge for minor
lines. The terrain was relatively level and,
in the earlier part of the 20th century,
schedules were not demanding, so that
comparatively light, often woodburning,
locomotives were sufficient. In the latter
days of steam, a small class of coalfired
Pacifics with good lines and particularly
commodious cabs worked the heaviest
passenger services. Local and semifast
services around Helsinki, the capital,
were served by the neat, most attractive
Class N1, built by Hanomag in Germany.

● **SWEDEN**
The "Golden Age" of Sweden's railways
may be said to be firmly linked to the
enormous supplies of iron ore in the
inhospitable mountains on the northern
borders of Sweden and Norway. Near the
town of Kiruna, at 509 m (1,670 ft) above
sea level Sweden's highest, established
mines work night and day. Some 16
million tons were produced in 1960, the
bulk being moved by rail for export.

Electrification of the lines at 16,000 volt
single phase ac 16⅔ Hz began in 1910

with the Frontier Railway between Lulea
and Rikseransen. By 1914, the first of the
massive electric locomotives 1＋CC＋1
for freight and B-B＋B-B were being
delivered by the builders ASEA/Siemens.
Electrification continued apace until, by
1923, some 450 km (280 miles) had
been completed. Even more powerful
locomotives were provided, ten -D- for
freight, producing 1,200 hp and capable
of working in multiple, as well as two
2,400 hp B-B＋B-B passenger machines.

For general electrification, SJ, the
Swedish State Railway, decided on a
single class of locomotive to work
passenger and freight trains. 1-C-1,

whose gearing can easily be changed to
operate either 500-ton passenger-trains
at 65 mph or 900-ton freight trains at 45
mph. Electrification did not supplant
steam rapidly. Main routes were
electrified in the 1930s with considerable
success, including the Stockholm–
Gothenburg line.

In the early days, locomotives were
bought from Britain. Later, designers
adapted and developed them to suit local
needs. This may be why inside-cylinders
continued to be used long after most
mainland countries had adopted the
more convenient outside form. The
practice continued until in 1930 the

per cent by electricity. The remaining 27
per cent was diesel, but during the period
under consideration, up to 1950, diesel
traction had yet to become significant.

● NORWAY

Norway, politically linked with Sweden
under the Swedish Crown between
1814–1905, is the most mountainous of
Scandinavian countries. Its railway lines
spread out from the capital, Oslo, like
fingers, seeking natural routes to a
scattered population.

Norway's railways developed late and
in a scattered fashion. In the more
benign terrain north of Oslo, steam
traction was successful. British designs
were the basis for further development.

Locomotives had been bought from
the USA since 1879. When purchase of
new locomotives became necessary
during World War I, Baldwin Works of
Philadelphia, USA, were asked to supply
2-8-0s, ostensibly to Norwegian design.
Certainly, the boiler fittings and enclosed
cab were Norwegian, but the rest was

Swedish Motala works built a massive
inside-cylinder 4-6-0 for the private
Kalmar Railways operating in the south-
eastern province of Kalmar.

The private Traffic-Ab Grangesberg–
Oxelosunds Jarnvagar (TGO), basically
an iron-ore mining company, had three
noncondensing turbine locomotives in
its stock, which achieved a degree of
successful operation.

The three-cylinder locomotive was rare
in Sweden. In 1927, Nydkvist and Holm
of Trollhättan, Sweden, built a class for the
Bergslagernas Railway. This class's golden
days on the expresses between Gothenburg and Mellerud, on Lake Vanern,
ended with electrification in 1939.

As late as 1955, 10 per cent of train
miles were operated by steam and 63

SWEDISH STATE RAILWAY (SJ) 4-6-0	
Date	1918
Builder	Nyakvist and Holm, Trollhättan, Sweden
Client	Swedish State Railway (SJ)
Gauge	1,435 mm
Class	B
Driving wheels	1,750 mm
Capacity	2 cylinders 590 x 620 mm
Weight in working order	69.2 tonnes (excluding tender)
Maximum service speed	90 kph

● LEFT
The beauty of
polished wood
adorning bodywork
is a striking feature
of SJ Class Du 1-C-1
E109 as it waits with
its train of period
coaches at Malmø
Central Station,
in the southern
Swedish seaport,
in 1981.

● **RIGHT**
This HHJ Class H3 4-6-0 No. 21 is pictured assembling its train of vintage coaches at Klippan, southern Sweden, in 1981.

● **BELOW**
The massive scale of this direct descendant of the earliest "Iron Ore" railway electric locomotives is put into perspective by the people in the foreground. It was joining a parade in Stockholm, Sweden, in 1981.

pure Baldwin. Two 0-10-0 yard-shunters came from the same source in 1916, as well as three 2-8-2 for freight. In 1919, a 2-6-2T arrived, which now had the stamp of real Norwegian design.

Later classes show German influence. An unusual design of 1935 was a 2-8-4, a wheel arrangement previously seen only in Austria for an express-locomotive. The class were four-cylinder compounds for the Dovre line, across the Dovrefjell, the 2,285 m (7,565 ft) high central Norwegian plateau, between Dombås and Trondheim (formerly Trondhjem), the seaport and the country's third largest city. The first engine was called The Dovre Giant. However, much smaller and ageing 2-6-0s and 4-6-0s worked main-line and branch services into the mid-1960s.

Electrification, especially in the far north, followed the Swedish pattern. Because there was plenty of water for hydroelectric power, electrification began in 1922 between Oslo and Drammen, the seaport on a branch of Oslo Fjord.

At the same time, work was in hand to link the main centres to Oslo. Trondheim was first in 1921, followed by Christiansand, the seaport on the Skagerrak in 1938 and Stavanger seaport in 1944.

Almost all the route mileage of about 4,300 km (2,700 miles) is state-owned, about a third of which is electrified at 15 kv single phase 16⅔ Hz. Few narrow-

gauge systems operated by state and private companies have survived.

Narvik, which exports iron ore, is the terminus for the railway that cuts across the peninsula from the Swedish port of Lulea on the Gulf of Bothnia. It is one of the world's two most northerly railway stations.

● **RIGHT**
The latter-day Swedish State Railways (SJ) steam locomotive is well represented by Class B 4-6-0 No. 1367 as it hauls a special train at the southern Swedish town of Nassjo in 1981. Note the large, enclosed cab.

INDIAN RAILWAYS

Of all world railways influenced by Britain, those of India best reflected the British presence. Railway development proceeded further in India than in any other part of Asia and by the 1950s 64,400 km (40,000 miles) were operating, comprising broad-gauge trunk lines, connecting large centres of population, and a network of narrow-gauge lines.

In the 19th century, four gauges emerged on the Indian subcontinent: 5 ft 6 in; metre; 2 ft 6 in; and 2 ft. The variety of companies operating these gauges had ordered a diversity of designs, which, with the exception of some metre-gauge standards , were largely unco-ordinated. The Central Provinces (from 1950 Madhya Pradesh), for example, had three railway systems.

● ENGINEERING STANDARDS COMMITTEES

This led the British Engineering Standards Committee (BESA) to appoint

● LEFT
The inside-cylinder 4-4-0 express-passenger hauling version of the inside-cylinder 0-6-0, again with an LNER aura – in this case the Manchester, Sheffield and Lincolnshire Railway's Pollitt 4-4-0s.

a subcommittee, composed of several leading British locomotive mechanical engineers, to prepare a set of standard designs for the subcontinent. In 1905, eight locomotive types were suggested to cover all broad-gauge requirements across India. The designs were classic British products: inside-cylinder 0-6-0s and 4-4-0s with common boilers, Atlantics, 4-6-0s and 2-8-0 heavy goods.

In 1924, the newly appointed Locomotive Standards Committee (LSC) was asked to make a new set of designs, in accordance with the need for more powerful locomotives. The committee presented eight basic types. The main ones were three Pacifics, XA, XB and XC, for branch-, medium- and heavy-passenger work; two Mikados, XD and XE, for medium and heavy goods respectively; and XT 0-4-2Ts for branch-line work.

Standard designs for metre and narrow gauge were also produced. Following the prefix X for the broad gauge came Y for metre gauge, Z for 2 ft 6 in gauge and Q for 2 ft gauge.

● AMERICAN INFLUENCE

A dramatic change occurred during World War II, Britain could not supply sufficient locomotives for India's increased traffic requirements and many new designs were ordered from North

● LEFT
A typically British 2-8-0 classified HSM from India's South Eastern Railway. These were once main-line heavy-freight haulers on the Bengal & Nagpur Railway. This last survivor is pictured on tripping duties in the Calcutta area.

● **LEFT**
An XC Class Pacific 4-6-2 of Indian Railways. These engines bear a striking resemblance to Gresley's Pacifics. Both types were introduced in the 1920s.

● **BELOW**
The heavy-freight hauling version of the XC was the XE 2-8-2. It bore a striking resemblance to Gresley's P1s of 1925.

● **BOTTOM**
One of Indian Railways's standard inside-cylinder 0-6-0s. These proliferated throughout many of the broad-gauge systems of the subcontinent. In common with the X types, these engines bear a striking resemblance to LNER classes, in this case the Pom Pom J11s of Great Central Railway (GCR).

America. These designs contrasted dramatically with the British engines and set a precedent for the remainder of steam development in India, because of suitability and popularity.

Three notable designs appeared on the 5 ft 6 in gauge: the AWC, which was an Indian version of Major Marsh's famous S160 of World War II; the class AWE, which was an Americanized version of the XE 2-8-2; and a lighter mixed-traffic Mikado 2-8-2 classified AWD/CWD. These three classes totalled 909 locomotives, 809 (89 per cent) of them being the light Mikado from mixed-traffic work. All entered service between 1943–9.

INDIAN XE CLASS 2-8-2	
Date	1930
Builder	William Beardmore Dalmuir, Vulcan Foundry, Lancashire, England
Client	East Indian Railway
Gauge	5 ft 6 in
Driving wheels	5 ft 1½ in
Capacity	Cylinders 23 x 30 in
Total weight	200 tons

CHINESE LOCOMOTIVE TRADITIONS

Railway development came late in China, and an incredible locomotive-building programme and standardization of types occurred in the years following World War II.

● EARLY DEVELOPMENT WITH FOREIGN LOANS

As recently as 1930, China had fewer than 16,000 km (10,000 miles) of railway. During the early years of the 20th century, China's railways were developed by a number of organizations, but

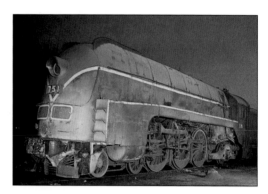

● LEFT
This streamlined Pacific classified SL7 is of a type built in Japan by Kawasaki and at the works of the South Manchurian Railway. These engines worked the high-speed Asia day-train between Dairen (the Japanese name for Dalian) and Mukden (modern Shenyang). The class was introduced in 1934.

invariably they turned to American imported locomotives of modest proportions. America's vigorous drive to promote the export of locomoties proved effective in China. The similarity in size between America and China, along with the varied terrain which the two countries

USATC S160 2-8-0	
Date	1943
Builders	American Locomotive Company (Alco); Baldwin Locomotive Company; Lima Locomotive Company
Client	United States Army Transportation Corps of Engineers (USATE)
Gauge	4 ft 8½ in
Driving wheels	4 ft 9 in
Capacity	2 cylinders 19 x 26 in
Total weight	125 tons

● LEFT
In the years following World War II, a number of Major Marsh's classic S160 2-8-0s were transferred to China in a programme to rebuild the country's railways.

had in common, rendered the American
locomotive relatively easy to sell and well
suited to the task in hand.

● **THE SOUTH MANCHURIAN
RAILWAY**
The most developed part of China was
Manchuria, and the South Manchurian
Railway, although Japanese owned, was
almost entirely American in its
equipment and operation as a result of
America having provided most of Japan's
railway. In 1931, Japan took over
Manchuria and with it the North
Manchurian Railway. Locomotives
operated in Manchuria were locally made
as well as imported from Japan.

The advancement of railway and
industrial operation in Manchuria led to

the South Manchurain Railway's
introducing the streamlined "Asia" train
in 1934, which operated a fast air-
conditioned service between Dalian and
Shenyang, or Makden as it was then
known. Streamlined Pacific locomotives
were built for this service both in Japan
and South Manchuria.

● **RAILWAYS UNDER CHAING
KAI-SHEK**
Under the nationalist government of
Chiang Kai-shek, development of
railways was proceeding in other parts of
the country in the 1930s. In 1937, the
outbreak of the Sino-Japanese War ended
new building. As this war went on, 80
per cent of China's railways were either
destroyed or fell into Japanese hands.

However, China's central government
continued to build lines in the west, in
areas not occupied by the Japanese.

● **KMT: RAILWAYS UNDER
COMMUNISTS**
Japan's surrender in 1945 found China's
railways in an appalling state. Aid came
through the United Nations Relief and
Rehabilitation Adminstration (UNRRA)
scheme, which again brought huge
numbers of American locomotives to
Chinese soil. The ongoing Chinese Civil
War caused further damage.

By the time of Mao's victory in 1949,
the railways were in terrible disarray.
Only half of the system was active. The
following decades provided some stability
under a powerful national identity and a
centrally planned economy. The railways
flowered under this regime. Herein lay
the seeds of China's "Golden Age" of
railways, expanding from the 1950s to
the present day.

SOUTH-EAST ASIAN RAILWAYS

This section covers the railways of
Peninsular Malaysia, from 1957 the
successor-state to the British-controlled
Federation of Malaya; of Thailand
proper and Peninsular Thailand, which
joins Peninsular Malaysia at the Kra
Isthmus; of Indonesia, the Philippines
and Taiwan.

● PENINSULAR MALAYSIA

In 1909 the last link of the line between
two island cities of the then-British
colony called the Straits Settlements,
Penang and Singapore, respectively at the
north and south ends of Peninsular
Malaysia, was opened. Termini were on
the mainland, at ferry ports serving the
islands. The engines used on this line
were the Pacifics, which, although small
by British and continental standards,
were robust machines weighing about
76 tons. With a 4-6-4 wheel
arrangement, the locomotives had large
headlights and cowcatchers.

In 1938, three-cylinder Pacific
express-passenger locomotives were
introduced on the Malayan metre-gauge
line between Singapore, Kuala Lumpur,

capital of Perak State, and Prai, the
railway terminus and seaport on the
mainland, opposite George Town on
Penang Island. Part of this line ascended
the 1,000 m (3,300 ft) high Taiping Pass
near Ipoh, the commercial centre of the
Kinta Valley tin-mining region of Perak.
These heavy gradients called for a special
type of locomotive. The three-cylinder
4-6-2 Pacifics had a relatively small boiler
but at high pressure provided the latent
energy needed for developing a high
tractive power.

The Pacifics were used on long runs
but there were branch lines on which a
tender-engine was unsuitable. For these,
a 4-6-4 two-cylinder tank-engine was

● ABOVE
One of South-east Asia's most remarkable
systems is the stone railway at Gunung Kataren
in northern Sumatra, Indonesia. The line
conveys stones from a riverbed to a crushing
plant for use as track ballast. Built to 60 cm
gauge, this veteran came from Orenstein &
Koppel in 1920.

● LEFT
Three standard Japanese 3 ft 6 in gauge designs
working in Taiwan. Left, a Taiwan Government
Railway Class DT595 2-8-0 (Japanese National
Railway 9600 Class); centre, a Class CT192
Mogul (JNR Class 8620); right, a Class DT673
Mikado (JNR Class D51) – 1,100 of these mixed-
traffic 2-8-2s were built between 1936–45.

A 4-6-0 built for metre-gauge Royal Siamese
State Railways in 1919 by North British of
Glasgow, Scotland.

4 - 6 - 0	
Date	1919
Builder	North British Glasgow, Scotland
Client	Royal Siamese State Railways
Gauge	Metre
Driving wheels	4 ft
Capacity	Cylinders 14½ x 22 in

used. It was fitted with cowcatchers at
both ends so that it was suitable for
running in both directions. Like the
Pacifics, these 4-6-4Ts were fitted with
Caprotti valve gear.

● **THAILAND**
In Siam (Muang-Thai to Thais and
since 1949 Thailand), in the rice-
growing and jungle country, the metre-
gauge railway was laid with relatively

light rails on a soft road bed. Powerful
locomotives were needed, and in
1925 26 Pacific 2-8-2s were bought from
the USA. They were woodfired,
and routes were arranged so that the
engines would travel out and back to
their home station on one tenderful
of fuel. The round trips were
193–225 km (120–140 miles) long.
This arrangement meant frequent
engine changes *en route*.

● **ABOVE**
A battered, hybridized, American-built
Mikado, believed to have been constructed
by Alco in 1921, at work on the metals of
the Ma Ao Sugar Central railway on the
Philippine island of Negros. These
locomotives draw freshly cut sugar cane
from the fields to the mills.

● **RIGHT**
A Thai railways metre-gauge Pacific 4-6-2, No.
823, which, with the MacArthur 2-8-2s, was
one of Thailand's last steam locomotives.

AUSTRALASIAN RAILWAYS

New South Wales (NSW) entered the 20th century with a scheme to have main-line traffic handled by standard classes for passenger services, the P6 (later C32) Class 4-6-0; for goods traffic, the 1524 (later D50 Class) 2-8-0, of which 280 were built; and for suburban working the S636 (later C30) Class, numbering 145 units.

● **NEW SOUTH WALES**
In the mid-1920s, as traffic grew, 75 C36 Class units took over major passenger services. From 1929, 25 4-8-2 D57 Class units were introduced for heavyfreight. With extreme traffic during World War II, 30 new C38 Class Pacifics were built, becoming the foremost express-locomotive. With the need for new goods locomotives after the war, 42 4-8-4+4-8-4 Garratts were obtained to carry the brunt of the load prior to the arrival of diesels.

● **TASMANIA**
Tasmania also used Garratts – the 2 ft gauge K Class of 1910 being the first Garratt in the world. The 3 ft 6 in lines followed, with the L Class 2-6-2+2-6-2 for goods traffic and the M Class 4-4-2+2-4-4s for passenger traffic.

● **SOUTH AUSTRALIA**
In South Australia, ten 4-6-2 passenger, ten 2-8-2 goods and ten 4-8-2 mixed-traffic locomotives entered service in 1926. These were of American design but built in England. On the narrow gauge, the T Class were the mainstay of the traffic, almost to the end of steam.

● **WESTERN AUSTRALIA**
Western Australia introduced 57 F Class 4-8-0s in 1902. These were accompanied by 65 E Class 4-6-2s for passenger services. Larger Pacifics entered service

from 1924 onwards. Following World War II, the fleet was augmented by 60 light-line Beyer Peacock 4-8-2 W Class and 25 heavy 2-8-2 V Class from Robert Stephenson & Hawthorn.

● **AUSTRALIAN NETWORK AND THE TCR**
The development of Australia's railway network was complicated but striking. The gauge was not uniform (New South Wales was mostly the standard 4 ft 8½ in, South Australia mostly broad 5 ft 3 in gauge and all Queensland was narrow 3 ft

● LEFT
K167, an example of Australia's Victorian Railways K Class Consolidations introduced in 1922, pictured with a tour-train at Bandiana, near the New South Wales (NSW) border, in 1965.

● LEFT
After 1924, the P96 Class was reclassified as the C32 class. With regular floods in the Hunter Valley, in eastern NSW, this class was able to maintain traffic in conditions no diesel-electric could handle. The cover over the crosshead keeps out dust in the almost desert country in the far west of NSW.

● LEFT
Imported from the North British Works, Glasgow, Scotland, in 1950, this Pmr726 Pacific is pictured outside the Midland workshops in 1968. Unsuccessful at speed, these locomotives did excellent goods-traffic work.

• **RIGHT**
The pride of Australia's NSW Railways, No. 3801, introduced in 1943, waiting to depart with an air-conditioned passenger-train in 1963.

SAR RX 4-6-0	
Date	1909
Builder	SAR Islington/NBLC Walker (SA)
Client	NSWGR
Gauge	4 ft 8½ in
Wheels	5 ft 9 in
Capacity	Cylinders 18 x 24 in
Weight	201 tons

• **RIGHT**
In 1899, South Australian Railways (SAR) started converting 30 R Class 4-6-0 locomotives to Rx Class by providing higher-pressure boilers. An additional 54 were newly built in 1909. This example, RX93, is pictured at the Mile End depot in 1965.

written off in 1957. The Pacific was further developed, eventually to the Ab class of 1915, of which 141 were built, and to a tank-engine, the Wab class. The Ab Class is claimed to be the first locomotive in the world to have been capable of 1 hp for each 100 lb of weight.

Tank engines played a major part on the lines of this small nation, the 4-6-4T W Class of 50 units being one of the more prolific. Garratts were also tried in 1928 but failed, due less to design faults than to the light drawgear on New Zealand rolling stock and the short crossing loops, making economical running almost impossible. Heavier conventional locomotives followed.

6 in gauge). Of the continent's some 45,000 km (28,000 miles) of railway, all but about 3 per cent, 1,290 km (800 miles), was state-owned by the 1950s. Of that length, 1,694 km (1,052 miles) were occupied by the Transcontinental (East-West) Railway completed in 1917. The TCR crosses South Australia and Western Australia, linking Port Augusta, at the head of the Spencer Gulf, and Perth with its port of Fremantle on the Indian Ocean. It crosses the Great Victoria Desert and the Nullarbar Plain, serves the goldfields of Kalgoorlie and the agricultural industry, and runs link lines to Port Pirie and to Alice Springs in the Northern Territory.

• **NEW ZEALAND**
New Zealand's main claim to fame is the development of the world's first true Pacific locomotive, 13 of which were supplied by Baldwin in 1901. These engines had a long life, the last being

• **BELOW**
Designed for traffic on light lines, this example of a J Class was one of 40 delivered to New Zealand at the start of World War II. A modified Ja Class supplied in 1946 is in front. The two locomotives are pictured at Fielding-Marton in 1972.

AFRICAN RAILWAYS

The years before the start of World War I were exciting and dynamic on South Africa's railways, many designs being produced. The 20th century brought a foretaste of the giants to come, powerful 2-8-2s, 4-8-0s and 4-8-2s being put into traffic with some racy Pacific designs.

● **UNION OF SOUTH AFRICA**

The immense distances and sparsely populated country called for strong locomotives, many of which had four-wheeled leading bogies to cope with cheaply laid track beds.

South African Railways (SAR) were formed in 1910 by the amalgamation of Africa's main railway companies. These were the Cape Government Railway (CGR), the Natal Government Railway (NGR) and the Central South African Railway (CSAR).

The country's first articulated locomotives were 2-6-6-0 compounds built by the American Locomotive Company (Alco). The type was introduced on to Natal's heavily graded, sharply curved routes.

Just as the giant Mallet conquered

● **BELOW**
Garratts on the Greytown Line in Natal, South Africa. One of SAR's pugnacious GMA Class 4-8-2+2-8-4 Garratts prepares to leave New Hanover, Natal, with full freight for Greytown. These powerful secondary Garratts, descended from the GM Class of 1938, climbed 1:40 gradients with only 60 lb weight.

● **ABOVE**
In contrast with the typical four- and six-coupled tanks of British industry, South Africa's engines were fully fledged mainliners to haul trains over undulating tracks to SAR connections often many miles from collieries. This North British-built 4-8-2T is one of a standard class exported from Glasgow, Scotland, to South Africa for industrial use.

● **LEFT**
SAR 3 ft 6 in-gauge 4-8-2s of the 1930s.

America, so the Garratt articulated conquered Africa. South Africa's railways were one of the largest users of Garratts from their introduction to the country in 1920. They quickly proved themselves superior to the Mallet on a network that ran through difficult terrain abounding in heavy gradients and curves with relatively lightly laid track.

The Garratt's boiler and firebox are free of axles and so can be built to whatever size is needed. A deep firebox allowed for ample generation of steam and full combustion of gases. By placing the engine's wheels and cylinders under a front water unit and with the rear coal units situated either side of the boiler, the engine's weight is spread over a wide area. With the front and rear units articulated from the boiler, a large, powerful locomotive can be built capable of moving heavy loads over curved gradients and

SAR "BIG BILL" 4-8-2

Date	1925
Builder	Baldwin, American Locomotive Company (USA), Breda (Milan, Italy), North British (Glasgow, Scotland)
Client	South African Railways (SAR)
Gauge	3 ft 6 in
Wheels	5 ft
Capacity	Cylinders 24 x 28 in
Weight	173 tons

● **FAR LEFT**
The SAR Class 15CA, 4-8-2 "Big Bills" were the first large American engines imported to South Africa. They had a profound influence on locomotive development. This Italian-built example is seen leaving Panpoort, Transvaal.

● **NAMIBIA (FORMERLY SOUTH WEST AFRICA)**
In the years following World War II, 100 2-8-4 Berkshires were put into operation for branch-line work, particularly over the 45 lb rail lines in South West Africa (Namibia since independence in 1990). They had cylindrical bogie tenders for long-range operation in waterless areas. The type displaced the ageing Class 7 and Class 8 4-8-0s of half a century earlier.

lightly laid lines. SAR used more than 400 Garratts, mostly British-built.

The 1920s also saw the introduction of large 4-8-2s and Pacifics of pure American construction. These set the precepts for the giants that followed, such as the 15F Class and 23 Class 4-8-2s. These formed the mainstay of steam motive power from the 1930s until the end of steam operations.

● **ABOVE RIGHT**
The Mallett was little used in South Africa but this 2-6-6-2, four-cylinder compound Class MH was one of five built by North British in 1915. At their introduction, they were the largest locomotives in the world on 3 ft 6 in gauge track.

● **RIGHT**
A South African Railways (SAR) Class 23 4-8-2 heads northwards from Bloemfontein, capital of Orange Free State. These American-inspired engines of 3 ft 6 in gauge were constructed in the late 1930s by both British and German builders and totalled 136 examples.

● LEFT
A former
Tanganyika Railway
ML Class 2-8-2,
complete with Geisl
ejector and air
brakes – and one of
Tanganyika
Railway's last
designs.

● OPPOSITE
TOP LEFT
The plate from a
locomotive built for
Rhodesian Railways
by Beyer Peacock of
Manchester,
England.

● **ZIMBABWE**

Railways were essential to the rich development potential of landlocked Zimbabwe (Southern Rhodesia until 1964, Rhodesia 1964–78). Routes extended to the Indian Ocean ports, eastwards to Beira in Mozambique, southwards through South Africa to Durban in Natal. A third route was opened up northwards, across the Victoria Falls at Hwange (until 1982 Wankie) and on through the copper belt. This route reached the Atlantic Ocean ports via the Bengeula Railway in Angola. By 1920, when Rhodesia Railways (RR) was formed, a unified 3 ft 6 in gauge was in operation.

Motive power was not dissimilar from that of South Africa, with 4-8-0s and 4-8-2 Mountains. As the national wealth of this vast region was developed, however, the demand for heavier trains became

huge and articulated locomotives vital. After a Kitson-Mayer phase, the Garratt phase was introduced to standardize the system. Almost half the locomotives built for Rhodesian Railways were British-built Garratts, embracing all duties from branch-line work, through heavy freights to expresses with the racy 15th Class 4-6-4+4-6-4s. These handled mixed-traffic duties and reached speeds of 70 mph with passenger-trains.

● **EAST AFRICA**

In East Africa, the British-built Kenyan and Ugandan lines and the German-built

● LEFT
Following the lead
by the USA the wide
firebox appeared
early on Britain's
locomotive exports,
especially those
bound for African
countries. A typical
example was the
Rhodesian Railways
12A Class 4-8-2. The
example shown is
No. 190, built in
1926 by North
British, Glasgow,
Scotland.

● RIGHT
A former Rhodesian
Railways 16th Class
Garratt 2-8-2+2-8-2,
built by Beyer
Peacock of
Manchester,
England, in 1929,
working at the
Transvaal
Navigation Colliery,
South Africa.

railways of neighbouring Tanzania (formerly Tanganyika) were metre gauge. The Ugandan railway in its early years used early Indian metre-gauge types, notably E Class 0-4-2s and the celebrated F Class 0-6-0s. Invariably, motive power

● **RIGHT**
A typical African plantation-train during the early 20th century at Lugazi, Uganda. The unidentified engine, with ornate spark-arresting chimney, is of European origin.

blossomed and embraced a Mallet stage and some Garratts, although the 4-8-0 was adopted as a general standard, many examples being to Indian BESA designs.

By the time the Kenya & Ugandan Railway (KUR) was formed in 1926, extremely powerful 2-8-2s worked the line linking the Kenyan Indian Ocean port of Mombasa and the Kenyan capital at Nairobi. The network also had a wide variety of Garratts, although these remained in a minority compared with the conventional locomotives, many of which were used on lighter sections of this vast area of Africa.

● **ANGOLA**
The 1,347 km (837 mile) long Angola Railway (Benguela Railway) was built by the Portuguese to link their then west and east coast possessions in southern Africa, respectively Angola and Mozambique. From the west, it runs from the Atlantic Ocean ports of Lobito and Benguela, to the Democratic Republic of Congo (formerly Zaire),

linking to Port Francqui (Ilebo), the Copper Belt of Zambia (formerly Northern Rhodesia) and Zimbabwe, and on to the Indian Ocean ports of Sofala (formerly Beira) and Maputo (Lourenço Marques until 1975) in Mozambique, and Durban, then on to the Cape.

It achieved world renown for the eucalyptus-burning Garratts, which worked over one of the sections climbing the steep coastal escarpment inland from the Atlantic. These red-liveried mammoths shot columns of fire into the sky at night and were regarded by some as one of the railway sights of the world.

NORTHERN AFRICAN RAILWAYS

Railway development in Africa was essential to open up the industrial potential of the continent's interior and provide vital lifelines for the movement of materials. Africa has benefited vastly from her railways but their piecemeal, often parochial, building defied the obvious ideal of a Pan-African system. Had the railways been built with this vision, Africa would be an infinitely more prosperous continent than she is today.

● ALGERIA

Algeria's railways were built and engineered by the French from the mid-19th century. A large network of lines of various types emerged, including through links with neighbouring Tunisia and Morocco. The standard gauge, fed by metre-gauge lines, saw many 0-6-0s. Moguls and standard De Glehn compounds of types commonly seen in Europe.

In the 1920s, 2-10-0s appeared for hauling heavy mineral trains. Famous types working in Algeria included some Prussian G8s and three-cylinder G12s. Most celebrated, however, were the Algerian Garratts. These, built in France in 1932, were the most powerful express-passenger-locomotives ever to

EGYPTIAN STATE RAILWAYS (ESR) ATLANTIC 4-4-2	
Date	1906
Builder	North British, Glasgow, Scotland
Client	Egyptian State Railways (ESR)
Gauge	4 ft 8½ in
Driving wheels	6 ft 3 in
Capacity	Cylinders 17 x 26 in

● **BELOW**
These British-styled Atlantics were delivered to ESR in 1906 from the North British Works in Glasgow, Scotland, for operation on Egypt's standard-gauge network.

operate outside the USA.

By the 1950s, a rail network of more than 4,800 km (3,000 miles) penetrated all parts of Algeria. Two lines stretched into the Sahara to link with motor routes stretching to then French West Africa.

● TUNISIA

Tunisia had both standard- and metre-gauge lines, although no standard-gauge locomotives were delivered into the country after 1928. During World War II, American S160 2-8-0s, British Hunslet Austerity 0-6-0STs and some British Great Western Dean goods were all introduced for military operations.

● MOROCCO

Morocco's railways were also French-dominated, the country having become a French protectorate in 1912. Through-services were run between Marrakech in

● **LEFT**
Two 0-6-0 well-tanks made by Orenstein &
Koppel at the Nsuta Manganese System in Ghana,
West Africa. The engines' Works Nos. 10609/10
respectively were exported to Ghana (until 1957
the British colony called Gold Coast) in 1923.

the west and Tunisia in the east, a
distance of 2,400 km (1,491 miles).

● **EGYPT**

The Egyptian State Railway (ESR) is the
oldest in Africa and blossomed following
British occupation of the Nile Valley in
1882. The railway was built and run by
the British. Though the ESR operated a
vast diversity of types, British operating
methods and many British designs were
in evidence. Much of Egypt's express-
passenger work was handled by the
Atlantic 4-4-2s, backed by either 0-6-0s
or Moguls for mixed-traffic work.

World War II's North African
Campaign demanded movement of really
heavy freight trains. Many British Stanier
8F 2-8-0s were sent, of which 60 were
adopted by the ESR after the war.

Egypt's rich locomotive tradition
ended with a class of oil-burning, French-
built Pacifics delivered as late as 1955.

● **SUDAN**

Egypt's standard-gauge lines contrast
with the 3 ft 6 in gauge network of
neighbouring Sudan where railway
building began around the turn of
the century. One of the earliest systems
ran from the Nile Valley to the Red Sea
then southwards through the capital,
Khartoum. Although much of this early
railway building had a military purpose,
the beginnings of a national railway were

● **ABOVE**
The spinning driving wheels of a Class 500
4-8-2 of Sudan Railway.

● **BELOW**
A mixed train on Sudan State Railways headed
by a standard oilburning Mikado 2-8-2 built
by North British, of Glasgow, Scotland.

established. Sudan has a great will to
operate a good, viable railway system.
Additions to the network were being
made as late as 1960.

Pacifics and Mikados, many with light
axle loadings, were a mainstay of Sudan's
motive power. Sudan also operated
4-6-4+4-6-4 Garratts pulling 1,600 ton
trains between Atbara, Khartoum and
Wad Medani. In contrast, English-
looking 0-6-0Ts handled shunting and
local tripping work. The last of these was
not built until 1951, notwithstanding
Sudan received diesel-shunters as early
as 1936.

The pièce de résistance of
conventional Sudanese motive power
came with the 42 500 Class 4-8-2s
delivered by North British, of Glasgow,
Scotland, in 1954.

● **WEST AFRICA**

In West Africa, Britain, France and
Germany all introduced railways to their
colonial possessions.

SOUTH AMERICAN RAILWAYS

South America's railways are of great diversity, reflecting the vast geographical contrasts of a continent that ranges from the tropical rain forests of the Amazon, to the passes of the Andes standing at 4,266 m (14,000 ft), through to the verdant beef-rearing flatlands of the Argentine pampas.

● ARGENTINA

Argentina had by far the greatest density of railways, with over 100 different types of locomotive operating over five different gauges. The British-owned railways of Argentina constituted the largest commercial enterprise ever to operate outside an investing nation. With many of the country's railway systems operated by Britain, Argentina was a huge recipient of British products. British-built steam locomotives fired on Welsh coal gave Argentina one of the world's most successful economies, exporting vast tonnages of meat, grain and fruit.

● URUGUAY

The railways of neighbouring Uruguay were also British-owned. Beyer Peacock of Manchester, England, was a principal builder over many years. Manchester was connected with the vast Fray Bentos meat corporation based on Fray Bentos town in Uruguay.

● BRAZIL

The vastness of Brazil, with its network of 5 ft 3 in and metre-gauge lines and a huge diversity of secondary routes, plantation and industrial railways, also ensured an incredibly rich locomotive heritage. American-built locomotives predominated with British classics on the metre-gauge Leopoldina system.

● PARAGUAY

Neighbouring Paraguay's standard-gauge main-line railway linked the capital and chief port, Asunción, with Encarnación

● LEFT
Mixed freight to Fray Bentos, in Uruguay. The Uruguayan Railway's last-surviving T Class 2-8-0 named Ing Pedro Magnou is heading a train bound for the meat-canning port on the Uruguay River. This 2-8-0 has a distinctive Scottish Highland Railway aura about it.

● OPPOSITE
A 5 ft 6 in gauge survivor of the Chilean Railway's 38 Class on pilot duties at San Bernardo works, outside Santiago in Chile. It is probably the last survivor from Roger's of New Jersey, USA, having come from those works in 1896.

386 km (240 miles) away on the Argentine border. This railway was also British-owned and operated. The main motive power for much of the present century has been provided by woodburning Edwardian Moguls, exported from the North British Works in Glasgow, Scotland.

● BOLIVIA AND CHILE
The railways of Bolivia, South America's other landlocked nation, connected Chile, over the Andes to the west, with Brazil and Argentina, over the humid lowlands to the east. The country's locomotive heritage was diverse, with a rich mixture of European, American and British schools of design.

● TRANS-ANDEAN
RAILWAY (TAR)
The Trans-Andean Railway (TAR) completed in 1910 links Valparaiso, Chile's greatest seaport, with Buenos Aires, the Argentine capital, crossing the Andes and desolate Patagonia at the Uspallata Pass between Mendoza in Argentina and Santiago in Chile. The near 3 km (2 mile) long Trans-Andean RR tunnel crosses at the pass's highest point, at 3,986 m (13,082 ft), near the Western Hemisphere's highest peak, 6,958 m (22,835 ft) high Mount Aconcagua. The link cut the 11-day

BUENOS AIRES & GREAT SOUTHERN 11B CLASS 2-8-0	
Date	1914
Builder	Beyer Peacock, North British and Vulcan Foundry
Client	Buenos Aires & Great Southern Railway (BAGS)
Gauge	5 ft 6 in
Driving wheels	4 ft 7½ in
Capacity	Cylinders 19 x 26 in
Total weight	105 tons

● LEFT
The last surviving Kitson-Meyer 0-6-6-0 – known as "The Dodo of the Atacama" – at work in Chile's Atacama Desert. These locomotives once brought gold and nitrates to Pacific coast ports.

journey by boat via the Magellan Strait to 40 hours overland. The line climbs hills so steep that part of it uses cog-wheel apparatus.

● COLOMBIA, ECUADOR
AND PERU
Colombia, Ecuador and Chile drew their locomotive traditions mainly from American builders. Peru had a mixture of American and British designs.

There were no locomotive-building traditions in South America or Africa. Both these continents were entirely dependent on the building traditions developed in Britain, Europe and America.

● OPPOSITE MIDDLE
A woodburning Edwardian Mogul from North British, of Glasgow, Scotland, heads along the standard-gauge main line from the Paraguayan capital Asunción to Encarnación on the Argentine border. This railway is the last all-steam worked international main line in the world.

● RIGHT
A 2-8-2, No. 183, of Guatemalan Railways, at Gualán in 1971.

The 1950s to the Present Day

The second half of the 20th century saw the decline of the railway as the premier form of transport. Competition from roads and airlines was intense, and vast amounts of railways were closed worldwide. Half-way through the period, the steam locomotive disappeared from much of the world, and in Western countries it became almost extinct. However, railway administrations sought to stave off competition with super hi-tech trains, and today we are seeing a vigorous international movement away from roads and back to rail. Increasing congestion and population are helping railways to make this resurgence.

BRITISH MAIN-LINE SHUNTERS AND INDUSTRIALS

The evolution of British main-line steam shunting-locomotives ended in effect in the 1950s. It fell to the Great Western Railway (GWR) to end the tradition formally with its 1500 Class/9400 Class 0-6-0-Ts. Building of the 9400 Class continued until 1956 when it totalled 210 engines. These were the last examples of a pre-nationalization design built by British Railways.

With many 0-6-0Ts inherited from the "Big Four" companies, British Railways had little need for any more shunting-tanks. Downgraded goods-engines became evermore available and

● LEFT
American-built diesels are being used on Britain's railways, on the main lines and in industrial service. This example, built for Foster Yeoman, is preparing rakes of aggregates at the company's Merehead quarry.

● BELOW LEFT
Several Great Western Railway (GWR) 5700 Class 0-6-0 pannier tanks passed into industrial service, to receive a further lease of life, like this one working at a colliery in South Wales.

gravitated to shunting yards in hundreds. The contemporaneous advent of diesel-shunters in the 1950s saw the standard British Railways diesel-electric 350-hp 0-6-0 produced in profusion from Derby Works, in Derby, Derbyshire. Many remain in service, fulfilling the modest shunting opportunities left on the main-line system.

● DIESELS REPLACE STEAM SHUNTERS

It had long been recognized that diesels were superior for shunting. Their ability to switch on and off for work often involving long idle periods showed a clear advantage. Also, the even torque provided sure-footed starts with heavy loads.

Since 1966, there has been a huge fall in the number of shunting-engines. Certainly fewer diesel engines are needed than steam. Far more significant, however, has been the erosion of sidings and marshalling yards as freight has been transferred from rail to road. Instead of the shunter being an everyday sight with thousands operating nationwide, sight of one now is a rare occurrence that often draws comment.

● **RIGHT**
A 16- in Andrew Barclay 0-4-0 saddle-tank draws a rake of freshly lifted coal out of the washery at Pennyvenie Mine, near Dalmellington, Ayrshire, Scotland.

● PRIVATE USE DECIMATED

Steam-shunters survived in industrial environments many years after disappearing from main-line service. The last did not entirely disappear until the mid-1980s. Although diesels, including some early British Railway engines, readily infiltrated industrial networks too, the massive decline in Britain's heavy industry and increasing dependence on roads decimated the number of private organizations using their own loco-motives. Those remaining, at collieries and power stations mostly, adopt the merry-go-round principle in which main-line trains serve the industry direct.

Fifty years ago, thousands of steam locomotives were working in hundreds of British collieries. Today there are no steam locomotives and only a handful of active collieries.

● **LEFT**
Cadley Hill Colliery, near Burton on Trent, Staffordshire, central England, was part of the Derbyshire Coalfield and one of the last locations in Britain to use steam locomotives. In this view, with Drakelow Power Station in the background, a standard Hunslet Austerity 0-6-0St (right) shunts beside Progress, a Robert Stephenson & Hawthorn 0-6-0 saddle-tank with inside-cylinders.

CLASS 08 DIESEL SHUNTER

Builder	Derby Locomotive Works, Derby, England
Client	British Railways
Gauge	Standard
Engine	English Electric 6-cylinder 350 brake horsepower (bhp) (261 kW)
Total weight	50 tons
Maximum tractive effort	35,000 lb
Maximum speed	15–20 mph

● **RIGHT**
Penzance, Cornwall, is one location of the British Railway network that retains a shunting-engine – a standard 08 Class Diesel Electric 0-6-0.

BRITISH MAIN-LINE FREIGHT

In the 1950s, many 2-8-0s firmly controlled main freight hauls on the newly formed British Railways. The most numerous were the Great Western Railway's 2800s; the LNER's 01, 02 and 04 classes; Stanier's LMS Class 8F 2-8-0 and their Ministry of Supply version from World War II. In all, these totalled about 2,000 locomotives. The 2-8-0 was supported by a vast array of 0-6-0s and 0-8-0s, which in themselves handled trains little short of 1,000 tons, especially the 0-8-0s of the former North Eastern and London's North Western railways.

The 0-10-0, widely used in Europe, was avoided in Britain. Its light axleload was of little benefit. Its potential power and adhesion for hill-climbing were not generally necessary. The 2-8-0's greater flexibility was preferred.

Similarly, the 2-8-2 and 4-8-0 were not applied. The 2-8-2's wide firebox capacity did not have to be exploited, because of the good quality coal available. The 4-8-0's powerful hill-climbing capacity was not needed on Britain's main lines. Outside the mainstream of

● **LEFT**
A British Railway's standard Class 9F 2-10-0s, No. 92084, reposes at Cricklewood Depot, north London, in 1960. This class totalled 250 engines.

● **LEFT**
An ARC's Class 59 Co-Co diesel-electric built in the USA by General Motors. Heavyfreight locomotives for Britain in future are likely to be American-built and of similar proportions to these aggregate-haulers.

● **BELOW**
Brush of Loughborough's Class 60 Co-Co diesel-electric No. 60061 Alexander Graham Bell heading oil-tanks along the West Coast main line beneath the 25 kV a.c. catinery. The 100 Class 60s, an advanced diesel-electric design, perform heavy haulage with trainloads up to 3,000 tons.

typically heavyfreight designs were some mighty 2-8-0 tanks Churchward produced, to work coal-trains from the valleys of South Wales to the docks.

● **NATIONALIZATION BRINGS STANDARDS**
Fast mixed-freights were pulled by Moguls, 2-6-2s or 4-6-0 types generally regarded as mixed-traffic designs. The LMS Crabs and Gresley K3s were typical Moguls. The V2s were the main design of 2-6-2. The 4-6-0s were epitomized by Stanier's Black 5s of the LMS, Thompson's B1s of the LNER and Collett's Halls of the GWR. The antecedent of the 4-6-0 fast mixed-traffic goes back to the early years of the century with Robinson's Fish engines and Fast Goods types.

Following nationalization of Britain's railways in 1948, 12 standard designs – the Standards – were prepared for the

● **RIGHT**
British Railways Class 56 Co-Co diesel-electric locomotives were introduced in 1977 to handle heavy, slow-speed merry-go-round trains. The first 30 were built in Romania. A further 75 were built at Doncaster, South Yorkshire, and Crewe, Cheshire. The Class 56s have a 16-cylinder Ruston four-stroke diesel engine. The type has become a main heavyfreight hauler on the British Railways network.

CLASS 47 CO-CO DIESEL ELECTRIC

Date	1962
Builder	Brush of Loughborough, Leicestershire, and BR Crewe Works, Crewe, Cheshire, England
Client	British Railways
Gauge	Standard
Engine	Sulzer 1920 kW (2,580 hp)
Total weight	125 tons
Maximum tractive effort	60,000 lb
Maximum speed	95 mph

entire country. Among them was the Class 9F 2-10-0 heavy-mineral engine. So the evolution of the British goods-engine had at the eleventh hour aspired to ten-coupled traction some 50 years after the type had become prevalent in America and 40 years after its inception in Austria and Germany.

The trusted British 0-6-0 drudge had finally turned into a highly sophisticated engine. The 9F presented a perfect climax to British freight-locomotive development. Considering the inside-cylinder 0-6-0's major role over 125 years, it is amazing that its absolute

displacement came within such a narrow space of time – the Southern Railway's Q1s appearing only 11 years before the first 9Fs.

The last 9F 2-10-0 was built in 1960. What a contrast these ultimate British freight haulers made with Stephenson's Locomotion No. 1 of 1825.

The diesel engine was invented in 1892 by French-born, German-educated engineer Rudolf Diesel (1858–1913). The first diesel engines were used in ships in 1903. The first diesel locomotive was built at the works of Sulzer in Switzerland in 1913.

● **RIGHT**
The Class 47 Co-Co diesel-electric's versatility is shown in this scene at Harbury Cutting, as one heads a Rail-freight Distribution container-train operating between Birmingham, West Midlands, and Southampton Docks, Hampshire.

BRITISH DIESEL MULTIPLE UNITS (DMUs)

The diesel multiple unit (DMU) descended from steam railcars working on the LMS and LNER in the 1920s and 1930s. These consisted of a single coach with a driving-compartment at either end and a steam-engine encased in a compartment at one end of the coach.

Britain's diesel-cars were introduced by GWR in 1933 for excursion traffic, branch-line and local services. Initially they worked between Paddington in west London and Didcot, about 80 km (50 miles) away in Oxfordshire. In 1934 they were used in an express service, mainly for businessmen on the 155 km (100 miles) between Birmingham in central England and Cardiff in Wales. The trains comprised two railcars with a restaurant-car between. This formation anticipated the first generation of DMUs in having two motor-units with a trailing car between and the later InterCity 125s with a power-car at both ends.

CLASS 158 EXPRESS DMU	
Date	1990
Builder	British Rail Engineering Ltd. (BREL), England
Client	British Rail
Gauge	Standard
Engine	One Cummings 260 kW (350 hp) or 300 kW (400 hp), alternatively Perkins 260 kW (350 hp)
Maximum service speed	90 mph

● ADVENT OF DIESEL-RAILCAR

The advent of the diesel-railcar proper was in the 1950s, as part of the British Railways 1955 Modernization Plan. The theory was that diesel-units could serve more stations efficiently, effect rapid starts and use high speeds between stations separated by only a few miles. No sooner had DMUs taken over many steam-stopping services than a vast

● **ABOVE**
A brand-new Turbo Class 165 for working the Chiltern lines between London Marylebone Station and Birmingham reposes outside the Aylesbury depot, Buckinghamshire. These trains were introduced in 1992 as part of the Chiltern lines' total route modernization.

● **LEFT**
A Class 158 two-car BREL express unit. This design has bridged the gap between local/cross-country work and express services and is used on many long-distance runs across Britain.

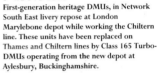

number of stations were closed nationwide under Beeching.

Early, steel-bodied DMUs ran as two-, three- or four-coach units. Two-car ones generally comprised two motor-units. Three-car ones had a trailing unit in between. Four-car ones had a motor-unit at both ends. The diesel engine sat beneath the motorized cars, providing direct drive.

Many designs appeared in the 1950s and 1960s, particularly from the works at Derby and Swindon, Wiltshire, and from private builders such as Metro Cammell, Birmingham Railway Carriage and Wagon Co. and Cravens. These early units were known later as Heritage DMUs. Their numbers ever dwindle but several classes remain in service.

● SECOND GENERATION

The second-generation DMU was introduced in the mid-1980s as the Sprinter series. These have sliding doors, hydraulic transmissions and offer great advance in riding qualities over the earlier trains. The main classes are the 150s and the 156s. Both are usually seen in two-car formations and have a Cummins 285 hp engine beneath each car.

In contrast came the Pacers embraced by Classes 141, 142 and 143/144. These are lighter, four-wheeled vehicles with each car motorized. The absence of bogies made these units rougher to ride in and probably accounts

for why they have not been popular.

The pièce de résistance of British DMUs is the Class 158 express unit. This first appeared from British Rail Engineering Ltd (BREL) in 1990. The 158s consist of two car units with an advanced bogie design and a 350 hp engine per car. They perform well on medium- and long-distance runs, are extremely comfortable and have a 90 mph top speed.

This second generation of DMUs has gone into widespread service nationwide and all but replaced traditional locomotive-hauled trains.

● **ABOVE LEFT**
First-generation heritage DMUs, in Network South East livery repose at London Marylebone depot while working the Chiltern line. These units have been replaced on Thames and Chiltern lines by Class 165 Turbo-DMUs operating from the new depot at Aylesbury, Buckinghamshire.

● **ABOVE RIGHT**
A Class 141 Leyland Pacer in West Yorkshire (Public Transport Executive [PTE]) livery. These units were built from Leyland National Bus parts on four-wheeled underframes at the Derby works, Derby, in 1984.

● **BELOW**
A green-liveried Heritage DMU "bubble car" heads an afternoon local service between Bletchley, Buckinghamshire, and Bedford, in the Midlands. Classified 121, these units date from 1960.

BRITISH ELECTRICAL MULTIPLE UNITS (EMUs)

The electrical multiple unit (EMU) predated the diesel multiple unit (DMU) by many years for the City & South London Railway, which used EMUs when it opened in 1890. Power-collection was from a third rail carrying 450 volts. Apart from London's Underground, it was the Southern Railway – following the 1923 Grouping – which truly exploited the EMU's potential with an expanding network of electrification based on a third-rail system at 600 volts d.c.

In 1923, Britain's railway companies had been reorganized into four groups – the "Big Four": London, Midland & Scottish (LMS); London & North Eastern (LNER); the Great Western (GWR) and the Southern Railway (SR).

EMUs' high power:weight ratio provides the rapid acceleration needed on busy suburban services. Most EMUs consist of four-car sets including a motor-coach. As traffic demands, these trains can be run as either four-, eight- or 12-coach combinations.

NEW GENERATION

As main-line electrification spread across Britain from the late-1950s, a new

● **LEFT**
Among British vintage overhead EMUs are Class 302s. One is pictured leaving Fenchurch Street Station, London, for Essex on the London-Tilbury, Southend-on-Sea section. These date back to the 1950s.

● **ABOVE**
A former Network South East Class 415/6. These are among the oldest units left on Britain's railways. They are slam-door stock with 750 volt d.c. third rail and date back to 1959.

● **BELOW**
Class 323s were introduced in 1992 for the West Midlands Public Transport Executive (PTE) and Greater Manchester PTE areas. They have aluminium bodies, thyristor control and sliding doors.

generation of EMUs emerged with overhead pantographs collecting from 25 kV a.c. More recently dual-voltage units have appeared, capable of running on 25 kV a.c. overhead and 750 volt d.c. third rail. In this category, Thameslink Class 319 and 319/1s operate between Bedford, in the Midlands, and Brighton, the Sussex seaside resort, through the heart of London.

In the 1950s, DMU and EMU features were combined to produce several classes of trains with a diesel-engine in the motor-coach to generate electricity to drive the traction motors. These diesel electrical multiple units (DEMUs) run on sections of non-electrified railway.

SUPERFAST EXPRESSES

In common with the DMU, the EMU soon developed into express units, the Brighton Belle being an early example. More recently, the Wessex Electrics have been introduced and operate superfast services between London Waterloo and Southampton in Hampshire and Bournemouth and Weymouth in Dorset. Later, the Networker Express Class 365, with aluminium bodies, advanced bogie design and regenerative braking, were introduced. These are 100 mph express units of comfort and sophistication.

● **RIGHT**
An express Class 325 parcels unit for postal services, with roller-shutter doors, heads south through the Lune Gorge with a West Coast postal train. These units operate on 25 kV a.c. overhead, 750 volt d.c. third rail.

● **BELOW**
Class 465 Networker EMUs replaced ageing units on Kent Link services. The new units have aluminium bodies, sliding doors and regenerative braking. They entered service in the early-1990s when building of new trains was at an all-time low. In 1996, the Class C1365 Networker Express was launched by Connex South Eastern. These 100-mph trains have dual-voltage capability, 2+2 seating layout (2+3 on Kent Link), a toilet for the disabled and carpeting throughout.

● **BELOW**
The Wessex Electrics Class 442 is a most prestigious EMU. These 100 mph units were built for the Waterloo-Bournemouth-Weymouth services and also worked to Portsmouth Harbour, Hampshire. Unusually for British EMUs, many are named. These comfortable riding units were introduced in 1988 as a partial refurbishment of older stock, a precedent likely to be followed in preference to building new trains.

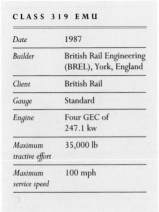

● **BELOW RIGHT**
A ThamesLink dual-voltage Class 319 climbs the steep gradient into Blackfriars Station, London, with a Bedford-to-Brighton service. These 100 mph units work on 25 kV a.c. on the Midland main line and on 750 volt d.c. on the London-Brighton section.

Class 325 express postal units were introduced in 1995. Apart from their dual voltage, these 100 mph trains are compatible with diesel-locomotive haulage over non-electrified sections, giving access to the entire railway system.

Many units on the 750 volt d.c. lines of southern England are ageing. In 1996,

Adtranz proposed the Networker Classic, a "half-life, quarter-cost solution" to unlock the potential of existing vehicles more than 25 years old by refurbishing the underframe, traction system and running-gear with the latest body design, including automatic sliding doors and crashworthy front ends.

CLASS 319 EMU

Date	1987
Builder	British Rail Engineering (BREL), York, England
Client	British Rail
Gauge	Standard
Engine	Four GEC of 247.1 kw
Maximum tractive effort	35,000 lb
Maximum service speed	100 mph

BRITISH STEAM STANDARDS

On nationalization of the "Big Four" railway companies – LMS, LNER, GWR and SR – in 1948, the new administration inherited hundreds of different locomotive types. Many of these had come down from the multiplicity of private companies that existed before the 1923 Grouping. This was untenable for a new, centralized administration and so it was proposed to build 12 standard types – the Standards – to fulfil most functions across the network.

● 1955 MODERNIZATION PLAN

Within four years of the Standards' introduction, the Modernization Plan for 1955 decreed the end of steam in favour of diesel and electric traction. This resulted in the Standards adding even more design variety. The new engines were designed on experience gained by the locomotive exchanges of 1948, in which the Big Four's leading types were tested across one another's territories to ascertain best-performance characteristics. Mechanically and

● LEFT
British Railways Standard 80000 Class 2-6-4Ts were based on earlier LMS engines by Stanier and Fairburn. Powerful, with a turn of speed, they were to be found on many parts of Britain's railway network. The class totalled 155 examples.

BR BRITANNIA PACIFIC 4-6-2	
Date	1951
Builder	Crewe Locomotive Works, Crewe, Cheshire, England
Client	British Railways
Gauge	Standard
Driving wheels	6 ft 2 in
Capacity	Cylinders 20 x 28 in
Total weight in full working order	150 tons

aesthetically, the new designs showed a distinct departure from traditional British practices, towards those of America.

The 12 types comprised three Pacifics (the Britannia for fast express work, the Clans for fast mixed-traffic work and the solitary Duke of Gloucester intended as forerunner of a new generation of heavy express-passenger-locomotives), two classes of 4-6-0s, three of Moguls, one powerful 2-6-4 tank, two 2-6-2 tanks and the Class 9F mineral-hauling 2-10-0s.

Except for Duke of Gloucester and the 9Fs, the new Standards were all mixed-traffic designs, because by this time the concept of different locomotives for freight and passenger work had all but

● **RIGHT**
British Railways Standard Pacific No. 71000
Duke of Gloucester reposes outside the
paintshop at Crewe Works, Cheshire.

● **BELOW**
British Railways Standard Class 4 4-6-0s were
for light passenger and general duties. The
class numbered 80 engines. Their clean,
modern lines, with distinct American
characteristics, are shown in this picture.

● **OPPOSITE BOTTOM**
British Railways Standard Britannia Class
Pacific No. 70042 Lord Roberts at Willesden,
west London, in 1962.

appeared at the Festival of Britain in
1951, attracting much interest and
admiration. This was justified by the
Britannias' performance over their
relatively short lives. They proved
extremely fast engines and put in
scintillating performances, not least on
the former Great Eastern main line
between London Liverpool Street and
Norwich, Norfolk.

Perhaps the biggest disappointment, at
least initially, was the Duke of Gloucester,
sluggish in service and heavy on coal. This
engine passed into preservation, having
been rescued from Woodhams Scrapyard
in Barry, Glamorganshire, South Wales,
and renovated to full working order.

Computer calibrations of the Duke's valve
settings proved, in the light of contemporary experience, that these were incorrectly
set during the engine's main-line years, and
the modifications made under preservation
have enabled the Duke to climb the
notorious Shap Bank with a 450-ton train
at a speed hitherto unknown and to top
the summit at 51 mph. This gives insight
into the potential of steam and of this
express-passenger design destined to
remain as a solitary engine.

● **BELOW**
British Railways Standard Class 3 Mogul, No.
76005, one of a class of 115 engines for light
intermediate work, at Bournemouth Shed,
Dorset, in the mid-1960s.

disappeared. In principle, the 9Fs were
the exceptions to this rule. In practice,
their balanced proportions enabled them
to undertake fast running with passenger-
trains. Stories abounded of them
reaching 90 mph – until their use on
such work was forbidden.

● **BRITANNIA AT THE FESTIVAL
OF BRITAIN**
In terms of easy accessibility to moving-
parts and labour-saving devices, the
Standards were an improvement on most
previous designs. In terms of overall
performance, they were little different
from their Big Four counterparts on
which they were largely based.

The first engine, No. 70000 Britannia,

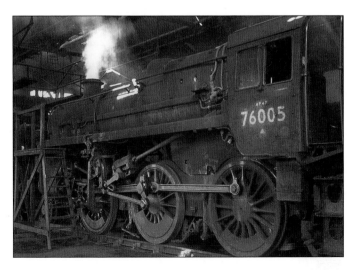

BRITISH DIESEL

The decision to dieselize came rather late in Britain. Not until 1955, when the government announced the Modernization Plan, was the end of the steam age seriously suggested. Even then, prolific railway experts like Cecil J. Allen confidently said steam would last until the end of the century.

The modernization programme was rapidly implemented. This resulted in many classes of diesel appearing, not all of which proved satisfactory. From the outset, diesel-electric was the preferred mode, following extensive trials of the LMS's 1947-built 10000/10001. The brief visit to the concept of diesel-mechanical, as epitomized by H.G. Ivatt's 4-8-4 No. 10100 introduced in 1951, and visits to gas turbines were not continued.

Diesel-hydraulic gained acceptance, especially on former Great Western lines, but the classes concerned, revered as they were, had a short life.

● EARLY EXPERIMENT

Another early experiment was the blue English Electric Deltic, prototype for the

● LEFT
H.G. Ivatt's twin diesel-electrics Nos. 10000/10001 appeared in the late 1940s and paved the way for main-line dieselization. This proved to be a milestone in the evolution of British locomotives. A unit is pictured receiving attention in Derby works, Derbyshire.

● LEFT
The Class 47 Co-Co diesel "Maid of all Work" has been a familiar sight on Britain's railways since the early 1960s, with hundreds still operating. Here, one leaves Birmingham in the Midlands at the head of a cross-country express.

● BELOW
One of the oldest diesel types left on British Railways is the Class 31 Brush Type 2s, introduced by Brush Traction at Loughborough, Leicestershire, in 1957. Over the years, they have been used on a wide variety of duties but are now almost entirely relegated to engineers' trains.

Deltics on the East Coast main line. These were highly admired, extremely successful and proved worthy successors to Gresley's A4 Pacifics.

Fine general-purpose mixed-traffic haulers are the Brush Sulzer Class 47s, which proved worthy successors to the 842 Stanier Black 5s. The 47s proved themselves equally at home with 90 mph passenger-trains or 1,000 ton freight-hauls. About 500 went into service; many remain active.

Other notables include Class 40 English Electrics, which moved most trains on the West Coast main line before electrification, and the Sulzer 12-cylinder Peaks introduced in 1959, which also proved themselves on passenger and freight. The 40s and Peaks are history but the Class 37, a 1950s design built from 1960 onwards, remains an important class engaged on such diverse services as EPS sleeping-car trains, locals, all types of mixed-freight operations and engineers' service trains.

BR CLASS 37 CO-CO DIESEL ELECTRIC

Date	1960
Builder	English Electric Company, Vulcan Factory, Newton-le-Willows, or Robert Stephenson & Hawthorn, Darlington, Durham, England
Client	British Railways
Gauge	Standard
Engine	English Electric 1,300 kW (1,750 hp)
Total weight	108 tons
Maximum tractive effort	55,500 lb
Maximum service speed	80 mph

● **ABOVE RIGHT**
English Electric Type 3 Class 37 Co-Co diesel electrics were built in 1960-65 by the English Electric Co. at its Vulcan Foundry, Lancashire, and by Robert Stephenson & Hawthorn in Darlington, Durham. They truly are maids of all work, fulfilling many functions. One of their most prestigious services is the sleeping-car run through the Scottish Highlands to the tourist attractions of Fort William and Inverness.

● **MIXED-TRAFFIC CONCEPT**

The concept of mixed-traffic locomotives established by the British Railways Standard steam designs has continued through the diesel age, but since 1976 the classes 56, 58 and 60 have been put into operation mainly for mineral- and aggregate-haulage.

The next batches of new diesels for Britain's railways are tipped to come from North America when EWS begin their mighty restocking of British freight-motive power. The new engines may follow the lead begun with Foster Yeoman and ARC's Class 59 General Motors Co-Cos.

● **LEFT**
A Class 50 Co-Co English Electric Type 4 diesel. Built in 1967–68 by the Vulcan Foundry at Newton-le-Willows, Lancashire, these engines originally worked the northern reaches of the West Coast main line between Crewe, in Cheshire, and Carlisle, in Cumbria, but ended up on the South Western main line between London Waterloo and Exeter, Devon.

● **LEFT**
The InterCity 125, one of the most successful trains in British railway history, revolutionized long-distance passenger services. Introduced in 1976, the 125s have a maximum speed of 125 mph, hence their name. A set on the Midland line is seen passing Milepost 92½, south of Leicester, with a Sheffield-to-London train.

BRITISH MAIN-LINE ELECTRIC

Although it is fashionable for electrification to be thought of as the ultimate railway modernization, it is a form of motive power extant in Britain since the 1880s. In the 19th century, two locomotive engineers, George Stephenson and F.W. Ebb, predicted that one day Britain's railways would run on electricity.

In 1905, the first freight-hauling electric locomotive appeared, on the North Eastern Railway (NER). After that, many adventurous schemes were proposed, including electrification of the NER's main line between York and Newcastle upon Tyne following World War I. However, the Depression in the 1930s, followed by World War II, prevented many projects being started. In 1948, only 17 main-line electric locomotives were inherited by British Railways.

● **GREAT CENTRAL MAIN LINE ELECTRIFIED**

In the early 1950s, a project was continued that had been held over in the war years. This was the electrification to 1,500 volt d.c. overhead of the steeply graded Great Central main line between the English industrial centres of Sheffield in West Yorkshire and Manchester in Lancashire. This highly acclaimed, much-

publicized project operated Bo-Bo locomotives for freight and Co-Co for passengers.

Simultaneously, in the mid-1950s there was a development with Southern Region's electro-diesels. The traction motors were fed from either a third rail or by current generated from an on-board diesel engine, enabling them to run across non-electrified sections. Many of these Class 73s remain active today and can be seen on the Gatwick Express service from London Victoria to Gatwick Airport – London, in West Sussex.

● **WEST AND EAST COAST MAIN LINES ELECTRIFIED**

The West Coast main line, from London Euston Station, is Britain's busiest. It was an early candidate for electrification to 25 kV a.c. under the 1955 modernization scheme. The locomotives were designated mixed-traffic and designed to haul 475-ton trains at 90 mph on level track, with maximum speed of 100 mph, and 950-ton freight-trains at 42 mph, with a 55-mph maximum. The West Coast fleet's mainstay are Class 86s, dating back to 1965. The 86s and later

● **RIGHT**
The 30-year-old Class 86 electric, built by English Electric at the Vulcan Foundry, remain the mainstay of services on the West Coast main line. Here, one approaches Crewe from the south, beneath the 25 kV a.c. overhead catinery.

● **RIGHT**
Driving-van trailers (DVTs) used on Britain's
East Coast and West Coast main lines simulate
the design of Class 91 electrics. On both
routes, southbound trains are headed by
DVTs, as in this London-bound service waiting
to leave Crewe, Cheshire.

● **OPPOSITE MIDDLE**
In the mid-1990s, Class 92 Bo-Bo electrics
were introduced for through-services between
Britain and Europe. The picture shows No.
92.019 at Crewe Station, Cheshire.

BR CLASS 91 BO-BO ELECTRIC

Date	1988
Builder	British Rail Engineering Ltd. (BREL), Crewe Works, Cheshire, England
Client	British Railways
Gauge	Standard
Traction motors	General English Electric (GEC) G426AZ
Total weight	84 tons
Continuous Rating	4540 kW (6090 hp)
Maximum speed	140 mph

87s are augmented by powerful Class 90s
introduced in 1987.

Completion of the East Coast main-
line electrification brought the Crewe-
built Class 91s with an outstanding
140-mph top speed. These are Britain's
most powerful locomotives capable of
running across the East Coast racing-
ground to reach Edinburgh, Scotland, in
under four hours from King's Cross
Station, London.

Almost all West Coast and East Coast
main-line electric services have the
locomotive at one end and a driving-van

trailer (DVT) at the other. These are
basically a luggage-and-parcel van with
a driving console that enables the train to
be driven in either direction without
turning around.

Soon after completion of the 91 class
came the dual-voltage Class 92s for
operating freight- and passenger-trains
through the Channel Tunnel between
Britain and France. Apart from being
another technical triumph, the 92s open
up the possibility of running through
freight-trains from many parts of Britain
directly into Europe.

● **RIGHT**
A GEC-designed
Class 91 Bo-Bo
electric at King's
Cross Station,
London. These
powerful
locomotives
revolutionized
services on the East
Coast main line.

BRITISH LIGHT RAIL

Britain's first electric tramway ran in Blackpool, Lancashire. It was the only British urban tramway to survive the abandonment completed nationwide in Britain by 1962. This traditional system continues to modernize its infrastructure and trams. It is one of only three systems in the world to use double-deck cars.

● TRAMWAYS AND MASS-TRANSIT SYSTEMS

In addition to tramways, mass-transit systems were built in London and Glasgow, Scotland. London Underground is one of the world's largest metro systems, with two sizes of rolling stock used, on subsurface and tube lines respectively. The Glasgow underground is a city-circle line built for cable traction but electrified in the 1930s. New rolling stock was delivered as part of complete modernization in 1978–80.

● TYNE & WEAR METRO

After a decade when it seemed that most of Britain's towns and cities would have

● BELOW
Supporting the regeneration of Birkenhead's docklands in Merseyside is a Heritage tramway featuring traditional double-deck trams, but built in Hong Kong to the British style.

to make do with buses and increasing traffic congestion, the late 1970s saw planning start for flexible and cost-effective light-rail systems (LRS). In Tyneside, north-east England, the closure of run-down local rail services offered the Passenger Transport Executive (PTE) the opportunity to create a rail-based

integrated system in 1980–84 by the introduction of light rail and new subways under the city centre. The successful Tyne & Wear Metro has been extended to Newcastle Airport, and also from Sunderland to South Hylton, using the disused Sunderland to Durham line.

● LONDON'S DLR

A different version of light rail was installed in London's Docklands in 1984–7. The Docklands Light Railway (DLR) was built as a fully segregated system (mostly on new or existing viaducts) with third-rail current collection and automatic train operation. Designed to carry 2,000 passengers an hour in single cars, the system soon had to be rebuilt to carry up to 12,000 passengers an hour with multiple-unit trains. The line now extends from Tower Gateway to the Royal Docks Victoria, Albert and King George V on Plaistow Marshes; from Canning Town to Beckton and King George V; to Lewisham; and to

● LEFT
Blackpool's Promenade tramway is just the place for a summer ride on an open-top tram. No. 706 is the only double-decker rebuilt to its original, 1935, condition.

SOUTH YORKSHIRE LOW-FLOOR TRAM

Date	1993–4
Builder	Siemens-Duewag, Germany
Gauge	1,435 mm
Power supply	750 v or kV
Bogie arrangement	B-B-B-B with 4x277 kW motors
Overall length	34.75 m
Width	2.65 m
Body height	3.64 m. Floor height 480 mm (880 mm over bogies)
Unladen weight	46.5 tons
Passengers	Seated 88; standing 155
Maximum speed	80 kph

● **LEFT**
South Yorkshire Supertram's steep gradients are easily handled by its German-built low-floor trams. This scene shows the Woodburn Road crossing in the background.

● **BELOW LEFT**
London's Docklands Light Railway (DLR) expanded when the towering office complex at Canary Wharf was built. The complex is served by this station incorporated in the tower.

● **BELOW RIGHT**
The Tyne & Wear Metro in north-east England has taken over local rail services, around Newcastle upon Tyne, including this former freight line to Callerton. It is seen here at Fawdon. The cars were built by Metro Cammell and based on a German design.

Stratford in East London. The system is operated by Serco Docklands Ltd, a company formed jointly by Serco and the former management company, the London Docklands Development Corporation (LDDC).

MANCHESTER METROLINK

In Manchester, light rail was created in 1990–93 by the PTE taking over the rail lines to Bury, Lancashire, and Altrincham, Cheshire, and linking them with new street-track through the city centre. The system was built and operated by the Metrolink consortium, using articulated trams made by Firema, Italy.

● **SOUTH YORKSHIRE, WEST MIDLANDS AND CROYDON**

In South Yorkshire, a tramway was created in 1992–5 to link Sheffield city centre with outer suburbs and the Meadowhall retail centre. The system's steep gradients required articulated trams with all axles motored. German-built, they are the first trams in Britain to feature low-floor boarding and alighting at all doors. After a slow start, caused by population shifts, poor traffic priorities and bus competition, Sheffield Supertram saw a 40 per cent rise in use in the second half of 1996.

BRITISH TRAIN PRESERVATION

Britain's railway preservation movement was created on 11 October 1950 when a meeting in Birmingham presided over by L.T.C. Rolt declared its intention to save the Talyllyn Railway in Brecknockshire, Central Wales (now Powys). There were no precedents for such action and tremendous opposition came from many sources declaring "enthusiasts could never run a railway". This pioneering endeavour's success is well known among railway enthusiasts.

GREAT WESTERN KING CLASS 4-6-0	
Date	1927
Builder	Swindon Locomotive Works, Wiltshire, England
Client	Great Western Railway (GWR)
Gauge	Standard
Driving wheels	6 ft 6 in
Capacity	4 cylinders (16 x 28 in)
Total weight in full working order	136 tons

● **BELOW**

Before Deltics were introduced, A4s held sway on the East Coast main line. Here, preserved, is No. 4498 Sir Nigel Gresley, named after the famous locomotive designer. Sir Nigel Gresley (1876–1941) was chief mechanical engineer of England's Great Northern Railway (GNR) and its successor LNER. He designed Mallard.

● **RIGHT**

Former British Rail Class 55 Co-Co Deltics were a production version of the Deltic prototype locomotive of the mid-1950s. They worked the heaviest long-distance trains on the East Coast main line for many years. Their popularity rendered them a perfect subject for preservation.

● **BELOW**

Great Western Railway's King Class 4-6-0 express-passenger-engine. Apart from one engine in 1908, GWR did not use Pacifics. Nothing larger than the 4-6-0 was needed, because of the high-quality Welsh coal they burned and the relative flatness of their routes. Several have been preserved. No. 6000 King George V, the original engine of 1927, pictured during "GWR 150" celebrations in 1985.

PRESERVATION AND THE LEISURE INDUSTRY

So began a movement that over the next 50 years created a vast new leisure industry and saved part of the railway heritage in living form for future generations to enjoy.

Once the 1955 railway modernization programme took effect, class after class of Britain's locomotive heritage was scrapped. A limited selection of locomotives was earmarked for static display in museums, but this would have done little justice to the heritage, and the joy and wonder of seeing steam trains in action would have been but a dream.

Nationwide, thousands of enthusiasts united to save locomotives, rolling stock and sections of railway. Following the Beeching programme, innumerable closed branch lines were available. Over the years, dozens became the subject of preservation schemes. The movement gained momentum at the ending of steam operation on British Railways on 11 August 1968, after which it was announced that no preserved locomotive would be allowed to run on the national system.

STEAM EXCURSIONS

Today, Britain has more than 100 centres where steam-trains can be enjoyed. They attract millions of visitors every year. More than 2,000 locomotives have been preserved.

Railway preservation is a creative, on-going process. As the first generation of diesels began to slip into history, examples were saved and put to work on preserved lines – often beside the very steam-locomotives they had replaced.

The decision to ban steam was rescinded in 1971. Many historic locomotives returned to the main line, including examples borrowed from the National Railway Museum in York. In 1985, a total of 235 steam-excursions operated on British Rail, attracting many people to linesides and promoting awareness of the railway among the general public.

A visit to any preserved line is an unforgettable experience, for enthusiast or lay person alike. These centres achieve authenticity and fascinate all ages.

The union of free enterprise and enthusiasm provided a catalyst for achieving the impossible. Britain's railway preservation movement has been little less dynamic in spirit than Victorian industrialists of a century earlier. The number preserved contrasts with the "handful of stuffed and mounted exhibits" proposed by the Government when the dismantling of the railways began.

EUROSTAR

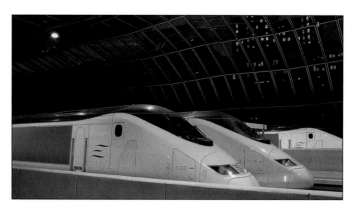

The idea that steam is exciting while modern traction is dull and lifeless is disproved for ever by Eurostar. This train combines the romance of the 1930s' streamlined era and the cutting edge of technology. London's St Pancras International Station is as magnificent as its Victorian counterpart and the Channel Tunnel, within the 37.5 km (24 mile) terminal-to-terminal fixed link between Folkestone and Calais, is one of the world's greatest civil-engineering feats.

● WORLD'S MOST COMPLEX TRAIN

The connecting of Britain's 16,000 km (10,000 miles) of railway with Europe's 185,000 km (116,000 miles) in 1993 has

● **ABOVE**
Three Eurostar units in repose at the former terminal at Waterloo International, London, England.

● **BELOW**
A Eurostar train speeds through the countryside of northern France on the high-speed line.

provided a much-needed and massive boost for railways. Eurostar competes with airlines between the cities of London, Paris and Brussels.

Eurostar is the world's most complex train. It operates on four different signalling systems and three different power-supply systems – 750 volt d.c. 25 kV a.c. in Britain; 25 kV a.c. in the

● **LEFT**
A Eurostar train from London approaches the Channel Tunnel. The Dolland's Moor freight complex is in the background and a new Class 92 locomotive in the left foreground.

● **BELOW**
Eurostar trains waiting to leave Waterloo International for France and Belgium.

● **BOTTOM**
Eurostar design details.

EUROSTAR

Date	1992
Builder	GEC Alsthom at various works
Clients	British Rail (BR); Société Nationale des Chemins de Fer Français (SNCF); Société Nationale des Chemins de Fer Belges (SNCB)
Gauge	Standard
Traction motors	Six XABB 6PH
Maximum service speed	187.5 mph

tunnel, France and on high-speed lines in Belgium and 3,000 kV d.c. on Belgium's conventional network.

● HIGH-SPEED LINK

Eurostar trains comprise 18 coaches. The trains, at 394 metres (1,293 ft), are almost a quarter of a mile long. Eurostar runs at 186 mph on Europe's high-speed lines but is restricted to below 100 mph in Britain.

Eurostar's coaches are joined by bogies. No bogies are set beneath the passenger seating. This and pneumatic suspension ensures a smooth, quiet ride. The train is comfortable and has footrests, reading-lights and air-conditioning. First-class has areas for business meetings.

There are two bar-buffets and a trolley service. Eurostar trains are serviced in London at the dedicated depot at Temple Mills, which is located near Stratford International station.

● OVERNIGHT TRAVEL REVOLUTION

The Eurostar service will be augmented by two developments. Firstly, day trains will run between Edinburgh, Manchester, Birmingham and Paris. Second, night trains will operate with sleeping-cars. These services will revolutionize long-distance overnight travel in Europe. Passengers will be able to go to bed in departure cities and awake at their destination next morning.

AMERICAN SWITCHERS

Switchers, that is engines to transfer rolling stock from one railway track to another, are relatively small, lightweight locomotives in the 300 hp to 1,500 hp range, designed to work at slow speeds, often on poor or winding track.

● FIRST SUCCESSFUL DIESEL-ELECTRIC

The first successful application of diesel-electric locomotives was as switchers. Central Railroad of New Jersey, USA, operated the first commercially successful diesel-electric in 1925. By the 1940s, builders were constructing low-horsepower diesel-electric switchers for yard switching, industrial switching and passenger-terminal work. General Electric (GE), Baldwin, the Electro-Motive Division (EMD) of General Motors, American Locomotive Company (Alco), Fairbanks-Morse, Whitcomb, Porter and Davenport all built switchers in the 1940s and 1950s.

● CHANGING DEMAND

As traffic patterns changed between the 1950s and 1970s, fewer switchers were needed. American railroads discontinued

● BELOW
Southern Pacific Lines embraced the switcher longer than other Western railroads and ordered larger numbers of EMD's SW1500s. The 1,500 hp SW1500 was eventually replaced in EMD's catalogue by the MP15, also rated at 1,500 hp.

● ABOVE
Baldwin switcher S-12 No. 16 is lettered for the Feather River & Western railroad. Baldwin built more than 550 S-12 diesel-electric switchers of 1,200 hp between 1951-56.

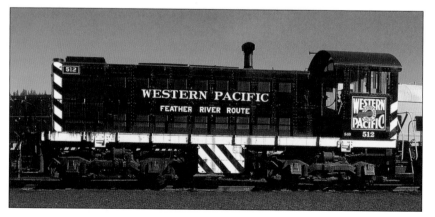

● LEFT
A former Alco S-1 switcher of the United States Army poses as Western Pacific Railroad's No. 512. More than 500 S-1s were built for use in the USA and Mexico between 1940-50. The locomotive features a six-cylinder 539 prime mover that delivered 660 hp.

● RIGHT
Western Pacific Railroad's NW2u shows off a coat of orange paint at Portola, California. Electro-Motive built 1,119 NW2 switchers of 1,000 hp. Many were later rebuilt, using the "u" designation.

many passenger-trains and thus had a greatly reduced need for switchers at terminals. Carload-freight declined as railroads switched to intermodal operations, that is using different modes of conveyance in conjunction. By the mid-1970s, railroads had stopped ordering large numbers of new switchers. Instead, they either rebuilt existing switchers or downgraded older road-switchers.

● SWITCHER MODELS

Electro-Motive began building switchers in the 1930s. An early model that gained popularity was the 1,000 hp NW2 made in 1930–49. The SW1, a 600-hp switcher, was made between 1939-53. Other SW-type switchers, ranging from the 700-hp SW7 to the 1,500-hp SW1500, were made through the 1970s. In the mid-1970s, EMD introduced its 1,500 MP line of switchers.

Alco made many S Series low-

SW8 DIESEL-ELECTRIC	
Date	1950–54
Builder	General Motors (Electro-Motive Division)
Engine	8-cylinder 567B
Capacity	567cc per cylinder
Power	800 hp

horsepower switchers between 1940–60. General Electric built switchers for many years before entering the heavy road locomotive market in 1960. Its most popular switchers were its 44-ton and 70-ton models.

In the 1990s, builder Morrison-Knudsen entered the new-switcher market with conventionally powered diesel-electrics and natural gas-powered locomotives. By 1996, it had not sold more than a handful of locomotives.

● RIGHT
An SW8 of the Wellsboro & Corning Railroad leads a train south of Gang Mills, New York. The EMD's 800-hp SW8 was built between 1950–54. Many short lines prefer switchers to larger road-switcher locomotives.

AMERICAN TRAINS IN THE 1950s

American freight railroads have relied on diesel-electric locomotives to move the bulk of their tonnage since America saw the end of steam in the 1950s. Builders have implemented many improvements in locomotive design in the last 40 years. Locomotive-builders – now just General Motor's Electro-Motive Division (EMD) and General Electric (GE) – have been working on single-engine, single-unit locomotives with ever-greater pulling power.

● **HORSEPOWER RACE**

In the 1950s, EMD's GP9 road-switcher and F9 carbody locomotives were state-of-the-art designs, each developing 1,750 hp with a 567-series 16-cylinder prime mover and traditional d.c. traction motors.

In the early 1960s, EMD increased the 567 prime mover's horsepower by adding a turbocharger, featured on its GP20 and SD24 models. Meanwhile, General Electric entered the new heavy-haul diesel-electric locomotive market

● **LEFT**
General Electric (GE) surpassed its main competitor, EMD, in new-locomotive sales with the introduction of the DASH-8 line. One of Santa Fe Railroad's 4,000 hp DASH 8-40Bs rests in Corwith yard, Chicago, Illinois.

● **ABOVE**
Brand-new EMD SD70MAC locomotives in Chicago. Burlington Northern Railroad prefers these powerful a.c.-traction locomotives for coal-train service in Wyoming, USA.

● **BELOW**
The carbody-style locomotive, popular in the 1940s and 1950s, was displaced by the more versatile road-switcher type. Only a few railroads now use this older style, including LTV Mining, which has a fleet of antique EMD-made F7As.

with its U25B. The U25B road-switcher developed 2,500 hp with its 16-cylinder, 7FDL-series prime mover. Following GE's entry into the market, a horsepower race was on. To meet North American railroad's demands, EMD, GE and Alco (which has since, in 1969, ceased locomotive production) began to develop both four- and six-axle road-switcher locomotives of ever-increasing output. EMD's most popular models were: the four-axle 2,000-hp GP38, the six-axle 3,000-hp SD40 and the 20-cylinder, 3,600-hp SD45. GE peaked with the 3,600-hp U36C. Both builders dabbled in high-horsepower dual-prime mover eight-axle monsters, but this big locomotive's limited flexibility resulted in weak sales.

● **DESIGN IMPROVEMENTS**

The 1970s saw many electrical improvements. The 1980s brought microprocessor control. In the mid-1980s, GE introduced the DASH-8 line, a successful 4,000-hp design that put GE at the forefront of the locomotive market. In the mid-1990s, improvements in

● **RIGHT**
GE introduced the a.c. traction motor with its AC4400CW, a model that closely resembles earlier, d.c. traction locomotives. This model proved popular with Western railroads, which use them mainly to haul heavy mineral-trains in the mountains.

SD45-DIESEL-ELECTRIC

Dates produced	1965–71
Builder	General Motors (Electro-Motive Division)
Engine	20 cylinder 645 cc per cylinder
Power	3,600 hp

microprocessors enabled both builders successfully to apply a.c. traction motor technology to North American freight locomotives. This was the most significant improvement to American locomotive design since the advent of the diesel-electric. By using a.c. traction, locomotive builders were able to improve dramatically the tractive effort of a single locomotive. In 1996, the first 6,000 hp a.c. traction locomotives were being tested and sales of 4,000–5,000 hp a.c. locomotives dominated the new locomotive market.

● **ABOVE**
In 1996, the Union Pacific Railroad (UPR) took delivery of EMD's latest a.c.-traction locomotives, the "upgradeable" SD90MAC. These locomotives have a 4,000 hp prime mover and can accept a 6,000 hp prime mover that is being developed.

● **RIGHT**
A new EMD SD75M, featuring a safety cab and colourful warbonnet paint-work, rests between runs at Corith Yard, Chicago, Illinois. Despite a trend towards a.c. traction motors, the Santa Fe Railroad has remained committed to the traditional d.c. motor.

AMERICAN SHORT LINES

American short-line railroads are those smaller carriers that operate fewer than 350 route miles (560 km) and produce revenue of less than $40 million.

● MANY NEW SHORT LINES

Since the mid-1970s, many new short-line railroads have been formed. These new lines are mainly branch and secondary main lines disposed of by larger railroads in recent downsizing. Traditionally, healthy short lines had a choice of buying secondhand locomotives from larger railroads or new ones from builders. Through the mid-1970s, builders offered a variety of low and medium horsepower, switchers, road-switchers and speciality diesel-electric locomotives that appealed to short-line needs.

● EMD SWITCHERS AND "GEEPS"

General Motors (Electro-Motive Division), the main builder of new locomotives, offered a line of switcher-type engines featuring a short wheelbase that were popular with both short lines and larger railroads for use in yards and on secondary track. This range began with the 600 hp SC and SW locomotives

● **TOP**
New Hampshire & Vermont (NHV) Railroad operates on several branch lines formerly operated by Boston & Maine and Maine Central. It uses Alco RS-11s and EMD GP9s. NHV RS-11 switchers are pictured at Whitefield, New Hampshire.

● **BELOW**
Green Mountain Railroad (GMR) runs freight- and passenger-trains in Vermont. Usually, EMD's GP9s handle freight-trains and its Alco RS-1 road-switcher is used on passenger-trains.

● **ABOVE**
Many American short lines operate with obscure locomotives. Massachusetts Central railroad has a rare EMD NW5, one of only 13 built. This 1,000 hp road-switcher was originally owned by Southern Railway.

CENTURY-425	
Dates produced	1964–6
Builder	American Locomotive Company (Alco)
Engine	251C
Gauge	4 ft 8 1/2 in
Power	2,500 hp
Capacity	16 cylinders

in 1936 and ended with the 1,500 hp SW1500 and MP15 in the mid-1980s. Another EMD locomotive popular with short lines was the GP series commonly known as "Geeps", particularly the lower-horsepower, non-turbo-charged 1,500 hp GP7, 1,750 hp GP9 and 2,000 hp GP38.

● LEFT
In the 1970s, the Santa Fe railroad converted many of its EMD-made F7 cab-units to road-switchers designed as CF7s. The Massachusetts Central Railroad bought one CF7 from Santa Fe in 1984. The CF7 has been popular with short lines looking for secondhand locomotives.

● SHORT LINES PRICED OUT OF NEW LOCOMOTIVES

As the price of new locomotives began to climb, more short-line railroads began to buy used and remanufactured locomotives. Also, as the large railroads disposed of branches, they had less need for the types of locomotives required for branch-line service, glutting the used market with switchers and "Geeps". By the late 1970s, few short lines were placing orders for new locomotives; instead, they operated with hand-me-downs. As a result, short lines are operating with a great variety of old, secondhand locomotives, long discarded from main-line service. As a

group, short lines feature the greatest diversity of locomotives in the USA. Locomotives built by Alco, which ceased production in 1969, and many other curious and obscure models can be found working on short lines around the USA.

● ABOVE
Sierra Railroad was one of the last short lines to use Baldwin locomotives regularly. To operate its 80 km (50 mile) railroad, it owned several Baldwin S-12 diesel-electrics. Many short lines held on to Baldwins long after larger railroads discarded them.

● LEFT
New Hampshire & Vermont GP9 No. 669 switchers at Whitefield, New Hampshire. NHV, like many modern short lines, operates "first-generation" diesels – those that replaced steam locomotives – on lines let go by larger railroads.

AMERICAN PASSENGER TRAINS

The diesel-electric made its passenger début in 1934 with the Burlington Northern railroad's Pioneer Zephyr and Union Pacific Railroad's M-10000 City of Salina.

● PIONEER ZEPHYR INTRODUCES THE PASSENGER DIESEL

After World War II, American railroads began ordering diesel-electrics in quantity for general passenger service. As with the freight market, the General Motors Electro-Motive Division (EMD)

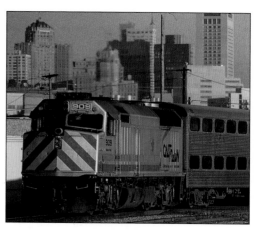

● LEFT
Cal-Train operates commuter-rail services between San Francisco, San Jose and Gilroy, California. The agency uses EMD's 3,000-hp F40PH locomotives in push-pull mode. The locomotives always face outbound (south).

FL9 DIESEL-ELECTRIC/ELECTRIC	
Dates produced	1956–60
Builder	General Motors (Electro-motive Division)
Engine	20 cylinders 567C or 567D1
Power	1,750 hp or 1,800 hp
Capacity	567 cc per cylinder

dominated the market for new passenger-locomotives. Its most popular models were its E series, streamlined locomotives featuring twin 567 prime movers and A1A trucks. Each truck had three axles but the centre axle was not powered. The E7, rated at 2,000 hp, was introduced in 1945; the E9, rated at 2,400 hp, was introduced in 1954 and remained in production until 1963. While other builders also produced passenger locomotives – notably Alco with its PA series – none was particularly successful in the USA. The PA was well liked by enthusiasts for its superior aesthetics but generally disliked by railroads for poor performance and high maintenance.

EMD also made four-axle F Series locomotives for passenger service. Western railroads preferred F units, mainly because of their pulling ability in heavily graded territory.

Beginning in 1956, the New Haven Railroad (NHR) took delivery of FL9s (dual-mode diesel-electric/electric) from EMD for use in electrified territory around New York City. These versatile locomotives use a diesel engine or electric third rail.

● THE AGE OF AMTRAK

Amtrak, America's National Railroad Passenger Corporation, an American government-owned body set up in 1970,

● LEFT
Amtrak maintains several dual-mode FL9 diesel-electric/ electric locomotives for service between New York City and Albany, New York. The now-defunct New Haven Railroad (NHR) ordered 60 of these specialty locomotives between 1956–60.

● OPPOSITE
Amtrak locomotives in Chicago, Illinois, await assignment. On the left, No. 828 is a General Electric AMD-103. On the right are EMD-made F40PHs.

● RIGHT
In the Northeast Corridor – between
Washington, DC and New Haven, Connecticut
– Amtrak operates AEM7 electrics in a high-
speed service up to 130 mph.

● RIGHT
In the Northeast Corridor – between
Washington, DC and New Haven, Connecticut
– Amtrak operates AEM7 electrics in a high-
speed service up to 130 mph.

assumed responsibility for most intercity
passenger runs in 1971. By the 1980s,
governmental operating agencies relieved
most railroads of commuter-train
responsibilities. A new generation of
motive power was developed for Amtrak
and the commuter lines. In the early
1970s, EMD made a passenger version of
its successful SD40 freight-locomotive,
but the six-axle passenger SDP40Fs, with
full cowl hood, proved largely
unsatisfactory for passenger service.
Many were later sold to the Santa Fe
railroad for fast freight service. In 1976,
EMD introduced the F40PH, a turbo-
charged 3,000 hp, four-axle locomotive
well received by Amtrak and the
commuter lines. Several hundred were
sold in the USA and Canada. Meanwhile,
General Electric offered its six-axle
3,000 hp P30CH, with limited success.

● **ELECTRICS AND TURBOLINERS**
Amtrak's Northeast Corridor is mostly
electrified. In the 1970s, General Electric
made about 30 E60 electrics to replace
40-year-old former Pennsylvania Railroad

● LEFT
Two General
Electric Genesis
AMD-103s lead
Amtrak's California
Zephyr westbound
at La Grange,
Illinois.

GG1 electrics operating on that route. In
the early 1980s, EMD licensed the Rc4
electric locomotive from the Swedish
company Allmänna Svenska Elektriska
Aktiebolaget (ASEA), and from that
design made more than 60 high-hp
AEM7 electrics for high-speed service on
the Northeast Corridor.

Amtrak has had limited success with
articulated turboliners. In the mid-
1970s, it placed seven streamlined Rohr
Turboliners in service in its Empire
Corridor, between New York City and
Niagara Falls. Each set has a 1,140 hp
power-car at both ends.

● **THE NEXT GENERATION**
In the early 1990s, Amtrak began taking
delivery of several new types of locomotives. It received about 20 utilitarian-
looking 3,200 hp DASH-8 32PBs from
General Electric, followed by several
varieties of GE's Genesis Locomotive.
The Genesis is a semi-streamlined
product that uses a monocoque
(frameless) body and a GE prime mover.
Amtrak and commuter-operator Metro-
North also use dual-mode Genesis
locomotives for service in the third-rail
electrified territory around New York
City. On its Californian routes, Amtrak
uses EMD's F59PHIs, streamlined
passenger locomotives exhibiting what
EMD deems the "swoopy look".

AMERICAN METRO-ELEVATED LINES

Traditional elevated lines, using steel structures to carry electrified rapid-transit tracks above city streets, can still be found in New York City, Philadelphia and Chicago.

● TRADITIONAL ELEVATED LINES

All of these elevated lines are operated in conjunction with a subway/heavy-rail metro system. In New York and Philadelphia, use of elevated lines is restricted to outside the central, commerical area – downtown. This leaves Chicago as the only remaining American city with a traditional elevated rapid-transit structure at its centre. Its skyscrapers and antique route present an incongruous mix of architecture.

In the mid-1980s, Boston, Massachusetts, replaced most of its Orange Line elevated structure with a

● LEFT
An outbound D train heads towards Coney Island, Brooklyn, Long Island, New York City, in a frigid December in 1993. The New York City Transit Authority (NYCTA) has several thousand rapid-transit cars in its fleet and operates the most extensive rapid-transit system in North America.

● LEFT
An inbound train from Flushing, Queens, New York City, heads for Times Square, Manhattan, in 1993. This is one of many elevated lines operating in the borough of Queens.

● ABOVE
Chicago's famous "Loop" is the last traditional elevated rapid-transit line to operate in the heart of an American city. A set of Morrison-Knudsen cars negotiates the "Loop" on 4 July 1995.

modern metro-rail system, leaving the Lechmere-North Station section of Green Line Light-Rail route as the only significant elevated structure in the area.

● MODERN HEAVY METRO-RAIL TRANSIT

Some American metropolitan areas that did not have traditional elevated lines are today served by modern heavy-rail metro transit systems. Like the traditional elevated lines, these systems use electrically powered multiple-unit transit vehicles (usually powered by third rail) on a variety of gradient-separated right-of-ways – underground (subway), in open cuts or on concrete elevated structures. The most extensive modern systems are the Washington D.C. Metro and, serving the greater San Francisco metro area, the Bay Area Rapid Transit, known as BART.

**CHICAGO TRANSIT
AUTHORITY (CTA)
SERIES 2000 CARS**

Date produced	1964
Builder	Pullman Car & Manufacturing Company
Weight	47,400 lb
Propulsion	General Electric
Seating	47/51 seats

● **RAPID TRANSIT CARS**

New York City and Chicago operate the largest rapid-transit fleets in the USA. In recent years, New York has modernized its rolling stock with new cars from north American builders such as Bombardier, and by having its older cars rebuilt. In the late 1980s and early 1990s, many of New York City Transit cars were built by MK Rail in the former Erie Railroad shops at Hornell in rural western New York state.

New York, with its new and rebuilt cars, has successfully eliminated the colourful graffiti that covered most of its fleet in the 1970s and 1980s. Its cars' spray paint-resistant surfaces are now nearly graffiti-proof.

Chicago's fleet of cars represents a host of different builders. Following discontinuation of streetcar service in the 1950s, Chicago rebuilt most of its large fleet of President Conference Committee (PCC) streetcars for rapid-transit service on elevated and subway lines. In 1964, Chicago took delivery of 180 new cars from Pullman. In 1969, it ordered 75 new stainless-steel cars from the Budd Co. In the 1970s, Chicago took delivery of 200 cars from Boeing-Vertol and another 600 cars from Budd. Chicago's most recent order was in the early 1990s, for 256 cars from Morrison-Knudsen.

● **ABOVE**
Into the 1950s, New York City operated a fleet of antique open-platform cars on one remaining Brooklyn elevated route, the Myrtle Avenue Line.

● **ABOVE LEFT**
On Independence Day 1995, in Chicago, Illinois, a red, white and blue set of cars made by Boeing-Vertol heads south on the Howard Street line.

● **BELOW**
Chicago has one of the largest networks of traditional elevated-metro rail lines. A 3200 Series car made by Morrison-Knudsen heads downtown on the Howard Street Line.

161

AMERICAN LIGHT RAIL

In the mid-1970s, San Francisco, California, and Boston, Massachusetts, ordered new light-rail vehicles to replace worn President Conference Committee cars (PCCs). This represented the first orders for new cars in several decades and began to reverse a long decline in American light-raise use.

● **AMERICAN LIGHT RAIL REVIVAL**

The new cars, built by Boeing-Vertol, had design flaws. There were no further orders for them. By the mid-1990s, fewer than 20 years after most of the Boeings were delivered, both cities were buying replacements.

● **CANADIAN LEAD FOLLOWED BY SAN DIEGO**

The real light-rail revival came in 1978 at Edmonton, Alberta, Canada, when the city inaugurated its 4½ mile (7 km) line. This was the first all-new light rail system in recent memory. The system used 14 six-axle Siemens-Duewag U2 light-rail vehicles (LRVs). The USA followed Canada's lead in 1980 when the San Diego Trolley (SDT) began operating in California. Like the Edmonton system,

MASSACHUSETTS BAY TRANSPORTATION AUTHORITY (BOSTON) TYPE 7	
Dates produced	1986–8
Builder	Kinki Sharyo
Client	MBTA (Boston)
Voltage	600 kV d.c.
Axles	Six
Weight	84,800 lb
Propulsion	Westinghouse
Seating	50 seats

● **ABOVE**
San Francisco's brightly painted, rebuilt PCCs have proved popular with tourists. The cars were regauged to operate on the San Francisco Municipal Railway's light-rail lines. Usually, the PCCs are assigned to the F-Market line, which does not use the Muni-Metro subway. This car is painted to represent Boston's MBTA scheme of the 1950s.

● **OPPOSITE BOTTOM**
An LRV made by Kawasaki, Japan, negotiates the broad-gauge single-track Media Line at Media, Pennsylvania, in suburban Philadelphia, in 1992. Philadelphia was the only city to buy these non-articulated cars.

● **BELOW**
A Type 7 car built by Kinki Sharyo of Japan prepares to turn at Cleveland Circle in Boston, Massachusetts, in 1993. Boston uses three different kinds of LRVs on its system.

● SAN FRANCISCO RE-EMBRACES THE PCC CAR

In 1995, San Francisco re-established its long-dormant F-Market line, using rebuilt PCC cars from Philadelphia, Pennsylvania. The cars were completely overhauled by M-K Rail, a division of Morrison-Knudsen, at Hornell, New York, and regauged for San Francisco tracks. To celebrate the PCC design, each car was painted differently, using traditional liveries from American cities that had formerly operated this traditional type of streetcar. The idea made this one of the most colourful fleets of regularly operated streetcars in the USA. San Francisco's once large fleet of PCC cars were mostly retired by the mid-1980s when new Boeing-Vertol cars arrived.

Some American cities have started a trend using low-floor cars. Portland, Oregon, was the first US city to use them, taking delivery of 46 Type-2 cars from Siemens Transportation Systems in 1993.

the SDT line, running from the commercial centre to the Mexican border at San Ysidro, was an entirely new light-rail system and also used six-axle U2 cars, painted bright red. The SDT system proved popular. Extensions and new routes have since been built.

● VARIETIES OF LIGHT-RAIL VEHICLES

Since then, nearly a dozen new light-rail systems have started operating. The latest is in Dallas, Texas, which started operating in June 1996. Its 18 km (11 mile) system uses yellow-and-white cars built by Kinki Sharyo/Itochu International.

LRVs used in the USA have few uniform standards and even the gauge varies somewhat. Most cities use the standard 4 ft 8½ in gauge, but New Orleans in Louisiana and Philadelphia and Pittsburg in Pennsylvania use 5 ft 2¼ in and 5 ft 2½ in.

Many builders' cars are in service. They range from traditional American companies, such as Perley Thomas with vintage streetcars built in 1923–4, used in New Orleans, to Bombardier which built cars for Portland, Oregon's light-rail system, and also include many foreign companies such as Italy's Breda and Japan's Kinki Sharyo.

TOURIST LINES IN AMERICA

In the past 20 years, dozens of railroads have begun operating tourist-trains. Some of these lines are strictly passenger-carriers, often catering to specialty markets such as luxury dinner-trains.

● **POPULARITY OF TOURIST LINES**
Other tourist trains are short-line railroads looking to supplement freight revenue. The type of motive power used on these lines varies greatly but tends towards the historic, to appeal to the travelling public. Some lines use steam-locomotives, others vintage diesel-electrics. Many lines that use diesels paint them in elaborate schemes reminiscent of the schemes used in the 1940s and 1950s.

● **CALIFORNIA'S NAPA VALLEY WINE TRAIN**
Napa Valley Wine Train is one of the most successful operations. It runs several trips a day through the Napa Valley and caters for up-market patrons. Guests have dinner and wine-tasting aboard vintage heavyweight passenger cars hauled by FPA-4 diesel-electronics

● **LEFT**
The Green Mountain Railroad (GMR) operates its freight- and passenger-trains with a fleet of well-maintained historic locomotives. In 1993, EMD's GP9 1850 leads a freight up the gradient at Ludlow, Vermont. The GP9 was popular in freight and passenger service.

● **LEFT**
The East Broad Top Railroad (EBTR) in central Pennsylvania offers an authentic railroad experience. It uses vintage equipment appropriate for its line. It has four operational 36 in gauge Baldwin Mikados. No. 15 is pictured at Rockhill Furnace.

● **BELOW**
In 1989, the Boone Scenic Railway (BSR) took delivery of a brand-new JS Class Chinese-made Mikado, seen here atop the railroad's high bridge, north of Boone, Iowa. The brightly painted steam locomotive is popular with train-riders.

made by Montreal Locomotive Works (MLW), Alco's Canadian subsidiary. Four of these engines, acquired from the Canadian passenger-rail authority Via Rail, entered service in 1989. They have a burgundy-and-gold paint scheme that reflects the colours of California's wine country. Several tourist lines acquired FPA-4s from Via Rail when it upgraded its locomotive fleet and disposed of many of these older models.

● **GREEN MOUNTAIN RAILROAD**
The Green Mountain Railroad (GMR), a successful short line in rural Vermont, USA, has augmented freight revenue by operating a seasonal excursion-train. For this service it maintains a vintage Alco RS-1 diesel – the precise model used by its predecessor Rutland Railway in passenger service in the 1940s and 1950s. It also uses General Motors Electro-Motive's GP9s when passenger-

FPA-A	
Dates produced	1958–9
Builder	Montreal Locomotive Works (MLW) (Alco)
Engine	251B
Power	1,800 hp
Capacity	12 cylinders

trains are heavily patronized, particularly in autumn when the coloured foliage attracts hundreds of riders daily.

● NEW STEAM PROVES POPULAR

The Boone Scenic Railroad (BSR) operating a former interurban line in central Iowa, USA, has taken a novel approach towards passenger-trains. In 1989, it took delivery of a brand-new JS Class Chinese-made Mikado. Several other American tourist lines have also ordered new steam locomotives. For Boone, which derives all its revenue from excursion-trains, the new steam locomotive has been a great success. Other tourist lines operate with traditional American-built steam locomotives restored for tourist service.

● **ABOVE LEFT**
A Northern Pacific Railroad (NPR) Ten-Wheeler 4-6-0, Class S-10 328, leads a passenger-excursion train across Wisconsin Central's St Croix River bridge in Wisconsin. This Alco-built locomotive 1907 is the only remaining NPR 4-6-0.

● **RIGHT**
In autumn 1989, the Napa Valley Wine Train began dinner-train service in the scenic Californian valley. Four streamlined Via Rail, FPA-4 locomotives provide power. They were bought from the Canadian passenger transport authority.

AMERICAN TRAIN PRESERVATION

Preservationists have rescued and restored nearly 150 steam locomotives to serviceable status in the USA and Canada. Authentic locomotives and replicas from all periods of development are represented – a complete range in age and size, from a re-creation of Peter Cooper's diminutive Tom Thumb of 1830 to World War II-vintage super power, such as Union Pacific Railroad's massive Northern type 4-8-4, No. 844.

● **STEAM LOCOMOTIVES**

Colorado's preserved narrow-gauge railroads operate vintage steam locomotives. The Cumbres & Toltec, which operates over the 3,048 m (10,000 ft) high Cumbres Pass through the San Juan Mountains of southern Colorado to Toltec in Arizona, maintains three classes of Denver & Rio Grande Western Mikado Type 2-8-2, Classes K27, K36 and K37. The Baltimore & Ohio Railroad (B&OR) Museum, Baltimore, Maryland, has a collection of steam locomotives, including the Tom Thumb replica. The Federal Government

● **TOP**
Chicago & Northern Western railroad's No. 1385, a Class R1, Alco-built 4-6-0 Ten-wheeler, is preserved in operating condition at the Mid-Continent Railway Museum, North Freedom, Wisconsin.

● **ABOVE**
Illinois Terminal GP7 No. 1605 displays a lively paint scheme. The GP7 was Electro-motive Division's first popular road-switcher. This locomotive and many others are preserved in operating condition at the Illinois Railway Museum, Union, Illinois.

has spent millions of dollars preserving vintage steam locomotives from around the USA and Canada, at Steamtown, in Scranton, Pennsylvania. Steamtown, once a private foundation, is now run by the American National Park Service.

Despite the many restored locomotives, considerable work is left for preservationists. Alas, for every serviceable locomotive there are probably a half-dozen others in poor shape and great need of attention.

● **LEFT**
Colorado's Cumbres & Toltec Scenic Railroad operates several former Denver & Rio Grande Western Class K36 narrow-gauge Mikado 2-8-2s. It maintains a Class K28 and a Class K37 for occasional use.

NORTHERN PACIFIC RAILROAD (NPR) 4-6-0, CLASS S10 NO. 328

Date produced	1907
Builder	American Locomotive Co. (Alco)
Driving wheels	57 in
Capacity	2 cylinders 19 x 26 in
Steam pressure	190 lb
Weight	153,000 lb
Tractive effort	26,000 lb

● **ABOVE RIGHT**
The Portola Railroad Museum, Portola, California, specializes in preserving diesel-electric locomotives. No. 6946, a Union Pacific Railroad DDA40X, the largest class of diesel ever built, is one of the museum's most impressive displays. EMD built 47 DDA40X for Union Pacific Railroad between 1969–71.

● **PRESERVED DIESEL-ELECTRIC AND ELECTRIC LOCOMOTIVES**
In the past 20 years, effort has been exerted to acquire and preserve significant examples of diesel-electric and electric locomotives. Several museums are now almost exclusively dedicated to such preservation.

The first commercially successful diesel, a box-cab built by Alco-General Electric-Ingersol Rand in 1926 for the Central Railroad of New Jersey, is preserved at the B&OR Museum. Several examples of the largest type of diesel-electric ever built, EMD's monster, eight-axle, 6,900 hp DDA40X, are preserved in the west. Union Pacific Railroad, sole operator of the big locomotives, still owns and operates one in excursion-service. On rare occasions, UPR still operates it for freight.

Electric locomotives are preserved, too. Several fine examples of the Raymond Loewy-styled Pennsylvania Railroad GG1 are on display. One of the largest collections of preserved railroad equipment – steam, diesel-electric, electric and traction – is located at the Illinois Railway Museum, Union, Illinois, where there is a DDA40A, Pennsylvania GG1 among hundreds of other items.

● **RIGHT**
Northern Pacific Railroad's "Ten-wheeler" 4-6-0 No. 328, made by Alco is operated by the Minnesota Transportation Museum, Osceola, Wisconsin. It has a limited summer-excursion schedule. When the steam locomotive is not running, vintage diesels are used.

CANADIAN FREIGHT TRAINS

● BELOW
Two Ontario Northland RS-3s await assignment. These MLW-built engines are almost identical to RS-3s built in the USA by MLW's parent, Alco.

Canadian railroads had a more conservative approach to motive power than had their American counterparts. Canadians preferred tested, established locomotive models rather than innovative ones and continued to rely on steam locomotives through the 1950s.

● THE 1950S

While Canadian railroads' transition to diesel-electrics copied the USA, they began serious conversion to diesel later and were far less experimental in choice of models. In the late 1950s and 1960s Canadian Pacific and Canadian National began taking delivery of mass-quantities of essentially stock American diesel-electric designs. General Motors Diesel Ltd (GMD) and Montreal Locomotive Works (MLW), Alco's Canadian subsidiary, were the main builders. Baldwin and Fairbanks-Morse also marketed their products in Canada.

Canadian railroads bought a few streamlined F units but largely dieselized freight operations with road-switcher-type locomotives had a solid market with Canadian Pacific and Canadian National. Both railroads acquired many MLW S-Series switchers.

● CANADIAN LOCOMOTIVES TAKE ON A DISTINCTIVE LOOK

In the late 1950s, Canadian locomotives took on a distinctive appearance, distinguishing them from their American counterparts. Mechanically, they were the same. For example, Canada bought MLW's 1,800 hp RS-18 that featured a slightly different hood-style from Alco's RS-11 preferred by American railroads. The locomotives were identical in most other respects. MLW continued to make diesels after Alco discontinued American production in 1969. Through the 1970s, MLW built distinctive Canadian locomotives

based on Alco designs. In 1979, Bombardier acquired MLW and continued to build locomotives into the mid-1980s. It has since left the new locomotive market.

● CANADIAN SAFETY-CABS

In the early 1970s, safety-conscious Canadians began ordering road-switcher hood-unit locomotives with full-width, four-window "Canadian safety-cabs", or "comfort cabs". These reinforced cabs were designed to protect the crew in derailments or collisions. Canadian railroads also began equipping locomotives with "ditch-lights", bright headlamps near the rail, for increased visibility. For many years, these were trademarks of Canadian motive power. American lines have since emulated Canadian practice and safety-cabs and ditch-lights are now standard features on North American locomotives.

● LEFT
Canadian National (CN) acquired SD701 locomotives from General Motors in 1995. In 1996, CN began to receive its first SD751s, part of an order for more than 300.

● THE 1990S

In the mid-1990s, Canadian National and Canadian Pacific began ordering what were essentially stock locomotives from GM and GE, although some assembly was done in Canada. In 1995, Canadian Pacific ordered a fleet of GE AC4400CWs for heavyfreight service in the Canadian Rockies. While Canadian Pacific had experimented with a.c. traction, this investment represented the first commerical application of the new technology in Canada. Meanwhile, Canadian National has remained firmly committed to traditional d.c.-traction motors. Instead of trying a.c. locomotives, it ordered more than 300 General Motors six-axle SD701 and SD751 locomotives.

● BELOW
The wide-nosed "Canadian safety-cab", or comfort cab, and ditch-lights were once trademarks of Canadian National locomotives. Now they are standard features on most North American freight locomotives. Here, a quartet of CN GP40-2s with comfort cabs leads a northbound freight.

RS-18

Dates produced	1956-68
Builder	Montreal Locomotive Works (MLW) (Alco)
Engine	12-cylinder, 251B
Power	1,800 hp

● OPPOSITE
A Canadian Pacific (CP) MLW RS-18 switches at St Martin's Junction, Quebec, in 1993. The Canadian-built RS-18 was not significantly different from the American-built RS-11.

CANADIAN PASSENGER TRAINS

Steam locomotives were used in passenger service in Canada until the early 1960s.

● 1950S TO 1980S

In the 1950s, Canadian National and Canadian Pacific began acquiring passenger-diesels. Both railroads used Canadian-built General Motors Diesel (GMD) FP7s. FP9s and passenger-equipped road-switchers. These locomotives were in most respects the same as

FPA-A	
Dates produced	1958–9
Builder	Montreal Locomotive Works (MLW) (Alco)
Engine	12-cylinder, 251B
Power	1,800 hp

● **LEFT**
Via Rail, the Canadian passenger-train operating agency, ran a fleet of Montreal Locomotive Works FPA-4s inherited from Canadian National. Four FPA-4s at Central Station, Montreal, Quebec, in 1984.

● **BELOW LEFT**
Via Rail's LRC locomotives did not always haul the specially designed tilting LRC train sets. In 1985, an LRC locomotive leads a conventional train in Toronto, Ontario.

● **BELOW**
Toronto's GO Transit was an early user of push-pull commuter train sets. On the end opposite the locomotive is an auxiliary cab. This provides head-end power in addition to comfort for the engineer. Some of GO Transit's auxiliary cabs were built from old F-units.

their American counterparts. Canadian National also used FPA-2s and FPA-4s, the MLW passenger version of Alco's FA freight locomotives. The E unit, popular in the USA, did not catch on in Canada, although Canadian Pacific owned a few.

● TORONTO COMMUTER OPERATIONS

In 1966, Toronto's commuter agency GO Transit ordered specially built road-switchers from General Motors, called GP40TCs, for its passenger runs. The GP40TC is essentially a modified version of the 3,000-hp GP40 freight locomotive, equipped with a headend power generator to operate electric heat and lights on passenger cars.

GO Transit was an early proponent of push-pull commuter trains. Rather than run traditional trains with the locomotive always on the front, GO Transit equipped the rear of its trains with auxiliary power-cabs. The auxiliary cabs, built from the shells of old F-units, provide head-end power and comfortable operating cabs. By using an aux-cab, GO Transit obviated need for a specially equipped locomotive to provide head-end power.

● LIGHT, RAPID, COMFORTABLE

The Canadian passenger agency Via Rail took on the operation of most long-distance passenger-trains in 1997. Looking for a better way to haul passengers, it decided to acquire modern "tilt" trains. Between 1981–4 Via Rail took delivery of LRC trains, powered by 31 specially designed locomotives built by Bombardier's Montreal Locomotive Works. The LRC locomotives proved problematic and are no longer made.

● ABOVE LEFT
Canadian National box-cab electrics lead a commuter-train at Val Royal Station, Montreal. CN's suburban commuter service to Deux Montagnes, Quebec, uses overhead electrification. The traditional electrification and electric locomotives, some nearly 80 years old, were replaced in 1995 with a modern system.

● ABOVE RIGHT
In the late 1980s, Via Rail began replacing its ageing carbody-style locomotives with new F40PHs from General Motors.

● BELOW
Ontario Northland Railroad operated its Northlander passenger-train with FP7m locomotives and secondhand Trans-European Express articulated train sets acquired in 1977.

CANADIAN LIGHT RAIL

Canada's three main light-rail systems are in Calgary and Edmonton, in Alberta, and in Toronto, Ontario. Both the Alberta systems were built new in the late 1970s and early 1980s. The Toronto system evolved from a traditional streetcar system.

Toronto and Montreal both operate underground electrified metro-rail systems. The Montreal system uses an unusual rubber-tyre propulsion. Vancouver, British Columbia, features an elevated metro-rail system called SkyTrain, which uses computer-controlled unmanned cars operating from a 600 volt d.c. third rail.

EDMONTON'S U12 LIGHT RAIL VEHICLES (LRVS)

Dates produced	1978–83
Builder	Siemens-Duewag
Voltage	600 volts d.c.
Axles	Six
Weight	71,585 lb
Propulsion	Siemens
Seating	64 seats

● **EDMONTON**

Edmonton inaugurated its 7 km (4½ mile) line in 1978. By 1992, the system had expanded to 10.6 km (6½ miles). In the 1900s, Edmonton operated a streetcar system. This was discontinued after World War I, in favour of highway transportation. Edmonton's light-rail system began operations with 14 six-axle articulated Siemens-Duewag U2 light-rail vehicles (LRVs).

● **CALGARY**

Calgary followed Edmonton's lead and opened its 12 km (7½ mile) all-new light-rail line in 1981. By 1992, Calgary's

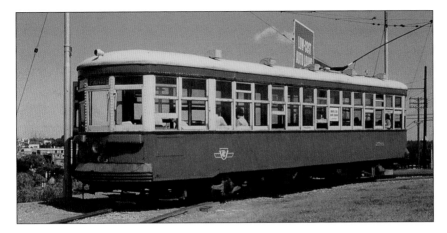

● **LEFT**
In the 1960s, Toronto still operated venerable Peter Witt cars, which seem particularly antique compared to a modern CLRV.

● **OPPOSITE**
Toronto operates 196 four-axle CLRV cars built between 1977–82. A TTC car pauses at Dundas Avenue, Toronto, in 1985.

● **BELOW**
Toronto once boasted a large fleet of President Conference Committee (PCC) cars. In the past two decades, most were replaced with CLRVs.

system was operating more than 27 km (17 miles), with extensions planned. Calgary operates a fleet of more than 80 six-axle articulated Siemans-Duewag U2 cars. It has also operated two experimental U2 cars that feature a.c.-traction motors. Most North American light-rail systems use traditional d.c.-traction motor technology. In the USA, the Baltimore, Maryland, light-rail system also uses a.c. traction.

● **TORONTO**
Toronto relied on a large fleet of President Conference Committee cars (PCC)s. In 1977, the city began replacing traditional PCCs with new Canadian Light Rail Vehicles (CLRVs). By the early 1990s, Toronto was operating nearly 100 four-axle single-unit CLRVs and more than 50 six-axle articulated CLRVs. Like cities in the USA, Toronto was looking at low-floor cars for future operation.

CUBA'S RAILWAY NETWORK

Cuba has an almost unbelievable diversity of classic American steam locomotives, left suspended in time following Fidel Castro's revolution in 1959.

Some of them came from former lines in the USA and their builders' plates read like a who's who of American locomotive history: H.K. Porter, Rogers, Davenport, Alco, Vulcan Ironworks and Baldwin. Small wonder that over the past ten years Cuba has become a focus for steam lovers worldwide, as traditional outposts of steam in Eastern Europe, South Africa and India have declined.

All of Cuba's steam-locomotive fleet work on the island's vast sugar plantations but, in the course of work, often

● BELOW
At the Boris Luis Santa Coloma mill network on Cuba, the flat crossing at Robles has a classic American signal-box on stilts. A Baldwin Mogul built in January 1920 completes the picture.

● RIGHT
A German-builder's plate on a Cuban locomotive.

travel over the national railway system's main lines. Far from being the small locomotives found on many of the world's sugar plantations, Cuba's engines are, in many cases, fully fledged mainliners and typical of the engines that many American roads were operating in the early years of this century.

A remarkable variety of gauges exists on Cuba, too, including standard, 3 ft, 2 ft 10½ in, 2 ft 6 in and 2 ft 3¾ in.

A remarkable number of centenarian engines is active, including Baldwins of 1878, 1882, 1891, 1892 and 1895, and a pair of Rogers of 1894.

Cuba looks likely to remain reliant on steam locomotives for many years to come, one of the most exciting bastions of classic steam power into the new century.

● **RIGHT**
This Mogul, built by
H.K. Porter in 1919,
was pictured
trundling a yellow
caboose, that is
guard's van, across
the rails of the Carlos
Manuel de Cespedes
sugar mill in
Camaguey Province,
Cuba.

● **FAR RIGHT**
The wreckage of
Baldwin 2-8-0
No. 1542 Manuel
Fajardo at Obdulio
Morales sugar mill's
locomotive shed in
Sancti Spiritus
Province, near the
spot where its boiler
exploded. The boiler,
wasted at the front
tube-plate, had been
welded. The result
was disastrous. The
driver, oiling the
motion, was blown to
pieces and only his
legs were found. The
fireman, in the cab,
was thrown about
15 m (50 ft) across
the depot yard.

4-4-0 WESTINGHOUSE	
Builder	Baldwins, New York, USA
Client	Havana Central Railroad
Gauge	4 ft 8½ in
Type	4-4-0
Driving wheels	5 ft 8 in
Capacity	Cylinders 18 x 24 in
Weight	119,600 lb

● **OPPOSITE**
Baldwin-built 2-8-0 No. 1390 eases a rake of
freshly cut sugar cane down the Arroyo Blanco
line at the Rafael Freyre sugar mill in Holguin
Province, Cuba.

● **ABOVE**
Cuba has several Fireless engines. This huge
0-4-0, built by Baldwin in September 1917,
works at the Bolivia sugar mill, in Camaguey
Province.

● **ABOVE**
Cuba has no coal reserves, so the island's
locomotives are oilfired. The cab interior of a
Baldwin 2-8-0 raising steam at the E.G.
Lavandero sugar mill.

SOUTH AMERICAN STEAM

South America was a major area of importance during the worldwide decline of steam from the 1950s and remained so until the mid-1980s.

The area is fascinating because of its diversity of locomotive types, operating terrain and gauge.

● ARGENTINA AND URUGUAY

Argentina displayed the British school of design. It had more locomotives than any other South American country – about 1,000 active as late as the mid-1970s. Five gauges operated over 80 different locomotive types. One of the world's most exciting steam lines is Argentina's 75 cm (2 ft 6 in) gauge Rio Gallegos, a

● ABOVE
A 4-8-0 15B Class of Argentine Railways. Britain's Vulcan Foundry exported 30 of these two-cylinder engines to Argentina in 1949. Mixed-traffic engines, they gained distinction in hauling seasonal fruit over the 1,200 km (750 mile) run from the Rio Negro Valley to Buenos Aires, working 1,000-ton loads on passenger-train timings.

● LEFT
In the 1950s, the Yorkshire Engine Co. of Sheffield sent two Moguls to Paraguay. The engines have a distinct LMS air about them as shown in this picture of No. 152 Asunción in the shed yard at San Salvador.

coal-carrying line 52 degrees south, near the Strait of Magellan. This route operates 2-10-2s, hauling 1,800-ton coal-trains, and is one of the steam sights of the world.

Uruguay, across the River Plate from Buenos Aires, was another stronghold of classic British designs, rivalling India in faithfulness to the domestic product.

● BRAZIL

Brazil has long been a land of discovery for rare and unrecorded locomotive types, because of its vast terrain and the relative remoteness of much of the country. Brazil's best-known steam-line is the metre-gauge Doña Teresa Cristina in the south-east where the world's last Texas Type 2-10-4s work. Formerly, they worked across the Mato Grosso, the highlands in eastern Mato Grosso state. These giants of American steam superpower, scaled down to metre-gauge operations, contrast with a plethora of sugar-plantation systems in the area around Campos, north of Rio de Janeiro, and in the north-eastern state of

Pernambuco behind the Atlantic Ocean
port and state capital Recife (formerly
Pernambuco). These sugar usinas hosted
a fascinating variety of metre-gauge
veterans, many from Brazil's former
main-line railways such as the Leopoldina,
Mogiana, Paulista and Sorocabana.

● **CHILE, PERU AND PARAGUAY**
Chile's waterless Atacama Desert was
host to the last Kitson Meyers, weird,
double-jointed beasts that bent in the
middle and had a chimney at both ends.
These engines were an articulated

predecessor of the more successful
Garratt engine.

The Kitson Meyer's rarity was
complemented by the incredible veterans
found farther north in Peru where an
1870 classic American Rogers 4-4-0 was
active at Puerto Eten.

The wilds of the Paraguayan Chaco
were host to a fascinating stud of veterans
that hauled *quebracho* from the interior to
ports along the River Paraguay for
conveying to the Atlantic Ocean at
Buenos Aires. The logs were once a
major source of tannin, used as tanning
agents and in medicines. The flame-
throwing woodburners of the Chaco
contrasted well with the standard-gauge
main line from Asunción to Encarnación
with its woodburning Edwardian Moguls,
from North British Glasgow and
Hawthorn Leslie 2-6-2Ts.

Thus, diversity and exotica have been
left over from the great age of steam.
Although, by the 1990s, much of the
diversity had disappeared, survivors will
linger on in ever-diminishing pockets
into the new century.

15B CLASS 4-8-0	
Date	1949
Builder	Vulcan Foundry, Lancashire, England
Client	Argentine Railways (Ferrocarriles Argentinos; FA)
Gauge	5 ft 6 in
Driving wheels	5 ft 8 in
Capacity	Cylinders 19 x 28 in
Total weight in full working order	154 tons

MODERN SOUTH AMERICAN LOCOMOTIVES

In the past, many South American countries had closer ties with Europe and the USA than with each other. This resulted in at least six different railway gauges being built on the continent.

● **SNAKING BULK TRAFFIC IN PERU**
Peru's railways climb the upper slopes of the highest Andean summits but adhesion only is used, resulting in spectacular sights as long mineral-trains snake up and around grand mountains. Diesel is the established form of motive power. Peru has more than 1,350 km (839 miles) of standard gauge and just 300 km (186 miles) of 3 ft gauge.

Peru's oil-burning steam locomotives were replaced by diesel-electrics, the most numerous being General Motors (GM) Type JJ 26 CW-2B 3,300 hp Co-Cos built by Villanes of Brazil.

● **RESTRUCTURING IN CHILE**
Chile has just under 2,576 km (1,600 miles) of 5 ft 6 in gauge and more than 1,600 km (1,000 miles) of metre-gauge

● **ABOVE**
An Alco-built 1,000-hp diesel-electric, No. 107, shunting on a multigauge track in the station yard at Mérida, Yucatan, Mexico. The locomotive belongs to the Ferrocarriles Unidos del Sureste.

● **BELOW**
Argentina's changing motive-power character is shown at Constitution Station, Buenos Aires. A diesel-electric stands beside a Class 8E three cylinder 2-6-4 suburban tank, one of the most successful locomotive types ever delivered to the country.

track still in use after restructuring of the railway system. The metre-gauge lines to the north of Santiago are diesel-operated but the standard-gauge Southern Railway, extending from Santiago south to Puerto Montt, an area of German settlement, has been electrified. Electric locomotives of Swiss origin are being built in Chile. Diesel has taken over the narrow-gauge routes.

ARGENTINE CLASS 8E 2-6-4T SUBURBAN

Date	1923
Gauge	5 ft 6 in
Client	Buenos Aires & Great Southern Railway
Driving wheels	5 ft 8 in
Capacity	3 cylinders 17 x 26 in
Pressure	200 lb sq in
Axle loading	19 tons
Weight in full working order	101 tons

● **BELOW**
The nameplate and numberplate of one of the
two Moguls delivered to Paraguay from
Yorkshire Engineering Co., named Asunción
after the country's capital city Nuestra Señora
de la Asunción founded in 1538. The sister
engine was No. 151, named Encarnación, after
Encarnación de Diaz, the agricultural centre
opposite Posados, Argentina, with which it is
connected by ferry.

The E32 Co-Cos from GAI of Italy are
Chile's most numerous passenger-electric
locomotives. Most diesels are from GM
in Argentina. The DT600, DT1300,
DYDT5100, D7.100 and D1600 classes
account for more than two-thirds of
Chile's diesels. The most numerous
diesel classes on the 5 ft 6 in gauge are
GAIA 1350, GAIA 1050 and Alco
RSD16. Metre-gauge diesels are supplied
by General Electric (GE), the most
numerous class being the G22CO with
more than 100 units in service. The
201 km (125 miles) of electrically-
operated track is entirely serviced by
Russian-built locomotives.

● **DIESEL TAKE-OVER IN
ARGENTINA**
Argentina has more than 22,500 km
(14,000 miles) of 5 ft 6 in gauge, nearly
3,220 km (2,000 miles) of 4 ft 8½ in
gauge and more than 14,500 km (9,000
miles) of other gauges. Much of the rail
system radiates from Buenos Aires.
Because of British influence in the early
days, most equipment is British in
appearance. Diesel has all but taken over,
yet steam is still active on the Esquel and
Rio Gallegos lines of Patagonia. On main
lines, Fiat-type diesel railcars are

● **ABOVE**
A 2-8-0 of Mexico's Southern Pacific Lines
threads a freight-train along the West Coast
route, which stretches 2,104 km (1,307 miles)
from Guadalajara, Mexico's second-largest
city, to the border of the United Mexican
States (UMS) and the USA.

● **BELOW**
An electric locomotive pulls a freight-train
through the Argentine-Chilean Pass at
Caracoles, near Socompa in Chile's
Antofagasta Province.

common, although freight traffic on
the many electrified lines is mainly
hauled by British outline diesels. Lines
carrying the heaviest commuter traffic
around Buenos Aires have been
electrified for many years.

● **HEMATITE, STEEL AND SÃO
PAULO IMPACT ON BRAZIL**
Brazil is South America's largest and
most industrial country. The two main
gauges are 5 ft 3 in and metre. Bulk
freight has increased and made new
export routes a priority, because of vast
hematite deposits, which is the chief
source of iron, in Minas Gerais state, the
steel industry of Volta Redonda town in
Rio de Janeiro state, Brazil's first steel-
making town from 1942, and the
manufacturing potential of the fastest-
growing city in the world, São Paulo,
itself a great railway centre. Track upgrading and electrification has been in
progress for the past 15 years. Diesels
work the various narrow gauges and the
non-electrified main lines. There are just
more than 1,932 km (1,200 miles) of
5 ft 3 in gauge, 24,150 km (15,000
miles) of metre-gauge with just more
than 885 km (550 miles) electrified.
Freight account for 99 per cent of traffic.

EUROPEAN SHUNTERS

In the days of steam, locomotives for shunting or gravity marshalling-yard work were sometimes specifically designed but many, also, were those pensioned off from main-line duties. To an extent, this practice still applies but from the 1950s increasing attention was paid to efficiency and fitness for purpose.

● **SHUNTING WITHIN STATION LIMITS**

These shunters come in many shapes and sizes, depending to a degree on whether what is required is casual shunting at a relatively small station or transfer work with moderate loads on the main line from time to time.

For the lighter duties, locomotives are usually four-wheeled and range from about 50 hp to about 300 hp. Propulsion can be diesel or electric. In Switzerland, alternative power sources are provided in the same locomotive and can be selected. For example, in sidings where there is no overhead-line equipment, the diesel engine provides power to the electric-traction motors. Some are fitted for remote radio control, enabling the driver to operate from the lineside, thereby performing the role of the traditional shunter. Small machines can be driven by people without the lengthy, rigorous training needed for a main-line driver, and, when not driving, they perform other station work.

Larger locomotives tend to be six-wheeled or Bo-Bo, diesel or electric. Diesel is usually preferred for its flexibility.

● **MARSHALLING YARDS AND TRIP FREIGHTS**

The bulk of marshalling-yard and trip-freight work is done by Bo-Bos where the prime power source is a diesel motor or overhead electric supply often giving an output of more than 1,000 hp. At gravity marshalling yards, standard locomotives with special low gearing for propelling wagons over the hump are sometimes used. In more recent years, some gravity-yard shunters have been fitted with radio to permit operation from the control tower. Other specialist shunters include a normal locomotive semi-permanently

● **RIGHT**
The trend to make small shunters more versatile is increasing. They have been fitted, for example, with radio control. A new application is accumulators, fitted to this electric-shunter of Switzerland's Spiez-Erlenbach-Zweisimmen Railway so that it can work in non-electrified sidings. Tea 245.021 is at Zweisimmen in 1995.

● **BELOW**
This Deutsche Reichsbahn Class 101 No. 512, almost the classic small diesel-shunter, acts as carriage-shunter at Riesa, Dresden, Germany, in 1991. It was later No.311.512 on the unified German railway system (DBAG).

● **RIGHT**
Older main-line locomotives are downgraded to light duties, performing trip-freight and shunting work as needed. Class 1200 of Portuguese Railways – Companhia dos Caminhos de Ferro (CP) – built by Sorefame in Portugal in 1961–64, do such work in Southern Portugal. Nos. 1213 and 1210 are pictured resting at the railway-junction town of Tunes, Algarve, in 1996.

ELECTRIC SHUNTER: BERN-LOETSCHBERG-SIMPLON RAILWAY (BLS)

Date	1943
Builders	mechanical: Swiss Locomotive and Machine Works (SLM) electrical: SA des Ateliers de Sécheron
Gauge	1,435 mm
Class	Ee 3/3
Axle (wheel) arrangement	030 (Whyte notation 0-6-0)
Catenary voltage	a.c. 15 kV, 16.7 Hz.
Weight in working order	38 tonnes
Rating	One hour, 462 kW (about 619 hp)
Maximum service speed	40 kph

coupled to a similar power-unit without cab or related console. Such units are sometimes called "cow and calf".

Larger, non-specialized shunters can work "trip freights" between their own yard and others in the vicinity, or to factory sidings.

● **LARGE PASSENGER STATIONS**
At most large passenger stations, the "station pilot", often in gleaming condition, is a familiar sight as it deals with empty stock or remarshals trains. The locomotives are often members of the same class, or a variant of those found in marshalling yards. Sometimes the only difference is the fitting of extra, or different, braking equipment or couplings.

● **ABOVE**
Hungarian State Railways (MAV) has a sizeable class of modern Bo-Bo electrics built by Ganz Mavag from 1983 onward. Their 820 kW (1,100 hp) enables them to cover a wide range of duties, including carriage pilot, heavyfreight shunting and trip-freights. No. V46. 054 is pictured at the river-port of Szeged (Szegedin), on Hungary's border with then Yugoslavia, in 1993.

EUROPEAN FREIGHT

Reconstruction of Europe after World War II and growing international trade brought a huge resurgence in rail freight. This traffic had to be integrated with equally large volumes of passenger-trains and so locomotives had to be able both to handle heavy loads and to run at relatively high speeds.

Carriage of many classes of freight by rail has steadily declined. New business, however, is arriving as road-freight tractors and trailers are transported by rail across national boundaries, sometimes with drivers accommodated in sleeping-cars on the train. Intermodal traffic, with either swap-bodies or vehicles designed to operate on rail or road, is not a new concept but it is being further developed. The transport of standard-gauge wagons on special metre-gauge bogies or transporter-wagons continues to cut the cost of time delays and trans-shipment, especially in Switzerland.

● ELECTRIC LOCOMOTIVES

As the mixed-traffic locomotive's development progressed along similar lines, the superficial appearance of the motive power on each rail system varied normally only to the extent of front-end body shape and the ventilation grilles' style and position.

Most adopted the Bo-Bo formation. In countries where heavy trains tackle steep gradients, however, locomotives with the Co-Co arrangement were introduced. In more recent years, developments in multiple working and remote radio control have enabled the use of two or more compatible locomotives at the head and a locomotive cut into the train. This is, among other things, to relieve weight on the drawbar between the locomotive and the train's

● LEFT
A new country and new livery have brought a striking change to former Deutsche Reichsbahn Class 242, which was bought by Lokoop, a Swiss consortium, and hired out. The engine, working on the Swiss Südostbahn in 1996, is pictured at Schindellegi in a livery advertising transport to a nearby mountain resort.

● ABOVE
Class 140 of German Railways (DBAG) was devised as a freight version of a similar passenger-class. It first appeared in 1957, and to 1973 nearly 900 were built. They handle anything from empty-carriage workings to medium-tonnage freights. No. 140 009-2 is pictured at Murneau, south of Munich, Bavaria, in 1994.

● LEFT
In sharp contrast to the bustle of the French scene, a freight-train in southern Portugal waits to leave the junction station of Tunes, Algarve, headed by Alco-built A1A-A1A diesel-electric No. 1503 in 1996.

● RIGHT
Two locomotives look excessive for this light freight-train at Venlo, Limburg Province, in the Netherlands in 1989, but Netherlands Railways-NV Nederlandse Spoorwegen (NS)-diesel-electric No. 6401, built in 1955, is part of the train that is in the charge of NS 2213. It is ironic that it is hauling a member of the class destined to lead to its withdrawal.

FRENCH STATE RAILWAYS (SNCF) CLASS BB 22200

Date	1976
Builder	Alsthom/MTE
Gauge	1,435 mm
Axle arrangement	BB
Catenary voltage	d.c. 1,500 v, a.c. 25 kV single phase (dual voltage)
Wheel diameter	1,250 mm
Weight in working order	89 tonnes
Rating	4,360 kW
Maximum service speed	160 kph

front vehicles. Longer trains also improve line capacity and therefore economic performance of the line.

● DIESEL LOCOMOTIVES

Diesel power, with locomotives working in multiple on heavy trains, is the only practical course on non-electrified lines or where traffic is lighter. The available tractive effort is generally lower than electric locomotives, but continuing use of diesels widely throughout Europe can be foreseen because of the flexibility of operation coupled with, usually, a mixed-traffic availability and, in some cases, lighter axleloading.

● BUILDERS

All the larger and some of the smaller countries of mainland Europe have the capacity to build both diesel and electric locomotives. However, the case now is that few builders design, manufacture and erect a complete locomotive. Credit for the design or manufacture of a particular class of locomotives often goes to the company or works which does the final erection. In practice, the design may well be that of the erecting company but components – bodies, motors, electrical equipment and other items – are likely to have been provided by other locomotive manufacturers.

● LEFT
French National Railways (SNCF) BB22288 Louhans leaves the extensive marshalling yards of Villeneuve-St Georges, south-eastern Paris, with a long train of empty car-transporters in 1996.

EUROPEAN RACK
RAILWAYS

Rack railways are specially built to climb
steep gradients in mountainous areas.

● TOURIST LINES

Most but not all tourist lines exist to
convey skiers in winter and walkers, or
just sightseers, in summer high into
mountains. Other lines enable the tourist
to reach points from which spectacular
views can be obtained.

Track gauge varies from 800 mm to
standard gauge. Propulsion is generally by
an electric power-car pushing a control-
trailer up the grade but the touristic value
of the steam locomotive has not been lost
on some operators who, in recent years,
have ordered new steam locomotives
using oilfiring and needing only one man
in the cab. For obvious reasons, the track
of each is relatively short. Examples of
both types of line are illustrated.

● **LEFT**
Austria's metre-
gauge Achenseebahn
uses both
Riggenbach rack-
and-pinion and
adhesion to climb
from Jenbach, in
Austria in Tirol, east
of Innsbruck, to the
lake that gives the
railway its name.
The locomotives
date from 1899.
No. 2 and its vintage
coaches are pictured
leaving Jenbach in
1980.

● **LEFT**
Switzerland's 800 mm gauge Brienzer-Rothorn
Bahn, between Brienz, on Lake Brienz in Bern
Canton, and Rothorn, has put into service three
new steam locomotives of revolutionary design
but conventional external appearance. These
are oilfired and can be operated by one man.
The first, No. 12, was delivered in 1992 and is
pictured at Brienz in 1995.

● **BELOW LEFT**
The Monte Generoso Railway has been operated
successively by steam, diesel and from 1982
electricity. The train is pictured having just
arrived at the summit station, which was being
modernized in 1989.

ELECTRIC RAILCAR –
MONTE GENEROSO
RAILWAY

Date	1982
Builder	Swiss Locomotive and Machine Works (SLM)
Client	Monte Generoso Railway
Gauge	800 mm Abt Rack
Class	Bhe 4/8
Axle arrangement	Four of the eight axles of the two-car unit are driven
Catenary voltage	d.c. 650 v
Weight in working order	34.1 tonnes
Rating	810 kW (about 1,086 hp)
Maximum service speed	14 kph

● **CONVENTIONAL RAILWAYS WITH RACK AID**

The main aim of conventional railways with track assistance is to provide communication between towns and villages for passengers and freight convey-ance. Often, tourist areas are served as well. Indeed, if this were not so, the viability of many lines often operating in relatively sparsely populated regions would be at risk.

The track gauge is generally metre and the trains appear at first sight quite conventional with an electric-locomotive hauling a moderately long train of coaches. Other trains might be hauled by single or double electric power-cars, in effect locomotives with passenger or baggage accommodation in the body. If track configuration permits, speeds of more than 75 kph are achieved over the adhesion sections but on rack sections about less than half of that can be expected.

● **INDUSTRIAL LINES**

A most spectacular example of industrial lines was the "Iron Mountain" railway from Vordernberg, in the Styria, Austria, to Eisenerz. Of standard gauge, there were some passenger services but its main purpose was to bring iron ore from Eisenerz, a mountain consisting almost entirely of iron ore, to a huge iron and steel works at Donawitz, west of Leoben in Styria. Steam was the motive power until the last few years of its existence when specially fitted diesel locomotives joined a rack locomotive purpose-built for the line. These achieved only a modest degree of success. Passenger traffic declined to the point where it could be handled by a single four-wheel, rack-fitted diesel-railcar.

This Austrian Federal Railways – Österreichische Bundesbahnen (ÖBB) – line closed in 1986 because of a fall in demand for steel coupled with the fact that it was cheaper to import ore from outside Austria. The last ore-train ran under diesel power on 27 June 1986. No fewer than seven steam locomotives have been preserved. Five of them are Class 0-6-2 Ts dating from 1890, the most popular with the crews, and one of which stands on a plinth in the town square. One is a 0-12-0T and one a 2-12-2T, built in Germany in 1941 and now standing on a plinth at Vordernmarkt Station.

EUROPEAN DMUs

The diesel multiple unit (DMU), the most flexible of all means of rail passenger transport, is used in Europe on all gauges and in many configurations.

● SINGLE RAILCARS

Single railcars range from a unit capable of coupling to another power-unit, to a control-trailer or just to a freight-wagon or passenger-coach. Operating alone, a single railcar can often be sufficient to maintain the passenger traffic on a narrow-gauge line, such as the Austrian Federal Railways 760 mm gauge line linking the Neider-Österreich (NÖ) towns of Gmünd and Gross Gerungs in the Greinerwald, or standard-gauge routes like the picturesque cross-border route between the Austrian Tirol town of Reutte and the German resort and winter sports centre Garmisch-Partenkirchen in the foothills of the Bavarian Alps.

● **ABOVE**
Netherlands Railways (NS) diesel-electric Class DE IIs were built by Allan, in 1953 and extensively rebuilt in 1975–82 by NS. This unit had just arrived at Arnhem, in Gelderland Province, in 1989.

● **BELOW**
The modern appearance of this rebuilt X4300 Series unit of French National Railways (SNCF) belies the fact that the class was introduced in 1963. In 1988, a typical representative, from Dinant, Belgium, awaits its return working at Givet, in the Ardennes Department of north-eastern France, near the border with Belgium.

The ability to strengthen the train quickly, to cope with known or sudden peaks of traffic, by adding a powered vehicle to run in multiple without reducing its line speed, is invaluable on services which share, for part of the route, the tracks of a main line where lengthy track-occupation by slow trains is unacceptable. Such units are capable of 120 kph.

On branch lines or secondary routes with a relatively infrequent service, any cut in speed from hauling unpowered trailers is not serious. However, many modern trailing-vehicles offer relatively

● **RIGHT**
In Bavaria, German Railways No. 614-012 pictured about to leave Hersbruck and head south for Nuremberg in 1985. These sets have self-tilting suspensions.

GERMAN FEDERAL RAILWAYS (DBAG) CLASS 614

Date	1971
Builder	Orenstein & Koppel/Uerdingen
Client	DB
Gauge	1,435 mm
Class	614 three-car set
Power unit	One MAN diesel-engine in each power-car, driving all wheels on one bogie via hydraulic transmission
Weight in working order	123 tonnes total (all three cars)
Rating	670 kW
Maximum service speed	140 kph

little resistance, so speeds can be relatively high, an important factor where the bus is the potential rival for traffic.

● **UNITS OF TWO OR MORE CARS**
The duties of units of two or more cars can range from branch-line work through local passenger to semifast and, in some cases, high-speed intercity services.

At the lower end of the speed-and-capacity scale are two-car sets in which only one vehicle is powered. At the other end of the scale are sets with two power-cars between which run one or more trailers.

These units are usually used on standard-gauge lines but also run with medium-distance semifast traffic on local and branch-line services. Recent developments in Germany with two-car tilting sets were sufficiently successful for

progress to be made to a further class having suspension of Italy's Pendolino type, with a maximum authorized speed of 160 kph. Their value has been particularly appreciated on lines such as the Bavarian one from Nuremberg to Hof, which suffers from stretches of frequent curvature. There, tilting trains can be permitted higher speeds than trains with conventional suspension.

● **ABOVE**
Coachwork made by Budd of USA seems popular with Portuguese Railways for its DMUs. These sets dating from 1989 work Rápidos – expresses stopping at main stations – as well as local trains. One curves away from the railway junction of Tunes, Algarve, in 1996.

● **BELOW**
Austrian Federal Railways (ÖBB) have revolutionized speed and comfort on lesser-used lines with modern Class 5047 railcars built from 1987 onward. Passenger-loads have risen as a result. No. 5047-028 a backdrop of mountains at Reutte-im-Tirol in 1994.

EUROPEAN EMU

The electric multiple unit (EMU) dates back to the turn of the century. In its simplest form, d.c. motors were controlled by robust mechanical tap changers made for relatively low maintenance costs, which balanced the high cost of line power supply. A bonus was that units could be coupled electrically and driven by one person. The main attraction, however, was probably that turnround times at terminuses were significantly cut because no locomotive change was required.

Operators of underground railways and metros found the system attractive not least because, in the restricted environment, a d.c. electric supply could be provided relatively cheaply by third rail.

This simple system saw few dramatic changes until the 1950s when the development of electronics and hi-tech engineering transformed the scene in nearly every aspect of EMU design and construction.

● THE MODERN EMU – LOCAL AND INTERMEDIATE TRAFFIC

In mainland Europe, the Netherlands can probably claim the most concentrated

● ABOVE
In contrast with the angular design of recent years, this Austrian Federal Railways two-car EMU epitomized the flowing lines adopted by several European countries from the 1950s. No. 4030.309, one of a batch built by Simmering-Graz-Pauker between 1956–9, is pictured about to leave St Margrethen, Switzerland, for a cross-border run into Austria's Vorarlberg Province, to Bregenz on Lake Constance in 1994.

● BELOW
These units, readily strengthened by adding trailers, set a standard for the modern thyristor-controlled EMU able to handle suburban and regional services equally well. They are used throughout Switzerland's Federal railway network. Similar versions have been bought by private railways. A unit is pictured arriving at Lausanne's main station in 1993. A French Train Grande Vitesse (TGV) – a high-speed train – and a former Swiss TEE unit now in grey livery are present.

use of EMUs. Few lines are not electrified and the proximity of towns and villages in this densely populated land calls for trains with high-capacity seating and good acceleration and braking.

In 1975, the Netherlands railways coined the term "Sprinter" for a two-car unit. Two- and three-car variants soon followed. The name was quickly copied by British Rail. In Belgium and around the big cities of France, Germany and Italy the EMU is important. The Swiss Federal Railway briefly flirted with EMUs in the 1920s, some of which are still used on departmental duties, but moved from locomotive haulage of short-distance trains to sophisticated EMUs from the mid-1950s. The latest units can be formed of two power-cars with up to three intermediate trailers and are termed Neue Pendel Zug (NPZ). Variants can be seen on the private railways where, in many instances, they form the backbone of the fleets. Thyristor control is well established following the usual difficulties experienced in many countries with development models. Reliability is now such that many of the numerous metre-gauge systems operate power-cars with similar technology.

Austria boasts a similar and sizeable class of attractive three-car sets built between 1978 and 1987 for suburban and middle-distance work.

NEUE PENDEL ZUG (NPZ) – SWISS FEDERAL RAILWAYS

Date	Four prototypes, 1984. Production, 1987-90
Builders	Mechanical: Flug und Fahrzeugwerke AG, Altenrhein, Switzerland; Schweizerische Locomotiv und Maschinenfabrik (SLM), Winterthur, Switzerland; Schindler Waggon AG, Pratteln, near Basel (Basle), Switzerland Electrical: A.G. Brown-Boveri & Cie, Baden, Baden-Württemberg, Germany
Gauge	1,435 mm
Class	RBDe4/4 (now Class 532)
Axle arrangement	All four axles driven on each power-car
Catenary voltage	a.c. 15 kV, 16.7 Hz
Weight in working order	70 tonnes (including driving-trailer)
One hour rating	1,650 kW (about 2,212 hp)
Maximum service speed	140 kph

● THE MODERN EMU – EXPRESS SERVICES

Few genuine EMUs have been designed specifically for long-distance express-services, but in 1965 Austria Federal Railways introduced a class of six-car sets with a permitted speed of 150 kph. All included a dining-car for some of the most prestigious services, including the run between Zurich in Switzerland and Vienna. No longer in the forefront of express travel, they have been refurbished and are usefully employed on expresses over the Semmering Pass.

● **ABOVE**
The Netherlands has long gone its own way with design. To some, Plan ZO/Z1 (ICM 1/2) "Koploper" three-car units are ugly. However, they are practical: the door beneath the driver's raised cab enables passengers to have unobstructed gangway-access to all vehicles.

● **ABOVE RIGHT**
The rounded outline of the 1950s is carried through in this four-car EMU of Trafik AB Grängesberg-Oxelosund Jarnvag, a Swedish private railway operating west of Stockholm. It is standing at Katrineholm in 1981. The X20 Class was built in 1956–7. It was ahead of its time, because the power-car is in the train rather than being a motored driving-vehicle.

● **RIGHT**
The Austrian 4020 Class EMU is similar in appearance to the Swiss NPZ but differs in technology. Between 1978–87, 120 units were built. They have proved most successful in S-Bahn and medium-distance work alike and were built by Simmering-Graz-Pauker, with electrical parts by Brown-Boveri, Elin and Siemens. Four traction motors produce 1,200 kW, about 1,608 hp, for each three-car unit, to permit a 120-kph service speed. No. 4020-116 sits beneath mountains at St Anton in 1990.

EUROPEAN DIESEL – MAIN-LINE

● BELOW

● BELOW
Diesel locomotive No. 232-231 stands, in 1992, at Brandenburg, former residence of Prussia's rulers, now in Lower Saxony, on a double-deck shuttle train to Potsdam. Brandenburg and Potsdam are respectively 60 km (37 miles) and 27 km (17 miles) south-west of Berlin.

Main-line diesels began to become prominent in the 1950s as steam started to decline. Some countries had seen at first hand diesels operated by the American Army just after World War II. The first large diesels were modelled on American lines. In some cases, virtual copies were made under licence or using imported components. One look at a large Belgian diesel shows from whence came the inspiration. Other examples were in Scandinavia where the Nohab Company of Trollhättan, Sweden, set a style that, externally at least, showed a transatlantic influence, which spread even to countries in the then Eastern Bloc.

The diesel's field of operation was almost universal for freight-trains. Some classes are geared specifically for this work. In passenger service, they tended to work on secondary lines or main lines that could not justify electrification costs. The locomotives can be classified by transmission type.

● ELECTRICAL TRANSMISSION
Electrical transmission is the more popular. A diesel-engine drives a generator to power electric-traction motors. The system is relatively simple, robust and easy to maintain. Proponents of hydraulic transmission, however, claim less precise control and lower efficiency.

The 5100 Class Co-Co of Belgium's national railways, the Société Nationale des Chemins de Fer Belges (SNCB), is powered by an engine producing 1,580 kW (about 2,118 hp) at 650 rpm built by Cockerill/Baldwin and has a 120-kph service speed. Germany, however, is where one of the most popular and sturdy classes of diesel-electrics is in widespread use. It originated at the October Revolution Locomotive Works in Lugansk (Voroshilovgrad, 1939–91), Ukraine, part of the former USSR. A batch of Co-Co locomotives, now Class 230, was built in 1970 for what was then the Deutsche Reichsbahn (DR) of East Germany. Another batch, Class 231, arrived in 1972–73. A final batch of 709 locomotives was delivered between 1973–82. With a massive diesel engine delivering 2,950 hp and a 120 kph top

● ABOVE
This diesel-electric of the Grand Duchy of Luxembourg's railways, the Société Nationale des Chemins de Fer Luxembourgeois (CFL), was built by Brissonneau & Lotz, of Aytre, in 1958. In 1995, standing at Esch/Alzette, in Luxembourg, at the border with France, it shows clear signs of French origin. Its duties include heavy trip-freights in Luxembourg's industrial south.

● ABOVE
The Austrian Federal Railways (ÖBB) Class 2043 and similar Class 2143 are, at 1,100 kW or 1,475 hp, of modest power by European standards. Yet they are the most powerful locomotives in Austria and find work on several non-electrified secondary lines.

DEUTSCHE REICHSBAHN CLASS 132

Date	1973
Builder	October Revolution Locomotive Works, Voroshilovgrad (Lugansk), USSR
Gauge	1,435 mm
Class	132 (now 232 on DBAG, unified German railways)
Axle arrangement	Co-Co
Weight in working order	123 tonnes
Rating	2,200 kw (appox 2950 hp)
Maximum service speed	120 kph

speed, they proved ideal for passenger and freight use.

With the reunification of Germany in 1990, their diagrams gradually spread across the country with favourable comment from drivers of the Deutsche Bundesbahn (DB), operating in what was the former West Germany. An uprated version, Class 234, has a 140 kph top speed. Many of the locomotives are being re-engined and appear to have a long life ahead.

Diesel-electrics have great importance to smaller nations where heavy traffic between major sites of population and commerce is offset by the need, on social if not economic grounds, to provide services over lightly laid secondary routes. An example is Portugal whose machines range from 117 tonne Co-Cos rated at nearly 3,000 hp to modest 64 tonne Bo-Bos producing about 1,300 hp.

● HYDRAULIC TRANSMISSION

The Deutsche Bundesbahn, now German Federal Railways (DBAG), favoured, for its large diesels, hydraulic transmission made by Voith, of Heindenheim, Brenz. This works like automatic gearboxes in cars. Between 1968–79, four classes of Bo-Bo machines were built, culminating in Class 217. Of this, there are two types. One is fitted with the Pielstick 16 PA 4V 200 engine producing 3,000 hp and a 140 kph top speed. Their weight in working order is 78.5 tonnes, compared with the Class 234's 123 tonnes.

Austrian Federal Railways (ÖBB) also favours Voith transmission in its relatively small 1,475 hp machines whose work is decreasing as lines are electrified.

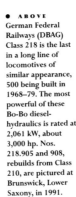

● **ABOVE**
German Federal Railways (DBAG) Class 218 is the last in a long line of locomotives of similar appearance, 500 being built in 1968–79. The most powerful of these Bo-Bo diesel-hydraulics is rated at 2,061 kW, about 3,000 hp. Nos. 218.905 and 908, rebuilds from Class 210, are pictured at Brunswick, Lower Saxony, in 1991.

● **RIGHT**
The unmistakable French lineage of this Portuguese Railways Class 2601 stands out in 1996 as a diesel-electric Bo-Bo built by Alsthom passes Santa Clara, in Beira Litoral Province, south-west of Coimbra, Portugal's former capital.

EUROPEAN MAIN-LINE ELECTRICS

World War II left mainland Europe's railways heavily damaged. Many administrations could see that electrification was the way forward but a neutral country, Switzerland, led the way.

● SWITZERLAND TURNS TO HYDRO-ELECTRIC POWER

Switzerland has no natural resources for power apart from abundant water. In the war, coal for steam-engines was practically unobtainable, so engineers

turned to the source already harnessed, hydroelectric power (HEP). The country had used electric locomotives and railcars for many years but there was now a need for powerful, relatively fast mixed-traffic machines with a high power weight ratio and good adhesion. This pointed to providing motors on all axles.

In 1944 it was the Bern-Loetschberg-Simplon (BLS) railway that set the trend. It did so with a small class of eight Bo-Bo locomotives weighing only 80 tonnes, having four, fully suspended, single-phase

motors driving all four axles. Current at 15 kV, $16\frac{2}{3}$ Hz from overhead-line equipment enabled the locomotive to operate at an hourly rating of 3,238 kW.

● UNIFIED GERMAN SYSTEM

West Germany's large, efficient fleet of steam locomotives operated into the 1970s on main-line duties but here, too, Bo-Bo locomotives of similar dimensions to the BLS machine were introduced, Class 110 in 1956 for mixed-traffic work and Class 140 in 1957 mainly for freight

● **ABOVE**
SNCF Class BB2600 dual-voltage "Sybic" 26053 heads an express-train.

● **TOP RIGHT**
A Deutsche Bundesbahn Class 120 is waiting to leave Munich Main Railway Station, Bavaria, in 1989 at the head of a train of Netherlands Railways double-deck coaches then on trial. A prototype batch of five of these advanced-design locomotives with three-phase motors entered revenue service in 1979. The production batch did not come on stream until 1987. These 60 machines have a one-hour rating of 6,300 kW, about 8,445 hp, and a maximum service speed of 200 kph.

● **RIGHT**
In 1995, a direct descendant of the trend-setting Bern-Loetschberg-Simplon (BLS) railway Bo-Bo of 1944 stands at Interlaken West Station at the head of the Thunersee from Berlin. It is one of a class of 35. With an hourly rating of 4,990 kW, about 6,690 hp, it has a maximum service speed of 140 kph.

● **LEFT**
Deutsche Bundesbahn (DB) 11 081-6 heads
north out of historic Boppard, in the Rhine
Valley south of Koblenz. This class of 227
locomotives is an improved version of the
prolific Class 110.

batches established a development line,
which might be said to lead to the
impressive BB26000 Class, the Sybic, an
acronym for "Systeme Bi-courant". These
dual-voltage machines operate either on
1500 V d.c. or 25 kV single-phase a.c.
They went into service in 1988 and
gradually proved themselves. They are
so successful that their numbers are
increasing rapidly towards a projected
target of more than 300 units. They
weigh 91 tonnes, have a rating of 6,400
kW and are authorized to travel at
200 kph.

France's Trains Grande Vitesse (TGVs)
– high-speed multiple unit trains – reach
high speeds. The SNCF holds an official
electric-traction record for on 28 March
1955 Co-Co, 1,500 V d.c. locomotive
CC 7107 achieved 330.9 kph
(205.6 mph) with a 100-tonne load.
Next day, this record was equalled by Bo-
Bo 9004 with an 81-tonne train.

but often seen on passenger-trains.
Several hundred of these and variants are
working in western Germany. In eastern
Germany, a class was developed using
thyristor control. This went into batch-
production in 1982, proving so
successful that it is widely used across
the unified German system – the DBAG
– as Class 143. The locos weigh 82
tonnes and have a one-hour rating
of 3,720 kW.

● **FRANCE USES DUAL VOLTAGE**
In France, development after the war was
different, not least because the various
constituents of the system that had finally
embraced all the main railways in 1938,
the Société Nationale des Chemins de
Fer Français (SNCF), had, where
electrification had been tried, used
noncompatible traction current. No
classes of locomotive had been made in
large numbers although several small

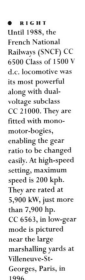

● **RIGHT**
Until 1988, the
French National
Railways (SNCF) CC
6500 Class of 1500 V
d.c. locomotive was
its most powerful
along with dual-
voltage subclass
CC 21000. They are
fitted with mono-
motor-bogies,
enabling the gear
ratio to be changed
easily. At high-speed
setting, maximum
speed is 200 kph.
They are rated at
5,900 kW, just more
than 7,900 hp.
CC 6563, in low-gear
mode is pictured
near the large
marshalling yards at
Villeneuve-St-
Georges, Paris, in
1996.

The need to produce a modern main-line electric locomotive to cope not only with express-traffic on level ground but also with heavy gradients in Austria's mountainous regions, led Austrian Federal Railways (ÖBB) to buy a batch of ten thyristor-controlled locomotives of the Swedish Railways Class Rc2 in 1971. Class 1044 was quickly developed by the railway authorities and introduced into service in 1974. No. 1044-092, pictured at Jenbach, in Tirol, east of Innsbruck, is one of the batch with a 160-kph service speed and a one-hour rating of 5,300 kW, just more than 7,100 hp. A later version has a 200 kph service maximum. One machine is approved for 220 kph.

● AUSTRIAN AND HUNGARIAN DESIGNS

Austria, so often challenging in steam design with the Gölsdorf locomotives and the Giesl ejector, has a most successful Bo-Bo Class 1044 that owes something to an earlier maid of all work, Class 1042, but also to the Swedish Rc2.

Hungary, too, has the numerous Class V43. This leans on German technology, in that the first small batch was built by Krupp, of Essen, Germany. Ganz, a world-renowned locomotive works, in which Hunslet of Britain has a financial interest, is keeping pace with modern locomotive technology.

● SWITZERLAND'S LOK LEADS FIELD

Switzerland, however, is again leading the field with a very "hi-tech" design developed by the Swiss Locomotive and Machine Works (SLM) of Winterthur. Known as Lok 2000, the technological advances are so many that a small book would be needed to do it justice. A notable feature is its quietness when running. Swiss Federal Railways Schweizerische Bundesbahnen (SBB/CFF/FFS) know it as Class Re 460. The BLS has a variant – and the most powerful version – Class 465. A broadgauge variant is in service on Finland's railway system. Examples have run trials in other countries.

The machines entered service on the federal railways in 1991, generally performing well. Teething troubles, however, slowed the progress of their introduction into general service. With problems solved, the class of 119 locomotives is operating widely throughout the country.

The Netherlands, a relatively small country, has an extensive railway network, part of which is in the European international system. Class 1600 and the almost identical Class 1700 are built by Alsthom, France, based on the French National Railways (SNCF) Class BB 7200. The Class 1600s entered service in 1981, the 1700s in 1990. Capable of 200 kph, they are restricted to 160 kph. Here, in 1989, No. 1643 has just brought an express-train into the border town of Maastricht in Limburg Province.

LOK 2000

Date	1992
Builders	Mechanical: Swiss Locomotive & Machine Works (SLM), Winterthur, Switzerland Electrical: ABB Transportation Systems, Baden, Zurich, Switzerland
Client	Swiss Federal Railways
Gauge	1,435 mm
Class	Re460
Axle arrangement	Bo-Bo
Catenary voltage	15 kV
Length over buffers	18,500 mm
Weight in working order	84 tonnes
Number of traction motors	Four
Rating	1,100 kw (8180 hp)
Maximum service speed	230 kph

● **RIGHT**
Lok 2000 No. 460 015-1 of Swiss Federal Railways waits at Lausanne in Vaud Canton in 1993 after bringing in an express-train from Basel.

● **LEFT**
Belgium has a dense network of lines and demands a powerful mixed-traffic locomotive able to handle anything from light "push-and-pull" trains, through freights to expresses. The Class 21, introduced in 1984, comprises 60 machines rated at 3,310 kW, about 4,437 hp, with a 160-kph maximum service speed. They were built in Belgium by La Brugeoise et Nivelles SA and are almost identical to the chopper-controlled more powerful Class 27. No. 2157 is pictured in 1992 leaving Ghent Sint Pieters Station in the East Flanders provincial capital of Ghent on its way to the depot at Dendermonde, East Flanders.

● **RIGHT**
Italy has long produced striking and seemingly unconventional designs of locomotives. In the Class 656 Bo-Bo-Bo with its articulated body, F.S. Italia has one of the most successful designs of recent years. It is based on well-tried technology for it derives from the 636 Class dating back to 1940. Provided speeds above 150 kph are not required, these locomotives handle expresses almost anywhere in Italy. They first entered service in 1975. By 1989, 608 had been built. Here, No. E 656-469 waits to take over a train at Domodossola, in Novara Province of the Piedmont Compartimento, in 1996.

EUROPEAN LOCAL PASSENGER – LOCOMOTIVE-HAULED

Until the late 1960s, it was possible to enjoy the sights and sounds of steam-hauled local passenger-trains soon to be displaced by electric and diesel traction. Because of the increased use of multiple units (MUs) with their favourable weight-per-person ratio and flexibility, many local services lost the familiar locomotive at the train's head.

The locomotive remains in use on such services for two main reasons. Firstly, and more obvious, certain lines have a mixture of relatively light passenger- and freight-traffic so that both functions can be fulfilled by a locomotive.

● "PUSH-AND-PULL" TRAINS

Second, in heavy passenger-traffic areas, displacement of locomotives by MUs, which often hauled trains of obsolescent coaches, meant that relatively modern machines would either have to be scrapped or sold at bargain prices. One solution was to select a class of

● **ABOVE**
Extensive improvements are being made to the line as German Railways (DBAG) Class 143 228-5 runs into Belzig-bei-Potsdam, south-west of Berlin, with a rake of double-deck coaches in 1992.

SWISS FEDERAL RAILWAYS CLASS 450	
Date	1989
Builders	Mechanical: Swiss Locomotive & Machine Works (SLM), Switzerland Electrical: ASEA Brown Boveri
Client	Swiss Federal Railways
Gauge	1,435 mm
Class	450
Axle arrangement	Bo-Bo
Catenary voltage	a.c. 15 kV, 16.7 Hz
Weight in working order	78 tonnes (locomotive only)
Rating	One hour, 3,200 kW (about 4,290 hp)
Maximum service speed	130 kph

● **LEFT**
Swiss Federal Railways (SBB) No. 450 067-4 on S-Bahn service at Zurich Main Station in 1994.

● **LEFT**
The striking S-Bahn livery suits this German Federal Railways (DBAG) Class 218 as it sits beneath the impressive roof of Cologne Main Station in North-Rhine Westphalia in 1986.

displaced locomotives. It was common practice on the former Deutche Reichsbahn to use electric locomotives where appropriate, and diesels elsewhere, coupled to rakes of double-deck coaches.

● **MODERN SWISS DESIGNS**
In Switzerland, in 1989, purpose-built locomotive Class Re450 was matched to three double-deck coaches, one of which was a driving-trailer. Initially, they operated in the environs of the Switzerland's largest city, Zurich. As the S-Bahn network is extended, however, they can be found far from the city. Multiple-unit working is common, and it is not unusual to see three sets coupled together. The locomotives were the first in a new era of rail technology in electrical, mechanical and body design. They were built by the Swiss Locomotive and Machine Works (SLM) and operate on 15 kV 16⅔ Hz supply. Four, three-phase, nose-suspended motors produce nearly 4,300 hp for a weight of only 78 tonnes.

locomotives with adequate power and good acceleration, refurbish them, fit remote-control equipment so they could be driven from a driving-trailer and match them to a set of high-capacity refurbished coaches. After receiving a colour scheme that matched with or blended into the livery of the MU fleet, the "new" sets were in business. Because they are driven by one person and from either end without uncoupling the locomotive, they can take their place in intensive local services.

Both diesel and electric locomotives are fitted for "push-and-pull" working. Indeed, this is now a feature of express services, too. Another advantage is that replacement is simple, if the locomotive requires maintenance.

A good example of such working can be found in Germany's industrial Ruhr and around Cologne in North-Rhine Westphalia. However, the reason the local "push-and-pull" working was adopted in other areas and countries was not because a use had to be found for

● **ABOVE**
Diesel-electric Co-Co No. 5105 of Belgian National Railways (SNCB) rolls into Sint Pieters Station, Ghent, East Flanders, with a commuter train in 1992.

● **ABOVE**
French-built steeple-cab Bo-Bo electric No. 3618 of Luxembourg Railways, the Société Nationale des Chemins de Fer Luxembourgeois (CFL), runs into Esch/Alzette, Luxembourg's second city, in the south of the country, in 1995.

EUROPEAN LIGHT RAIL AND METRO

Mainland Europe had few truly light-rail systems in the early 1950s, apart from street tramways. As for electrified metros, the most famous must surely be the Paris *chemin de fer métropolitain*. The Métro, opened in 1900 – although one of the oldest in the world in Budapest, Hungary, was opened on 23 May 1896. Probably the most ornate in the world is the one in Moscow, opened in 1933. Similar rolling stock to that in Moscow can be seen in Budapest.

● **LIGHT RAIL**

There were many tramway systems in Europe after World War II, some of them of an interurban nature. In the combatant countries, most were

● **LEFT**
In complete contrast to the Strasbourg tram, delightful reminders of a past, more ornate period can be found in small trams still tackling the narrow streets and hills of the old city in Lisbon, the Portuguese capital.

THE "EUROTRAM" IN STRASBOURG	
Date (year into service)	1994
Builder	ABB Transportation, York, England
Client	Compagnei des Transports, Strasbourgeois, Strasbourg
Gauge	1,436 mm
Class	Eurotram
Axle arrangement	Variable
Catenary voltage	750 volt d.c. Power is fed to traction-inverters in the car
Maximum rating	38 kW (50 hp) per motor
Speed	21 kph

● **LEFT**
This tram is operating on an entirely new system in Strasbourg, France, the first 12.65 km (8 miles) of double-track having been officially opened on 26 November 1994. It runs on reserved track, in-tunnel or, as in this 1996 picture, in pedestrianized streets.

● LEFT
One of Europe's most extensive tram systems is in Budapest, Hungary. A modest underground heavy metro and a web of tram routes, some with reserved track, combine to provide an efficient, cheap means of getting around the city. Moskva tét in Buda is a focus of many tram routes. Car 4158 with its sister tram is pictured in 1993, about to start its Route 61 run.

damaged, some badly. Trams were put back on the streets as quickly as possible because they were and are one of the most efficient means of moving many people fast, especially in heavily populated areas.

Numerous old vehicles survived for many years until recovering manufacturing industries were able to supply the demand for new and more efficient vehicles. Smaller towns tended to replace trams with buses, particularly in France. Others turned to trolley-buses and various experimental schemes were tried, including guided buses and even Mag-lev. In Germany, the Langen-type suspended railway between Barmen and Elberfeld in Wuppertal, an industrial city in North-Rhine Westphalia, not only survived but continues to operate with comfortable modern double-cars.

Probably two tram builders made the most impact on the postwar scene, Duewag of Germany and CKD, of Prague (Praha), Czech Republic, with Tatra cars. Both produced robust reliable vehicles, which are widely used in many countries.

More recently, demand for easier access to public-transport vehicles has led to the development of sophisticated low-floor cars, some incorporating elegant and advanced bogie designs allowing low floors throughout the vehicle. General advances in control equipment used on heavy rail have readily found use on tramways.

● LEFT
Vienna is served by an expanding underground railway system. However, one of the best ways to get a feel for the city is to take the frequent trams. Routes 1 and 2 operate in opposite directions around the Ringstrasse. Standard Series E2 No. 4311, on Route 65, is pictured in 1987 standing at Karlsplatz, near the interchange with the underground.

● LEFT
Some systems fall between light-rail and heavy-metro categories. One is that in Utrecht, a bustling city and major rail junction in the Netherlands' eponymous smallest province. This unit, one of 27 built between 1981–3 by SIG of Neuhausen, Switzerland, although called a tram, operates more like a true heavy metro and has an 80-kph service speed. Here, it is pictured near Utrecht's main railway station in 1989.

● LEFT
Austria's private railways have for many years taken advantage of the availability of good secondhand equipment. The rolling stock waiting to leave the terminus of the Salzburger Stadtwerke Verkehrsbetriebe (SVB) near the main station in Salzburg in 1986 originated on Germany's Cologne-Bonn private railway (KBE). Today, the SVB terminus is in an underground complex, and services are operated by a fleet of light Bo-2-Bo units.

The impression of 20 years ago that the tram was noisy, rough riding and uncomfortable has changed to such an extent that suitable devices have had to be devised to warn pedestrians of their quiet approach, especially in areas restricted to public transport. Where track is well laid and maintained, the ride can be as good and often better than on heavy rail.

An ideal arrangement to take advantage of the relatively high-speed capability of the modern tram is the use of reserved track and, in some instances, redundant heavy-rail formations for part of the route. In others, light-rail vehicles are used for urban and suburban services over tracks carrying normal main-line trains such as the Swiss Federal Railway line from Geneva to La Plaine.

● ABOVE
The use of light-rail type vehicles on main-line tracks is spreading. Switzerland's section of line between Geneva and La Plaine is electrified at 1,500 volt d.c. for through-working to Geneva by standard French locomotives. Swiss Federal Railways have introduced these lightweight EMUs to replace time-expired main-line stock.

● BELOW
An EMU train on suburban service in Paris.

● **RIGHT**
The popularity of lightweight, low-floor units to replace the main-line type of construction is leading to their widening use on metre-gauge railways in Switzerland, especially where the route is substantially in an urban-style environment with frequent stops. Unit Be4/8 33 is pictured at the outer terminus of the Wynental und Suhrentalbahn line, at Menziken, south of Aarau, in 1996, about to leave for Aarau, an important station, in Aargau Canton, on the federal railways' main line from Zurich to Bern.

● **BELOW**
Another German interurban line is the Wuppertal Schwebebahn running 13.3 km (8 miles) from Oberbarmen to Vohwinkel. Its articulated cars were built from 1972–4 by MAN. They are suspended from massive girderwork dating back to the turn of the century. The route is over a river for a considerable way and elsewhere follows the course of roads.

wide tunnels built by cut-and-cover method, incorporating closely spaced stations with many interchanges with other Métro lines whose tentacles spread deep into the suburbs.

Where lines emerge into daylight, they may be on viaducts or bridges spanning the River Seine, some giving fine views. The narrow multiple-unit sets in places grind around sharp curves or have to tackle steep gradients. The opportunity should not be missed to ride on one of the lines, which uses pneumatic-tyred wheels for traction and guidance, with conventional flanged wheels on rail as a fail-safe.

Using the Métro and the modern, quick RER system, which goes deep into the surrounding countryside, is the finest way to get around Paris, a remark true for all cities and conurbations that have increasingly adopted the Métro concept as a transport system for the future.

● **METRO SYSTEMS**
Such systems are generally used in large cities or densely populated conurbations, usually to provide a high-frequency, high-capacity service. In some instances, the routes are wholly or substantially in-tunnel. In other cases, tramway or heavy-rail routes have been linked or diverted to run partly in tunnel. In many instances, the term has been used on reorganized and refurbished heavy-rail routes to provide the ensuing improved services with a "brand name", a growing practice.

● **PARIS MÉTRO**
For overall utility and its mixture of retained antiquity coupled with modern technology, the Paris Métro is hard to beat. Under the streets of Paris, it has

● **ABOVE**
Germany's Oberrheinische Eisenbahn-Gesellschaft (OEG) is an example of an interurban system. It operates through four states – Bavaria, Rhineland-Palatinate, Baden-Württemberg and Hesse. It has 61 km (38 miles) of metre-gauge routes from the spa town of Dürkheim, through the commercial and manufacturing cities of Ludwigshafen am Rhein and Mannheim to Heidelberg. Trains run in or alongside roads, in pedestrianized areas and on the reserved tracks. Unit 109, built by Duewag of Düsseldorf and Uerdingen in 1974, stands in the station at Viernheim, a suburb of Mannheim, in 1986.

INTERNATIONAL EUROPEAN SERVICES

● BELOW
The latest Pendolino development is the ETR 470 Cisalpino. These dual-voltage trains are operated by an Italian-Swiss consortium. Services began in September 1996 from Milan to Basle and from Milan to Geneva. A train from Geneva to Milan is pictured snaking into Lausanne in 1996.

Initially, electrically powered international services were little different from the days of steam. Locomotives hauled their rakes of, usually, the best stock the originating country could provide, to the border-station where one locomotive was removed and another from the next country was added. This was not always easy. For example, at Venlo in Limburg Province of the Netherlands, the electrical system differs radically from that in Germany and the international platforms are provided with special wiring that can be switched to either power-supply. It was found convenient to use a diesel-shunter to attach and detach the main-line locomotive.

● **GERMANY, AUSTRIA, HUNGARY AND SWITZERLAND**

In Germany, Austria, Hungary and Switzerland there was and is little difficulty in through-working because the electrical supply is common at 15 kV a.c., 16.7 Hz. These countries share the German language, to a greater or lesser degree, so the main constraint is that of differing signal aspects and operating regulations, which can be overcome by training.

The French already had much experience because the railways, electrified from early days, used 1,500 volt d.c. and 25 kV single-phase a.c. In 1964, they plunged into the multicurrent field with a class of locomotives designed to cope with most situations. These had the capacity to work on 1,500 volt–3,000 volt d.c., 15 kV single-phase and 25 kV three-phase a.c. They were thus able to cross all their rail frontiers, although in practice they worked mainly Paris-Brussels-Amsterdam.

However, the complete unit, incorporating power-cars, came to the fore. Austrian Class 4010 six-car sets, introduced in 1965, working in multiple, operated an express-service from Zurich to Vienna, although they have been supplanted by locomotive-hauled stock because of inadequate passenger-capacity. Such units still work to Munich, Bavaria.

● **FRANCE DEVELOPS TGVs, GERMANY ICEs**

More recent developments are the French Trains Grande Vitesse (TGVs) – "high-speed trains" that have become multicurrent, running into neighbouring Belgium and Switzerland. From these have developed the Thalys, that is, TGVs running the Paris-Brussels-Amsterdam services. These in turn have given rise to an experimental unit, still under trial in 1996, specifically for Thalys but capable of much wider use.

Germany has produced the Class 401 Inter City Express (ICE) units in large quantity. Broadly, these match the TGV in performance and, like them, use proven technology. Most Swiss standard-gauge railways' common electrical system

● ABOVE
Germany's DBAG multicurrent Inter City Express (ICE) uses conventional technology to achieve speeds of up to 330 kph. The "Thunersee" from Interlaken is pictured leaving Olten railway junction in Switzerland, for Berlin in 1996.

● **BELOW**
Conventional technology and new high-grade track brought success for France's Train Grande Vitesse (TGV). Journey-times were revolutionized with a 300-kph top speed, as this image of a TGV Atlantique at speed shows.

● **ABOVE LEFT**
The quadricurrent development of the TGV for the Thalys services (Paris-Brussels-Amsterdam) was still under trial when this picture was taken at Paris, Gare du Nord, in June 1996. TGVs painted in Thalys red livery were still operating revenue services in November 1996.

● **BELOW RIGHT**
The ETR 450 can be regarded as the first commercially successful tilting train. "Pendolino" is an accepted nickname for the type.

enables them to run lucrative international services such as the Thunersee from Berlin to Interlaken.

Franco-British co-operation in constructing and operating cross-Channel international expresses involves yet another electrical complication on the British side – 750 volt d.c. supplied from a third rail.

● **ITALY DEVELOPS PENDOLINO**
Italy has developed the tilting train to the extent that the concept, with which

several countries have experimented for some years, has become acceptable for public service. The Pendolino, as it is called, draws heavily on pioneering work by British Railways with its Advanced Passenger Train (APT). The aim is to be able to use existing infrastructure for higher speeds by relieving passengers of gravitational forces in curves. Other technological developments have enabled speeds and ride-quality to be improved even more.

THE PENDOLINO (ETR 450)	
Date	1987
Builders	Fiat/Marelli/Ansaldo
Gauge	1,435 mm
Class	ETR 450 (Elletro Treni Rapidi 450)
Axle arrangement	1-A-A-1
Catenary voltage	d.c. 3,000 volt
Weight in working order	400 tonnes
Rating	4,700 kW (about 6,300 hp)
Maximum service speed	250 kph

THE PRESERVATION OF EUROPEAN TRAINS

At the turn of the century, enlightened railways and historians realized the importance of preserving equipment that had helped to make railways one of the most important developments the world has seen. Equipment was put either into a museum or on to a plinth, in the latter case often being damaged beyond repair. Mainland Europe has several fine museums, those at Nuremberg in Germany, Mulhouse in France, Vienna in Austria and Lucerne in Switzerland among them.

● **RIGHT**
No. 298.51 pushing a snowplough reaches Grünberg in Oberösterreich (Austria) from Garsten on the 760 mm gauge line to Klaus.

● PRESERVATION – WORKING RAILWAY MUSEUMS

Static exhibits though informative are lifeless. Private individuals' efforts were largely responsible for restoring locomotives and rolling stock to working condition. Funds were raised, often slowly, to obtain unwanted and sometimes derelict items. On these, teams, usually of volunteers, laboured for months or years to achieve their aims. These were often either to run locomotives and carriages on sections of line bought after abandonment by original owners, or to persuade main-line or other companies to allow the stock to be run from time to time over their rails. For the latter, high standards had to be met and maintained. It is a great credit to the army of volunteers that all over Europe a pool of stock is available. However, from the 1970s onward, national railways and private companies began to realize the commercial and advertising potential of possessing and running their own nostalgic services. Locomotives emerged from static display to be restored by the companies and operated frequently in connection with line or station anniversaries.

● **RIGHT**
All three types of
motive power, visible
at Gmünd depot,
Austria, in 1987.

● **BELOW RIGHT**
Preservation
volunteers' skills are
shown in this
beautifully restored
electric-railcar of the
metre-gauge Martigny
Châtelard Railway
built in 1909 in
Switzerland.

AUSTRIAN FEDERAL RAILWAYS – ÖSTERREICHSCHE BUNDESBAHNEN (ÖBB) CLASS 16

Date	1911
Designer	Dr Karl Gölsdorf
Builder	Maschin Fabrik der Österreichisch- Ungarischen Staats- Eisenbahn Ges, Vienna
Client	Kaiserlich - Königlich - Österreichische Straatsbahrien (KKSTB)
Gauge	1,435 mm
Class	BBÖ 310 ÖBb 16
Axle (wheel) arrangement	1C2 (2-6-4)
Capacity	2 cylinders (390 x 720 mm) and 2 (630 x 720 mm). Compound
Wheel diameter	2,100 mm
Weight in working order	86 tonnes
Maximum service speed	100 kph

● **OPPOSITE**
Gölsdorf-designed No. 310.23 is pictured
being cleaned before taking part in Austrian
Railways' 150th anniversary.

● **RIGHT**
In Switzerland, a double-headed train snakes
into Filisur in 1988.

205

● LEFT
A Belgian stream-
lined 2B1 4-4-2 built
by Cockerill of Liege
in 1939 and a
Deutsche
Bundesbahn
No. 23.023 at
Utrecht, in the
Netherlands, in 1989.

● **TOURIST RAILWAYS**

Tourist railways take several forms. They range from narrow-gauge lines in pleasure-parks such as Vienna's Prater – an imperial park since the 16th century but now a public place, through lines specifically built to support tourism – to main lines and branches built for trade but which attract tourists.

Lines built with the tourist in mind are often in mountainous areas and take skiers, climbers and walkers to suitable points to start their activities as well as many passengers who ride the trains just to enjoy the view. Examples are too many

● ABOVE
In Hungary, on the Children's Railways in the hills above Budapest, a Mk 45-2002 arrives in Szenchenyi from Huvosvolgy.

● LEFT
The Flying Hamburger part-preserved unit was displayed at the Nuremberg 150th anniversary exhibition in Germany in May 1985.

● OPPOSITE
The beauty of the preservation of modern steam is epitomized by this then Czechoslovakian Railways Class 241 4-8-2 No. 498-022.

to mention in Switzerland; Austria's Achensee, Schafberg and Schneeberg; and in Germany the Drachenfels, at 320 m (1,053 ft) one of the Siebengebirge of the Westerwald, on the eastern bank of the Rhine where, according to legend, Siegfried slayed the dragon.

A group of Swiss lines illustrates railways fulfilling a general commercial need but attracting tourists. These are the metre-gauge systems of the Brig-Visp-Zermatt in Valais Canton, Furka-Oberalp in Uri Kanton and the extensive Rhaetischebahn in Graubünden Kanton, which together cover the Glacier Express route.

Finally, there are lines, usually narrow gauge, which have lost the bulk of their original passenger and freight traffic to the roads but still maintain limited services. Examples are the railways of the Harz Mountains in central Germany, Gmünd to Gross Gerungs in Austria's Neider-Österreich Province, and the "Little Yellow Train" in the Cerdagne, France.

● **ABOVE**
In Italy, beneath France's 4,807 m (15,781 ft) high Mont Blanc, the highest mountain in the Alps, a lightweight 1C (2-6-0) with inside-cylinders and outside-valve chests, built in 1910–22, waits at Pré Saint Didier to return to Aosta, the town at the junction of the Great and Little St Bernard Passes, in Aosta Province of Piedmont Compartimento.

COMMONWEALTH OF INDEPENDENT STATES (CIS)

In 1991, the former Soviet republics of the Union of Soviet Socialist Republics (USSR), the Soviet Union, formed a loose organization called the Commonwealth of Independent States (CIS). The CIS inherited more than 151,000 km of railways (94,000 route-miles) of 5 ft and more than 2,400 km of narrow-gauge railway. The narrow gauge is mostly 2 ft 6 in, with a small amount of metre- and 2-ft gauge. In addition, there are

● **LEFT**
A Class CS4T electro-locomotive stands on shed awaiting repair.

CLASS P36 4-8-4

Date	1954
Builder	Kolomna Locomotive Works, Russia
Client	Russian State Railways
Driving wheels	6 ft 0¾ in
Capacity	Cylinders 22–22⅝ x 31 in
Boiler pressure	213 lb per sq in

61,000 km (38,000 miles) of light industrial railways within the former Soviet Union.

The industrial, mineral, agricultural and forestry lines were not subject to state railway motive-power policy and stayed with steam rather longer, especially where waste from sawmills afforded a ready supply of fuel. TO-4, TO-6A and TO7 diesels have taken over where this cheap supply of fuel is not available.

● **WORLD RECORDS**
Freight traffic dominates rail operations with the 2,000,000 ton-miles produced annually being more than the rest of the world's rail traffic put together. The L Class 2-10-0 built after World War II has been an outstandingly successful goods-engine. More than 5,000 have been built. The L Class 2-10-0s followed the successful E series 0-10-0s, some 14,000 of which were produced in slightly

● **LEFT**
S2D 4-8-4 P36 No. 0250 train No. 1 Russia in Skovorodino (formerly Rukhlovo), a town in the Amur Oblast (administrative division) of Soviet Russia, on the Trans-Siberian Railway for which it is a junction. It connects with the Amur River, 56 km (35 miles) south, on the Sino-Soviet frontier.

● **LEFT**
A Russian EA Class 2-10-0 locomotive stands at Manzhouli, in the Inner Mongolian Autonomous Region, just inside China's border with Russia, across from the Russian railhead, a terminus of the Trans-Siberian Railway (TSR), at Zabaikalsk. Manzhouli is about 1,000 km (700 miles) north of Beijing, China's capital. It was on the former Chinese Eastern Railway (CER) in what was then known as northern Manchuria and, until China's Communist Party set up the People's Republic in 1949, was part of Heilungkiang Province. A Mongol trading town, in 1905 it was declared a foreign treaty-port town. When part of Japan's puppet-state of Manchukuo (1932–45), it was called Lupin.

● **BELOW**
A Class VL80S electric-locomotive stands on shed awaiting its turn of duty.

varying forms, making them the most numerous steam-class in world history.

The express-passenger streamline P36 Class 4-8-4 was the last main-line express-type built in the USSR, the first example appearing in 1950. This was a successful locomotive with many modern features and graceful lines. About 250 were built by Kolomna Locomotive Works, between 1954-56.

The S Class 2-6-2 standard express-locomotives, of which more than 4,000 were built, is the most numerous passenger-class in the world. It was introduced in 1910, and building continued until 1951.

● **PARTY CONGRESS PHASES OUT SYSTEM**
In February 1956 the Communist Party Congress declared that steam should be phased out. That year, all steam construction ceased.

Today, nearly a fifth of the standard gauge has been electrified. The basic freight-hauler on a.c. lines is the eight-twin-unit type VL80. The d.c. system uses VL10 Bo-Bo twin units – also made in a four-unit version.

Passenger electrics are supplied by the Skoda company from its works in the

Czech Republic. The most numerous is the CS4T Bo–Bo for a.c. lines.

Diesel-powered freights are hauled by TE3 and 21762 12-axle twin-unit locomotives. To cope with ever-longer trains, three-and four-unit sets have been built – the 3TEIOM, 4TEIOS and 4TE130S Series.

Diesel passenger trains use the Skoda-made TEP60 in one- or twin-unit sets. A TEP70 series of Co-Cos developing 4,000 hp per unit and weighing 129 tonnes has been introduced for longer, 25- to 30-car passenger-trains. These units have a maximum speed of more than 178 kph (110 mph).

● **BELOW**
This 2-10-0 Ty4 109 former Deutsche Reichsbahn Class 44 was a German Army engine in World War II and formerly S160 Tr203 229 of the United States Army Transport Corps (USATC). It is pictured at Malbork, Poland, in 1974. The city, a railway junction, was assigned to Poland in 1945. Formerly part of East Prussia, it had been known as Marienburg.

THE MIDDLE EAST

The former Hejaz Pilgrim Route to Mecca forms an important part of the railway networks of Syria and Jordan. The route, built to the 3 ft 5¼ in gauge, still sees steam operation in both countries. Syria also has a standard-gauge network, which originated with the Baghdad Railway. This passed through Aleppo, north-west Syria. The former Prussian G8 0-8-0s and British War Department 2-10-0s used on these lines all disappeared in 1976. The system has been diesel-operated ever since.

Jordan Railways operates between Der'a in Syria on the border with Jordan, southwards towards Saudi Arabia. The Pilgrim Route originally went as far south as Medina, but the northern reaches in Saudi Arabia have long since been abandoned. Mecca, the ultimate destination, was never reached. In 1975, Jordan Railways opened a branch to Aqaba on the Gulf of Arabia extension of the Red Sea. Jordan's last steam locomotives were a batch of Japanese Pacifics. Its steam survives as Mikado 2-8-2s.

IRAQI STATE RAILWAYS METRE-GAUGE Z CLASS 2-8-2	
Date	1955–6
Builder	Esslingen, Baden-Württemberg, West Germany
Client	Iraqi State Railways
Gauge	Metre
Driving wheels	4 ft
Capacity	Cylinders 18 x 24 in
Total weight	68 tons

● **ABOVE**
One of the Moguls built by Borsig of Berlin in 1911 for the Baghdad Railway rolls on to the pier at Hisarönü on the Black Sea coast of Turkey in Asia.

● **OPPOSITE ABOVE LEFT**
A scene on Syria's Hejaz Railway between Damascus and Der'a in Syria, on the border with Jordan. The engine is No. 91, a Hartmann 2-8-0 built to the Hejaz 1.05 metre gauge.

● **BELOW LEFT**
A quartet of modern diesels standing outside Haifa depot, Israel.

● **BELOW RIGHT**
A 2-8-0 engine built by Borsig of Berlin in 1914, pictured at Der'a from which it worked the twice-weekly mixed-traffic train branch to Busra in southern Syria.

● JORDANIAN PHOSPHATES

Another railway organization in Jordan is the Aqaba Railway Corporation (ARC). This began operations in 1979, to carry phosphates from mines at Al Hassa and later from Wadi el Abyad to Aqaba. General Electric 100-ton 2,000-hp Co-Co diesel-electrics are used and are powerful units for the Middle Eastern gauge.

Abdul Aziz ibn Saud (1880–1953), the first King of Saudi Arabia (1932–53), was keen on railways. He promoted a standard-gauge line about 600 km (370 miles) long to connect Ryadh – the joint capital with Mecca – with Ad Dammām,

the town on the Gulf opposite Bahrain, and the related oilfield at Damman. Diesel-electric Bo-Bos and Co-Cos were used from the outset. In the 1970s, a consortium worked on plans to re-open the Jejaz southwards from Jordan. Many field-surveys were made, but work did not proceed.

● ACCESS TO MEDITERRANEAN SEA

Iraq's railways comprise a mixture of metre- and standard-gauge systems. Iraq has an outstandingly keen will to develop its railways, by modernizing and by building new lines. One such is

westwards from Baghdad through Syria, to provide access to the Mediterranean Sea. Investment in powerful diesel-locomotives has been made for standard-gauge lines, using 3,600 hp engines. Iraqi Railways has about 450 diesel-electrics in service, mainly on standard gauge. It retains 75 steam locomotives on its books for metre-gauge use in the south.

Iran phased out steam in the 1950s in favour of General Motors (GM) diesel-electrics.

Israel's 900 km (560 mile) railway system is also fully diesel-operated.

● **ABOVE RIGHT**
A Jordanian Railways Hejaz 2-8-2 engine built by Jung in 1955 at the shed in Amman, the Jordanian capital, in 1979.

● **RIGHT**
A brace of Syrian 1.05 metre-gauge 2-6-0 tanks built by SLM of Switzerland in 1894 raise steam at Sergayah on the Syrian-Lebanese border before returning to Damascus, the Syrian capital, with excursion-trains.

INDIAN STEAM TRAINS

India's final steam-development phase was irretrievably influenced by American designs, which flooded into the country in World War II. The American engines' simple, robust construction, free steaming and accessibility to moving parts suited Indian conditions. When new standard designs were required for the broad gauge, to replace the ageing British X Series, India turned to American practice.

CLASS WT 2-8-4T	
Date	1959
Builder	Chittaranjan Locomotive Works, Chittaranjan, West Bengal
Client	Indian Railways
Gauge	5 ft 6 in
Driving wheels	Diameter 5 ft 7 in
Capacity	Cylinders 20 x 28 in
Total weight in full working order	123 tons

● **WP EXPRESS-PASSENGER ENGINE**
After talks with Baldwin in the mid-1940s and before independence in 1947, the WP express-passenger engine was conceived specifically for Indian conditions. The first batch was delivered in 1947. They proved successful, well-balanced, free steaming and – because of their 18-ton axleload – capable of rolling heavy trains at 60 mph. Building continued over a 20-year period and the class totalled 755 engines.

A heavyfreight version was introduced in 1950, classified WG. These had the same boiler, motion and other parts standard with the WP but smaller driving wheels and larger cylinders. Again, they were a complete success, and the class had reached 2,450 examples when building ended in 1970.

As the years passed, WGs often worked turnabout with WPs on express-passenger duties for increasing numbers of diesel engines, and electric engines were used on India's heaviest freight-trains. It is a tribute to the American engines' design that there was little tangible difference between them.

The suitability of American engines after World War II resulted from changing conditions in India. Maintenance, track condition and general standards of workmanship not being

● **LEFT**
Indian Railways operated 30 of these massive 2-8-4 tanks, designed in India for heavy suburban services. Their coupled wheels and cylinders were the same dimensions as the WP Pacifics, but the boiler was smaller. This example, taking water at Rajahmundry, did cross-country traffic work around the Godavari Delta, Andhra Pradesh State.

● **OPPOSITE**
WPs were standard express-passenger power across India over the last 30 years of steam but no two were ever exactly alike. Many had delightful ornamentation and decoration.

what they once were. A lighter Pacific was needed for the more restricted routes in the North West and 104 examples of the WL Class went into service. These engines, built in 1955–68, have a 17-ton axleload.

● **END OF STEAM**

A similar locomotive standardization applied on India's huge network of metre-gauge lines with the introduction of the YP Pacific and related YG 2-8-2 in the early 1950s. The metre-gauge YL 2-6-2s – with an axleload of eight tons – appeared in 1952 to complete a trio of standard designs.

As dieselization and electrification advanced, India, popularly regarded as the world's last great steam country, began to lose its steam heritage. Steam ended on the broad-gauge main lines in 1995. By the end of 1996, the metre gauge was but a shadow of its former self. On the erstwhile narrow gauge, diesels and closures had taken their toll, almost decimating a fascinating, extremely diversified group of veterans.

● **TOP**
Each year, Indian Railways held a locomotive beauty competition. Each regional railway was invited to submit an ornately embellished WP for the grand judging in Delhi, India's capital. Here, engine No. 7247, the Eastern Railway's exhibit, leaves the depot at Asansol, West Bengal, before proceeding to Delhi.

● **ABOVE**
This depot scene on the 5 ft 6 in gauge lines shows a WP Pacific (left) and a WG Class 2-8-2 (right). These post-World War II Indian Standards totalled more than 3,000 locomotives.

● **LEFT**
Northern India's sugar-plantation lines have many vintage locomotives running on 2 ft gauge systems. Most locomotives are of British or Continental European origin, augmented by a batch of Baldwin 4-6-0s built for military service in Europe in World War I and pensioned off to India for further use. A veteran takes water on the Katauli system.

INDIA GOES ELECTRIC

India's first electric-trains were operating before the famous X Series standard steam locomotives entered service in the late 1920s. By the 1930s, extensive electrification was operating over the two main lines from Bombay on the Great Indian Peninsular Railway (GIPR). This was encouraged by the long climb to the Deccan Plateau through the Ghats. Two routes, one to Calcutta, one to Madras, involved a 600 m

INDIAN RAILWAYS (IR) ELECTRIC LOCOMOTIVE CLASS WAM4	
Date	1971
Builders	Chittaranjan Locomotive Works, Chittaranjan, Damodar Valley, West Bengal OR Bihar State, India
Client	Indian Railways
Gauge	5 ft 6 in
Line voltage	25 k V a.c.
Wheel arrangement	Co-Co
Weight	113 tons

(2,000 ft) climb on 2.5 per cent grades. The locomotives were from Metropolitan Vickers 2-Co-1s for passenger operation and a C-C with coupling-rod drive for freight. Operations were on 1.5kV d.c.

● **THE DISAPPEARANCE OF STEAM**

India had a long transition period from steam to diesel and electric. It was to be another 65 years before main-line steam disappeared. One of the 4-6-0 passenger designs from the BESA Series early in the century was still being built in 1951.

By the mid-1950s the aim of Indian Railways was to advance electrification and diesel as a general policy. Electrification was the preferred mode, the country having an abundance of coal and, at that time, no indigenous oil industry. Electrification of main long-distance lines was sound investment in a country with so vast a population and a railway system that was

the lifeline of a surging economy. By 1961, 718 km (446 miles) of broad-gauge line were electrified. This rose to 3,540 km (2,200 miles) over the following decade.

Electrification of suburban services in Calcutta, both Howrah and Sealdah, used the 25 kV a.c. system, which was to become an Indian standard. The standard diesel-electric locomotive WDM1 from America was followed by many standard WDM4s, which were Alco-designed and built at the diesel-locomotive works at Varanasi, Uttar Pradesh State. Later, electric-locomotives adopted many features of these six-motor workhorses.

● **INDIAN-BUILT ELECTRIC-LOCOMOTIVES**

In 1962 the first Indian-built electric-locomotive appeared from Chittaranjan Locomotive Works near Asansol in West Bengal. The WCM-type, 3,600 hp engine

● **RIGHT**
A brand-new Class WAG 6C Co-Co 25 kV a.c., resplendent in blue-and-white livery.

● **BELOW LEFT**
One of 1,200 electric multiple units owned by India's Northern Railway pictured on the line between New Delhi and Palwal, a place of great antiquity important to Aryan traditions, in Haryana State, south-east of Delhi.

● **BELOW RIGHT**
A Class WAP 1-25 passenger Co-Co of India's Northern Railway about to depart.

was for the Central Railways d.c. line. In 1964, India's first a.c. electric-locomotive was the WHE1 Bo-Bo, designed by a European consortium.

By the 1970s, Indian Railways operated 600 electric-locomotives and more than 1,100 diesels, 700 of which were standard WDM2 2,500 hp Co-Cos. A year later, Chittaranjan built its last steam locomotive, a YG Class 2-8-2 for the metre gauge. India's first key route to be electrified was the main line between Delhi and Calcutta. Next came Delhi-Madras, Delhi-Bombay, Calcutta-Madras-Bombay. By 1987, about 8,000 km (5,000 miles) had been electrified.

● **SELF-SUFFICIENCY**
The days when India imported vast packages of locomotives and rolling stock, mainly from Britain, are

history. The country is self-sufficient in all aspects of railway production, with hi-tech plants and skilled production. The locomotive industry developed in India since the 1960s has enabled steam to be phased out on the

broad gauge. Metre-gauge systems with YP and YG Pacifics and Mikados remaining in certain areas, especially the Western and North-East Frontier Railways, were expected to be phased out in 1997.

● **LEFT**
This locomotive built by Alco waits for the right of way.

CHINESE LOCOMOTIVES

The Steam Age has been in decline across the world since the 1950s. By 1970 steam had disappeared from large areas, notably North America, Britain and most of Europe. In the mid-1970s, the fact that China was still building steam-locomotives at the rate of more than one a day was worldwide news reported extensively by the media.

● DATONG AND TANGSHAN

China's main building centre was at Datong, west of Beijing, in Shanxi Province, close to the border with the Inner Mongolian Autonomous Region. The area is noted for hot summers and bitterly cold winters when temperatures drop to minus-20 degrees Celsius.

Datong, opened in 1959, built steam-engines based on a 1950s design from the Soviet Union. It produced two standard classes: the Qianjin (Forward) Class, QJ 2-10-2, freight, first produced in 1965, and the JS 2-8-2 for general purposes. Some of these engines were

being sent to new lines as railway building continued apace in China.

Shortly after activity at Datong was discovered by the West, news came of another works, producing locomotives for industrial use. It was located in Tangshan, a coalmining and industrial centre about 260 km (160 miles) east of Beijing, in Hebei Province. Tangshan had produced the Shangyang (Aiming at the Sun) or SY Class locomotive, but had been largely destroyed by an earthquake

in 1976. The quake was unparalleled in modern history, with a 242,000 death-toll from a population of 1.06 million. The city was rapidly rebuilt and steam-locomotive production continued. Tangshan has built about 1,700 SY Mikados.

Datong finished building steam in the late 1980s. In summer 1996, however, continued building at Tangshan was confirmed, albeit on a reduced scale.

● ABOVE
A QJ Class 2-10-2 locomotive is assembled in the erecting shop.

● LEFT
A brace of QJs resides amid the smoky gloom of the steam-testing shed at Datong works. Both locomotives have spent the day running trials on the specially constructed test-track.

● STEAM BUILDING

Other works built steam locomotives for China's 762 mm gauge forestry lines. These are standard 28-ton 0-8-0 engines. Isolated building of these may have continued.

To witness steam-building is unforgettable. A vast shop contained 20 or more boilers in varying stages of construction. Inner and outer fireboxes contrasted with boiler shells. All was illuminated and silhouetted in ghostly patterns by the welders' blinding flashes and set to a deafening cacophony of heavy drilling. The memories flooded back – Crewe, Derby, Doncaster, Swindon it mattered not, as if by time-machine the witness was back among the living vitality of the Steam Age, and something for many years suspected was confirmed: the Steam Age was every bit as fabulous as remembered.

(QJ) CLASS 2-10-2	
Date	1957
Builder	Datong & Dalian
Client	China Railways
Gauge	4 ft 8¹/₂ in
Driving wheels	1,500 mm
Capacity	2 cylinders 650 x 800 mm

● **TOP LEFT**
Welding an inner-firebox at the Datong Locomotive Works, Datong, Shanxi Province, China.

● **TOP RIGHT**
Welding-operations on cylinders and smokebox saddle for a QJ Class 2-10-2 engine.

● **ABOVE**
Measuring tolerances of machining on a QJ Class 2-10-2's driving-axle.

● **LEFT**
QJ Class 2-10-2 driving wheels in the foreground. The locomotive behind is waiting to leave the erecting shop for steaming trials.

CHINA'S WORKING STEAM

An industrial SY Class 2-8-2, built at Tangshan, tips molten slag down the slag bank at Anshan Iron and Steel Works. Anshan, in Liaoning Province, is China's steel capital.

Steam's rapid decline in India in the 1990s has left China by far the biggest user. In 1996, China had about 6,500 steam-locomotives at work. This is far more than the rest of the world put together. When India had 6,500 active locomotives, they comprised more than 150 different types. China's centralized planning has meant there have been just five types – only three main-liners, one industrial and one narrow-gauge type predominate.

● MAIN-LINERS

Of the main-liners, most are QJ class 2-10-2s of which about 3,000 are active. These are followed by the JS Class 2-8-2 with about 1,300 examples, backed up by a mere 25 survivors of the once-numerous JF Class 2-8-2. The SY Class 2-8-2 industrial accounts for another 1,700 engines. On 762 mm gauge lines about 500 standard 0-8-0s bring the total to some 6,500 locomotives. In contrast with the ubiquitous QJs are the JF Mikados, now rapidly disappearing from main-line service. These were the forerunners of the JS Class and once numbered more than 2,000 locomotives. The earliest ones date back to 1918.

Most of China's rail-connected heavy industries use SY Class 2-8-2s. Many are

● LEFT
The daily workmen's passenger-train heads across the 700 mm gauge rails of the Anxiang in north-eastern China.

● OPPOSITE
A trio of QJ Class 2-10-2s bask amid the sooty magic of the steam-locomotive sheds at Shenyang, Liaoning Province, north-eastern China.

SY CLASS INDUSTRIAL 2-8-2 (PICTURE NUMBER 2)

Date	1969
Builder	Tangshan Locomotive Works, Hebei Province, China
Client	Industrial users across China
Gauge	Standard
Driving wheels	1,370 mm
Capacity	2 cylinders 530 x 710 mm
Total weight in full working order	143 tons

relatively new engines but are, in essence, typical light-American Mikados, the type of engine common on many American roads before World War I.

The odd main-line rarity does occur in industrial locations. In November 1996, it was confirmed that at least one KD6 Class 2-8-0 remained active. This engine is one of the famous United States Army Transportation Corps (USATC) S160s, more than 2,000 of which were built in America to the British loading gauge for World War II operations around the world.

● **UNIQUE 2,000-TON TRAINS**

China is also the only country in which steam locomotives can be seen out on main lines heading 2,000-ton trains. The mighty QJ Class often run in pairs and are put through their paces over the steep gradients presented on many main lines.

● **QJS WORKING NEW LINES**

The concept of China as a steam paradise was heightened on 1 December 1995 when a new 950 km (590 mile) long railway opened across the Inner Mongolian Autonomous Region. It is completely QJ-worked, has six

locomotive-sheds and is semaphore-signalled over much of its distance. The line runs between Tongliao, a town in the region's far east, and Jining, east of the region's capital Hohhot. The Jingpeng Pass sees double-headed QJs working up a 50 km (31 mile) bank through six tunnels, around horse-shoe curves and over a 90-degree curved viaduct.

● **ABOVE LEFT**
The pride of the Harbin shed was Zhoude, the QJ Class locomotive named in honour of Chinese Communist revolutionary hero Marshal Zhu De (1886–1976) who became Commander-in-Chief of the People's Liberation Army (PLA) and second in the Communist Party's hierarchy only to Mao Tse-tung. Zhoude is commemorated on the smokebox-doors' brass bust.

● **ABOVE RIGHT**
An industrial SY Class 2-8-2 resides in silhouette among the smoky gloom of the engine-shed at Anshan Iron and Steel Works.

MODERN CHINA

Since the establishment of the People's Republic of China in 1949, China's national system has more than doubled its track route mileage and increased its passenger and freight traffic by ten and 20 times respectively.

● CONTINUED GROWTH

From 2001 to the end of 2005 more was spent on railways and other fixed assets than in the previous 50 years. This level of investment is due to continue with the development of high-speed links. Steam will remain for some years: coal is cheap and plentiful, whereas oil is not, and the annual intake of new electric- and diesel-powered locomotives is insufficient to keep up with the expanding traffic, so that steam is being replaced only slowly.

Both standard- and narrow-gauge steam locomotives are still being made although in small numbers. By the 1980s, Chinese railway building had reached unprecedented levels. Getting at the coal had become China's most pressing transport need. Shanxi Province has a third of China's coal reserves and

● **LEFT**
Mainland China has only three cities with tramway systems – Changchun, Anshan and Dalian. This scene at the rundown depot in Changchun shows the decline that has set in and caused many parts of this once prolific network to be abandoned.

millions of tons were lying on the ground awaiting conveyance. At present, coal accounts for well over 50 per cent of freight on China's four major rail trunk lines. These are:

- Beijing – Guangzhou.
- Shenyang – Lanzhou – Lianun Gang.
- Beijing – Shanghai.
- Harbin – Dalian.

Lanzhou (Lanchow) is in Gansu (Kansu) Province. Llanyun Gang (Lienyun Harbour) is in Jiangsu (Kiangsu) Province. Harbin is in Heilongjiang (Heilungkiang) Province. Dalian (Talian) is in Liaoning Province.

Many diesels have been built since the late 1950s and by the 1980s 20 per cent of China's railway traffic was diesel-

● **ABOVE LEFT**
In Liaoning Province, the shape of things to come on the main line between Shenyang and Dalian, which until the late 1980s was one of China's most famous steam-operated main lines. A freight-train heads away from Shenyang and passes beneath the Fushun line at the Hunhe River. Fushun, north-east of Shenyang, works China's largest opencast coalmine.

● **LEFT**
A China Railways Co-Co diesel hydraulic locomotive, Class DFH3, heads a passenger-train between the cities of Jilin and Changchun, in Jilin Province, north-eastern China. Changchun was developed by the Japanese as capital of their puppet-state of Manchukuo (1932–45).

A brace of China Railway's DF4 class diesel-electric locomotives head a freight-train past Zoujia on the Changchun to Jilin line in January 1994.

CHINESE RAILWAYS CLASS DF4 DIESEL ELECTRIC

Date	1969
Builder	Dalian Locomotive Works, Liaoning Province, China
Client	Chinese Railways
Gauge	4 ft 8¹/₂ in
Wheel arrangement	Co-Co
Weight	138 tonnes
Maximum speed	100 kph

hauled. A large fleet of locally built 3300 Dong Feng (East Wind) 4 freight Co-Cos is expected to reach more than 4,000 units by the end of the century. In the early 1980s, General Electric (GE) supplied more than 200 Type C36-7 4,000 hp Co-Co diesel electrics for freight-haulage. A repeat order for 200 locomotives three years later was placed with the same company.

● DEMAND EXCEEDS SUPPLY

A 5,000 hp Dong Feng Co-Co is the standard passenger diesel locomotive. Expansion of diesel and electric traction is inadequate to keep up with demand, so Class QJ 2-10-2s and Class JS 2-8-2 continue to be used.

Priority in the early 1990s was to electrify the double-track coal-line from the railhead in Shanxi Province to the port of Qinhuangdao, Hebei Province, as well as the 322 km (200 mile) coal route from Datong, Inner Mongolia, south to Taiyuan, capital of Shanxi Province.

The building of new lines and further electrification is to increase the coal-carrying capacity, because China's domestic needs are 70 per cent met by coal. Coal is also a top foreign revenue-earner with millions of tonnes being exported yearly. To serve the newly electrified lines, Chinese builders have supplied 138-tonne Shaoshan SS3-type electric-locomotives. Demand is so great, however, that 80 microprocessor-equipped, thyristor-controlled, 138-tonne, 4,800 kV Co-Cos have been bought from Japan, as well as 100 electric-locomotives from Russia.

● LEFT
Harbin, the capital of Heilongjiang Province in north east China, once had a tramway network. By the late 1980s, this was down to one line. This picture was taken at Harbin tram depot in the final year of operation.

JAPANESE FREIGHT

Japanese railways were largely built to the 3 ft 6 in narrow gauge, to save money crossing often mountainous terrain. Gauge and terrain meant slow services. Then, road services started to compete. New motorways, often built along shorter, more direct routes, allowed shorter journey-times. The railways had to respond and the solution devised for the passenger service was the Shinkansen.

● EFFICIENT MOVEMENT OF LARGE TONNAGES

The solution for freight-traffic was not so positive but followed the practice in most other countries of focusing on what railborne traffic could do best, the efficient movement of large tonnages over a limited number of routes. This can be either block-loads of bulk commodities such as stone or ore, or containerized-traffic where handling-costs can be minimized. Despite this concentration on particular types of

● BELOW

JR Freight locomotives on-shed at Shin Kawasaki depot. Right, EF 66 29, a 1968-built mixed-traffic locomotive. Several locomotive classes have the same body style, being built to work under different catenary voltages. Left, EF 200 8, an early 1990s design. As the legend on the side indicates, this uses inverter technology.

traffic, freight is still loss-making. Traffic fell from 68.6 million tonnes in 1985 to 58.4 million tonnes in 1991. The number of marshalling yards has been cut, from 110 to 40 in 1986. Freight-train-kilometres were cut by 25 per cent in 1985 alone.

● BREAK-UP OF JAPANESE RAILWAYS

As part of the break-up of Japanese railways, which started in 1987, JR Freight was formed to operate all freight services. The company owns its own locomotives (1,069 in 1994), wagons and terminals, paying passenger-companies for the use of their tracks.

Only a couple of the private railway companies operate freight-trains. The Chichibu Railway, serving Chichibu, 50 km (30 miles) north-west of Tokyo, runs more freight than any other private company, linking a limestone quarry and a cement works to the JR network.

● ABOVE
JR diesel DE10 1521, a shunting and trip-working locomotive. These 1966-built diesel-hydraulic locomotives have the unusual wheel arrangement AAA-B. They work at many of the few stations that still have a freight-terminal. The engine is pictured at Fuji, Honshu, in 1994, which is below the 3,775 m (12,388 ft) high sacred mountain, Japan's highest peak, known as Fuji-no-Yama, 113 km (70 miles) south-west of Tokyo. Its volcano last erupted in 1649.

● BELOW
Electric locomotive EF 65 22 on a container-train at Odawara on the original Tokaido line, in 1994. This locomotive class was introduced in 1964. It shares body design with other classes, as well as with exported designs, notably locomotives built under licence in Spain. Odawara is a town in Kanagawa Prefecture, south-eastern Honshu, the largest of Japan's four chief islands and considered as Japan's mainland. Odawara is 80 km (50 miles) south-west of Tokyo (ancient Edo or Yedo). Tokaido is the great coastal road along the Pacific Ocean between Tokyo and Kyoto, Japan's capital until 1869 and a great manufacturing centre, along the Kanto Plain beneath the Kanto Mountains. Tokaido means "Eastern Sea Route".

CLASS EF 66 ELECTRIC LOCOMOTIVE

Year into service	1968
Builders	Mechanical: Kawasaki Heavy Industries, Japan Electrical: Tokyo Shibaura Electric Co., Tokyo, Japan
Gauge	1,067 mm
Catenary voltage	1,500 kV d.c.
Wheel arrangement	B-B-B
Rated output	3,900 kW
Weight in working order	100 tonnes
Maximum service speed	120 kph

JAPAN'S "BULLET TRAIN"

Japan's "Bullet Train", called Shinkansen – Japanese for New Super Express – was developed to provide fast, regular and reliable passenger-services between main conurbations.

All the routes were to be newly built and segregated from the rest of the network. This allowed them to be constructed to standard gauge rather than to the narrow 3 ft 6 in (1,067 mm) gauge of the national railway system. The lines were to be designed for high speed, the initial expectation being to operate eventually at 250 kph.

● TOKAIDO LINE

The first route, the Tokaido line on Honshu, opened in 1964 in time for the Olympic Games that year. It ran between Tokyo and, about 400 km (250 miles) away, Osaka, Japan's second city in size and the industrial metropolis of the Orient, via Nagoya and Kyoto. Three further routes subsequently opened on Honshu:

- The Sanyo line running south across the country from Osaka.

- The Joetsu line crossing the country from Tokyo to Niigata to the north.
- The Tohoku line running north from Tokyo to Morioka.

A branch has been built off the Tohoku line, to Yamagata, a silk-industry centre. However, this route is an upgrading and regauging of an existing line, not the full high-speed line of the other routes.

● FIVE SERIES OF TRAINS

The Shinkansen has five series of trains. The 0-Series are the original sets, which now run the stopping-services on the Tokaido and Sanyo lines. The 100-Series run the semi-fasts and the 300-Series the fast – Nozomi – trains, both on the Tokaido/Sanyo lines. The 200-Series run the Joetsu and Tohoku services and are distinguished by a green rather than a blue stripe along their sides. The 400-Series are short, narrow sets, which look distinctly different from the others and run the Yamagata service. The E-2 Series are double-deck sets for use on the Joetsu and Tohoku routes and have been christened "Max".

The Shinkansen are fitted with an in-cab signalling system. This can be

SHINKANSEN 0-SERIES TRAIN

Date	1964
Builders	Mechanical: Niigata Tekko; Hitachi Mfg Co; Kawasaki Heavy Industries, Japan Electrical: Hitachi Mfg. Co.; Tokyo Shibaura Electric Co., Mitsubishi Electric Co., Japan
Gauge	1,435 mm
Catenary voltage	a.c. 25 kV, 60 Hz
Powered axles per unit	All axles driven
Rated output per unit	11,840 kW
Maximum service speed	220 kph

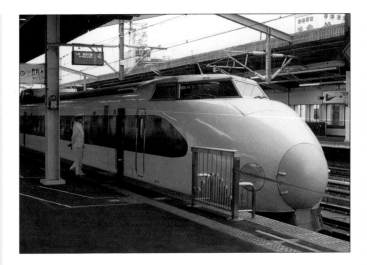

seen in a driving-simulator unit at Tokyo Transport Museum. The original lines operated at 220 kph, increased to 240 kph on the northern routes. Nozomi trains run at 270 kph. It is planned to run the next generation of stock at an increased speed of 320 kph, experimental sets having run much faster.

There is a dense service pattern. For example, ten trains leave Tokyo on the Tokaido line between 08.00-09.00 hrs, six terminating at Osaka, one continuing to Okayama seaport, two to Hiroshima and one service going through to Hakata. The fastest service covers the 515 km (320 miles) to Osaka in 2 hours 32 minutes, with two intermediate stops, and overtakes four trains *en route*.

● **ABOVE**
A 200-Series Shinkansen 222-18 at Utsunomiya, 97 km (60 miles) north of Tokyo, in 1994. The gentleman in white is a train crew-member. This station is the terminus of the JR branch line to Nikko, one of Japan's main centres for temples and shrines, a city and mountain resort at 609 m (2,000 ft) in the Nikko Mountains of central Honshu Island.

● **BELOW**
A 0-Series Shinkansen at Shin Fuji in 1994, one of many stations, which allow fast trains to overtake the stopping-services. The much-photographed section of route, with Mount Fuji as a backdrop, is just north of this station.

JAPANESE MULTIPLE UNITS

Japanese Railways (JR) have a long history of electrification. By 1991, 11,700 km (7,300 miles), 58 per cent of the total JR network, were electrified. Intensive operation of many lines has led to significant use of multiple unit trains. Although only 58 per cent of the lines are electrified, electric multiple units (EMUs) outnumbered diesel multiple units (DMUs) by a far greater proportion. In 1991, there were 3,189 diesel-powered passenger-coaches (13 per cent) and 20,548 electric-coaches (87 per cent).

Multiple Units exist in each segment of Japan's railways – both private and JR, suburban, outer-suburban and long-distance (and high-speed if Shinkansen are included), as well as in the luxury-train market. The EMU's variants and history are vast.

The two most common EMU designs, of which there are many variants, are the suburban set and the outer-suburban set. The Odakyu EMU represents the many small builds of specialist EMUs. The

Class 165 EMU described in the technical box represents about 20 classes of trains built during 1959–71 for the railway's different electrical systems and with small changes in detail. This example runs in three-coach sets. Other variants run in sets of up to ten coaches.

● **DISTINCTIVE DESIGNS**

Private railways run a variety of EMUs. Some have a JR pedigree, either secondhand or to similar designs. Many railway companies, however, have developed their own often distinctive designs.

Because electrification focused on busier routes, most lines around the main conurbations are operated by electric traction. DMUs, being limited to through-services from lesser-used routes, are seldom seen in such built-up areas. Diesel-powered services tend to increase the farther you travel from Tokyo. They are concentrated on the northern and south-western ends of the main island, Honshu, and on the two islands of Hokkaido and Kyushu, respectively Japan's second- and third-largest islands.

● RIGHT
Shonan monorail EMU 505 approaching Ofuna, south of Yokohama, Honshu, in 1994. This line, built in 1970, connects JR's Tokaido line with Enoshima resort area. It has steep gradients and two tunnels. It is a means of transport, not a tourist or showground operation.

JAPANESE RAILWAY (JR) CLASS 165 ELECTRIC MULTIPLE UNIT (EMU)

Date	1962
Builders	Mechanical: Nippon Sharyo Seizo Ltd, Kinki Nihon Sharyo and Hitachi Mfg Co., Japan Electrical: Hitachi Mfg Co., Mitsubishi Electric Co., Tokyo Shibaura Electric Co., Japan
Gauge	1,067 mm
Catenary voltage	d.c. 1,500 kV
Configuration	Two power-cars per three-car unit
Wheel arrangement	Four powered axles per power-car
Rated output	480 kW per power-car
Weight in working order	108 tonnes per three-car set
Maximum service speed	110 kph

● ABOVE

An express-EMU of Odakyu Railway (OER) approaching Shinjuku Station, inner Tokyo, in 1994. The OER, like many private railways, has several express EMUs, in addition to its large fleet of suburban trains. It serves a resort area south-west of Tokyo. Shinjuku Station is the world's busiest station, being served by JR, two private railways and several underground lines.

● ABOVE

JR outer-suburban EMU No. 401-76 at Ishioka, 64 km (40 miles) north-east of Tokyo, in 1995. This is representative of a widely used design, the 1960 multivoltage (1,500 volt d.c. and 20 kV, 50 Hz) version of the Class 165. The livery represents a group of routes, similarly to suburban trains. Background: DMUs of the Kashima Railway, Honshu.

● BELOW

Electric-railcars Nos. 109 and 108 of the Hakone Tozan Railway near Gora, Honshu. This 15 km (9 mile) line climbs 450m (1,477 ft) by means of three dead-end reverses and up gradients of up to 8 per cent. These trains, from 1927, were operating in 1994. Hakone is a mountain resort with hot springs and wonderful views of Mount Fuji, 32 km (20 miles) to the north-east.

● **THE KASHIMA COASTAL RAILWAY ON HONSHU**

All train categories exist as DMUs, ranging from two-axle railbuses, through rural all-station stopping-trains, to luxury-express units. Vehicle design has tended to follow that of EMUs, with small modifications to allow for engines.

Many of Japan's private railway companies are commuter operations which were electrified many years ago and operate large fleets of EMUs. However, some of these companies also operate DMUs, not only for rural stopping-train services but for other services as well. An example is the Kashima Coastal Railway (KRT) on Honshu. It runs DMUs on an 80 km route east of Tokyo, built in 1985, using both a high-capacity design and a streamlined version for its express services.

JAPANESE LONG-DISTANCE PASSENGER SERVICES

Japan's narrow-gauge railways and often mountainous terrain have prevented its railways competing successfully with the increasing competition of motorways and airways. The main response for passenger-services was the Shinkansen. However, long-distance passenger services still exist, although far fewer than 40 years ago. This is often the result of the opening of high-speed lines, which cause inter-city services to be remodelled to feed into the Shinkansen. Where new lines are unlikely, there are moves to increase speeds from the usual 120-kph maximum to 160 kph.

Long-distance services are in two categories: the usually EMU-operated day services and the locomotive-hauled overnight services.

The day services tend to be of limited frequency. They require compulsory seat-reservations and payment of a supplementary fare. A variety of EMUs, and some DMUs, are used on these services. Some feature passive tilt, to take

● **LEFT**
JR Blue Train sleeping-cars passing Yarakucho, Tokyo, in 1994. The streamlined body style was very modern when these were introduced.

● **LEFT**
JR EMU No. 189 508 passing Oji, near Tokyo, in 1994.

● **BELOW LEFT**
Japan Railways (JR) electric-locomotive EF 66 44 passing Yarakucho, Tokyo, towards the end of its overnight haul of a Blue Train in 1994. Note the headboard with the train's name.

curves faster. Double-deck stock, with its extra carrying capacity, features increasingly in new designs.

● **BLUE TRAINS**
The overnight trains, usually "Limited Expresses", are largely operated by a fleet of Blue Trains. These consist of coaching stock, predominantly sleepers, introduced since 1958. The sleeping-cars come in several forms. The difference between A- and B-sleepers is the bunk width. Some trains include dining-cars. Only a few include the addition of seated accommodation. These trains can be hauled by any locomotive. Those painted red with a shooting star on the side are reserved for sleeper services. "Ordinary Express" overnight trains, sometimes

● RIGHT
JR EMU No. 185 107 passing Hamametsucho, Tokyo, in 1994. Note the train's name display.

JAPAN RAILWAYS (JR) CLASS 185 ELECTRICAL MULTIPLE UNIT (EMU)

Date	1980
Builders	Mechanical: Niigata Tekko, Kawasaki Heavy Industries, Japan Electrical: Hitachi Mfg Co., Tokyo Shibaura Electric Co., Mitsubishi Electric Co., Japan
Gauge	1,067 mm
Catenary voltage	1,500 volt d.c.
Cars per unit	Four
Powered axles per unit	Eight
Rated output per unit	960 kW
Maximum service speed	110 kph

● LEFT
An accompanied car-carrying train of JR being loaded at Hamametsucho, Tokyo, in 1994. Note the unusual side-loading method. Car-drivers join the train at the same location.

with sleeping accommodation, are an endangered species.

Certain overnight trains also include wagons for accompanied cars. These are unusual for their method of loading – sideways on a pallet by fork-lift truck.

Private railways operate express stock, often with compulsory seat-reservations and supplements, but distances involved do not compare with JR's services.

● RIGHT
On Honshu Island, JR EMU No. 250-04 operating near Kogetsuenmae, between the Tokyo manufacturing suburb of Kawasaki and Japan's chief port, Yokohama, in 1994. These trains include seats from which passengers can see forward above the driver. This EMU is on the Tokaido line where it runs parallel with the Keihin railway, providing a fine train-watching location.

JAPANESE LIGHT RAIL AND METRO

● BELOW
The Keihan interurban company runs a light-rail service out of Kyoto, Honshu. Nos. 89 and 90 made by Kinki Sharyo of Japan in 1967 are equipped with folding steps for stops on the street section. They are pictured passing a true high-floor interurban.

Japan is a paradise for students of electric mass transit. It is well serviced with light railways and metros to carry its vast population from place to place. More than 100 tramways, metros and interurbans exist, most linked with one of the extensive privately owned electrified railway networks. Definition is difficult, because interurbans can run down the street like tramways; metros can carry interurban trains; and railways, which started off as interurbans, today provide a dense network of express, limited-stop and stopping-trains to carry people into Japan's crowded towns and cities. In terms of transit interest, some say Japan has everything Switzerland can offer and more. With most of the 120 million population crammed into

● BELOW
Kochi, on Shikoku, Japan's fourth-largest island, is a seaport city but the outer end of its tramway displays a rural village aspect. It is single-track with passing loops. The Hitachi Co. built Tram 201 in 1950.

25 per cent of the land area, efficient rail transit is of the utmost importance. The biggest cities have underground or elevated metro systems.

● METROS AND TRAMWAYS

Tokyo's extensive metro has been developed partly with private capital. The result is two separate networks, three different gauges, with overhead and third-rail current-collection. Patronage is heavy, with ten-car trains and, at peak periods, pushers employed at some points to ensure train-doors close on the crush of passengers. In addition, some private railways running into Tokyo operate underground in the city. Through-operation of private railways on to urban metros can be found in Kobe and Osaka on Honshu and with JR trains at Fukuoka, the seaport on Hakata Bay, Kyushu Island. Sapporo's Metro on Hokkaido Island features rubber-tyred trains and elevated tracks, which are covered over as protection from heavy winter snow. Sapporo was laid out in 1869 by the Japanese government as a colonizing centre for Hokkaido Island and replaced Hakodate as the island's capital.

Car 7513 is pictured on the Arakawa tramway of Tokyo Metropolitan Transport Bureau, a 12 km (8 mile) long survivor of the citywide 1,372 mm-gauge system. All stops have high platforms. The tram was built in 1962 by Niigata Engineering.

Tramways have been in decline for some years. Those in larger cities were replaced by metros. Buses replaced trams in other places. There was little development elsewhere. Hiroshima, on Honshu, is the only city that has modernized an extensive network. The city was rebuilt after receiving the world's first atomic bomb on 6 August 1945, which ended World War II. It includes an interurban line with through-operation on to the city tramways.

However, in the 1990s there are signs of an upturn in tramway fortunes. Hakodate, the seaport city of Hokkaido Island, on the Tsurgaru Strait, and Kitakushu, across the Strait of Shimonoseki opposite Honshu, have retrenched but other systems have bought new rolling stock or rebodied older cars, segregation and traffic-management are making operation more efficient and further closures seem unlikely.

● **BELOW**
The town of Gifu in central Honshu, north-west of Nagoya, shows the interaction of trams and interurbans on street and segregated track. Articulated tram Nos. 875 and 876, which formerly worked in Sapporo, runs on the urban section of the Mino line where through-operation on to the interurban requires dual-voltage cars. Mino is 20km (12 miles) north of Gifu.

● **ABOVE**
The 1,067 mm gauge tramway of Toyohashi city, on Honshu, south-east of Nagoya, has three lines totalling 23 km (14 miles). Tram 3105 pictured approaching the railway-station terminus is secondhand from the tramways of Nagoya. It was built in 1943.

Japan's most northerly city, Sapporo on Hokkaido Island, has kept one tram-route to feed the metro. Car 255 was built in 1958 by the local railway workshops for the 1067 mm gauge system.

● TRAMWAYS

On Honshu, Tokyo's tramway is a single, largely segregated line in the southern suburbs, the survivor of a citywide system. There is also a privately operated outer suburban tramway on a private right of way. The system at Gifu, central Honshu, is a fascinating mixture of street operation and rural interurban (at different voltages) provided by a private company. Kochi, the seaport city on

HIROSHIMA ARTICULATED-TRAM

Builder	Alna Koki/Hiroshima
Gauge	1,435 mm
Power supply	600 volt d.c.
Bogie arrangement	B-2-2-B with two 120 kW motors
Overall length	26.3 metres
Unladen weight	38.4 tons
Maximum speed	80 kph

Shikoku Island, has a reputation for acquiring individual, secondhand trams from European systems. These are rebuilt to run as a tourist attraction within the regular service. On Honshu, Osaka's city trams were abandoned in 1969, but a suburban tramway, subsidiary of a private railway, continued operating. Other tramways have been continuously upgraded over the years and, although still legally tramways, they can be difficult to distinguish from interurban railways. One such tramway is at Enoshima, one of Honshu's popular seaside resorts.

● HOME OF THE MONORAIL

Japan is also known as the home of the monorail. These offer proper urban-transit facilities in Chiba, a prosperous commercial town on the eastern shore of Tokyo Bay, and Kitakyushu. There is also the original line between Tokyo and

Japan's most modern city-tramway serves Hiroshima, Honshu, completely rebuilt since World War II. Car 3702 is one of an increasing number of modern articulated-trams. It was built in 1987 by Alna Koki.

● LEFT
The Hankai tramway in south Osaka, Honshu, comprises two standard-gauge lines totalling 18.7 km (12 miles). Car 169, pictured here at Ebisucho terminus, is one of many veterans from 1928 still in everyday service.

Haneda domestic airport, and a link between Ofuna, south-west of Yokohama, and Enoshima. More recently, several guideway systems have been built, usually featuring rubber-tyred cars and automatic train operation on elevated shuttle lines to new development. Examples on Honshu are the Portliner in Kobe, Newtram in Osaka, NTS in Hiroshima and VONA in Nagoya.

Japan, with its huge home market for electric-rail vehicles, supports many rolling-stock producers. Electrical equipment features the latest in power electronics. Among large orders for railways and metros, the producers are happy to process small but quite frequent orders from tramway undertakings. There has also been secondhand dealing within the country.

● LEFT BEHIND

Most systems operate single-bogie trams but a few articulated-cars can be found in Gifu, Hiroshima, Kagoshima, the seaport on the south of Kyushu Island, and

Kitakyushu. A sign that Japan accepts it has been left behind in tramcar development and that new ideas can come from overseas is the recent announcement by Kumamoto, a city on Kyushu Island, that it has negotiated a local-assembly package for a German design of a low-floor tram of the type developed by AEG before it became part of ADtranz.

● BELOW LEFT
Rubber-tyred guideway systems are appearing in many Japanese cities. An example is the Astram line, built in Hiroshima in 1994.

● BELOW RIGHT
The tramways of Hakodate on Hokkaido Island and of Tokyo on Honshu Island have in common the 1,372 mm gauge. Hakodate has received secondhand trams from the capital, but Car 3003 is a 1995-built tram constructed by Alna Koki for use on Hakodate's two-route system.

THE PACIFIC RIM

Some of the smaller countries that surround the Pacific Ocean have relatively limited railway networks.

● **LEFT**
Singapore Mass Rapid Transit Corporation (SMRT) metro sets Nos. 3126 and 3111 at Yishun in 1990. Yishun is the terminus of the north-south line.

● REPUBLIC OF KOREA

The Korean National Railroad (KNR) of South Korea has just more than 3,000 km (1,860 miles) of track, built to standard gauge, of which more than 400 km (250 miles) had been electrified by 1987. The country's major route is between the capital Seoul and the major port of Pusan. KNR is unusual in that both freight- and passenger-traffic have been growing, although this has not been enough to ensure continued profitability. New lines and extensions continue to be built as the economy expands. Electrification is being gradually extended but most services remain diesel-hauled, except Seoul's suburban services. These are interconnected with the metro, thus requiring electric multiple units (EMUs) that can operate at both 25 kV a.c. and 1,500 v d.c.

Increasing competition from coach and air services led to acceleration of the Seoul-Pusan service, with the

● **LEFT**
Standard-gauge 800 hp, diesel-electric locomotive No. 38-150 of Vietnam Railways shunting at Luu Xa in 1989. Note the mixed-gauge track.

● **BELOW**
KNR express diesel multiple unit (DMU) No. 132 at Yongsan in 1995. These units, introduced in 1987, run with two power-cars and five intermediate trailers. Yongsan, a southern district of Seoul, is a good location at which to observe the railways. The suburban service goes underground between here and the main station.

introduction of 150-kph diesel-sets. Improvements are continually being made to several routes by the introduction of centralized train control (CTC), which enables more efficient and consistent control of a route, thus allowing an improved, faster service.

● MALAYSIA AND SINGAPORE

Singapore does not have its own national railway system. The sole main-line railway is a line over the Johore Strait Causeway that joins the island with Malaysia, terminating at Singapore Station, and a freight-only branch to the docks. A through-service operates from Singapore to Kuala Lumpur (KL), the Malaysian capital. A luxury-tourist service also operates from Singapore via KL to Butterworth, opposite George Town, Pinang Island, Malaysia.

Singapore has a significant mass transit network. The first section of the standard-gauge, third-rail electrified metro opened in 1987. The metro has tunnelled sections in the city centre

● RIGHT
Vietnam Railways metre-gauge 2-6-2T steam-locomotive No. 131 444 at Haiphong in 1989. French influence can be seen in the locomotive, Chinese in the rear coach.

and elevated structures through the suburbs.

Malaysia has a metre-gauge network totalling more than 1,600 km (1000 miles). Its main route runs from Singapore via KL to Butterworth. Electrified suburban services were introduced in KL in December 1995. The 18 three-coach EMUs were based on a British design, built in Hungary with Dutch electrical systems and fitted out in Austria.

Passenger-loads have been rising, but there was a steady fall in freight tonnage in the 1980s.

● LEFT
An Indonesian State Railways PJKA F10 Class engine, No. F1012, at Blitar, Java, in 1971. Between 1912–20, Java and Sumatra took delivery of 28 of these mighty 2-12-2Ts. This engine was built by Hanoang in 1914.

KOREAN NATIONAL RAILWAYS (KNR) 8000 CLASS ELECTRIC LOCOMOTIVES	
Date	1972
Builders	Mechanical: Alsthom Electrical: AEG and ACEC
Gauge	1,435 mm
Catenary voltage	25 kV, 60 Hz
Wheel arrangement	Bo-Bo-Bo
Rated outputs	5,300 hp
Weight in working order	132 tons
Maximum service speed	85 kph

● VIETNAM
Vietnam's small railway network covers fewer than 3,000 km (1,860 miles). It is mainly metre gauge but does have a couple of standard-gauge routes, including the regauged line between Hanoi, the capital, and Haiphong, the

port and industrial centre. The railways were devastated by the Indo-Chinese Wars (1940–75) and continued investment levels are still limited. Despite these problems, a completely new line between Hanoi and Ha Dong was opened in 1986.

● RIGHT
Korean National Railways (KNR) electric-locomotive No. 8001 at Chongnyangnii Station, Seoul, in 1995, just arrived with a long-distance passenger train. The French pedigree of these locomotives is obvious.

HONG KONG SYSTEMS

The territory of Hong Kong boasts three tramways, two on Hong Kong Island and one in the New Territories (NT). On the island, the funicular-railway Peak Tram between Garden Road and Victoria Gap, 397 m (1,303 ft) above sea level, with 1:2 gradients, celebrated its centenary in 1988. It has since been modernized. The north-shore tramway on the island was opened in 1904 and runs double-deck cars. The Hong Kong Tramways line, built to 1,067 mm gauge, runs for just under 17 km (11 miles) along the northern side of the island, through the Central District business, administrative and shopping areas of the capital, Victoria. All trams are two-axle cars operating off a 500 volt d.c. power

supply. They were all rebuilt in the tramway's own workshops in the past ten years and now carry new bodies on old trucks. The 163 trams comprise the only all-double-deck fleet in the world. There was a fear that the Victoria tram line would close when the parallel Mass Transit Railway (MTR) metro line was opened. However, while there was a

distinct drop in tram traffic, the tram's advantage for short journeys and as a metro-feeder has kept it in business. This is shown by the service pattern. Broadly, the tramway is a single-line of route but there are, typically, six separate routes operated between different turning-circles. Only a small proportion of trams operate over the full route.

• **ABOVE RIGHT**
A 12-coach commuter-train of the Kowloon-Canton Railway (KCR) near Fanling, NT in 1996 is externally similar to MTR units. Internally, however, it is far more comfortable, with higher seating capacity on transverse seats.

• **RIGHT**
In Hong Kong's New Territories (NT) Light-Rail Transit (LRT) Car 1022 is pictured at Yau Oi on route 720 to Tin Shui Wai in 1996. Note the 910 mm high platforms provided where there is street running.

TUEN MUN LIGHT-RAIL TRANSIT (LRT) CAR	
Date	1988
Builders	Mechanical: Cars 1001–70 Comeng, Australia. Cars 1071–90 Kawaski Heavy Industrial, Japan. Cars 1201–10 Duewag, Germany (bogies) Electrical: Thyristor Control, Siemens, Propulsion, AEG, Germany
Operator	Kowloon Canton Railway Company
Gauge	1,435 mm
Catenary voltage	d.c. 750 volt
Overall length	19.4 m (63 ft 8 in)
Weight in working order	27.444 tonnes
Rating	390 kW (523 hp)
Maximum service speed	80 kph

The fleet has two special vehicles, Nos.
28 and 128, used for tourist services
such as the daily Dim Sum tours. These
also have new bodies, albeit designed, by
the addition of brass fittings, to look old-
fashioned. All service-cars carry
advertising livery. It provides more than 10
per cent of the company's total revenue.

Apart from the double-deck cars
tramway, there are three public rail
systems in the territory.

KOWLOON – CANTON RAILWAY

The Kowloon-Canton Railway (KCR) links
the territory with Canton, the capital of
Canton Province of China.

Construction of the 34 km (21 mile)
long British section between Tsimshatsui
at the tip of Kowloon and Lo Wu on the
Sino-British border in the NT began in
1905. The line was opened on 1 October
1910. The whole 179 km (111 miles)
was opened on 5 August 1911.

From 14 October 1949 to 4 April
1979 there were no through-passenger
services except for infrequent, secret
visits by Chinese leaders. Services
terminated either side of the border. In
the British sector, diesels replaced steam
for all traffic, but electrification and
modernization, completed on 15 July
1983, saw the introduction of electric
multiply units (EMUs) for passenger work.

MASS TRANSIT RAILWAY (MTR)

The first section of the Mass Transit
Railway (MTR) linking the island and
Kowloon by a submerged-tube tunnel
opened in 1979. It is 15 km (9.3 miles)
long and largely underground. A 10.8 km
(6.7 mile) branch goes to the NT
industrial town of Tsuen Wan. The units
were supplied by Metro-Cammell of
Britain. They operate on an overhead-
line current of 1,500 d.c. and are

● **LEFT**
In 1996, a Mass
Transit Railway
(MTR) train speeds
along one of the few
open sections. This
is on the Tsuen-Wan
line serving this
industrial centre in
the New Territories
(NT).

designed for maximum loading, their
seating being lengthwise down the sides
only. A four-car set can carry 3,000
people of whom only 400 can be seated.

TUEN MUN LIGHT-RAIL TRANSIT (LRT)

The territory's population explosion
transformed the rural NT. New towns
have been built and modern public
transport is essential. The history is
complex but the result is the Tuen Mun

Light-Rail Transit (LRT), a 31.75 km
(19.7 mile) network operated by single-
ended cars sometimes paired in multiple.
The 1201 Series are called "drones",
because they are powered but do not
have full driving capability. The first phase
– 23 km (14 miles) between Tuen Mun
in Castle Peak Valley and Yuen Long –
was opened on 18 August 1988. The
system is run by the Kowloon-Canton
Railway Corporation (KCRC).

● **LEFT**
Hong Kong
Tramways tram
No. 90 en route in
1991. Such sections
of street running
have much delayed
trams in frequently
congested traffic.

AUSTRALASIA

With the coming of the 1950s, the writing was on the wall for those fiery steeds that had served railways for more than a century: growling tin boxes on wheels were on the horizon. Steam locomotives were still built for Australian Railways for a few more years, however. Class BB13 1/4, No. 1089 was the last for Queensland in 1958. These final steamers, still needed by the community to overcome the problems created by the years of World War II, had very short lives.

● DIESEL-ELECTRICS

With the arrival of diesel-electrics, much individuality disappeared from the railway systems as they began to buy what were basically standard overseas designs, just like those in the automotive trade. These designs were modified to suit local gauge, track and climatic conditions, but between systems they varied by little more than colour schemes. A few steam-builders tried to enter the field. Beyer Peacock with Metropolitan Vickers of Manchester produced 48 2-Do-2 locomotives for Western Australia Railways (WAR) in 1954, this arrangement giving a lightweight distribution over the track. With a few

● **ABOVE**
Tasmania, with a sudden rise in load sizes, had to obtain more powerful locomotives. The Z Class at 1,850 hp doubled the power of existing main-liners. These four Co-Co units entered traffic in 1972 and were a development of the Western Australian Railways (WAR) R Class. They were built locally under licence to English Electric and were followed by even more powerful units. The example's yellow colour scheme was intended to give better visibility at level crossings.

● **ABOVE RIGHT**
J & A Brown's 2-8-0 locomotive No. 23 was built at the Great Central Railway's Gorton Works in 1918. It is pictured hauling coal out of Sockrington en route to Port Waratah.

● **BELOW**
An Australian heavy-hauled diesel-electric locomotive.

exceptions, the market soon rationalized itself to four main brands, mostly built under local licence – English Electric, Alco, General Motors-EMD (EMD) and General Motors of America (GM).

● FIRST MAIN-LINE DIESEL ELECTRICS

The first main-line diesel-electrics to go into service in Australia were 32 V Class Bo-Bos supplied by English Electric in Britain to the tiny island-state of Tasmania, which had joined the Australian Commonwealth in 1901. These were hood units with a cab at one end. With major water problems on the long desert run over the Nullabor Plain in South and Western Australia, Commonwealth Railways (CR) soon followed with 11 A1A-A1A GM units built under licence by the then-local firm of Clyde Engineering in 1951. These were single-ended, full-width units with a streamlined cab. At the same time, New South Wales (NSW) Railways imported

● **RIGHT**
New South Wales
(NSW) Railways, to
try to revive ever-
decreasing country-
passenger traffic,
took the British
high-speed train
(HST) design and
modified it for local
conditions. The
Paxman engines
were retained but
stainless-steel
construction was
used for the trains.
The 19 Bo-Bo units
of 2,000 hp were
geared for 160 kph
running. Here, a
northbound XPT
crosses Boanbee
Creek Bridge on the
north coast in 1990,
about nine years
after the first XPT
train entered
service.

40 A1A-A1A hood units, the 40 Class, from Alco in Canada. Overseas use of Bo-Bo units was common but Australia systems chose six-wheel bogies because of load limitations on the lighter track. From then on, the replacement of steam was rapid. NSW continued to favour Alco units, built locally, until the collapse of Alco in America in the late-1970s.

● **STATES SELECT BUILDERS**
Victoria soon became a GM state. Tasmania chose English Electric; South

Australia, a mix of Alco and English Electric; Commonwealth Railways, GM; Western Australia GM and Queensland a mix of English Electric and GM. Because American designs eventually outnumbered the others and English Electric units were incompatible with the American, the building of EE locomotives in Australia ceased in 1976.

One local builder made an impact on the market, producing Bo-Bo diesel-hydraulic locomotives – Walkers Ltd of Maryborough, near Brisbane,

Queensland: Emu Bay Railway bought four main-line units in 1963 and another seven in 1970; Queensland Railways (QR) bought 73 for shunting in 1968; the NSW Railways 50 in 1970 and WAR five in 1971. With the railways abandoning anything but block-loads, these shunters had a very short life as such. However, still being serviceable, most were sold off, and many were eventually converted to 2 ft gauge and put into service on the extensive Queensland sugar cane networks.

● **RIGHT**
Commonwealth Railways (CR) followed the
WAR lead with its traffic increasing, in
breaking the then 2,000-hp barrier. It ordered
17 3,000 hp CL Class locomotives in 1970.
Following earlier policy, CR stayed with GM-
EMD products. CR, unlike WAR, ordered a
full-width streamlined body. Here, CL31 leads
a mix of other classes on a heavy ore-train at
Cockburn, south-west of Broken Hill, South
Australia, in 1988. By then, CR had become
Australia's National and swallowed the
railways of South Australia and Tasmania.

● LEFT
A State Railways
standard Class 2-8-2T
engine, No. 26,
pictured on the South
Maitland Railway.
Made by Beyer
Peacock, these
engines were nick-
named "Bobtails".

● BELOW
An advertisement by the Vulcan Foundry,
showing one of the 60 J Class 2-8-0s supplied
to Victorian Government Railways.

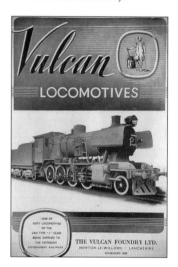

As to the trackwork in various states, not until 1987 did governmental lines consider anything more powerful than 2,000 hp. That year, WAR ventured into more power with 25 L Class Co-Co GM hood units, probably influenced by the private iron-ore lines in Western Australia, where superpower and record loads were seen as early as 1965. Since then, 4,000 hp has been reached on governmental lines with NSW obtaining 31 Co-Co units from GM-EMD in Canada, the 90 Class. The iron-ore lines are still ahead, with 29 GE Dash 438-hp locomotives having been imported from the Erie Railroad, USA.

Electrification did not advance far in most states. Queensland, however, with its tremendous mineral traffic, went into it in a big way. Since 1986 about 186 locomotives of the Bo-Bo-Bo wheel arrangement have entered traffic. This arrangement is unusual for Australia. These are all of 3,890 hp. Many have Locotrol transmitters, allowing trains to be run with several locomotives leading and several in the middle of loads. Loads often exceed 10,000 tonnes.

● NEW ZEALAND'S EXPERIENCE
New Zealand has passed through a similar period. It started with three

English Electric classes from 1952. These included one of the unusual wheel arrangement of 2-Co-Co-2, the Df Class, again a matter of distributing weight. However, GM gained the upper hand here also, in 1955, with the introduction

● LEFT
Coal is one of the main commodities handled by New South Wales (NSW) Railways. Two 4-8-4+4-8-4 (AD) 60 Class Garratts roar through Cockle Creek with a bulkload in 1970.

of 146 Da Class A1A-A1A units. Most locomotives being imported, New Zealand shopped around. In 1968, Mitsubishi, Japan, supplied 64 Bo-Bo-Bo diesel-electrics to dieselize South Island.

With more power needed on North Island, 1972 saw the introduction of 49 Dx Class Co-Co units from GE. At 2,600

hp, three were large units for the 3 ft 6 in gauge. In 1993 work started on upgrading these units to 3,200 hp as the Dxr Class. New Zealand Railways has now been privatized, and sold to America's Wisconsin Central Railway (WCR), which has turned it into a progressive, profitable enterprise.

● **PRIVATIZATION**

The announcement of the intended sale of the National Rail (NR) freight system left an uncertain future for 120 NR Class, 4,000 hp Co-Cos recently ordered from GM and for their builders Goninan & Co, which delivered the first of these powerful locomotives.

STATE RAILWAY
AUTHORITY, NEW
SOUTH WALES (NSW)
CLASS 48

Date	1959
Builders	Alco/Goodwin/GE/AEI
Client	NSW State Railway
Driving wheels	Co-Co
Total weight	75 tonnes
Rated power	708 kW
Maximum speed	120 kph

● **LEFT**
In South Australia a 48 Class Alco locomotive, No. 872, works a goods-train at Minnipa on the isolated narrow-gauge Port Lincoln Division, Eyre Peninsula.

AUSTRALIAN LIGHT RAIL AND METRO

Australia is one of the most urbanized countries in the world, with 70 per cent of its population living in towns and cities. The cites are concentrated in the coastal regions in the east and south. Thi is where the major cities – Sydney (New South Wales), Melbourne (Victoria), Brisbane (Queensland) and Adelaide (South Australia) – have developed. An exception is on the other side of the continent, Perth (Western Australia).

● TRAMWAYS NOT METROS

None of Australia's major cities has a dedicated metro system, although the electrified urban-rail networks in both Melbourne and Sydney fulfil a similar role to some extent, with city-centre underground loops linked to suburban lines.

● **RIGHT**
Adelaide Tram
No. 376 dates from
1929. It is pictured on
the street track
through the shopping
centre at Glenelg
seaside suburb. The
pantograph is part of
recent modernization.

Tramways appeared in 13 Australian towns and cities in the late 19th and early 20th centuries. After World War II, uneconomic tramways in smaller towns were replaced by buses. In the 1950s and 1960s, all major cities apart from Melbourne followed the British trend to wholesale tramway abandonment. In Adelaide, one tram route has survived, the reserved track linking the city centre with Glenelg seaside suburb. This is

operated by light modernized trams of 1929 vintage. Proposals for a new light-rail line in Adelaide were superseded by the project for the O-Bahn guided busway, opened in 1983. Debate continues about new rolling stock for the Glenelg line and its extension across the city centre to northern Adelaide.

● SOUTHERN HEMISPHERE'S LARGEST TRAMWAY

Melbourne's 238km (148 mile) tramway is the largest in the Southern Hemisphere. It has seen significant expansion in recent years as well as new rolling stock to replace most of the

MELBOURNE CLASS Z TRAM

Date	1974–7
Builders	Comeng/ASEA
Client	Melbourne Tram
Gauge	1,435 mm
Power supply	600 volt d.c.
Bogie arrangement	Bo-Bo with four 52 kW motors
Maximum speed	70 kph

● **LEFT**
Melbourne's Z Class trams were the first
modern cars to enter service in quantity. Tram
No. 110 is seen on the recent extension to
Latrobe University.

● **RIGHT**
A prototype double-deck train for Victorian Railways, destined to operate on Melbourne's suburban system, runs into Heatherdale Station in the eastern suburbs.

● **BELOW**
Bourke Street in Melbourne shows articulated-trams on light-rail service operating through a pedestrianized area.

● **BOTTOM**
"Toast-rack" Tram No. 17 returns to the depot after private-hire duty on this heritage tramway running through the streets of Bendigo (formerly Sandhurst) in Victoria State. Bendigo was a Gold Rush town, founded in 1851.

traditional centre-entrance bogie trams. However, some of these are being refurbished for further use, including those on the City Circle line, which offers free travel around the central area. Changes from trolley-pole to pantograph current-collection and to one-man operation across the system are nearing completion. Most routes use modern bogie-trams and articulated-cars. The latest extensions and the recent conversion of rail lines to the St Kilda and Port Melbourne districts are built to light-rail standards.

In Sydney, a new tramline has been constructed to link the central railway station with the Darling Harbour redevelopment district. This was partly privately financed and is worked by Australia's first low-floor trams, the articulated Variotram design from ADtranz. Darling Harbour is also the site of a privately owned monorail offering a tourist link to the city centre's edge.

● **MUSEUM MOVEMENT**
The tramway-museum movement is well established in Australia. The operations in Adelaide (St Kilda), Ballarat in south-central Victoria and Sydney (Loftus) include alignments in or beside the public highway. In Bendigo, central Victoria, the tramway museum runs a daily heritage service carrying passengers between tourist attractions using street track through the town centre.

SOUTHERN AFRICA

Steam-locomotive deliveries to the Republic of South Africa (Union of South Africa, 1910–61) continued until the late 1960s.

● SOUTH AFRICA'S KAROO DESERT

The most dramatic post-World War II design was the 90 Class 25 condensing 4-8-4s of 1953. These were based on the 15F Class 4-8-2s, with large boilers, cast-steel integrated bed-frames and roller bearings throughout. Also built were 50 condensing engines classified 25NC.

The condensers, used for services on the main line through the arid Karoo desert of Cape Province, could save up to 85 per cent of their water consumption, a far cry from the early days when water had to be taken into the desert by train. The condensers had no conventional exhaust beat, only the whine of turbine-driven fans, which exhausted hot gases from the smokebox. The long banks of condensing elements in the engine's tender made the locomotives 33 m (108 ft) long.

● LAST GREAT GARRATTS

The next year, 25 GO Class 4-8-2+4-8-4 Garratts were delivered from Henschel of Germany as a lighter variation on the GMA type. The Republic's last Garratts were for the 2 ft gauge lines delivered in 1967–68, built by Hunslet Taylor, of Alberton, SA. These were the last Garratt

SAR CONDENSER 25 NC CLASS 4-8-4	
Date	1953
Builder	Henschel, Germany; North British, Glasgow, Scotland
Client	South African Railways (SAR)
Gauge	3 ft 6 in
Driving wheels	5 ft
Capacity	Cylinders 24 x 28 in
Total weight in full working order	234 tons

● **ABOVE**
South Africa's Red Devil 4-8-4 represented an attempt to improve steam-locomotive potential in the face of the avowed policy to eliminate steam-traction.

● **LEFT**
Painted in Imperial Brown, to match the coaching stock, Locomotive No. A371 glints in the sun at Figtree, south-west of Bulawayo, Zimbabwe (formerly Rhodesia), in 1993.

locomotives built. In contrast with the foregoing designs, a batch of 100 heavy-duty 0-8-0 shunting-locomotives was delivered from Krupp in 1952–53.

● **RAPID MODERNIZATION**
Motive-power modernization occurred as rapidly in South Africa as it had in so many other countries. The Republic was the preferred location for steam operations throughout the 1970s and most of the 1980s, attracting huge numbers of enthusiasts to see big steam locomotives in glorious landscape with idyllic weather conditions.

It had been hoped that the 25 NC 4-8-4s would be retained in Cape Province on the main line between De Aar, an important railway junction of main lines from Cape Town, Port Elizabeth and Kimberley, the world's diamond centre. The engines were relatively new and performing excellently. This was not to be and the changeover from steam has coincided with a partial rundown of the

railway itself. On a happier note, South Africa retains enough steam operations to entice the visitor. These include some of the world's last Pacific 4-6-2s, active in industrial service on the goldfields.

● **BELOW**
A Landau Colliery Class 12A 4-8-2 heads a loaded train from the colliery to the connection with the South African Railway (SAR) main line. Landau, in common with many Transvaal collieries, used locomotives of main-line proportions. The 12As hauled 900 ton-trains over the steeply graded route.

● SOUTH AFRICA AND NAMIBIA

South Africa has abundant cheap coal but no oil, so electrification was the preferred form of motive power. An early candidate was predictably the suburban service around Johannesburg, in Transvaal, Africa's largest city south of Cairo, and in the Witwatersrand, the world's richest goldfields, and Cape Town, South Africa's legislative capital and the first white settlement in southern Africa (1652). The lines of Namibia (formerly South West Africa) were the first to be dieselized, as early as the late 1950s, because of the waterless terrain. Prevalent among South Africa's diesel fleet are the D34.400 Class/35.200 Class of diesel-electric Co-Cos. Among electric locomotives are Class 6E1 Bo-Bos. Unlike the previous steam fleet, the nation's diesels and electrics are being built mainly in South Africa.

Vast tonnages are being conveyed compared with loads in steam days. The main freight line in Cape Province is the 865 km (537 mile) route from the Iron

● ABOVE
A former EAR Governor Class Garratt 4-8-2+2-8-4, with an 11-ton axleloading, plies across the frail line between Voi, the Kenyan railway junction on the Mombasa-Nairobi line, and Moshi, the Tanganyikan town on the slopes of Mount Kilimanjaro. This engine, No. 6024, is the Sir James Hayes-Sadler. The Governors, named after British colonial governors, comprised a class of 29 locomotives, all built in 1954, of which 12 were made under licence from Beyer Peacock, by Franco-Belge in Paris.

● BELOW
A Zambian freight-train arriving at the Victoria Falls on the Zambezi River at the Zimbabwe-Zambia border.

and Steel Corporation's mine at Sishen in Griqualand West to Saldanha on the coast north of Cape Town. This section is electrified on a 50 kV, single-phase a.c. system, and 9E Class Co-Co locomotives with an output of 5,070 hp haul trains up to 2.4 km (1½ miles) long. A motorcycle is carried on the leading locomotive for use when inspection of the train is needed.

● PROGRESS IN ZIMBABWE

In neighbouring Zimbabwe, steam-traction continued until the late 1950s when the last of the huge 20th Class 4-8-2+2-8-4 Garratts was delivered. Since then, steady progress towards diesel-electrics of both Bo-Bo and Co-Co types has been made. These mixed with the steam fleet through the 1980s. It was thought this situation would continue. By 1996, however, all but a handful of the steamers had been withdrawn. Almost all of Zimbabwe's steam fleet over its last 20 years of operation were of the Garratt type.

● DRAMATIC END IN EAST AFRICA

A similar situation occurred over the territories covered by the former East African Railway Corporation (EARC). Steam ended dramatically with the 34

● ABOVE
In Tanzania, an EAR Class 31 Tribal 2-8-2 heads away from Tabora, a modern town founded in 1820 by Arabs. These engines have an 11-ton axleloading for the lightly graded lines of East Africa and were built by the Vulcan Foundry, Lancashire, England, in the mid-1950s. The class is named after East African tribes. This engine is No. 3129, Kakwa.

MOUNTAIN CLASS GARRATT

Date	1955
Builder	Beyer Peacock, Manchester, England
Client	East African Railways (EAR)
Gauge	Metre
Driving wheels	4 ft 6 in
Capacity	4 cylinders 20½ x 28 in
Total weight in full working order	222 tons
Tractive effort	83,350 lb

● LEFT
A mighty Class 59 4-8-2+2-8-4 Garratt climbs the steep coastal escarpment above Mombasa on the Indian Ocean at the start of its 535 km (332 mile) journey to Nairobi, the Kenyan capital. During this steeply graded journey, the Mountain Class engines take 1,200 ton trains and climb almost one mile in altitude, Nairobi being on a plateau 1,500 m (5,000 ft) above sea level. The engine shown is No. 5933, Mount Suswa.

Mountain Class 4-8-2+2-8-4 Garratts of 1955. These 252 oilfired giants with a 21-ton axleloading worked from the Mombasa-Nairobi line. They were 32 m (104 ft) long and had a boiler of 7 ft 6 in diameter, more than twice the width of the tack gauge, and an 83,350 lb tractive effort. Incredible though this is for metre-gauge operation, a 372-ton 4-8-4+4-8-4 locomotive was proposed with a 25-ton axle loading but the attraction of diesel-electrics prevented these Garratts from being built. Delivery of Tribal 2-8-2/2-8-4 Types continued until the mid-1950s when all-out dieselization began across the then British-controlled territories of Kenya, Uganda and Tanganyika.

● STEP TOWARDS PAN-AFRICAN
NETWORK
One of the most dramatic events in Africa was the Tanzania-Zambia Railway – known as TAZARA and TANZAM – built in the 1960s to a 1,067 mm gauge. With a 1,860 km (1,155 mile) route length the line runs from Dar es Salaam to Kapiri Mposhi in the Zambian Copperbelt, north of the Zambian capital Lusaka. China provided the finance,

technical support and Bo-Bo diesel-hydraulics. This route serves export and import traffic between the Indian Ocean and Botswana, Malawi, Zaire, Zambia and Zimbabwe. The vision's potential has not been reached because of endemic economic and political problems but the railway is a tangible step towards the Pan-African railway network the continent so desperately needs.

● BELOW
In 1953–4, Beyer Peacock, of Manchester, England, delivered very British-looking locomotives to the then Southern Rhodesia (at that time part of the central African Federation with Northern Rhodesia and Nyasaland). One of them, a Rhodesian Railways 14A Class 2-6-2+2-6-2 Beyer Garratt, pauses in Matabeleland for refreshment at Balla Balla on its way from West Nicholson to Bulawayo.

NORTHERN AFRICA

Desert condition in Algeria made dieselization inevitable, and steam disappeared in favour of American diesels in the 1950s. Electrification had begun in 1932 on iron-ore lines with about 40 electric-locomotives active.

● NORTH AFRICA – ELECTRIFICATION AND DIESELIZATION

In Morocco (El Maghreb el Aqua, the "Far West"), electrification began as early as 1927. Today, 50 per cent of the nation's railways are electrified. The system is modern, having overhead 3 kV d.c. Non-electrified sections are all diesel-operated.

Tunisia operates an intensive suburban service from Tunis, the capital, on standard and metre gauges. The country has a long-term statutory commitment to reopen lines and build new lines of metre and standard gauge.

Egyptian railways have been dieselized during the past 20 years. Freight has declined but passenger traffic is healthy. Investment in double-tracking, reopening of abandoned lines and the building of new lines is all taking place. About 350

● **ABOVE**
Trams at Helwân, the town and baths on the Nile in Lower Egypt, opposite the ruins of Memphis.

● **RIGHT**
A Class 500 4-8-2 of Sudan Railways, one of 42 engines built in the 1950s by North British of Glasgow, Scotland. Although 3 ft 6 in gauge, they have a 35,940 lb tractive effort, almost identical with that of an LMS Stanier 8F 2-8-0. The engine is pictured heading across the line between Kosti, in the Blue Nile Province, south of Khartoum, and Khana.

● **BELOW**
The Location Locomotive Works of Ghana Railways displays a contrast of diesel-electrics.

diesel-locomotives are on the books of Egyptian State Railways (ESR).

The 42 oilfired Class 500 4-8-2s supplied to Sudan by North British works, Glasgow, Scotland, were that builder's last big steam order and also the last placed by Sudan Railways.

Dieselization of main-line trains began in 1959 with a class of English Electric Co-Cos, which bear a striking resemblance to British Rail's Peaks. No sections are electrified. Sudan Railways is mainly diesel-operated but does use steam for some line work, particularly in the south with Class 500s and lightly axleloaded Pacifics and Mikados.

● **RIGHT**
An Algerian National Railways (SNCFA) 3 kV d.c. Co-Co electric-locomotive. These operate over a 256 km (159 mile) route between Tèbessa, near the Algerian-Tunisian border, and 'Annaba on the Mediterranean Sea.

● **BOTTOM LEFT**
An industrial diesel working in Ghana, West Africa. Before independence in 1957, the territory was known as Gold Coast.

● **BOTTOM RIGHT**
A Co-Co English Electric diesel of Sudan Railways waits to leave Khartoum with the 15.50 hrs freight-train to Sennar Junction between the White Nile and the Blue Nile in 1981.

ALGERIAN RAILWAYS CO-CO ELECTRIC

Date	1972
Builders	Mechanical: LEW Electrical: Skoda
Client	Algerian National Railways (Société Nationale des Chemins de Fers Algériens) (SNCFA)
Gauge	Standard
Line current	3 kV d.c.
Rated output	2,700 hp
Length	18,640 mm
Weight	130 tons

● **WEST AFRICA – OBLIVION AND WILLPOWER**

Sierra Leone is the largest, most-populated country to have lost its railways altogether. The system comprised 515 km (320 route miles). As recently as 1955, 4-8-2+2-8-4 Garratt locomotives were supplied by Beyer Peacock of Manchester, England. In later years, the system also received diesel-hydraulics. After Sierra Leone's independence from Britain in 1961, the railway fell rapidly into oblivion.

The same could have happened in Ghana but a national will to retain the railway against massive economic and operational odds prevailed and the system is fighting back from the brink of ruin. All the once-elegant steam locomotives have vanished, to feed Ghana's large steel plant at the seaport town of Tema. Diesel locomotives operate all services. Some Ghana Railways engineers feel that the simplicity of steam locomotives was better-suited to Ghanaian conditions than more complex diesel-electrics. This sentiment is often expressed in developing countries.

West Africa's largest railway network was in Nigeria. The plenitude of oil, however, meant massive competition from road transport. This greatly eroded the railway's premier place. In the 1980s, the system was down to only 50 operable main-line diesels. As in Ghana, the railway is making a comeback with foreign aid.

WORLD STEAM SURVIVORS

It could have been little realized by Richard Trevithick in 1804 that the pristine machine crawling out of the Pen-y-Darren Ironworks in South Wales would have such enormous an effect worldwide or that steam locomotives would still be active 200 years later.

● PRESERVATION AND CONSERVATION – CHINA'S ROLE

So significant was the steam locomotive to the development of world transport, industry and commerce, that railways were laid almost everywhere. From the 1850s, when railways became widely established, until 1950, the steam locomotive was largely unchallenged as the dominant form of transportation. The very depth of the heritage means there are far more locomotives still in existence than is popularly believed.

Over the past few decades, many countries have come to realize the attraction of steam-railways and now run their own tourist-trains. These, combined with the enormous preservation effort, particularly in Britain, America, Europe and Australasia, ensure that steam is kept alive.

● ABOVE
Locomotive No. 8 is a 0-8-0 tender-tank of 1927 built by Orenstein & Koppel. This veteran works at the Meritjan sugar mill, Kediri, Java, Indonesia, and burns bagasse, that is the pulp remaining after extraction of juice from sugar cane or similar plants.

● BELOW
An oilburning 5 ft 6 in gauge, inside-cylinder 0-6-0 of Pakistan Railways heads a special passenger-train in Punjab.

● LEFT
The Hawaii Philippine Co.'s 3 ft gauge locomotives on the Philippine island of Negros are known as "Dragons". Dragon No. 6, a Baldwin 0-6-0 of 1920, is pictured trundling a rake of sugar-cane empties back into the fields.

● INDIA AND PAKISTAN

In January 1997, an expedition to India found an incredible list of types including former Great Indian Peninsular Railway (GIPR) Ghat bankers, both 2-8-4Ts and 0-8-4Ts; British-built XE 2-8-2s of 1928 and a Kitson Pacific – all of 5 ft 6 in gauge. On the metre gauge, there were two F Class 0-6-0s, a type dating back to 1874, and two Sharp, Stewart 2-4-0s of 1873, contrasted with more recent metre-gauge classics like the last of the MacArthur 2-8-2s of World War II. On the 2 ft gauge, a Bagnall 0-4-0ST was operating at a brickworks on a system, which could have existed in rural Wales at the dawn of the Industrial Revolution.

● SOUTHERN AFRICA AND SOUTH-EAST ASIA

Even great steam countries of yesteryear like South Africa and Rhodesia (now Zimbabwe) still offer many lingering survivors, especially in industrial environments. It is still possible to make rewarding visits to these and other African countries including Mozambique and Sudan.

In south-east Asia, Java's sugar plantations offer a fabulous variety of battered, multi-hued veterans of continental European, British and American origin. The American engines on the Philippine island of Negros remain active albeit in dwindling numbers. Main-line steam continues in Vietnam and North Korea.

● EASTERN EUROPE, THE CIS AND LATIN AMERICA

Industrial engines survive in Eastern Europe and in the former Yugoslavia. There are also many discoveries to be made in Russia where engines are known to exist as stationary boilers, carriage-

● RIGHT
A Rhodesian Railways 14A Class 2-6-2+2-6-2 Garratt with a freight-train romps along the main line north of Bulawayo, Zimbabwe's main industrial centre, in Matabeleland. These light Garratts were for secondary-route operation and have an axleload of only 13¼ tons. The type was delivered from Beyer Peacock, of Manchester, England, in 1953–4.

RHODESIAN RAILWAYS A CLASS 14A GARRATT	
Date	1953
Builder	Beyer Peacock, Manchester, England
Client	Rhodesian Railways
Gauge	3 ft 6 in
Driving wheels	4 ft
Capacity	4 cylinders 16 x 24 in
Total weight in full working order	132 tons

● LEFT
The United States Army Transportation Corps (USATC) 0-6-0Ts of World War II were one of the most famous military designs of the 20th century and served in many countries. All came from three American builders – H. K. Porter, Vulcan Works and Davenport Works. Here, one of the examples that passed to Greece is pictured shunting at Salonika, the Macedonian port.

heaters, shunters or in the industrial environment with some isolated main-line working, too.

As indicated in preceding sections, pockets of steam survive throughout Latin America. Cuba is the last bastion of classic American locomotives, few of which are more recent than the 1920s. The island has become one of the world's great steam attractions — a working museum to be admired and enjoyed.

Genuine working-steam has disappeared from Western Europe, North America, Australia, New Zealand, Japan and most of the Middle East but there is still much to see, research and enjoy. It will be many more years before the last fires will be dropped and man's most animated and influential creation passes in to extinction.

● BELOW
A Pakistan Railways 5 ft 6 in gauge AWD Mikado, one of the most important locomotive classes on the Indian subcontinent in post-World War II years.

● ABOVE
The last Uruguayan B Class 2-6-0 tank, attached to a six-wheeled, outside-framed tender. She was built by Beyer Peacock, of Manchester, England, in 1889.

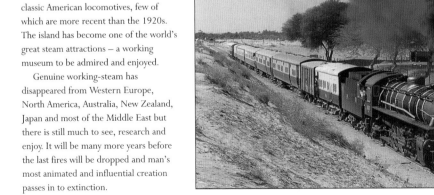

Great Railway
Journeys
of the World

MAX WADE-MATTHEWS

Great Journeys of the West

This section of the book will take the reader from the thrilling 3,200 km (2,000 mile) trip from Chicago to Oakland in North America to the 27 km (17 mile) jaunt back in time between Bedford and Bletchley in rural Bedfordshire, England. We will ascend the high mountains of Peru and Switzerland; and descend under the English Channel as we travel through one of the wonders of the modern world – the Channel Tunnel.

Rail journeys for pleasure began in the late nineteenth century with growing prosperity and the adoption of the workers' holiday. In many parts of Europe and America are to be found towns that came into prominence in the latter half of the nineteenth century for the simple reason that they had the good fortune to find themselves connected to the growing railway network. Many of the journeys detailed in this section are still in operation; others, however, are now part of history and can only be travelled in the pages of a book such as this.

● OPPOSITE
A summer view of the train from the Look-out in
Agawa Canyon, Ontario, Canada.

● ABOVE
Superliners in Amtrak's Chicago coach yard.

TORONTO TO VANCOUVER

Only one transcontinental train journey for passengers is still operating across Canada, over a length of 4,467 km (2,776 miles). This is from Toronto to Vancouver by the Canadian National route under the auspices of the VIA Rail Corporation.

The train runs three times a week as the Canadian, a name taken over from Canadian Pacific, which inaugurated it in 1954 with the first streamlined sleeper train in Canada. Three days and three nights are spent by the Canadian on its journey, which is a mixture of tour land-cruise and point-to-point transportation. Passengers in the former category pay quite large sums for superior accommodation and brilliantly restored public rooms and diner.

Although transcontinental trains used to run from Montreal, the starting-point

for the journey today is Toronto, and the route lies by way of Capreol (close to Sudbury, Ontario), then across hundreds of kilometres of pre-Cambrian shield to Sioux Lookout, later winding through the Manitoba Lake District to Winnipeg, 1,958 km (1,217 miles) from Toronto. After a stop of one hour, the Canadian heads west across rolling prairies to Saskatoon, Saskatchewan, and Edmonton, Alberta, before climbing into

● **TOP**
An exterior view of Vancouver's Pacific Central railway station.

● **ABOVE LEFT**
An interior view of one of the Canadian's domed park cars. From these seats, passengers can drink in the full beauty of the diverse Canadian countryside.

● **LEFT**
VIA's Canadian on the tracks of the Canadian Pacific between Montreal and Vancouver.

● LEFT
The east-bound Canadian, *en route* from Vancouver to Toronto, takes a break at Banff, Alberta.

● BELOW
The concourse of Toronto's Union Station.

the foothills of the Rocky Mountains.

Jasper is high amid these mountains, and here the train halts for 70 minutes while some of the cars are attached to the Skeena, which has come from Edmonton on its way to the Pacific at Prince Rupert. The main part of the Canadian carries on through the Rockies, going over Yellow Head Pass and down to Kamloops. The final part of the journey is beside the Fraser River (with the tracks of the Canadian Pacific Railway on the opposite bank) down to Vancouver, which is reached at 08.30 Pacific Time on the third morning after leaving Toronto. Inevitably some of the best scenery is passed at night, but the high points of the Rockies are viewed in daylight. At one time, Canada had three transcontinental

routes, which it could not support economically. These came down to two when Canadian National was formed from earlier private systems (Grand Trunk, Canadian Northern and Grand Trunk Western). As recently as 1967 there were four transcontinental trains each day, all from Montreal.

While air competition hurt these trains, the greatest damage was done by the completion of the Trans-Canada highway in 1968, leading to the reduction in service to just one train thrice weekly. However, thanks to support from tour operators in the USA and particularly Britain and Germany, the Canadian now seems profitable in its new dual role as tour train and short-haul passenger service. For tour passengers, meals in the refurbished diner, use of the vista domes, lounges and sleeping cars newly equipped with showers, are included in the fare.

● ABOVE LEFT
The Canadian leaves Montreal's Windsor Station on the first part of its journey across the Canadian continent.

● LEFT
The Canadian winds its way through a background of autumnal colour.

INFORMATION BOX

Termini	Toronto and Vancouver
Country	Canada
Distance	4,467 km (2,776 miles)
Date of opening	1885

SAULT SAINTE MARIE TO HEARST

Running from south to north across Ontario, the Algoma Central & Hudson Bay Railway (ACR) is a private company dating from 1899. The starting-point is Sault Sainte Marie (known as the Soo) at the eastern end of Lake Superior, the world's largest lake. Its main line, 476 km (296 miles) long, ends at Hearst, still more than 240 km (150 miles) from the sub-Arctic bay. It passes through mountains that are the highest in Canada

● RIGHT
Part of the train trip is by the shore of the mighty Montreal River.

INFORMATION BOX

Termini	Sault Sainte Marie and Hearst
Country	Canada
Distance	476 km (296 miles)
Date of opening	1899

east of the Rockies. The daily passenger-train threads its way through a landscape of canyons, forests, lakes and fast-flowing rivers. On spring, summer and autumn weekends, this is the longest and busiest passenger-train on the North American continent.

The great train runs as an excursion because so many people want to visit Agawa Canyon in the heart of Algoma Country. While about three cars continue to Hearst, another 18 to 20, including the restaurant cars and one diesel

locomotive, are uncoupled and stay on the floor of the canyon for about two hours. Hikers and picnickers can enjoy the area until the southbound train from Hearst arrives to join up the heavy load, hook on the waiting diesel and run back to the Soo, 183 km (114 miles) to the south. Originally the railway was built for iron-ore traffic coming from the Helen Mine near Michipicetin, to which a branch was extended, while the main route to Hearst sought to carry general freight, especially lumber.

● LEFT
During the autumn, Algoma Central County is ablaze with colour. Here is an autumnal shot of the Agawa Canyon train tour crossing the Montreal River by a trestle bridge.

● RIGHT
The train snakes
through the
autumnal beauty of
the Agawa Canyon.

● BELOW
As well as travelling in the public coaches,
passengers can also hire their own car. Here is
one of the private cars – "Michipicoton" –
which was built by Pullman of Chicago in 1910.

● BELOW RIGHT
The train also runs in
winter, the warmth of
the coaches keeping
the ice and sub-zero
temperatures at bay.
Here we see it making
its way through the
deep snow.

spectacular trestle affords stupendous
views. There is a twisting climb to
Hubert, 461 m (1,512 ft) above sea level
and the summit of the line.

While the section to Agawa Canyon
carries holidaymakers *en masse*, the
northern part of the line numbers big
game hunters and fishermen among its
customers. In the autumn, when foliage
colours are fantastic, and moose and deer
are "in season", the train, which stops on
flag request along the way, is called the
Moose Meat Special.

The Algoma Central possesses 25
diesel locomotives painted in maroon,
cream and grey, while the passenger cars
are in a very attractive maroon.

Although it is allied to the Algoma
Steel Corporation, the railway is a
separate entity and enjoys steady
profitability. A large proportion of
Algoma Central's profit comes from its
well-advertised passenger service. It is
not unusual for 1,200 to 1,500
passengers to ride to Agawa Canyon on a
summer Sunday, paying about $30
Canadian (£14) each for the excursion.

It helps that there are no roads
competing with the railway, except at
Hawk Junction, 265 km (165 miles)
from the Soo. The line's isolation is
interrupted at two points: Franz, where
there is a junction with Canadian
Pacific's main line (now freight only), and
Oba, where the Canadian National
crosses it. Both are hamlets, and only at
Oba, a flag stop, can a change be made
for passengers when VIA's Canadian
comes through three times a week.

Great rivers are crossed on fine trestle
bridges, including those over the Goulais,
South and North Chippewa, and the
Batchewana. The biggest of these crosses
the Montreal River at Milepost 93. This

VANCOUVER TO SQUAMISH

● BELOW
Preserved ex-Canadian Pacific Royal Hudson
class locomotive No. 2860 at Squamish. This
4-6-4 locomotive was built in 1940 by the
Montreal Locomotive Works.

The route from North Vancouver to
Squamish is on the British Columbia
Railway (known as BC Rail or BCR),
which is primarily a freight railway. The
section travelled is, at 61 km (38 miles),
only a small fraction of the company's
network, which totals over 2,172 km
(1,350 miles). Passenger services are
limited to a daily service each way
between North Vancouver, Lillooet and
Prince George. The train named the
Cariboo Prospector, takes 13 ½ hours to
travel 745 km (463 miles). In addition,
there is a school train between Seton
Portage and Lillooet. In the summer
months, there are two tourist-oriented
services: a weekday service north from
Whistler and the Royal Hudson service
described here.

The BCR, which was called the Pacific
Great Eastern Railway until 1972,
connects to the Canadian National railway
(CN) and so to the rest of the Canadian
rail network at North Vancouver Junction.
There is also a connection to the
Vancouver Wharves Railway, which, as its
name implies, serves the port area.

The section of line from Squamish to
Vancouver only opened in 1956, quite a

● LEFT
The Royal Hudson
train, soon after
departure from
North Vancouver,
seen from Prospect
Point. Lions Gate
Bridge is just out of
sight to the right.

● LEFT
BCR diesels 4642+762+4615 at the north end
of Squamish yard waiting to depart on a
northbound freight. No. 4642 is a 4400 HP
General Electric DASH 9 built in 1995; 762 is a
3000 HP General Motors SD40 of 1980; 4615
is a General Electric 4000 HP DASH 8 of 1990.

INFORMATION BOX

Termini	Vancouver and Squamish
Country	Canada
Distance	61 km (38 miles)
Date of opening	1956

● **LEFT**
Shannon Falls seen from the water, a couple of miles south of Squamish.

construction of a 132 km (82 mile) electrified branch (the Tumbler subdivision) in 1983.

The Royal Hudson runs Wednesdays to Sundays from June to September and takes two hours for the northbound trip. The train is named after the class of steam locomotive used to haul it, a type which were built by the Montreal Locomotive Works in 1939 for the Canadian Pacific Railway. Hudson is the name for the locomotive's wheel arrangement, 4-6-4. The Royal prefix comes from the occasion when one of the class (No. 2850) was used to haul the royal train during a visit of King George VI and Queen Elizabeth to Canada in 1939. Upon withdrawal, 2860 became the property of the British Columbia

while after the railway reached Squamish from the north. This was because the railway's main purpose was to link the logging and mining areas with the sea, and there are port facilities at Squamish for large bulk carriers. The BCR has expanded relatively recently, with the

● **BELOW**
Royal Hudson No. 2860 passing Porteau Cove in June 1996. The road, known as the Sea to Sky Highway, runs close to the line for most of the way from Horseshoe Bay to Squamish and provides several excellent photographic opportunities.

Government, who currently lease it to BCR. In addition, BCR leases the 2-8-0 3716, built by MLW in 1912 for Canadian Pacific, as a reserve for these trains. Locomotive No. 2860 is resplendent in polished maroon and black, with a polished, unpainted metal-clad boiler and firebox, and royal crowns on each side above the cylinders.

The journey starts from BCR's North Vancouver station (depot). Adjacent to the station is the small shed used to store and maintain the steam locomotives. Across the tracks, there are extensive freight-yards and a diesel locomotive

depot. The train is made up of 12 coaches, mostly ex-CN stock of 1954, painted Tuscan Red. In the middle is an open-sided observation coach named Britannia, which was built in 1920. In June 1996 the weather was too chilly for all but the hardiest of passengers! The last vehicle is a parlour car, called Mount Cascade, which can be used on payment of around twice the normal fare.

The train leaves the station slowly, heads west and passes the freight-yards. At the end of these, it passes under the approaches to Lions Gate Bridge. This

was reputedly built with money from the Guinness brewing family to help in opening up the north shore, where they owned land. An excellent photographic location is the viewing area at Prospect Point on the Stanley Park Drive on the opposite bank, close to the bridge. The line keeps a short way from the waters of English Bay as it passes through residential areas and skirts Ambleside Beach. It then passes through the 1,280 m (4,200 ft) Horseshoe Bay tunnel, cutting off the "corner". Leaving the tunnel, the train heads north for the remainder of the journey. Just visible is the Horseshoe Bay ferry terminal, used by car ferries to Vancouver Island. Soon after this, the railway comes back down to the water's edge and rarely leaves it before reaching Squamish. Across the Sound there are views of great forests and snow-capped peaks.

The line, while curving considerably, is largely flat with only short gradients. The highest point is in Horseshoe Bay tunnel, 51 m (167 ft) above sea level, around 16 km (10 miles) out. Between North Vancouver and Squamish, there are passing-points at Brunswick, Porteau and Britannia.

A BCR track patrol vehicle passing Porteau Cove. This precedes the Royal Hudson by around five minutes to ensure that the line is free from such obstructions as fallen rocks.

downtown area, away from the main line. Squamish is home to the BCR workshops and main locomotive depot, and has a large area of sidings. It is also the home of the West Coast Railway Heritage Museum, which is by the north exit to the yards, a couple of kilometres from where the Royal Hudson stops. For those interested, there is a bookable add-on coach excursion to visit the museum during the Royal Hudson's layover.

The town of Squamish, population around 12,000, is not a tourist destination. However, it is a regional centre with a wide range of small shops and pleasant restaurants. The town is overshadowed by towering, rocky hills, those to the east being part of Garibaldi Provincial Park, the 816 m (2,677 ft) Mount Garibaldi being around 19 km (12 miles) to the north. The valley of the Cheakamus River, which drains into Howe Sound at Squamish, heads north to Whistler amid increasingly mountainous scenery.

At Porteau, the railway skirts a small bay in which some old ships have been scuttled to provide interest for divers. Porteau is also one of the best photographic locations. Eight kilometres (5 miles) further on, at Britannia Beach, there is the British Columbia Museum of Mining, at what was the largest copper producer in the British Empire. The scar on the scenery caused by the mine is visible from a considerable distance.

At Squamish, the Royal Hudson is reversed on to a siding adjacent to the

BCR Budd diesel railcar BC-33, built in 1957, at BCR's North Vancouver station soon after arrival on the southbound Cariboo Prospector.

The lighthouse at the confluence of Howe Sound and English Bay, with the skyline of downtown Vancouver in the background.

WHITEHORSE TO SKAGWAY

The White Pass and Yukon Railway has had a chequered history. That history, however, is an integral part of the story of this exciting land, just as much as that of the great Canadian Pacific, and riding this down-to-earth line is one of northern Canada's great experiences.

The 117 km (72 mile) narrow-gauge railway connects Yukon's capital, Whitehorse, to the historic port of Skagway and the coastal shipping that calls there. In doing so the line passes through the territory of Yukon, British Columbia and Alaska. It was constructed to transport thousands of gold seekers and their supplies from Skagway through the coastal mountains to the beginning of the river route to the Klondike gold fields. Work began in May 1898, and the railway's last spike was driven at Carcross on 29 July 1900, the conclusion of 26 months of blasting, chipping, shovelling and hardship suffered by construction crews whose number fluctuated from 700 to 2,000. A narrow, moss-filled

INFORMATION BOX

Termini	Whitehorse and Skagway
Country	Canada
Distance	177 km (110 miles)
Date of opening	1900

● **ABOVE LEFT**
A photograph of the interior of the passengers' parlour car.

● **LEFT**
A view of the line stretching into the horizon.

● **BELOW LEFT**
A train passing through woodland on the descent to Skagway.

ledge beside the track, marked by a stone inscription, is a mute reminder of the trudging steps of the thousands of men and women who succumbed to the lure of gold.

When the gold rush died away, the Yukon population dwindled; and during the dark days of the 1930s, the trains operated only once a week, but the steam locomotives and the rotary ploughs kept the line open. Afterwards the line was used by tourists as well as for the transportation of ore; when some of the vintage parlour cars of 1883 were still in use. They made strange bedfellows with the heavy steel mineral wagons and multiple diesel locomotives that formed the rest of the trains. Then it became a goods-only line for a period. Today, only

● **RIGHT AND FAR RIGHT**
Views of the trackside, from the cab, as the train heads north.

● **BELOW RIGHT**
The track reaches its maximum height at Log Cabin, BC.

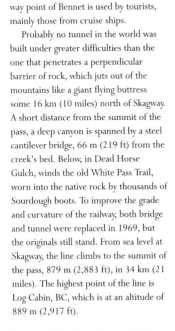

the route between Skagway and the half-way point of Bennet is used by tourists, mainly those from cruise ships.

Probably no tunnel in the world was built under greater difficulties than the one that penetrates a perpendicular barrier of rock, which juts out of the mountains like a giant flying buttress some 16 km (10 miles) north of Skagway. A short distance from the summit of the pass, a deep canyon is spanned by a steel cantilever bridge, 66 m (219 ft) from the creek's bed. Below, in Dead Horse Gulch, winds the old White Pass Trail, worn into the native rock by thousands of Sourdough boots. To improve the grade and curvature of the railway, both bridge and tunnel were replaced in 1969, but the originals still stand. From sea level at Skagway, the line climbs to the summit of the pass, 879 m (2,883 ft), in 34 km (21 miles). The highest point of the line is Log Cabin, BC, which is at an altitude of 889 m (2,917 ft).

From terminal to terminal, the journey takes about eight hours, and the views of the mountains and lakes are superb. Just 64 km (40 miles) from Skagway is a frame building called the

Bennet Eating House, where trains from both directions used to meet. Here passengers descend to sit down to a lunch, included in the ticket, of stew, beans, sourdough bread and apple pie.

THE SAN FRANCISCO MUNI

● RIGHT
A Muni herald.

San Francisco is one of America's most scenic and most compact cities, and it is famous for its eclectic flavour and wonderful weather. The San Francisco Municipal Railway – better known as just the Muni – operates the city transit system, an integrated network of buses, electric buses (trolley coach), light rail, light-rail subway (Muni Metro) and the world-famous cable-cars. The Muni is one of the best ways to experience the city, and most of San Francisco is within a four-block walk of a transit line.

The Muni's cable-car routes are the most interesting rides in the city. The cable-car originated in San Francisco as a way of moving people by rail over its

exceptionally steep hills. There were many different routes operated by several companies. While other American cities also operated cable-cars, including New York City, Chicago and Seattle, today only San Francisco's remain. The three cable-car routes are a big tourist attraction, and at the peak tourist season it is not unusual to wait an hour or so to ride. The Powell & Hyde line is the most interesting line and the most popular. Both the Powell & Hyde and Powell & Mason routes begin at the corner of Market and Powell Streets near the downtown area. The Powell & Hyde line runs to Fishermans Wharf, passing through Chinatown and over both Russian Hill and Nob Hill. The best time to ride the cable-cars is on an early weekday morning in the winter. While you'll need a warm jacket, you might find yourself the only rider on the car! A vastly more attractive prospect than fighting the summer noontime hoards. The cable-cars are a very pleasant way to view the city, and are fun to ride.

The Muni operates six light-rail lines, five of which use modern equipment and feed into the Muni Metro subway downtown. The remaining route is the F-Market line, which runs from the Transbay bus terminal downtown along Market Street to Castro using historic PCC (President Conference Committee)

● ABOVE RIGHT
Muni PCC 1056 is painted in the scheme used by streetcars in Kansas City, Missouri. Like all the cars in regular service on the F-Market line, this PCC came from Philadelphia, Pennsylvania.

● RIGHT
A Boeing-Vertol LRV pops out of the Muni Metro on to Duboce Street. This J-Church car will take the turn on to Church. N-Judah cars also use this portal, but continue due west on Duboce up into the Sunset Tunnel and then to the Pacific Ocean.

INFORMATION BOX	
Terminus	San Francisco
Country	USA
Distance	48 km (30 miles)
Date of opening	1873

● LEFT

San Francisco's extraordinarily steep hills are the reason for the cable-cars: no conventional form of transport could negotiate these grades successfully. A Powell & Mason car rolls past the San Francisco Academy of Art on Powell Street in downtown San Francisco.

● ABOVE
Interior of a rebuilt PCC used on the F-Market line.

● BELOW
The San Francisco skyline at sunrise.

30th Street. Some cars turn back here, while others continue to Balboa Park via San José Avenue on a new line opened in the early 1990s. At present the Muni has a fleet of ageing Boeing-Vertol light-rail vehicles – an unsuccessful design used only in San Francisco and Boston – but it has a fleet of new Breda LRVs on order.

cars. In the early 1990s the Muni acquired secondhand PCCs from Philadelphia, had them rebuilt and painted each one differently. Each car wears the colour scheme of an American city transit system that once ran PCCs. One car is painted for Boston, another for Kansas City, etc. These cars entered regular revenue service on the F-Market route in 1995. The differently coloured cars make quite a spectacle coming up the street and are well worth riding.

Of the five light-rail lines operating into the Muni Metro, the J-Church line is the most interesting. It leaves the subway at Duboce and Church Streets, then follows Church for several blocks before winding up a steep grade on a private right of way through Dolores Park, which offers a spectacular view of the San Francisco skyline. The line rejoins Church after cresting the hill and runs to

CHICAGO TO SEATTLE
THE EMPIRE BUILDER

James J. Hill was a giant of American railroading. Small in stature, one-eyed and bearded, he was described by the legendary Lucius Beebe as piratical. By 1901 he was in control of three railroads, which served the then wilderness of the Pacific Northwest: the Great Northern, the Northern Pacific and the Burlington. These became known as the Hill Railroads. His crack train was the Oriental Limited, which ran from

Chicago and the Twin Cities (Minneapolis-St Paul) to Seattle, where his own steamships linked the Pacific North-west to Japan and China. Much later, in 1929, when the Asiatic connection had faded, a splendid transcontinental train was named for him as the Empire Builder.

The Great Northern Railway worked as a separate entity to the Northern Pacific Railway, which also served Seattle

from the Twin Cities. But by 1971, with the coming of the quasi-nationalized Federal Corporation AMTRAK, only the Great Northern route – closest to the Canadian border – carried a passenger-train. This is still called the Empire Builder and is arguably the finest transcontinental ride in the States.

Since 1980, the train has been composed of the latest "superliner" equipment with day coaches, diner, sightseeing lounge and sleeping cars, all 5.2 m (17 ft) above track level. The first 687 km (427 miles) from Chicago to St Paul are over the Burlington. From St

● RIGHT
A view from the
Empire Builder as it
heads through
Flathead River
Indian Reservation,
Montana.

**● OPPOSITE
FAR LEFT**
Amtrak's eastbound
Empire Builder
passes through
Grizzley, Montana,
against a backdrop
of the Rocky
Mountains.

**● OPPOSITE
LEFT**
An Amtrak
Superliner coach,
part of the Empire
Builder at Chicago
Union Station.

● BELOW
Amtrak's eastbound Empire Builder
approaches its station stop at Columbus,
Wisconsin.

Paul it is 2,888 km (1,795 miles) to
Seattle, making a total journey of 3,575
km (2,222 miles).

From the start at Chicago's Union
Station there is a smart run to
Milwaukee, beer capital of America.
Then the train follows the Mississippi
River almost all the way to the Twin
Cities, with enchanting daylight views of
the great river on its upper reaches. The
really wide open spaces begin soon after
Minneapolis. In the small hours of the
first night, there is a stop at Fargo, the
town where the firm of Wells-Fargo —
the forerunner of today's American
Express — was founded. Next morning
the train passes Rugby, a flag-stop, where
there is an obelisk outside the station
marking the exact centre of the North
American continent.

After passing over yet more plains,
through Glasgow and Havre, the train
reaches Browning, Montana, where the
Rocky Mountains begin in dramatic style.

As the train climbs, passengers see to the
north a 2,500 m (8,000 ft) mountain
known as Triple Peak Divide, from which
the melting snows run off to three oceans
– the Atlantic, Pacific and Arctic. The
Empire Builder proceeds through the
scenic wonderland of Glacier National
Park, crossing the Continental Divide at
Marais Pass, which, at 1,596 m (5,236 ft),
is the lowest summit of any rail route

through the Rockies. James Hill sent a
surveyor called John Paul Stevens to find
out if this legendary low pass really
existed. Travelling alone, the first white
man to enter the region, he found it in
bitter winter weather. A statue of Stevens
may be seen on the right-hand side of the
train going west.

There are more mountains and river
scenery to Spokane, "Capital of the
Inland Empire", where the Portland,
Oregon, portion is detached. On the way
to Seattle, the main train passes through
the 12.5 km (7 ¾ mile) long bore of
Cascade Tunnel – the longest in the
Western Hemisphere – which was
opened in 1929. Breakfasting passengers
experience the train winding down from
Washington's Cascade Mountains and are
often treated to views of elk and deer on
the final stretch towards Seattle.

● LEFT
Marais Summit on the
former Great
Northern main-line in
northern Montana
hosts Amtrak's Empire
Builder and 30 to 40
daily Burlington
Northern Santa Fe
freight-trains. The
larger-than-life statue
is of John P. Stevens,
the man who surveyed
the line in the late
19th century.

PUEBLO TO DURANGO
THE SAN JUAN EXPRESS

● **BELOW**
A 16mm "fisheye" view of C&T Class K36
No. 487 with passenger-train behind at
Chama, New Mexico.

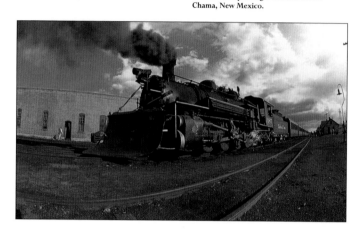

The Denver and Rio Grande Railroad
had the largest 36 in gauge system in the
United States and even operated a
sleeping-car and dining-car train over a
534 km (332 mile) route as the San Juan
Express. This ran until the beginning of
the 1950s from Pueblo, Colorado, via
Alamosa, Colorado, and through
northern New Mexico to Durango,
south-western Colorado.

Some of this track remains and is
operated by steam-trains over two
sections – the 72 km (45 mile) Durango
to Silverton, and the 103 km (64 mile)
Antonito to Chama, New Mexico. The
former line was run for many years as a
tourist route by the Rio Grande before
passing into private hands, and has
become the foremost preserved line in
America, with patronage from the public
increasing year by year. The Antonito to
Chama line is a joint undertaking of the
states of New Mexico and Colorado,
leased to Kyle Railways.

A useful fleet of 2-8-2 locomotives
survived the sad time when diesel engines
replaced steam all over the nation, and
nine splendid steam engines in sound
order work the lines. The coaching stock
on the Durango-Silverton line is partly
original, while the Chama-Antonito line

level. From the train windows in this area, one can look down to see a cattle drive, with horsemen and countless steers, moving through a valley, looking no bigger than ants.

Durango is over 1,800 m (6,000 ft) up, and the line to Silverton climbs all the way through the San Juan mountains, at its most spectacular in the Animas Canyon, to reach nearly 2,750 m (9,000 ft) at the chilly old silver-mining town (which is how Silverton got its name). The train journey to Silverton takes about 3 1/2 hours through the wilderness. The train waits at Silverton for 2 1/4 hours before returning downhill to Durango in about 15 minutes faster.

On the Cumbres and Toltec trip, some 6 1/2 hours are spent travelling one way, including a picnic lunch stop at Osier near the summit. Both for this open-air venue and for travel in gondola cars, passengers must wrap up warmly, even in summer. The westbound train is called Colorado Limited, and the eastbound is called New Mexico Express. Return trips are made by buses the same day or the next day by train.

uses converted boxcars. As many as three trains each way daily are run on the Silverton line in peak season, with one a day at other times of the year, apart from around Thanksgiving in November to the New Year when there is no service, apart from one holiday train, until the spring snow melts. There is a daily train over the Chama-Antonito line from mid-May to mid-October.

This is high-country railroading. The Chama-Antonito line, whose proper title is the Cumbres and Toltec Scenic Railroad, climbs over the Cumbres Pass to reach 3,055 m (10,022 ft) above sea

MANITOU SPRINGS TO PIKE'S PEAK

In 1806, Army Lieutenant Zebulan M. Pike, a United States military surveyor, came across a dramatic Rocky Mountain peak in what was then unknown Colorado Territory. He never climbed it but "established" the height at 5,500 m (18,000 ft). Ten years later an army team did climb to the summit, which was found to be 4,300 m (14,110 ft). Seventy-five years later, a steam railway wound its way up with the aid of a cog.

Cog railways were an American invention, the first being the White Mountain Line up to the summit of Mount Washington in New Hampshire – a mere 2,134 m (7,000 ft), but the windiest place on earth. The Swiss engineer Niklaus Riggenbach was an apprentice during the construction in 1866. All trains up this pioneer cog line are still steam powered.

On the Pike's Peak climb, a steam locomotive pushed a car upwards, and remained in operation from the 1891 opening until final retirement in September 1958. From 1938 onwards, though, some of the climbs were shared with a curious petrol-powered (gasoline-powered) railcar, which only carried 24

passengers compared to 50 aboard the steam car. Since 1964, Swiss-built diesel-electric units (each carrying 80 passengers) have been in use, at first two of them, but later joined by two more from the Winterthur builders. In 1973, the Swiss works produced two diesel-electric sets – the first articulated ones to be used on a cog railway. They carry 216 passengers, and the volume of traffic on a clear summer's day is shown by the fact that sometimes as many as 16 trains are run. The round trip is just under four hours and trains operate, subject to visibility, from May to October.

The Manitou and Pike's Peak Railway is standard gauge, starting from the resort town of Manitou Springs, at the mouth of Englemann Canyon, through which the cog railway begins its journey. The old Colorado Midland railway used to bring passengers close to the cog line's depot, but today they come by bus. In early days, there was also an interurban tramway from Colorado Springs.

Passengers bound for the summit see the retired old Baldwin Tank No. 5. All

● LEFT
Swiss units at Manitou Springs, the bottom
terminus of the railway.

4,300 m (14,110 ft) above sea level. This
is a desolate spot with limited shelter, and
it is the highest point reached by rail on
the North American continent. Exactly
14.3 km (8.9 miles) from the Manitou
Springs depot, the views on a clear day are
described by the cog company as "showing
the grandest scenery on the Globe".

The stopover is usually 40 minutes, by
which time the chilled and breathless
passengers, satiated with views that take
in Denver, 113 km (70 miles) away, and
most of the 30 Colorado Rockies' peaks,
which are higher than Pike's, must return
to the train. In August 1911, a man and
his wife failed to return, having taken a
short walk, inadequately clad. They were
found frozen to death.

the other steam engines have been saved
and dispersed to museums. At 2,003 m
(6,571 ft), the start is already quite high,
but on its way through the canyon the
gradient increases to 1:4, and at the first
station, Minnehaha, the line reaches
2,540 m (8,332 ft). Then comes Son-of-
a-Gun Hill, also at 1:4, to Halfway
House. Passing through Lion Gulch on
easier gradients, the railway attains the
3,048 m (10,000 ft) mark at Mountain
View, where a dramatic panorama unfolds.

The climb continues, twisting and
turning, past Grecian Bend, Big Hill and
Windy Point to reach Summit House,

● ABOVE
A train waits at the
summit of Pike's
Peak. Train services
operate from May
(depending on snow
conditions) to late
October.

● LEFT
Pike's Peak summit
terminus, which is
4,300 m (14,110 ft)
above sea level.

ST ALBANS, VERMONT, TO WASHINGTON DC
THE VERMONTER

Vermont is among the most beautiful and pastoral regions in the eastern United States. It is bordered on the east by New Hampshire and on the west by New York State. It is known for its dairy farms, its maple syrup and its ski resorts. Following the discontinuance of the nocturnal Montrealer in 1995, a train that had run between Washington DC and Montreal, Quebec, Amtrak began operating a daylight train between Washington and St Albans, Vermont. Appropriately named the Vermonter, the train is funded by the state, and it is one of the most popular new trains in the north-eastern United States. It features a distinctive baggage car carrying the name of the train, and stops at rural towns in Massachusetts, New Hampshire and Vermont. Without the train, these communities would have no public transport.

Between St Albans, Vermont, and Palmer, Massachusetts, the Vermonter operates over the New England Central, a short-line railroad run by RailTex, a large short-line operator based in Texas. The New England Central began operations in February 1995, only a few months before the Vermonter, on trackage that

● **ABOVE**
The Vermonter pauses at Amherst, Massachusetts, on a sunny Sunday afternoon.

● **BELOW**
The southbound Vermonter approaches the short, narrow tunnel at Bellows Falls, Vermont.

was formerly operated by the Canadian National through its Central Vermont subsidiary. The Vermonter has the distinction of being one of the few daily Amtrak trains to operate over a short-line freight railroad (as opposed to a larger Class I railroad), and one of the few Amtrak trains to operate in "dark territory" – a section of track not protected by automatic block signals. This is not to say operations are casual or haphazard: a strict system of track occupancy authority is in place. The Vermonter safely shares the tracks with New England Central's couple of daily freights.

South of Palmer, the Vermonter operates to Springfield over Conrail's busy Boston Line – a route used by several

INFORMATION BOX	
THE VERMONTER	
Termini	St Albans, Vermont, and Washington DC
Country	USA
Distance	975 km (606 miles)
Date of opening	1995

● **RIGHT**
The Vermonter, Amtrak train No. 56, runs swiftly along the Connecticut River backwater near Vernon, Vermont.

● **BELOW LEFT**
On New Year's Day 1997, the southbound Vermonter crosses the high bridge at Millers Falls, Massachusetts.

● **BELOW RIGHT**
On a crisp clear October afternoon, the Vermonter approaches Amherst, Massachusetts.

other Amtrak trains. From Springfield to New Haven, it uses the Springfield Branch of the North-east Corridor, and then follows the main stem of the Corridor – Amtrak's most travelled route – all the way to Washington. However, the most interesting section of the trip is the New England Central portion. The train stops in Amherst, Massachusetts, a small college town, and once the home of the famous poet Emily Dickinson. In Vermont, the train serves Brattleboro, Bellows Falls, Windsor, White River Junction, Randolph, Montpelier, Waterbury, Essex

Junction and St Albans. Bellows Falls is the site of a short tunnel, which passes directly below the town centre.

In the summer and early autumn, the Bellows Falls station is shared with the privately operated Green Mountain passenger-train which carries sightseers on a round trip to Chester, Vermont. Between Bellows Falls and Windsor, the tracks cross over the Connecticut River into New Hampshire, and the train stops at Claremont – currently the only point in the Granite State served by a passenger-train. From the train, passengers can see

Mt Ascutney, one of the tallest mountains in Vermont, and wooden-covered bridges, for which the region is famous.

The northbound train, No. 56, departs Washington in the early morning and arrives in St Albans in the evening, while the southbound train, No. 55, features the same schedule but in reverse. It arrives in Washington about the same time as its counterpart arrives in St Albans. The Vermonter requires reservations. Amtrak revises its schedules every six months, and prospective passengers should consult the carrier before riding.

BOSTON TO CHICAGO
LAKE SHORE LIMITED

The Western Railroad of Massachusetts – one of the first mountain railroads in the world – crossed the Berkshire Hills to connect Boston with the Erie Canal at Albany, New York. The line was surveyed by American railroad pioneer George Washington Whistler in the 1830s and completed in the early 1840s. To maintain a reasonable ascending grade on the east slope of the Berkshires, Whistler followed the course of the west branch of the Westfield River, crossing the river several times using large stone-arched bridges. Although the ruling westbound grade was kept to 1.67 per cent, on its completion it was one of the longest adhesion grades in the world. Especially powerful locomotives were required to bring trains through the hills.

In 1867 the Western Railroad merged with the Boston & Worcester to form the Boston & Albany, and in 1900 the New York Central leased the route. Ownership of the line has since changed several times, but to local residents it is known as simply the "B&A". Today, Whistler's railroad makes up the most scenic portion of the route traversed by the Boston

● **LEFT**
Amtrak's Lake Shore Limited climbs Springfield Hill against the dramatic backdrop of a brooding, stormy November sky.

● **BELOW LEFT**
One of George Washington Whistler's famous stone-arch bridges over the Westfield River, near Middlefield. This is one of several bridges abandoned in 1912 when the railroad was realigned.

section of Amtrak's Lake Shore Limited, trains 448 and 449. This train operates daily between Chicago Union Station and South Station in Boston, Massachusetts. Between Chicago, Illinois, and Rensselaer, New York, the Boston section is combined with the New York section.

Bound for Boston the Lake Shore leaves Rensselaer around lunch-time for a relaxing run over the Berkshires. To climb out of the Hudson River valley, the train uses a section of track to a junction at Post Road, which was abandoned in the early 1970s after Penn Central (then the owner of B&A) discontinued the passenger service. Since all freight traffic

INFORMATION BOX

LAKE SHORE LTD

Termini	Boston and Chicago
Country	USA
Distance	1,636 km (1,017 miles)
Date of opening	1840s

uses the Castleton Cutoff west of Post Road to Selkirk, the old passenger line to Albany was deemed redundant. However, after Amtrak reintroduced a passenger service, the old track was put back. East of Chatham, New York, the tracks pass over the New York State Thruway, and a short while later through the famous

● **LEFT**
Amtrak No. 448 exits from the east portal of the State Line tunnel on a clear summer morning. This famous short, curved tunnel is located only about a mile from the New York-Massachusetts state line.

direction on both tracks. On the east slope, near the village of Middlefield, several of Whistler's stone arches are visible through the trees on the north side of the tracks. These bridges were abandoned in 1912, when the railroad was realigned to reduce the gradient. At Chester, the remains of an engine facility, complete with roundhouse and cooling tower, can be seen on the south side of the tracks. The westbound run out of Boston is less revealing because, except in the long days of summer, the train unfortunately runs through the most interesting scenery at night.

State Line tunnel – so named because it is located near the New York-Massachusetts state line. This is a twin-bore tunnel, although at present only the south bore is used. The north bore was abandoned in the late 1980s.

East of the station stop at Pittsfield, Massachusetts, the track begins the climb up to Washington Summit, elevation 445 m (1,459 ft) above sea level – the highest point on the old B&A. It is not unusual for the Lake Shore to overtake a slow-moving eastbound freight climbing the grade. The railroad is bi-directional double track over Washington Mountain, so trains may safely operate in either

● **ABOVE**
An Amtrak Heritage sleeping car, typical of those used on the Lake Shore Limited.

● **RIGHT**
Amtrak No. 448 winds down the grade on the east slope of Washington Hill, east of Middlefield, Massachusetts.

CHICAGO TO OAKLAND
THE CALIFORNIA ZEPHYR

Connecting Chicago and Oakland, California, is one of Amtrak's most popular western trains, the California Zephyr. On the way it traverses some of the most spectacular scenery in the West, from the towering Colorado Front Range to the California coast. It runs up around the "Big Ten curves" west of Denver, crests the divide via the famous Moffat Tunnel, runs through the deep rugged Gore and Glenwood Canyons, across the Utah Desert and over Soldier Summit to Salt Lake City. Then it passes through the Nevada deserts, over California's Donner Pass, across the Central valley and along the Carquinez Straits to Oakland.

While some routes may have a scenic highlight, the route of the California Zephyr is defined by the scenic splendour it passes through; it has not one highlight but rather a continual succession of great vistas. Among the best are those found when climbing high above the Plains up into the Front Range, where the city of

Denver is seen in the distance against a seemingly infinite horizon. However, the most spectacular view is on the west slope of Donner Pass. After crossing the Smart Ridge, which separates the Yuba River Basin from that of the American

River, the railroad follows the American River Canyon; while the river drops deep into the cavernous ravine, the railroad rides high on the north side, along the right of way laid out in the 1860s by the Central Pacific's chief supporter and

● **ABOVE LEFT**
Amtrak No. 5 crosses Yuba Pass after a winter storm. The City of San Francisco was snowbound at Yuba Pass for three days in the early 1950s.

● **LEFT**
The westbound California Zephyr crosses Smart Ridge, leaving the Yuba River Basin and entering the American River Basin, west of Donner Pass.

● LEFT
Amtrak No. 6 climbs along the Truckee River
at Floriston, California.

great visionary genius, Theodore Judah.
At American, just east of the village of
Alta, California, the tracks ride the very
edge of the canyon, 610 m (2,000 ft)
above the river. From this spot on a clear
night, the lights of Sacramento nearly
113 km (70 miles) away can be seen.

Although the original California
Zephyr began operations in 1949, this
train was discontinued in 1970. The
present-day California Zephyr uses much
of the original route, except that it goes
over Donner Pass rather than via Feather
River Canyon. Amtrak's reincarnated
California Zephyr began operation in the
mid-1970s, but did not start operation,

via the Denver and Rio Grande Western
line over the Front Range, until 1983. It
runs with Amtrak's typical western
equipment: the high-level Superliners,
which may be hauled by its ubiquitous
Electro Motive F40s (200-400 series), the
boxy General Electric P32 "Pepsi Cans"
(500 series) and the aesthetically
controversial streamlined General Electric
Genesis diesels (series 1-99 and 800s).

● ABOVE
Cosmic sunrise over Donner Lake in June
1990. Amtrak runs high above this serene
mountain lake on the right of way located by
Theodore Judah in the 1860s.

● BELOW
Amtrak No. 5 passes through the Colorado
Rockies on the Dotsero Cutoff – a line that
was finally completed in the 1930s to connect
the Denver & Salt Lake with the Denver & Rio
Grande Western.

INFORMATION BOX

THE CALIFORNIA ZEPHYR

Termini	Chicago and Oakland
Country	USA
Distance	3,218 km (2,000 miles)
Date of opening	1949

SEATTLE TO LOS ANGELES
THE COAST STARLIGHT

The Coast Starlight, connecting Seattle with Los Angeles, is Amtrak's premier West Coast train. It offers first-class accommodations and features splendid scenery all along its route. On the way it traverses several mountain ranges, including the Oregon Cascades and California's Coast Range, and south of San Luis Obispo, California, it runs along the Pacific Ocean for many miles. Amtrak advertises the Coast Starlight as "superior service": first-class passengers are treated in comfort to complimentary wine tasting and champagne.

South of Eugene, Oregon, at the village of Oakridge the Starlight begins its ascent of the Oregon Cascades. Southern Pacific completed its Cascade Route in the mid-1920s, when it opened its Natron Cutoff between Black Butte and Eugene. Today this is among the most impressively engineered lines in the West. A few miles out of Oakridge the tracks wind over a tall trestle at Heather, amid tall evergreen trees. The tracks twist their way up the mountain and pass through a series of long snowsheds and tunnels.

● **LEFT**
Amtrak No. 11, the Los Angeles-bound Coast Starlight, rolls down the Embarcadero at Jack London Square in Oakland, California. Two General Electric P32 diesel-electric locomotives, which are nicknamed "Pepsi Cans", lead the train.

● **BELOW LEFT**
Amtrak No. 11 climbs up through Cruzatte, Oregon – high in the Cascades – on its way to California from Seattle and Portland.

INFORMATION BOX

THE COAST STARLIGHT	
Termini	Seattle and Los Angeles
Country	USA
Distance	2,235 km (1,389 miles)
Date of opening	1894

Near Cruzatte, the tracks pass from a tunnel into a snowshed, then out across a tall curved trestle over the cascading Noisy Creek, into another snowshed, then through a long curving tunnel. As breathtaking as the scenery is in the summer, it is downright awesome in the winter, when the trees are heavily laden with pristine snow, and the snowsheds protect the tracks from avalanche. Unfortunately, the southbound Starlight usually crosses the Cascades at night in the winter, although the northbound makes a daylight run.

Amtrak does not serve San Francisco directly, but instead provides a bus service from its new Emeryville Station. Passengers wishing to ride into San Francisco by rail can change for a Cal Train "commute" at San José. In Oakland, the Starlight runs down the Embarcadero through Jack London Square, where the train stops at Amtrak's new Oakland station. The street here is a memorable experience. There are few places where Amtrak's high-level Superliner cars share the right of way with automobile traffic! To reach San Luis Obispo from the agricultural Salinas

valley, the Starlight crosses the Cuesta Grade, a steep, tortuous 22.5 km (14 mile) stretch of railroad that winds its way through some of California's prettiest scenery: rolling grassy hills punctuated by perfectly placed oak trees. The grass is iridescent green for a few weeks in March and April, and golden brown for the rest of the year.

The ride along the coast brings the Starlight through Vandenberg Air Force Base, land otherwise restricted to militia. You will not find many photographs of the train in this isolated spot. North of

● ABOVE LEFT
Coast Starlight advertisement at the new Amtrak station in Oakland, California.

● ABOVE RIGHT
On a misty June day, the Seattle-bound Coast Starlight descends Southern Pacific's Cascade Line near Fields, Oregon.

Santa Barbara, the tracks pass over a tremendous trestle at Gaviota and along several popular beaches. The southern end point is Los Angeles Union passenger terminal, one of the last great American passenger terminals. It was completed in 1939 and blends Spanish-Moorish architecture with 20th-century Art Deco motifs.

● ABOVE
Amtrak's Coast Starlight has just passed through Tunnel 5½ in the Salinas valley. Before the tunnel was drilled the railroad ran around the mountain on a circuitous alignment (visible to the left of the tunnel).

● LEFT
The Pacific Ocean glints in the morning sun.

BELLOWS FALLS TO CHESTER, VERMONT
THE GREEN MOUNTAIN FLYER

The Rutland Railway once connected Bellows Falls, Rutland and Burlington, Vermont, with Ogdensburg, New York; it also had a line running south from Rutland to Bennington, Vermont, and on to Chatham, New York. The Rutland discontinued all operations in the early 1960s and portions of the line were abandoned.

Today the Green Mountain Railroad operates a segment of the former Rutland Railway, and a very short portion of the former Boston & Maine Railroad in south-central Vermont between North Walpole, New Hampshire (directly across the Connecticut River from Bellows Falls, Vermont), and Rutland, Vermont. This colourful short-line railroad maintains the spirit of the old Rutland Railway by using Rutland's shield and green and

● **LEFT**
The Green Mountain Flyer departs Chester, Vermont, bound for Bellows Falls.

● **LEFT**
The Green Mountain Railroad logo is reminiscent of the old Rutland herald.

● **BELOW**
On a brilliant autumn morning, Green Mountain Alco RS-1 405 leads the Green Mountain Flyer at Brockway Mills, Vermont.

● **RIGHT**
When the passenger-train is running heavy, it rates one of the powerful Green Mountain's GP9 locomotives.

● **BELOW RIGHT**
At the end of the day, the Green Mountain Flyer rests at Bellows Falls, Vermont.

yellow colour scheme on its rolling stock. From late spring through early autumn Green Mountain operates a tourist train called the Green Mountain Flyer.

The train runs twice a day on Tuesday through Sunday (daily in foliage season) between the Amtrak station in Bellows Falls (also serves the daily Vermonter) and Chester. The train runs with vintage passenger-cars including two historical former Rutland cars, still bearing the name of their former owner.

The Flyer is reminiscent of a typical backwoods branch-line passenger-train of an earlier period, giving passengers a refreshing change from the modern Amtrak trains that are most prevalent in the United States today. Green Mountain operates several Electro Motive GP9

diesel-electric locomotives, which it purchased secondhand from other railroads, as well as a vintage Alco RS-1 diesel-electric, which dates from the mid-1940s and was once owned by the Rutland. Often Green Mountain operates the Flyer with the RS-1, and the train appears even more the way a traditional Rutland passenger-train might have looked 50 years ago.

The scenery along the line is outstanding. Passengers may board the Flyer at either end of the line, and both Bellows Falls and Chester feature splendid stations. Leaving Bellows Falls,

the railroad briefly follows the Connecticut River and then winds its way inland. At Brockway Mills the tracks cross a deep gorge on a high-deck bridge. Along the way several of Vermont's quaint covered bridges and a number of old rustic barns are visible. Vermont is most enjoyable in the early autumn when the days are crisp and clear and the foliage turns to brilliant colours, and there is no better way to view the scenery than to ride the Green Mountain Flyer. Special trains are run on October weekends, the peak period for autumnal colours, all the way to Ludlow, Vermont.

INFORMATION BOX

THE GREEN MOUNTAIN FLYER

Termini	Bellows Falls and Chester, Vermont
Country	USA
Distance	21 km (13 miles)
Date opened for passenger traffic	1984

CHICAGO METRA'S "RACE TRACK"

Chicago's Metra operates a comprehensive network of suburban commuter lines with more than a dozen routes over half a dozen different railroads. Its busiest route is the former Chicago, Burlington & Quincy line to Aurora – a suburb about 56 km (35 miles) west of the the downtown area.

The route, known colloquially as the "Race Track", is owned by Burlington Northern Santa Fe. It carries approximately 50,000 weekday Metra

● RIGHT
An express makes a station stop at Stone Avenue, La Grange.

INFORMATION BOX

Termini	Chicago and Aurora, Illinois
Country	USA
Distance	61 km (38 miles)
Date of opening	1853

passengers on more than 80 daily commuter trains, handles several daily Amtrak long-distance passenger-trains, including the Southwest Chief and the California Zephyr, and carries between 40 and 60 daily freight-trains operated by host railroad Burlington Northern Santa Fe, plus those by Canadian National and Southern Pacific/Union Pacific.

The combination of heavy passenger-traffic and heavy freight-traffic makes this triple-track main-line one of the busiest in the United States, and one of the most

interesting to watch and ride. Aurora-bound trains serve Chicago Union Station, one of four large passenger terminals in Chicago. The operation of the triple track is handled by Centralized Traffic Control, allowing trains to use all three tracks in both directions.

In the evening rush hour, when the bulk of passengers are leaving the city, local and express-trains depart Chicago Union every few minutes. Local trains normally use the outside track on the north side, while the express-trains use

● LEFT
An F40M "Winnebago" races westbound at Stone Avenue. These locomotives are unique to Chicago.

● **RIGHT**
A westbound express dashes down the centre track at La Grange, Illinois.

the centre track and inbound trains the outside track on the south side. To avoid interference during the peak passenger times, freight-trains are either held in yards in either Chicago or Eola, or west of Aurora.

Metra normally uses bi-level "gallery cars" hauled by Electro Motive Division F40s or F40Ms. The F40s are America's most common passenger locomotives, while the F40Ms – nicknamed "Winnebagos", after the popular motor

home – are unique to Chicago Metra. All Metra trains are operated in a push-pull fashion, with the locomotive facing westward. Eastbound trains are operated from a control cab in the leading passenger car. Running time between Chicago and Aurora varies from 1 hour and 20 minutes on a local run to just 52 minutes on an express train.

One way to enjoy the action on the "Race Track" is to ride a midday Metra train from Union Station to one of the

suburban stops – Hollywood (Brookfield Zoo) and Stone Avenue, La Grange, are recommended – and spend the afternoon watching the railroad. On a typical weekday, there will be plenty of freight- and passenger-trains. At weekends Metra service is limited. Other interesting Metra routes include: Metra Electric to University Park – the former Illinois Central electric lines; Rock Island District to Joliet, Illinois; and any of the three former Chicago & North Western routes.

● **ABOVE**
A nice place to soak in the action, one of the busiest lines in the United States is the Zoo Stop at Hollywood, Illinois. More than 100 trains pass through here every day.

● **RIGHT**
The Burlington Northern Santa Fe hosts Canadian National freight-trains on its triple-track main-line between Aurora and Chicago. Between four and eight CN trains use this line every day.

MILWAUKEE TO EAST TROY

Beginning in the 1890s, interurban electric railways were in use across the United States. Employing relatively lightweight construction, they often operated along country roads and in city streets. A great many interurbans operated in the Midwest, connecting such large cities as Chicago and Milwaukee with rural outlying towns. In addition to their passenger operations, many interurbans carried freight, using small electric locomotives. However, the interurban era was short-lived. The advent of the automobile put a swift end to many of these marginally profitable lines, and most were abandoned in the 1920s and 1930s.

The Milwaukee Electric Railway & Light Company, which operated a 320 km (199 mile) long interurban electric empire in south-eastern Wisconsin,

● **ABOVE**
The East Troy Electric Railroad serves several industries in East Troy by means of the Trent Spur. An excursion using open-bench car 21 celebrates the inauguration of electric service in 1996.

● **LEFT**
The East Troy Electric Railroad herald.

● **BELOW**
A car rolls through Beulah on its way from East Troy to the Elegant Farmer.

● **RIGHT**
One of East
Troy's most
popular cars is
Duluth-Superior
Transit "Gate
car" No. 253, a
typical American
streetcar. The
interior of the car
has been
meticulously
restored.

● **BELOW LEFT**
Former Milwaukee Electric Railway & Light
Company steeple-cab L9, and former Chicago,
South Shore & South Bend interurban coach
No. 1130 in front of the old substation, now a
museum, at East Troy, Wisconsin.

● **BELOW RIGHT**
One of East Troy's interurban cars rolls
through the Army Lake Road crossing near
Mukwonago, Wisconsin. Much of this rural
line follows the highway on the 8 km (5 mile)
run between East Troy and Mukwonago.

● **BOTTOM**
A former Chicago, South Shore & South Bend
interurban takes the siding at Beulah for two
eastbound cars heading for the Elegant
Farmer. This old interurban route is single
track with passing sidings at several locations
to allow "meets" between passing trains.

opened its line to rural East Troy,
Wisconsin, in 1907. While Milwaukee
Electric abandoned passenger service to
East Troy in 1939, this line survived for
many years as an electric freight line. The
village of East Troy maintained the line to
serve local industries. Today it is one of
the last electrified remnants of the interurban era. It is operated by the East Troy
Electric Railroad and provides weekend
passenger excursions in conjunction with
the Wisconsin Trolley Museum between
May and September, using traditional
interurban equipment. It is still a freight-
hauler too, although in the 1990s it has
only carried 20–30 cars per year.

Passengers may board at either East
Troy or the Elegant Farmer, near
Mukwonago, Wisconsin. The 16 km (10
mile) round trip runs along a county highway through pastoral farming country
and takes a little more than an hour. East
Troy operates a fleet of vintage electric

interurban equipment, including cars
that operated on the Chicago, South
Shore & South Bend. It also operates
streetcars from several North American
cities, including Duluth, Minnesota and
Philadelphia. The pride of its fleet is car
No. 21, a single-truck open-bench

streetcar replica, typical of street railway
operations at the turn of the century. At
East Troy an old electric substation is part
of the museum and the car-barn is just a
block away. Adjacent to the museum is
J. Lauber's Ice Cream Parlor, where one
can order traditional ice cream sodas.

INFORMATION BOX

Termini	Milwaukee and East Troy, Wisconsin
Country	USA
Distance	8 km (5 miles)
Date of opening	1907

BOONE SCENIC RAILROAD

Iowa, located in the central portion of the United States, is largely an agricultural state. Near the centre of Iowa is Boone, once an important railroad town on the Chicago & North Western's busy main line between Chicago, Illinois, and Council Bluffs, Iowa. This was once a crew change and an important freight switching yard. Sadly there has been no regular passenger-service on this important main line in many years.

Amtrak crosses Iowa on the old Chicago, Burlington & Quincy (now operated by Burlington Northern Santa Fe) many miles to the south. A few miles west of Boone is the gigantic Kate Shelley High Bridge – named after a young woman who risked her life to warn a train of a washed-out bridge – which spans the valley of the Des Moines River. Today the Kate Shelley bridge handles 40–60 daily freight-trains operated by the Union Pacific Railroad (UP acquired the Chicago & North Western in 1995).

On the west side of Boone is the Boone & Scenic Valley Railway, a popular tourist line that operates steam, diesel and electric trains seasonally along the

● **ABOVE**
Every morning before it hauls passengers, Boone & Scenic Valley's steam-engine runs light (without cars) to the tall trestle in order to blow down its boiler – a procedure intended to remove mineral impurities.

● **LEFT**
Charles City & Western interurban car No. 50 is reminiscent of the sort of electric equipment that once ran on the Fort Dodge, Des Moines & Southern through Boone. The Boone & Scenic Valley runs the vintage electric at weekends in the summer.

● **OPPOSITE**
Boone & Scenic valley's Mikado takes on water between runs on a hot June day. Boone is proud of its railroad heritage and every year hosts "Pufferbilly Days" in September.

● **ABOVE LEFT**
Boone & Scenic Valley's Chinese-built 2-8-2
Mikado type marches into Boone, Iowa.

● **ABOVE RIGHT**
An eastbound Union Pacific coal-train crosses
the Kate Shelley High Bridge. Although the big
bridge has two tracks, it can only support the
weight of one train at a time.

INFORMATION BOX

Terminus	Boone
Country	USA
Distance	11 km (7 miles)
Date of opening	1906

right of way of the Fort Dodge, Des
Moines & Southern, known as the Fort
Dodge Line – the largest of the Iowa
interurbans. Iowa was once criss-crossed
by lightweight electric interurban lines
that carried freight and passengers. While
most of these lines have been abandoned,
a few segments remain in place, primarily
as freight operations. This particular line
operated under wire until the mid-
1950s, when it was converted to diesel
operation. In later years it was taken over
by the Chicago & North Western and
operated as a freight-only branch line.
Several years ago, Boone & Scenic Valley
acquired the picturesque route from the

C&NW and began operating passenger
excursions. Since that time, Boone
Scenic has re-electrified a short section
of its line into town and operates an
interurban car reminiscent of those that
traditionally operated here.

In the summer the main attraction is
Boone's steam-train, hauled by the
brightly painted Chinese 2-8-2 Mikado
type locomotive No. JS8419. This
locomotive was ordered new by the
railroad from the Datong works in 1988,
and it was delivered in 1989 for the
specific purpose of hauling passengers.
The steam-train operates along the right
of way of the old interurban north-west
out of Boone, along the bucolic valley of
the Des Moines River. The engineering
highlight of the trip is Boone Scenic's
high bridge, a 48 m (156 ft) tall trestle,
which crosses a creek that feeds into
the Des Moines River. Trains cross the
bridge very slowly to allow passengers to
admire the view.

During the summer the railroad
operates three steam trips at weekends
and one round trip on weekdays. Diesel-
powered trips are offered at other times.
For an extra fare, passengers can ride in
the elevated cupola of a traditional
American caboose. The electric portion
of the line is also generally operated
during summer weekends.

LOS MOCHIS TO CHIHUAHUA
THE COPPER CANYON

In 1961, with the opening of the newest
transcontinental railway in North
America, the tremendous spectacle of
canyons deeper and longer than Arizona's
Grand Canyon was made available to
travellers. However, they could only see it
by rail, for there were no roads and
certainly no airfields amid the wild Sierra
Madre mountains of Mexico.

The Chihuahua Pacifico Railway is a
success. In its 36 years of existence, it has
carried millions of passengers – many of
them from overseas. It runs for 655 km
(407 miles) from Los Mochis on
Mexico's west coast tidewater to the city
of Chihuahua, passing through 87 tunnels
and across 36 bridges. At one stage, it has
to negotiate a triple loop to gain altitude.
The summit is attained at kilometre post
583, some 2,502 m (8,209 ft) above sea
leavel, near the halt of Divisadero where
the Barranca (meaning copper) Canyon
divides from the almost equally awesome
Ulrique Canyon.

Originally planned at the end of the
last century as a freight route for Texas
and central America to serve the deep-
water Pacific ports of Mexico, the railway
took some 60 years to complete. Only

surveyors and missionaries had ever been
to these remote canyons, populated by a
tribe of Tarahumara Indians who lived in
caves in the canyon walls. The
Tarahumara retain their traditions, and
are mostly unable to speak Spanish,
although they have a school at Creel, a
logging township on the railway where a
few basic roads exist. Travellers by train
may see some of the more venturesome
Tarahumaras selling souvenirs at stalls

beside the tracks at Divisadero, where all
trains stop for 20 minutes to allow
passengers to enjoy the wonderful views.

Two passenger-trains run each way
daily, providing what is reckoned by
experts to be among the world's five top
scenic train rides. They are usually well
patronized, and both make early morning
starts to provide a daylight ride over the
full length of the line. Foreign visitors to
Mexico are often in a majority in the first

THE COPPER CANYON

Termini	Los Mochis and Chihuahua
Country	Mexico
Distance	655 km (407 miles)
Date of opening	1961

● **LEFT**
The arrival, from the Pacific, of El Tarahumara
at Divisadero station. The train is named after
the indigenous people of the canyons.

class, where meals are served. There are also freight services, usually one by day and one by night, serving the deep-water port of Topolobampo, some 20 km (12½ miles) beyond the growing city of Los Mochis.

Once a week, a set of special cars called the Sierra Madre Express are attached to the Mexican trains coming down from Nogales and are coupled to the first Chihuahua-Pacifico train over the Copper Canyon line. This takes place at Sufragio, the junction of the new line with the Ferrocarril Pacifico. Usually two sleepers, a lounge, restaurant and dome car (all restored from US equipment of the 1950s) constitute the Sierra Madre Express, all of which make a very heavy load to haul up from sea level to 2,500 m (8,000 ft). Detached at Divisadero, these American cars lay over in the sidings, passengers sleeping aboard. They will have begun their "train cruise" in Arizona, and the special fares are high.

● **TOP LEFT**
The Rio Chinipas bridge is the highest on the line.

● **TOP RIGHT**
A parked US cruise train at Divisadero station.

● **ABOVE RIGHT**
Trains at Divisadero, Copper Canyon. On the left is the lounge car Arizona, which is part of the Sierra Madre train.

● **RIGHT**
The Copper Canyon. This is one and a half times deeper and longer than Colorado's Grand Canyon.

SANTOS TO SÃO PAULO

The São Paulo Railway in Brazil was described as Britain's most successful transportation investment abroad. Incorporated in 1856 as the San (this was a wrong interpretation, which the company retained all its working life) Paulo Railway, it was built to link the port of Santos with the healthy uplands of Brazil, mainly – in early days – for the coffee growers. It contributed greatly to the growth of São Paulo, now one of the biggest cities in the world and one of South America's most industrialized urban areas.

This unique line is a 5 ft 3 in gauge railway that is literally hoisted up the Serra do Mar, a mountain precipice, by an endless rope. It was always a full-scale main line with excellent rolling stock, first-class steam locomotives, restaurant cars and an efficient working practice. The whole journey was only 80 km (50 miles) in length, 19 km (12 miles)

through swamps at the coastal end and 53 km (33 miles) along a plain at the top, with 8 km (5 miles) of steep rope haulage in between. The best trains took just two hours for the journey, including up to 45 minutes "on the rope" if more than six coaches had to be hoisted (these were done three at a time). When diesel units were introduced after World War II, times were cut since the whole unit could

be hoisted in one go. The 99-year lease ran out in 1955, when the name of the railway, now under Brazilian ownership, was changed to Estrada de Ferro Santos a Jundia. The railway had been profitable from the start and the take-over was cordial, with huge amounts paid to shareholders at the end. But since then circumstances have changed, with the construction of a Canadian-financed

● **ABOVE**
Santos railway station where the journey begins.

● **LEFT**
One of the 0-4-0 tram-like steam brake-vans on the Santos a Jundia section of the line. As can be seen the engines produce a lot of smoke, so much so that they sometimes appear to be on fire.

● **RIGHT**
The journey starts at the beautiful seaside resort of Santos. Travellers must often be loath to leave the sandy beach.

● **BELOW LEFT**
São Paulo's Estación de la Luz (Station of Light). This 1936 scene shows the train to Santos about to depart. The locomotive would run the first 53 km (33 miles) to the start of the incline.

● **BELOW RIGHT**
Three coaches of a Santos-São Paulo train going up an incline with a breaking locomotive attached.

highway, the Anchieta, which sweeps up the escarpment to São Paulo, and on which cars and buses make the trip in under 90 minutes. There are now only two passenger-trains each way daily, all second-class, taking 115 minutes. They are still patronized because the fare is low compared to the buses. The ownership is now with Rede Ferroviaria Federal, São Paulo, a government department. After 1927, five new inclined planes were built on a gentler gradient (about 1:11), which speeded ascent and descent. Ropes are renewed every two years and re-spliced every six months. A trained gang re-splices a rope in 40 minutes. None has ever broken. The height above sea level at the top of the incline is 792 m (2,598 ft). The beautiful roofed Estación de la Luz (Station of Light) in São Paulo is still there as a reminder of the days of great prosperity and 12 per cent dividends.

INFORMATION BOX	
SAN PAULO RAILWAY	
Termini	Santos and São Paulo
Country	Brazil
Distance	80 km (50 miles)
Date of opening	1856

SANTA ROSA DE LOS ANDES TO LAS CUEVAS, ARGENTINA

● BELOW
A veteran steam branch-line train between Loncoche Junction and Villarica in the Chilean Lake District.

Although the Trans-Andine railway was projected in 1854, work did not begin until 1887, and the line was not finally opened until 1910. Built to provide a rail link over the Andes between Chile and Argentina, the line now terminates at the border between the two countries.

The first section of this metre-gauge line, which goes 34 km (21 miles) from Santa Rosa de Los Andes to Rio Blanco, rises some 640 m (2,100 ft). On this stretch the trains average about 29 kph (18 mph). The second section of the trip, from Rio Blanco to the frontier, about two-fifths of the way through the 3,028 m (9,934 ft) long Uspallata tunnel, is just under 36.5 km (23 miles) long and rises 1,730 m (5,676 ft). In this 71 km (44 mile) stretch of line, there are six rack sections and no less than 26 tunnels with a total length of 3,183 m (10,443 ft) – not counting the Uspallata. The electric trains average about 18 kph (11 mph) on this stretch. The Uspallata

tunnel, between the peaks of the 7,040 m (23,097 ft) Aconcagua and the 6,187 m (20,298 ft) Tupungato , lies at an altitude of 3,200 m (10,500 ft).

One of the locomotives used on the line was a Shay type, built by Lima in 1904. It was carried on two four-wheeled bogies with the tender on another four-wheeled bogie. This engine took light trains up the rack grades and

INFORMATION BOX

Termini	Santa Rosa de Los Andes and Las Cuevas
Countries	Chile and Argentina
Distance	71 km (44 miles)
Date of opening	1910

● LEFT
A view of the Paso de los Liberadores (the Pass of the Freedom Fighters) in the Andes on the Chilean/Argentinean border.

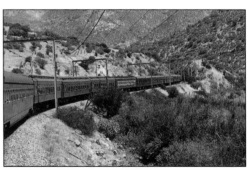

worked the section between Portillo and the Summit tunnel. There were also two 2-6-2T rack and adhesion engines, made by Borsig of Berlin. A 0-8-0+0-6-0T Meyer is kept at Los Andes mainly for use in snow clearance.

The main problems encountered on the route were, in winter, snow, which can reach as much as 6.4 m (21 ft) deep, and, in summer, rock falls and avalanches. Indeed, owing to the many landslides that have occurred over the years, the rail route over the Andes has now been closed for good – there is neither money nor incentive to restore it, especially as a road now crosses its path and, ironically, uses the rail tunnel beneath the great statue of Christ.

When the Trans-Andine train did run, it was at Las Cuevas, 3 km (2 miles)

into Argentina, that the Chilean crew with their Swiss-built Brown-Boveri electric locomotive would hand over the train to their Argentine colleagues with their Czech-built cog-wheel diesel unit. Once the start of a 1,088 km (676 mile)

journey to Argentina's Santiago Alameda station, the line is now mainly only used during the winter sports season, when the resort of Portillo, altitude 2,743 m (9,000 ft), suddenly comes to life with the influx of winter sports enthusiasts.

● **ABOVE LEFT**
A spacious Chilean State Railways restaurant car.

● **ABOVE RIGHT**
A main-line express, the "Trans-Andino Combinación" near Llay Llay, en route to Los Andes.

● **LEFT**
The Laguna del Inca (Inca Lake), which is seen as the train progresses on its journey.

● **LEFT**
A Swedish-built electric locomotive shunts coaches for the "Trans-Andino Combinación" at Llay Llay.

ASUNCIÓN TO ENCARNACIÓN

It has truly been said that a Paraguayan train journey is one of the most high-rated rail experiences in the world. Although Paraguay has other railways, only one, the Ferrocarril Presidente Carlos Antonio López, carries passengers. One of the abiding memories of a trip on the line is the firework display that comes from its fleet of 100 per cent wood-burning locomotives. This is a truly unforgettable experience.

The first section of the line, from Asunción to Paruguar, was opened in 1861. In 1889 it was acquired by the London-based, British-controlled Paraguay Central Railway. The line, which reached Encarnación in 1911, was nationalized in 1961. Originally built to the 5 ft 6 in gauge, in 1911 it was reduced so that it could be connected to

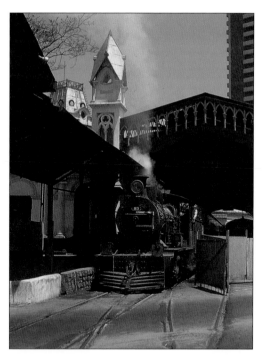

● **LEFT**
A train for Encarnación waits to leave the grand station in Asunción.

● **BELOW**
A North British, 2-6-0, No. 103, at Parguar Station.

● **OPPOSITE BOTTOM LEFT**
Train no. 286 passes through the streets of Asunción. This picture was taken just before the train was hit by a bus! Thankfully there were no casualties.

● **OPPOSITE BOTTOM RIGHT**
Engine No. 51, one of the original North British-built Moguls of 1910, at San Salvador at the head of an overnight train from Encarnación to Asunción.

One of the North
British-built wood
burners surrounded
by wood at Colonel
Belgrado.

● BELOW
A steam tram built by Borsig of Berlin for
working around the docks of Buenos Aires.
After a long life in the Argentinian capital, this
veteran was pensioned off to the sugar fields
of neighbouring Paraguay, and during its
workaday chores it regularly sallies forth on to
the international main line linking Asunción
to Encarnación.

Argentina's standard gauge. Although the
railway is run down and the line in poor
condition, a trip over the line should be
very high on the list of any South
American traveller.

The 376 km (234 mile) journey, which
lasts from 14 to 18 hours, commences at
Asunción's multi-colonnaded colonial-
style station and heads in a south-easterly
direction across undulating countryside to
Villarica. Thereafter the landscape
changes to flat pampas and swampland for
the rest of the journey to Encarnación.
Here the through train to Argentina leaves
the station to proceed down the length of
a street towards the ferry terminal at Paca
Cua. The coaches are then lowered on to

the train ferry by a steam-operated winch
and cable. The ferry, which can carry six
coaches at a time, crosses the Paraná
River to Posadas, Argentina.

The twice-weekly train is usually
hauled by one of the country's British-
built locomotives, from the North British
of Glasgow or the Yorkshire Engineering
Company's Meadow Hall works in
Sheffield. There are still Edwardian
2-6-0s in service. This sole passenger
line in the country, where passenger
comfort is an unheard-of concept, is
operated with only nine passenger-cars.
There used to be a sleeping car, but it
was withdrawn in 1972. The restaurant
car, which used to be fitted to the train,
has also been out of use for some years,
so that during the journey food has to be
purchased from itinerant vendors along
the track.

The future of this unique railway is in
doubt. The new road bridge over the
Parana River at Encarnación now brings
road and rail traffic directly from

Argentina, rendering the ferry defunct.
At present, all services are suspended,
ostensibly for track up-grading, and it is
hoped that the railway will eventually
work again. This must be open to
question, however, as traffic has dwindled
progressively over recent years. At
present the locomotive fleet of vintage
rolling stock remains intact, as it waits for
a tomorrow that may never come.

INFORMATION BOX	
Termini	Asunción and Encarnación
Country	Paraguay
Distance	376 km (234 miles)
Date of opening	1861

JULIACA TO CUZCO
THE HIGHEST RAILWAY IN THE WORLD

Crossing the Andes meant constructing the highest railway in the world. Because of its altitude, the Peruvian Central Railway presented civil engineers with major problems, for, in a confined space and short distances, they had to build railways over passes that exceeded Mont Blanc in altitude. The solutions they adopted were tight curves, zigzags and rack sections.

Operating the lines was also fraught with difficulties: steep gradients, lack of local sources of fuel, heavy wear and tear on locomotives and rolling stock, and frequent landslides and washouts. Even the change from steam to diesel was, initially, a step backwards, because diesel units were prone to power loss in the rare atmosphere, and there were cases of trains being unable to take the gradients.

The three lines of the the Southern Railway of Peru serve the *altiplano*, a windswept plain 3,901 m (12,798 ft) above sea level. Of standard gauge, they run to Mollendo on the Peruvian coast through the country's second city, Arequipa, to the town of Juliaca on the altiplano. Here the line divides. A short section continues to Lake Titicana and around its shores to the port of Puno, while a 339 km (211 mile) line from Juliaca runs north to Cuzco, the ancient Inca capital, crossing a summit of 4,314 m (14,153 ft) at La Raya.

A glance at the map of Peru shows that the route of the Central Railway forms a lop-sided T, with Lima at its base, running up to La Oroya at the junction of the cross-piece. The main line runs from

INFORMATION BOX

THE HIGHEST RAILWAY IN THE WORLD

Termini	Juliaca and Cuzco
Country	Peru
Distance	339 km (211 miles)
Date of opening	1908

● **LEFT**
A Hunslett 2-8-0 No. 108 at an isolated mountain stop on the Huancayo to Huancavelica line.

Lima through La Oroya to Huancavelica, its terminal, on the right. To the left, a privately owned railway runs from La Oroya to Cerro de Pasco, site of Peru's copper mines. The Southern and Central Railway systems are unconnected.

The Central Railway is regarded as one of the wonders of the Americas, and the engineering of the route involved immense problems. The deep Rimac valley between Lima and La Oroya, the only feasible route to the central region of the country, narrows to a maximum width of about 198 m (650 ft). Within its limits, the engineers had to find a way of climbing nearly 3,960 m (12,992 ft) within a distance of less than 76 km (47 miles). The twists and turns that the railway needs to gain height have made the railway considerably longer at 117 km (73 miles).

To keep the gradient down to 1:23, the line has to utilize the whole width of the valley, crossing frequently from one side to the other. Even this would be impossible without the use of the famous zigzags to gain height. Between Chosica and Ticlio, the highest point of the line at 4,783 m (15,692 ft), there are six double and one single zigzags, 66 tunnels, including the 1,177 m (3,861 ft) long

● **LEFT**
A Tren Turista pulls up at the halt for Machu Picchu. In the absence of roads, the railway is the only method of reaching this popular site.

● **BOTTOM LEFT**
A Tren Turista on the Quillabamba-Cuzco-Juliaca line stands at Cuzco station.

● **BOTTOM RIGHT**
A Baldwin 2-6-0 No.103 at Huancayo in 1980.

Galera, and 59 bridges, including that over the Verrugas, which, at 175 m (574 ft) long, when built in 1890, was the third longest in the world.

Construction of the line, which began in 1870, presented problems in addition to the geographical ones. A mysterious disease killed off thousands of workers in 1877, and Peru went bankrupt, which effectively held up completion until 1929. The chief reason for the Central

Railway has been freight-carrying, particularly since 1897 when the La Oroya copper mine opened. However, the incredible journey still remains attainable to travellers. Except for those unfortunates who suffer from altitude-sickness and have to be given oxygen by the white-coated attendants on the train, all will marvel at the ingenuity of the men who built this railway amid some of the most rugged landscapes on earth.

GUAYAQUIL TO QUITO

The chief component of the Ecuadorian State Railway is the Guayaquil to Quito line (misleadingly nicknamed the "Good and the Quick"), which connects the two major cities of the country; the former on the coast, the latter high up in the Andian mountains.

Construction work began in 1871, but it was not until 1908 that the contractors completed the rare 3 ft 6 in gauge line. To traverse the 463 km (288 miles) and 3,609 m (11,840 ft) altitude, tight curves and zigzags were incorporated. It has never been a commercial success and its resulting

● LEFT
Passengers board a first-class train on the Ibarra to San Lorenzo line.

● LEFT
Travellers on the *tren mixto* (mixed train) ready to leave Sibambe.

INFORMATION BOX

Termini	Guayaquil and Quito
Country	Ecuador
Distance	463 km (288 miles)
Date of opening	1908

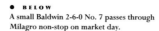

● BELOW
A small Baldwin 2-6-0 No. 7 passes through Milagro non-stop on market day.

near-bankruptcy has given it a poor reputation for chaotic administration, breakdowns and derailments. Its lines are antique, and the fact that the railway is continuing to operate tends to raise more amazement than the fact that it was ever built. But for anyone interested in travelling on impossible railway lines, who is not put off by an uncomfortable ride punctuated by possible disasters, the G&Q must be a prized experience. It has sometimes been called "the world's mightiest roller coaster".

Guayaquil, Ecuador's second city, has its railway station at Duran, a long way out of town and on the opposite side of the Gyayas River estuary. The spectacular line to Quito begins its zigzagging course within a narrow gorge before climbing the famous Mariz del Diablo (Devil's Nose), a perpendicular ridge rising to a height of 3,230 m (10,597 ft). Another

engineering challenge, this almost
insurmountable obstacle was finally
conquered by the construction of a series
of switchbacks on a 5¹/₂ per cent grade.
First one way and then the other, the
train zigzags higher and higher to gain an
altitude of 3,609 m (11,840 ft) at
Urbino, a small town lying near the foot
of the 6,705 m (21,997 ft) volcano of
Chimborazo.

The northbound line from Quito runs
to San Lorenzo on the coast. At least the
line does, if not many services use it. It is
erratic, to say the least, and a bus –
sometimes – now takes over from the
trains if the passenger load warrants it
or if there's not enough freight for a *tren
mixto*. Even today the *Thomas Cook
Overseas Timetable* finds itself unable to
prise proper timings of the service out
of the administration.

The train, when it decides to put in an
appearance, is a little monster called an
autocarril. Basically this is a vehicle that
was born as a British Leyland lorry and
ended its life on flanged wheels and a
fixed course. Although the ticket
stipulates a reserved seat, there are in
fact no seats to reserve.

On one occasion the River Mira cut
the line in two by sweeping away the
bridge. This meant that for a while the
passengers had to alight and cross the
river on a temporary rope structure, four
at a time. A few kilometres on, along ill-
laid and worn track, the train comes to a
waterfall that descends directly on to the
track to drench passengers who have
failed to close their windows.

The total curvature of this line is no
less than 16,200 degrees – the equivalent
of more than 45 complete circles. The
entire line is adhesion-worked and
accounts for no less than 40 per cent of
the country's total rail length.

● **ABOVE**
Looking down
Devil's Nose as the
train enters
Sibambe.

● **LEFT**
A large Baldwin
2-8-0 No. 44 leaves
Bucay on a *tren mixto*
(mixed train), which
has plenty of room
on top.

301

DUBLIN TO CORK

The principal railway route in the Republic of Ireland is that which joins the country's two main cities, Dublin and Cork. It was built by the Great Southern & Western Railway and, like so many of the major trunk lines in the British Isles, it was a product of the railway mania of the 1840s.

Even by the standards of the time, the project was an ambitious one. At 265 km (165 miles), this line was longer than any comparable scheme in Britain. Given the much less favourable economic conditions in Ireland at the time – construction of the route was undertaken during the dark years of the Great Famine – the fact that the line was completed on schedule was a remarkable achievement. The line opened to a temporary station on the outskirts of Cork in October 1849, five years after the passing of the Act of Parliament authorizing the railway.

INFORMATION BOX

Termini	Dublin and Cork
Country	Ireland
Distance	265 km (165 miles)
Date of opening	1849

● **ABOVE**
The Dublin to Cork express speeds its passengers between two of Ireland's largest cities.

● **ABOVE LEFT**
The CIE logo used from the 1960s.

● **LEFT**
The train leaves the town and heads out into the beautiful Irish countryside.

The line starts from Heuston (formerly Kingsbridge) station in Dublin. The magnificent building that fronts the station, containing offices and the board room used by the three organizations that have run the line over the decades, was designed by the architect Sancton Wood and opened in 1844. This is in marked contrast to the rather dingy train shed, which lurks behind the frontage and, rather pointedly, is not physically connected to it.

The route is relatively level except for short sharp gradients at either end. Leaving Dublin, trains are soon speeding across the Curragh of Kildare where thoroughbreds can be seen exercising on the gallops alongside the track. After passing through Portarlington, Ballybrophy and Thurles, trains reach Limerick Junction where, until track changes were made in 1967, every train serving the station since its opening in 1848 had to reverse to get into its platforms. Here the line from Limerick to Rosslare crosses the Cork line on the level, the only such occurrence that is met in Ireland today.

At Mallow the route that serves County Kerry branches off, and the tracks for Cork cross the River Blackwater on a viaduct that replaced the original one, destroyed in the Troubles of the 1920s – one of the few notable engineering feats of the line.

● **ABOVE**
A remarkable survivor from the dawn of the railway age in Ireland is preserved under cover in Cork station. This is 2-2-2 locomotive No. 36, built by Bury, Curtis & Kennedy in Liverpool for the commencement of services on the Dublin to Cork line in the 1840s. It remained in service, covering about half a million miles in its time, until 1875. It was not scrapped but remained at Inchicore works in Dublin until the 1950s, when it was renovated and put on display in Cork.

Approaching Cork the line plunges into one of the longest railway tunnels in Ireland at over 1,189 m (3,901 ft) in length. The tunnel virtually brings a train to the platforms of Cork station. The stiff gradient through the tunnel provided a daunting start for Dublin-bound trains in the days of steam. The line continues through the curving platforms of the station to the final terminus at Cobh. Cobh was known as Queenstown, and was once a stopping-point for the great Atlantic liners; it was also the last port of call for the ill-fated *Titanic* in 1912.

Now a frequent service of fast express trains runs throughout the day. The trains are powered by the latest General Motors diesels, and they generally operate at speeds approaching 160 kph (100 mph). There is, however, a reminder of the line's earliest days in the foyer of the station at Cork in the form of a steam locomotive No. 36. A 2-2-2. This train was built by Bury, Curtis & Kennedy Company in Manchester for the opening of the line in the 1840s, and is a remarkable survivor from the dawn of the Railway Age in Ireland.

DROMOD TO BELTURBET

Ireland was sadly lacking in deposits of coal and iron ore, the raw materials that fuelled the Industrial Revolution in the 19th century. One place where both these elements could be found was at Arigna in County Roscommon. Though the surrounding districts in the county of Leitrim were thinly populated and consisted of poor boggy land often inundated by the area's many lakes and streams, the prospective mineral wealth of Arigna led to plans being made in the 1880s for a narrow-gauge railway to connect Belturbet, County Cavan, in the north to Dromod, on the main Dublin to Sligo railway, in the south. A branch was planned from Ballinamore, midway along the route, to Arigna.

Most journeys along the line began at Dromod, where the narrow-gauge station adjoined the main-line one. The mixed train consisting of a tail of wagons and a carriage with a veranda and open platform at either end – shades of the

● LEFT
4-4-0 tank No. 2, originally named Kathleen, one of the locomotives built for the opening of Cavan & Leitrim Railway in 1887 simmers in the shed yard at Ballinamore in the late 1950s. When the line closed, No. 2 was preserved and now resides in the Ulster Folk & Transport Museum at Cultra near Belfast.

● ABOVE
At Belturbet the C&L shared a platform and station with the standard-gauge Great Northern branch. Trains on Ireland's two gauges are seen in this April 1956 view.

● LEFT
This Cavan to Leitrim train is being hauled by a 0-4-4 tank complete with cow-catcher.

● OPPOSITE BOTTOM
The deplorable state into which the locomotives had been allowed to fall is graphically illustrated in this view of Ballinamore shed in March 1959, just before the line finally closed.

INFORMATION BOX

Termini	Dromod and Belturbet
Country	Ireland
Distance	53 km (33 miles)
Date of opening	1887

● **LEFT**
One of the locomotives transferred to the
C&L from the Cork, Blackrock & Passage
line, when this closed in the 1930s, is seen
here at Ballyconnell.

● **BELOW**
The view from the train on the roadside
tramway to Arigna, which religiously followed
the undulations and curves of the road for
most of the way.

Wild West – threaded north through an area of small lakes and boggy land, with sharp curves and stiff gradients impeding progress. At the main stations, passengers were left to drum their fingers as the engine rambled off to shunt the goods yard. After 26 km (16 miles) the line's hub and headquarters at Ballinamore was reached. Here the main line was met by the branch from Arigna. For much of its 23 km (14 miles), the line, always known as the tramway, ran alongside the public road. It criss-crossed the road on ungated level crossings and stopped at road side halts distinguished only by name boards poking out of the hedges, and at one point passed over Ireland's longest river, the Shannon, here little more than a mountain stream.

From Ballinamore, the main line turned east to Belturbet, where the 3 ft gauge shared a station with a branch of the great Northern Railway. Just outside the station, another of the great rivers of Ireland, this time the Erne, was bridged by a fine stone viaduct.

In later years there was just one train conveying passengers on this section. The journey from Dromod took three hours for the distance of 53 km (33 miles). This was a line on which passengers

would not have wanted to be in a hurry!

It was the carriage of Arigna's poor-quality coal that kept the Cavan & Leitrim in business up to 1959. Taken over by the Great Southern railway in 1925, as other narrow-gauge lines in the Irish Free State closed from the 1930s to the 1950s, their locomotives were transferred to the Cavan & Leitrim to cope with the sometimes hectic coal traffic. By the end, it was a veritable working museum and attracted rail fans from far and wide.

The memory of the gallant little line survived undimmed, and in the 1990s a new Cavan & Leitrim Railway Company was formed. Based at the southern terminus at Dromod, preservationists have re-laid part of the track and ultimately hope to run trains some 8 km (5 miles) to the next town of Molhill. This recreation of the railway, which has already brought the sight of a working 3 ft gauge locomotive back to County Leitrim, will rely on tourists and railway enthusiasts, not coal, for its revenues.

LONDONDERRY TO BURTONPORT

At its peak in the 1920s there were over 800 km (500 miles) of narrow-gauge railway open for service to the public in Ireland. The epic of these 3 ft gauge lines was the run from Derry to Burtonport on the tracks of the Londonderry & Lough Swilly Railway Company (L&LSR) in north-west Donegal.

The L&LSR began life as a standard-gauge line but converted its existing route from Derry to Buncrana to 3 ft gauge when a new narrow-gauge line from Derry to Letterkenny was opened in 1883. At this time the British Government was engaged in a policy of attempting to open up some of the more impoverished and remote districts in the west of Ireland by subsidizing the construction of railways in areas where they were of doubtful commercial viability. This was seen by some cynics as an effort to kill with kindness the agitation for Home Rule in Ireland.

Whatever the political motivation, it is hard to believe that serious investors could have been persuaded to put up the money for the extension of the L&LSR's Letterkenny line, which was promoted in 1898. It was to run through some of the

bleakest and poorest land in all of Ireland, and to terminate at the fishing harbour of Burtonport on the west coast of County Donegal. A separate company, the Letterkenny & Burtonport Extension railway, was formed to build the 80 km (50 mile) link, which opened in 1903 at

● ABOVE
The final engines supplied to the L&LSR were also unique and magnificent machines. Nos. 5 and 6 were 4-8-4 tanks built by Hudswell Clarke of Leeds, the only locomotives of this configuration to run on any gauge in the British Isles. They weighed 51 tons and had a tractive effort greater than many standard-gauge engines in use in Ireland at the time of their introduction in 1912.

● LEFT
4-6-0T No. 3 arriving at Letterkenny with a goods train from Derry, June 1950. The buses shown in the photo were operated by the L&LSR and continued in service decades after the trains ceased to run.

INFORMATION BOX	
Termini	Londonderry and Burtonport
Country	Ireland
Distance	119 km (74 miles)
Date of opening	1883

● **RIGHT**
4-8-0 No. 12 waits to head a train back to
Derry from Burtonport in June 1937. The
bleak rocky landscape seen in the picture is
typical of the area served by the line.

a cost to the public purse of some
£300,000. The line avoided most of the
tiny habitations it was supposed to serve
– allegedly to enable locals to find some
employment in ferrying goods and
passengers from these villages to their
distant stations.

The 119 km (74 mile) journey from
Londonderry to Burtonport took around
five hours in carriages that were unheated
in winter. It had been a difficult line to
construct, with whole sections of the
formation sinking into the boggy ground
before the track could be laid. Its main
engineering feature was the 347 m
(1,138 ft) long Owencarrow viaduct,
which was so exposed to gales howling in
from the Atlantic that in both 1906 and
1925 trains were blown off it. The 1925
accident resulted in the deaths of four
passengers. To work the line, two 4-8-0
tender engines were supplied by
Hudswell Clarke in 1905, by far the
largest narrow-gauge locomotives ever to
run in Ireland, and the only machines of
this type ever to operate in the British
Isles on any gauge.

The partition of Ireland severely
affected the fortunes of the L&LSR. The
city of Derry was in Northern Ireland,
while its natural economic hinterland in
County Donegal was now across an
international boundary in another
country. Fuel shortages occasioned by
World War II postponed the inevitable
for a few years, but the line beyond
Letterkenny finally closed completely in
1947, ending this heroic chapter in the
history of Ireland's minor railway.

● **ABOVE**
The Burtonport line soon spawned the largest locomotives ever to run on the
narrow gauge in the British Isles. Nos. 11 and 12 were 4-8-0 tender engines,
introduced in 1905, which looked more like the sort of engines found in India or in
southern Africa. No. 12 is seen near Derry with a Burtonport train in the 1920s.

● **RIGHT**
The line to Letterkenny and Burtonport left
the Derry to Buncrana at Tooban Junction,
an isolated spot near the shores of Lough
Swilly. 4-6-2 tank No. 10 is seen at the
junction on a special train in June 1953.

LEICESTER TO LOUGHBOROUGH

In May 1840 the Midland Counties Railway came to Leicester. On the fourth of the month, crowds were assembled at the town's new Campbell Street station as four first- and six second-class carriages, hauled by Leopard, arrived from Nottingham. After a short stop for the officials of the railway who lived in Leicester to take their places, the train pulled out of the station *en route* to Derby, where they dined at the King's Head before returning to Leicester.

The next day the station and all the surrounding area was crowded with spectators to witness the public opening. In spite of the cold, more and more people were arriving as the time of departure of the first train drew near. At seven-thirty the train, with its 50 passengers for Nottingham and Derby, started on its epic journey, reaching Syston, a distance of 9.5 km (6 miles), in 12 minutes.

The train reached Loughborough at eight o'clock where, once again, vast crowds were waiting to see the train, which arrived in Nottingham at nine o'clock. The following week the line was

● **RIGHT**
Built in 1894, two years after Thomas Cook's death, this terracotta building, Franco-Flemish in style, was the firm's Leicester office. At second-floor level, on four bronzed relief panels, are depicted four of the major events in Cook's career.

● **BELOW RIGHT**
The first of the panels shows the train involved in the 1841 excursion. Note that the passengers are travelling in what were affectionately known as "tubs".

● **LEFT**
The statue of Thomas Cook, the father of tourism, outside Leicester's London Road station. The work was commissioned by Leicester City Council in 1992 to mark the centenary of Cook's death.

● **BELOW**
Thomas Cook's grave in Leicester's Welford Road Cemetery.

● **LEFT**
The entrance to Campbell Street station, Leicester, as it appeared in December 1843 to mark the arrival of Queen Victoria. The station, built in 1841, was replaced by the present London Road station in 1892.

INFORMATION BOX

Termini	Leicester and Loughborough
Country	England
Distance	16 km (10 miles)
First advertised rail excursion	5 July 1841

● **LEFT**
A view of Loughborough Midland station.

● **BELOW**
A Class 43 leaving Loughborough on the Midland Main Line. It was on this line that Thomas Cook's historic first railway excursion took place.

extended to Sheffield, a journey of 70 miles which took just over four hours.

In July 1841 Thomas Cook organized his first conducted tour. This was the first advertised excursion train in England – if not the world. With the co-operation of John Fox Bell, Secretary of the Midland Counties Railway, Cook arranged a special train to take people from Leicester to the quarterly temperance meeting at Loughborough. Bell not only agreed to the special train, but also gave Cook a contribution towards the preliminary expenses and agreed to a half-price third-class fare of one shilling. On the morning of Monday 5 July, 570 people got into the nine open carriages, which had been provided for them. These carriages, called "tubs", were seatless open trucks in which the passengers stood unsheltered from the weather. As well as the crowds of people at Campbell Street station to witness the departure, all the bridges along the route were lined with hundreds of people eagerly waiting for a look at the train.

Thus began, in the heart of the English Midlands, the company whose name has become synonymous with travel. By 1865 Cook's business had grown so big that he was organizing tours to the Continent and the USA and had had to relocate his head office from Leicester to London.

FORT WILLIAM TO MALLAIG

The start of this, arguably the most scenic rail journey in Britain, is Fort William, a town that nestles under the lofty peak of Ben Nevis. At 1,343 m (4,406 ft), this is Britain's highest mountain.

Soon after leaving the station, the train crosses the River Lochy, and then, at Banavie, the swing bridge over the 97 km (60 mile) long Caledonian Canal. Started by Thomas Telford in 1803, the canal traverses the Great Glen from Fort William to Inverness.

At Corpach, there is a pulp-paper mill, which is of note inasmuch as it is

mainly responsible for the line remaining open. The West Highland line was used to deliver timber and then collect the finished product from the factory. After skirting the northern shore of Loch Eil,

still with Ben Nevis in view, one soon arrives at Locheilside at the western end of the loch. This station, like others on the route, is still painted in the blue of the original Highland line. Having

● LEFT

An LNER on the West Highland line between Fort William and Mallaig.

● BOTTOM

The George Stephenson leaves Banavirwith on the 11.05 from Fort William to Mallaig.

lake in Britain. Another 4.8 km (3 miles) brings the train to its destination, the small fishing port of Mallaig. During the summer, some trains are still steam-hauled by the locomotive *The Jacobite*.

In the 1970s and 1980s, the pleasure of the journey was enhanced if passengers, on payment of a supplementary fare, travelled in the observation saloon, where there was a running commentary on the various points of interest on the route. These wooden-bodied Gresley observation cars were the last two in service on British Rail. Although extremely popular, they were withdrawn when the turntable at Mallaig was dismantled, making it impossible for them to be turned. However, one car was fully restored and returned to service on the Great Central Railway in Leicestershire in 2007; it is now in regular public use on the Great Central Railway, and other carriages await restoration.

travelled another 3 km (2 miles) through a narrow glen, the train reaches the Glenfinnan viaduct. It was near here that the Young Pretender, Bonnie Prince Charlie, unfurled his standard in 1745.

Built by Robert "Concrete Bob" MacAlpine, the 21 arches stand 30 m (100 ft) above the ground, the concrete structure curves in a crescent across the Finnan valley. During its construction a cart-horse and its driver were killed when the horse stumbled as it backed to tip its load into one of the shafts. The result was that cart, horse and driver were entombed in the wet concrete. A plaque recording the fatality can be seen on the viaduct.

After leaving Glenfinnan, the train travels through a wooded glen and emerge on the shores of Loch Eilt. From Lochailort station, there is a series of

short tunnels before a viaduct takes the train across Glen Mamie, after which it soon meets the Atlantic at Loch nan Uamh (Loch of the Cave). There are then a few more short tunnels before reaching Arisaig, from where the island of Eigg can be seen.

The line now turns north and at Morar crosses the River Morar. The river, which flows from Loch Morar, is 310 m (1,017 ft) deep, and as such the deepest

INFORMATION BOX

Termini	Fort William and Mallaig
Country	Scotland
Distance	67 km (41³/₄ miles)
Date of opening	1901

EDINBURGH TO WICK/THURSO

Soon after leaving Edinburgh, the Forth and Clyde canal is crossed and the train eases slowly round a sharp right-handed curve to Larbert and Stirling, whose large station, still with semaphore signals, was built by the Caledonian Railway. The ground now becomes undulating, and there are distant mountains to be seen. Soon after leaving Stirling, the River Forth is crossed and an 8 km (5 mile) climb at 1:100 begins.

After leaving Perth, 111 km (69 miles) from Edinburgh, the most spectacular part of the run to Inverness begins. After the long climb to the summit of the line at Druimuachdar, 452 m (1,483 ft) above sea level, there is a lengthy undulating section through verdant farming country and woodland.

● **LEFT**
Named after Scotland's largest lake, Loch Lomond, locomotive No. 37412 speeds its passengers through the Scottish lowlands *en route* to Inverness.

● **BELOW**
The Loch Lomond snakes its way past one of the lochs on its way to the Scottish Highland city of Inverness.

INFORMATION BOX

Termini	Edinburgh, Wick and Thurso
Country	Scotland
Distance	Wick 540 km (335 miles), Thurso 529 km (329 miles)
Date of opening	1871

Blair Atholl, approached over a castellated bridge, was important in the days of steam traction because banking locomotives were shedded at a small depot still visible to the left of the line. The 29 km (18 mile) length of the line, which raises the railway 315 m (1,033 ft) to the highest rail summit in the UK apart from Snowdon, imposed a great strain on locomotive crews and on the

steam-raising capacity of boilers. Even now, although the HST makes light of the climb, heavy trains hauled by diesel locomotives struggle in bad weather.

The Highland Railway originally reached Inverness down the Spey valley through the Boat of Garten, a junction with the Great North of Scotland Railway, and Grantown on Spey. This 97 km (60 mile) route was shortened by 42 km (26 miles) by constructing a line from Aviemore through what was then wild country over the Slochd Pass, 401 m (1,315 ft) above sea level.

The train leaves Inverness round a left-handed curve and soon crosses the river Ness on a bridge replaced fairly recently after the original collapsed in severe flooding. A spirited run along the Beauly Firth provides fine views to the right before the train swings away from the water through the Muir of Ord to Dingwall. The line now heads north-west, following the coastal plain before swinging north-east to Tain on the picturesque Dornoch Firth, where it starts to climb alongside the Kyles of Sutherland to Culrain.

There follows a sharp climb at 1:70/72 as the line passes through a rocky gorge and past the small town of Lairg on its way to a summit 149 m (489 ft) above sea level, after which it swings east and drops down through pleasant scenery past the small Loch Fleet to reach the coast again at Golspie. A little further on is Dunrobin Castle, the seat of the Dukes of

Sutherland, which had its own private railway station and a shed to house the duke's own locomotive and carriage.

The railway follows the coast for another 24 km (15 miles) and, after Helmsdale, begins to climb again, in places as steeply as 1:60, toward the bleak but impressive uplands. At Forsinard, where a small group of houses and some trees cluster around the station building, the railway parts company with

the track, which goes straight on down Strath Halladale. The line swings sharply east, rising to 216 m (709 ft) at County Marsh summit, after which it descends until, 6.4 km (4 miles) further on, it is a surprise to come upon a station, Altanbreac. It then continues down to the wide coastal plain and the rail junction of Georgemas, where trains were divided, one section going to Wick and the other to Thurso.

● **ABOVE LEFT**
This small shop proclaims itself to be the first and last on mainland Britain. The house built by Jan de Groot (corrupted to John o' Groat) is nearby.

● **ABOVE RIGHT**
The striking blue of the erstwhile Caledonian Railway adorns No. 828, once belonging to that railway, as it waits at the Boat of Garten to take its train to Aviemore on the main line to Inverness.

● **LEFT**
A view from the castle of Edinburgh's world-famous Princes Street. The park between the castle and the street is on the site of a long dried-up loch.

SETTLE TO CARLISLE

The Settle to Carlisle line, which transports the traveller from the Yorkshire Dales through the desolate mountain scenery of the north-west, is one of the most scenic in England. For most of the journey, which takes in 14 tunnels and 19 viaducts, the line runs at an altitude of over 305 m (1,000 ft). One of the tunnels, the 137 m (450 ft) deep Blea Moor tunnel, is a massive 2,404 m (7,887 ft) long.

The Yorkshire village of Settle, where the journey starts, lies about 137 m (450 ft) above sea level. Although work began on the line in 1869, it was not until 1876 that the first passengers were able to enjoy the stupendous views that the line commands. The building of the line was not without incident, as can be seen from the plaque in the village church. Erected by the Midland Railway, it commemorates the men who lost their

● **LEFT**
No. 4498 Sir Nigel
Gresley leaves Rise
Hill tunnel on the
approach to Dent
station.

● **BELOW LEFT**
The West Yorkshire
Dalesman, hauled by
locomotive No.
5305, approaches
the summit at Ais
Gill Cottages *en route*
to Carlisle.

lives while building the 27 km (17 miles) of track between Settle and Dent Head.

The first 21 km (13 miles) of the line travels through the Ribble valley to an elevation of 320 m (1,050 ft). After 18 km (11 miles) the train crosses the Ribblehead viaduct. Built out of limestone and red brick between 1870 and 1874, at 32 m (105 ft) high this handsome viaduct is one of the highlights of the journey. The remoteness of the

INFORMATION BOX	
Termini	Settle and Carlisle
Country	England
Distance	115 km (71 miles)
Date of opening	1876

The Ribblehead viaduct, built between 1870 and 1874 out of limestone and red brick. At 32 m (105 ft) high, this is one of the high points of the journey.

The Flying Scotsman heads the Cumbrian Mountain Express. It is seen here at Great Ormside heading south *en route* from Appleby to Hellifield.

line can be gauged from the fact that Blea Moor signal box stands some 1.2 km (³/₄ mile) from the nearest road, and that Dent station is 6.4 km (4 miles) and 213 m (700 ft) above the village it serves. In winter the weather can be worse than anywhere else in England, with prolonged bouts of heavy snow. To prevent the snow from drifting on to the line, fences have been erected in the exposed mountain areas.

From Appleby to Carlisle the train passes through the Vale of Eden. Never encountering gradients of over 1:100, the line is laid some 15–30 m (50–100 ft) above river level. This makes it less liable to flooding, an important factor as the annual precipitation in this area can be over 2.5 m (100 in) per year.

The end of the journey is Carlisle station, which, in the early part of the century, with many railway companies jointly using it, was bustling with activity. Once an important artery between the city of Leeds and the north-west, the line is now one of the country's foremost lines for seeing, and travelling by, preserved steam locomotives.

The Settle and Carlisle is one of the finest preserved lines in Britain. A journey on these tracks is a trip back in time that every rail enthusiast should experience at least once in their lifetime.

LONDON EUSTON TO GLASGOW

This is one of the most historic lines in Britain, including, as it does, major lengths of Robert Stephenson's London & Birmingham and Joseph Locke's Grand Junction Railway. Although the title of Royal Scot was not bestowed until 1927, the train that bore the name was one of the oldest established in Britain, having first pulled out of Euston for Glasgow in June 1862. Up until 1914 the train left London Euston at 10.00, stopping at Willesden Junction, Rugby, Crewe (where it divided, with one section going on to Edinburgh) and Symington, reaching Glasgow eight and a quarter hours later.

In the summer of 1927, the LMSR made the Royal Scot a train for through passengers between London, Glasgow and Edinburgh only. The double-headed train, hauled by a Claughton 4-6-0 and a George the Fifth 4-4-0, stopped only twice – once at Carnforth, 380 km (236 miles) from Euston, where two 4-4-0 compounds took over for the run over Shap and Beattock summits to the second stop, Symington, 209 km (130 miles) further on, where the Edinburgh part of the train was detached. In 1928, hauled by Royal Scot 4-6-0 No. 6113 Cameronian, the Glasgow train made a non-stop run of 645.8 km (401.3 miles), a British record for any type of locomotive.

The most scenic part of the journey is the stretch north of Wigan, which starts with a sharp climb of about 3 km (2 miles) at 1:104, and then one at 1:119 to the summit of Coppull. Although the

● **ABOVE**
A southbound Glasgow to Euston train leaves Proofhouse Junction, south of Birmingham's New Street Station.

● **LEFT**
A scene at Wolverhampton's No. 1 Lock as a Euston to Glasgow InterCity train, hauled by a Class 86 electric locomotive, enters the station.

● **RIGHT**
A Euston-bound train near Ecclefechan, Galloway, on the first part of the journey.

● **BELOW LEFT**
A southbound Glasgow to Euston train beside the M1 in Northamptonshire.

● **BELOW RIGHT**
An RES (Rail Express Systems) liveried Class 86 heads southwards through Cumbria on the West Coast main line.

next section of the track was conducive to high-speed running, speed restrictions were necessary owing to subsidence (erosion) caused by mine workings. At Boars Head the subsidence was so severe that the windows of the station waiting-room sunk to the level of the platform.

After the almost level track through the Lune Gorge comes one of the steepest main-line inclines in Britain – the 6.4 km (4 mile) long 1:75 climb to Shap summit, 279 m (915 ft) above sea level. From the summit there is a 51 km (32 mile) long run of unbroken downhill running to Carlisle.

Until the 1923 regrouping, Carlisle station was one of the most colourful in the British Isles, with many companies' locomotives in their bright liveries to be

seen. These included the crimson of the Midland, the blue of the Caledonian, the bright green of the North Eastern and the yellow of the North British.

After crossing the into Scotland at Gretna, much of the ten tonnes of coal with which the train started off had been used and the "coal-pusher", a piston

operated by steam that shoved the coal forward from the rear of the tender, was set to work. A sign that the coal-pusher was in action was a jet of steam trailing from the top of the tender.

Just beyond Wamphray began the most gruelling climb on any British main line. Although most trains had to take on rear-end assistance, the Royal Scot charged unaided up the formidable 16 km (10 mile) long 1:74 grade to Beattock Summit, 318 m (1,043 ft) above sea level.

From here the train descended into Glasgow Central station, which opened in 1879. Although remodelled some 12 years later, it was still found to be inadequate for the growing traffic, and in 1906 it underwent further changes, to more than double the station's capacity.

INFORMATION BOX

Termini	London, Euston and Glasgow, Central
Countries	England and Scotland
Distance	645 km (401 miles)
Date of opening	5 July 1841

LONDON KING'S CROSS TO EDINBURGH WAVERLEY
THE FLYING SCOTSMAN

The name Flying Scotsman entered railway language on 1 January 1923. When the first expresses from London to Edinburgh began in 1862, the journey took 10½ hours; today it takes 4 hours and 35 minutes. Up to 1935, Ivatt's Atlantics were usually at the head of the train between London and Leeds; an A3 Pacific between Leeds and Newcastle; and a Heaton Pacific between Newcastle and Edinburgh.

London's King's Cross station was designed by Lewis Cubitt and built by John Jay in 1852. Today this station is one of the smallest London termini with only eight main-line and two suburban platforms. As the train leaves King's Cross, it passes St Pancras train shed. Designed by W.H. Barlow, the 210 m (689 ft) long, 30 m (98 ft) high building has a glass and iron roof, which spans 74 m (243 ft). When this magnificent feat of engineering was built, it was the widest in the world.

After passing through nine tunnels, the train travels over the stately Welwyn viaduct. Designed by Lewis Cubitt, the structure contains 40 solid brick arches, which reach 27 m (89 ft) at their maximum height over the Mimram valley.

All the original GNR stations between King's Cross and Doncaster, such as Stevenage, Hitchin, Huntingdon and Peterborough, were built using local materials by the Leicester-born Henry Goddard. Shortly after leaving Peterborough, the train reaches the

24 km (15 mile) long Stoke Bank, the summit of which, 105 m (345 ft) above sea level, is the highest point reached by the train this side of the border.

Travelling north the gradient steepens from 1:440 to 1:178 until, at the top, the train enters the 805 m (2,640 ft) long Stoke Tunnel, after which it descends to the town of Grantham. This is the stretch of line on which, in July 1938, Gresley's Mallard reached the world steam record of 203 kph (127 mph).

There are several flat crossings on this part of the line. One of these, just before Retford, was the scene of an accident in which the driver of a down express saw a goods train ambling straight across his

path. Having no time to brake, the quick-thinking driver accelerated and cut the goods train in two, thereby saving his train at the expense of only two or three goods wagons.

After leaving Doncaster, the train runs along a curving viaduct into Wakefield, before beginning its 3 km (2 mile) climb of 1:122 to Ardsley. Following a descent of 1:50 the train enters Leeds Central terminus, from which, after a short halt, the train retraces its steps for a short way before bearing right to strike up the 1:100 8 km (5 mile) long Headingley Bank. Just past the summit, the train plunges into Bramhope Tunnel. At 3.42 km (2 miles and 234 yd) long, Bramhope Tunnel is the seventh longest tunnel in the country. Beyond it, the gradient alters sharply to a downhill 1:94.

The train approaches Newcastle over the Tyne by the High Level Bridge. Designed by Robert Stephenson for both road and rail, this was the first major bridge-building work on which James Nasmyth's steam-driven pile-driver was used. Begun in April 1846, with a total weight of over 5,000 tons, this is the earliest example of a dual-purpose structure. The upper deck was for the railway, the lower for the road.

The next big bridge to be crossed is the 658 m (2,159 ft) long Royal Border Bridge, also built by Robert Stephenson, which was opened by Queen Victoria in 1850. Over 2,000 workers were engaged

● **ABOVE LEFT**
This picture clearly shows the two famous arches that are a feature of King's Cross station, London.

● **ABOVE RIGHT**
An InterCity train passes Durham Cathedral, the last resting-place of St Cuthbert.

● **BELOW**
350 miles to go until London.

INFORMATION BOX

THE FLYING SCOTSMAN

Termini	London King's Cross and Edinburgh, Waverley
Countries	England and Scotland
Distance	650 km (404 miles)
Date of opening	1 January 1923

in building the fine 28 redbrick semicircular arches, each with a span of 18.7 m (61 ft 4 in).

After crossing the border, the railway hugs the coastline as it ascends the 6.4 km (4 miles) of 1:190 up to Burnmouth. On passing Grantshouse the train enters the Penmanshiel tunnel, which was closed temporarily in 1979 after a fall had killed two men who were working in the tunnel.

The train enters Waverley station through the Carlton tunnel, opened in June 1846. Edinburgh's first station was confined to the narrow valley between the old and new towns of the city, and became congested. A new station, covering 23 acres, said to be the second biggest in Britain, was opened in 1900.

LONDON PADDINGTON TO SWANSEA – *THE RED DRAGON*

● **BELOW**
A Class 143 Regional Railways train outside
Ragnor, near Cardiff.

The Red Dragon service, between London Paddington and Swansea (Abertawe), was first run in the winter of 1950–51. Departing Swansea at 08.45, the train made stops at Cardiff (Caerdydd) and Newport (Casnewydd-ar-Wysg), before completing the final 214 km (133 miles) of the journey to Paddington, non-stop in 165 minutes, arriving at 13.05. The return trip was 30 minutes longer. Leaving Paddington at 17.55, it made additional stops at Swindon and Badminton, so that Swansea was not reached until 22.45.

Reading station was the first of Brunel's one-sided stations, and one of the last survivors. All that remains of the original is the building on the southernmost platform. It was here that one of the first accidents on the Great Western occurred. While the station was being built, Henry West, a carpenter, was fatally blown from the roof by a "whirlwind".

About 14 km (9 miles) from Reading the train crosses Basildon Bridge, which was built in 1839 and extended in the 1890s. Its four redbrick 19 m (62 ft)

arches cross the Thames uniting Berkshire and Oxfordshire. The line soon returns to Berkshire by means of Moulsford Bridge.

At the western end of Steventon, 18 km (11 miles) further on, the line crosses "The Causeway". One mile long, this is a raised flood path lined with trees and 17th- and 18th-century houses. A further 16 km (10 miles) brings us to Uffington, famous for its "White Horse", which can be seen from the train. This is 114 m (374 ft) from nose to tail and is believed to have been first cut into the hillside about 100 BC. Although called a horse it is more than likely that it was meant to be a dragon, for nearby is Dragon Hill on which, so folklore tells us, St George slew the fabled beast.

Swindon station, 124 km (77 miles) from Paddington, was originally built in 1841–42. A feature of the station was the hotel and dining-room connected to it by a covered overbridge. The original agreement was that all trains passing through should have a ten-minute refreshment stop here. Swindon was the site of Brunel's Great Western works, which were completed in 1843. The last

INFORMATION BOX

THE RED DRAGON

Termini	London, Paddington and Swansea
Countries	England and Wales
Distance	307 km (191 miles)
Date of first run	1950

steam engine built at the works was
Evening Star, which entered service in
May 1960.

Badminton station, 160 km (100
miles) from Paddington, was specially
built for the Duke of Beaufort, who
demanded that any train had to stop at
his request – until, that is, an Act of
Parliament put a stop to his right. It was
here that the eponymous game was first
played. A few miles out of Badminton,
the train goes under the Cotswold Hills
through the 406 m (1,332 ft) long
Chipping Sodbury tunnel.

First sketched out by Charles
Richardson in 1865, the Severn tunnel,
after twice being flooded out, was finally
completed in 1886 at the cost of nearly
£2 million (then $3.2 million).
Connecting Wales to England, at 4,064 m
(13,333 ft) long it is the largest main-line
railway tunnel in Britain. The tunnel

● BELOW
A driver's-eye view from the cab of an
InterCity 125 as it approaches the up train on
the line between Paddington and Swansea.

● BELOW
The "Welcome to Wales" sign that greets
passengers as the train leaves the Welsh side
of the Severn tunnel.

shortened the route from London to
South Wales by 40 km (25 miles) and led
to the popular belief that the initials
GWR stood for the "great way round".

Just before Newport the line crosses
the River Usk. The first bridge, one of
Brunel's wooden viaducts, was damaged
by fire during construction. Remarkable
as it sounds, out of the many wooden
viaducts built by Brunel, this was the only
one to suffer such a fate. It was later

rebuilt, but this time in wrought iron.

Cardiff Central station, 233 km (145
miles) from Paddington, was first built in
1850. To create a site for the station, the
River Taff had to be diverted. The station
was modernized in the 1920s. On leaving
the Welsh capital, the line turns inland
until it regains the coast near Margam,
after which it skirts Swansea Bay, passing
through Port Talbot and Neath before
arriving at Swansea.

● OPPOSITE
The English portal
of the Severn tunnel,
connecting Wales
and England.

● RIGHT
A scene near
Sonning Cutting.
Although passengers
in the train do not
get a good view of it,
Sonning Cutting is
an engineering
achievement at
18 m (60 ft) deep
and nearly 3 km
(2 miles) long. It was
built in the autumn
and winter of 1839
and opened in
March 1840.

LONDON EUSTON TO HOLYHEAD
THE IRISH MAIL

The London & North Western Railway's Irish Mail was the world's first named train. Known unofficially as the "Wild Irishman", it departed from Euston station for the first time in August 1848. After passing through the 1,080 m (3,543 ft) long Primrose Hill tunnel, the train entered Acton Lane station (named Willesden Junction in 1866), which was built in 1842. Owing to its two groups of completely separate high-level platforms, and the fact that nobody knew at which platform any particular train was to arrive at or depart from, the station was unofficially nicknamed "Bewildering Junction" by its passengers.

Some 27 km (17 miles) into the journey the train passes through the Watford tunnel. 1.65 km (1 mile and 57 yd) long, the tunnel was built so that the railway line did not cross over the land of the Earl of Essex.

After another 56 km (35 miles) the train passes over the Wolverton viaduct. Over 200 m (660 ft) long with six arches, each with an 18 m (60 ft) span, the viaduct is at the centre of an

● LEFT
A 20th-century InterCity train passes the 13th-century Conway Castle.

embankment 2.4 km (1½ miles) long and 15 m (49 ft) high. After a further 16 km (10 miles), Kilsby tunnel is reached. At 2,216 m (7,270 ft) in length, when it was built, at a cost of £290,000 (then $460,000), it was the longest railway tunnel in the world.

Passing Birmingham New Street, Manchester, Crewe and Chester, the train then runs along the North Wales coast. After going through Rhyl and Colwyn the line goes under the steep slope of the almost precipitous headland of Penmaen Mawr. As there was not enough room

between the mountain and the shore, in some places the rock had to be blasted and in others sea walls had to be built up to enable the line to be laid. A tunnel 211 m (693 ft) long was cut through the headland and, in some places, where the line ran close under the steep mountain face, covered ways were built as a precaution against falling stones.

During its construction, in October 1846, a north-westerly gale, combined with a spring tide of 5 m (16 ft), destroyed a large part of the work on the westward side of the headland. It was

● LEFT
An InterCity train approaching Crewe from the south.

The Britannia Bridge. Built by Robert Stephenson, the 420 m (1,380 ft) long bridge over the Menai Strait was opened in 1850. Two million bolts were used in its construction.

● BELOW
The Irish Mail seen here in preservation on the Great Central Railway, in Leicestershire.

then decided to cross the section by means of the big, curving, open viaduct that brings the train into Bangor. Work on the viaduct was eventually finished in 1849.

In the days of steam, in order to permit non-stop running between Chester and Holyhead, just before Bangor, near Aber, the speeding train would scoop up water from troughs laid between the tracks. Laid down in 1860, these were the world's first railway water troughs.

Next comes the Menai Strait tubular railway bridge leading to Anglesey. Built by Stephenson, the bridge spans 335 m (1,100 ft) of water near to Britannia Rock, from which it gets the name of Britannia Bridge. Stephenson's first plan

was to construct it out of cast iron. However, this was rejected by the Admiralty, who insisted that under no circumstances was the navigation of the Strait to be interrupted. After toying with various plans, in March 1845 Stephenson finally decided on the tubular wrought-iron beam with openings of 140 m (459 ft) and a roadway, formed of a hollow wrought-iron beam, about 6 m (20 ft) in diameter.

Built by a team of about 1,500 workers, the bridge has four spans, two of 140 m (460 ft) over the water and two of 70 m (230 ft) over the land. It was

opened for the public on 18 March 1850. Before the opening of the bridge, passengers had to disembark in Bangor and cross the Menai Strait by coach via Telford's suspension bridge.

The short run over Anglesey passes Llanfair PG, or, to give it its 58-letter name, coined by the local innkeeper in the 19th century, Llanfairpwllgwyngyll-gogerychwyrndrobwllllantysiliogogogoch. Renowned for having the world's longest railway sign, the station was re-opened in 1973. Then the train soon reaches Holyhead — and the ferry that conveys passengers to Ireland, the Emerald Isle.

INFORMATION BOX

THE IRISH MAIL

Termini	London, Euston and Holyhead
Countries	England and Wales
Distance	425 km (264 miles)
Date of first run	1 August 1848

LONDON PADDINGTON TO PENZANCE

One of the most exciting and interesting rail journeys in England is that from London Paddington to Penzance, at the south-westerly tip of Cornwall. When the line opened, in August 1859, not only did almost all the trains stop at all stations, but passengers also had to change at Exeter and Plymouth. On arrival in Truro, a horse-drawn bus took them on to Falmouth, where the travellers boarded the West Cornwall narrow-gauge railway for the 33-minute ride to Penzance. The fastest time for the whole journey was some 14 hours and 50 minutes.

1862 saw the introduction of the Flying Dutchman, a train which did the journey from Paddington to Churston,

on the Torquay branch of the South Devon Railway, at an average speed of 89.6 kph (56 mph), making it possible to reach Penzance in 10 hours and 19 minutes. The following year the line was extended from Truro to Falmouth,

● **BELOW**
Cornish Riviera Limited. The first train of this name ran in 1904.

thereby making the equine transport redundant. By 1867 the broad gauge was extended to Penzance.

In 1890 the Great Western introduced the Cornishman express, which, by cutting out a number of intermediate stations, was able to reach Penzance in 8 hours and 42 minutes. After the conversion from broad to standard gauge in 1892, the Flying Dutchman was able to cut a further 15 minutes off its time, so becoming the fastest train in the world.

In 1896 the Cornishman posted a time of 3 hours and 43 minutes for a

● **OPPOSITE ABOVE**
When the station was built Paddington was still just a village. In the booking hall is a diminutive statue of Isambard Kingdom Brunel which was unveiled in May 1982.

● **OPPOSITE BELOW**
One of the few Brunel stations left, Dawlish station, built in 1846, is lovingly preserved. Here an InterCity train leaves the station *en route* to Penzance.

● **ABOVE LEFT**
A section of the dramatic coastal track between Dawlish and Teignmouth.

● **RIGHT**
An InterCity train crosses the Huntspil River at the Somerset Levels. This is one of the wettest areas in England with an average annual rainfall of 101 cm (40 in). Much of the area is below sea level and liable to periodic flooding.

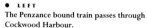

● LEFT
The Penzance bound train passes through Cockwood Harbour.

Cutting, 18 m (59 ft) deep and 6.5 km (nearly two miles long), is another remarkable achievement, built in 1839 and opened in March 1840. The excavation was fraught with difficulties as torrential rain flooded the area and reduced the site to a quagmire.

One of the features of the line was Brunel's celebrated one-sided stations. With both platforms on the same side, but a short distance apart, the design obviated the necessity for passengers to cross the line. Examples of these, now totally rebuilt stations, which must have caused chronic operating difficulties, include Reading, Taunton and Exeter.

After the 998 m (3,274 ft) long Whiteball Tunnel, which marks the boundary of Somerset and Devon, there is a flat coastal run, taking in the five tunnels between Dawlish and Teignmouth – Kennaway, Phillot, Clerk's, Coryton and Parsons. In 1905 these tunnels were widened to accommodate double tracks.

Newton Abbot was where Brunel set up his atmospheric railway. The concept of this was that, instead of being hauled by steam engines, the carriages were

non-stop run to Exeter – then at 310 km (194 miles) the longest non-stop route in the world – cutting the time to Penzance to 7 hours and 52 minutes.

In July 1904, by running non-stop to Plymouth, the time was reduced even more when the Limited express reached Penzance in 7 hours dead. In May 1914, the time was cut to 6¹/₂ hours and, in 1927, with the introduction of the King Class, the most powerful engines in the British Isles, the Cornish Riviera reduced the time by a further five minutes to 6 hours and 25 minutes.

Soon after departing Paddington Station, which was designed by Brunel and opened in 1854, the train passes over the 274 m (899 ft) long Wharncliffe Viaduct. Built in 1838, the eight 21 m (69 ft) brick spans tower 20 m (65 ft) above the ground. The next point of interest on the route is Sounding Arch Bridge, which was built in 1838 and widened in 1891. Considered to be one of Brunel's finest bridges, it cost £37,000 (then $59,200) to build and consists of two of the largest, flattest arches ever built in brick, each with a span of 39 m (128 ft) with a rise of only 7.4 m (24 ft 3 in). It is this bridge that is depicted in Turner's painting, *Rain, Steam and Speed*.

Although passengers in the train do not get a good view of it, Sonning

● ABOVE
On getting off the train, visitors to Penzance are welcomed by this bilingual greeting in both English and Cornish.

● BELOW
The holiday is over. The train to Paddington leaves Penzance.

The 12.25 Great Western train from London to Bristol, showing the Great Western's new livery, at Swindon.

propelled by a vacuum caused by compressed air being pumped through a pipe between the rails.

Separating Devon and Cornwall is the 338 m (1,109 ft) long Royal Albert Bridge, which spans the River Tamar, the world's only chain-link suspension bridge to carry express trains. Widely regarded as Brunel's masterpiece, the two main tubular spans, each 137 m (450 ft) long and weighing over 1,077 tonnes (1,060 tons), are supported by three piers that allow a clearance of at least 30 m (100 ft)

above the water. The central underwater pier is anchored on hard rock 24 m (79 ft) below the high-water level and was built by masons working in a pressurized diving bell – the first such use in civil engineering. It took seven years to build and was opened by Prince Albert in May 1859, four months before Isambard Kingdom Brunel's death.

Over the 85 km (53 miles) between Plymouth and Truro, the train crossed 34 of Brunel's timber viaducts, now replaced by masonry ones. The viaducts,

which crossed the many deep and narrow valleys of the area, were constructed in two standard spans of 20 m (66 ft) for the Cornwall and Tavistock lines and 15 m (50 ft) for the West Cornwall structures.

The line reached Penzance in March 1852, when it opened to standard-gauge trains. Fifteen years later, in March 1867, the Great Western's broad gauge reached the town. The present station, which has a charming sign welcoming visitors in the now almost dead language of Cornish, was built about 1865.

● **ABOVE RIGHT**
The Mayflower entering Exeter St Davids station.

● **LEFT**
The train crossing the sea wall at Dawlish. The town of Dawlish is often the victim of fierce storms. One such, in 1974, washed away most of the down platform.

LONDON VICTORIA TO DOVER
THE GOLDEN ARROW

Although the Southern Railway (and its predecessor the South Eastern & Chatham Railway) had maintained a service from London Victoria to Paris, it was not until 15 May 1929 that the title Golden Arrow was bestowed upon the train. The first trains were hauled by 4-6-0 Lord Nelson Class and were exclusively for first-class Pullman passengers; however, two second-class cars were added in the 1940s . After World War II, the Lord Nelson Class was

● **LEFT**
The Golden Arrow travelling through Ashford, Kent.

● **BELOW LEFT**
The Golden Arrow coming into Headcorn station. This view is taken from Fritten Road Bridge.

replaced by Oliver Bulleid's Merchant Navy Class 4-6-2s. Bulleid, a New Zealander by birth, was the Chief Mechanical Engineer of the Southern Railway. Then, in 1951, Britannia 4-6-2 Standard Class 7s were introduced to the service. One of these, No. 70004, William Shakespeare, was exhibited at the 1951 Festival of Britain.

The Golden Arrow was one of the first trains in England to be fitted with a public address system, through which the international passengers were addressed in English and French.

Another feature of the train was the Trianon cocktail bar, reminiscent of a high-class club, where the rich were able to sup their way to the Continent. The exclusive first-class train lasted only two years, for by May 1931 the weight of the

INFORMATION BOX	
THE GOLDEN ARROW	
Termini	London Victoria and Dover
Country	England
Distance	113 km (70 miles)
Date of first run	15 May 1929

● **RIGHT**
The Golden Arrow
seen here between
Tonbridge and
Sevenoaks.

● **BELOW RIGHT**
King Arthur Class
4-6-0 No. 30794 Sir
Ector de Maris stands
at the night ferry's
traditional platform 2
at London Victoria.

● **BOTTOM
RIGHT**
The up Continental
boat express leaving
Dover Marine station
after collecting
passengers from the
cross-channel ferry.

Depression had persuaded the railway
company that their only course of action
was to admit second-class passengers.

Sporting a Union Flag and Tricolour,
the Golden Arrow departed London
Victoria at 11.00 a.m. The journey began
with a 1:62 climb on to the Grosvenor
Bridge. Subsequent gradients included
2.4 km (1½ miles) at 1:102 leading to
Penge tunnel, and 3 km (2 miles) at 1:95
to Bickley Junction, with slow running
round the curve to Orpington.

After passing Tonbridge the train was
faced with 6 km (4 miles) at 1:122 and 3
km (2 miles) at 1:144, the latter through
the Sevenoaks tunnel. From here to
Dover Marine, which was reached at
12.38, the line was fairly level and speeds
of 96 kph (60 mph) were possible.

The ferry, Canterbury, crossed the
English Channel in 75 minutes. After
transferring to the awaiting Flèche d'Or,
a four-cylinder Nord Pacific of the
French Northern Railway, the travellers
completed the last 296 km (184 miles)
from Calais to Paris in 190 minutes,
arriving in the French capital at 17.35.
You can still travel by rail and ferry from
Victoria to Paris, but not by steam.

BEDFORD TO BLETCHLEY

A rail journey from Bedford to Bletchley, two stations that connect the Midland main line with the West Coast main line, may not sound as romantic as a trip on the Orient Express, but the "friendly line", as many locals call it, is one of the finest journeys in the kingdom.

Since the first train ran on 17 November 1846, operated by the London & North Western Railway, the line has been vital to the people of the area. A journey along the route engineered by George and Robert Stephenson, now denominated the Marston Vale line and operated by National Express, is like a trip back to the 1930s. The 27 km (17 mile) journey,

which takes 50 minutes, is completely rural, with no mass urbanization to be seen. There are three manned level crossings and no fewer than six signal boxes that still operate semaphore

signals. The Fenny Stratford box houses a fine collection of old paintings and sepia photographs showing the area as it was.

At the beginning of the 20th century, the line was covered by a railmotor service. These were an early form of multiple unit and consisted of a self-propelled coach fitted with a steam boiler in one end. Because the passengers entered and left the coaches by means of steps, it was not necessary to build conventional platforms at the halts along the way. Today the trains are operated by Heritage DMUs. This is one of the last lines to use these units, which date back to the 1960s.

The journey begins at Bedford Midland station, which is on the Midland main line with services to Luton and Gatwick airports. The first part of the journey passes through Bedford St Johns, Kempston Hardwick, Stewartby (formerly Wootton Pillinge) and Millbrook. Here there is a crossing where the levers are housed in the open air by the side of the box. The crossing keeper has a collection of wheel hub caps that have fallen off cars as they ride over the bumpy crossing.

Part of the route goes over land belonging to the Duke of Bedford. The 10th Duke was a great supporter of the building of the line. He did, however,

● **ABOVE RIGHT**
Evening shadows lengthen as the two-car Class 117 DMU ambles through glorious countryside near Millbrook with a Bletchley to Bedford service.

● **RIGHT**
A Bletchley-bound train pauses at the delightful rural station of Fenny Compton, next to the A5 Watling Street, with a Bletchley to Bedford service. Note the semaphore signals and the high escarpment sweeping towards Ampthill in the background.

INFORMATION BOX	
Termini	Bedford and Bletchley
Country	England
Distance	27 km (17 miles)
Date of opening	1846

insist that all the station buildings on his estate (Fenny Stratford, Woburn Sands, Ridgmont and Millbrook) should be of half-timber design. Woburn Sands, the coal depot for the line, was also important for its brickyard, and the railway was used to transport the bricks.

A feature of the journey used to be the London Brick Works, whose many tall chimneys were counted by generations of children. There are now only ten, which can still be seen from the train. The old clay pits, now filled with water, create a moonlike landscape. Some of these sites were used as landfill for London's waste, which was carried down the line as far as Forders Sidings.

● **ABOVE**
The Derby Lightweight two-car DMU Class 108 stands in the bay at Bedford station with a Class 319 Thameslink EMU in the background.

● **ABOVE RIGHT**
The traditional country station atmosphere of the 1930s is conjured up in this typical scene as a two-car Class 108 unit stands at Aspley Guise station.

● **RIGHT**
"Ten Chimneys". A two-car Class 117 DMU ambles past the high escarpment near Lidlington with a Bedford to Bletchley service.

LONDON TO COLOGNE

● BELOW
Electric BoBo locomotive No. 86.250 stands at
the head of its train in Liverpool Street station
in London.

There are three rail routes from London to
Cologne, one is via the Hook of Holland,
one is via Ostend, and the third is through
the Channel Tunnel.

● VIA THE HOOK OF HOLLAND

This used to be one of the pleasantest
ways to go to Cologne. A boat train,
usually with the best stock the railway
could muster and a gleaming locomotive
at the head, left London's Liverpool
Street station each evening. On arrival at
the special station at Harwich, where
facilities have been greatly improved
recently, passengers passed through
passport and customs controls and
walked straight to the ship. This route
can still be followed, but since June 1997
night ships for rail passengers have been
discontinued and replaced by catamarans
operating day services only.

The railway station at the Hook of
Holland is on the dockside. Connecting
international express trains ceased a few
years ago and the route via Venlo now
requires a couple of changes to get to
Cologne. Frequent local services run to
Rotterdam, which is a major port.

● LEFT
The König Albert
was one of the
vessels that ferried
passengers from
Dover to Ostend in
the 1950s.

INFORMATION BOX

Termini	London and Cologne
Countries	England, Belgium, Netherlands and Germany
Distance	via Ostend 595 km (370 miles); via The Hook of Holland 545 km (339 miles)
Date of opening	via Ostend 1861; via The Hook of Holland 1893; via the Channel Tunnel 1994

● LEFT
The Hook of Holland rail/ship station by
night. The large ships will soon be replaced
by large catamarans.

The terrain in the Netherlands is only difficult for rail construction to the extent that numerous rivers, many of them navigable, must be crossed. On the line to Venlo is the longest rail bridge in the Netherlands, at 1.07 km (3,510 ft), over the Hollandsch Diep at Moerdijk. Other places of rail interest are Tilburg, where the main workshops of the Netherlands railways are situated, and Venlo, on the border with Germany, an industrial centre that not only provides a wide variety of Netherlands motive power but also sees the hand-over of trains to German locomotives.

The route through Utrecht is the one now normally used to get to Cologne from Rotterdam. There is a good connecting train every hour to Utrecht, a major rail junction.

● VIA OSTEND

London's Victoria station was the starting-point to this once classic route to the continent, with boat trains depositing passengers virtually alongside ships. Today an electric multiple unit (EMU) runs to Ramsgate, and the bus provided by the shipping line carries passengers to the harbour. The night crossing used to bring them to Ostend early enough to catch the 06.34 train, giving passengers an arrival at Cologne by 10.42. The harbour at Ostend is host to myriad small

● BELOW
The smart way to get to Brussels and into Germany is to come from England by Eurostar from St Pancras International station in London. A train arrives at Brussels Midi station, where connections can readily be made to most parts of Europe.

● LEFT
A Sprinter on local services stands at Rotterdam Central station.

craft and fishing boats, and the town can offer a variety of places to sample continental fare. Just outside the station, a coastal tramway, part of the much diminished "Vicinal" system, runs southwards to De Panne and northwards to Knokke.

The elegant building and seven platforms of Ostend station are right alongside the quay. In addition to the usual local and inter-city services, international trains commence their journeys here, although the numbers have declined in recent years. At Ghent, the largest town in 13th-century Europe, there is a large railway station with an

● RIGHT
Cologne's Hauptbahnhof is overshadowed by
the city's Gothic cathedral.

● RIGHT
Cologne's Hauptbahnhof is overshadowed by
the city's Gothic cathedral.

impressive old main building. In the
early morning and evening rush hours its
many tracks are very busy. A good range
of motive power and a variety of EMUs
plus the occasional freight train provide
constant interest.

And so to Brussels where the third
railway route to Cologne is met.

● **VIA THE CHANNEL TUNNEL**

The new London Eurostar terminal at
St Pancras is now the starting point for
trains serving Paris, Lille and Brussels.
The vast single-span roof has been
restored to accommodate the 400-metre-
long trains that will run on the first
high-speed line linking London to the
European high-speed rail network.
The interior of the trains bears a close
resemblance to the TGV on which it is
based. Once under way, the ride quality
is superb. It is so quiet and smooth that
the speed is hard to determine.

The train makes a slow start from
London, weaving its way through the
suburbs for many kilometres until it can

sprint along the fairly straight route
through Kent, passing hop fields and
oast-houses on the way to the entrance
to Dollands Moor sidings, where the live
current ceases to be collected from a
third rail and is taken from the overhead
line equipment. This operation is carried
out without stopping, and the train is
soon running at the maximum permitted
speed of 160 kph (100 mph) for about
20 minutes through the tunnel.

The train emerges in France with the
very extensive sidings for the car and
goods vehicle shuttle services away to the
left. The TGV line to Lille is joined and
having passed the specially built station
there is a locomotive depot to the right
and a large TGV and general repair
depot to the left. As the high-speed lines
in Belgium are completed it is possible
to see and appreciate the impressive
engineering feats which have been
undertaken in this ambitious project.

Brussels also has a fine Eurostar
terminal at the Midi station. From the
many platforms of the main station,
trains go to all parts of Europe. Below,
trams and a metro system serve the
environs of this bustling capital city.

The Belgium Government was far-
sighted when it supported the joining of
stations north and south of the city by a
tunnel – something yet to be achieved in
Paris or London. Brussel Centraal, as the
name implies, serves the city centre,
where there are many fine buildings. The
Gare du Nord is situated in the French-
speaking part of the city, in an area which
was once rather disreputable but is now
being sanitized by the construction of
many modern buildings.

● **RIGHT**
For passengers with some time to spare there is plenty to see and do in Brussels. Maybe a cup of coffee, or something stronger, in the Grande Place.

● **OPPOSITE BELOW**
The majority of short-distance inter-city and local passenger-trains are in the hands of EMUs in Belgium. Aum 75 Class 4-car unit heads a rush-hour train at Gent St Pieters.

● **BELOW**
The old Marloiban station in Utrecht has been turned into a fine railway museum. Railways in the Netherlands bought many locomotives from the UK. This outside-framed 2-4-0 No. 32 was built by Beyer-Peacock in 1864.

● **BOTTOM**
German Railways No. 140. 741 stands at the Dutch/German border at Venlo. It has taken over from its German counterpart and will soon set off for Cologne.

There are numerous trains from Midi station to Cologne, taking just under three hours, but this timing will be greatly reduced when the planned new lines have been completed. The approach by rail to Liège is down a very steep gradient, and even today a special electric locomotive is kept to bank heavy trains going in the Brussels direction. The station is very busy, with trains coming from all points of the compass, including the picturesque line to Luxembourg. The line climbs away from Liège following a sinuous course with some pleasant scenery on the way to Aachen. Beyond Aachen, the journey is largely through rural agricultural areas, passing the significant town of Düren. Increasing industry and urbanization heralds arrival at the outskirts of Cologne with large carriage sidings to the right and a massive locomotive depot at the left.

Cologne's main station is at a high level on the banks of the River Rhine. Its huge arched roof shelters passenger-trains of all descriptions, and traffic has increased to such an extent that the Hohenzollern bridge across the river now has a modern double track set of spans opposite the spans of the road and tramway part of the bridge that was destroyed in World War II.

PARIS TO ISTANBUL
THE ORIENT EXPRESS

What became the Orient Express sprang upon eight countries in 1883. Founded specially by Georges Nagelmackers, a Belgian mining engineer, La Compagnie Internationale des Wagons-Lits (The International Sleeping Car Company), the world's first multi-national, had been running through sleeping cars with wide buffers from Paris to Vienna since 1876. "Et des Grands Express Européens" was added to the name in 1883 when the train first linked Paris with Bucharest, as it still does today, via Munich, Vienna and Budapest. The journey took 77 hours one way and 81 the other – local time was unsynchronized.

Istanbul passengers were taken on to Giurgiu, ferried from Romania across the river Danube to Rustchuk in Bulgaria and then had another seven-hour train journey to the Black Sea port of Varna. From here an Austrian Lloyd liner took the travellers on the final part of their 82-hour journey.

From 8 August 1888, the train abandoned Giurgiu and diverted at Budapest to Belgrade and Nis in Serbia. It then travelled up the Dragoman Pass through the Northern Passara mountains by cornice and tunnel, on a gradient of 1:37, to Bulgaria; down to Sofia, up again

● **ABOVE**
The Military Orient Express in 1919. All the seats on this Allied military train were held by the French Army (note the tricolour on the tender), but civilians were admitted if seats were available. It is seen here crossing the River Limmat near Zurich.

● **BELOW**
The Orient Express as seen on the French Eastern Railway on 4 October 1883. The train of two passenger cars and a sleeper is being hauled by a 500 Class 2-4-0.

INFORMATION BOX

THE ORIENT EXPRESS

Termini	Paris and Istanbul
Countries	France to Turkey
Distance	3,212 km (1,996 miles)
Date of opening	1883

to Tatar Pazardjik, and through the mountains over the newly opened line to the city of Plovdiv, the furthermost point of the Oriental Railway from Istanbul. This journey took 67 hours and a few minutes.

Passengers from 1888 enjoyed the comfortable sleeping cars with velvet curtains, plush seating, lavatories at the car ends, and a tinkling hand-bell in the corridors, which summoned them to five-course French *haute cuisine* in the dining cars. Renamed the Orient Express in 1891, it made cursory frontier stops

● **ABOVE RIGHT**
One of the head attendants waits to welcome passengers aboard the Orient Express.

● **ABOVE**
The Pullman coat of arms.

● **RIGHT**
A British Pullman, taken at Kensington Olympia around 1987. The train manager stands in front of the dining car.

to change engines. The clientele always included government couriers, chained to their diplomatic bags, but often royalty and diplomats also used the train. Indeed the story goes that a Romanian count caught the train just to enjoy the menu, remarking, "The express takes four hours to cross me" – meaning his vast estate!

Leaving Gare de l'Est, Paris, the train had an easy run up the Marne valley through Champagne vineyards, Epernay and Chalons, where, later, the Calais car was attached. The train then crossed the River Moselle at Nancy and continued on its way to the then German frontier at Deutsch-Avricourt.

The route across Alsace passes through the notable 1,678 m (5,505 ft)

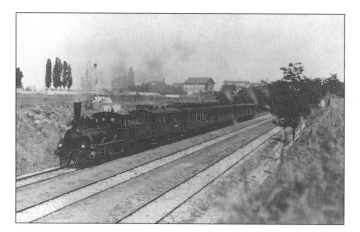

● LEFT
The Orient Express in Turkey about 1910. The train here is being hauled by an Oriental Railways Austrian-built 4-4-0. Note the "cow-catcher" on the locomotive.

The Orient Express was stopped abruptly in 1914 by the outbreak of World War I, when both sides used were forced to commission their passenger coaches for use as ambulance trains.

In 1916 the Germans started the rival Mitropa Company, using requisitioned Wagons-Lits cars, running the Berlin-Istanbul Balkan Express, to reach their Turkish allies. After the 1918 Armistice was signed in Wagons-Lits Dining Car No. 2419, destroyed by Hitler's SS troops in 1944, the Orient Express restarted with difficulty in 1921. In 1923, due to the Rheinland Occupation, the train was diverted via Zurich (Switzerland) and the 10.24 km (6 miles 650 yd) long Austrian Arlberg tunnel, which had been completed in 1884. This became a permanent route.

The Swiss-Arlberg-Vienna Express, renamed Arlberg-Orient Express in 1932, ran to Budapest via Hagyeshalom from Vienna, and to Bucharest via Sighisoara. A Paris-Athens sleeper ran

long Homarting-Arzviller twin tunnels – the twin carries the Marne-Rhein Canal. Eight km (5 miles) beyond Strasbourg (Strassburg) the Orient Express crossed the Rhine at Kehl, over a steel bridge destroyed in World War II, into Baden-Württemberg.

After travelling through Stuttgart, Augsburg and Ulm the express arrived in Bavaria's capital, Munich. Originally the express entered Austria at Simbach, but was soon diverted past Lake Prien to Salzburg and so on to Vienna, where, from 1894, it was joined by the Ostend-Vienna express.

The Orient Express then ran on through Bratislava to Budapest. The next section of the route, through to Bucharest, was via Szged and Timisoara, over the now disused 30 m (99 ft) high Biatorbagy viaduct, where, in 1931, the train was dramatically blown up by Hungarian fascists.

The Istanbul train ran south from Budapest, crossing the Danube at Peiterwarden bridge, and the Serbian frontier at Subotica. From here it was an easy run, through fields of sunflowers, to Nis-Plovdiv and the junction for Greece.

From Plovdiv, the Oriental Railway followed the Maritza valley near the Bulgarian frontier and so, after crossing the river several times, once over the

1,270 m (4,167 ft) long, 173-span bridge at Pithion, the train ran along the dramatic Aegean coastline to Thessalonika. It was on this stretch of the line that Ian Fleming's *From Russia with Love* was filmed. Then there are 1:66 gradients over the snow-clad hills to the Sea of Marmora and journey's end at Istanbul's Sirkeci station.

In 1900 Wagon-Lits tried a Berlin-Breslau (Wroclaw) to Istanbul express that avoided Vienna. This experiment, however, sadly only lasted two years.

twice a week and a Paris-Istanbul service
ran three times a week.

Disrupted again by World War II
(there was a Zurich–Istanbul service for a
time), the Orient Express was restarted
in 1947 with ordinary coaches, one or
two sleepers and the occasional dining
car. In 1950, Captain Karpe, US Military
Attaché at Bucharest, was murdered on
the train as it was passing through a
tunnel near Salzburg, in Russian-
occupied Austria.

The Budapest-Belgrade sector ceased
in 1963 when the Tauern-Orient sleeper
was started from Ostend to Athens. This
ended in 1976. The Tauern tunnel,
which is 8.53 km (5 miles and 557 yd)
long, was completed in 1909.

Today Wagons-Lits Austria still staff
the Vienna-Paris sleeper, while a
Hungarian Railways (MAV) dining car
serves classic dinners between Budapest
and Salzburg. Romanian Railways run the
Budapest-Bucharest sleeper.

CALAIS TO ISTANBUL
THE SIMPLON-ORIENT EXPRESS

● **BELOW**
The 1900 timetable cover showing the dining car surrounded by compartments of (left) the Orient Express and (right) the St Petersburg-Cannes express.

In 1906, Wagons-Lits started the Simplon Express (SE) from Paris to Lausanne (Switzerland). The route took in the recently opened 19.8 km (12 miles 557 yd) long Simplon Tunnel (Europe's longest until 1991), Milan (Italy) and later Venice (Italy) and Trieste (at that time part of Austria). However, Vienna would not let it proceed farther east, which was precisely the SE objective.

At the end of World War I, the Allied governments at the Treaty of Versailles created the Simplon-Orient Express (SOE). They asked Wagons-Lits to run the route, which connected liberated Romania, Yugoslavia and Athens with the West, thereby avoiding Germany, Austria and Hungary. They also compelled the Germans to restart the Orient Express.

COMP.ᵉᴵᴺTERNATIONALE DES WAGONS-LITS & DES GRANDS EXPRESS EUROPEENS

AGENCES DE LA COMPAGNIE

● **LEFT**
A replica of car No. 2439. The original, in which the Armistices of 1918 and 1940 were signed, went by road to Germany, where it was destroyed on the orders of Hitler.

● **BELOW**
The Simplon-Orient Express at the Turkish frontier in 1950.

INFORMATION BOX

THE SIMPLON-ORIENT EXPRESS

Termini	Calais and Istanbul
Countries	France to Turkey
Distance	about 3,460 km (2,150 miles)
Date of opening	1906

The Athens-Salonika main line, with its numerous tunnels and viaducts through and over the Greek mountains, opened in 1917. The second track tunnel was opened in 1921.

The line from Calais Maritime to Paris Gare de Lyon opened in 1870 and crossed the 30 m (99 ft) high Chantilly viaduct. From Paris the Simplon Express followed the Seine valley to the Laroche-Migennes engine-changing stop, after which there was an easy rising gradient to

● **OPPOSITE**
The Venice Simplon-Orient Express travelling through the Arlberg Pass near the picturesque village of Pettnau.

● LEFT
The Venice Simplon-Orient Express at Pettnau on the Arlberg in July 1984. The train is headed by ÖBB 1020 and 1010 Class locomotives.

After crossing the Orbe on the 30 m (100 ft) high Le Day bridge, at Daillens, the train joined the Swiss main line, electrified in 1906, from Neuchâtel to Lausanne, continuing along Lake Geneva through Montreux and following the Rhône valley to Brig at the mouth of the Simplon Tunnel. This last section was electrified in 1906.

The line emerged at Iselle, Italy, from where the Swiss-operated line drops 358 m (1,175 ft) in 28 km (17 miles) through the Trasquera tunnel, Iselle station, the 2,968 m (9,738 ft) long Varzo Spiral tunnel, five smaller tunnels and the 1,092 m (3,583 ft) long Preglia tunnel, to join the Italian railways at Domodossola. Passing Lake Maggiore, the train followed the flat line, built in

the Blaizy-Bas summit and a 4,100 m (13,451 ft) long tunnel before descending to Dijon. Here, turning east from Burgundy, it climbed from 288 m (945 ft) at Mouchard to 900 m (2,953 ft) at the mouth of the 6,100 m (20,013 ft) long Mont d'Or Tunnel, opened in

1915, which goes through the Jura mountains to Vallorbe (Switzerland). Before the tunnel was built, the trains ran via Pontarlier to Vallorbe on a line, which is now disused but whose claim to fame is that, in 1974, the film *Murder on the Orient Express* was made on it.

1848, from Milan to Venice, passing Lake Garda and Verona. After reversing at Venice the train crossed the causeway to Venice-Mestre, where the line rejoined the coast outside Trieste.

The Simplon-Orient Express, with its teak cars, took three nights and four days each way. Although all passengers had to change at Trieste, westbound passengers could sleep in the standing train and catch the connection to Paris the following morning.

From Trieste, where all passengers had to change, the line climbed from sea-level to 302 m (991 ft) at Poggioreale del Carso, the present frontier.

The SOE route through Ljubljana (Laibach) and Zagreb (Agram) ran daily to Vinkovci-Belgrade and Nis, where it divided – one part going to Istanbul (three times weekly) and the other to Athens (twice weekly). The Istanbul train also had connections to Bucharest, which it reached by using the notorious Vinkovci-Subotica branch line that crossed the Yugoslav-Romanian frontier over the Danube near the Iron Gates. Fuel shortages sometimes caused delays,

indeed it is said that on one occasion the passengers had to put money together to buy wood for the engine!

The famous blue-and-gold all-steel sleepers first appeared in 1926, four years after the Train Bleu (Calais-Nice-San Remo). By 1929 there was a daily service from Paris to Istanbul, which included a dining car, Calais-Istanbul sleepers and Calais-Trieste sleepers. In 1930 the SOE became the main prop of the Wagons-Lits London-Cairo service (known as the Taurus Express).

The train was re-organized in 1932, with the Ostend-, Amsterdam-, Berlin-, Prague-, Vienna-, and Paris-Orient or Arlberg-Orient sleepers joining the train at Belgrade on different days. This provided three daily Istanbul sleepers and two services daily (four from Thessaloniki) to Athens.

Romantic, dazzlingly mysterious, the train was used by all the Balkan grandees. King Boris used to drive the Simplon-Orient's engine in Bulgaria. British agents

● ABOVE
This rare picture shows the Venice Simplon-Orient Express on a diversion on the old Arlberg-Orient Express line via Zell am See. This was caused by a damaged bridge at Kufstein. The train is seen here in the 180 degree turn near Hopfgarten in Tyrol in July 1990.

● RIGHT
The Venice Simplon-Orient Express stands at Jenbach station in the Austrian Tyrol. A storm is brewing over the mountains.

included Lord Baden-Powell, later founder of the Boy Scouts movement. It was on the train, just after World War II broke out, that Royal Navy agents murdered a German agent. Many novels were written about the train, perhaps most famously Agatha Christie's *Murder on the Orient Express* and Graham Greene's *Stamboul Train*. Mystery also reflected the route's atmosphere, in which there were always difficulties with the local customs, who sealed one dining car's cupboard supplies and broke the seals on another at each border.

Wagons-Lits kept reserve supplies of block ice, coal and vehicles along the route, maintaining an almost out-of-this-world glamorous elegance on board. In summer the baggage van had a shower in it. Wagons-Lits ran daily dining cars for Lausanne-Trieste-Svilengrad, Nis-Thessaloniki, Amfiklia-Athens and a kitchen van for Uzunkopru-Istanbul.

World War II did not stop the Simplon-Orient's glamorous journeys. The warning that "Les Oreilles de l'ennemi vous écoutent" (the equivalent of the British World War II poster

"Walls have Ears") was pasted in the cabins – the listening enemy ears still travelling in the Berlin car, which lasted until 1940. The train was finally stopped in 1942, and individual sleepers with neutral Turkish staff served most of the overnight sectors until the SOE re-started in January 1946 (to Istanbul) and 1949 (Athens). After the war, dining cars became a rarity.

The Simplon-Orient Express ended in 1962, and, with much media coverage, the last Paris-Istanbul sleeper ran on 22 May 1977.

GORNERGRAT TO ST MORITZ
THE GLACIER EXPRESS

Most people start this journey at Zermatt or St Moritz, but to miss seeing the Matterhorn while standing amid the snow 3,000 m (10,000 ft) up, with a panoramic view of other mountains, is to miss one of the finer sights in Europe.

It is not essential to take the Glacier Express itself to enjoy the wonderful scenery, but there are a number of advantages such as the provision of air-conditioned Panorama coaches and a restaurant car in which one can experience the novelty of having a wine glass with an angled base so that the stem and bowl remain upright on the steep gradients. It is recommended that, if at all possible, a seat is obtained on the right-hand side facing forward on this part of the journey.

There is pasture land in the valley from here to Randa. Look out for the houses built behind the huge boulders that fell from the mountains many years before. The Weisshorn, 4,506 m (14,783 ft) is off to the left. Between Randa and Herbriggen is a new section of rack line

- **LEFT**
A heavy express from Chur to St Moritz with coaches from the "Glacier Express" is about to plunge into the tunnel in the vertical rockface 213 feet above the Landwasser river.

- **BELOW LEFT**
A train from Chur to Arosa eases round the bend in the road by the Obertor gate in the city walls of Chur to join road traffic on the narrow Plessurquai alongside the river.

- **BELOW RIGHT**
The Gornergratbahn rack railway train is completing its descent to Zermatt. An electric taxi makes its almost silent way to a hotel.

Swiss Federal Railways main line down the Rhône valley. A short, brisk run on level ground brings the train to Brig. Watch out on the left for the trains of the Bern-Loetschberg-Simplon railway clinging to the valley side on their way to and from the Lötschberg tunnel.

Like most other towns strategically situated near the entrance to mountain passes, Brig has a long history and today watches over the northern entrance to the Simplon railway tunnel beneath the pass of the the same name, which links Switzerland with Italy. It has strong commercial and industrial interests and a growing tourist trade.

At Brig the train reverses in the station square outside the impressive Federal Railways building. A locomotive of the

constructed in the past ten years to circumvent the area where the whole mountainside collapsed, fortunately without causing any loss of life. This can be seen to the left where the route of the old line can still be seen in places.

The valley descends in steps at one place near Kalpetran, the line sharing a narrow gorge with the river. It then appears that the broadening valley with pastures and small vineyards heralds the end of spectacular views for the moment. Not so, for suddenly the train is perched on the edge of a deep cleft cut by the river, and following the contours, wheel flanges screaming.

Ahead and to the right appear two bridges leaping across the chasm. Both were built to carry the road from

Stalden-Saas, which the train is now approaching, to Saas-Fee.

The valley becomes wider and more populous, and at the large town of Visp the line shares a station area with the

● **ABOVE LEFT**
Andermatt looking toward Hospental and the distant Furka Pass.

● **LEFT**
The young Vorderrhein rushes alongside the line as both descend toward Hospental. In the far distance, road and rail zigzag up the mountainside from Andermatt heading for Disentis.

INFORMATION BOX	
THE GLACIER EXPRESS	
Termini	Gornergrat and St Moritz
Country	Switzerland
Distance	279 km (173 miles)
Date of opening	1926

The imposing Swiss Federal Railways station at Brig forms a fine backdrop to the station shared by the Furka-Oberalp and Brig-Visp-Zermatt railways. The "Glacier Express" reverses here.

● RIGHT
Horse-drawn transport vies for business with battery-electric taxis outside the Zermatt station of the Brig-Visp-Zermatt railway. The station has been rebuilt since the picture was taken.

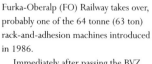

● BELOW RIGHT
The clear waters of the Matter Vispa tumble alongside a Zermatt to Brig train as it approaches Täsch station.

using rack-and-pinion gear to climb. Be ready to look out to the right on emerging from the tunnel, for there is a wonderful view back down the valley toward Brig.

Lax sees the end of the rack for the present. Fiesch is a pretty tourist town in a sheltered location, from here the railway executes a 180 degree climbing turn on rack away from the town to reach Frgangen and yet another cable-car to Bellwald and the Fiesch glacier. One of the most picturesque parts of the journey follows as the train passes through or near many charming old villages, with their wooden houses packed closely together for shelter from the elements, watched over by an ancient church. Look out for the ancient wooden barns, which are raised above the ground on supports capped by large flat stones to prevent rats and mice from reaching the stored grain and fodder above.

At Oberwald, the present-day railway parts company from the old line. The latter passed Gletsch, with splendid views of the Rhône Glacier, the source of the

Furka-Oberalp (FO) Railway takes over, probably one of the 64 tonne (63 ton) rack-and-adhesion machines introduced in 1986.

Immediately after passing the BVZ locomotive depot at the station, the train swings right to cross the Rhône, known locally as the Rotten, on a girder bridge. Another sharp right turn, and the train is running alongside one of the main streets in Naters, just across from Brig. The valley narrows and is shared by road, rail and river.

Grengiols has the highest viaduct on the FO, it spans 31 m (102 ft) above the valley floor. When the train has crossed the viaduct, it enters a spiral tunnel still

● LEFT
The autumn tints are still on the trees as one of
the new and powerful locomotives of the
Rhaetischebahnen climbs with its train away
from Tiefencastel on its way to St Moritz.

and, of course, there are the regular
passenger-trains. About two-thirds of the
way through the tunnel, the train is
under the watershed of the Rhône and
Reuss rivers.

The line emerges near Realp and
follows the broad Urseren valley, passing
Hospental close by on the right.

Andermatt is a well-known holiday
centre and the junction for what used to
be the Schöllenen Bahn, now part of the
FO system. This runs down a steep rack
line in the narrow gorge to Göschenen

river, and entered the old tunnel to
emerge in a wild valley where the winter
conditions are so severe that through rail
services to Andermatt and beyond can be
suspended. Happily, a preservation
society is in the process of re-opening the
line between Gletsch and Realp for
summer use.

The present line uses a new tunnel,
much lower down the mountains. It was
opened on 26 June 1982 after a ten-year
construction period and with a length of
15.442 km (9.59 miles). Single-track
with two passing loops, it is the longest
metre-gauge tunnel in the world. Special
trains ferry cars and their passengers
through the tunnel in winter and summer

● ABOVE
Thusis is an important
rail and road
interchange point on
the line between Chur
and St Moritz. Its new
station reflects the
innovative style of the
Rhaetischebahnen.

● LEFT
Arosa is reached in
less than an hour by
a spectacular branch
of the Rhaetischebahn
from the station
square at Chur.

on the Federal Railways main line
through the Gotthard pass and tunnel.
Glacier expresses cross at Andermatt,
and much shunting is necessary to
change the restaurant car from one train
to the other.

The climb out of Andermatt is both
surprising and rewarding. A seemingly
impassable mountainside faces the train,
which heads straight for it, engages the
rack and swings right, climbing across the
face of the wall and giving views of the
valley to the right. Then it reverses

347

direction, opening up even wider views
down the Urseren valley, now to the left.
There are no fewer than four such
reversals before reaching Nätschen, which
is 407 m (1,335 ft) higher than
Andermatt. Still climbing, the train
passes through a long avalanche shelter to
emerge with the Oberalp lake to the right
and, just ahead, the station of
Oberalppasshöhe at 2,033 m (6,670 ft)
the highest point on the FO.

Between Tschamut and Dieni is the
small and isolated chapel of St Brida,
built in 1736. From here on there is no
need for rack assistance as the valley
broadens out with pleasant views. Sedrun
is one of the access points for the
construction of a new tunnel beneath the
Gotthard pass which will revolutionize
times on perhaps Europe's most
important north-south axis.

Disentis's station has the attraction of
being the meeting-point between the FO
and Rhaetische Bahn (RhB) where, again,
a locomotive change takes place with
haulage probably being put into the
hands of one of the fairly new 60 tonne
(59 ton) Ge4/4 machines. The going is

● **LEFT**
A sharp eye is
needed to spot this
bridge on the old
road toward the
Albula pass. The
relatively soft nature
of the rock has
allowed the
Hinterrhein to cut
such a narrow
passage.

● **BELOW LEFT**
Filisur gives a brief
respite to trains
climbing to the
Albula tunnel. The
"Glacier Express"
for St Moritz is
pulling into the
station where trains
connect to Davos.

now easy through pasture dotted with
woodland. The next important feature is
the Rhine gorge, which is entered around
Castrisch, some 2 km (1¼ mile) beyond
Ilanz. It was formed in prehistoric times

by a landslide which filled the valley to a
depth of 300 m (984 ft) through which
the river gradually forced its way. The
unusual rock formations are best seen
from the left-hand side of the train.

The majority of passengers on the
through trains are heading for St Moritz,
and the coaches for that destination are
detached from the train at Reichenau-
Tamins and added to another train that
has started at Chur.

Chur, the capital of the canton, is also
the terminus of the standard-gauge
Federal Railways and has a depot and
workshops. The large station, recently
rebuilt to incorporate the bus station, is
shared by the RhB.

On the way back to Reichenau, the
Ems Chemie works at Domat-Ems is
seen to the left. For passengers coming
direct from Zermatt, there is a further
reversal at Reichenau, and after crossing

● **RIGHT**
The line between Disentis and Chur passes
along a deep valley cut by the Vorderrhein
through the prehistoric Flims landslip.

the Hinterrhein the train swings left to
follow its course all the way to Thusis.

As the train climbs away from Thusis,
on the right one can glimpse the
fearsome Viamala gorge cut by the
Hinterrhein, while on the left there is a
good view back down the valley. The
Schyn gorge cut by the Albula River is
now followed right to Preda.

The line holds to the left side of the
valley. Suddenly, round a curve, the
remarkable Landwasser viaduct appears,
carrying the tracks 65 m (213 ft) above
the valley floor before plunging into a
tunnel cut into the rock face.

Filisur is the junction for the shuttle
trains to Davos and the starting-point for
one of the most gruelling climbs in
Europe for trains relying on adhesion
only. It involves brilliant engineering,
with the line now clinging to a vertical
mountainside, then spiralling across the
narrowing valley to gain height and then
into spiral tunnels, one upon the other.
Between Bergen and Preda at the Albula
tunnel, the line rises from 1,376 m
(4,514 ft) above sea level to 1,792 m

● **LEFT**
In February, the
snow is beginning to
melt on the rooftops
of the ancient city of
Chur, the capital of
the Kanton of
Graubünden.

● **BELOW LEFT**
The upper valley of
the Vorderrhein
near Tschamut-Selva
in the grip of winter.

(5,879 ft) in about 12 km (7.5 miles)
with a ruling gradient of 1:28.6. The
Albula tunnel is the highest in Europe,
with the summit in the tunnel at 1,820 m
(5,971 ft). It was built between 1898 and
1902 under impossible conditions and
has a length of 5,864.5 m (3½ miles).

Samedan is a rail junction for
Pontresina and the Bernina line and has a
locomotive depot and workshops. It is
only a short distance to St Moritz, passing
through Celerina. The railway ends at St
Moritz by the lake used for langlauf in
winter. Above the lake are the hotels and
restaurants of one of the most famous
resorts in the world, a fine centre for
exploring Switzerland's mountain scenery.

PILATUS
A ROUND TRIP FROM LUCERNE

● **BELOW**
The banner at Alpnachstad proclaims that the Pilatusbahn is the steepest rack railway in the world. Even the platform at the station is on a steep gradient.

Few visitors to Lucerne in central Switzerland can have failed to notice the imposing bulk of Pilatus, a massif of limestone virtually in the suburbs of the city. The massif comprises a number of peaks, the highest of which is Tomlishorn, 2,129 m (6,985 ft) high.

The mountain had an attraction for tourists long before the coming of the famous Pilatus railway, and several famous people have made the ascent, including Queen Victoria in 1868. Even then, she could obtain refreshment after the ascent, because two hotels had been built near the summit in 1860.

The success of the standard-gauge rack-and-pinion railway from Vitznau to the summit of the Rigi mountain prompted an application to the Federal Parliament in 1873 by the Vitznau-Rigi board to build a rack-and-pinion line up Pilatus. This implied using gradients no steeper than 1:4, the limit imposed by the Swiss authorities on the grounds that the vehicles might lift off the rack were the inclination to be greater. The line would have followed the route already

● **BELOW**
The banner at Alpnachstad proclaims that the Pilatusbahn is the steepest rack railway in the world. Even the platform at the station is on a steep gradient.

INFORMATION BOX

Terminus	Lucerne
Country	Switzerland
Length	4.27 km (2.65 miles)
Date of opening	1889

● **BELOW LEFT**
A small plume of cloud adorns the summit of Pilatus, seen from a ship on Lake Lucerne, which is heading for Alpnachstad at the foot of the mountain several kilometres away.

● **BELOW RIGHT**
Even the steep steps of the station platform at Alpnachstad fail to convey an adequate impression of the severity of the gradient on which the car stands.

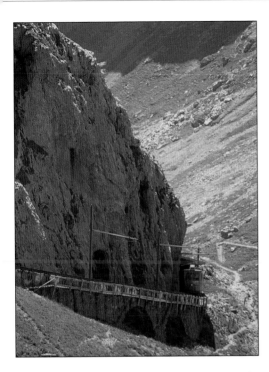

● LEFT
An ascending car nears the upper station just below the summit of Pilatus.

● BELOW
A metre gauge train on the Brünig line of the Federal railways is arriving at Alpnachstad from Luzern.

● BELOW
The car to the left has just departed from Alpnachstad station. Those to the right are waiting to pick up passengers.

used by porters and horses. It was soon realized that this was so circuitous that the heavy construction costs would make it unlikely to return a profit. A shorter route would also be much steeper, and an obvious one was from Alpnachstad by the shores of Lake Lucerne, calling for a gradient of almost 1:2. The Locher rack-and-pinion system based on a concept by the famous mountain railway engineer, Riggenbach, utilizes a pair of vertically mounted pinions which engage in teeth on either side of the rack rail, thus providing a drive and preventing lateral movement. Beneath the teeth on the pinions, discs larger in diameter than the toothed wheels rotate beneath the broad base of the rack rail, thus preventing vertical movement. The conventional wheels on locomotives and carriages merely provide stability on the 800 mm gauge track. Turnouts are always complex on lines such as this, but the Pilatus is special. At six locations, heavy-duty

traverses slide curved track into the appropriate positions, while at two other points, one near the summit, the whole turnout is rotated horizontally.

The line, 4.27 km (2½ miles) long, opened on 4 June 1889 and runs from

Alpnachstad at 441 m (1,447 ft) above sea level to the upper station at 2,070 m (6,791 ft). Between 1886 and 1909, 11 combined steam locomotives and carriages operated the services until electrification at 1550V d.c. on 15 May 1937. One of the steam units is preserved at the transport museum in Lucerne.

Eight electric units were introduced at the start of electrical operation, followed in 1954 by a freight unit, which was provided with a "swap body" to convert it for passenger work, as required, in 1962. One more passenger unit arrived in 1968, and in 1981 another freight unit, diesel-powered, was delivered.

It is suggested that the journey is started at the ship terminus just in front of the main railway terminus at Lucerne and that a ship, possibly one of the old paddle steamers, is taken to Alpnachstad. In summer, there are six or seven sailings a day, and one can enjoy a meal and a drink while admiring the scenery and observing the considerable activity on Lake Lucerne. The alternative is to take the Swiss Federal Railways (SBB) Brünig line metre-gauge train to Alpnachstad.

Both train and ship deposit the passenger close to the Pilatusbahn station. The bright red trains await at a platform angled to correspond with that

of the train. It is advisable to choose the lowest compartment and, if possible, to obtain a seat on the far side facing downhill. Although sitting alongside the rock face on much of the lower part of the journey, you will be on the spectacular side on the upper section, where the line is perched on ledges as it nears the summit. Moreover, it is possible to look back down the line for the whole journey. Although facing rearward is advised, the journey is described as if facing forward. Shortly after the train departs, the depot and workshop are seen to the left. The depot is the only place where the tracks are on the level. Rail access is gained by one of the traverser type turnouts. Very soon the houses, the ship and the Brünig railway line look like small-scale models. Then the line enters beech woods, crosses a small mountain road and begins to dive in and out of a series of short tunnels.

After about eight minutes, the train crosses the Wolfort viaduct, which spans a deep gorge, providing a sudden view to the right and below across the arm of Lake Lucerne on which Alpnachstad is situated and toward the Glärner Alps. The train passes through more short tunnels, after which the nearby scene broadens into pasture dotted with contented cows and alpine flowers. Here at Aemsigen Alp is the passing loop and an opportunity to watch the traverser turnouts in action.

Craggy outcroppings of rock start to appear. The line follows the route of an ancient watercourse and levels out a little before reaching the Mattalp pasture, decked with flowers in summer and often with its own contingent of cows, bells

● **ABOVE LEFT**
The car seen at the cab window is descending and has been passed at the only loop there is on the line.

● **ABOVE RIGHT**
The car has just left the shelter of the summit station at Pilatus.

● **RIGHT**
One of the spectacular views from the top of Pilatus. The cables carry the car on the aerial ropeway, which descends toward Kriens near Lucerne.

jangling as they munch contentedly on
the grass. There are few trees here,
merely some stunted pines.

Through a tunnel and what a
sensation! The train is crawling up a
ledge on the sheer rock face of the
Eselwand. Far below, little moving dots
proclaim the presence of walkers on the
mountain tracks, while above lies the col
on which is situated the summit station.
If there is a following train, it may be
possible to watch the changing of the
route by the rotating turnout before your
train enters the covered station.

The saddle of the mountain has been
levelled, and the hotels there provide
restaurants and cafeterias as well as
accommodation. There are numerous
safe and well-made paths giving easy
access to viewpoints, which, in fine
weather, are difficult to beat. One can also
watch arriving and departing trains edging
along the Eselwand in the distance.

An interesting way to return to
Lucerne is to take the large cable-car at
the summit, which, immediately on
departure, crosses an abyss on the east

face of the mountain before dropping
down to Fräkmüntegg. The descent is
quite steep, the car losing 650 m
(2,133 ft) in a distance of 1,450 m
(4,760 ft). There, transfer is made to a
Gondelbahn, the little cars of which

swing just above the tree-tops to Kriens
on the outskirts of Lucerne. Arrival is
close to a trolley-bus route, which runs
to the centre of Lucerne, passing on the
way part of the route of the Kriens-
Luzern-Bahn, an industrial railway.

LONDON ST PANCRAS TO BERNE
EUROSTAR AND TGV

This journey is one of the most technically exciting train routes of modern times. It begins at London's recently restored St Pancras International terminal for the Eurostar trains, which run regularly via the Channel Tunnel to terminals at Brussels and Paris.

The newly-restored terminal opened on 14 November 2007, at the same time as the opening of Britain's first high-speed line, meaning that the journey from London to Paris may now take as little as 2 hours 15 minutes. A new purpose-built terminal in Kent, Ebbsfleet International, opened that same month, offering easy access from London and the M25.

The international group responsible for design adopted the principles employed in the French TGV (Train Grande Vitesse), but numerous changes were necessary. The trains needed to operate in the much more restricted loading gauge found in Britain; electrical supply was to come from three different systems, including current collection from a third rail in Britain; there were to be four signalling systems; and stringent safety standards were demanded for operation through the tunnel.

The exterior design was British, one consequence of which is that future TGV and the "Thalys" have a central

● **ABOVE AND LEFT**
The original purpose-built Eurostar terminal at Waterloo station, London.

INFORMATION BOX

Termini	London St Pancras and Berne
Countries	England to Switzerland
Distance	1008 km (626 miles)
Date of opening	Eurostar (London to Paris) 1994; TGV (Paris to Berne) 1987

driving position and one window at the front of the cab. The interior design was a joint Franco-Belgian operation, and the result appears to be that the Eurostar has more space than the TGV, in spite of being dimensionally smaller.

There were many mechanical and electrical problems to be solved. For example, safety requirements for the tunnel demanded that passengers could be moved from one end of the whole train to the other. That ruled out employing two units, so that the Eurostar has just two power cars, situated at each end of the 20-vehicle formation, with additional motored bogies under the first and last passenger coach to make up to some extent for the loss of the power that two equivalent TGV sets would have had.

Bogies had to be reduced in overall dimensions; the high overhead contact line in the tunnel called for a higher-reaching pantograph; carriage steps had to be designed to match automatically the differing heights of platforms in three countries, and the complex signalling requirements had to be met.

It is a credit to the international teams that this was all achieved between conception in 1987 and the start of regular services in November 1994.

The dedicated high-speed line is still relatively new, and the Eurostar trains have always had to slot into the slower traffic serving the south-east region. In the urban area of London, lines built in the earliest days of railways tended to be sinuous, but at least it gave the traveller the opportunity to glimpse the widely changing patterns of life to be found in any major city. Once into the Kentish countryside, there was the opportunity to increase the speed to 160 kph (100 mph), especially on the fairly straight section from Tonbridge to Ashford.

Certain Eurostar trains stop at the rebuilt station in Ashford, which also

● **LEFT**
A typical sight at
Paris termini today
are sets of TGV such
as this one at the
Gare du Nord in
March 1996.

● **BELOW**
A timeless street
scene in Montmartre,
Paris, as people shop
for fruit.

serves local and inter-city trains. This
facilitates rail interchange and the
gathering of passengers who have come
by car and who would not have found it
convenient to board in London.

It is a fairly short distance to the
point at which the train swings left from
the former British Rail lines to those of

Eurotunnel. The expanse of tracks,
sidings, depots and loading docks for
cars and heavy goods vehicles is called
Dollands Moor. It is here that the shoes
collecting current from the third rail are
lifted and the pantograph is raised,
although passengers will be unaware
of it. The Channel Tunnel is 49.93 km

(31.03 miles) long and is the second
longest rail tunnel in the world, as well
as the tunnel with the longest underwater section. It lies 137.4 m (451 ft)
below mean sea level.

French cab signalling passes
instructions to trains in the tunnel and
on the TGV lines beyond. Maximum
speed in the tunnel is restricted to 160 kph
(100 mph), and the riding is so smooth
that, without any exterior point of
reference, it is hard to detect movement.

Passage through the Channel Tunnel
takes some 20 minutes and, on emerging
from the tunnel into France, the
immense yards of the Coquelles terminal
can be seen to the left. The line to Paris
passes through a newly built exchange
station at Fréthun, and soon the Eurostar
is running on the high-speed tracks
through fairly level terrain with sweeping
curves. On this stretch, an announcement is usually made that the train is
running at its maximum authorized
speed of 300 kph (186.4 mph).

Facilities for departing Eurostar
passengers at the Gare du Nord generally
leave much to be desired. Those passing

through Paris on their way to Switzerland can either take a taxi (and make sure that it is an official one) to the large and impressive Gare de Lyon or take the relatively new underground link, which gets one there quicker and much more cheaply in some 15 minutes.

Finding the Swiss TGV – and it will probably be Swiss-owned, albeit in standard TGV livery – can be daunting among all the other TGVs, but once on board you can spot the differences between Eurostars and TGVs, which, for example, are wider and higher. The start from the Gare de Lyon is relatively cautious as the TGVs share the tracks

with numerous EMU, locomotive-powered push-and-pull services, both often formed of double-deck coaches, and the occasional locomotive-hauled express. As speed picks up, the train passes the immense marshalling yards at Villeneuve St Georges.

At Lieusaint the TGV joins the "Ligne à Grande Vitesse" (LGV), for the most part a new formation and alignment, purpose-built to permit the high-speed performance of these trains to be exploited. This is the Sud-Est LGV to Lyons, Valence and, ultimately, Marseilles.

The services to Berne and Lausanne follow the line only as far as Passilly,

from where there is a short link to the old main line at Aisy. Travel on the LGV is so smooth that the train's speed is hard to judge. There is little chance to study the local scene, however, because of the speed and the fact that the line is often in a cutting.

From Aisy to Dijon the alignment is good enough to maintain a good pace, and soon, a little to the right and below, Dijon comes into view. The TGV swings down the long grade, a stern test for man and machine northbound in the days of steam, and enters the busy main station, which is on a rather constricted site. The best trains take only 99 minutes

● **LEFT**
A TGV in orange livery passes the exit of the huge marshalling yards at Villeneuve St Georges in the suburbs of Paris. Several TGV services now bypass this section of line using a new and much quicker route designed for TGVs, partly in tunnel, to reach southbound TGV lines.

● **RIGHT**
View of the Münster in Berne from the Kirchenfeld bridge over the Aare.

● **BELOW RIGHT**
Some light railways in Berne terminate in the streets. This train has arrived from Worb, a large village outside Berne, and is waiting in Helvetia Platz to return to Worb. The service has recently been extended to a terminal the other side of the River Aare at Casino Platz.

plain until it approaches the formidable mountain barrier of the Montagne du Lermont. The narrow defile through the mountains is guarded by the ancient town of Pontarlier, with its impressive castles perched high above rail and road as the Franco-Swiss border is approached.

The first village on Swiss soil is Les Verrières. A little further on and to the right, St Sulpice and Fleurier can be seen below in the Val de Travers, where the Scots engineer, MacAdam, saw the potential of the tar substance mined there as a surface for roads. The line winds through delightful scenery until, suddenly, panoramic views across Lake Neuchâtel are revealed to the right, the lake surface below dotted with yachts, small craft and passenger boats on regular services.

Neuchâtel, whose castle can be seen to the right on the approach, is an ancient city lying on the important main line between Basle and Lausanne/Geneva. Its large station mainly handles trains belonging to the Federal Railways

to travel the 315 km (195.7 miles) from Paris to Dijon.

Soon after leaving Dijon, the TGV swings left away from the broad valley of the Saône and climbs toward the mountains, giving extensive views to the right. These give way to more restricted views as the track gets higher and woods and rocky cuttings close in.

Frasne, on a high plateau, is a junction. The main line runs straight ahead to Vallorbe, just over the Swiss border, from where it swings down with good views across villages and agricultural land until reaching Lake Geneva (Lac Léman) at Lausanne. The other line branches left and meanders across the

Certain services to Berne require a change at Frasne in France to one of the electric multiple units (EMUs) previously used on the Swiss Federal Railways Trans-Europe-Express, now in a new livery, which has earned them the nickname "Grey Mouse". The connecting train is seen at Frasne.

(SBB/CFF/FFS), but the livery of the Berne-Loetschberg-Simplon Railway (BLS) is also present. It is that company's metals that are used to cross the generally level and fertile broad plateau to Berne, where the TGV service terminates in the curving and rather gloomy station, well situated near the centre of this small and very pleasant capital city.

The journey from London to Paris has until now taken 4 hours and 32 minutes. With the new High Speed 1 (formerly known as the Channel Tunnel Rail Link) it is now possible for the journey to take as little as 2 hours and 15 minutes.

● ABOVE
One of the electric multiple units arriving at Frasne station.

● RIGHT
In the foreground is one of the many decorated fountains to be found in the heart of the old city of Berne.

BUDAPEST TO LAKE BALATON

Budapest boasts three main-line termini, two of grand proportions and often featuring in period films, and Déli Pályaudvar (spelt Pú in timetables), a modern structure without much cover over the platforms. The station is close to Castle Hill and the large tram interchange at Moszkva tér and is thus convenient, although other services start at B. Kelenföld, a large suburban station. First-class travel is advisable and reasonably early arrival at the station is recommended, not only to get the right tickets but also to get a seat.

The train is likely to be hauled by one of the ubiquitous class V43 electric locomotives in a pleasing light-blue livery. The first batch of seven were built by Krupp in Germany, but the rest are from the well-known Hungarian firm of Ganz-Mavag. They are dual voltage but here operate on a supply of 25kV/50Hz providing an hourly rating of 2130 kW.

Loads are relatively light, and speeds, by Western European standards, are

● **ABOVE**
Buda seen from the Fisherman's Bastion on Castle Hill.

moderate, but this has the advantage for the interested traveller that the passing scene may be studied, whether it be architectural, agricultural or human.

The train sets off through the industrial and dormitory suburbs of Buda, keeping to the west of the Danube. It threads its way through the complex of lines serving people and industry before entering flattish countryside with small towns and villages, some of the latter surrounded by small fields worked

INFORMATION BOX	
Termini	Budapest and Lake Balaton
Country	Hungary
Distance	399 km (248 miles)
Date of opening	1861

● **ABOVE LEFT**
A Russian-built CoCo diesel electric locomotive stands at Balaton central station, waiting for its next duty on a service to Keszthely.

● **LEFT**
The terminal station at Déli Pályaudvar is the starting-point for the journey to Lake Balaton. One of the ubiquitous Class 43 BB electric locomotives, mostly built in Hungary between 1963 and 1982, is the usual motive power for the main-line trains.

● **RIGHT**
The cool courtyard
of this café in old
Buda provides a
welcome relief from
the dry heat of mid-
summer.

"privately". In open areas one may see a
collective farm enlivened by a few trees
but surrounded by flat, tilled soil, but
this style of farming is mostly found on
the Great Plain to the east.

Streams meander near the line, with
areas of marsh as well as tall grasses and
some woodland. The 47 km (29 miles)
from Budapest brings the traveller to
Lake Velence, some 10 km (6 miles) long

and shallow. It is seen to the right of the
train, and its proximity to the city has
attracted the usual lakeside cafés and
stalls as well as holiday homes. The north
end is a wildlife sanctuary, access to
which requires a special permit.

Soon after, one reaches the large town
and junction of Székesfehérvár, where
connections from the north of the
country are made. Only 10 km (6 miles)

further on, and 77 km (48 miles) from
Budapest, is Szabadbattyán, the junction
where the lines to the north and south of
Lake Balaton divide. This train is going
south of the lake, and it is around here
that the distant hills of Bakony Vértes can
first be seen at the right.

It is not until after Balatonalig, 102 km
(63 miles) from Budapest, that the blue
waters of the lake, dotted with sailing
craft, come into view on the right. It is
the largest freshwater lake in west and
central Europe, 77 km (48 miles) long
and very shallow. It is no more than 1.5 m
(5 ft) deep on the south side as far out as
1 km (.625 mile) from the shore, and it
is said to be only about 3 m (10 ft) deep
in the middle.

The north shore of Lake Balaton is
significantly different from the south.
After leaving the hills and lake shore
round Keszthely, the railway curves
inland across a small plain to Tapolca, an
industrial town and rail junction whose
prosperity began with the mining of
basalt. The line then swings back to the
more pleasant narrow coastal plain.

The line is now approaching the
north-eastern end of the lake, which it
follows closely before turning sharply
inland to the junctions at Casjäg and
Szabadbattyán, where the outward route
is rejoined.

● **ABOVE LEFT**
A close view at
Keszthely of 2-6-2
No. 324-540, of a
class dating from
1909, which has just
finished a special
journey with a train
of vintage stock.

● **RIGHT**
The hub of the tram
system in Buda is at
Moszkva tér, seen
here in an "off-
peak" period!

FIER TO VLORE, SHKODER TO DURRES

This account of a journey describes a visit made to Albania in the early 1990s during the Communist regime of Enver Hoxha, the fanatical dictator of that small nation. Entry to the country was then exceedingly difficult; the only possible way was to attempt participation in a group tour run by a limited number of, usually, politically minded agencies. Upon arrival, moreover, the riot act was read to all Western visitors; virtually everything worth doing was not only forbidden but "punishable by execution". There was one exception: for travelling the state railway without government permission the penalty was a mere 25 years' hard labour. So one covered the country by rail.

Until the national railway network was inaugurated in 1946, there were only two lines: a 31 km (19 mile) Decauville track taking bitumen from the mine at Selence to Skele, the port 3 km (2 miles) south of Viore; and a much shorter line between

Shkozet and Lakaj, south of Durres. Today passenger-trains run twice daily between Shkoder in the north and Durres, the chief port, via Lezhe and Lac; six times daily between Durres and Eibasan (with one extending to

● **ABOVE**
Vlore Junction. It is from here that asphalt and cement are transported to Durres.

● **BELOW LEFT**
A freight-train waits in the rail yard at Durres.

● **BELOW RIGHT**
A train waits to depart from Tirana station.

INFORMATION BOX

Termini	Fier and Vlore; Shkoder and Durres
Country	Albania
Distance	*c.* 700 km (435 miles)
Date of commencement of construction	1946

Pogradec); and twice daily between
Durres and Fier; in all some 700 km
(435 miles) of track.

A line has long been under
construction to link Fier with Vlore, and
now, with the help of "volunteer" labour,
it is at last complete. However, the
much-vaunted connection of the

Albanian rail network to the European
system south of Titograd in Montenegro
has still not materialized. Nor has the link
with Bar in Yugoslavia yet been made.
Thus the Albanian Railways network
remains isolated and detached.

The track is in poor condition, but in
1991 the rolling stock was renewed from

Italian sources. Previously most of it
originated from Romania, Hungary and
the then Czechoslovakia, and the
condition was deplorable, with broken
seats and overflowing toilets. In fact, even
while in operation, the seats and fittings
were being used for fuel by chilly
passengers and, without the metal
replacements, by now there would
doubtless have been nothing but the steel
bogies left!

Only one class of travel is available,
trains are diesel-powered, and because of
the mountainous terrain the builders of
the line had considerable obstacles to
overcome.

The taking of photographs of anything
to do with the railway or its routes
carried severe penalties, which made the
photographs shown on these pages
extremely difficult to obtain. As it was,
on a second visit, the author was finally
arrested for boarding a forbidden train in
possession of a camera and was taken
before the Ministry of the Interior in
Tirana for a severe reprimand and threat
of expulsion before being released.

TUNES TO LISBON

The journey commences in Tunes and is a wonderful way to experience the fertile landscape of Portugal. Tunes is a town that has avoided so far the refurbishment or modernization that has afflicted other parts of the network. Much of the investment has come from EU sources, and the accompanying requirements and dictates do not always sit easily with the relaxed local way of life. Welcome track improvements have been made, together with track rationalization and the withdrawal of freight-yards. Expensive and impressive refurbishment of stations has been coupled with de-staffing and the appearance of graffiti and vandalism.

As a junction serving single-track routes to Barreiro, along the Algarve through Faro to the Spanish border and the Algarve branch to Lagos, Tunes sees considerable activity. At times six or more locomotives and four trains may be in the station at once, with complicated shunting of stock between various services. The three-coach train to Lisbon, headed by a French-designed 3,000 hp locomotive, is soon under way, rattling

● **BELOW**
No. 1933 on train IC582, passing the vineyards in the hills south of Sao Bartolomeu de Messines, having travelled some 11 km (7 miles) from Tunes.

across the turnouts and over the broad level crossing at the Barreiro end of the station. This distinctive crossing, which has a road junction in one arm between the Lagos and main lines, is still operated from a hut by a woman crossing-keeper who shows flags or lights to the train crew as they pass.

The journey provides a great variety of generally sparsely populated landscape ranging from fertile pastures to quite bleak hillsides, that in summer would offer little protection from the sun. Having crossed the flat pastures and small orchards near Tunes, the train soon starts its sinuous course through the first range of hills. Fresh vegetation contrasts with the white walls of isolated farms and the reddish-orange of the soil. In places, grey rock cuttings and cactus bushes add variety.

As the train climbs higher, pockets of mist hang in the hollows, and clear streams and rivers curl around the contours of the hills. Near Sao Marcos da Serra, 27 km (17 miles) from Tunes, the train crosses the Ribeira de Odelouca, from whose banks a deafening chorus of frogs can be heard. Formerly, the hills around here were the harmonious domain of sheep and cork oaks, but increasingly the harsher culture of eucalyptus is becoming dominant. Near

● **RIGHT**

● **OPPOSITE TOP**
The attractive tile-decorated station at
Grandola shows signs of life as the train IC580
rolls in to a stop.

● **RIGHT**
IC583 raises dust from the ballast as it
accelerates through the isolated station of
Santa Clara-Saboia. A line of wagons awaits
the next load of timber in the adjacent siding.

● **RIGHT**
Train IC583, behind
a 1931 Class
locomotive, disturbs
the rural tranquillity
and interrupts the
chorus of frogs,
having crossed the
Ribeira de Odelauca
some 25 km (16
miles) from Tunes.

Pereiras, the train crosses an impressive
stone-arched viaduct, the 123.5 m (405
ft) long Ponte de Mouratos, one of the
tallest structures on the line.

After the train has growled its way
round more curves and through the

station, the landscape, although
undulating, becomes more open. Next
we come to Santa Clara-Saboia, its
attractive station some distance from
either of the communities it purports to
serve, after which the train heads

● **BELOW**
In the tranquil setting of the valley of the
Mouratos, a 1931 Class diesel heads a well-
laden IC582 across the imposing Ponte de
Mouratos viaduct.

● **LEFT**
The fortified town of
Alcacer do Sol is
seen across the
floodplain of the Rio
Sado as a train
approaches the
274 m (900 ft) long
bridge over the
river. One of the
more distinctive
crops in the area
is rice.

towards the short Tunel da Horta. The
line remains fairly sinuous, providing a
vista of an impressive villa near Torre Va.

More open terrain allows the train to
gather speed. Lighter soils lead to further
variety of vegetation, with pine-woods
and heathland interspersed here and
there. At Alvalade, 111 km (69 miles)
from Tunes, the train encounters orange
orchards and in places lupins abound,
while white egrets, storks and buzzards
can sometimes be seen.

Having left the plain, the train
encounters a lush rolling landscape of
fields and meandering rivers. Broom,
flat-topped pines and firs being tapped
for resin attract the eye before an even
more impressive sight is met. At Alcacer
do Sal, the line takes a broad sweep

● **LEFT**
Two of the
ubiquitous 1201
Class rest between
duties at the Lisbon
end of Tunes
station.

● **BELOW LEFT**
SOREFAME-built
No. 1939 thunders
across the points to
the south of Santa
Clara-Saboia, with
IC582 *en route* to
Barreiro.

around the hilltop town and castle before
crossing the Rio Sado on a girder bridge.
Until a few years ago this view was
absolute perfection, but today it is
marred by a major highway that shares
the locality.

The lazy Rio Sado meanders towards
its estuary, which incorporates one of the
prime wetland nature reserves in the
country. Mudflats, marshland, water
meadows and low wooded hills provide a
rich prospect for both humans and birds.
The line swings away from the water
eventually, and we are back to a sandy
landscape of large fields fringed by cork
oaks and pine.

At Pinheiro, 191 km (119 miles) from
Tunes, the station buildings are well
maintained but somewhat remote from
the tracks – and positively distant from
the community they purport to serve.
Not surprisingly, services are sparse; only
two northbound trains per day are
booked to stop and search for passengers.

From here, the train takes the more
northerly route via Valdera, whereas on
the return journey in the evening it
serves the historic town of Setubal.
Having joined the line serving Vendas

● **RIGHT**
The Fridays-only
Algarve to Porto
sleeping-car express
approaches the
Tunel da Horta,
some 50 km (31
miles) from Tunes,
behind a British-
built 1801 Class.

● **BELOW
RIGHT**
The train IC580
basks in the
morning sun, as it
waits to pass inter-
regional service
IR871 at Grandola.
Not surprisingly
with such a
relatively light load,
the locomotive 1937
has made good time.

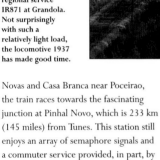

displays, not always providing relevant
information, have changed the old
ambience somewhat. There has been talk
of moving the tracks nearer to the new
piers, but not, one hopes, at the expense
of the old station structure.

The ferries provide a frequent and
pleasant voyage across the Tejo (Tagus),
especially if you are able to secure some
of the limited open deck space. The
upper deck was formerly reserved for
first-class passengers, but these days the
accommodation is open to all. Sitting in
the sun at the stern for the half-hour
crossing serves as a welcome appetizer
for lunch. One can watch the activities of
other ferries and catamarans criss-
crossing the harbour and survey the naval
dockyard and commercial yards at
leisure. Dominating all, on a clear day, is
the impressive suspension bridge high
above the waterway.

All too soon the journey is over.
However, just as the Algarve exerts its
annual charms, so too does Lisbon, and
there is no finer way to link the two than
by inter-city express from Tunes and
ferry from Barreiro.

Novas and Casa Branca near Poceirao,
the train races towards the fascinating
junction at Pinhal Novo, which is 233 km
(145 miles) from Tunes. This station still
enjoys an array of semaphore signals and
a commuter service provided, in part, by
elderly ALCO diesels dating from 1948.

On the final stage of the rail journey
to Barreiro, the driver maintains both a
high speed and frequent blasts on the
horn as this area has many official and
unofficial level crossings, as well as
people who use the trackside as an
extended footpath. Barreiro itself boasts
a major locomotive works and extensive
sidings for both locomotives and rolling
stock. The station has an attractive overall
roof and associated metalwork, but
surprisingly few platforms considering
the area it serves.

Until recent years, the ferries to
Lisbon used to depart from jetties

immediately adjacent to the station.
However, as part of a major new
investment, they now leave from opposite
the bus station, a short walk away. New
turnstiles, ticket machines and dot matrix

CALAIS TO MILAN
ACROSS EUROPE BY MEDLOC

Any reference to rail journeys from the Channel coast to Italy conjures up delightful visions of the Orient Express speeding across frontiers while passengers dine on *cordon bleu* meals in Pullman comfort. My own experience, however, as a serviceman in the aftermath of World War II, could hardly have been in greater contrast.

In late March 1946, after a spell of home leave, I reported back to a transit camp outside Southampton, anticipating a return voyage by troopship to Port Said. But the ways of the Military are ever unpredictable, and after whiling away a fortnight, a party of us were bundled aboard a Waterloo-bound train at Southampton Central, hauled by nothing more prestigious than an N Class 2-6-0. On arrival we were promptly transferred to Victoria station, where I had my first glimpse of a West Country Pacific before departing on a semi-fast to Dover Priory. The next day, after a mercifully smooth Channel crossing, we docked at Calais alongside the war-torn remains of the Gare Maritime.

● **LEFT**
The Sacré Coeur in Paris.

● **BELOW LEFT**
A view of Savona station in 1975, showing a four-car EMU.

● **OPPOSITE BELOW**
Not a museum or a palace, but the exterior of Milano Centrale station, the end of one stage and the beginning of another on the 1946 Medloc marathon.

Here I should explain that, to expedite the transit of service personnel between the UK and various Continental destinations, the railway Operating Division of the Royal Engineers had organized the "Medloc" (Mediterranean line of communication) service of troop trains. I was about to experience Route B, which went from Calais to Milan, with feeders onwards to Southern Italy. Route A, meanwhile, linked Dieppe with Toulon, and Route C went from Calais to Villach in Austria. As Route B was discontinued shortly afterwards, I count myself fortunate since, despite the discomforts, it was an unforgettable and unrepeatable journey.

What better locomotive to tackle the gradients between Dijon and Vallorbe than one of the fleet of ex-PLM Mountains? No. 141-F-177 of this large locomotive family is portrayed at Périgueux in 1962.

● **BELOW LEFT**
Haulage of a British troop train was an unusual assignment for a Swiss Federal Railways locomotive, but an Ae4/7, as shown here at Lucerne, was so employed on the Medloc special in April 1946.

● **BELOW RIGHT**
An SNCF Class BB8100 passing through Villeneuve-St-Georges.

The train in which we were to spend the next 37 hours consisted of 11 FS (Italian) corridor coaches – somewhat lacking in such luxuries as upholstery – plus two vans and a silver-painted FS NAAFI car, decorated with army insignia and named Lancastrian for the essential supply of "char and wads" (tea and cake). I was eager for my first sight of a French locomotive, and I was delighted when the former Nord Collin Pacific No. 231-C-43, of a type renowned for pre-war haulage of the Flèche d'Or, backed on to the train. Also in view in the dock

area were numerous War Department 2-8-0s awaiting repatriation.

We left Calais around 13.00 and made slow progress, hindered by the vast amount of reconstruction work arising from the ravages of war, along the main line towards Paris. Engines were changed

at Amiens. At Boves we had a meal halt, where we were fed and watered beside the line. Another lengthy stop was made at Creil, where a line of 141R Mikado 2-8-2s, newly delivered from America, stood outside the locomotive depot. After the war, a fleet of over 1,300 of

INFORMATION BOX	
Termini	Calais and Milan
Countries	France, Switzerland and Italy
Distance	Calais-Milan: 2,392 km (1,486 miles)
Date of opening	1866

● LEFT
The Piazzo della Scala in Milan.

SNCF Region 5 (PLM) steam traction. There were Mountains (4-8-2s), including one resplendent in olive green, and a selection of mixed traffic 2-8-2s dating from 1919 onwards, although, curiously, only one example of the fleet of over 300 Pacifics was seen at close quarters. Other attractions included the distinctive French signals, notably "chequerboards" controlled from high cabins designated "Poste 1", "2" etcetera, and goods rolling stock including elderly vans with brakemen's cabins perched high on the ends.

A 2-8-2, No. 141-E-173, took over for the more demanding section to

these rugged machines was to prove of immense help to the SNCF during the years of transition to widespread electrification.

From Creil we diverged from the main line as darkness fell, and my scanty notes tell me that our route thereafter took us through Epluches, Ermont, Eaubonne and round the outskirts of Paris via the North-South Ceinture link line. There were tantalizing glimpses of vast marshalling yards and strange locomotives under the arc lights, including one of the Mallet 031-130TB tanks used for local heavy-freight trains and shunting.

A period of fitful sleep followed – the unyielding seats and persistent draughts were not conducive to slumber, though one enterprising fellow-traveller took to the luggage rack – and daybreak found us making steady progress south-eastwards along the former PLM main line towards Dijon. Superbly engineered, the line closely followed the course of the Yonne and Armençon rivers. This route would in years to come provide a race track for fast expresses such as the Mistral; our speed, however, was restricted to a maximum of around 80 kph (50 mph). Even in a bleary-eyed state, one's interest was soon aroused when passing places such as Laroche-Migennes and Les Laumes-Alésia, both with well-stocked

locomotive depots and busy yards.

During a long halt at Dijon, an important junction where the lines to the Mediterranean and to Switzerland part company, I feasted my eyes on a variety of

● LEFT
The US Army S160 2-8-0s were invaluable in the haulage of troop trains in Italy during and after the war. This example, as FS No. 736.205, sadly ended its days at Milano Smistamento.

Vallorbe, leaving Dijon at 08.30 and
reaching the Swiss frontier at 15.00.
There was a break in the journey when
we backed up a branch line at Villers-les-
Pots for a meal of stew eaten from our
mess tins at another line-side fast food
outlet. On this section, locomotives
recorded included a 4-8-0 with V-shaped
fronts to the cabs. Most impressive to
British eyes were local passenger 4-8-4
tanks, as big as a pair of LNER N2s
coupled together.

At Vallorbe, a Swiss Federal Railways
Ae4/7 4-8-2 electric locomotive took
over. The next 241 km (150 mile) stretch
was the highlight of the journey. We went
down to Lausanne, then along Lake

Geneva and eastwards through the Rhône
valley to Brigue. The superb scenery
along this section of the route was bathed
in bright sunshine and made a lasting
impression, and a nice touch was that
some of the good citizens of Lausanne

were kind enough to hand us chocolates
while our train waited under the station's
overall glass roof. Even with the addition
of a steam-heating van to an already
heavy train, the 3,120 hp steed gave a
lively performance, non-stop to Brigue,
with the level-crossing bells sounding
merrily as we sped past.

At this time, steam traction had not
been banished from Swiss rails, and a trio
of 4-6-0s and a neat little 2-6-0 had been
observed outside the depot at the end of
Lausanne's platforms. Elsewhere,
however, the scene was all electric with
glimpses of metre-gauge lines at the
stations of Montreux, Aigle and
St-Maurice. As twilight fell we threaded
the Simplon tunnel, emerging at the
other end into Italy.

During a prolonged stop, another
meal was consumed at Domodossola
before departure for Milan at 21.00
behind FS Pacific No. 601.010. This
locomotive, rather more impressive in
looks than in performance, was one of
only 33 built just prior to World War I.
With modifications in the 1930s, most
FS main-line passenger work was
entrusted to the more numerous and
dependable Compound 2-6-2s.

Little was seen during the run to
Milan, where we arrived in darkness at
the great 22-platform terminus at the
unsociable hour of 02.00.

MYRDAL TO FLÅM
THE FLÅM RAILWAY

● **BELOW**
Preserved electric locomotive No. 9.2063 of
1944, on display at Flåm. Adjacent is the old
station building, which houses a small
museum about the Flåm railway.

The Flåm Railway, part of the Norwegian
State Railway system, or Norges
Statsbaner (NSB), runs between the
towns of Myrdal and Flåm, a distance of
20 km (12 miles). The railway's claim to
fame lies in the fact that Myrdal is 865 m
(2,838 ft) higher than Flåm, making this
line one of the world's steepest non-
rack-operated railways. Since the late
1950s, NSB has been selling an excursion
ticket called "Norway in a Nutshell" for a
round trip from Bergen by train, boat
and bus via the Flåm railway. This is the
journey described.

However, before boarding a train, a
little history of the Flåm railway.
Flåmdalen – the Flåm valley – starts from
Myrdal with a 350 m (1,148 ft) drop,
and it is this that causes the major
engineering work as the railway must
negotiate it by tunnels, ledges and hairpin
curves. The first survey for the line was
in 1893, which produced a proposal for
an 18 km (11 mile), 3 ft 6 in gauge rack
railway with gradients of 10 per cent on
the rack section. However, after

● **BELOW**
NSB electric locomotive No. 11.2110 at Flåm
on the stock of the overnight sleeper service to
Oslo. This is the Flåm branch's only through
train to the rest of the network, the coaches
being attached to the overnight Bergen to
Oslo train. The Flåm branch is one of the last
outposts of the Class 11 locomotives.

government approval, the plan was
modified to the current, standard-gauge,
electrified adhesion route in 1923. The
purpose of the line was to link the
Bergen to Oslo line, itself completed in
1909, with the Sognefjord. This route
was already popular with tourists,
although the limit was one person per
chaise on the uphill journey, limiting the
number of people that could be handled.

The Flåm railway has a ruling gradient
of 5.5 per cent for 80 per cent of the
line's length. There are 20 tunnels
totalling 5,692 m (over 3$\frac{1}{2}$ miles), which
is over a quarter of the line. The
minimum curve radius is 130 m (427 ft).
All trains operating over this line are
fitted with five different braking systems,
each of which alone can stop the train.
Unsurprisingly, maximum speed is
limited, to 40 kph (25 mph), giving a
journey time of 53 minutes. However,
the scenery is so spectacular, that this
seems too short a time, not too long!

It had been intended to open the
railway in 1942, but wartime measures
meant it was opened in August 1940,

● **RIGHT**
A view from Stalheim Hotel, towards
Gudvangen and the Nærøyfjord. The pass road
leaves the new road where it crosses the
stream in the middle of the photograph, and
then crosses the stream a little to the right.

although steam-operated. The electric
locomotives ordered, on the other hand,
were delayed by the war, not arriving
until 1947. These locomotives,
designated Class E19, survived until
1984. One has been put on display at
Flåm station.

Despite threats of closure in the
1960s, traffic on the line has grown,
reaching 315,000 in 1992. The passenger
service is seasonal, with only four trains
operating each way in winter, but 12
services each way in summer.

The day's journey starts from the
terminus station in Bergen, Norway's
second city. This is an imposing stone-
fronted and very solid-looking building
with a curved roof over the four main
tracks. The journey to Myrdal is by

● **RIGHT**
A view from Stalheim Hotel, towards
Gudvangen and the Nærøyfjord. The pass road
leaves the new road where it crosses the
stream in the middle of the photograph, and
then crosses the stream a little to the right.

INFORMATION BOX	
THE FLÅM RAILWAY	
Termini	Myrdal and Flåm
Country	Norway
Distance	20 km (12 miles)
Date of opening	1940

● **RIGHT**
Fylkesbaatane's boat
Skagastol arriving at
Flåm. Its previous
use as a car ferry
can be discerned,
the raisable bow
continuing to be
used for embarking.

stopping train, which is formed of a
suburban electric multiple unit (EMU).
These are not as comfortable as the long-
distance trains, but the low seat-backs
and large windows allow good views of
the passing scenery.

While the journey to Myrdal is not as
spectacular as the Flåm railway, nor the
countryside as barren as that on the
central part of the Oslo to Bergen railway,
there are some very attractive views on
the first 86 km (53 miles) to Voss. Best
of all is the stretch between Takvam and

● LEFT
NSB three-car EMU No. 69625 at Myrdal,
having worked from Bergen.

Stanghelle, where the railway follows one of the minor fjords.

From Voss, the railway starts to climb. The line to Oslo will reach 1,300 m (4,265 ft) above sea level at its highest point, but this journey only goes as far as Myrdal, 867 m (2,845 ft), two hours and 135 km (84 miles) from Bergen.

Myrdal is situated between two tunnels and seems to exist purely for the purposes of a railway junction. The only visible habitations are a few houses, quite probably built by the railway. The steepness of the Flåm railway is obvious from the start, when one sees the way the railway track disappears downhill from the end of the platform. During the journey, anyone walking up and down the carriage – literally – will realize just how steep the track is, one end of the 24 m (79 ft) coach being 1.4 m (4½ ft) below the other.

The first view comes after one kilometre (⅔ mile) at Vatnahalsen, where the Kjosfossen power-station lake and waterfall can be seen below. Three kilometres (2 miles) later, the train stops

at Kjosfossen to allow passengers to leave the train and photograph the waterfall, now pouring down from several hundred feet above.

A couple of kilometres (1.24 miles) later, the highest settlement in the Flåmdalen comes into view. At several points, between tunnels and snow shelters, spectacular views are available, both down and upwards, where you can see parts of the route taken by the railway. In particular, the "window" out from one of the tunnels inside the rock face can be seen above the snow shelter on the lower level of the line. At Berekvam, slightly under half-way, there

is a passing loop, the only place on the line where trains can pass each other. Below Dalsbotn, Flåm church can be seen along with some farms in the flatter valley floor. Soon after Hareina, the gradient slackens as the valley floor is reached, and the last couple of kilometres are relatively flat, passing through farmlands, but still overhung by the towering sides of the fjord. The "port" of Flåm is finally reached after negotiating a narrowing and curving of the valley, such that the fjord cannot be seen from the train on the journey down from Myrdal.

The area around Flåm station is clearly aimed at tourists, with a number of gift shops and restaurants. However, a short walk brought relief from the throng! The two-hour connection is more than adequate to see the area around the railway station and, with a little effort, there may be enough time to walk some way up the valley towards the Flåm church. Some of this time should be spent on a visit to the interesting Flåm railway museum, situated in the old station building, which explains the history of this extraordinary railway.

● RIGHT
A view of Flåmdalen from below Dalsbotn, seen from a train on the Flåm railway. Flåm church is in the small settlement in the middle of the view. The Aurlandfjord is off to the right after the valley narrows.

Preserved electric locomotive No. 9.2063, of the type built for the Flåm line, is displayed on the station platform. The adjacent small railway depot is home to an unusual battery shunting locomotive.

Gudvangen is on the Nærøyfjord, a branch off the Aurlandfjord. The village appears to be little more than a couple of farms, a jetty for the ferries and a tourist shop and restaurant, albeit in an attractive setting.

From here our trip continues by coach to Voss. The coach trip is dramatic in itself. The first section is along the valley at the end of the fjord, but the coach turns off the main road to take the pass road up to Stalheim. This road is very narrow and steep and has frequent hairpin bends. These are a struggle for the coach, even without the distraction of downhill traffic. This is fortunately light, as a new road tunnel has been constructed to avoid this section. The views from the coach are spectacular, but are as nothing compared to those from Stalheim. This is a hotel perched on a saddle between two valleys. On one side is the steep drop down to Gudvangen; on the other, the much shallower drop towards Vinje.

The run on to Voss is much less dramatic. The scenery is no less attractive, although the height of the land allows only a minimal amount of vegetation to grow, which shows one a different side to the country. Voss is a lakeside town and skiing centre, with an imposing church. It used to be the junction for a branch line to the Hardangerfjorden, since closed. Finally, a train is joined for the return to Bergen.

Great Journeys of the East

This section takes the reader on some of the most exciting rail journeys in the world, from the romance of the Trans-Siberian Express to the fabulous luxury of the South African Blue Train. The reader will experience the deserts of Iran and the plush jungles of Ghana where, if not attended to, within months the flora and fauna overgrow the railway line itself. This section also brings to life historical figures such as Lawrence of Arabia whose destruction of the railways in Saudi Arabia still has not been repaired, and we go to China, the last bastion of the steam locomotive.

India is not forgotten as we travel the length and breath of the sub-continent, riding on trains ranging from the luxurious Palace on Wheels to the "toy train" that takes us up the foot-hills of the Himalayas to the town of Darjeeling. We visit Australia where we remember the pioneers of the 19th century through whose efforts the railways of that vast continent were laid, and lastly New Zealand for, among others, its spectacular Transalpine journey.

● **OPPOSITE**
The Eastern and Oriental Express near
Kanchanaburi, Thailand.

● **ABOVE**
The afternoon train leaves Pachegaon station, in
India, which amounts to little more than a sign
board set amid the scrub.

CASABLANCA TO GABES

The trains on this line will take the rail traveller all along the Mediterranean coast of North Africa from Morocco's Casablanca, via Tangier, to Gabes in south-eastern Tunisia, some 1,778 km (1,105 miles) in all. French from 1840 to 1960, Algeria was treated as a *département* of France, and its railway – the Société Nationale des Transports Ferroviaires (SNTF) – was constructed and run accordingly. Built to standard gauge, the trains ran with a pre-war speed and efficiency admired by many countries. The system is basically coastal, to provide a link between Casablanca in Morocco and Tunis, at one time all French.

Neither Moroccan nor Algerian Railways are the slightest mite house-proud. Some of the trains are a disgrace. From Fez to the Algerian border, compartments are a mass of sprawling bodies trying to get some sleep on wooden seats.

Pink *wadis* show in the dawn. Taza Haut brooded on a hill and, nearby, an amazing conglomeration of buildings

● **ABOVE**
Ouja railway station on the border between Algeria and Morocco.

called the Kasbah of Taourirt scowl at the train. Ouja is the border town, a dull but not unpleasant place of wide streets and solid European-style houses.

Rusty train wrecks lay beside the line to Oran. Tiemcen, however, shows a face of Andalusian elegance and Moorish arcades. Sidi-bel-Abbas smells of Foreign Legionnaires. The most Moorish-looking building in Oran is the chaotic railway station, where a corner seat on the train may be won by starting a rumour that it is to arrive at an adjacent platform.

● **ABOVE**
The Casablanca to Tangier express waits at Sidi Slimane.

● **LEFT**
The through diesel express of Moroccan Railways on its way from Marrakesh to Tangier via Casablanca and Rabat.

In Tunisia, however, things change dramatically and abruptly. The trains are reasonably clean and in better order, even though the general feeling is that foreign tourists are not expected to use such lowly vehicles. On the train to Tunis, the customs officers have the habit of searching bags by the simple expedient of turning them upside down.

The 190 km (118 miles) of line between the border and the capital is narrow – metre-gauge – which explains the change of train. Though a fraction of the size of its massive neighbour, Tunisia can boast a track mileage of 2,200 against Algeria's 2,570.

In the south of the country, at Sfax, one has to change trains again. However, the onward connection to Gabes is poor, and the trains that eventually arrive seem as reluctant as the traveller is eager to reach the end of the line.

As in many industrial countries, the railway route into the capital is not the most attractive. The line sneaks in by the back door through the dingiest of industrial complexes. Onwards to Constantine and its amazing rock formations and a deep ravine traversed by slender bridges. The next main station is Annaba – once known as Bône. The trains that creep out of Annaba are equipped with third-class coaches, which are fit only for the knacker's (junk) yard, several compartments being both windowless and seatless. Souk-Ahras is the border town, some 16 km (10 miles) from the Tunisian frontier. Here, on the fringe of war, the border police sport brigand-style uniforms and swaggers.

● **ABOVE**
A modern passenger train passes Bab Tisera (Sidi Kacem) *en route* from Casablanca to Fez.

● **RIGHT**
A passenger train arrives at Rabat.

CAIRO TO ASWAN
THE STAR OF EGYPT

Although the all-sleeper express has lost its name today, tourism up the River Nile is 120 years old. Thomas Cook & Son (more particularly his son John) organized tourist river steamers on the Nile from about the mid-1870s. They were based in Cairo, which was connected with Egypt's main port Alexandria by the first railway in the Middle East, built in 1855. It included a bridge over the Nile outside Cairo, also used by the Star of Egypt on leaving Cairo Main. Wagons-Lits, creators of the Orient Express, celebrated their Silver Jubilee in 1898 by expanding simultaneously into Russia and Egypt.

Here the cars were painted white to reflect heat and had double roofs, while dining cars, built by Ringhoffer in Prague, had primitive air-conditioning, with blocks of ice cooling the air circulating between the skins of the roof. The great rival of Cook, whom they bought up in 1928, but lost during World War II, Wagons-Lits started sleepers with a diner in 1898 from Cairo to Luxor. At least until 1908, the lines which ran on up the Nile to Aswan remained narrow-gauge. The 1908 night train left Cairo on

● **RIGHT**
A typical village market, or souk, of which many are seen on the journey.

● **BELOW**
Part of the frieze on the Thomas Cook office building in Leicester, depicting Cook's first full Egyptian tour begun in 1884.

● **BELOW**
An Egyptian Railways 1,500hp Bo-Bo waits to take its carriages to pick up Cairo-bound passengers at Aswan.

Mondays, Wednesdays and Saturdays, returning from Luxor on Tuesdays, Thursdays and Sundays.

The line leaves Cairo, crosses the Nile on the Alexandria line bridge and then turns upstream along the Nile's left bank through Assyut. It crosses the Nile at Nag Hamadi, and thereafter follows the right bank to Luxor and on to Aswan.

In 1906 Lord Dalziel bought from the executors of George Mortimer Pullman their British operations together with the exclusive rights to the name Pullman on railway cars throughout Europe and

● LEFT
A French-built turbo train on the Cairo to Alexandria run in Egypt.

Egypt. Lord Dalziel gave these rights to Wagon-Lits, of which he was a director, in 1907. Wagons-Lits started using Pullmans in about 1925 and those for Egypt were shipped, newly built, direct from England. Lord Dalziel died in 1928, a few weeks after Wagons-Lits had swallowed up Cook, in the pretence that it was a merger.

Further Pullman cars were sent out in 1929, when the Sunshine Express, an all-Pullman day train from Cairo to Luxor, was started. New sleeping cars now ran in the night train, named Star of Egypt. At Aswan it continued to El Shallal, above the cataracts and the Aswan Dam, connecting with steamers to Wadi Halfa, in the Sudan, where the Sudanese Railways line to Khartoum avoids a big bend in the river. When the new Aswan Dam was built, the Aswan terminus was forced to move to El Sadd el Ali.

● ABOVE
A mechanized maintenance train in Egypt.

● BELOW
For much of the journey, the train travels by the Nile, seen here near Cairo.

The Sunshine Pullman ended its life in 1939, but the sleeping cars were revived after the war, and the Star of Egypt continued until around 1958-9 when Wagons-Lits was sequestered. The Egyptians found they could not really manage without them, and the Egyptian Republic Railways allowed them back, setting up a joint company to run the train. The Hungarian sleeping cars that ERR had bought were relegated to slow trains, and the modern-day all-sleeper train, with lounge car, now has German vehicles built in the 1980s by Messerschmidt MBB. A supply car replaces the diner, and meals are served in the cabins.

At present one train suffices on the route – most people either cruise on the Nile or fly. Thomas Cook still run the Nile cruise ships, but mostly these belong to other companies. Now the journey by all-sleeper train, which terminates at Aswan, takes some 16 hours – the 1938 journey was half an hour faster.

INFORMATION BOX

THE STAR OF EGYPT

Termini	Cairo and Aswan
Country	Egypt
Distance	960 km (597 miles)
Date of opening	1908

NAIROBI TO KAMPALA

When construction of the then East African Railway began in 1898, it appeared to be going "from nowhere through nowhere to nowhere", and so they called it the "Lunatic Line". But there was a purpose. The aim, besides building a railway line through unknown East Africa to the once remote inland country of Uganda, was to help put down the detested Arab slave trade.

Victorian crusading enterprise in East Africa was chiefly directed at Uganda. Kenya was an afterthought. The crusade needed a railway so, with the matter-of-fact approach characteristic of the times, a railway was driven all the way from Mombasa on the Indian Ocean. If the track had to rise many metres up and down again, what did it matter? So it was successfully driven across hundreds of kilometres of bush alive with marauding wild animals, disease-carrying swamps and the lunar trough of the Great Rift itself, to Lake Victoria.

The line reached Kisumu after unbelievable feats of human endurance and engineering, and was later pushed forward to Kampala and beyond. From

● **ABOVE**
Locomotive No. 5932 "Ol' Donya Sabuk" seen here hauling a Mombasa to Nairobi freight at Athi River.

INFORMATION BOX	
Termini	Nairobi and Kampala
Countries	Kenya and Uganda
Length	1,338 km (831 miles)
Date construction commenced	1898

the coast, the line snaked through the uplands, infested by lions that killed some 200 construction workers, to reach a well in the deserted Kikuyu country. It came to the great Rift Valley escarpment, down which trains had to be lowered on an inclined plane assisted by rope haulage, and then continued over the Mau Summit to Kisumu on the shores of Lake Victoria. Here a prefabricated ship was launched, and Kampala, capital of Uganda, became accessible to the outside world via a journey of under five days. Nowhere else in the world, and at no time in history, has a journey been so dramatically shortened from six months'

● **ABOVE**
Derailed on the soggy Kasese Extentions, this locomotive was back in service within three months.

● **LEFT**
A train approaches Jinja bridge near the Ripon Falls, the source of the Nile.

● **RIGHT**
An East African
Railways Class 59
4-8-2 + 4-8-2
Mountain Class
Garratt pulls heavily
away from Voi at the
edge of the Tsavo
game reserve in
Kenya with a heavy
freight from
Mombasa, bound
for the Kenyan
capital, Nairobi.

● **BELOW LEFT**
An East African Railways Class 59 4-8-2 + 2-8-4
Garratt locomotive, built by Beyer Peacock of
Manchester in 1955, rounds the spiral that
forms part of the steep climb up the coastal
escarpment from Mombasa on the Indian Ocean.

Notwithstanding the many stops at the
wayside stations, the train did its best to
make up for lost time. Each station was a
colourful pageant of people, though few
seemingly had any business with the
railway; it was just that the station was
the community centre – the place where
the action was. At Jinja we crossed the
River Nile.

It was raining when we reached
Kampala and, climbing the stairs towards
the exit, I was intercepted by what I later
learned was a plain-clothes agent of the
security service. The ensuing
developments form no part of this rail
narrative but, briefly, entailed my being
arrested as a likely spy (for showing an
interest in the railway), my interrogation
in Kampala's grizzly central police station
and prison, which took place over several
days and nights, and my final release.

I was put aboard (i.e. left clinging to
the step of a packed coach of) the
seemingly very last train allowed through
to Nairobi, where I arrived none the
worse for my ill-fated Kampala visit
except for a deficiency of sleep and a
good meal.

dangerous walking to a four-day ride in
what was then comparative comfort. At
the same time, the line opened up both
Uganda and Kenya and was instrumental
in the development of East Africa's major
metropolis, Nairobi.

By early 1997 all rail services except a
once-weekly international one terminated at the Kenya-Uganda border, but
on this particular journey, 20 years or so
earlier, the train was the last non-
intercontinental through service to
operate for some time. A military crisis
had arisen, and President Idi Amin's
army was poised to invade Kenya.

Deciding to press on regardless, the
journey had to be confined. The train out
of Nairobi was a lesser animal than that
of the Mombassa-Nairobi Express, but
adequate enough. And when one has the
stupendous sight of the Rift valley *en
route*, a reasonably clean and openable
window is all that you really require.

On the floor of the Rift valley lies the
town of Nakuru and, to the south of it,
Lake Nakaru, an expanse of shallow,
saline water, the shores of which are the
sacred nesting ground of over 10,000
flamingos.

Unfortunately, the train was kept
standing at the Kenyan border station of
Malaba for five hours, following which it
drew into Tororo. Between these two
points the train was virtually empty – a
somewhat lonely experience in a
potential war zone. But the coaches filled
up at Tororo.

● **BELOW**
East African Railways Class 59 4-8-2 + 2-8-4
Garratt No. 5922 "Mount Blackett" climbs the
steep coastal escarpment away from Mombasa
with a Nairobi-bound freight.

A NETWORK IN DECLINE

Rail travel in Ghana is now, alas, almost a thing of the past. In its heyday, however, passenger travel was luxurious with restaurant and sleeping facilities on many trains. By 1985, owing to the general decay of the system as well as the permanent way, steam was extinct. This was much to the chagrin of the railway workers, who liked the simplicity of steam; diesel locomotives are much more difficult to maintain. This has resulted in much of Ghana's railway being almost at a complete standstill, with hardly any passenger trains running at all.

Although the total route length of railway in Ghana was only 953 km (592 miles), a journey on its tracks was an unforgettable experience. The system was in the form of a letter A, with Kumasi at the apex, the two feet at Takoradi and Accra, and the chord of the A connecting Huni valley and Kotoku. One of the notable features of the network is the excessive curvatures. A prime example of this is the section between Kumasi and Takoradi, where there are about 504 curves in a section of 270 km (168 miles).

It was the discovery of gold that caused the British to begin building the first railway in the country, which was then called the Gold Coast. Starting from the coastal village of Sekondi in 1899, the line progressively embraced the communities at Tarkwa, Dunkwa and Obuasi, and in September 1903 it finally reached the Ashanti kingdom of Kumasi, an incredible 265 km (165 miles) inland. The original Sekondi station is still there, with its Gents clock from Leicester still on the wall – long since stopped.

INFORMATION BOX

Termini	Accra, Kumasi and Takoradi
Country	Ghana
Distance	953 km (592 miles)
Date of commencement	1899

● **TOP**
British steam locomotives lie derelict in the overgrown yard at the Location works.

● **ABOVE LEFT**
A decrepit diesel-electric locomotive undergoing overhaul at the Location works.

● **LEFT**
The historic railway station at Sekondi, which would have made the perfect site for a national railway museum, complete with defunct clock from Gents of Leicester.

Ghana's coast is hemmed in by a belt of jungle 240 km (149 miles) deep, and building the railway through the gloomy forests and the vast tracts of fever-laden jungles of the interior was a superhuman achievement, costing many lives as workers fell victim to diseases. In many places there was less than 30 m (100 ft) of clear view ahead. There were many depressions filled with swamp water, concealed from sight by the overgrowing scrub. Another, not so obvious, problem, was caused by the pegs that the engineers placed 30 m (100 ft) apart to indicate the centre of the proposed track. As these stakes were cut from green wood, they soon started to sprout, causing the survey line to be obliterated in a short space of time.

Extensions to the network made the Gold Coast Railways the pride of Africa. Apart from opening up the gold fields, the railway helped to exploit Ghana's vast potential for cocoa, which developed the Cadbury empire, while manganese from Nsuta, bauxite from Awaso, and timber from Kumasi all flowed down the west line to the coast for export. The circuitous line from Accra to Kumasi was begun in 1909 but did not reach Kumasi, 583 km (362 miles) away, until 1923.

One of the more impressive bridges on the network was that at Ancobra, on the 31 km (19 mile) long branch line from Tarkwa to Prestea. The bridge, supported on 12 m (39 ft) high concrete piers, has four spans, the central one

being 55 m (180 ft) long. In 1985, when the railway photographer and historian Colin Garratt visited Ghana, he found Accra's railway station mouldering in an aura of decay. The huge marshalling yards had been turned into a fruit and vegetable market, the sidings were rusty and unused, and the only passengers were market women who had come to the city from the country to sell their produce in the capital.

Garratt appealed for the heritage to be conserved – Sekondi station would have been ideal. However, all was destroyed in exchange for instant revenue from the sale of scrap to the steelworks at Tema. Thus Ghana lost the chance of a fine cultural/tourist opportunity.

● **ABOVE LEFT**
The infrastructure of Ghana's railways degenerated into such a poor condition as to threaten survival of the whole network. During the 1980s, huge numbers of volunteers were mustered to form work gangs in a desperate bid to save the network.

● **ABOVE RIGHT**
Industrial history, all imported from Britain, in the forge at the Location locomotive works – a piece of industrial Lancashire grafted on to the primeval jungle.

● **BELOW**
The abandoned locomotive depot yard in Accra has long since been illegally taken over by marketeers. Forming a backdrop to the merchandising is (left) a Hunslit 0-8-0 tank engine along with a Vulcan Foundry 4-8-2.

CAPE TOWN TO PRETORIA
THE BLUE TRAIN

The first luxury train to run the 3 ft 6 in gauge route from Cape Town to Pretoria was started in 1903. This was operated by the Cape Government Railway and the Central South African Railway. In 1910, on the formation of the Union of South Africa, all the country's independent lines amalgamated to form South African Railways, and the train was named the Union Limited. Although the train was a luxury one-class express, which required supplementary fares, it was extremely popular, so much so that in the 1930s more coaches had to be added and the smart Pacifics, which were used to haul the train, were replaced with 4-8-2s.

The twice-weekly train was renamed the Blue Train (Bloutrein) in April 1939. It was, of course, not the first time a train had been so named, for the Train Bleu had been running from Paris to the Côte d'Azur since the 1920s. This change of name coincided with the introduction of new blue-and-cream carriages with clerestory roofs; the locomotives, however, continued to be in the black of South African Railways. The compartments were super deluxe,

● **LEFT**
The Blue Train at Johannesburg station.

● **BELOW LEFT**
A head-on view of the Blue Train.

INFORMATION BOX

THE BLUE TRAIN

Termini	Cape Town and Pretoria
Country	South Africa
Distance	1,607 km (999 miles)
Date of first run	1910

● **BELOW LEFT**
The Blue Train traversing the Hex River valley.

● **BELOW RIGHT**
The Blue Train is not without luxuries, such as facilities for a wash and brush up.

dust-proofed and air-conditioned with blue leather upholstered seats, loose cushions and writing tables with headed notepaper. At the rear of the train was an observation car. In spite of the 3 ft 6 in gauge the body width of these coaches was 3 m (10 ft).

Such was the popularity of the train that, in spite of the high prices, reservations had to be made far in advance. To provide room for the various on-board services, including fully equipped bathrooms, only 100

passengers could be catered for on each journey. The train was electrically hauled by blue locomotives between Pretoria and Kimberley, and again between Beaufort West and Cape Town, and scheduled to do three round trips weekly from October to March and one from April to September.

President Nelson Mandela inaugurated the "new" Blue Train in June 1997. Built from the undercarriage of the original Blue Train sets, these two new trains feature only two grades of on-

board accommodation – luxury and deluxe – as opposed to the previous four.

The luxury suites differ from the deluxe in that they are more spacious and offer larger bathrooms – deluxe ones have private shower or bath, luxury ones all have baths. There is 24-hour butler service, laundry service and two lounge cars, and while all the suites are equipped with televisions and telephones, the luxury suites in addition have CD players and video recorders. There is also live footage on TV from a camera positioned in the front of the train, giving passengers a "driver's-eye" view of their journey.

With this impressive level of upgrading of the Blue Train, capacity on board has inevitably been reduced from 107 to 84. The Blue Train no longer serves Johannesburg, routing via Germiston instead as it travels between Pretoria and Cape Town. There are several departures throughout the year between Pretoria and Victoria Falls.

● **ABOVE**
The Blue Train running through the beautiful Hex River valley.

● **LEFT**
The Blue Train with the unmistakable Table Mountain in the background.

CAPE TOWN TO VICTORIA FALLS

Railways in the Cape Colony date back to 1857, when a pioneering line was opened from Cape Town to Wellington – a 72 km (45 mile) journey. In 1873 the first trains completed the 1,036 km (644 miles) from Cape Town to Kimberley across the Karoo, and as Cecil Rhodes progressed through Africa, the iron road was laid northwards, the 235 km (146 mile) section from Kimberley to De Aar being laid in an impressive 20 months between March 1884 and November 1885. The route of the Pride of Africa is from Cape Town, via Beaufort West, De Aar, Kimberley, Klerksdorp, Johannesburg, Pretoria, Mafeking (border), Gaborone, Plumtree (border), Bulawayo, and Hwange to Victoria Falls.

The modern flat-roofed station at Cape Town seems an improbable place to

● **LEFT**
The observation car of the Pride of Africa allows unimpeded views across the African bush. Comfortable armchairs make this an ideal venue to watch the passing scenery, while the open platform gives photographers superb views of the passing landscapes.

INFORMATION BOX	
Termini	Cape Town and Victoria Falls
Countries	South Africa to Zimbabwe
Distance	3,200 km (2,000 miles)
Date of completion of first section	1873

embark on one of the world's most entrancing railway journeys, but on Platform 24 stands no ordinary train. Drawn up like guards on parade, the Pride of Africa, resplendent in bottle-green livery, evokes the sublimity of a truly grand occasion. At the head of the train, a pair of Class 6E1 3,000V DC Bo-Bo electrics, in the rather old-fashioned rusty-brown colours of South African Railways, look purposeful and

● **LEFT**
A double-headed train crosses over the Kaaiman River bridge.

● **BELOW**
Locomotive No. 519 returning from the cement
works at Gwanda, Zimbabwe.

● **BOTTOM RIGHT**
An impressive line-up of Garratts at Bulawayo shed.

● **BELOW**
Rovos Rail owns four steam locomotives. No. 439, Tiffany, is the oldest,
built in 1893 and restored by Dunns Locomotive more than 90 years
later. Numbers 2701, 2702 and 3360 are all Class 19D locomotives.

ready to haul their charge over the 708
km (440 miles) to Beaufort West, from
just over sea level at Cape Town to over
1,219 m (4,000 ft) across the Karoo.

The dignified welcome for the
passengers is in stark contrast to the local
Metro trains busily heading off into the
suburbs, their human cargoes packed
tighter than sardines. Rohan Vos, owner
and visionary behind the Pride of Africa,
is often on hand to give a few handy hints
on how to get the most out of the pan-
African odyssey, before he bids the train
farewell, toasting the travellers with fine
South African sparkling wine.

Nestling beneath the distinctively flat-
topped massif of Table Mountain, Cape
Town enjoys one of the most spectacular
settings on earth. As the Pride of Africa
begins its journey northwards, it soon
leaves the compact patchwork of red-
and white-roofed houses and modern
office blocks behind as the tracks follow
the mighty circle of Table Bay with its
encircling ocean before heading inland.

In the wine country of Paarl and the
Hex River valley, tangled vines grow in
the foothills of starkly chiselled
mountains. These are modest farmsteads,
their white porticoes guarded by
cypresses at the end of rutted dirt roads.
Here and there, roosting in the scrub,

ostriches preen their feathers among
indifferent sheep and horses.

Africa has been a magnet for
adventurers ever since Xenophon's men
took time out to hunt the wild ostrich,
and in our own times Rohan Vos has
single-handedly created one of southern
Africa's most romantic travelling idylls.
Rovos Rail is his dreamchild, and in 1986
he started lovingly restoring ancient,
abandoned railway coaches and proud
steam locomotives.

Dating from 1919, each sleeping car,
observation car, bar and lounge car, as
well as the atmospheric Victorian and

Edwardian dining cars, combines the
opulence of pre-war style with subtle
modern innovations. Sleeping
accommodation is in suites with double
or twin beds, together with private
showers and toilets.

As the sun all but disappears, leaving a
last explosion of light along the earth's
rim, the train arrives at Matjiesfontein.
Here an hour-long visit can be made to
the historical hamlet where, over one
hundred years ago, Laird Logan set up a
small refreshment hotel to revictual the
hungry and thirsty travellers of the Cape
Government Railways. The graceful

hotel, named after Lord Milner, provides an opportunity to take the evening air and enjoy a small draught of the famous Castle beer.

As the train continues its journey, the Karoo's horizon becomes scarlet, the sky salmon, the earth blood – it is the drunken dusk of the desert. Passengers become ensconced in the observation car, aperitif in hand, watching the African night creep up on the train.

Coach No. 148, Pafuri, was originally built in 1911 as an A-17 type dining car comprising a small bar, a 24-seat dining section, and a kitchen. In 1924, she was converted into a full 46-seater, responding to an increasing percentage of

passengers taking meals on the great trains of Africa, such as the Diamond Express, the Imperial Mail and the African Express.

Today's passengers enjoy evoking the nostalgia of the great days of travel in this most romantic of settings, surrounded by seven pairs of carved roof-supporting pillars and arches. Later, the travellers fall asleep to the rhythmical, hypnotic motion of the train's wheels. Despite the narrow 3 ft 6 in gauge of South Africa's railways, the ride is surprisingly smooth.

Unnoticed at Beaufort West the current changes to a.c., and now two Class 7E Co-Co locomotives are attached

to haul the train to De Aar. During the night, the 235 km (146 mile) stretch of non-electrified line from De Aar to Kimberley is reached, and a pair of Class 34 Co-Co diesel electrics put in charge.

The following day sees the train arrive at the fine old Victorian station of Kimberley. This city of diamonds is set in the flat, austere landscape of the Karoo. History is rekindled as lunch is enjoyed in the famous Kimberley Club, wistfully recapturing the spirit of the reign of Rhodes and Jameson, who clinched so many deals on these premises. Now with two powerful, high-speed 3,000V d.c. Bo-Bo Class 12Es in command, the Pride of Africa speeds towards Pretoria.

The following day, after a sightseeing tour of Pretoria, the 17-carriage train heads north through groves of orange, papaya and avocado, past depressing townships where flocks of children run down to the tracks smiling and waving. In the observation and lounge cars the rail-borne safari begins in earnest as sightings of impala, kudu and zebra give us a foretaste of this unforgettable close encounter with Africa.

Crossing into Botswana at Mafeking the Pride of Africa undergoes one of a series of no fewer than seven locomotive changes between Pretoria and Victoria

Falls. The mood on board is one of anticipation as passengers savour Cape crayfish and Karoo lamb washed down with Chardonnays and Cabernets.

The steepest gradient encountered is 1:50, as the train makes its assault on the steep-sided mountains that separate the lush, fertile Hex River valley and the elevated, arid Karoo. The climb of 533 m (1,750 ft) over 82 km (51 miles) is the most spectacular section of the journey; its highest point lies just south of Johannesburg at 1,834 m (6,017 ft). The series of four tunnels in the 16.4 km (10.2 mile) long Hex River tunnel system are ranked as the fourth largest in the world and are by far the single most outstanding feature of the journey between Cape Town and Victoria Falls. The tunnels are dead straight, and the longest of them, the northernmost, is spectacular when viewed from the observation car – you can still see the entrance as you leave the exit.

The last complete day on the train is filled with spectacular views of the African bush. After crossing into

Zimbabwe at Plumtree, an afternoon visit is made to Bulawayo. Home to Lobengula, King of the Matabele nation in 1870, the city went on to become synonymous with mining. Here a Class 15 Garratt articulated steam locomotive takes charge. This huge 28-wheeler hauls the Pride of Africa through the night along one of the longest stretches of straight railway line in the world – the 116 km (72 miles) between Gwaai and

Dete on the eastern edge of the Hwange National Park. Musi-oa-tunya ("smoke that thunders") – the African name for the Victoria Falls – heralds journey's end. The screaming of the wheels as the train rounds the final curve adds to the dramatic sense of theatre that this 3,218 km (2,000 mile) pan-African adventure has created. Truly, the Pride of Africa is an iconoclast, following in the footsteps of empire.

CAPE TOWN TO PRETORIA
THE TRANS KAROO

The Trans Karoo is named after its crossing of the Karoo Desert, which covers around one third of South Africa, and is larger than Great Britain and Ireland. Although the Karoo is not of the sand dune type, it proved to be a difficult barrier to cross. Another kind of barrier is the altitude of the Highveld on which Johannesburg is situated; the city is over 1,524 m (5,000 ft) above sea level. The combination of these two factors continues to make operation of trains between these principal towns of the Republic of South Africa (RSA) a continuing challenge, even after electrification of the line.

The lack of water in the desert led to the introduction of a feature unique to South Africa, the condensing tender. These elongated vehicles contained steam-condensing equipment and were used with many Class 25 steam locomotives to reduce water consumption by recycling as much steam as possible. The result was that the British-built locomotives could travel over 1,100 km (700 miles) on one tender of water.

Modernization has shortened the Cape Town to Pretoria journey from the 30 hours taken in 1978, and the Trans Karoo now runs daily rather than five days a week as it did then. However, a second train over the route, running to a schedule 12 hours later on four days a week, has been deleted. The reduction in passenger rail travel has been repeated across the country and is well illustrated by the long lines of stored passenger-coaches outside Cape Town.

The Trans Karoo runs daily between Cape Town and Pretoria via De Aar, Kimberley and Johannesburg, taking 26 hours for the 1,600 km (1,000 mile) journey. The famous Blue Train continues to operate over the same route three days per week, but is now aimed at the luxury travel and tourist market, whereas the Trans Karoo operates the "genuine" passenger service.

The Trans Karoo departs the large Cape Town terminus station from platform 24, which is reserved for this and the few other long-distance services.

● **RIGHT**
SAR Class 6E electric locomotive No. E1184 outside Beaufort West depot sporting the latest Spoornet livery. These 3,340 hp locomotives were built in 1970–1 by Union Carriage and Wagon Co. (UCW), at Nigel, Transvaal, with equipment from AEI in Manchester, England. Double-headed members of this class haul the Trans Karoo from Cape Town to Beaufort West and from De Aar to Pretoria.

● **BELOW**
The SAR steam locomotive dump at Millsite. The large locomotive in the centre of the picture is one of the large Bayer-Garratt articulated locomotives.

INFORMATION BOX

THE TRANS KAROO

Termini	Cape Town and Pretoria
Country	South Africa
Distance	1,600 km (1,000 miles)
Commencement of building	1892

● **OPPOSITE BELOW**
A steam-hauled Trans Karoo passing Millsite. The locomotives are 4-8-4s of class 25NC, Nos. 3476 and 3404. These locomotives were constructed in 1953–4 by North British in Glasgow, Scotland, and Henschel of Kassel, Germany.

● **BELOW**
The Karoo near Beaufort West. The background hills are of a shape common in the desert.

The train the author travelled in was made up of 15 coaches, a car-carrying van, a steam-heating van and two electric locomotives of Class 6E. The weather was cool enough for wisps of steam to be seen emanating from the steam-heating van. The locomotives would be changed a couple of times *en route*, at Beaufort West and De Aar. A Class 7E was used between these points as this route is electrified at a different voltage, 25kV a.c. as opposed to 3,000V d.c. from Cape Town and into Pretoria. The Friday departure from Pretoria as far as Klerksdorp, and the Saturday return, were steam hauled using double-headed 4-8-4s of Class 25NC.

First impressions of the train are not helped by the tatty appearance of the paintwork, which belies the state of the interior. Inside, the coaches are clean and simply but effectively furnished. The train was formed with three classes of accommodation. The first and second class were sleeper coaches marshalled each side of the restaurant cars. The third class, mainly day coaches, was separated from the rest of the train by a door that remained firmly locked throughout the trip. There are on-board showers located at the end of each sleeping coach.

The restaurant car (actually two coaches, one containing the kitchen and staff quarters, the other the seating area) provides good food, although the approach to service seems to be of the same vintage as the coaches. In addition, there is a very effective trolley service of drinks and snacks. The train crew, who were on duty for the entire journey, included an armed guard. This is not so much due to the high crime levels as to control drunken passengers.

The train first heads through the Cape Town suburbs and then into the Cape wine areas of Stellenbosch and Paarl. This area is characterized not only by the vineyards, but also by the famous white-painted, Dutch-style farmhouses. Of particular note is Huguenot Station in an area named after the early French settlers. This is built in the Cape Dutch style, but it has very British influences in the footbridge and signals. The Cape wine area is within the Cape Town electrified suburban rail network, which is served by brightly coloured suburban EMUs.

After initially travelling north, the train turns in a north-westerly direction,

● ABOVE
SAR coaches at Pretoria. The blue-and-grey Interpax coaches are of the type used on the Trans Karoo.

● BOTTOM
Typical Karoo scenery between Touwsrivier and Matjiesfontein.

● BELOW
An SAR electric locomotive of Class 7E on a freight train at Beaufort West. These 4,340 hp locomotives were built by UCW and the "50 Cycles Group" (a consortium of European electrical equipment manufacturers) in 1978–9. This class hauls the Trans Karoo between Beaufort West and De Aar.

which is the wrong way for Johannesburg, and it is this diversion to find a crossing-point in the coastal mountains that makes competition with road transport so difficult. After Herman, the line curves towards the mountains and follows a winding pass before descending into the Breede valley. This is an area of farmlands and orchards; a very English-looking landscape, except for the shapes of the distant hills.

After De Doorn, four hours out of Cape Town, a couple of very lengthy tunnels take the train to the start of the Karoo. One of the first things to notice is

Millsite, a few minutes before arrival at
Krugersdorp. Adjacent to the SAR
locomotive depot is the main store of
withdrawn and stored steam locomotives.

The morning run through the
Johannesburg suburbs showed a stark
contrast with Cape Town. Nearly every
house has high railings, usually with razor
wire, and several stations have guards
armed with shotguns.

The train proceeds from
Johannesburg, to end its journey at the
imposing Pretoria station. Opposite
stands the Victoria Hotel, now owned by
luxury train operator Rovos Rail. This is
a traditional colonial-style hotel, in
contrast to the buildings around it. Rovos
Rail also operates between Cape Town
and Johannesburg, but its service is even
more expensive than the Blue Train.

● BELOW
SAR suburban EMUs, including No. 13150, in
Cape Town carriage sidings, showing the old
and new liveries. The yellow livery is branded
"Metro". No. 13150, of Class 5M2A, was built
by UCW in the 1960s, one of a type that was
constructed by two builders between 1958
and 1985. The mountain in the background is
Devil's Peak, with Table Mountain behind
and to the right.

an ostrich farm complete with a rail-
connected loading dock. Another is the
sturdy shrubs covering the desert. These
have varied flower colours, and their
density thins out as the train gets farther
into the Karoo. The only "wildlife" visible
from the train are some very hardy sheep.
The other dominating features are the
interesting shapes of the hills, which tend
to be flat-topped and sheer-sided with a
surface of shattered rock and no
significant vegetation.

Two lasting memories of crossing the
desert are worth recording. After
travelling through a rare rain shower,
there was a magnificent rainbow against
the darkened sky and the strangely
shaped hills. Secondly, a stop at a passing
loop in the middle of the night. Not only
was the air very cold, but the author has
never seen a night sky so clear and starry,
and with no man-made light visible from
the horizons.

While the very necessary inclusion of
the heating van was unusual in October,
not everyone seemed aware of the
arrangement. The van was taken off the
train at Beaufort West. After this, the
train became exceedingly cold in the
desert night, not properly warming up
until the sun was well up.

The few trains that passed us on this
Sunday were all containerized freights. It
was clear that most sidings at local
stations were out of use, as road traffic
has taken over the local and short-haul
freight, leaving only the long-haul and
large-volume freight to the railways.
However, much of the route showed
signs of modernization, as curves and
gradients had been eased, and new
tunnels built to avoid difficult sections of
the route, indicating that the railway does
have a future.

The Johannesburg end of the journey
is dominated first by farm land, and then
by the mining industry, with many spoil
heaps visible until you are almost into the
city. One site worth looking out for is at

ISTANBUL TO BAGHDAD
THE TAURUS EXPRESS

Started in 1930, the Taurus Express (Toros Ekspresi in Turkish) linked London to Cairo and Berlin to Baghdad. Only the English Channel and the Bosporus needed ferries. With Germans in charge of operations, it followed the route of the Baghdad Railway, a Turkish enterprise that had been funded with money from the Deutsche Bank. Once controlled by the French, the Baghdad Railway was taken over in 1880 by the British and in 1888 by Turkey.

From Istanbul the Ottoman Anatolian Railway retained its French title, handing over to the Baghdad Railway at Konya, an Islamic centre famous for the Mevlevi

● **ABOVE RIGHT**
The imposing walls of the Citadel at Aleppo.

● **RIGHT**
Poster of the Simplon-Orient Express for the inauguration of the Taurus Express route via Ankara in 1930.

Order of Whirling Dervishes. Like Rome or Canterbury, the city has a holy atmosphere.

In the south of Turkey, the railway ran through the rich Cilician Plain that feeds most of the otherwise rocky desert with its patches of civilization. It was opened from Adana to Mersin via Yenice in 1886, but was taken over by the Deutsche Bank in 1906.

The CFOA started originally as a narrow-gauge line in 1873, along the north coast of the Marmora Sea and across the Ak Ova plain. After Arifiye, 36 m (118 ft) up, the line climbed through the Baleban gorge, then across

INFORMATION BOX	
THE TAURUS EXPRESS	
Termini	Istanbul and Baghdad
Countries	Turkey and Iraq
Distance	2,566 km (1,595 miles)
Date building commenced	
1893	

● **FAR LEFT**
The first Wagons-Lits
sleepers in Asiatic
Turkey, seen here on
the Anatolia Express
in 1927. These cars
were put into service
on the Taurus
Express in 1930.

● **LEFT**
An SG type sleeping-
car compartment,
built in Birmingham,
England, for the
Taurus Express. A
feature of the
compartment are the
holders for fob
watches.

the smallish Akhisar plain where tobacco,
corn and mulberries grew. It then
ascends 294 m (965 ft) through a narrow
gorge, whose walls are about 90 m
(300 ft) above the railway, to Bilecik, a
steam-lovers' paradise. Here worked
western Turkey's last huge steam banking
2-10-2 tank-engines, which hauled trains
16 km (10 miles) up another 390 m
(1,280 ft) at a 1:40 gradient to Eskesehir
on the Central plateau.

From Eskesehir, where Turkey's main
railway works is situated, a branch line
turned east to Angora (famous for its
wool), which was reached by rail in
1892. The city was renamed Ankara in
1921 by Attaturk, when he made it his
nation's capital. The British ambassador,
not wanting to relocate to Ankara, hired
some sleeping cars and a diner from
Wagons-Lits and lived in them during the
week, returning to his palatial Istanbul
Embassy at the weekends.

In 1927 Wagons-Lits created the
Anatolia Express, which went as far as
Ankara, the Russians not wanting
German-influenced railways extending
too far eastward. In 1895, influenced by
Germany's *Drang nach Osten*, a railway to
connect Konya and Baghdad was started
simultaneously from both termini. By the
time World War I broke out, the line had
reached Samora (now in Iraq), 290 km
(180 miles) south of Monsul and 121 km
(75 miles) from Baghdad.

● **ABOVE**
Only two all-Wagons-Lits trains existed after
the war: the Train Bleu in France and the
Ankara Express in Turkey. The latter, hauled
by a Henschel 2-8-2, is seen here arriving at
Istanbul in 1957.

● **BELOW**
A view of the city of Aleppo, stretching out,
taken from the walls of the Citadel.

● **ABOVE**
A visit to Egypt is not complete without a cruise. Here we see a cruise ship and a felluca on the Nile at Cairo.

From Konya the line crossed the 64 km (40 mile) long Konya plain, followed by the Karaman plain to Cakmak, where it climbed from 61 m (200 ft) to 366 m (1,201 ft) in 29 km (18 miles), mostly at 1:40. The summit was at Kardesgedigi, where the 1935-built line from Ankara was joined. Thereafter the Taurus Express ran by Ankara, and Konya was only a secondary route.

Now, as the train began its great drop through the Cilician Gates to Yenice, from 1,468 m (4,816 ft) to 34 m (112 ft) in 105 km (65 miles), the Taurus mountains were on all sides. Pozanti, the only town for miles around, is 32 km (20 miles) from the top. From Andna, the Germans decided that the flat line on the coastal plain through Antioch would be too close to the sea (fearing seizure by the British), so they took an inland route from the Cilician Plain. This climbed back up to 732 m (2,402 ft), where they built the 1,495 m (4,905 ft) long Amanus tunnel, which took the train to Fevsipasa. Here the Taurus Express turned south through Meydan Ekbez to Aleppo. From Aleppo the line ran on towards Tripoli, which was the main supply line to Palestine.

In 1927, Attaturk formed the Turkish State railways, which, in 1919, took over from the French from Pozanti to Favaipasa. The French formed two

companies – the Cenup, or Turkish Southern, and the Syrian-Baghdad lines. Both were worked and run by the same management between Aleppo and Tel Kotchek, 76 km (47 miles) beyond the Syrian frontier at Nusaybin. Until 1939, travellers to Baghdad left the train at Tel Kotchek, now El Yaroubish, which had a Wagons-Lits rest house, and motored to Kirkuk, the terminus of the narrow-gauge line to Baghdad. The Baghdad Railway was extended to Sanora in 1940. After 1940 the Taurus Express became a through train with sleepers and a diner, for the 2,566 km (1,595 miles) from Istanbul to Baghdad. This service ended in 1966.

Before World War II the Taurus ran three days a week to Tel Kotchek and three days a week to Tripoli, with a connecting sleeper from Aleppo on the days when the train ran to Tel Kotchek. At Tripoli the passengers transferred to Model A Ford motor cars. To avoid the heat they drove to Beirut early in the morning and rested for about four hours before going on to Haifa, avoiding the mountain barrier by driving along the beach – there was no road.

At Haifa, Wagons-Lits ran a sleeping car to Kantara East in Egypt, crossing from Palestine at Rafa, after passing

● **ABOVE LEFT**
The impressive Sphinx at Giza, just outside Cairo.

● **LEFT**
The Istanbul to Ankara express near Kaysari.

happy with the results. Basra, once in Iran, is now of course an Iraqi city, but the hate continues, and this was going great guns when I arrived in Khorramshah and wanted to reach Basra. I got there in the end by walking for miles across a no man's land of a desert, delayed lengthily and not very pleasantly by innumerable checkpoints and gun-toting soldiers.

A bevy of friendly Iraqis took charge of me in Basra, a city I found to be a hotchpotch of other people's developments: Carmathian, Mongol, Turk and European, with a thin veneer of Muslim. At the railway station I ran the station-master to ground, was invited to tea and finally — he learning of my inability to change my Barclays-issued traveller's cheque into local currency (Barclays being pronounced a "Lackey of Israel") — was given a first-class ticket valid for the air-conditioned deluxe overnight express to Baghdad.

From Basra to the Iraqi capital it is 611 km (380 miles), and the distance was covered in nine hours, which is a good rate of knots for a Middle Eastern train. For some way the route follows the Euphrates River and passes within two miles of Ur, of the Chaldees fame. We also flashed by a short platform

designated "Babylon Halt" which apparently even the little local trains pass with a derisive whistle.

My berth was almost up to European standards, and after weeks of rough living

and travelling on lesser trains and even lesser buses and lorries, it seemed like paradise. In the morning the train drew into West station, the Grand Central of the Iraqi capital.

● **ABOVE**
A Syrian-built 2-6-0 tank dating back to the 1890s heads away from Damascus with a Sunday excursion train.

● **LEFT**
After the day's intense sun the evening's mellow light brings relief to the border country between Syria and Lebanon as a Swiss-built 2-6-0 tank heads towards Damascus with an evening passenger-train.

405

DAMASCUS TO MEDINA

Every Muslim male is required to visit Muhammad's birthplace in Mecca at least once in his lifetime if he can. During the 19th century, the journey was hazardous in the extreme. The Arabs were reluctantly under Ottoman rule, and bands of vulnerable Turkish pilgrims were murdered as they journeyed through the desert. Eventually the Sultan of Turkey authorized the building of a railway between Damascus and Mecca to carry pilgrims in safety. Construction began in 1901, and seven laborious years later Medina, where Muhammad is buried, was reached 1,302 km (809 miles) to the south. This line, the Hedjaz, takes its name from the area alongside the Red Sea in Arabia where the holy city lies.

Trouble dogged every mile; marauding Arabs attacked the workers; the heat was intolerable, and violent sandstorms frequently caused work to be stopped. The Arabs, frantic that their holy city would be defiled, refused to allow the

railway past Medina. In wild fervour they invaded the railway construction camp and massacred the work-force. The line was destined to go no further, and pilgrims had to continue on foot over the remaining 370 km (230 miles) to Mecca.

The railway only carried pilgrims for seven seasons until the outbreak of World War I. The Turks allied with Germany, and Arab nationalists, supported by the British under Colonel Lawrence, partly succeeded in driving the Turks from the Hedjaz. To prevent enemy

reinforcements from getting through, Lawrence blew up large sections of the line. Indeed, so great was the damage that trains were forced to terminate at Ma'an in Southern Jordan. Today, almost 70 years later, not only does the southern section remain abandoned despite various attempts to reopen it, but many of the abandoned locomotives still lie half-buried in the sand.

The line now passes through three countries, and all would benefit by its reinstallation. In 1963 a consortium of

● **ABOVE**
A 2-8-2 crossing the desert, about 48 km (30 miles) from Amman. Although passenger traffic was ended by the Syrians in 1983, the line reopened for passenger traffic in 1987.

● **LEFT**
Nippon Pacific No. 82 storming up the bank out of Amman.

● **RIGHT**
A 2-8-2 pauses at
Mafraq near the
Syrian border. There
is a twice-weekly
service between the
two countries, both
for freight and
passengers.

British engineers began work. The task
was daunting. The section from Ma'an to
Medina is 845 km (525 miles) long and,
apart from being plagued by the elements
(and damage incurred by Lawrence),
48 km (30 miles) of embankment had
been washed away by the violent rains
that sweep over the Arabian desert every
five years. Half the route needed attention
with much of the track unserviceable.

Much work had been done by 1967,
when the Arab-Israeli War broke out and
Saudi officials ordered work to stop.
Work on the line was never resumed, and
the railway was again abandoned with
only the 467 km (290 mile) 3 ft 5$^{1}/_{4}$ in
gauge line section from Damascus to
Ma'an remaining in operation.

● **LEFT**
A 2-8-2 crosses a
viaduct at a town
near Amman.

● **BELOW**
Nippon Pacific No.
82 on the viaduct on
the outskirts of
Amman.

INFORMATION BOX

Termini	Damascus and Medina
Country	Jordan to Saudi Arabia
Distance	1,302 km (809 miles)
Date of opening	1908

MOSCOW TO VLADIVOSTOK
THE TRANS-SIBERIAN EXPRESS

It was in 1858 that proposals were first made for a Trans-Siberian Railway that would connect Moscow and European Russia to the Pacific. Owing to the Crimean War, however, it was not until 1875 that an official plan was put forward. During the ensuing years other plans were proposed until, in 1891, the Russian Government finally gave its official approval, and Crown Prince Nicholas cut the first sod in Vladivostok. The railway, one of the world's greatest engineering achievements, was seen by the Russian Government as a means of consolidating the Russian hold on Siberia and the Pacific provinces by both developing the Eastern economy and exerting a political influence on China.

● **LEFT**
Yaroslav station, Konsomol Square, Moscow. Built by the architect Franz Shekhiel in 1906, this is the western terminus of the Trans-Siberian Railway.

● **BELOW**
The Kremlin and the River Moskva in Moscow.

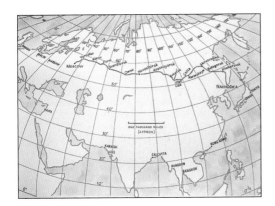

● **FAR LEFT**
Map showing the
route of the Trans-
Siberian Railway.

● **LEFT**
People queuing at a
food and drink
kiosk at Gorky Park,
Moscow.

● **BELOW LEFT**
The Rossia waits at
Khabarovsk.

Although work began in 1891, through rail communication was only established in 1903. This did, however, include the train ferry over Lake Baikal – the deepest lake in the world. In the winter, when the ice became too thick for ice breaking, rails were laid on the ice itself and the train was run over the lake. The line round the southern shore of the lake was not blasted out of the solid rock until 1905. Such was the terrain of this 68 km (42 mile) section that no fewer than 38 tunnels had to be bored. In places, the shore of the lake is almost vertical and up to 1,200 m (4,000 ft) high. The toughest gradient is just east of Ulan Ude, where a sharp incline of 1:57.5 is encountered.

At first, part of the route was laid across Manchuria (and known as the Chinese Eastern Railway) direct from Chita via Harbin to Vladivostok. This section over Chinese soil was necessary because the comparatively flat land of Manchuria made the line both cheaper and shorter. However, after the Russo-Japanese War, which strained the line to capacity by carrying large numbers of troops and supplies from European Russia to the Far East, a connection was built from Chita via the Amar valley and Khabarovsk. Although considerably longer than the direct route across Manchuria, it did ensure that the whole route was over Russian territory.

Although the line, which begins at Moscow, goes through Omsk, Irkutsk (on the shores of Lake Baikal) and Khabarovsk before terminating at Vladivostok, was originally built as single track, by 1913 most of it had been

● **RIGHT**
The Trans-Siberian
Express, one of the
world's greatest
engineering
achievements, and a
railway legend.

● **LEFT**
The archways and
tower of the River
Station, Moscow.

● **BELOW LEFT**
The railway bridge,
built between 1896
and 1901, over the
River Ob at
Novosibirsk. It
consists of seven
main spans and is
814 m (2,670 ft)
long.

● **BELOW
RIGHT**
The Trans-Siberian
Express at Chita.

converted to double track. It was not
until the 1950s, however, that the whole
route was double-tracked. By the mid-
1970s, three-quarters of the line (from
the European end) had been electrified.

One of the most interesting features
of the line is the number of bridges. On
the western portion of the line alone
there are eight bridges of over 305 m
(1,000 ft) in length, including those over
the Irtish, the Ob and the Yenisei, all of
which are over 610 m (2,000 ft), while at
Khabarovsk, on the North Manchurian
frontier, there is another exceptionally
long bridge across the River Amur.

Between the two world wars, the
through passenger service was provided
by the Trans-Siberian Express, which had
a special sleeping car and dining facilities.
There was also the Blue Express, which
included ordinary "hard" and "soft"
accommodation as well as a sleeping car.
These trains, which were relatively light,
with only eight or nine carriages, took
just under ten days to complete the
9,611 km (5,973 mile) journey from
Moscow to Vladivostok, at an average
speed of only 40 kph (25 mph).

In 1913, an English traveller called
Pearson wrote a detailed account of the

journey, which began at Moscow's Yaroslav station. His train, headed by a highly polished Pacific locomotive, was composed of long green-and-gold carriages. The corridors were carpeted, and the dining car was decorated with an impressive ivory-white ceiling, large plate-glass windows and panelling. In those days the train also included a travelling bathroom, a chemist's shop and reading and games rooms.

Nine days on a train might not be everybody's ideal trip. Yet there are rail enthusiasts who say they dream of riding the Trans-Siberian Express. The author's experience of it when the country was still the Soviet Union, was not entirely the stuff of dreams. Although the four-bunk soft-class (Westerners were forbidden to travel hard-class) compartments were spacious and clean, there was a radio loudspeaker, which exuded the sort of thing expected from Stalinist Russia. The quality of everything, from coat-hangers to reading matter, was extremely poor. Moreover, the electric locomotive was Czech, and

● **ABOVE**
Travellers at the railway station, Moscow.

● **LEFT**
The "Rossia" Trans-Siberian Express (left) in company with the Peking Express. Both trains had been halted by an accident on the line, just west of Irkutsk.

● **BELOW LEFT**
A traditional Russian wooden house.

the silvery coaches were East German. Indeed, it would not be too far wrong to say that it was only the tea, served in the carriages from an old-fashioned samovar, that was genuinely Russian.

INFORMATION BOX
THE TRANS-SIBERIAN EXPRESS

Termini	Moscow and Vladivostock
Country	Russia
Distance	9,611 km (5,972 miles)
Date of opening	1903

BRUSSELS TO HONG KONG

There is no such animal as a Trans-Siberian Express listed in the Russian Railway timetables or, for that matter, in any issue of the *Thomas Cook Overseas Timetable*. What you will see, however, is a Train No. Two, which travels between Moscow's Yaroslav station and Vladivostok's Main station. There are also other numbered trains with names like Zabaikal, Rossia and Tomich, which cover major sections of the 9,297 km (5,777 mile) line.

All these could be termed "Trans-Siberian Expresses", though to cover the route of the so-called Red Arrow Express – a collection of different trains running between Brussels and Hong Kong – the Zabaikal, linking Moscow to Irkutsk, was used on this section of the journey.

● LEFT
The Irkutsk to Moscow coach nameplate on the Zabaikal Express.

● BELOW
The train speeds through the Polish countryside.

To attain Moscow from Brussels, the Ost West Express is the most convenient vehicle. This train leaves the Midi Station at 15.55 and arrives at Moscow Smolenskaya at 22.05 two nights later. It is now considerably faster and more comfortable than it used to be during the Communist era, when gruelling checks by border guards in the then German Democratic Republic, Poland and the then Soviet Union held up progress for hours – in addition to the still continuing

● **RIGHT**
Berlin's Frauen
Kirche has been left
as it was after being
bombed in the
Second World War
as a reminder of the
horrors of war.

INFORMATION BOX

Termini	Brussels and Kowloon
Countries	Belgium to Hong Kong
Distance	21,384 km (13,290 miles)
Date link completed	1949

Siberia is autumn, when the seemingly endless landscape of birch trees turns to the colour of burnished gold. Crossing great rivers, such as the Ob and the Yenisei, on immense bridges makes for the most emotive sights.

Four days out, by which time the fare in the restaurant car has been reduced to mainly bortsch, macaroni and Russian champagne, the express reaches Irkutsk, capital of Siberia, and a not unattractive city with some timber houses of the Chekhov era still surviving. Here the

chore of bogey-changing that is effected at Brest to adapt the train to the wider Russian gauge.

On the Trans-Siberian line, the long-distance expresses are reasonably comfortable, with soft- and hard-class berths that can be used as beds. Tea is always on tap from coach samovars and is brought to compartments by the attendants. The best time to traverse

● **LEFT**
A Russian train
approaches a
country station.

through coaches bound for Ulan Bator,
the Mongolian capital, or – once weekly
– right through to Beijing, are
transferred to what was termed the
Irkutsk-Ulan Bator Express. Maybe
things have changed for the better, but
the train used to be as dirty as the
blankets issued for sleeping. From Ulan
Ude, on the Russian-Mongolian border,
the train was headed by a rust-pink –
more rust than pink – diesel unit of
Mongolian Railways to deflect
southwards from the shores of Lake
Baikal, snaking into the low hills and
across rolling plains, the habitat of wild
camels, wild horses and the Gobi bear.
Occasional wind-swept villages of
hexagonal *yurts* draw the eye. The line
here is non-electric.

Ulan Bator's most attractive building
is its small and well-kept station. The city

itself is a dull one, centred on the
standardized Soviet-style parade-ground
square bordered by grim government
buildings but enlivened in recent years by
a pink stock-exchange. Though there is
only one through train a week to Beijing,
there are two a week from Ulan Bator to
the Chinese capital.

● **BOTTOM**
A view from the train window of the
countryside of Outer Mongolia.

The author's onward journey towards
China was made in Chinese rolling stock.
This was a step up in the comfort stakes,
with shaded table lamps, jasmine-
flavoured tea in flasks, dainty seat
coverlets and chintzy curtains.

At Erlan, 36 hours later, the train
bogeys have to be changed back to fit
China's standard gauge, an operation that
can be watched by passengers so inclined.
Then, powered by a new and electric
locomotive, the train enters the Chinese
province of Inner Mongolia.

Railway construction in China has
been considerable in recent years. By the
time of the so-called liberation in 1949,
only 11,000 km (6,835 miles) of rail
track were still open to traffic, the
remainder having been destroyed by
many years of internal conflict. The total
rail system now exceeds 55,000 km

Beijing, is not the largest city in the country – that accolade goes to Shanghai – but the trappings of capitalship lie firmly upon the city's shoulders. The main station is a surprisingly modest establishment, constantly overcrowded. From Beijing southwards the train is electric powered, and for another 36 hours one can enjoy eminently comfortable living quarters and often delicious scenery to match. The 2,400 km (1,500 mile) route lies through sprawling cities and over prodigious rivers, such as the Yangtse, where trains clatter endlessly across great bridges.

Before Canton, round-topped peaks give the lie to the idea that Chinese landscape paintings are figments of Chinese imagination, and provide an intensely beautiful finale to the journey. Here the line cuts through the gorges of the Pei Kiang and a water-logged territory of rice paddies peopled by half-submerged peasants and water buffalo.

The ride from Canton to Hong Kong is the smoothest of all. And there is nothing like a three-week rail journey to give the luxurious comforts of this unique Anglo-Chinese city an added lustre.

(34,000 miles) and while, before 1949, seven provinces had no railways at all, now only Tibet is without rail communication – though the line to Lhasa has long been under construction.

Datong is a familiar name on account of its huge factory that produced those giant Chinese steam locomotives, but, alas, it is no longer doing so. Visitors were once lucky enough to be shown around the works when these monsters were in full production and, if they were very lucky, even allowed to drive a newly produced locomotive undergoing its operational testing. China's capital,

QUETTA TO ZAHEIDAN
ACROSS THE BALUCHISTAN DESERT

● **BELOW LEFT**
The village of Skardu.

● **BOTTOM**
One of Pakistan's diesel-electrics, which haul international services.

The lonely line that connects Quetta to the southern Iranian town of Zaheidan is known by some as the Nushki Extension Railway though it runs hundreds of kilometres past Nushki, across the border and 80 km (50 miles) into Iran. It leaves Quetta's main line at Spezand and continues parallel to the mountain ranges forming the frontier with Afghanistan. The line was laid during World War I, when the British and Russians "policed" the territory between the Caspian Sea and the Persian Gulf.

Between Dalbandin and Nok Kundi, a distance of 167 km (104 miles), the region is wholly without habitation, virtually devoid of vegetation and a hell upon earth. The line crosses long stretches of desert covered with sharp black stones broken only by patches of

coarse sand. For eight months of the year the heat is intense, and the "120-day wind" whips this sand into tight little whirlwinds that lacerate the skin. The whole desert is covered with sulphur dust, and water, when it is obtainable,

tastes like a concentrated mixture of common and Epsom salts. When there is any rain at all, the whole year's fall may occur within an hour. The river beds, bone dry for 90 days out of 100, then hurl the water, laced with quantities of stone, at the exposed railway. To overcome this disconcerting event, the engineers built Irish bridges, or "dips", and the drivers of the steam-hauled trains crossing them were expected to use their discretion as to whether they could pass through without water getting into their fireboxes and putting the fire out.

Then there are the *do-reg*, or marching sand-hills. These are crescent-shaped sand-hills formed by the wind and constantly on the move. Again the line is the target and, from time to time, diversionary track has to be laid to take

the railway round the back of the *do-reg* to avoid several thousand tonnes of sand. The sand-hills move in parallel lines for many miles across the *dasht*. Their speed is 500–600 m (1,600–1,900 ft) per year, so the duplicated tracks are left in position and trains use whichever one happens to be clear of sand.

Sometimes the marching sand-hills cover the track, and then all the male passengers from the stranded train spend hours re-laying the track. Spare lengths of rail, shoes and sleepers lie alongside in readiness for just an emergency. These,

then, are just some of the vicissitudes of a trans-Baluchistan journey.

Hours behind schedule, the journey will be resumed across the terrible landscape. At a remote habitation, the

train halts for what seems to the weary passengers an interminable period while the crew is changed.

At Mirjaveh, on the Iranian border, there is a long passport check and general evacuation to the hut for the issue of Iranian railway tickets for the last 80 km (50 miles) to Zaheidan, which is reached – if there are no delays such as those mentioned above – some 30 hours after departure from Quetta.

● LEFT
Young boys working
in the fields at
Tongul.

INFORMATIONBOX	
Termini	Quetta and Zaheidan
Countries	Pakistan and Iran
Distance	650 km (404 miles)
Date of opening	1916

LINDI KOTAL TO PESHAWAR DOWN THE KHYBER

It is probably only the British who become charged with emotion at the mere mention of the Khyber Pass. Its fame is based on history rather than scenery, and the comparatively recent and universally known story of the Khyber is exclusively British – though the armies of Alexander the Great and the Mogul emperors Babur and Humayan also used its defiles.

The British-built line climbs to about 1,070 m (3,500 ft) on wide-gauge track without rack-and-pinion assistance, and even with two engines it is heavy going. From Lindi Kotal there was a once-weekly train to Peshawar run at no charge, simply as a gesture by Pakistan Railways to prove to the fiercely independent tribesmen that the line, in spite of them, was open and the Pakistan Government was the boss.

The old coaches were a morass of humanity intent upon going along for the free ride. With not an inch of space available, the author found a seat astride the right-hand front buffer of a steam locomotive made by the British Vulcan

● **LEFT**
Passengers stretch their legs in the heat of the afternoon.

● **BELOW LEFT**
Locomotive No. 2495 steams through a cutting in the red hills of western Pakistan.

● **BELOW RIGHT**
Tribal musicians meet travellers at the Khyber Pass.

INFORMATION BOX

Termini	Lindi Kotal and Peshawar
Country	Pakistan
Distance	64 km (40 miles)
Date of opening	1902

foundry in 1923. Two Pakistani passengers had already seated themselves on the other buffer, and a necklace of humanity encircled the boiler.

The 64 km (40 mile) ride that followed was a spectacular and unforgettable journey. The descent of the Khyber is the steepest non-rack stretch of track in the world. It is made in the form of a letter Z, the train changing

● **LEFT**
The train takes a curve in this typical western Pakistan landscape.

● **BELOW LEFT**
The Pakistan/Afghan border at the Khyber Pass.

● **BELOW RIGHT**
An armed guard stands by the regimental coats of arms in the Khyber Pass.

direction at each apex and, on the steepest sections, safety track is installed to divert runaway trains into the hills. Until one became accustomed to the motion, one felt extremely insecure astride the metal seat. To maintain balance, it was necessary to grip the greasy ironwork with one's knees with hands clamped to the buffer flanges like limpet mines. The great hissing, threatening boiler licked the passengers with jets of steam, while one's imagination worked overtime painting mind pictures of what the relentless wheels would do to anyone who had the misfortune to fall off.

The train travelled at no great pace through a series of short tunnels and beneath empty forts, which gave a walnut topping to every brown hill. The Khyber's narrowest defile was commanded by the oldest of these – Ali Masjid – built high on a cliff, and near to it was a showcase displaying regimental badges, British, Pathan and Indian.

All around was an alien landscape, burnt brown and exuding that air of latent hostility so different from the green meadows of England. Here was magnificence for sure, but its constituents were sharply formed crags varying in shades of colour from deep

red to sandy yellow, punctuated by jagged pinnacles of rock.

The plain below the pass was suddenly upon the train, the brown and barren hills abruptly deflated. Fortified villages, their high mud walls blank apart from firing slits, remained in evidence, their unseen occupants presumably still ready to repulse attack from wherever it might come. At one point, where the line doubled back on itself, one could see the Khyber mountain looking impregnable to man and train; not a gap or defile showed anywhere. The train limped into Peshawar, the once-in-a-lifetime vice-regal ride at an end.

KALYAN TO HOWRAH
ACROSS INDIA BY TROOP TRAIN

One of the great experiences in life is to travel across a mighty land mass such as the Indian subcontinent, as it was known in 1945. This account is based on notes made at the time, but the expanded version was lost to the military censor because of the railway details it contained. Some things have changed dramatically since then, but the long history and traditions of the many peoples of that great land mass will ensure that much also remains the same.

It was not a journey made voluntarily, but as a soldier under orders, heading for the advance HQ of the Allied Land Forces in South-east Asia – wherever that might be. In the meantime, the railway and its surroundings were there to be enjoyed or endured as the case may be.

The author had landed at Bombay some weeks before and had travelled several times between there and Kalyan, using trains that were generally hauled by massive 2-C0-1 electric locomotives, built in 1925 by Metropolitan Vickers of the UK for the Great Indian Peninsular Railway standard (5 ft 6 in) gauge and operating on a line voltage of 1,500 d.c.

INFORMATION BOX

Termini	Kalyan and Howrah
Country	India
Distance	2,129 km (1,323 miles)
Date of travel	1945

● BELOW LEFT
A train load of cotton in a timeless scene.

● BELOW RIGHT
A train crosses a bridge while a young woman sits by the river with her water pot.

It was probably one such that was hauling the troop train, consisting of 14 coaches and two vans, a load of some 567 tonnes (560 tons) tare, which left Kalyan at 1100 hours on 8 March 1945.

The line was fairly level and straight as it passed through rather arid country, which allowed for speeds up to 113 kph (70 mph). Although I was travelling in third class, it was not overcrowded and the compartment was large. Windows that came right down and shutters to keep out the glare of the sun, coupled with the speed of the train, made things

● **BELOW**
A contemporary photograph of a scene that is
virtually unchanged since 1946.

● **BOTTOM**
A train steams through the Indian countryside.

● **BELOW**
A train crosses a river using one of the many
bridges on the Indian rail network.

reasonably comfortable, although the
well-shaped wooden seats encouraged
movement from time to time. There was
no through corridor connection, which
meant that lengthy stops were required
so that one could collect the meals
provided and wash personal utensils and
mess tins in the vats provided.

At the approach to the Western Ghats,
just beyond Khardi, hard climbing began,
with the line twisting and turning and
passing through several tunnels. It got
colder, and wonderful views opened up
of the plain below, followed by
spectacular engineering as the line clung
to steep valley sides.

At Igatpuri, electricity gave way to
steam haulage, and it is possible that
traction was put in the hands of a Class
XA1 4-6-2 built by Vulcan Foundry in
the UK in 1929. From here the line
undulated over a rather barren plain
dotted with villages until arrival at
Deolalih, a feared posting for army
troops, which gave its name to doolally, a
nickname for a form of madness.

Soon after departure from Deolalih,
the train began the long drag of some
80 km (50 miles) at gradients of 1:200 to
1:120 to the 914 m (2,999 ft) summit of
the line. At that time of the year, in the

dry season, the scene was forbiddingly
barren but enlivened by hawks circling
above looking for prey.

During the night, the train stopped
at Sonepur, at a station that proclaimed
that it had the longest platform in India,
and then at the major city of Nagpur,
where locomotives were changed, the
system from here on being the Bengal
Nagpur Railway.

By morning, the train was descending,
twisting and turning past sheer rock

faces. Toward the end of the day, the
countryside became more green until
jungle pressed upon the line. By night, it
can be very cold, but the temperature
soon rises with the sun and the hot,
steamy conditions were such as to
encourage us to sit with our feet over the
footsteps of the carriage, which provided
some interesting experiences when the
train crossed high bridges over rivers or
dried water-courses with an
unobstructed view of the ground below.

As night fell, flat country was again
encountered. In the night, the sight of
the enormous Tatanagar steel works left a
lasting impression. By morning, the train
was on double track some 80 km (50
miles) from Calcutta in low-lying, dank
and misty marshland, cold in the early
light. Lines proliferated, and we passed
local trains crammed with people with
others on the outsides and on the roofs
of carriages.

Howrah station, 2,129 km (1,323
miles) and 44 hours from Kalyan, was a
sea of people, with porters vying to carry
passengers' luggage to waiting rickshaws
and taxis. As the crossing of India came
to a close, one was left with wonderful
memories of a truly unique rail journey
set in unbelievable scenery.

DELHI TO COCHIN

Amid the chaos that characterizes all
Indian railway stations, New Delhi's
contains an air-conditioned haven that is
the Foreigners' Booking Office, where
comparative order is preserved. From
here you can set out, armed perhaps with
that open-sesame of Indian rail travel, the
Ind-Rail Pass, on a journey south on the
second longest rail route in the country.

The vehicle for much of the way is the
Kerala Express. The train is not one of
the "super expresses" that ply between
Delhi and Bombay, but, while never
generating great speed, its progress is
reasonable enough. At intervals small
flasks of tea and hot meals – ordered
prior to delivery (vegetarian or
"European") at ridiculously low cost – are
served, and, come nightfall, the
compartment seats are turned into bunks.

The route is not initially a spectacular
one, the urban centres being Agra,
Gwalior, Jhansi, Bhopol, Nagpur, Gudin,
Coimatore and Cochin. The last of these
is in the province of Kerala, its distinctive
woods, lakes and coconut plantations
making a sudden and picturesque change
from the parched flatlands of central
India. At Trivandrum, the Keralan capital,

● **ABOVE**
The station in New
Delhi, India's capital
city since 1931.

● **LEFT**
Panan bridge under
construction.

● **BELOW LEFT**
A group of railway
workers zip along
the tracks near
Cochin station,
southern India

a bed may be acquired for the night in a
dormitory of that British-inspired and
now firmly Indian concept called a
railway retiring room. The cost again is
infinitesimal and, should one be averse to

the continual noises of snoring and
hawking, private rooms are also available.
Pillows, sheets and pillowcases are issued,
and a lockable bedside cupboard is
provided. A very welcome hot shower is
also supplied.

From Cochin, a beautiful city of
Portuguese ancestry overflowing on to a
trio of islands, you can, if you choose,
forgo the famed beaches of nearby

INFORMATION BOX

Termini	Delhi and Cochin
Country	India
Distance	2,100 km (1,305 miles)
Commencement of building	
1853	

The bustling station at Rameswaram station, the ferry port for Sri Lanka.

Kovalam, take the short train ride to Cape Comerin, the extreme southern tip of India, where three oceans meet.

Another ride can be taken southward to Rameswaram on the Madras-Rameswaram Express, which can be joined at Coimbatore. Rameswaram, with its sacred shrine, is a ferry port for Sri Lanka, just across the Palk Strait. The town is approached by the gigantic, recently built Panan bridge, over which the train slowly trundles. The same train, a day later, will take the traveller back as far as Madurai, to view its massive temple, prior to joining a night train to the garden city of Bangalore.

From Bangalore, one travels on to Mysore and northwards to, eventually, Coa and Bombay on a variety of trains with varying characteristics and degrees of comfort. Prior to Bombay it is worth pausing at Pune – Poona of British Army fame – which is the site of another narrow-gauge mountain line, the Matheran Hill Railway.

The return to Delhi is on the crack Rajdhani Express, which, by the standards of the Indian railway system, is of sublime comfort and high speed. On it, attendants make the beds, and afternoon tea, dinner, early morning tea and breakfast are all included in the price of the ticket. However, after travelling for weeks on lesser trains, you might find this rather a dull one, lacking the charm of the true India.

DELHI TO JODHPUR
THE PALACE ON WHEELS

● **BELOW AND BENEATH**
The Fort of Jodhpur, one of the locomotives
that hauls the Palace on Wheels.

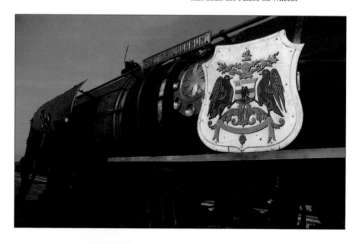

Though the Raj is no more, the romance
of the train lives on in India – or at least
it does for many foreign visitors, Britons
predominating. To cater for these
nostalgic longings, Indian Railways in
conjunction with the Rajasthan Tourist
Board produced a train to resurrect a
glamorous past. They called it the Palace
on Wheels. Alas, this palace of a train is
no more, but another in the same vein
has taken its place. The "Palace" was
assembled from appropriate coaches
unearthed from sources throughout the
subcontinent, many rusting away in
obscure sidings and some once owned by
long-deposed maharajas. Restored to
their former glory, they became the pride
and joy of Indian Railways.

What set the final seal of authenticity
were the two superb steam locomotives
chosen to head them. To complement the
image of the golden coaches, these giant
monsters with their shining brass-work,
glistening pistons and proud coat of arms
at the front of the boiler were christened
Desert Queen and Fort of Jodhpur.
Crews were hand-picked from the cream

of drivers for this, the most prestigious
train in all India.

On the inaugural journey, the coach,
bearing the insignia of the Jaipur State
Railway, was one which had once carried
the Maharaja of Bikaner, while a more
recent incumbent had been Mrs Gandhi,
the late Indian Prime Minister. It was the
most opulent and historic saloon of all,
with pink upholstery, silver-embroidered
curtains, teak wall panels and traditional
carpeting. The suites consisted of a
bedroom, amply proportioned, with a
wide bed, a wardrobe and a bedside
table, and a comfortable lounge,
generously equipped with sofas and

INFORMATION BOX	
THE PALACE ON WHEELS	
Termini	Delhi and Jodhpur
Country	India
Distance	250 km (155 miles)
Date of first run	1982

● **BELOW**
A driver's-eye view of the track ahead of the
Palace on Wheels.

armchairs. Two servants attired in
turbans and smart Rajastani costumes
were constantly at the guests' beck and
call. Included in the train's make-up
were a restaurant car serving gourmet
dinners and fine wines, a lounge,
observation car and library.

Rajasthan is a state made for such a
train. Much of it is desert or semi-desert,
but the towns of Jaipur, Udaipur,
Jaisalmer, Jodhpur and Bharatpur are
fairyland cities: pink-stoned, rock-
pinnacled lakeside oases, dominated by
fortresses and palaces, each flaunting an

epic history engraved upon dramatically
beautiful buildings.

Having rumbled through the night,
the Palace would arrive at its destination
where, after breakfast in bed, guests were
invited to emerge on to the platform
strewn with flowers, to be welcomed by a
pipe band, elephants in regalia and
troupes of dancing girls. Suitably
garlanded, they would be whisked away
for the tour of the day, broken by a
superb lunch in a palace.

A none-too smooth metre-gauge
track, emphatically not continuously

welded, made sleep a little elusive for
those not lulled by train travel, but this is
to quibble. From the one-time centre of
the Raj – Delhi – a traveller could begin
a journey such as he or she was unlikely
ever to experience again.

● **OPPOSITE
BOTTOM**
The Palace on
Wheels waiting at
Rajasthan station.

● **RIGHT**
The Desert Queen,
one of the
locomotives that
hauls the Palace on
Wheels.

SILIGURI TO DARJEELING

The railway that takes passengers from the heat of the Bengal plains to the blissful mountain balm of Darjeeling involves a climb of no less than 2,164 m (7,100 ft) in a distance of 88 km (54¹/₂ miles). Before the railway was built in 1879, exiles from the heat had to take the cart-road, which had been built by the Government at an astronomical cost.

The track is 2 ft gauge and, remarkably, while train loads have to be restricted, is worked wholly by adhesion. The steel rails, which weigh 41 lb per yard, are laid on wooden sleepers. Because the track has to be lifted so much in such a short distance, heavy gradients and sharp curves are unavoidable. On the journey there are banks ranging from 1:19 to 1:31 and curves of 15 m (50 ft) radius.

For the first 11 km (7 miles) to Sookna the going is easy, as the ascent is only 1:281. It is on this stretch that the

213 m (699 ft) long Mahanuddy bridge, comprising seven 30 m (100 ft) spans, is crossed. It is when the train leaves Sookna that the climb begins in earnest, for in the next 7.6 km (4³/₄ miles) the track ascends 265 m (869 ft). At the end of this section, the ascent was so sudden that originally the track had to describe a sharp loop through a deep cutting. However, in 1883 part of the

INFORMATION BOX

Termini	Siliguri and Darjeeling
Country	India
Length	88 km (55 miles)
Date construction commenced	
	1879

● **ABOVE** The train stops for a break and passengers take the opportunity to stretch their legs.

LEFT The little engine is inspected as it sits at the station.

OPPOSITE MIDDLE LEFT AND OPPOSITE MIDDLE RIGHT Various angles of the engine, which seems almost toy-like, that carries passengers from Siliguri to Darjeeling.

● **OPPOSITE BOTTOM** At an altitude of 2,258 m (7,408 ft), Ghoom is the second highest station in the world.

● **RIGHT**
The sign welcoming visitors to the town
of Darjeeling.

mountainside slipped into the cutting,
completely filling it, and the track had to
be realigned.

Between Rungtong, at 428 m
(1,404 ft), and Tindharia, at 860 m
(2,822 ft), a distance of just over 12 km
(7 1/2 miles), the gradient stiffens to 1:29.
Just past Rungtong there is a sudden rise
of 42 m (138 ft), which is overcome by
what is practically a double loop that
involves sharp curvatures. Then, a little
further on, just before Tindharia, the
ingenuity of the builders is illustrated by
a "reverse". The line, climbing at a 1:28
gradient, enters a curve of 244 m
(800 ft) radius, where it reaches a dead
end at 754 m (2,474 ft). The train backs
up a second curve at 1:33, to another
dead end at 762 m (2,500 ft). After a
further climb at 1:28, the line reaches an
altitude of 773 m (2,536 ft).

The next section of the line, the
6.4 km (4 miles) between Tindharia and
Gybaree, encounters the heaviest average
gradient of the journey – 1:28. It is on
this section that "Agony Point" is
reached. Not only is the ascent steep but,

because of the tight squeeze for space on
the upper part of the loop, the train
virtually overhangs the hillside as it
negotiates a precipitous curve of 18 m
(59 ft) radius.

After this challenging stretch, the
route becomes less arduous, and once
Gybaree is reached the gradients become
slightly easier, a mere 1:32, for the 6.4
km (4 miles) to Mahanuddy, at 1,256 m
(4,120 ft) above sea level. After Sonada,
66 km (41 miles) into the journey, comes
one of the least exacting stretches of all –
the 1:36 climb to the summit at Ghoom,
2,258 m (7,408 ft) above sea level. From
here, the line descends to the city of
Darjeeling and journey's end.

KALKA TO SIMLA

The Simla Mail does not go to Simla at all. To reach this one-time British hill station, one has to leave the main line at Kalka and transfer to the white-painted railcar for the five-hour haul up through the green hills. As the passengers take their seats in this undramatic little train, carriage attendants solicitously wrap rugs around their legs, as it is still only five o'clock in the morning.

For much of the way the line runs close to the road, their paths crossing at frequent intervals. To enable trains to climb the 1,524 m (5,000 ft) to Simla, 3 km (2 miles) of viaducts and 107 tunnels had to be constructed over a track length of 96 km (60 miles), such is the terrain. Two hours out, and the train halts at the

INFORMATION BOX	
Termini	Simla and Kalka
Country	India
Length	96 km (60 miles)
Date of opening	1903

little station of Barog, where the railcar waits while its passengers partake of a leisurely breakfast before setting off again into the tumbling clouds.

Occasionally the cloud and mist are rent by shafts of light to reveal a valley floor hundreds of metres below, ignored

by the busy little train, which has more important things than views on its mind as it hoots indignantly at buffalo and goats straying on to the track.

The Solan brewery halt is both a brewery and a station. The brewery came first, erected in the 19th century by a British company, which found good spring water here in the hills of Himachel Pradesh. In 1904, when the railway was built, the line cut right through the brewery, and passengers thereafter were treated to the rich aroma of malt and hops at the station approaches.

With each engaging of the gears, the little railcar gives a slight leap forward, reminiscent of the effects of "Kangaroo Petrol" when one is learning to drive a

car. In fact, the sight of this vehicle puts
one in mind of a light blue Ford truck
that has escaped from a museum. There
are actually four such vehicles in service,
built in 1927 and reconditioned in 1982.

The longest tunnel on the line is No.
33 at Barog, at a height of 1,144 m
(3,753 ft) above sea level (at Kalka,)
through which the train proceeds at the
maximum permitted speed of 29 kph
(18 mph). Including the viaducts, there
are 869 bridges which gives an indication
of the engineering problems faced during
the construction of the line.

The car will halt at any station *en route*
by request and – since there is no WC
aboard – anywhere along the line for
those passengers in urgent need.

However, above Solan station there is
something called a "Relieving Lodge",
which presumably caters for more
onerous bodily functions. Simla station,
presents such a magnificent view down

the mountains that the traveller feels
amply rewarded for the 4^1/$_2$ hour ride.

● **BELOW**
The Kalka to Simla railcar standing at Kalka
station.

PULGAON TO ARVI

The Pulgaon to Arvi line, originally a narrow-gauge branch from the Great Indian Peninsular Railway, will go down in history as the last genuine narrow-gauge line in India. It leaves the Bombay to Nagpur 5 ft 6 in broad-gauge main line at Pulgaon, where it has its own little station next to the main-line one, to meander through remote cotton-growing country to the town of Arvi some 33 km (20 miles) away. Immediately alongside Pulgaon station is a massive 19th-century British cotton factory, a truly "dark satanic mill", which is blessed with a fabulous steam hooter poignantly reminiscent of the industrial north of Victorian England. It is likely that the origin of the line lay in conveying cotton from the outlying areas to this mill. India's only other surviving narrow-gauge, 2 ft 6 in main lines are the tourist-operated Darjeeling Himalayan Railway and the famous tourist line in the south

INFORMATION BOX

Termini	Pulgaon and Arvi
Country	India
Distance	33 km (20 miles)
Date of opening	1917

● **TOP**
The morning train, No. 643, leaves Pulgaon and passes a bullock-drawn cart of cotton bales heading for the factory next to the station.

● **ABOVE LEFT**
The ZP Pacific's driver in reflective mood at Arvi prior to working the evening train back to Pulgaon.

● **LEFT**
The afternoon train heads across the river at Kubgaon on the final leg of its journey to Arvi.

● **RIGHT**
If running to time,
the last train of the
day reaches Rhona
Town at sunset.

● **BELOW
RIGHT**
The timelessness of
waiting for trains in
India is epitomized
by this rural scene at
Sorta – the travellers
all being resigned to
a long dreary wait.
Should a bus come
along in the mean-
time, many will take
it rather than wait
for the train.

based on Ootacamun (known as the
"Ooty"). At one time the line had three
daily mixed trains each way, along with an
old Armstrong Whitworth diesel railcar of
1934. Today, with two daily trains each
way, the line is distinctive in being worked
by ZP Class Pacifics of traditional British
design but built by Nippon in Japan in
1954. These sprightly locomotives,
originally built for the Satpura lines but
transferred in 1976, are some of the last
Pacific locomotives in the world, certainly

the last in India with the exception of the
metre-gauge YP Class.

The appalling difficulties facing
maintenance engineers with the shortage
of spare parts means that only one
locomotive is in steam at any one time,
and the line has no crossing loops,
although formerly a loop did exist at
Rhona Town.

The line is a last vestige of a form of
transport that was once common in many
parts of the world and retains all the

characteristics of a classic country railway
of the late 19th century. Four trains a day
are scheduled to run: No. 643 leaves
Pulgaon at 08.00 and arrives in Arvi at
10.20; No. 644 leaves Arvi at 10.40 and
reaches Pulgaon at 12.25; No. 645 leaves
Pulgaon at 14.30 and reaches Arvi at
16.50; and No. 646 leaves Arvi at 17.30
and arrives in Pulgaon at 19.15.

There are nine stations on the route:
Pulgaon, Sorta, Virol, Rhona Town,
Dhanori, Pargothan, Pachegaon, Kubgaon

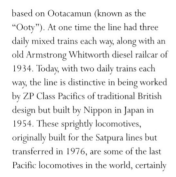

● **ABOVE**
Poor coal is a perennial problem. These huge
lumps of clinker have been shovelled out of
the firebox following the fire grate becoming
clogged and the engine failing to steam.

सोर्टा
SORTA

● **RIGHT**
Railway supremacy is asserted at this level crossing near Rhona as ZP Class Pacific No. 2 hustles its two coach train over the main road.

● **BELOW RIGHT**
The afternoon train from Pulgaon to Arvi overtakes a pair of carts bringing cotton in from the surrounding fields.

● **BOTTOM LEFT**
Monkeys play around the station name board at Arvi.

● **BOTTOM RIGHT**
The water pump outside the station at Pargothan attracts women from the surrounding villages. Here they are busily filling their urns as the morning train to Pulgaon prepares to depart for Arvi.

crossings. This classic roadside tramway is picturesque and rustic, travellers being solely village people and mostly heavily laden ones who use the train to carry their bags of produce.

The trains consist of two bogie coaches and on the outward journey from Pulgaon the engines go tender first; upon reaching Arvi the coaches are shunted round to ensure that the brake remains at the rear of the consist.

It is said that one tonne of coal is burnt on the engine on each trip, which seems excessive for such a small locomotive so lightly laden. It is possible that, as with so many rural Indian lines that were worked by steam, coal is thrown down at strategic points along the track to favoured recipients in return for rupees!

The quality of the coal is another reason for sloth on the line, as much of it turns to clinker and clogs up the firebox, necessitating regular stops for "blow-ups". If coal is unavailable, all trains are cancelled. Likewise punctuality is treated very liberally – lateness can be caused either by mechanical problems or,

and Arvi. The line passes through remote countryside, and many of the stations are simple tin shacks in the middle of nowhere, the villages they serve being some some distance away. Rhona Town serves a sizeable community which has a large cotton mill, as does Kubgaon.

The line is paralleled throughout by a road, which is generally well surfaced and over which frequent buses ply their trade. They provide serious competition for the railway and prevent it from being profitable. The only supremacy the railway can claim lies in the many level

seemingly, the whims of the engine crew who have a frequent tendency of stopping for tea at Pargothan.

In today's world, the sheer joy of a railway such as this is always going to be under threat, and early in 1997 diesel servicing facilities were installed and ZDM4A No. 198 arrived from Kurduwadi. There was no immediate question of the diesel taking over, as many spare parts had to be obtained, and ZP Pacific No. 2 continued as before. Fortunately, despite the line's incredible unprofitability, Indian Railways have extended the contract with the British owners to operate the line up to 2006.

● ABOVE
Travelling musicians entertaining passengers during the station stop at Sorta.

● BELOW
The picturesque rural nature and general remoteness of this country line can be gauged from this scene of the scrub and bush, which characterize much of the land.

COLOMBO TO KANDY

This picturesque, and often thrilling railway line was built between 1858 and 1868 to link Colombo, the present capital, with the former capital of what was then Ceylon, Kandy, in the mountains 488 m (1,601 ft) above sea level and 121 km (75 miles) distant. The system expanded to 1,530 km (951 miles) at the standard gauge of 5 ft 6 in and 138 km (86 miles) at the narrow gauge of 2 ft 6 in, the latter mainly up the valley of the Kelani River. Mileage has now been reduced to 1,390 km (864 miles) for the standard gauge and 63 km (39 miles) for the narrow gauge, which is being converted to mixed gauge. Another short narrow-gauge line, from Nanu Oya to Ragalla in the mountains, has closed.

However, in 1991, an extension of the broad gauge for 121 km (75 miles) from Matara to the pilgrim town of Kataragam on the south coast was begun, and there are proposals to extend this into the mountains to join up with Badulla, the railhead beyond Kandy and Nuwara Eliya. An 11 km (7 mile) branch from Anuadhapura to Mihintale in the north was due for completion in 1997.

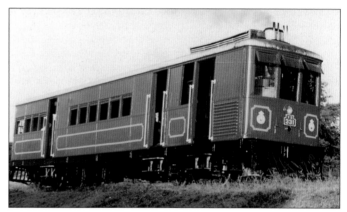

Steam traction was the mainstay of the railways until the 1970s. By then the high cost of imported coal had led to the early development of British-built diesel traction, both locomotives and DMUs, an attractively styled version of which worked the frequent local services along the pictureque coastline from Colombo to the resort of Mount Lavinia. Japanese-built DMUs bought in 1990 now operate the local services.

Colombo's main railway station is at Fort and is a "through" station. Five platforms served the broad gauge and there was one for the narrow gauge. It always was busy, but suburban traffic has

● **LEFT**
Another less technically advanced form of transport in rural Sri Lanka is the ox cart.

INFORMATION BOX	
Termini	Colombo and Kandy
Country	Sri Lanka
Distance	121 km (75 miles)
Date of opening	1868

increased by 30 per cent since 1980. Just to the north of Fort lies the important station of Maradana, with no fewer than six platform faces for the broad gauge and three for the narrow. It is the junction where the narrow gauge heads off down the Kelani valley. About 1.2 km (³/4 mile) further on, the large locomotive depot and repair shops at Dermatagoda at the right of the line provided eight long tracks for broad-gauge and two for narrow-gauge locomotives. This was by far the largest depot on the island and, for such a relatively small system, the

● **OPPOSITE TOP**
Colombo's House of Assembly, the seat of Sri Lanka's parliament.

● **OPPOSITE MIDDLE**
This railcar, No. 331 of Class V2, operated on the 2 ft 6 in gauge lines.

● **BELOW LEFT**
There were four batches of Class B8c dating back to 1922. Two of the batches were built by Hunslet Engine Co. of Leeds, England, and this machine was from the batch delivered in 1927. With an axle load of only 9.2 tonnes (9 tons), they were suitable for use on lightly laid track.

● **OPPOSITE BOTTOM**
The 2 ft 6 in gauge line from Colombo up the Kelani valley saw locomotives such as this neat J1 Class 2-6-2T No. 220.

● **RIGHT**
A familiar sight by the side of the line in Sri Lanka are the tea pickers working in the plantations.

● LEFT
Another familiar sight by the side of the line in
Sri Lanka are the rice paddy fields.

the mainland of the Indian subcontinent.
It is also the end of the double-track
section, and the train for Kandy turns
away to the east, gently climbing to
Rambukkana, 11 km (7 miles) further on
at a height of 95 m (312 ft).

The 29 km (18 mile) section from
Rambukkana to Peradenya is one of the
most spectacular in Sri Lanka. Travellers
are advised to sit on the right-hand side
of the train to take advantage of the ever-
changing scene. A large 4-8-0 banking
locomotive of Class A1 is placed at the
rear of the train to assist on the 19 km
(12 mile) climb at 1:44, made more
difficult by numerous sharp curves down
to 201 m (660 ft) radius.

The route leaves the jungle floor and
climbs on ledges frequently cut from the
almost vertical rock faces. The expanding

number of different types of locomotive
that had to be maintained, ranging from
diminutive narrow-gauge 4-4-0T to
Beyer-Garratts, must have put a strain on
the skills and resources of the engineers.

The double-track main line generally
heads north-east through level
countryside with paddy fields, coconut
plantations and small villages with palm-
thatched huts. Areas of uncultivated land
are often ablaze with the blooms of wild
flowers, and brightly coloured birds
complete the scene. At Ragama, the
branch line along the west coast to
Puttalam goes off to the left.

By Ambepussa, 56 km (35 miles) from
Colombo, the train has begun to climb
away from the wide coastal plains through
coconut plantations until its arrival at
Polgahawela, 74 km (46 miles) from
Colombo at an altitude of 73 m (240 ft)
above sea level. This is the junction for
the main line northward, which finishes at
Kankesanturai, where there is a ferry to

● RIGHT
Class B1a 4-6-0 Sir
Thomas Maitland
was built in England
in 1927 by Beyer
Peacock and is seen
in a much more
colourful livery than
that used in 1945.

● RIGHT
Class B2c 4-6-0 No.
213 is one of several
engines delivered
from 1915 onward
and comes from a
batch manufactured
by Vulcan Foundry
in England in 1922.
It is essentially a
main-line
locomotive, and,
until the arrival of
Class B1, it was the
pride of the line.

● **LEFT**
A typical scene in Sri Lanka's hill country.

views, first into the valley below and then into the far distance, are incomparable. "Sensation Curve" is rightly named for it is on a ledge with a 305 m (1,000 ft) sheer drop to the valley floor below. It is best seen from a train going toward Colombo, for it then appears that the line is going to take off into space.

Kadugannawa, 104 km (65 miles) from Colombo and 515 m (1,690 ft) above sea level, is where the banking locomotive is removed. The line then falls 41 m (136 ft) in the 9.6 km (6 miles) to Peradeniya Junction station, where the route to Newara Eliya and Badulla turns south while the other line turns north-east for the 6.4 km (4 miles) to Kandy. It is well worth pausing at New Peradeniya station to visit the nearby Botanical Gardens and wander through the extensive grounds.

The station at Kandy, 121 km (75 miles) from Colombo, had three terminal roads and one which continued through the station to Matale, 26 km (16 miles) distant and a centre for the cattle trade. Lightweight 4-6-0 steam locomotives were shedded here, together with two Sentinel Steam coaches, which worked local trains to Matale and Peradeniya.

● **BELOW**
Travellers will want to take time off in Kandy to visit the world-famous Temple of the Tooth. Here we see the temple across the lake of the same name.

● **ABOVE**
The Class B10 4-6-0 had the very light axle load of only 7.6 tonnes (7.5 tons) enabling it to work over lightly laid lines such as that to Matale. The class dates back to 1901.

TUMENJAN TO PYONGYANG

"What do you want to go *there* for?" exclaimed the Russian engine-driver in amazement. "Don't you know there are *Communists* there?" He made it sound as if Russia had never had anything to do with Communism itself.

I was ensconced in the cab of the leading heavy diesel unit of the two deemed necessary to haul one battered coach along the single-track line that runs southwards from Ussuriysk, the junction for Vladivostok, the city of which could be seen in the distance, to Pyongyang, the capital of North Korea. There were no more than half a dozen passengers on the train, and, beyond Ussuriysk and the eyes of authority, I was actually permitted to drive the train as far as Khazan, border town of the then USSR, China and North Korea. At this politically sensitive spot, it was deemed prudent for me to return to the carriage.

Tumenjan is the North Korean entry station on this remote line, and the red

● **LEFT**
One of the freight-yard working steam locomotives at Nampo station.

banners and giant portraits of the "Great Leader" proclaimed entry into the hard-line Stalinist state where such propaganda drips from every village, town and city wall – even some of the mountain flanks.

INFORMATION BOX	
Termini	Tumenjan and Pyongyang
Country	North Korea
Distance	*c.* 800 km (500 miles)
Date of opening	1899

Pyongyang's main station is a cross between a cathedral and an opera house in a city risen from the ashes of the 1950–53 Korean War to resemble a metropolis straight out of a Jules Verne fantasy (with a metro outshining even the architectural magnificence of Moscow's). Regretably, the marbled platforms of the station are closed to the rank and file who have to wait for their trains outside in the open.

Korea, as a whole, first opened its railway in 1899, and a 6,400 km (3,977 mile) network was developed during the Japanese annexation between 1910 and 1945. At partition in 1948, the network

● **LEFT**
A general view of Pyongyang.

RIGHT
Views of the North Korean mountains can be seen as the train travels through the countryside.

RIGHT
Views of the North Korean mountains can be seen as the train travels through the countryside.

One of the towns served by the railway is Nampo, site of the 8 km (5 mile) long West Sea Barrage, a major engineering project of which North Korea is justly proud. It was here that I was allowed to ride in the cab of one of the freight-yard's working steam locomotives – the dirtiest I have seen for quite a long time. While some of the lines have been electrified in North Korea, the majority of trains are still diesel-hauled.

I left the country on the Pyongyang to Beijing express, crossing the Yalu River on the massive steel-lattice swing bridge into China's Manchuria, with far less rumpus than had one General Douglas MacArthur in the early 1950s.

and stock were divided on a ratio of 2:1, North Korea getting the greater share. The war destroyed much of the network, but this has now been rebuilt and improved upon – particularly in South Korea, which has outstripped in route-length its fractious neighbour.

As in all one-time Communist states, a permit is necessary for movement beyond a certain radius. This means that only those passengers engaged in labour for the State can travel worthwhile distances, which at least eliminates the scourge of overcrowded trains. Besides the line to Pyongyang from the Russian border, the only other lines run from the capital to the Chinese border at Dandong and southwards to Haeju and Kaesong, the town nearest the heavily fortified demarcation zone centred upon the village of Panmunjom (which, oddly, Western visitors are permitted to visit, albeit under guard, to stand just centimetres away from the actual line of demarcation separating the two halves of the country).

LEFT AND BELOW
The North Korean–Russian border station of Tumenan.

SHENYANG TO HARBIN

The Chinese, in the midst of their modernization of the railways, are justifiably amused, not to say perplexed, that foreigners should want to travel thousands of miles to gape at their remaining steam-engines. Railway construction came late to Imperial China, forbidden (it is said) by successive emperors. By the 1880s, when the USA already possessed some 145,000 km (90,000 miles) of track, China had a mere 18,000 km (11,000 miles). However, once the ban was lifted the country took to railway construction with gusto. And no part of China is more rail-minded and enthusiastic about trains than Manchuria, a vast region, larger than France and Germany combined, that the Chinese call Dongbei.

Between 1876 and 1949, some 21,000 km (13,050 miles) of railway were built, though only half of it was operative following the civil war that led to the Communist take-over. Today's rail system exceeds 60,000 km (37,284 miles) with many single-track sections doubled.

It is in Manchuria, where there are huge deposits of brown coal, that steam

traction can still be observed. Life on the Manchurian railways is often hard – in winter, when temperatures fall as low as –25°C (–13°F), locomotives can freeze to the rails. Yet even at such times earnest train buffs descend on the yards to take pictures with frost-affected cameras and enter copious notes into their pocket notebooks. In fact so many such visitors now arrive that today the workers are less mystified by all the attention.

The capital of Manchuria's Liaoning Province – one of three provinces – is Shenyang, the former Mukden. This is the scene of the "Mukden Incident", which arose when an explosion on the railway line triggered the Japanese occupation. Sixty km (37 miles) away, on a branch of the main Shenyang-Harbin line, sits the smaller city of Fushan, site of the prison, still operational, that held Pi Yi, the "Last Emperor", whose cell is open for inspection.

● **TOP**
A view of Harbin's vast marshalling yards from Sankong Bridge, with the city of Harbin in the background.

● **ABOVE LEFT**
Harbin railway station.

● **LEFT**
A China Railways QJ Class 2-10-2 storms up Wang Gang Bank out of Harbin with a heavy freight bound for Changchun.

INFORMATION BOX

Termini	Shenyang and Harbin
Country	China
Distance	*c.* 725 km (*c.* 450 miles)
Commencement of building	1876

For true rail buffs the Shenyang-Harbin line puts on a huge display of gigantic black steam locomotives, or at least it did in 1990. The route takes a full day to cover, and longer if one stops off to visit the sheds, where visitors are welcome.

The line was once the so-called Russian Manchurian Railway, and there is much in Harbin to remind one of the long gone Russian occupation. Between the small towns of Lungxiang and Lancha, about five hours' ride from Harbin, a narrow-gauge railway, using fussy little steam-engines, transports both visitors and timber between forest and town. On the main line the long-distance trains are adequate rather than luxurious, but at the railway towns *en route* the workers in the sidings and sheds are the friendliest imaginable, much heartened by the interest shown by visitors.

Harbin railway station is the third largest in China, with an average daily departure of over 200,000 passengers. With a floor space of 14,200 sq m (152,848 sq ft), it contains five waiting rooms, 28 booking offices, a restaurant, a department store, a left-luggage office and a hotel with over 300 beds.

● **ABOVE**
One of the magnificent Japanese-built streamlined Pacifics in the Railway Museum at Shenyang. During the 1930s these engines worked the Asia Express between Shenyang – then known as Mukden – and Harbin.

● **ABOVE**
The city of Anshan, China's iron and steel capital, shows a wonderful diversity of architectures combined with the landscaped parks in which China excels.

● **LEFT**
A QJ Class 2-10-2 races down Wang Gang Bank and into Harbin on a frozen afternoon.

● **LEFT**
In China public transport is practised to a fine art as the private motor car barely exists. The back-up for China's excellent public transport system is the humble bicycle, and bike jams are a regular feature of rush-hour travel.

Ulan Bator to Datong Across the Gobi Desert

● BELOW
Serenity may be found in the country's only functioning Buddhist temple.

The train out of Ulan Bator, made up of seven coaches plus a baggage car, is normally in pristine condition. Before departure, all the coaches are given a final clean by smartly dressed attendants. Inside the four-berth coaches, the upper berths make up as beds, while there is plenty of room to sit on the lower seats, each covered by an attractive clean cloth.

On leaving Ulan Bator, the views are at first rather uninspiring. There is a confusing mixture of austere housing, steam-draped heavy industry and *yurts* (tents) against a backdrop of low hills. Items of railway interest include an ancient working 2.8.0 steam locomotive, a preserved industrial or narrow-gauge engine and some 20 diesels. Once having left the capital behind, the train winds through a sparse landscape, with almost bare hills to the left and occasional clumps of forest on the right.

About half an hour into the journey, the train loops around a set of three aerials as it climbs on to a flat plateau. An hour or so later it encounters an almost volcanic outcropping, before curving left and accelerating down a gentle downgrade. The train now traverses a

INFORMATION BOX

Termini	Ulan Bator and Datong
Countries	Mongolia and China
Distance	1045 km (655 miles)
Date of opening	1929

● BELOW
A QJ Class 2-10-2 and a JS Class 2-8-2 are subjects of interest at an intermediate station.

seemingly endless hot flat plain until it reaches Choyr, where the landscape falls away gently to the right.

There are subtle changes in the terrain over the next couple of hours. A jagged rocky ridge in the left middle distance glows purple in the sunlight while the plain becomes gently undulating with dried grass and light soil on either side. The sinuous nature of the route, despite the level landscape, allows frequent views of the twin diesels, which haul the train, relatively slowly, through almost mesmeric terrain.

On the border, the Mongolian officials are all very smart and correct. A number of soldiers stand to attention along the platform. Formalities last between 23.40 and 01.00, and then the train is on the move once again, this time entering China or, to be pedantic, Chinese-dominated Inner Mongolia.

The welcome at the first Chinese station is very different from the arrivals experienced in the once-Soviet sphere of influence. The station is festooned with coloured lights, and cheerful music is relayed from loud-speakers, all in marked

contrast to both the desert and other
more drab administrations encountered
previously. The formalities can still be
lengthy, nevertheless, and some
passengers may miss the experience of
seeing the train being converted to run
on the Chinese gauge.

The line from Ulan Bator to Datong
was built by the Soviets to their broader
gauge of 5 ft but, following the cooling of
relations between them and China, the
Chinese re-laid their portion of the route
to the local (standard) gauge, viz. 1,435 4
ft 8^1/$_2$ in. This need to change gauge gives
the traveller the first opportunity to travel
behind steam. The locomotive hauls the
train about 1. 6 km (1 mile) to the shed
equipped to change bogies.

Apart from the engine crew, nearly all
the workers engaged in the operation are
female. The locomotive positioned, each
coach opposite a pair of jacks,
preparations are made to the bogies and
the brake gear. Then the coach is jacked
up, the bogies are rolled away, to be
replaced by a new set by overhead crane.
Finally the coach is lowered and fine
adjustments, if necessary, are made to the
position of the new bogies. Regular
practice has, however, made the initial
positioning of both coach and wheelsets
remarkably accurate. Once everything is
correctly positioned, and the requisite
connections have been made, the whole
process is repeated for the next coach.

During breakfast on the second day
the views of isolated forts and ruined
walls on the passing heights – remnants
of the defences of the Great Wall –
remind travellers that they are entering
China proper. The train follows a
winding river valley, as doubtless earlier
invaders would have done. They,
however, would not have encountered
increasing signs of industrialization as the

● **BELOW**
The train sweeps round a sun-baked village,
the passengers probably oblivious to the harsh
life of its inhabitants.

train appraoches Datong. Pollution
control is still a relatively foreign
concept, and the fumes from the various
factories, mingled with the smell of
night-soil in the more rural areas, make
for a potent mixture.

A succession of passing steam-hauled
freights provides evidence not only of
industry but also of how effective the
distribution system of the Chinese is
compared with that of the Russians.
Water melons, pears, apples, plums,
grapes, cabbages, peppers, beetroot,
swede, carrots and chillies are all visible
on the trains and for sale in these
northern regions in contrast to the
former Soviet Union. A journey across
the Gobi Desert in many ways remains
one in time as well as kilometres.

FUJI TO KOFU

A pleasant one-day jaunt from Tokyo is to ride on the metre-gauge Minobu line, which runs from the city of Fuji, near the base of the famous Mount Fuji, to Kofu. A circlular trip from Tokyo via Fuji and Kofu is easily accomplished with a little planning. Fuji is served by both the Tokyo-Osaka-Hakata Shinkansen high-speed line (also known as the Tokaido-San-Yo Shinkansen) and the metre-gauge Tokaido line of Japanese Railways (JR). Trains operating on the Minobu line use the same station as the Tokaido line, and passengers can make a cross-the-platform transfer here. The Shinkansen Shin-Fuji station is several blocks distant from the metre-gauge station, making transfer between trains more difficult.

The northern end of the Minobu line joins JR's busy metre-gauge Chou Line a mile east of the main station in Kofu, where another cross-the-platform transfer takes place. There is frequent

● LEFT
Interior of a JR EMU assigned to the Fujikawa express trains. This train was the Fujikawa No. 5, heading to Kofu from Fuji.

and direct service to Tokyo on this incredibly scenic main line, and a number of interesting streamlined trains run this way, including the Super Azusa and the Boso View – which despite its name is not a circus train!

Fuji is an industrial city on Suruga Bay and warrants a considerable volume of freight service on the Tokaido line in addition to frequent passenger service. While making a connection to the Minobu line, passengers may see one of many intermodal freights pass through the station or watch a diesel hydraulic-switch engine shunt cars in the nearby yard.

● ABOVE LEFT
After a five-minute stop at Minobu, a local train's conductor checks his watch before departing for Kofu. Most of the Minobu line is single track with passing sidings at key stations. Local trains are required to clear the way for Fujikawa expresses.

● LEFT
A Fujikawa express train races through Hadakajima on its way to Fuji. The Minobu line passes through fabulous mountainous terrain on its run between Fuji and Kofu.

● LEFT
A local train, bound for Fuji from Kofu, coasts
downgrade toward its station stop at
Hadakajima.

INFORMATION BOX

Termini	Fuji and Kofu
Country	Japan
Distance	97 km (60 miles)
Date of opening	Information unavailable

There are both local and express trains on the Minobu line. Local trains are usually equipped with JR's Spartan but very clean electric multiple units (EMUs) of the sort found in commuter service all around Japan. The seating is not of the best sort for a long trip, but the windows are clean. Express service is provided by considerably more luxurious multiple-unit trains, which run as the Fujikawa. A JR Green Pass will entitle foreign visitors to travel on these express trains; otherwise first-class tickets can be purchased from JR. The Fujikawa operates on a significantly faster schedule than the local trains; it attains a top speed of 85 kph (53 mph), and stops much less often, making the Fuji-Kofu run in just under two hours. Local trains can take a little more than three hours to cover the same distance.

Leaving Fuji, the Minobu line follows the Urui River and winds through residential neighbourhoods and industrial areas of the city. In addition to the local through trains, commuter trains also serve suburban Fuji on the lower end of the line. On a clear day, Mount Fuji is visible to the north of the tracks. Several miles out of town, the railroad leaves the Urui and follows the Fujikawa River, one of the most important waterways in

Japan. On the way up the scenic Fujikawa valley, the railroad passes through many short tunnels and provincial towns. The line is primarily single track, with short passing sidings at most stations allowing for well-timed meets between opposing trains. Towards Kofu the railroad drops down into a broad agricultural plain.

● ABOVE
The Minobu line features many tunnels,
including several long bores near Wariishi
Pass, located between Shimobe and Kofu.

● LEFT
A Super Azusa train departs the Kofu terminal
for Tokyo via the Chou line. Upon arriving at
Kofu from Fuji, passengers may continue on to
Tokyo on a number of interesting streamlined
electric trains, including the Super Azusa.

TOKYO'S YAMANOTE LINE

The Yamanote line makes a 32 km (20 mile) loop through Tokyo, connecting the city's principal rail terminals at Shinjuku, Ueno and Tokyo stations. Other lines operate immediately parallel to this extremely busy metre-gauge electrified commuter line, including the busy Tokaido, Chou, and Seibu-Shinjuku lines, making the Yamanote Loop route one of the busiest railway lines in the world. In many places, the right of way has between six and twelve main-line tracks.

Many long-distance trains, including Japanese Railway's (JR's) overnight sleeping car trains, run alongside the Yamanote commuters. Riding the loop, one might even see one of the new streamlined silver and purple Super Azusa trains pacing your train on an adjacent track! Service on the Yamanote line itself is provided by JR EMU commuter train sets painted light green (all of the Tokyo area commuter train routes are colour-coded) that run around the loop continuously. The trains run every couple of minutes between 6 a.m. and midnight.

● **BELOW**
A Yamanote line train leaves Shinjuku.

INFORMATION BOX

Termini	Shinjuku, Ueno and Tokyo
Country	Japan
Distance	32 km (20 miles)
Date of opening	Information unavailable

● **FAR LEFT**
At Shinjuku, on a platform adjacent to the Yamanote line, is one of JR's new Super Azusa train sets. Soon this metre-gauge streamliner will head out on the Chou line towards Kofu.

● **OPPOSITE BOTTOM**
A long Yamanote line train departs Habata station in the morning rush hour. These trains run on one- and two-minute headways at peak times, and are nearly always jam-packed right up to midnight.

● **LEFT**
The Shinjuku shopping district on a sunny weekday morning is a primary destination of many railway commuters. The Shinjuku region of Tokyo is served by many railway lines including the busy Yamanote line.

At Akihabara the Sobu line crosses the Yamanote line on an exceptionally tall elevated structure, with the Sobu line on the upper level. Far below one can observe the Shinkansen. Akihabara is known as "Electric City", and the latest electronic devices imaginable are available here, from electric toilet seats to singing alarm clocks!

Although the Yamanote line is run by JR as part of the commuter rail network, the level and quality of service resembles a rapid transit line more than that of a conventional commuter train line.

Most of the line is either elevated or depressed through Tokyo, offering many excellent views of the city. However, the Yamanote line's principal attraction is the astounding volume of rail traffic along this route. Shinjuku station on the west side of Tokyo presently ranks as the world's busiest railroad station, including two interurban electric terminals adjacent to it. At rush hour, on any week day, traffic through this terminal is virtually continuous.

At Ueno, a 12-track flying junction separates metre-gauge routes on to two levels. (The Shinkansen is below ground at this point.) It is not uncommon to find six trains moving in different directions through Ueno all at one time! Ueno station serves Ueno Park, the location of several museums and the Tokyo Zoo. The Tokyo Science Museum is only a block from Ueno station and features a preserved JR 2-8-2 Mikado-type steam locomotive and a semaphore signal.

The Shinkansen runs alongside the Yamanote Loop at several places on the east side of Tokyo. At traffic peaks these high-speed trains operate every five or six minutes, yet traffic on the parallel metre-gauge line is even more frequent.

● **RIGHT**
Ueno station in Tokyo, one of several large busy stations connected on the Yamanote line.

TOKYO TO NIKKO
BY TRAIN TO THE SHRINES

It is a cliché to state that Japan is a land of contrasts, but anyone visiting the country cannot help but come to that conclusion. A visit by train to Nikko is one of the many ways of experiencing this. Nikko is one of the major Japanese temple and shrine areas and, at approximately 150 km (93 miles) from Tokyo, is the nearest to the capital. The contrast is not only between the city noise and the calm of the temples, but also between the express train on the Tobu Railway, the Japanese Railways (JR) semi-rural branch line and a trip on the "Bullet train" (Shinkansen).

The round trip starts at Asakusa station in Tokyo. The area around the station, close to the Sumida River, is itself worth visiting, with its large number of craft goods shops and the large Sensoji Temple. This elevated station, integrated into the second floor of the Matsuya department store and at the end of a

● LEFT
Tobu Railway Spacia EMU 102-6 at Nikko. The streamlined styling is more for appearance than practical benefit, given the relatively low speeds reached.

bridge over the river, is the terminus of the Tobu Railway. The site is very cramped, and many of their trains now run through to the Eidan Hibiya metro line from a junction around 10 km (6 miles) out of town. There are only three six-coach platforms, and plans for a total rebuild are under discussion, not least to allow the Tobu's standard ten-coach

● ABOVE
Tokyo has two metro systems, a "private" company, TRTA, and the city authority's TOEI group. This is TRTA metro 05014 at Nakano, on the Tozai line. Asakusa station is served by the TRTA Ginza line.

● LEFT
Tobu Railway Spacia EMU departing Asakusa station, Tokyo, in December 1995. Note the curved approach to the station from the river bridge, on the right of the photograph.

● **LEFT**
Detail on the buildings at the Daiyuin Shrine.
The proximity of the forest can be seen in
the background.

● **BELOW**
Tobu Railway EMU 6267 arriving in Nikko.

● **BOTTOM**

JR's Nikko station building. The small garden
cum shrine on the left is fairly typical. Note the
JR practice of including the romanized version
of place-names on the station name-boards.

trains to use the station.

Nikko can be reached on the
suburban trains, but the quicker and
definitely more comfortable way is to
travel on one of the Tobu's "Limited
Express Spacia" trains, which are formed
of streamlined EMUs. There are six
through trains in the morning, taking an
hour and 40 minutes, followed by a half-
hourly service for most of the day,
requiring one change at Shimo Imaichi.
The Spacia trains come complete with
hostess and drinks service, and the seats
are a pleasant contrast to the longitudinal
seats on the suburban trains.

The Asakusa ticket-office can be
confusing to those who do not speak
Japanese, but a little observation will
identify the special queue for these trains.
Seat reservation is compulsory, but can
be bought on the day, and there should
not be too many problems getting a place

INFORMATION BOX

Termini	Tokyo and Nikko
Country	Japan
Distance	150 km (93 miles)
Date of opening	Infomation unavailable

● **LEFT**
JR outer-suburban
EMU 115-422 and
JR freight electric
locomotive EF65
540 at Utsunomiya.
The Tohoku
Shinkansen
platforms are in
the structure above
the platform on
the left.

● **BELOW**
JR's Utsunomiya
station. On the left is
the Nikko branch
train formed of
EMU 106-7. On the
right is outer-
suburban EMU
115-122.

on the next departure. Sign language is adequate to buy a ticket!

The main line of the Tobu Railway was built in the first decade of this century, and Nikko was reached in 1929 at a time of electrification and expansion. The present Asakusa terminus was opened in 1931. Through running of Tobu trains to the Tokyo metro, starting in 1962, was the first of its kind in Tokyo. The Tobu Railway is one of the largest private railways in Japan and carried over 945 million passengers on 463 km (288 miles) of route during 1994, totalling over four billion passenger kilometres (2.5 billion miles). Unlike commuter railways in other countries, but like most in Japan, the Tobu Railway is profitable, despite its cheap fares.

The line proceeds through the ever-expanding suburban sprawl of Tokyo for some time but eventually reaches the country area beyond. The landscape is attractive rather than dramatic, with the low hills, woods and paddy fields interspersed with farm buildings and small towns. However, as the journey

progresses, mountains come into view. Whilst the railway does not reach them, the mountains form a backdrop to the area around Nikko, with three peaks over 2,000 m (6,500 ft) within 20 km (12 miles) of the town.

There are no great engineering features on the line caused by the terrain. However, in order to avoid frequent level

crossings and to expand capacity in its evolution from a local line into a four-track commuter railway, significant stretches of elevated line have been constructed, on ugly concrete structures.

The Tobu station in Nikko is the closest to the town centre, although the JR station is only 200 m (650 ft) further away. The shrines are about 2 km

● **RIGHT**
The Shinkyo bridge, Nikko, a 1907 reconstruction of a 17th-century original. This can be seen from the road between Nikko and the shrine area.

● **BELOW RIGHT**
The "three wise monkeys" carving on the sacred stables at the Toshogu Shrine.

(1¹/₄ miles) from the railway stations, along a road lined with many shops aimed at the Japanese tourist market. The more adventurous could try some of the food shops, most of which make few compromises for the non-Japanese. There is also a bus service.

Around half-way along the road is the Nikko Information Centre, which is also the main outlet for the cheapest way to visit the temples: the two-shrines-one-temple ticket. The ticket offices at the sites will try to sell you individual entry tickets, a far more expensive combination. The attendant in the office seemed surprised that a foreigner had found his way there and knew about this ticket. However, the information is given in any good guidebook, which will also help you understand the history behind this religious site.

The area contains (despite the name of the ticket!) four main attractions: the Rinnoji Temple, the Daiyuin Shrine, the Futarasan Shrine and the Toshogu Shrine. The latter contains the original of the "hear no evil, see no evil, speak no evil"

carving and is the most visited. However, all four are recommended, and are listed in the suggested viewing order. The Toshogu Shrine, dating from 1617 and including a five-storey pagoda, is undoubtedly the most famous and, unfortunately, has the crowds to match. This contrasts with the Daiyuin Shrine, which few people seem to reach. All the buildings are set amongst a forest of tall trees, giving an appropriately serene atmosphere to a site with religious links going back to the 8th century.

The return journey starts with the JR branch line from Nikko to Utsunomiya, which opened in 1890. The service is frequent, if not entirely regular, and starts from a white, half-timbered building, which appears in style to be a cross between Japanese and English Victorian mock-Tudor architecture. The train usually consists of a suburban-style two-car EMU.

The first part of the 40-minute journey is through the countryside and small towns. The significant number of

● **LEFT**
The Senso-ji Temple complex includes the massive Hozomon Gate, seen here from the temple steps.

● **BELOW LEFT**
JR suburban EMU approaching Ueno Station, Tokyo. This train is on the upper level, the tracks visible on a lower level are used by long distance trains. The Shinkansen from Utsunomiya and the north is on a third, underground level at this station.

school students on my train showed that the railway was not just run for the visitors to Nikko. The scenery becomes more urban as Utsunomiya, a large town, is approached. Its station is in two adjoining parts: the main JR station and the elevated Shinkansen platforms. There is also a Tobu Railway terminus in the vicinity, also with services to Tokyo.

JR is now the poor relation on this route – although journey times are comparable, most people visiting Nikko now tend to use the Tobu line. However, JR did not give up without a fight, and the 1950s were characterized by the two companies vying to provide the best service and best rolling stock to gain the most passengers; by the mid-1960s, however, the Tobu had won.

The Shinkansen journey is on the Tohoku line, which runs between Tokyo and Morioka, to the north. Trains run from Utsunomiya to Tokyo approximately three times per hour and take around 55 minutes for approximately 108 km (67 miles). This journey will be taken using the unreserved seating on the Shinkansen, unless there was enough time to plan the schedule in detail a day or so in advance. The unreserved seats are only in specified coaches, and the ticket will indicate which. It is recommended to be near the front of the queue, which will be at exactly the right spot on the platform to be opposite the door when the train stops.

The Tohoku line opened north from the Tokyo suburban station of Omiya in 1982, 78 km (48 miles) from Utsunomiya, and reached Ueno in 1985; the final section into Tokyo being opened in 1991. The run to Tokyo is elevated for much of the way through largely built-up areas as far as Ueno, the main station on the north side of Tokyo. From here, the line is in tunnel to Tokyo station where, although meeting the Tokaido line Shinkansen, there is no end-on junction

as the power supplies and automatic signalling systems are different. There is also a big contrast between this station and Asakusa, where the journey started. However, whilst Tokyo station seems vast and very busy, it is not the busiest station in Japan, a distinction belonging to Tokyo's Shinjuku station.

This round trip, which provides something for those culturally minded as well as those interested in the railways, can be done comfortably in a day from Tokyo The relative cheapness of rail fares in Japan means the strong yen does not make the cost overly expensive. It should be noted that this itinerary is not sold as one ticket and rebooking will be required in Nikko, but my total lack of knowledge of Japanese did not prove a barrier to a fascinating day out.

- **ABOVE**
JR Shinkansen 221-204 arriving at Utsunomiya. The two central tracks allow non-stopping trains to overtake, a quite frequent occurrence which requires strict adherence to the timetable to avoid delays.

- **BELOW LEFT**
Close by the Tobu Railway's Asakusa station is the Senso-ji Temple. One of the buildings in the complex is this five-storey pagoda.

- **BELOW**
JR Shinkansen 221-25 at Tokyo, in the low-level platforms used by the Tohoku line. The green livery is unique to the Shinkansen on this route.

TOKYO TO OSAKA

Just after World War II, the Japanese proposed to build a straight line between Tokyo and Osaka that would allow trains to travel at 201 kph (125 mph). However, with the massive rebuilding that had to take place after the war, it was not until 1958 that an aerial survey of the route was made. The following year, within a week of Parliament approving the project, the ceremonial ground-breaking took place. In 1965, just 65 months later, the first full service between the two cities began.

To permit such high speed, the line was constructed so that no curve had a radius of less than 2.4 km (1½ miles). To avoid urban congestion and to minimize noise, the line is carried on viaducts with high parapet walls some 6.4 m (21 ft) above towns. There are no level crossings on the track, and valleys and estuaries are crossed on long viaducts. Where mountains block the way, no fewer than 66 tunnels, 12 of them over 2 km (1¼ miles) long, have been driven through the rock. To make allowance for the aerodynamic effect of two trains passing at combined speeds of over 400 kph (250 mph), the distance between the nearest rails of opposing track in the

tunnels has been increased from the standard 1.83 m (6 ft) to between 2.74 m (9 ft) and 2.89 m (9 ft 6 in). Because of the high speed, care also had to be taken when building the embankments to ensure that there was an adequate degree of compactness in the piled-up earth.

From 06.00 to 21.00, a Hikari (Lightning) train leaves Tokyo every 15 minutes and covers the 518 km (322 miles) in three hours and ten minutes – stopping only twice, at Nagoya and Kyoto – at an average speed of over 160 kph (100 mph). Each train consists of 16 cars and carries an average of 1,000 passengers per train.

Because of the tunnels and the high windows in the coaches, travellers do not get a chance to see much of the beautiful scenery the train passes. It is only when the line crosses the broad river valleys that they can appreciate the Japanese countryside and the distant mountains, including Mount Fuji, of which there are magnificent views.

Today the Tokyo-Osaka Shinkansen is the busiest of several Shinkansen routes, with trains departing Tokyo as often as

● **LEFT**
The interior of an older Shinkansen train set of the sort now used on local trains.

● **BOTTOM**
A Tokyo-bound express races through Shizuoka.

● **BELOW**
The fastest regularly scheduled train in the world is the 300 kph (186 mph) Nozomi 500, which makes one round trip from Osaka to Hakata daily. It is seen here stopping at Okayama on its eastbound run.

● RIGHT
A Tokyo-bound Nozomi train nears its destination. The wedge-shaped train sets are usually assigned to either the Nozomi or Hikari trains running between Tokyo, Osaka and Hakata.

INFORMATION BOX	
Termini	Tokyo and Osaka
Country	Japan
Length	518 km (322 miles)
Date of opening	1965

every six minutes at peak travel times. West of Osaka, the Shinkansen extends to Kobe, Okayama, Hiroshima and, by way of an undersea tunnel, to Hakata in the island of Kyushu. (The extension to Okayama opened in 1972, and to Hakata in 1975.) North of Tokyo, the Shinkansen extends to Niigata, Yamagata, Sendai and Morioka on separate routes. (The Morioka line opened in 1982.) Tokyo is the terminal for all lines, and there are no through trains between the western and eastern Shinkansen lines. However, there are regular express trains from Tokyo all the way to Hakata on the Osaka line.

Service is provided by three classes of trains: Kodama local trains, which make freqent stops; Hikari limited-express trains; and Nozomi extra-fare super-express trains. On the Tokyo-Osaka segment, there are now three generations of equipment in service, the newest dating from the early 1990s. The latest equipment is used for the Nozomi service. In March 1997 the Nozomi 500 entered service between Osaka and Hakata. This unmistakable train regularly operates at speeds of up to 300 kph (186 mph) and is now the fastest regularly scheduled train in the world. North of Tokyo, there is a pot-pourri of new train styles in service, including the double-deck "Max" trains.

● LEFT
One of the older Shinkansen train sets pauses to pick up passengers at Shizuoka. Many of these traditional "Bullet Trains" are now used as locals – albeit high-speed ones – while the newer equipment handles more glamorous Hikari and Nozomi express duties.

● BELOW
On a rainy April evening, two express trains pass at speed, while a local makes a station stop at Shizuoka. Service on the Tokyo-Osaka line is fast and frequent.

SINGAPORE TO BANGKOK
THE EASTERN AND ORIENTAL EXPRESS

The Eastern and Oriental (E&O) Express links Singapore, Kuala Lumpur and Bangkok. This luxury train started in 1993 and was the creation of James B. Sherwood, the owner of the Venice Simplon-Orient Express.

It is the world's first sleeping car train with a private shower and toilet in every cabin. The train consists of six standard double-bunk sleepers, seven State twin-bed sleepers and one Presidential double-bed sleeper with dressing-room. The whole totals 132 beds and is air-conditioned throughout with three dining cars, two service cars, a generator car, a bar car and an open-end observation car from which one can smell the jungle and hear the birds and the croaking frogs. The 22 cars are 433 m (1,421 ft) long and weigh 844 tons.

Built in Japan for the New Zealand Railways, the train is wholly redesigned by Frenchman Gérard Gallet, whose

INFORMATION BOX

THE EASTERN AND ORIENTAL EXPRESS

Termini	Singapore and Bangkok
Countries	Malaysia and Thailand
Distance	1,943 km (1,207 miles)
Date built	1909–18

VSOE-type rounded brass handles protect sharp angles in the bar car, with its pale ash panelling, lotus motif décor and clever mirrors. Here the piano tinkles, two fortune tellers attend and the tireless, helpful Thai staff serve drinks late into the night.

In the cabins, the genuine welcome of the Thai personal staff, the elegant diamond-patterned parquetry, set off with antique brass fittings, all convey a

highly civilized atmosphere to the guests. On leaving Singapore, afternoon tea is served, British Straits Settlements style. The sumptuous dining cars offer innovative Eurasian menus with fine wines. The brass torch and Pullman table lamps set off the lacquered Chinese or rare veneer panels, sparkling French glasses and gleaming silverware.

After passing customs at Singapore's Kappel station, the E&O enters Malaysia

● **ABOVE LEFT**
The observation car of the Eastern and Oriental Express, where passengers can admire the outstanding scenery alongside the track.

● **LEFT**
The Eastern and Oriental Express near Kanchanaburi, Thailand.

● **RIGHT**
The Eastern and
Oriental Express at
Kuala Lumpur's
magnificent station.

● **FAR RIGHT**
The Eastern and
Oriental Express
crossing the 800 m
(2,624 ft) long
bridge over the
River Kwai. This
multi-span steel
girder bridge spans
on stone pillars
approximately
4.5 m (15 ft) above
the water.

● **BELOW
RIGHT**
The Eastern and
Oriental Express
crossing the South
East Asian
countryside.

waiting-room flanked by topiary in the
form of elephants. Fresh supplies are
brought aboard here. Later, near Nakhon
Pathom, the express diverts some 70 km
(43 miles) to visit the infamous bridge
over the River Kwai.

Forty-two hours after leaving
Singapore, having travelled 1,943 km
(1,207 miles), the train arrives at
Bangkok's Hualampong station. Most
passengers end their journey here, but it
is possible to spend a third night aboard
by continuing 751 km (467 miles) north
to Chiang Mai.

over the 6 km (3³/₄ mile) long Johor
Bahru causeway. Thereafter, as many have
already experienced, the train makes a
leisurely, varied journey on narrow-gauge
tracks through the Malayan rubber
plantations and primitive jungle, and later
through Thailand's terraced farmlands,
dotted with Buddhist shrines.

The train reaches Kuala Lumpur,
394 km (245 miles) from Singapore –
and the world's most beautiful station –
one hour before midnight. From now on,
the line is on single track and the jungle
closes in. After luncheon on the second
day, the scene begins to change as Karst
Limestone mountains rise from the lush
plains near Padang Besar, where the
Keretapi Tanah Malayu Railways (KTM)
hand over to the State Railways of
Thailand (SRT). On a historical foot-
note, KTM first ran air-conditioned
sleeping cars from Butterworth to
Bangkok as early as 1936.

The next morning, after passing
through Thai terraced farmlands during
the night, the train stops on the east
coast at Hua Hin. It is here that the Thai
royal family spend their holidays, and the
station is magnificent, with its royal

SINGAPORE TO PENANG

Although the description of this journey has been compiled from notes made on several runs in 1946 when overall timings were low, it is described as if made on one occasion. Fortunately, the whole journey is still possible today, and long may it remain so.

On the day of departure, the "Day Mail" to Kuala Lumpur left from Singapore station at 07.00, not long after dawn. The station at Tanjong Pagar, somewhat out of the centre of the city, was built in 1932 in the European style of the day. At the time of writing, it is still in use and has an impressive high-ceilinged entrance hall with three storeys of offices on one side and a restaurant and hotel on the other. Murals in painted tiles depict scenes on the railway.

The train comprised 12 coaches and two vans and was hauled by a Class 564 Pacific built in 1945. The author's coach

was built in 1935 and rode very well. After departing on time, and the fireman having collected the single-line token from the signalman, the train swung round past the locomotive and carriage sheds at the right. On a siding were small 0-4-0 tank locomotives belonging to the Singapore Harbour Board awaiting disposal. An 0-6-0T of the Federated Malayan States Railway (FMSR), which had been bought to replace them, was on shed together with a couple of MacArthur 2-8-2s, still bearing their

● **TOP**
A MacArthur Class WD10G4 drawing a train out of the carriage shed at Singapore in March 1946.

● **ABOVE LEFT**
The trolley bus was popular in Singapore and Penang. This one, built between the two world wars and pictured in December 1946, is on a service in Georgetown, capital of the island of Penang.

● **LEFT**
On the journey, the traveller passes many villages of which this is typical.

● **LEFT**
Kuala Lumpur's
ornate railway station.

● **BELOW**
The signboard outside
the funicular railway
station on Penang
Island gives an
indication of the
height of the
mountains, whose
relatively cool climate
provides a welcome
escape from the heat
and humidity of
Georgetown.

● **BOTTOM LEFT**
View from the summit
station on the Swiss-
built funicular on
Penang Island on 17
December 1946. The
height is 762 m (2,500
ft) and the mainland
can just be discerned
in the background.

British War Department numbers, a
Japanese C58 2-6-2 and an ex-Javanese
C30 2-6-2T, as well as the resident
FMSR Class I 0-6-2T No. 173 built by
Kitson of Leeds in 1913.

To the left were the sidings serving
the large dock area. Then the train ran
through a mixture of settlements and
open country, now swallowed up by
concrete and steel. Soon the train
reached the famous causeway, 1,080 m
(3,543 ft) long. To the right could be
seen various naval vessels anchored at the
large base.

At Johore Bahru, seat of the Sultan of
Johore, the scene changes dramatically.
Some authors have implied that, because
the railway builders chose to keep the
ruling gradient at 1:100 and followed
contours and natural routes to avoid the
mountains in the interior, there was little
difficulty in construction – but this is not
so. As the land is situated near the
equator and is subject to torrential rains,
numerous watercourses cut across the
line of the railway. Because of the swamps
and tropical rain forest, there were few

INFORMATION BOX

Termini	Singapore and Penang
Country	Malaya
Distance	783 km (487 miles)
Date of travel	1946

established land routes to follow. The
railway had come before track and road,
as most trade went by sea and river.

Consequently, the line twists and
turns, crossing numerous steel bridges
and at times affording tantalizing
glimpses of settlements or sudden distant
views. In places, great rock walls rise
alongside the line and, whether riding in
the coach or taking advantage of the
restaurant/buffet car, an alert traveller
will find much of interest throughout
the journey.

Johore Bahru had a number of sidings
and a locomotive stabling point. Today it
is a frontier station with the usual

disruption to be expected at such places. Heading north, the line was fairly level and straight, passing through jungle alive with wildlife. The jungle had been cut back from the track by 50 m (164 ft) or more, as a security measure, but this was also useful in that it helped to keep natural debris off the line and improved the driver's line of vision. Where the jungle had been cleared, there was mile upon mile of rubber and palm tree plantations interspersed with villages. At Layang-Layang was a particularly extensive plantation with its own narrow-gauge railway system and exchange sidings with the FMSR.

Kluang, 113 km (70 miles) from Singapore, was a place of some importance to the railway and a passing-point. Here, two rail-mounted Jeeps (the famous, little, wartime, rough-country vehicles) lurked in the small, wooden, locomotive depot.

Gemas, 220 km (137 miles) from Singapore, was and is, the junction for the line that cuts across the country for 516 km (321 miles) to Kota Bharu on the east coast. In 1946, Gemas had two 296 m (971 ft) platforms, extensive sidings, a four-road locomotive depot with an 18.2 m (60 ft) turntable and a two-road carriage shed. Movement was controlled by two signal-boxes each with

60 levers, now replaced by a modern 80-lever frame. It was normal for locomotive crews to be changed here.

There is a short climb out of Gemas, and it is just 53 km (33 miles) to Tampin along the main line, which kept as closely as possible to the western side of the peninsula to avoid the central mountain range that rises in places to over 2,133 m (7,000 ft). Tampin was the junction for the 38 km (24 mile) branch to Malacca on the west coast, which was not re-laid after the war.

The next stretch was notable for tin mines and rubber plantations as well as paddy fields, a feature often to be found in areas cleared of jungle. At Seremban, some 61 km (38 miles) further north, was the junction for Port Dickson, which sees only freight traffic now.

In the 59 km (37 miles), to Kuala Lumpur, the whole nature of the scene changed. There were more signs of habitation, and the scars of tin mining became more evident, especially near Sungei Besi, which claimed to have the largest tin mine in the world.

At Salak South Junction a 30-lever signal-box controlled the entrance to the short Sultan Street and Ampang branches, the latter now used for oil traffic. Port Swettenham Junction, 4.8 km

(3 miles) further north, had a 40-lever signal-box covering the entrance to the 43 km (27 mile) long branch to the west coast harbour of Port Swettenham and the Brickfields branch, leading to Kuala Lumpur's large freight yards.

Kuala Lumpur's ornate main passenger station still exists, with four platform faces covered by an overall roof. In 1945, it housed the headquarters of the FMSR, which now occupies a nearby office block. The two 80-lever signal-boxes have been replaced by a single 80-lever modern box.

Some 900 metres (2,953 ft) to the south of the station on the west side was situated the 28-stall roundhouse with its 18.2 m (60 ft) turntable, pre-heating water plant, mechanical coaler, ash-plant and a workshop. Three large carriage sheds served by 13 tracks were adjacent to the roundhouse, together with a carriage-washing plant. Both these depots were severely damaged in attacks by the US airforce, and in 1946 the ash-plant and coaler were not functioning and the pre-heating plant was wrecked.

Sentul locomotive, carriage and wagon works was situated about a mile down the Batu Caves branch, which diverged

● **ABOVE LEFT**
A view of Singapore's Chinatown.

● **ABOVE RIGHT**
A Swiss-built funicular railway to Summit Road on Penang Island.

● **RIGHT**
The traveller will see many mosques from the train. One such is the Ubundian Mosque at Kuala Kangsar.

● **BELOW**
The craft in the foreground was one of the
means of getting from the Malayan mainland
to Penang Island. The ship in the background
was a "prize of war" and renamed *Empire Rani*,
17 April 1947.

● **BELOW**
Seen in December 1946, No. 402.03, one of
the powerful 4-6-4Ts of the FMSR, was used as
a "banker" for trains travelling over the
Taiping pass.

● **BOTTOM**
Famous throughout
the world for its
rubber, this is one of
the many Malayan
rubber plantations
which will be seen
from the train.

north-west about 1.6 km (1 mile) from
Kuala Lumpur station. The works was
divided into two sections by a 61 tonne
(60 ton) electrically powered traverser.
The section to the south was devoted to
locomotive repairs, with iron and brass
foundries, pattern shop, tin- and copper-
smiths' shops, stores and an electrical
sub-station. To the north were the C & W

shops, electrical and train lighting repair
shops, paint shop, saw mill, smithy and
boiler shops.

A short distance north of Kuala
Lumpur lies Kuang, the junction for a
23 km (14 mile) long branch to Batang
Berjuntai on which, at the half-way point,
was situated the coal mine at Batu Arang,
which provided steam coal for the FMSR.
From here to Tanjong Malim, the 61 km
(38 miles) of line ran through open
countryside but a depressing sight was
the wastelands created by abandoned
tin workings.

For the 124 km (77 miles) from
Tanjong Malim to the important town of
Ipoh, the line runs along the eastern edge
of the wide coastal plain and below the
foothills of the mountains. The 71 km
(44 mile) section to Tapah Road, the
junction for the 29 km (18 mile) branch
to Telok Anson, a port on the Perak
River, is largely through jungle. Tapah
Road was also one of the nearest points
of access to the mountain resorts in the
cool and highly scenic Cameron
Highlands to the west of the line.

A 24 km (15 mile) long branch heads
off westward to Tromoh. At Falim,
approximately 1.6 km (1 mile) down, lies
the locomotive depot for Ipoh, a
substantial six-road building with a
workshop and an 18.2 m (60 ft)
turntable. The two-storey station building
was imposing, and the station boasted no
fewer than five platforms.

For the author, the line from Ipoh to
Prai provided the widest variety of
scenery on the whole journey, for it
includes the climb to the summit of the
line through what was generally known as
the Taiping pass. From Kuala Kangsa, the
railway ascended gently through rubber
plantations, but at Padang Rengas the
serious climbing began. For all trains of
more than 152 tonnes (150 tons),
banking locomotives were provided,

● **RIGHT**
Penang's Kek Lok
Si Temple.

● **BELOW
RIGHT**
A pair of the
Singapore Harbour
Board 0-4-0STS at
Singapore shed in
December 1945. No.
5, on the right, is
believed to have
been built by Robert
Stephenson (Works
No. 3346/1907).

usually Class C² 4-6-4T from Taiping
locomotive depot. For 1.6 km (1 mile)
the grade is 1:80, and the scenery
became spectacular as the train twisted
and turned, passing now and again
through tunnels, the longest of which was
345 m (1,132 ft). Emerging from one of
these tunnels, the line crossed a viaduct
providing a splendid view of Gunong
Bondok and the valley of the Perak River.
The line descended for 8.5 km (5¼
miles) from the summit at Bukit Gantang
at the same 1:80 gradient, including in
this section the sharpest main-line curve
of 12 chains (241 m or 792 ft) radius.
The maximum banked load over the pass
was 660 tonnes (650 tons) if the train
engine was a Class S 4-6-2, which had
not only the maximum tractive effort of
13,370 kg (29,477 lbs) but also the
heaviest axle load of 16.25 tonnes (16
tons). The O Class were allowed 559
tonnes (550 tons).

Taiping, in the middle of the Larut
plain, was the centre for the local rubber
plantations and the once extensive tin
mining industry first established there

some 100 years ago. It was the junction
for the 12 km (7½ mile) long Port Weld
branch and there were a number of
sidings. Passengers were served by a
sizeable station with three platform
faces. Not far north of Taiping, the line
passes through low hills, and then there
is an 8 km (5 mile) long stretch of
straight track.

The 69 km (43 miles) from Taiping to
Bukit Mertajam is mostly level, and much

of the terrain is marshy. From Bukit
Mertajam, 775 km (481 miles) from
Singapore, the line to the Siamese
frontier at Padang Besar heads north, but
my train took the short westward branch
to Prai. This was double track, but made
single by the Japanese. From Prai, I hired
a native craft to take me across to
Butterworth, from where the FMSR
ferry was then running to the main town
on Penang Island, Georgetown.

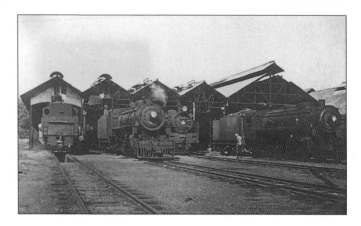

TANAHABANG TO RANGKASBITUNG

The account of this journey has been compiled from notes taken in August 1974. The journey is still possible today and is highly recommended.

Since the coaches were already packed with people, I decided to travel on the engine. There were 75 people already mounted on that locomotive – a modest 3 ft 6 in gauge secondary line diesel – of whom 23 were in the cab and the remainder on the front, sides and top. Undaunted I was hauled aboard.

Upon leaving the station, the train gingerly threaded its way through a maze of dwellings – colonization of the sidings and the disused rolling stock being considerable. One metre (3¼ ft) from the lines lay tightly packed dwellings, a mixture of tile, thatch and wood. We passed close to line-side stalls which, but for 7.6 cm (3 in), would have been collapsed by the engine.

INFORMATION BOX

Termini	Tanahabang and Rangkasbitung
Country	Indonesia
Distance	c. 70 km (43 miles)
Date of travel	August 1974

But this colourful scene, which stretched over a considerable distance, was tinged on this occasion with another pleasure, for the simple, delightful Indonesian state flag – the upper half red, the lower white – fluttered gaily and riotously from every building, wagon and stall. It was 18 August – Independence Day. During the week of celebrations even the locomotives bear flags, attached to special mounts incorporated on to the smokebox tops.

The journey was excruciatingly bad. The diesel crawled indolently along and stops were frequent. We had scarcely covered 16 km (10 miles) before even the locals were beginning to look drowsy. The driver was wedged up in a far corner of the cab from which he could see a little of the track ahead – presumably some agreement existed with the horde on the buffer beams that, should an

● LEFT
A typical sugar plantation scene on Java, showing the temporary track beds, which bring the wagons of loaded cane to the main-line railway. The locomotive, which patiently waits in the background, was built in Leeds, England.

● **RIGHT**
Indonesian
Independence Day
celebrations on 18
August 1974, and
the state flag flutters
gaily on the smoke-
box top of Class B51
No. 39, a two-
cylinder 4-4-0 built
by Werkspoor of
Amsterdam. This
scene at the
locomotive shed at
Rangkasbitung
features a C27 4-6-
4T in the back-
ground, an engine
also built by
Werkspoor and
dating back to 1919.

● **BELOW**
A typical Javan sugar plantation worker
suitably attired for protection from the razor-
sharp leaves and stems of the sugar cane.

emergency arise, they must bang on the engine's sides. Such conditions underline part of the malaise of the Perusahaan Negara Kereta Api (Indonesian State Railways), in that the only passengers who ever pay on a PNKA line are those unfortunate individuals who dutifully remain in the compartment or are unable to escape the ticket-collector either by climbing out on to the coach roof or by obtaining another, equally precarious place on the train by any of 20 or more hazardous methods.

The engine, of course, is the driver's preserve; few ticket-collectors ever infiltrate that domain. My compassion for the driver on this trip was put sharply into perspective when the hat came round. This was the driver's collection – half the price of the normal fare, no tickets issued and no questions asked. Had I really thought the engine crew would suffer such discomfort for nothing? Honour among thieves was

never better epitomized than by the way in which the hat finally did the round of the engine compartment and was dutifully returned to the driver full of the passengers' rupiahs.

A plume of rich brown smoke erupted from the loop ahead. We were crossing with an eastbound steam train. Despite the barrage of flags, I detected the

familiar outline of a Class 27 4-6-4T, built by Armstrong Whitworth of Newcastle upon Tyne in 1922, hauling an unbelievably well patronized six-coach Independence Day Special. Nearly five hours after leaving Tanahabang, the journey over the Javan paddy fields was over as the train crawled into the small town of Rangkasbitung.

● **LEFT**
A Class C12 06, seen
against one of Java's
famous sunsets,
following the
Independence Day
celebrations.

RANGKASBITUNG TO LABUAN

The unintended journey started with my inspection of a Werkspoor engine of 1909, a B51, which was standing idle in a siding at Rangkasbitung. Utterly fascinated, I entered the vacant cab. However, the Javan crew soon arrived and with an incomprehensible acknowledgement of my presence proceeded to back down on to a rake of decrepit rolling stock lying in the station. Suddenly the engine moved forward, and the unexpected journey began.

I had no idea where I was going and, although the crew were friendly enough, the language barrier made communication impossible. The epic way in which B5138 stormed out of Rangkasbitung that evening did justice to her Prussian lineage as, with trilling

● **BELOW**
The constant flurry of sparks that emanate from the chimneys of Java's steam locomotives is epitomized in this scene of a Class B50 2-4-0 built by Sharp Stewart of Manchester in 1885.

● **BOTTOM**
A typically decrepit Javan passenger-train, consisting of wooden-bodied four-wheeled coaches and hauled by B50 2-4-0 No. 14.

whistle, she charged through the suburbs and out of town.

Although the B51 burned a mixture of coal, wood and oil, during the journey's early stages the fireman was principally using coal. Dusk was rapidly advancing and soon our engine was pumping black exhaust into an azure sky, a pungently smelling frothy smoke, which continually swept round the cab and down the train. Our speed was greater than I had thought possible as the engine ferociously headed through the darkening landscape. The veteran's violent lurching over the rough track beds was stimulating enough, though on the few occasions when she was eased a pleasant aroma of coal smoke wafted back through the fire-hole door and into the cab.

INFORMATION BOX

Termini	Rangkasbitung and Labuan
Country	Indonesia
Distance	*c.* 55 km (34 miles)
Date of travel	August 1974

Darkness had fallen by the time we reached the first station – a wayside halt, which only merited our presence for a matter of seconds.

Soon the drama returned in all its affray. A hiss of steam escaping from the front end became audible and made an exciting foil to the throbbing rasps of exhaust. Speed mounted terrifyingly, and the engine became a mass of churning, pulsating machinery. The whistle screamed and wailed in long eerie bursts as we sped past lonely villages and small ungated crossings, but remote as we were and dark as it was, a few ox carts could invariably be discerned momentarily lit up by the swirling incandescence of B5138's fire.

Without warning she hit a downgrade, and the engine was really opened out. The roar became hypnotic. It was impossible to estimate our speed, the darkness outside revealing nothing from which a bearing might be taken. The crew, bathed in a shimmering orange glow, clung tenaciously to the cab sides. The fire, white hot, lit up the black exhaust trail, which raced in a swirling slipstream above the cab roof. It certainly felt as if we could to all intents and purposes have been hitting one hundred miles per hour (160 kph)!

I had come to Indonesia to find a locomotive dinosaur and by perfect fortune had found one in triumphant full cry – the last of her breed, a Prussian phantom and a living ghost of the great 19th-century steam age. With many kilometres now behind us it seemed that the country was beginning to flatten out and fireflies could be seen over the rice fields. It was about this time that our coal supply ran out, and the logs that had hitherto been ignored came into their own. The B51 responded in a flurry of sparks, brilliantly cascading in the paths of the fireflies. Suddenly, as the train sped onwards through different terrain, the fireflies were left behind, and, like the eclipse of a fireworks display observed with the awe of childhood, the magic was gone.

Soon we slowed down and speckled lights could be seen ahead. We had reached our destination.

● **ABOVE**
An Indonesian State Railways Class B51 4-4-0 takes water at Rangkasbitung. The Prussian ancestry of this German-built veteran of 1902 is in full evidence.

● **LEFT**
A brace of Class B51 4-4-0s – including No. 38 on which the footplate journey took place – raise steam in the depot yard at Labuan.

PORT AUGUSTA TO ALICE SPRINGS
THE GHAN

The heart of Australia has seen little potential for development beyond minerals and cattle stations. To serve the few hardy settlers who ventured into this harsh country in the early days, Afghans brought in the supplies with their camel teams. As the need for transport grew, the South Australian government commenced the construction of a narrow-gauge railway from Port Augusta in South Australia, first to serve the anticipated wheat and wool traffic in the false belief that "rain would follow the plough", and then to tap the minerals and cattle from further north.

The line to Hergott Springs, now Marree, was opened for traffic in 1884. This was the end of the famous Birdsville Track and a meeting-point for several cattle-driving routes. Three mixed trains a week handled the traffic. Beyond there, the line was constructed as Unemployment Relief and in 1891 reached Oodnadatta, 769 km (478 miles)

● **LEFT**
Following World War II, the Commonwealth Railways imported luxurious air-conditioned cars from Wegmann in Germany for the transcontinental service between Port Augusta and Kalgoorlie. These included a rounded observation car, seen here at Port Augusta in 1964.

INFORMATION BOX	
THE GHAN	
Termini	Port Augusta and Alice Springs
Country	Australia
Distance	1,240 km (770 miles)
Date of opening	1891

from Port Augusta. At first, one mixed train a week handled this extension, but this was soon reduced to one a fortnight, with trains averaging 19 kph (12 mph). In 1911 the Commonwealth Government became owners of the line, but did not take control of operations until 1916. They continued building the line, supposed to continue on to Darwin on the northern coast, stopping construction at Alice Springs, 471 km (293 miles) further north. The mixed

● **LEFT**
Early settlers believed that rain would follow the plough and called this place Farina, hoping it would become the heart of the wheat belt of South Australia. But rain did not follow, and the fields had to be abandoned. Little remained when this enthusiast special Ghan travelled the standard gauge of the 1964 period. Today, even the rails are gone as a new standard-gauge route further west bypasses this area.

● **RIGHT**
An NM Class steam locomotive of the
Commonwealth Railways, with a water gin,
heads a tour train through the scenic Pichi
Richi pass.

train that served this line became known
as "The Ghan" in honour of the previous
traders. This ran twice a week, while
another service known as the "slow"
travelled weekly.

Travelling on the Ghan was truly an
adventure. The first section of the line
through the Pichi Richi Pass was very
scenic; its magnificent river gum trees are
a notable feature of an area currently
exploited by rail enthusiasts running the
Pichi Richi Railway. The line continued
alongside and through the Flinders
Ranges, made famous by many painters
in Australia, and then through flat salt
bush country and on to Marree. Between
there and Alice Springs, the lightly
ballastered track was subject to sand
drifts and on occasions to sudden
downpours that caused washaways,
making the route impassable until repairs
could be effected. Passengers starting out
on what was supposed to be a three-day
journey could suddenly find themselves
marooned in the desert for up to several
weeks, with food drops from aircraft not
being uncommon.

As the narrow-gauge route through
the Pichi Richi pass and the Flinders
Ranges limited the loads hauled, a new
standard-gauge line was constructed to
join the old route near Brachina, beyond
which the line was standardized to
Marree. In view of the problems with the
line beyond Marree, it was decided in the
1970s to build a complete new standard-
gauge line from near Port Augusta on a
more direct route to Alice Springs
bypassing virtually all of the old route,
leaving everywhere beyond the Leigh
Creek coalfields to more or less disappear.

Today, with standard gauge reaching
Adelaide's suburbs, the only adventure on
this trip – weekly in summer and twice
weekly in the cooler months – is the taxi
journey out of town to the standard-
gauge terminal, no doubt put there to
discourage patronage. From there, you
ride a luxury air-conditioned train in
pampered comfort. The wonders of the
"Red Heart" of Australia are certainly
well worth seeing, but it is not
recommended in summer for those not
prepared for temperatures that can rise
as high as 50°C (122°F).

● **ABOVE**
The real railway adventure in Australia was "The Ghan", originally all
narrow gauge, running from Port Augusta in South Australia to Alice
Springs in the Northern Territory. The starting-point was the exchange
platform at Port Augusta.

● **ABOVE**
An early vehicle used in Government Railway days in the vicinity of the
Pichi Richi pass was a Kitson steam rail motor. Coffee Pot, as it is
affectionately known, has been restored and is again in periodic service
for tourist groups. Here it is undergoing servicing in the Quorn
workshops of the Pichi Richi Railway.

SYDNEY TO BRISBANE
THE BRISBANE EXPRESS

● **BELOW**
The express on the long and arduous ascent to
Toowoomba. The vehicle behind the second
locomotive is a water gin, which is used to
augment the supply in the engines' tenders.

In the 1960s, two trains running on
entirely different routes were both called
the Brisbane Express. For travellers in a
hurry, and with little interest in the
journey itself, there was the one using the
newer 1,035 km (643 mile) coastal route,
much of the journey being done in
darkness. This service was actually divided
into two, with the Brisbane Limited
Express doing the journey in 15½ hours
and the slower Brisbane Express following
in 17 hours and 50 minutes.

For the tourist, the older route had far
more to offer, and although it did include
a night section, enjoyable stretches of
scenic country were traversed in daylight.
By the 1965 timetable, an early
afternoon departure of 13.55 meant that
the descent of the Cowan Bank and the
crossing of the Hawkesbury River would
be done in good light, as would the run
along the shores of Brisbane Waters.
There was well inhabited country as far
as Wyong and then timbered hilly
country nearly to Broadmeadow, the
junction for trains to Newcastle. This was
coal mining country, and a considerable
amount of coal traffic would be seen on

INFORMATION BOX

THE BRISBANE EXPRESS

Termini	Sydney and Brisbane
Country	Australia
Distance	1,150 km (715 miles)
Date of opening	1888

the way to Maitland, where the shorter
coastal route branched off to the north.
The "Main" route continued westwards
through relatively flat dairy country to
Singleton, passing through there about
dusk. In the darkness, the line began a
gradual climb towards the foothills of the
Great Dividing Range via Murrurundi,
the depot town for push-up and assistant
engines used by heavy traffic crossing the
range from both directions. The ruling
gradient there was 1:40 on both sides,
and provided many a spectacle as
locomotives struggled up the 8 km
(5 miles) of steep bank to Ardglen tunnel.

To the west of the range, the line
dropped in easier stages to Tamworth
before climbing the Moonbi Range to the
Northern Tablelands. Daylight came in
the beautiful hilly country before
Tenterfield, the last major town before
the Queensland border. Less than 18 km
(11 miles) brought the train to the
border and the change-of-gauge station at
Wallangarra. Here the narrow-gauge
express to Brisbane waited to continue
the journey through more scenic hilly
country to some of the finest rural land

● **ABOVE**
The famous and familiar sight of Sydney Harbour Bridge.

● **OPPOSITE BOTTOM**
One of the world's best-known landmarks is Sydney Opera House.

● **BELOW LEFT**
The view from Sydney centre looking down William Street to King's Cross.

● **BELOW RIGHT**
Part of the climb facing the early Brisbane-Sydney expresses near Toowoomba in Queensland. The diesel-hauled goods train is carefully easing itself down the first part of the descent towards Brisbane, Toowoomba being just over the crest in the middle background.

in Australia, the Darling Downs. After 5¹/₂ hours, the train reached the beautiful city of Toowoomba, famous for the magnificent gardens created by the local inhabitants.

The descent of the mountains from Toowoomba was an immensely scenic but very time-consuming journey. Because of this, the Queensland Railways had a co-ordinated bus/rail service between Toowoomba and Helidon at the bottom of the range, and Brisbane-bound travellers could spend over an hour in Toowoomba, eating, sightseeing or

whatever. They could then catch the bus and rejoin the train at Heildon for the final run into Brisbane. This option, however, meant that they missed much of the beauty of that part of the journey. In the reverse direction, Toowoomba dwellers could get home an hour ahead of the train by using the bus. The arrival in Brisbane would be shortly after dusk at 18.26 – 28¹/₂ hours after leaving Sydney, a run of 1,150 km (715 miles). Today this journey is no more, as a considerable length of the line from Glen Innes to the Queensland border has been abandoned.

BROKEN HILL TO ADELAIDE
THE BROKEN HILL EXPRESS

For centuries, man has dreamed of the pot of gold at the end of the rainbow, and prospectors have trudged into the wilderness in search of their fortune.

Few areas could have been more dismal than the country near the South Australian-New South Wales border. However, as early as 1876, galena (lead sulphide) was found on the NSW side, and by 1883 the Silverton area was booming with mines and even smelters. In the same year, galena was discovered at Broken Hill. The South Australian Government, seeing the potential of the area, hastily built a narrow-gauge line from Peterborough (then Petersburg) to the border, reaching there in January 1887, but it was not permitted to cross the border by the NSW government. This led to the formation of the private Silverton Tramway Company, later known as Broken Hill's gold mine. By this time Silverton, a town with 36 hotels, was declining rapidly. However, Broken Hill, though now declining, has been a boom town for all this century.

Though in NSW, Broken Hill is included in the South Australian time zone, and most commercial business is

● **ABOVE**
Between Terowie and Adelaide, the broad-gauge Broken Hill Express could have been handled by a variety of locomotives, the most eye-catching being the streamlined 520 Class. For a short period, the 23 km (14 miles) between Terowie and the main junction town of Peterborough had a third trail added to eliminate a short journey on narrow gauge where the standard gauge reached Peterborough. Here No. 526 works a broad-gauge route to Adelaide, that spelt the end of this section, leaving the once important break-of-gauge town of Terowie to become a ghost town.

● **BELOW**
The Broken Hill Express travelled most of its journey in darkness. Enthusiasts wishing to re-create the journey in daylight arranged for South Australian Railway's Garratt No. 402 to haul the train, seen here passing the isolated Mannahill station heading north.

conducted with the closer capital city of Adelaide. To make this connection a regular train service connected the two cities, with the Broken Hill Express being one of the few passenger expresses in Australia hauled for many years by Garratt locomotives. The others were in Queensland. This was basically an overnight service, and the South Australian Railway (SAR) built up the tonnage with freight wagons, thereby making it a mixed train.

To the east of the border, the Silverton Tramway Company, with its 58 km (36 miles) of line, provided the locomotives and a percentage of the freight wagons. The original locomotives were Colonial Moguls, followed in 1912 by the A Class, very English-looking 4-6-0s. In 1951, the W Class 4-8-2 semi-streamlined locomotives, similar to those used in Western Australia, took over before being replaced by 673kW Co-Co diesel electrics from 1960 to 1970, when the standard gauge bypassed the private line.

Early traffic on the South Australian side was handled by Y or X Class Moguls, but with the growing traffic bigger locomotives were soon needed, with the Chief Mechanical Engineer designing the highly successful T Class 4-8-0s, 78 of which were built from 1903 onwards, with some remaining in service right to

INFORMATION BOX

THE BROKEN HILL EXPRESS

Termini	Broken Hill and Adelaide
Country	Australia
Distance	582 km (362 miles)
Date of opening	1887

● **ABOVE**
The Broken Hill Express was worked by the Silverton Tramway Company on the New South Wales side of the border and a South Australian Garratt on their side of the fence. Here we see a re-enactment of the border change.

the end of the steam era. These brought the train 225 km (140 miles) to Terowie, where one changed to the broad gauge, with an S Class 4-4-0 continuing the 225 km (140 mile) journey to Adelaide until the arrival of larger engines of the Webb era in the mid-1920s.

In 1953, the 400 Class Garratts arrived and rapidly took over the Broken Hill traffic. From 1959, the SAR began

● **ABOVE RIGHT**
The Adelaide skyline.

● **RIGHT**
This plant, called Black Boy, is common along the route of the Broken Hill Express.

acquiring 830 Class Co-Co diesel electrics, which eventually replaced steam on this semi-desert route. This standardization rang the death knell for the Broken Hill Express with the Indian Pacific eventually taking over the passenger traffic on the line and the broad-gauge services being withdrawn from Terowie.

According to a 1953 timetable, the Broken Hill Express would depart from Broken Hill at 19.48 behind a Silverton W Class, covering what was possibly the most scenic part of this semi-desert journey in darkness to the border, arriving at 21.21. Here a 400 Class Garratt took over for the run to Peterborough, where passengers for Port Pirie had to make an 03.58 change of train. From there the train reversed, with a new locomotive for the short run to Terowie, where Adelaide passengers changed to the broad gauge at 04.50. After a 20-minute allowance for refreshments, the broad-gauge train headed for an 09.20 arrival in Adelaide.

BRISBANE TO CAIRNS
THE SUNSHINE RAIL EXPERIENCE

Probably more than the other Australian states, Queensland relied on coastal shipping to service the large number of ports on its long coastline. This resulted in railways being built, but not along the coast. They were built as isolated lines running inland from the various ports. As passengers began demanding quicker and more reliable services from Brisbane to the northern centres, the Government began constructing lines to connect the various isolated sections. It was, however,

not until the end of 1924 that it was possible to travel all the way, 1,679 km (1,043 miles), to Cairns in the far north.

The lines were lightly built with low-level bridges not far above the river beds. To the Government's surprise, the railways gained a considerable amount of goods traffic, and rural industry, particularly sugar, expanded rapidly. In the beginning, a trip to the north took 52 hours, which included a 24-hour stay in Townsville along the way. Services were

soon improved, with the 1950 Sunshine Express departing Brisbane at 20.00 and arriving at Cairns two days later at 16.00.

However, time brought great changes. First came dieselization, and then the gaining of massive coal contracts by mines inland from the coastal ports. Lines had to be upgraded and realigned in many areas, new bridges built and Centralized Traffic Control introduced. Steam trains could handle a reasonable depth of floodwater when there was no

● **ABOVE**
No trip to Cairns in the far north of Queensland is complete without the final excursion to Kuranda, battling up the cliff faces with magnificent views of the coast, cane fields, rain forest, waterfalls and finally the enchanting market village of Kuranda.

● **ABOVE**
When steam was king in Queensland, the expresses between Brisbane and Cairns would have been worked by these beautiful BB18 1/4 Class Pacifics with their comfortable wooden coaches. A tour train stands at Nambour, typifying an express of the period. Parochial rail fans from interstate would often sing "I'll Walk Beside You" whenever Queensland trains were mentioned – hardly fair, as they provided a very efficient and reasonably speedy service in steam days and are now probably the most modern in the country.

● **ABOVE**
One of the attractions of Kuranda are the waterfalls.

● LEFT
The dieselized air-conditioned Sunlander express rumbles through the cane fields near Feluga in North Queensland in 1971.

appreciable current. With one leading, and another locomotive at the rear to steady the train, they could run down into a river and work their way across. This was completely out of the question for a diesel electric, so new high-level bridges were a must.

In the late 1950s, Queensland's magnificent Garratts brought 406 tonnes (400 tons) of coal to the coast. In the 1980s, six diesel electric locomotives, three leading and three in the middle of the train with Locotrol radio control, were bringing in over 10,000 tonnes (10,160 tons) at a time.

Electrification was the answer for this heavy traffic, and coal lines were electrified together with the coastal line from Brisbane to Rockhampton in 1989. Now luxury express trains such as the Queenslander cover the distance to Cairns in only 32 hours and 5 minutes.

With the connection of the isolated systems, to build maintenance depots for the new locomotives and railcars all over the State would have been a costly exercise, so most major work was carried out near Brisbane. Some person capable of lateral thinking, realizing that returning rail motors from the branch lines for periodic overhaul over this great distance was a slow and costly exercise, came up with the idea of using the trips to carry tourists, with local sightseeing trips laid on as a feature during the driver's rest periods.

While the expresses race over the distance in less than one-and-a-half days three times a week, the rail motor

exchange has developed into an exciting weekly six-day train tour, now with a loco-hauled train. It includes accommodation in quality hotels overnight and numerous trips to points of special interest, such as a boat tour to the Barrier Reef.

Unlike most lengthy rail journeys in Australia, there is no let up to the magnificent scenery for the full length of the railway line, be it Mother Nature or the rural properties, which are seen at their best in early spring. For the rail fan, too, there is the heavy traffic to be seen *en route*, and during the cane season, from August to November, a multitude of 2 ft gauge trains are busy rushing cane to the mills and sugar to the ports. Indeed, the highlights of the journey are not over on reaching Cairns. Further exciting rail trips can be started from there, such as the magnificent climb to Kuranda, rising along the cliff face past waterfalls, or, with the help of buses, tours can reach the Mount Surprise line and the famous Croydon-Normanton line.

INFORMATION BOX	
Termini	Brisbane and Cairns
Country	Australia
Distance	1,679 km (1,043 miles)
Date of opening	1924

● RIGHT
The train from Cairns approaches Kurunda.

PORT KEMBLA TO MOSS VALE
THE COCKATOO RUN

In a deal involving the establishment of a steelworks at Port Kembla in New South Wales, the Government agreed to construct a railway line up the steep mountainsides to connect the new industrial area with the Main Southern Railway at Moss Vale, thus providing a shorter and cheaper link to the interstate markets in the south. The new line, approximately 70 km (43 miles) in length, was opened in 1932 and has handled heavy goods traffic, mainly coal, limestone and steel products, ever since.

Passenger-traffic has been rather light, as much of the line is through a water catchment area where the entry of people, the worst polluters, is discouraged. This passenger-traffic was usually handled by rail motors or two- and three-car passenger-trains. Many of the travellers have been tourists, as this is the most scenic line in NSW, rivalled only by the now abandoned Dorrigo branch.

The line leaves the coastal Illawarra line at Unanderra and almost

immediately starts on a 1:30 gradient with magnificent views of the coast. This steep gradient is almost continuous until Summit Tank, some 20 km (12½ miles) up the mountainside. While the coast cannot be seen from the line at Summit Tank, time has always been allowed for tourists to walk a few steps to a lookout on the cliff edge for a view of the coast.

As this relatively short section of track became congested during World War II,

with heavy steam-hauled goods trains taking over an hour in the section, it became necessary to provide a crossing loop within the section. Due to the difficult terrain, the Dombarton crossing facility was unique in NSW. Trains ascended up the mountainside and branched off to the left into a level dead-end siding on a slight rise. This rise gave the train a start for rejoining the main line, on its left, on to another dead-end

● LEFT
In the days of government operation of passenger services on the route of the Cockatoo Run, this traffic was usually handled by railmotors or short trains hauled by a tank-engine. Here a C-30 Class tank-engine bites into the 1:30 grade with a few light carriages, a short distance out of Port Kembla in 1967.

INFORMATION BOX	
Termini	Port Kembla and Moss Vale
Country	Australia
Distance	70 km (43 miles)
Date of opening	1932

siding parallel to that used by the ascending trains. When the line was clear, the train backed into the first dead-end siding used by the ascending trains before again proceeding downhill. This parallel siding for descending trains also gave some protection to the other train in the case of a runaway. The line is also subject to rock falls, and concrete shelters similar to snowsheds have been erected in the worst sections to protect it.

Summit Tank, at 579 m (1,900 ft) above sea level, is a normal crossing loop and has a turntable for turning the third locomotive used to assist heavy goods, trains and allow it to return to the coast. From here the grade eases, with even a few downward stretches and with nothing worse than 1:60 compensated for curvature to the highest point near St Anthony's. Beyond here, it is relatively flat all the way to Moss Vale.

Dieselization improved running times and increased train loads, but it also brought problems. The slow continuous grind up the mountainside, with no activity required from the driver and the

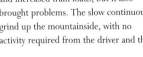

continuous rumble of the motor behind him, lulled drivers to sleep and resulted in two head-on smashes. This hastened the introduction of "vigilance controls" on locomotives, forcing drivers to react at quite short intervals, and thus keeping them alert. Today, the goods traffic continues, but passenger traffic is handled by an enthusiast group known as 3801 Limited who run trains four times a week. Steam haulage is used, except in the summer months when a diesel hydraulic locomotive substitutes.

● ABOVE RIGHT
Once off the train, there are some unique road signs to be seen.

● RIGHT
This journey passes some beautiful coastal scenery.

SYDNEY TO PERTH
FROM THE PACIFIC TO THE INDIAN OCEAN

Although railway construction in Australia proceeded in earnest from the 1850s, it was not until 1917 that it was possible to cross the continent from ocean to ocean, a distance then of 4,352 km (2,704 miles) by rail. When this journey became possible, Australia was caught up in a muddle of different railway gauges, making this trip quite an adventure for travellers who were rail enthusiasts, but something of a nightmare for those who were not. The current route is standard gauge and fairly direct, but in those days it was necessary to travel via Melbourne and Adelaide.

According to timetables published shortly after the opening of the transcontinental line, a traveller from Sydney would board his standard gauge train at 19.25 on, say, Sunday evening and travel throughout the night to the Victorian border at Albury, where at 07.23 he had 23 minutes to change to a broad-gauge train that would arrive at Melbourne at 12.51. Here there was another change, to a broad-gauge train

● **LEFT**
A triple restoration: the Great Zigzag on the western side of the Blue Mountains in NSW, with Queensland Railway's express passenger locomotive BB18 1/4 No. 1072 hauling a set of ex-South Australian narrow-gauge cars. The popularity of this restored feat of engineering has resulted in trains running daily through this spectacular countryside for the pleasure of tourists.

INFORMATION BOX

Termini	Sydney and Perth
Country	Australia
Distance	3,961 km (2,461 miles) since 1970
Date of opening	1917

departing at 16.30 and again travelling overnight to arrive in Adelaide, South Australia, at 09.55 on Tuesday. Fifty minutes later, he would be on yet another broad-gauge train (no through carriages on any of these services) northwards to Terowie, where half an hour was allowed for refreshments and a change to a narrow-gauge train. This then worked its way by a circuitous route to Port Augusta,

● **LEFT**
An XPT Intercity express speeds along the deviation, including ten tunnels, that was used to bypass the old zigzag at Lithgow. The viaducts and old formation now carry tourists in 3 ft 6 in gauge regular services.

arriving at 22.05 on Tuesday for the next change – this time a standard-gauge train for the journey across the Nullarbor Plains.

Over a day and a half would now be spent crossing this semi-desert, with the longest straight in the world, 478 km (297 miles), to reach the gold-mining town of Kalgoorlie at 13.38 on Thursday. Here he had a lengthier stop, no doubt for a little tourist activity, as the narrow-gauge express to Perth did not leave until 17.15, with an 09.47 arrival at Perth on Friday morning. The whole journey had taken just over four-and-a-half days, allowing for the two-hour time difference between the two sides of the continent. For the period, the trains were suitably comfortable, but these stops and changes – and the scramble for food, supplied at stations and not on the train – must have been somewhat irritating.

It was not until 1969 that the route via Broken Hill to Perth was completely standardized, and in 1970 the Indian Pacific service was inaugurated, cutting the journey down to 3,961 km (2,461 miles) and a running time of just over two-and-a-half days. Since then, a standard-gauge line has been laid almost into Adelaide and, unlike European railway systems that would provide through cars, for use from Melbourne through Adelaide to Port Pirie to attach to the train, the Indian Pacific takes a lengthy and time-consuming side jaunt from near Crystal Brook to Keswick in the Adelaide suburbs and back. This must cause frustration to through passengers.

Today, after departing from the Sydney terminal at 14.55, the train is soon through Sydney's inner suburbs and at Blacktown is on the "speedway", a fairly straight and level run on which trains are known to attain their best speeds. After crossing the Hawkesbury River beyond Penrith, the train begins the climb into the Blue Mountains. The current route is the third ascent of the mountains, the first having been a zigzag. This starts as a cut on the side of a cliff face with spectacular views. A 1:60 grade is fairly consistent as far as Valley Heights, where the real climb begins. Originally, this was continuous 1:30 with numerous 8 chain (20 m/66 ft) radius curves, but most of these curves have been improved to better than 11 chains and the grade to 1:33. Spectacular views continue to the western descent. Beautiful rolling agricultural country continues as far as Parkes, but by now the train is running in darkness. From there it is semi-desert almost all the way to Perth.

● **ABOVE**
Prior to the standardization of the east-west route across Australia, most travellers would have preferred the journey through Melbourne to the slow narrow-gauge journey from Broken Hill in NSW to Port Pirie in South Australia. Now, having lost this traffic, Melbourne is still a very busy railway centre, as seen in this view of the approaches to Spencer Street station.

● **BELOW**
As in many parts of the world, Australia has seen a decline in rail passenger traffic in recent years. Thirty years ago, many of the major expresses, especially at holiday time, had to be run in several divisions to cope with the loading. The Overland, making the connection between Melbourne and Adelaide on the east-west route, was one such train. The second division is seen here crossing the Murray River Bridge.

BROKEN HILL TO SULPHIDE JUNCTION

Although passenger expresses tend to dominate railway enthusiasts' records, there is one goods train that has achieved an equal fame. This was simply known as the W-44 block ore concentrate train from Broken Hill to Sulphide Junction.

Although the South Australian Railways had been reaping the revenue from silver, lead and zinc ore haulage from the rich Broken Hill mines since 1888, the New South Wales Railway did not enter competition until 1927. This was at the same time that the east coast was joined to the isolated Menindee to Broken Hill line. Sulphide Corporation had already established zinc smelters at Cockle Creek, near Newcastle, and had been taking the Broken Hill ore by train over 400 km (249 miles) to Port Pirie in South Australia. They then shipped it another 2,000 km (1,243 miles) by sea to Newcastle for further transfer to Cockle Creek. The new line made it possible to take the ore by train 1,252 km

(778 miles) direct to the smelter.

The first part of this journey to be affected was the semi-desert area between Broken Hill and Parkes, where steam haulage was rapidly replaced by 49 Class Co-Co units. These 875 hp units were specially pressurized to keep out the

dust on this 679 km (422 mile) first stretch over hot and dusty plains. The block train consisted of 16-bogie concentrate wagons and a brake van totalling 1,036 tonnes, (1,020 tons) with a typical departure from Broken Hill at 11.30 for arrival at Parkes 03.24 the next

● **ABOVE**
A New South Wales 3644 assists Garratt 6014 with a heavy Western goods at Borenore in 1966. Seventy-five of the 4-6-0 (C)36 Class, known affectionately as "Pigs", were built for express passenger-traffic from 1925 but ended their days on express goods. The 42 (AD)60 Class Garratts were the main goods power at the end of steam.

● **LEFT**
The journey takes the traveller through the Blue Mountains National Park.

INFORMATION BOX

Termini	Broken Hill and Sulphide Junction
Country	Australia
Distance	1,252 km (778 miles)
Date of opening	1927

morning. Here the story changes as the diesel was replaced by a Garratt steam locomotive assisted by a "Standard Goods" Consolidation or a 36 Class 4-6-0 express locomotive relegated from passenger services. The train now faced a ruling grade of 1:60 to travel the 86 km (53 miles) to Molong in 3 hours and 20 minutes, arriving at 10.00. Here there was another change, as the assistant engine came off and was replaced by a modified Garratt. These modified units had enlarged cylinders, while the addition of duplicate controls allowed the crew to face the direction of running when working in reverse.

This new Garratt was attached with the bunker leading to remove the smoke nuisance later in the journey when working hard through the Marangaroo tunnel. At 10.35 the two monsters thundered through clouds of automotive dust towards the 1:40 grades *en route* to Orange East Folk. The modified Garratt then continued unaided to Bathers, received assistance up the Raglan Bank, and then went on alone again to Lithgow.

Lithgow is the beginning of the crossing of the Blue Mountains, and in earlier days the climb was started with a zigzag. This was replaced in 1911 by a double track through ten tunnels. Nevertheless, the start of the climb was 1:42 around an 8-chain (20 m/66 ft) curve, and prior to electrification heavy goods trains had two Standard Goods and NSW's most powerful non-articulated locomotive, the 57 Class Mountain,

leading, with a further Standard Goods pushing from the rear – a sight and sound never to be surpassed.

W-44 had two 49 Class electric locomotives over this stretch, with one coming off at Newnes Junction and the remaining unit continuing onwards. At Katoomba, at the top of the 1:33 descending grade, the train was stopped and grade-control valves set before a safe journey down the mountains could be started. These grade-control valves permitted only a very slow release of the Westinghouse Brakes, giving the locomotive time to recharge the air reservoirs between brake applications on the long descent. On joining the Main Northern Line, an additional 46 Class assisted to the then end of electrification at Gosford. At 01.24 a modified Garratt with Standard Goods assistance departed on the final leg of the journey, arriving at Sulphide Junction at 03.28.

- **ABOVE**
One of the many fine views of the Blue Mountains to be experienced on the journey to Sulphide Junction.

- **RIGHT**
The final leg of the journey for the block train was on the Main Northern Line, but this section was run in darkness. Here another goods service on the same route sees a 60 Class Garratt taking over from a 46 Class electric locomotive just north of Gosford yard.

FERNTREE GULLY TO GEMBROOK
PUFFING BILLY

The main routes radiating from the Victorian capital, Melbourne, were broad gauge. With the great depression of the 1890s, the Victorian government sought cheaper ways of handling the traffic in remoter parts of the State, with the result that four branch lines were built to 760 mm gauge for these areas. However, with the double handling of all freight and the coming of motor road vehicles, these lines soon became liabilities. Cutbacks and closures commenced in 1944, with services no longer running to Walhalla, and the final closure was that of the Beech Forest line in 1962.

The line from Upper Ferntree Gully to Gembrook was closest to Melbourne and became a popular tourist entry to

the Dandenong Ranges. However, following several landslides about 10 km (6 miles) from Upper Ferntree Gully, railway services were abandoned from August 1953. The 29 km (18 mile) line had first been opened in December

INFORMATION BOX

PUFFING BILLY

Termini	Ferntree Gully and Gembrook
Country	Australia
Distance	29 km (18 miles)
Date of opening	1900

The Puffing Billy
Preservation Society's
2-6-2T locomotive No.
7A crossing a curved
wooden viaduct
shortly after leaving
Belgrave in Victoria,
while hauling one of
its regular tourist
services into the
Dandenong Ranges.

● OPPOSITE
BELOW
There are many types
of plants and flowers
which can be seen
from the train. One of
these is the Olinda
Rhodendron.

● OPPOSITE
AND BELOW
Animals can also be
seen such as the koala
and the kangaroo.

1900, and with a speed limit of 24 kph
(15 mph) the journey took two-and-a-
quarter hours.

However, in December 1954, a
Melbourne newspaper sponsored trips
between Upper Ferntree Gully and
Belgrave, about 5 km (3 miles) away, and
following public demand further trips
were run. In Easter of the following year,
the Puffing Billy Preservation Society was
formed with the aim of ensuring the
retention of the fan trips. These lasted
until February 1958 when, with the
expansion of the Melbourne
Metropolitan area, the Government
decided to widen the gauge to Belgare
and electrify the line.

The volunteers of the PBPS again
went into battle to attempt to restore and
re-open the balance of the abandoned
line. Through the work of the volunteers,
aided by the 3rd Field Engineer
Regiment of the Citizen Military Forces,
scouts etc., a new station and locomotive
depot was built at Belgrave and the line
restored to Menzies Creek, about 5 km
(3 miles) away. This included a 2-chain
(20 m/66 ft) radius deviation around the
landslide, which had caused the closure

of the line. Services recommenced in July
1962, and the society also established a
museum at Menzies Creek.

Since then the society has grown in
leaps and bounds, and work is in progress
from both ends to complete the line once
again to Gembrook. Passenger-traffic is
heavy and growing, with most of it being
handled by NA Class 2-6-2T locomotives,
an 1898 American Baldwin design,
although later engines of the same design
were built locally. Also serviceable is a

former timber line Climax, but this is too
slow for regular traffic. The society owns
a Victorian Railways narrow-gauge
Garratt, and a South African Garratt has
recently been acquired for conversion to
760 mm gauge to handle the growing
traffic. New carriages are currently being
built, so there is certainly confidence in
the future. A Taiwanese Shay has been
acquired for the museum, as well as a
large variety of narrow-gauge locomotives
from over Australia, which makes a visit
well worth while.

The route has a ruling grade of 1:30,
limiting the load of the NA Class
locomotives to 90 tonnes. Tight curves
abound, and much of the country is
heavily timbered. In places the suburban
sprawl can be seen, and later a few farms.
From Menzies Creek, the line descends
to Clematis, once known as Paradise
Valley, an area of rolling fields and stately
homes, before the downhill run takes it
to the banks of Emerald Lake and
Lakeside, the current terminus for the
tourist services. Unfortunately this part
of Victoria has been subject to some
disastrous bush fires, but the railway has
survived and continues to progress.

ZEEHAN TO STRAHAN
A WEST COAST SAFARI

Though the smallest state of Australia, Tasmania probably has the greatest variety of scenery, and any traveller thinking of assessing the State in a few days has much to learn. The north-west coast has a very English atmosphere about it, but heading southwards along the west coast we find rain forest in rugged mountainous country cut by deep ravines. This wild country, however, has meant more to Tasmania's economy than the rest of the State, for the area is rich in minerals, possessing huge deposits of tin, lead, silver, gold, copper and iron ores. As it is difficult country for road construction, access to the deposits was generally achieved by tramways or railways.

In its day Mount Bischoff was the largest tin mine in the world, and the Van Diemens Land Company connected the

area to Burnie with a horse tramway in 1878. This was soon converted to a 1,067 mm gauge railway, the first 59 km (37 miles) now being the northern end of the private Emu Bay Railway.

Galena (lead sulphide) deposits were found at Zeehan, and transport for the silver was also needed. The Government was finally persuaded to construct a line to the coastal port of Strahan, and in 1892 this 46 km (28 mile) line with a ruling gauge of 1:40 was opened.

Meanwhile, huge copper ore deposits had been found at Mount Lyell, and by

● **ABOVE**
The Mt Lyell Mining & Railway Company's line connecting their copper mine in Tasmania with the coast was through lush rain forest. This is a passenger's view ahead shortly before the line closed in 1963.

● **BELOW LEFT**
Tourists inspect the push-up engine, while the lead engine fills its tanks at the summit at Rinadeena.

● **BELOW RIGHT**
From the left, a tourist bus waits on a flat wagon to be shunted on to the train; a hired Tasmanian Railways diesel–mechanical locomotive waits with a goods-train bound for Zeehan; No. 6, an immaculate Dübs 4-8-0, and an Australian Standard Garratt waits with a goods-train that will follow behind.

INFORMATION BOX

Termini	Zeehan and Strahan
Country	Australia
Distance	46 km (28 miles)
Date of opening	1892

● RIGHT
One of the problems leading to the closure of the Mt Lyell railway in Tasmania was the cost of maintenance on the "quarter mile bridge" over the King River, seen here being crossed by a Drewry diesel locomotive.

1899 the Mt Lyell Mining and Railway Company had constructed a tortuous but very scenic 34 km (21 mile) line of which 7 km (4¹/₂ miles) was operated on 1:16 and 1:20 grades on the Abt rack principle to Regatta Point near Strahan, a journey of two hours' duration. The Emu Bay Railway, seeing business potential in this area, pushed their line southwards through dense forests and over various streams to reach Zeehan, 142 km (88 miles) from Burnie, in 1901.

As the Government had connected Strahan to Regatta Point in 1900, it was then possible to travel all the way from Burnie on the north-west coast to Mount Lyell, using three different carriers. Owing to the light track, speeds were seldom in excess of 16 kph (10 mph), but in 1912 when a fire, caused by arsonists, occurred in the Mount Lyell mine with 170 men underground, the train racing breathing apparatus, rescue equipment and personnel to the mine cut

five hours off the journey, resulting in the saving of many lives.

The copper and barytes from Mount Lyell was loaded on to shipping at Regatta Point, and the silver from Zeehan went on the Emu Bay railway, leaving the government line to decline rapidly, operated by one locomotive and a railcar. The line closed in 1960.

Tourism was growing on the west coast and the Mount Lyell Railway, probably the most scenic in Australia

with its rack line over mountainous rain forest country and the King River gorge alongside, soon attracted its share. Unfortunately the owners and the Government still decided to close the line in 1963. Today, eight diesel-hydraulic locomotives coupled together bring in Mount Lyell ore between Zeehan and Roseberry. Tour trains periodically travel the line, and a Dübs locomotive is currently under restoration with a view to recreating the "West Coaster" express.

● RIGHT
Just north of Rosebery on the Emu Bay Railway in Tasmania was the Pieman River bridge, here being crossed by a tourist special of Tasmanian Railway's coaches in their "blood and custard" colours being hauled by a 10 Class BBR diesel-hydraulic loco-motive during Easter 1965. With the damming of the river for hydro-electric purposes, the line has since been deviated to higher ground and a new bridge built.

PACIFIC COAST MOTORAIL

Since surfing became fashionable, a section of over 30 km (19 miles) of the Australian coastline just north of the New South Wales border from Coolangatta to Southport has been developed into the major holiday destination in Australia. Known as the Gold Coast, it caters for almost all levels of society, the temperate climate allowing it to be a resort all the year round.

Queenslanders had had access by a narrow-gauge train for many years, but, owing to the slow service, buses soon won this traffic and the line closed. However, with the Brisbane suburban electrification, a new line is being opened along part of the length of the coast.

The big influx of tourists come from the south – New South Wales and Victoria – though direct transport has been slow in coming to feed this area. Prior to the mid-1920s, Sydneysiders had to travel north to Brisbane by the main northern line, which crossed to the west

of the Great Dividing Range. Then they continued to the Queensland border, well inland from the coast, where a change was made to the narrow gauge to cross the Great Divide again and descend to Brisbane, where another train was caught to the Gold Coast.

The Clarence River was the main obstacle to a coastal journey. An isolated section of railway had been built from Lismore via Byron Bay to Murwillumbah, about 32 km (20 miles) south of the

border on the coast, prior to the turn of the century, but it was not until 1924 that the two sections of coastal line faced each other across the Clarence River at Grafton and a train ferry service was introduced. Although the standard-gauge track reached Brisbane in September 1930, the ferry continued until May 1932, when a double-deck road-rail bridge was built over the river.

The Department of Railways, however, did not see an early need for

● **ABOVE**
Hauled by two 442 Class locomotives, the Pacific Coast Motorail heads north from Lismore. The locomotives and the sitting cars at the end of the train are in a short-lived "candy" colour scheme, while the power car and sleeping cars are of stainless steel.

● **LEFT**
With the elimination of almost all locomotive hauled passenger-trains in NSW, the Pacific Coast Motorail was superseded by the XPTs. Here an XPT charges through regrowth timber country near Bonville in northern New South Wales.

● **RIGHT**
The 1990s saw the introduction of XPT inter-city services, speeding up the timetable considerably. Not only was the speed limit raised to 160 kph (100 mph) but also many of the smaller stopping-places were closed. Here we see a southbound XPT crossing Boambee Creek between the coastal resorts of Coffs Harbour and Sawtell.

● **BELOW**
The southbound Pacific Coast Motorail approaching Lismore.

more direct traffic to the Gold Coast, and intending travellers had to catch the Brisbane Express and change trains at the crack of dawn for a branch-line service to Murwillumbah, where a bus would complete the journey. Eventually the traffic potential of the holiday seekers was realized, and in the early 1970s a through service to Murwillumbah was introduced, which included car carriers for those wishing to travel around the extensive holiday area. This was known as the Gold Coast Motorail.

Whether owing to interstate jealousies or a desire to promote the northern coast of New South Wales, in the 1980s the train also unloaded cars *en route* at Casino and was renamed the Pacific Coast

Motorail. Today, with the almost complete elimination of locomotive-hauled passenger-trains, this service has gone. Now an XPT service runs the route, with a bus connection at Murwillumbah.

The Motorail service, with sleeping cars, departed Sydney at 06.25 with the

INFORMATION BOX	
Termini	Sydney and Murwillumbah
Country	Australia
Length	935 km (581 miles)
Date of opening	1932

first light of dawn creeping over at somewhere near Coffs Harbour. Here the mountains come almost to the coast, and the huge banana plantations, which cover the hillsides, could be seen from the train between the various tunnels.

The train turned inland and ran through hilly and well-timbered country northwards to reach South Grafton, a former meal-stop, where it crossed the river and continued north through undulating timber country to the town of Casino. Then came Byron Bay, the easternmost point of Australia. Further north, sugar cane country was entered, before the train finally descended to the Tweed River at Murwillumbah, where it arrived at 13.05.

CHRISTCHURCH TO GREYMOUTH
THE TRANSALPINE ROUTE

New Zealand is not well known for its railways. This is a shame, as some of the scenery traversed is the equal of anywhere else. The 233 km (145 mile) long Midland line is probably the most scenic route in New Zealand. Construction, by the English-financed New Zealand Midland Railway Company, commenced in 1885.

Unfortunately progress was slow and after ten years, with only about 60 km (37 miles) in service, the Government took possession of the line and continued its construction. In those days, with limited engineering equipment available, the most difficult task was the boring of the tunnel section from Arthur's Pass to Otira. After much consideration of alternative ways of crossing the mountain range this 8.6 km (5½ mile) long tunnel, with a descent at 1:33 from Arthur's Pass to Otira, was started in August 1908, but was only opened almost 15 years to the day later on 4 August 1923.

It had been a very difficult bore, with World War I adding to the problems that nature imposed. At the time of its

● **LEFT**
Between Otira and Arthur's Pass on the Transalpine route is an 8.6 km (5½ mile) long tunnel on a 1:33 grade. To assist trains through the tunnel, three Toshiba Bo-Bo electric loco-motives working in multiple are used through the tunnel. At Arthur's Pass the threesome prepare for the next journey.

opening, this tunnel was claimed to be the seventh longest in the world. With such a steep grade in such a long tunnel, working heavy trains through by steam was most uncomfortable, not to say dangerous, and so the tunnel was electrified at 1,500 volts d.c., and five Bo-Bo locomotives were imported from the English Electric Company.

This tunnel, however, was not the only one along the route. Another 16 tunnels occur in a very short section near Staircase along the scenic gorge of the

Waimakiri River, as do many spectacular viaducts and bridges, and a further two tunnels at the western end of the line.

Commencing a journey from Christchurch, a little over the first hour of the trip is spent travelling over the Canterbury Plains *en route* to Springfield, 71 km (44 miles) away. From here the Alps come into view and the line follows the Waimakariri River in its spectacular gorge. Four large viaducts and 16 tunnels are features of the next section to Avoca, 97 km (60 miles) from Christchurch. Soon mountain ranges become visible, and the line parts company with the Waimakariri River a little before Cora Lynn, 125 km (78 miles) from the start of the journey.

From here the train enters Arthur's Pass National Park, a popular tourist destination throughout the year. Arthur's

● **LEFT**
In 1923, to make more bearable the passage through the 8.6 km (5½ mile) long Otira tunnel, with its 1:33 grade, New Zealand Railways electrified the tunnel. With the original electric locomotives worn out, five replacement Bo-Bo units of 1286 hp were obtained from Toshiba in Japan. Normally these locomotives worked in threes, one being spare and one in the workshops for servicing. Here they are seen at the Arthur's Pass end of the tunnel.

The Transalpine route across the South Island follows the Waimakariri River for a considerable portion of the journey. This view is taken from the train.

INFORMATION BOX

Termini	Christchurch and Greymouth
Country	New Zealand
Distance	233 km (145 miles)
Date of opening	1923

Pass station, at an elevation of 737 m (2,418 ft), is the highest station in the South Island of New Zealand. Once through the Otira tunnel, rivers and lakes are a feature of the continuing scenery. Coral mining activity is evident near the west coast, as the gold rush that sparked interest in the west coast never really happened. At Greymouth, on the west coast, the present-day journey ends some 4 hours and 25 minutes after leaving Christchurch.

From 1939, in steam days, much of

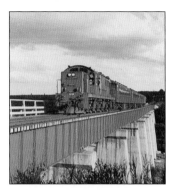

the traffic was handled by New Zealand's most powerful non-articulated locomotives, the Kb Class. Through the Otira tunnel the trains were hauled, generally triple-headed, by electric Eo Class locomotives. These old electrics were replaced in 1968 by five new Toshiba units, which are also worked with three coupled together. Steam had now been replaced by Mitsubishi diesel-electrics with a Bo-Bo-Bo wheel arrangement. These units are powered by Caterpillar diesels and are rated at 670kV.

● **ABOVE RIGHT**
Diesel electric locomotive Dj-1218 crossing the Kowai viaduct. This is the first viaduct on the Transalpine route, just before the railway enters the Waimakariri gorge.

● **RIGHT**
Dj 1218 hauls a tourist train across the Broken River viaduct on the Transalpine route. The view on one side of the train is unfortunately blocked out by the windshield needed to prevent trains being blown off the bridge in bad weather.

CHRISTCHURCH TO WELLINGTON – THE COASTAL PACIFIC EXPRESS

The route from Christchurch to Wellington travels through spectacular scenery which is the equal of anywhere else in the world. In 1991, there were only long-distance passenger services operating over five routes, and only one of these, Wellington to Auckland, had more than one train each way per day. In addition, Auckland and Wellington have commuter railways, the latter electrified. Subsequently, New Zealand Railways (NZR) has been taken over by Wisconsin Rail of the USA (who have also taken over most of the UK freight operation under the name English, Welsh & Scottish Railways).

This train journey is from Christchurch to Wellington by the Coastal Pacific Express. More accurately, it goes to Picton, from where the railway-owned inter-island ferry must be taken to reach Wellington. This journey exemplifies the problem facing long-haul services in New Zealand, for it takes nine-and-a-half hours by rail and boat, but only one hour by air. There is only

● **ABOVE**
The old "colonial" style is nicely represented in this street in Christchurch.

● **BELOW**
The sea reflects the blue of the sky in this placid scene near Christchurch.

limited consolation in the fact that the roads are not much quicker.

The journey starts from Christchurch station, a big 1960s building on a large site, both echoing the past rather than the drastically reduced present. Two of NZR's other passenger services also start from here, the Trans-Alpine Express going over Arthur's Pass in the New Zealand Alps to Greymouth and the Southerner Express to Dunedin and Invercargill.

Christchurch was home to one of the four areas of electrified railways in New Zealand, the short and now dieselized route through the tunnel to the nearest port at Lyttelton. The other electrified sections, all remaining, are the summit tunnel at Arthur's Pass, the central section of the Wellington to Auckland main line (the North Island Trunk) and the Wellington suburban network.

The Coastal Pacific follows the South Island Trunk, as it hugs the eastern side of the South Island. This line took a long time to build, as it was affected not only by the difficult terrain to be crossed, but

● **RIGHT**
Diesel locomotive DF 6162 at the head of the
Coastal Pacific Express at Kaikoura. Thirty
1,230 kW locomotives was delivered by
General Motors Canada in 1979–80.

also by various communities each
preferring different routes. The current
general route was decided upon in 1883,
although the first section along this route
had been opened in 1872. The final
detail of the route was revised several
times until the late 1930s. The through
route was only completed in December
1945, when the section between
Parnassus and Wharanui was opened.
The further delays had been brought
about by two world wars and economic
depressions, both local and global. The
track is laid to 3 ft 6 in Cape Gauge,
although some early sections had been
laid initially with a gauge of 5 ft 3 in.
Although only around 100 km (60 miles)
of the 348 km (216 miles) is by the sea,
it is visions of the rugged scenery on this
section that remain in the mind of the
rail traveller.

The railborne part of the journey
takes 5 hours and 20 minutes to reach
Picton, where there is a 50-minute
connection into the "Interislander" ferry.

● **ABOVE**
South-east of Blenheim there are views from
the train of Cook Strait, with the North Island
visible in the distance. The railway curves
around to pass through the cutting in the
centre of the picture.

● **LEFT**
A view of coastline from the train south of
Kaikoura. The route of the railway and coastal
road can be seen hugging the coastline around
the promontory.

INFORMATION BOX

Termini	Christchurch and Wellington
Country	New Zealand
Distance	348 km (216 miles)
Date of opening	1945

● LEFT
Diesel shunting locomotive DSJ 4032 at Picton.
This class of five locomotives was designed by
Toshiba in Japan, where the first one was built.
The other four were erected from imported parts
in NZR's Addington workshops in 1984.

of the line and various sites to be seen
from the train. Cream teas are available
as part of the food service, along with
cold snacks and a bar service. This
innovation obviated the need for the
trains to make long stops at certain
stations to allow passengers to visit the
refreshment rooms, a practice that had
continued right up until introduction of
the Coastal Pacific.

Leaving Christchurch, the route
crosses flat farmland before entering the
rolling hill country of North Canterbury.

The train consists of three coaches and a
baggage van hauled by a DF Class diesel
locomotive. The coaches are a batch of
vehicles modernized for what amount to
tourist services introduced in September
1988 by enlarging the windows, covering
the seats with lambswool, installing a
public address system etc. They were
painted in the long-distance passenger-
coach livery of blue with red-and-white
stripes. There is a hostess aboard the
train, giving a commentary on the history

● RIGHT
Gorse frequently
provides a startling
splash of colour on
the journey to
Christchurch.

● BELOW
The Cook Strait lives
up to its reputation
for rough seas.

The foothills of the central mountain
range are visible almost immediately.
Soon the traveller becomes aware of a
recurring feature of the journey, the
crossing of the estuaries of rivers flowing
down from the Southern Alps into the
Pacific Ocean. Some of these estuaries
are very wide and require long viaducts
to take the railway across. The Ashley
River, 35 km (22 miles) from
Christchurch and the second river
crossing, is one of the longest at 549 m
(1,801 ft). After around 80 km (50
miles), the train reaches the highest point
on the line, 135 m (443 ft) above sea
level, at Spye. Just before Parnassus, the
706 m (2,316 ft) bridge crossing the
Waiau River is the longest on this route.

● **RIGHT**
Picton station
building. Note the
old railway vans
being given a new
lease of life off
the track.

The Pacific coastal section, between Claverley and Wharanui is very attractive, hugging the rocky shore and including 20 tunnels in its 100 km (60 miles). The statistics for this stretch of line (plus the stretch to Parnassus) give some idea of the work involved – there are 43 bridges totalling 3.2 km (2 miles) in length; 2.9 million cubic metres (102 million cubic feet) of rock and spoil had to be excavated; and between Goose Bay and Kowhai the road had to be extended over the beach to make way for the railway. Hawkeswood cutting, just north of Parnassus is, at over one kilometre (^{2}⁄$_3$ mile) long and up to 19 m (62 ft) deep, the largest in New Zealand. It is near here that the train passes from Canterbury into Marlborough on crossing the Conway River.

After leaving the coast, the railway crosses the salt lakes of Lake Grasmere on a causeway. The section on to Blenheim includes a double-deck viaduct

● **LEFT**
DX 5500 stands at
the head of a short
main-line train with
coaches in an
attractive blue
livery. Behind it, in
this scene at
Wellington, is the
"Silver Fern"
express railcar.

near Seddon to cross the Awatere River, where the railway track takes the top deck, and the road takes the lower.

After Blenheim the line passes into one of New Zealand's major wine-producing areas. A little way north of Blenheim is the 293 m (961 ft) bridge across the Wairau River. The stretch through hills to Picton crosses the 129 m (423 ft) Waitohi viaduct, once the largest timber trestle bridge in the country, but now a concrete bridge. Picton, a small town that has flourished as a result of being the port for the inter-island ferry, is approached on a 1:37 gradient, the steepest on the route. This gradient is a result of the town's picturesque setting, surrounded by large hills, which form a major barrier for the railway.

Most stations no longer have freight facilities as a result of transport deregulation in the 1980s, and rail business is now dominated by container traffic. The increasing power available from newer locomotives is allowing an increase in train weights and a reduction

in the number of services.

The inter-island roll-on, roll-off ferries were introduced in 1962, with management passing to NZR in 1971. This service is marketed as the "Interislander". The four crossings each way per day carry road and rail vehicles and form an integral part of the New

Zealand railways freight network.

The port of Picton is a fair way from the open sea, on a side fjord off the Queen Charlotte Sound. While this does not have the towering mountainsides that the name suggests – for that one should visit Milford Sound on the south-west corner of the South Island – the hilly

country around the watercourse is attractive. Nearer the sea, seals can often be seen sunning themselves on the rocks.

The boat journey across the Cook Strait takes 3 hours and 20 minutes for the 52 nautical miles (96 km). One of the ferries used is the *Aratika*, originally built in France in 1974 as a train ferry but converted in 1976 to carry cars and passengers along with rail wagons.

While the approach to Wellington is by no means as scenic as the departure from Picton, it gives a different view of the city, the central area of which is steep enough to warrant a (Swiss-built) funicular. Foot passengers are met on the quay at Wellington by the "Interislander" shuttle bus and taken to the bus station outside Wellington railway station.

Anyone visiting New Zealand should try to make time to travel the Coastal Pacific Express. The scenery alone is worth the time; the glimpses of the "real" New Zealand, away from the tourist areas, are a bonus.

● **ABOVE**
The impressive rocky coastline at Castle Point near Wellington is a popular spot for visitors.

● **BELOW**
The attractive coastline near Wellington is further embellished by a geyser.

PICTON TO CHRISTCHURCH
THE COASTAL PACIFIC EXPRESS

● **BELOW LEFT**
Centre cab shunters exchange wagons
between ship and shore.

Historically, the important commercial
centre of Wellington, on New Zealand's
North Island, has been linked to the city
of Christchurch – seat of provincial
government and gateway to the vast
agricultural hinterland of Canterbury –
on the South Island, by a network of
coastal steamers.

The first proposal for a rail line to join
the two was mooted in 1861. A broad-
gauge line was commenced northwards
under the auspices of the Provincial
Government in 1872. It was later
converted to 3 ft 6 in gauge in 1877. A
line southwards from Picton was opened
in 1875. Further construction followed
as resources and political decisiveness
permitted, but, even by 1916, the
northern line had reached only so far as
Wharanui, 90 km (56 miles) from
Picton, while the southern section
penetrated as far as Parnassus, 133 km
(83 miles) from Christchurch. It was to
be another 20 years before meaningful

INFORMATION BOX	
THE COASTAL PACIFIC EXPRESS	
Termini	Picton and Christchurch
Country	New Zealand
Distance	rail 348 km (216 miles); sea crossing 80 km (50 miles)
Date of opening	1945

progress was made in closing the gap,
through the fearsome mountainous
terrain around Kaikoura. The line
opened throughout officially on
15 December 1945.

In 1954, a rail roll-on, roll-off ferry
altered the connecting sea crossing and,
in 1988, the service was transformed by
the introduction of rebuilt rolling stock.
The trip provides four main features of

● **LEFT**
No. 6110 at the head
of the southbound
Coastal Pacific
Express at Picton.
The locomotive is a
DF Class Co-Co
built by General
Motors, Canada, in
1979 and is rated at
1250 kW.

● **RIGHT**
Atanaga, an "Interislander" ferry, makes an impressive sight as she proceeds up the now sheltered waters toward Picton, South Island.

interest. After the sea crossing, memorable in itself, comes the ride through the hills of Marlborough, followed by the exhilarating passage through the harsher mountains around Kaikoura with the Pacific Ocean as an intimate companion, and finally the gentler landscape leading towards Canterbury Plain.

After the passage across the exposed waters of the Cook Strait, one enters the comparatively sheltered area of the Marlborough Sound. Here there is a multitude of islands and islets, some little more than wave-washed rocks, others massive crags or verdant mounds. Wildlife is abundant.

The final passage to the port in its sheltered setting is almost serene after the earlier bluster. The community of Picton, with its jetty, rail and freight yards and low-rise housing, is dominated by the surrounding ridges and peaks, not unlike a port serving the Western Isles of Scotland.

One can watch the unloading and loading of railway traffic from the ferry if one wishes or, perhaps more prudently,

● **LEFT**
Even in the partial shelter of Marlborough Sound, islets and cliffs are assaulted by wave and wind.

● **BELOW LEFT**
The deep cutting in Dashwood Pass is seen from further up the line. It forms part of an 8 km (5 mile), 1:53 climb.

retrieve one's baggage from the somewhat unsupervised free-for-all below. Once rightful ownership is secured, there is time to survey the train that will provide the rest of the journey.

The concept of a "luxury" service on the route had followed the successful introduction of a similar service between Christchurch and Greymouth through the alpine scenery of South Island. Several existing coaches were converted, receiving large (2 m x 1 m; 6 ft 6 in x 1 ft 4 in) panoramic windows, separated by narrow pillars, that provide excellent visibility. The seats, which face each other in pairs across a large snack table either side of the central aisle, have high backs and are sumptuously furnished in sheepskin. Wall to wall carpeting, large ventilators, curtains and an effective public address system furnish an attractive environment. Internal colours are pink and grey, while the external livery is mid-blue relieved by white-and-red bands. A buffet car provides both snacks and a full bar service. Uniformed attendants and a well-informed

● LEFT
Road and rail share the narrow coastal strip
between Pacific breakers and mountains,
which proved such an obstacle to the
construction of the line.

another long ascent, this time towards
the bleaker regions of Dashwood Pass,
the 8 km (5 mile) 1:53 climb being
presaged by a sweeping horseshoe curve.
The mountains here are softened by the
effects of the elements into smooth folds
rather than pronounced peaks, the more
sheltered pockets offering a refuge for
isolated clumps of low trees.

Another grade takes the train to the
unusual bridge over the Awatere River.
This is a combination bridge with the
railway carried on an upper deck and the
road below. The next point of note on
the trip is Blind River, the site of the
worst crash on the line in 1948 when six
people were killed. The train then crosses
over a long causeway, the vast salt lakes
on the approach to Lake Grasmere.

Near Wharanui, the long stretch of
coastal running begins. From here the
traveller can enjoy some one-and-a-half
hours of superb scenery before the stop
at Kaikoura. For much of the way, railway
and road are squeezed into a narrow strip
between beach and mountain. In the
approximately 100 km (62 miles) of line
to Oaro there are 20 tunnels, numerous
embankments and steep cuttings, sharp
curves and lonely bridges, of which there
are more than 40 along the central
section of line. One stretch of track,
known as the "Blue Slip", is notorious
for the highly unstable nature of the
ground through which it passes in
cutting: the local rock of blue pug
absorbs water easily, and the whole
hillside is heading slowly for the sea.

As gullies come down to the sea and
the train speeds on, there are glimpses of
remote valleys, sheltering between
flowing hills and rising gently to more
majestic and mysterious mountains. The
sinuous course of the line, which follows
the indentations of the sea, is interrupted

conductor making sensible use of the PA
all add to the ambience of the journey.

Once everyone is aboard, the train
winds out of Picton and commences a
steep 1:37 climb, and rumbles across the
sweeping 129 m (423 ft) Waitohi
viaduct. The town, itself originally known
as Waitohi, is overshadowed by tumbling
tree-clad foothills, jumbled peaks and the
waters of the sound. By Elevation, 4 km
(2½ miles) from Picton, the mountains
take on an Italianate or Austrian alpine

air, with strands of conifer and dusty
logging tracks, but the pastures below
with their scattered specimen trees owe
more to English parkland, albeit with
trees unfamiliar to visitors.

Before Blenheim, the train passes the
blue waters and gravel banks of the
Wairau on a long low bridge. Blenheim
itself serves as the gateway to the
increasingly well-known wine growing
regions of Marlborough. Beyond
Blenheim, the train commences yet

● **RIGHT**
Passengers take the opportunity to stretch
their legs during the stop at the attractive
intermediate station of Kaikoura.

as Kaikoura – its name is said to be from
the Maori *kai* (food) and *koura* (crayfish)
– is approached. This fishing centre and
former whaling community lies on a
peninsula about half-way between Picton
and Christchurch.

Here the train pauses long enough for
passengers to alight from the train and
stretch their legs, a reminder of when it
needed to stop for refreshments.
Onboard buffet facilities now make such
an extended halt redundant, but the old
building is still there and retains much of
its former charm.

Leaving the town on another curving
viaduct, there is a further period of
spectacular coastal running with a stretch
of line with nine tunnels in as many
kilometres. Beyond Oaro, at sea level
again, the train climbs steeply and
encounters the almost kilometre (^{2}/$_3$
mile) long tunnel at Amuri Bluff and the
adjacent Okarahia viaduct. Soon the
suburbs of Christchurch come into view
and this spectacular journey is sadly over.

● **ABOVE**
RIGHT
Canterbury has seen
many architectural
styles, and as yet
traffic has not
reached the urban
levels found
elsewhere.

● **OPPOSITE**
Clumps of low trees
find sheltered
pockets in the
windswept hills
beyond Blenheim.

● **RIGHT**
The ferry port of
Picton on South
Island nestles in the
lee of mountains at
the head of
Marlborough
Sound.

GLOSSARY

Articulation
The connection of two or more parts of the otherwise rigid frame using pivots, to increase flexibility and allow the locomotive to take sharper curves.

Axleloading
The weight imposed on the track by the locomotive's heaviest pair of wheels.

Bar-frame
A structure of girders, instead of steel plates, on which the wheels and boiler are mounted.

Big three
Baldwin, Alco and Lima, the three principal builders of locomotives in America.

Bogie
A truck with a short wheelbase at the front of the locomotive, pivoted from the main frame.

Brick arch
An arch of firebricks in the firebox, which deflects the hot gases and distributes them evenly among the flue tubes.

Caprotti valve-gear
A locomotive valve-gear for regulating the intake and emission of steam. It uses two pairs of valves operated by cams whose angle can be varied to adjust the cut-off.

Class
A category of locomotives built to a specific design.

Compound locomotive
A locomotive in which the expansion of the steam is carried out in two stages, first in a high-pressure and then in a low-pressure cylinder, arranged in series.

Condensing locomotive
A type of locomotive used in areas where water is not easily available, in which exhaust steam is condensed and recycled as feedwater for the boiler.

Conjugated valve-gear
An arrangement in three-cylinder locomotives by which the valve-gear of the inside cylinder is worked by a system of levers connected to those of the outside cylinders.

Coupled wheels
The driving wheels together with the wheels joined to them by the coupling-rod. This arrangement enables the power to be spread over several wheels, thereby reducing wheel-slip.

Cowcatcher
A semi-vertical plate or grid above the rails at the front of the locomotive designed to push obstructions off the tracks in order to prevent derailments. Called a "pilot" in America.

Cross-stretcher
A girder or plate joining the main plates of the frame to give rigidity.

Cut-off
The point in the piston stroke at which the admission of steam is stopped.

Cylinder
One of two, three or four chambers in the locomotive, each containing a piston, which is forced backwards and forwards by the admission of high-pressure steam alternately on each side of it through steam ports controlled by valves.

Diagram
The work schedule of the locomotive.

Double-header
A train pulled by two locomotives.

Firebox
The part of the boiler that contains the fire, with a grate at the bottom; the sides and top are surrounded by water spaces.

Fireless locomotive
A locomotive with a boiler charged with steam from a separate source.

Footplate
The floor of the cab on which the crew stands, or the running-plate.

Frame
The structure of plates or girders that supports the boiler and wheels.

Franco-Crosti boiler
A boiler with a pre-heater drum to heat the feedwater, by means of exhaust steam and hot gases piped from the smokebox.

Gauge
The size of the track, measured between the insides of the rails.

Grate area
The interior size of the firebox at grate level, used as a measure of steam-raising capability.

Heating surface
The total surface area of the firebox, flue tubes and superheater elements.

Outside-frame
A locomotive class in which the frame is outside the coupled wheels.

Outside valve-gear
A locomotive class in which the mechanism for opening and closing the steam admission valves lies outside the frame.

Piston valve
A valve for controlling steam admission and exhaust in the form of two short pistons, attached to a valve rod, which operate over steam ports with a cylindrical profile.

Plate frame
The main frame of the locomotive consists of two thick steel plates, slotted to accommodate the axleboxes of the driving and coupled wheels.

Route availability
The tracks available to any class of locomotive, determined by its weight and other dimensions.

Running-plate
The footway that runs around the sides and front of the boiler.

Saddle-tank
A saddle-tank or saddleback locomotive has a tank that straddles the boiler.

Side tank
A tank locomotive with its tanks on the main frame at each side of the locomotive.

Slide valve
A valve for controlling steam admission and exhaust shaped like a rectangular lid.

Smokebox
The front section of the boiler, through which hot gases from the fire escape through the chimney and exhaust steam is expelled through the blastpipe below. The door at the front allows cinders to be cleared out.

Superheater
Superheater elements subject the steam to an extra heating on its way to the cylinders, so that even though its temperature drops in the cylinders it will remain sufficiently hot not to condense.

Tank locomotive
A locomotive that carries its fuel and water in bunkers and tanks attached to the main frame, not in a separate tender.

Tracking
A term describing the locomotive's ability to negotiate curved or irregular track.

Tractive effort (TE)
The force that the wheel treads of a locomotive exert against the rails: a measure of pulling-power.

Type
A category of locomotives conforming in function and basic layout, including wheel arrangement.

Valve-gear
The linkage connecting the valves of the locomotive to the crankshaft.

Vertical cylinder
A locomotive in which the cylinders are mounted in a vertical position.

Walschaert's valve-gear
A valve-gear co-operated by a link, which is rocked to and fro by a return crank connected to the piston rod and a combination lever connecting the crosshead and the radius rod.

Wheel arrangements
The various combinations of leading, coupled and trailing axles are described by a three-figure formula known as the Whyte notation. The first figure refers to the leading wheels, the second to the coupled wheels and the final figure to the supporting wheels.

ADDRESSES

Your national tourist office may be able to give details of rail travel and visa requirements.

Albania
Hekurudhat Shqiptare
Ministria e Transporteve
Tirana
Tel:(42) 32389/62503
Fax:(42) 34647

Australia
Australian National Railways Commission
1 Richmond Road
Keswick
SA 5035
Tel:(8) 8217 4321
Fax:(8) 8217 4609

Puffing Billy Railway
PO Box 451
Belgrave
Victoria 3160
Tel:(3) 9754 6800
Fax:(3) 9754 2513

Brazil
Rede Ferroviaria Federal SA
Praça Procópio Ferreira 86
CEP 20224
Rio de Janeiro
Tel:(21) 291 2185
Fax:(21) 233 3040

Canada
Canadian Pacific
Windsor Station
Peel Street
PO Box 6042
Montreal
Quebec H3C 3E4
Tel:(514) 395 5135
Fax:(514) 395 5132

Leisurail
PO Box 113
Peterborough
United Kingdom
PE3 8HY
Tel:(1733) 335599
Fax:(1733) 505451

Algoma Central Railway Inc
PO Box 130
129 Bay Street
Sault Ste Marie 20
Ontario P6A 6Y2
Tel:(705) 946 7300
Fax:(705) 541 2989

Chile
Empresa de los Ferrocarriles del Estado
Av Libertador Bernardo O'Higgins 3322
Santiago
Tel:(2) 779 0707
Fax:(2) 776 2609

China
China Railway Foreign Service Corporation
PO Box 2495
Beijing
Tel:(10) 632 22265

Ecuador
Empresa Nacional de Ferrocarriles del Estado
Calle Bolivar 443
Quito
Tel:(2) 210262

Egypt
Egyptian National Railways
Ramses Bldg
Ramses Square
Cairo 11652
Tel:(202) 574 9474/9274
Fax:(202) 574 9074

India
Indian Government Railways
Rail Bhavan
Raisina Rd
New Delhi 110 001
Tel:(11) 388931

Indian Railways
SD Enterprises Ltd
103 Wembley Park Drive
Wembley
Middlesex, United Kingdom
HA9 8HG
Tel:(181) 903 3411

Indonesia
Perusahaan Jawatan Kereta Api
1 JL Perintis Kemerdekaan 1
Bandung
Java 40117
Tel:(22) 430063/443878

Iraq
Iraq Republic Railways
Central Station
Damascus Square
Baghdad
Tel:(1) 537 0011

Ireland
Irish Rail
Heuston Station
Merchant Quay
Dublin 1
Tel:(1) 836 6222

Japan
Central Japan Railway
Yaesu Centre Building 1-6-6
Yaesu, Chuo-ku
Tokyo 103
Tel:(3) 3274 9535

Jordan
Ministry of Transport
PO Box 582
Amman
Tel:(6) 551 8111
Fax:(6) 552 7233

Kenya
Kenya Railways Corporation
PO Box 30121
Nairobi
Tel:(2) 221211
Fax:(2) 340049

Malaysia
Pentadbiran Keretapi Tanah Melayu
Jalan Sultan Hishamuddin
50621 Kuala Lumpur
Tel:(3) 274 7452
Fax:(3) 230 3936

Morocco
Office National des Chemins de Fer
Rue Abderrahmane El Ghafiki
Rabat-Agdal
Tel:(7) 774747
Fax:(7) 774480

New Zealand
Trans Rail
Bunny St
Wellington
Tel:(4) 498 3303
Fax:(4) 498 3090

Norway
Norwegian State Railways
PO Box 1162 Sentrum
Prinsensgt 7-9
0107 Oslo
Tel:2315 0000
Fax:2315 7033

Pakistan
Pakistan Railways
Shahra-e-Abdul Hamid Bin Bades
Lahore
Tel:(42) 636 6274

Paraguay
Ferrocarril Presidente Carlos Antonio Lopez
Mexico 145 y Eligio Ayala
Asunción
Tel:(21) 445717
Fax:(21) 447848

Peru
Empresa Nacional de Ferrocarriles del Peru
Ancash 207
Lima 1
Tel:(14) 428 7929

Portugal
Caminhuos de Ferro Portugueses
Calçada do Duque 20
1294 Lisboa
Tel:(1) 888 4025
Fax:(1) 886 7555

Russia
Russia Railways
Novo Basmannaia 2
107174 Moscow
Tel:(095) 262 1628
Fax:(095) 975 2411

South Africa
Spoornet
Paul Kruger Bldg
Wolmarans St
Johannesburg 2001
Tel:(11) 773 2944

Sri Lanka
Sri Lanka Government Railway
PO Box 355 Olcott MW
Colombo 10
Tel:(1) 421281
Fax:(1) 546490

Tunisia
Société Nationale de Chemins de Fer Tunisiens
PO Box 693
Tunis 1000
Tel:(1) 249 999

Turkey
Türkiye Cumhuriyeti Devlet Demiryollari Isletmesi
Genel Mürdürlügü
Gar-Ankara 06100
Tel:(312) 311 0620/311 4994
Fax:(312) 312 3215

United Kingdom
Eurostar House
Waterloo Station
London
SE1 8SE
Tel:(345) 303030

The above addresses and telephone numbers are
correct at the time of going to press.

CONTRIBUTORS

George Behrend
Europe: Paris to Istanbul; Calais to Istanbul. Egypt: Cairo to Aswan. Turkey: Istanbul to Baghdad. The Middle East: Istanbul to Kars; Istanbul to Teheran. Malaysia and Thailand: Singapore to Bangkok.

Gary Buchanan
South Africa: Cape Town to Victoria Falls.

Tom Ferris
Ireland: Dublin to Cork; Cavan to Leitrim; Dromod to Belturbet. Northern Ireland: Londonderry to Burtonport.

Colin Garratt
India: Pulgaon to Arui. Indonesia: Tanahabang to Rangkasbitung; Rangkasbitung to Labuan.

Alex Grunbach
Australia: Port Augusta to Alice Springs; Sydney to Brisbane; Broken Hill to Adelaide; Brisbane to Cairns; Port Kembla to Moss Vale; Sydney to Perth; Broken Hill to Sulphide Junction; Ferntree Gully to Gembrook; Zeehan to Strahan; Pacific Coast Motorail. New Zealand: Christchurch to Greymouth.

Frank Hornby
Europe: Across Europe by MEDLOC.

Alan Pike
UK: Edinburgh to Wick/Thurso. Europe: London to Cologne. Switzerland: Gornergrat to St Moritz; Pilatus. Europe: London Waterloo to Bern. Hungary: Budapest to Lake Balaton. India: Kalyan to Howrah. Malaysia and Thailand: Singapore to Penang.

Graham Pike
Portugal: Tunes to Lisbon. China: Ulan Bator to Datong. New Zealand: Picton to Christchurch.

Christopher Portway
Canada: White Horse to Skagway. Peru: Juliaca to Cuzco. Ecuador: Guayaquil to Quito. Albania: Fier to Vlore, Shkoder to Durres. North Africa: Casablanca to Gabes; Nairobi to Kampala. Iraq: Basra to Baghdad. Russia: Red Arrow Express. Pakistan: Quetta to Zaheidan; Lindi Kotal to Peshawar. India: Delhi to Cochin; Delhi to Jodhpur; Kalka to Simla. Europe/Asia: Brussels to Hong Kong. North Korea: Tumenjan to Pyongyang.

Brian Solomon
USA: The San Francisco Muni; St Albans, Vermont to Washington DC; Boston to Chicago; Chicago to Oakland; Seattle to Los Angeles; Bellows Falls to Chester, Vermont; Chicago Metra; Milwaukee to East Troy; Boone Scenic Railway. Japan: Fuji to Kofu; Tokyo's Yamamite Line.

Max Wade-Matthews
Chile: Santa Rosa de Los Andes to Las Cuevas. Paraguay: Asunción to Encarnación. UK: Leicester to Loughborough; Fort William to Mallaig; Settle to Carlisle; London Euston to Glasgow; London King's Cross to Edinburgh; London Paddington to Swansea; London Euston to Holyhead; London Paddington to Penzance; London Victoria to Dover; Bedford to Bletchley. South Africa: Cape Town to Pretoria. Jordan: Damascus to Medina. Russia: Moscow to Vladivostok. India: Siliguri to Darjeeling. China: Shenyang to Harbin. Japan: Tokyo to Osaka.

Kenneth Westcott-Jones
Canada: Toronto to Vancouver; Sault Sainte Marie to Hearst. USA: Chicago to Seattle; Pueblo to Durango; Manitou Springs to Pike's Peak. Mexico: Los Mochis to Chihuahua. Brazil: Santos to São Paulo.

Neil Wheelwright
Canada: Vancouver to Squamish. Norway: Norway to Flåm. South Africa: Cape Town to Pretoria. Japan: Tokyo to Nikko. New Zealand: Christchurch to Wellington.

● **ABOVE**
The Glacier Express, on one of the world's most spectacular scenic railway journeys, Gornergrat to St Moritz, Switzerland.

● **ABOVE**
One of a group of Moguls built in 1899 by Beyer Peacock of Manchester, Lancashire, for Brazil's Leopoldina Railway.

ACKNOWLEDGEMENTS

The majority of the pictures in this book were provided by Milepost 92½. The Publishers would also like to thank the following people and organizations for additional pictures:

The World Encyclopedia of Locomotives

A E Durrant: pp38BL, 40BR, 235M, 238M, 240TL, 245T, 245M. Howard Ande: p4. Barnaby's Picture Library: pp178, 179TL, 179B. British Waterways Archive: p10T. Ian D C Button: p209B. H H Cartwright: p142T. Colour Rail: p66B. Roger Crombleholme: pp17T, 17B, 18, 19B, 20T, 20B, 21B. Richard Gruber: pp77T, 78B. Alex Grunbach: pp50, 51T, 51B, 120, 121, 238T, 239, 240B, 241, 242, 243. John P Hankey: pp24T, 24M, 25T, 28T, 29M, 30T, 32B, 34T, 35B, 74B, 75T, 76T, 77M, 79M, 85T, 87T. Ken Harris: p203TL. Maurice Harvey: p246BR. Michael Hinckley: p17M. Fred Hornby: pp104T, 105, 108T, 110BR, 111T, 112, 113, 189M, 192T, 194T, 198B, 207B. International Railway Journal: pp210BL, 214, 215T, 215M, 246BR. Frederick Kerr: p134B. Locomotive Manufacturer's Association: p69BR. Dennis Lovett: p16B. Arthur Mace: pp12B, 15TR, 65T, 65B. William D Middleton Collection: pp46B, 47T, 47B. Mitchel Library: pp31B, 35T, 35M, 41BR, 46T, 47M, 49T, 51M, 52M, 54–5, 119T, 123M, 126B. Alan Pike: pp39B, 52T, 100, 101B, 102B, 103B, 104B, 106, 107, 180, 181T, 181B, 182T, 182M, 183, 184, 185, 186, 187T, 187B, 188, 189T, 189B, 190T, 190BL, 191T, 192B, 193, 194B, 195, 196, 197, 199, 200, 201, 202, 204, 205, 206M, 206B, 207T, 211TR. Graham Pike: pp109L, 181M, 182B, 187M, 191B, 236, 237T, 237M. Popperfoto: pp25M, 31M, 34B, 37, 38BR, 49B, 56T, 56B, 94M, 95M, 125TR. William Sharman: pp60B, 61T, 70B, 71T, 148T, 148B, 149. Brian Solomon: pp25B, 26T, 26B, 30M, 30B, 32T, 33M, 33B, 72, 73M, 73B, 74T, 75M, 76B, 78T, 82T, 86B, 87M, 87B, 89B, 152, 153, 154, 155, 156, 157, 158, 159, 160, 161T, 161B, 162, 163, 164, 165, 166, 167, 168B, 169, 170, 171, 172, 173B, 509BR, 511B. Richard J Solomon: pp73T, 75B, 79B, 82B, 84, 85B, 86T, 88T, 88BR, 89T, 89M, 90, 91T, 91M, 92T, 93, 94T, 94B, 95T, 95B, 161M, 168T, 173T. Gordon Stemp: pp60T, 63B, 66B, 83T, 134T, 135T, 140B, 258. Michael Taplin:

pp146, 230, 231, 232, 233. J M Tolson: pp108B, 234M, 235T, 248T, 249BR. Verkehrsmuseums Nürnberg: pp38T, 39T. Max Wade-Matthews: p10B. Neil Wheelwright: pp110BL, 222, 223, 224, 225, 226, 227, 228, 229, 234T, 234B, 235B, 237B. Ron Ziel: pp28T, 79T, 83B, 92B, 119BR, 129B, 208B.

Great Railway Journeys of the World

Howard Ande: p255. Adrian Baker/Photobank: pp477M, 477B, 480B, 480T. Jeanetta Baker/Photobank: pp434T, 435T, 435BR, 437TL, 459T, 461B, 463T, 482T, 483B. Peter Baker/Photobank: pp380T, 380B, 381B, 436T, 437BL, 458B, 460T, 461TL, 462B, 482B. Paul Barney/Travel Ink: p473B. Nick Battersby/Travel Ink: pp396T, 397B. George Behrend: pp336, 337T, 338, 340, 342B, 343, 397M, 397TL, 398T, 399T, 400T, 402BL, 404T, 462T. Beyer Peacock & Co. Ltd: p390T. W G Boyden/F Hornby: p369ML. Gary Buchanan: pp386BL, 386M, 386BR, 387, 380T, 389T, 391B. Brian Burchell: p323T.

Carlos Reyes-Manzo/Andes Press Agency: pp294B, 295M. Trevor Creighton/Travel Ink: pp470B, 471T, 471BL. A E Durrant: pp298, 299BR, 380T, 391T. The Eastern and Oriental Express Press Office: pp376, 451TR, 451B, 456T. Abbie Enock/Travel Ink: pp398T, 398M, 399B, 400BL, 401B, 419. Tom Ferris: pp302, 303, 304T, 305-7. Alex Grunbach: pp468M, 470T, 471BR, 472, 473T, 474TR, 474L, 475T, 476, 477T, 478, 479, 480T, 481B, 483T, 484-489. Allan Hartley/Travel Ink: pp416T, 417. Frank Hornby: pp332M, 333T, 334T, 335T, 368, 369MR, 370T, 371. G Holland: pp474L, 475B. T Hudson: pp269TL, 294T. Brian Lovell: p454B. Office Nationale des Chemins de Fer, Rabat: pp378, 379. Ontario Government Tourism: p259TL. A W Mace: pp311T, 328T. Gavin Morrison: pp200M, 296, 297TL, 297BL, 300B, 389TR, 389B, 390B, 406, 407. David Patterson: pp256T, 257TR. Jeremy Phillips: p227M. Alan Pike: pp313, 332B, 333B, 333M, 334B, 335M, 335B, 344-349, 350, 351, 352, 355-361, 458T, 458M, 459M, 459B, 460B, 461TR, 462T, 463B. Graham Pike: pp257M, 364B, 365TR, 366B, 367, 442-443, 490, 492M, 492B, 493B, 494-499. Christopher Portway: pp256B, 265B, 299T, 299BL, 300T, 310TR, 362, 363, 409B, 411M, 412T, 414, 415B, 422-427, 438B, 439T. Seaco Picture Library: pp328B, 329T, 337B, 341T. William Sharman: pp310B, 311B, 314, 315B. Gordon Smith/Photobank: p482B. Brian Solomon: pp266, 267, 269TR, 269B, 270, 271, 274-289, 444-447, 454T, 454M, 455. South American Pictures: pp292 (David Lorimer), 293 (Tony Morrison). SX Picture Desk: pp256M, 257M. Gordon Stemp: p304B. David Toase/Travel Ink: pp408B, 409TR, 410T, 411T, 411B. Max Wade-Matthews: pp308M, 380M, 413T. A M Wellington: p293. Kenneth Westcott-Jones: pp10TL, 22R, 26, 27, 290, 291, 382, 383, 408T, 409M, 410B. Neil Wheelwright: pp260, 261, 262, 263, 372-375, 392-395, 447-455, 491, 492T, 493T. Thanks also to ianród éireann for supplying some of the pictures used for the journeys in Ireland.

T=top, B=bottom, L=left, R=right, M=middle, TR=top right, TL=top left, ML=middle left, MR=middle right, BL=bottom left, BR=bottom right, LM=left middle.

● **ABOVE**
This engine from Sharp, Stewart foundry in 1884, burning both coal and wood, issues shrouds of fire from its chimney.

INDEX

CONVERSION CHART

To convert:	Multiply by:
Inches to centimetres	2.540
Centimetres to inches	0.3937
Millimetres to inches	0.03937
Feet to metres	0.3048
Metres to feet	3.281
Miles to kilometres	1.609
Kilometres to miles	0.6214
Tons to tonnes	1.016
Tonnes to tons	0.9842